100 QUESTIONS
EVERY FIRST-TIME
HOME BUYER
SHOULD ASK

100 QUESTIONS EVERY FIRST-TIME HOME BUYER SHOULD ASK

With Answers from Top Brokers from Around the Country

SECOND EDITION

Ilyce R. Glink

THREE RIVERS PRESS

NEW YORK

Published by Three Rivers Press, New York, New York.
Member of the Crown Publishing Group.

Random House, Inc. New York, Toronto, London, Sydney, Auckland
www.randomhouse.com

THREE RIVERS PRESS is a registered trademark and the Three Rivers Press colophon is a trademark of Random House, Inc.

Originally published by Times Books in 2000.

Printed in the United States of America.

Library of Congress Cataloging-in-Publication Data

Glink, Ilyce R.
    100 questions every first-time home buyer should ask : with
answers from top brokers from around the country / Ilyce R. Glink —
2nd ed.
        p.   cm.
    Includes index.
    ISBN 0-8129-3235-8
    1. House buying.   2. Residential real estate—Purchasing.
3. House buying—United States.   4. Residential real estate—United
States—Purchasing.   I. Title.   II. Title: One hundred questions
every first-time home buyer should ask.
    HD1379.G58   1999
    643'.12—dc21   99–41015

987654

Second Edition

For my mother, Susanne,
who is the kind of real estate agent
every home buyer dreams of;
And for Sam, Alex, and Michael,
without whom my home would be just a house;
And in memory of Harry, Maddie, and Lexi Bull:
may their sunny smiles and happy hearts live on in us always.

Contents

Preface

As the title implies, this is a book for first-time home buyers.

It might also be used quite successfully by anyone who hasn't bought property recently. Indeed, if you haven't bought a home in the past five years, you will undoubtedly find that the game has changed. Others who might find this book helpful include buyers who bought homes within the past few years, but had trouble with the sellers, the financing, the brokers, the negotiation process, the inspection, the closing, or any of the other dozens of pieces that go into the complex game called real estate.

First-time buyers are a breed apart. Brokers say the moment first-time buyers walk into the home of their dreams and realize that it is affordable, a glow of complete satisfaction settles on their faces; it is the thrill of finally achieving the American Dream.

The idea for this book came to me as I was writing an article for the "Your Place" section of the *Chicago Tribune* many years ago. The article was supposed to include a few of the questions first-time buyers always ask. The brokers I interviewed told me all first-time buyers ask the same questions—over and over again. I easily culled a dozen questions from my interviews with brokers. And then another dozen. Over the years, I've added to, and refined, the questions on that list. This Second Edition has perhaps a dozen new questions, and another dozen that have been rewritten, but almost every *answer* has been rewritten entirely, because the real estate industry has changed monumentally since this book was first published.

One truth remains: Most first-time buyers don't remember to ask every question they should. In real estate deals, those unanswered questions are often the ones that may sink your purchase.

This new edition of *100 Questions Every First-Time Home Buyer Should Ask* leads you through the maze of purchasing property by answering the questions that pop up at different checkpoints along the way. You'll find plenty of information about shopping for a home and a loan on the World Wide Web, moving across state lines, and buying a brand new home. The Appendix includes a brand new state-by-state guide on where to file complaints against your mortgage lender and real estate agent or broker (just in case) and an enhanced General Resources Section. After this book goes to press, I'll continue to update these lists on my web site, thinkglink.com.

I've tried to phrase these 100 questions in a way that you would think about them and ask them. I've tried to explain the answers in a way you would understand and recognize. There are two ways to use this book. You can read it from cover to cover, starting with the Introduction, or you can pick it up when you have a question, find your question, and read the answer. I recommend you do both.

Good luck. And, happy house hunting!

ILYCE R. GLINK
Autumn, 1999

P.S. Buying a home is an extraordinary experience. If you'd like to share an anecdote or your own house-buying story, or if you have questions or comments, please write to me at P.O. Box 366, Glencoe, Illinois 60022. My e-mail address is IlyceGlink@aol.com and my web site address is ThinkGlink.com.

100 QUESTIONS
EVERY FIRST-TIME
HOME BUYER
SHOULD ASK

Introduction

So you want to buy your first home. Well, you're not alone, according to a recent report, more than 2 million first-time home buyers purchase property each year. More than 21 million first-time buyer families have purchased a home in the past decade.

In many areas of the country, first-time home buyers account for as many as two-thirds of all home buyers. And, they're expected to remain a large percentage of all home buyers throughout this decade. Why? As we start the millennium, interest rates are historically low. Also, many first-time home buyers are now feeling financially secure. The economy is strong, people have jobs, and believe they will have these jobs in the future. Finally, most first-time home buyers are composed of a couple, each of whom works. They are free to purchase a home the moment they saved enough money for the down payment; they, unlike the rest of the home-buying population, are not already tied down to a property. They do not have to sell before they buy.

My grandfather used to say that no line is too long if someone is standing in line behind you. Plenty of first-time buyers have walked this path before you, and millions more will walk it long after you close on your first home. There is some comfort in knowing that, this year, you and two million other first-time-buyer families will embark on the same voyage. Like them, you will be learning the entirely new vocabulary of real estate. You will learn to be selective in choosing a new home, smart in negotiating for that home, careful in inspecting it, and adept at piecing together the details for closing on it.

Real estate agents and brokers say that first-time buyers have a naïveté that is genuine and enjoyable. A broker in Florida says working with first-time buyers is like taking your children to Walt Disney World for the first time. Their excitement is contagious. It's exciting for a broker to work with someone who's thrilled about the prospects of homeownership. For all their questions, and for all the hand holding they require from brokers, first-time buyers reinvigorate the process of purchasing real estate. Few things in life give as much satisfaction as finally owning your own home.

Who Are You?

Would you recognize yourself in the following description?

According to Chicago Title and Trust's most recent survey, "Who's Buying Houses in America," the average first-time buyer earns $57,200 per year, is 32.2 years old, spent 2.3 years saving up for the down payment, and looked at nearly twelve homes over five months. The average down payment is equal to nearly 13 percent of the purchase price of the home (although a home can be purchased with 2 percent down, or even with zero down, in some cases).

(Here's a confession: When my husband, Sam, and I were looking for a house to buy, we looked at more than 100 homes, over four years, and in ten neighborhoods, before we found the 1880s farmhouse we bought in 1994. So don't feel bad if you end up looking at more homes than the "average" first-time buyer.)

The *median price* (it means an equal number of homes were sold above and below this dollar amount) of a first-time-buyer home continues to rise. In the most recent survey, the median cost was $142,200, compared with $135,400 the year before—a 5 percent increase. The average home price (the total amount paid for all homes, divided by the number of homes sold) grew to $165,400, from $157,800 the year before.

In recent years, nearly 17 percent of first-time buyers purchased new construction; 83 percent bought an existing, or used, home. Single-family homes remain the most popular choice. Nearly 80 percent of all first-time buyers purchase single-family homes.

Most first-time buyers (59 percent) are married. The percentage of two-income families who are first-time buyers is 77.3 percent, down from an all-time high of 80.8 percent in 1997.

Since this book was first published, the sophistication of first-time buyers has grown tremendously. With the advent of the

Internet, more information is accessible than ever before (perhaps even more than is necessary to successfully complete your purchase). Many home buyers are using the Internet to gain market, demographic, and sales information about cities and neighborhoods in which they're interested. They check out interest rates on-line, read real estate news feeds, and investigate companies with which they'd like to do business.

As more quality information becomes readily available, I believe the sophistication of home buyers, particularly first-time buyers, will continue to grow. Some real estate agents and lenders are wary of home buyers who possess knowledge about the process and about what they want, but most are glad to work with buyers who understand what's supposed to happen and how to get from showings to the closing. Agents and lenders who fail to encourage the understanding of first-time buyers will ultimately see their business dry up.

Jim, a longtime Chicago broker, has worked with hundreds of first-time buyers over the years. "First-time buyers are sophisticated, motivated people with money to spend," he says. "But they're sophisticated enough to know they need education and guidance. They know that while they're nervous about making the biggest purchase of their life, education is an antidote to fear."

Are You Ready to Buy a Home?

Think about your answer to that question. Are you really ready to make the commitment required by homeownership?

The answer is more complicated than you might imagine. There is a chasm of difference between a homeowner and a renter. Renters are free to pick up and move, provided their lease is up or they can find someone to sublet their rental apartment or house. Homeowners can list their property for sale, but they are vulnerable to the changing tides of the marketplace and must usually wait for their property to be sold before they can move on.

People rent for many reasons, including:

- They haven't saved up enough money for a down payment.
- They are in a job that may require them to move from location to location.

5

- They are unsure about where they want to live.
- They believe they can make more money in investments other than a home.
- They don't want to be tied down.
- They think they can't afford the home they really want.
- Their personal life is unsettled.
- They are unmarried, and they believe they shouldn't buy a home until they have found their soul mate.
- They are uneducated about the benefits of homeownership.

If you ask new home buyers why they bought, they might tell you:

- It's part of the American Dream.
- Their parents told them it's the single best investment they can make.
- They've saved up enough money for a down payment.
- They see it as an enforced savings plan (a portion of every mortgage payment is principal and contributes to the equity they have in the home).
- They're tired of "throwing money away" on a rented apartment.
- They don't want to deal with landlords.
- They just want a place to call home.

The Psychology of Homeownership

A strong psychological barrier separates owners from renters.

Frank and Julie have rented an apartment in Chicago for more than thirty years. Sue, a residential real estate broker and Julie's friend, asked her why she still rents, when, in the past thirty years, she could have bought a house or condo and completely paid off the mortgage. Instead, thirty years later, all Frank and Julie have to show for their $432,000 (30 years × $1,200 per month average rent × 12 months per year) are rent receipts. But Julie said she and Frank never could agree on where to live. He wanted to be downtown near his work, and she thought they'd eventually move to the suburbs. They liked their apartment building and decided that if it went condo, they'd buy then. It didn't, and there was always another excuse not to buy a place to live.

Are you psychologically ready for the responsibilities that come with buying and owning a home?

Buying a home means more than simply making a monthly mortgage payment. It also means paying taxes, maintenance costs, and insurance premiums. If you buy a condo, town house, or co-op, you're taking on the added responsibility of monthly assessments for maintenance of the commonly held areas of the property, such as the garage or party room. If you're a homeowner, you shoulder the burden of home maintenance yourself. If the roof leaks, you have to fix it. If the boiler breaks, you must replace it. There is no landlord to call.

As a homeowner, you also shoulder the burden of real estate taxes. Your dollars support the local school system, fire and police departments, and city government. When you buy a home, you also buy into your local community. If someone wants to put a trash dump adjacent to your house, you'd better be out there fighting against it to protect your property's value.

(After we moved into our 1880s farmhouse, we discovered that the village had a plan in place to widen our street. During the first five years we lived in the home, we fought the village. The road was completed just before this book was published. Not only was the road not widened, but parts of it were narrowed. The narrowing, resurfacing, and relandscaping of this road will undoubtedly increase the value of our home—and those of our neighbors—over time.)

You may live in your first house for a long time or you may sell within your first year of homeownership. Today, the first-time buyer market is exceptionally hot (there is strong demand for homes priced under $175,000), but that could change. If it does, the two-bedroom condo you bought in a bidding war three years ago could sit for 60 to 120 days before you receive a single offer. Becoming a homeowner means you are somewhat subject to the whims and tides of the market. Renters can leave at the end of their lease, or they can sublet their unit. Homeowners must either rent out their homes or sell. Neither is an attractive option under pressure.

But the benefits of homeownership compensate nicely for most of its hardships. In addition to having a place to call your own, you receive tax breaks from the federal government. You may deduct the interest you pay on your mortgage, plus any points paid to obtain your loan. You may also take a deduction for your real estate property taxes. If you work out of your home, the tax benefits include a deduction for the costs associated with owning and maintaining the portion of the home you use exclusively for business. When you sell the home, you can take the first $250,000 (up to $500,000 if you're married) in capital gains profits tax-free. That's right; that profit is completely tax-free, as long as you've lived in your home for two of the last five years. You don't even have to tell Uncle Sam about the sale, unless your profit exceeds the allowable amount.

Perhaps the best reason to own a home is that, traditionally, homeownership has been an excellent financial investment. Real estate has often been used to hedge against inflation, but, during the 1990s, real estate prices increased anywhere from 10 to 100 percent, or more, per year in many neighborhoods across the country. For many people, real estate far outperformed the stock market!

Gains like these can't be counted on every year, but real estate appreciation does tend to outpace inflation. In addition, paying down a mortgage offers homeowners an enforced savings plan. Every mortgage payment is part interest and part principal, and that little bit of principal, called home equity, adds up over time. When you sell, it becomes cash in your pocket.

One study showed that the younger you are when you purchase a home, the wealthier you'll be later in life. Perhaps this is because homeowners tend to spend a fair bit of time thinking about their finances. When you have financial obligations, like a regular mortgage payment due each month, you had better know where that cash is coming from!

If you've already decided that you're "in the market" to buy a home, this book ought to help. It tells you what questions to ask, and it answers those questions in easy-to-understand English. There are no stupid questions when it comes to buying (or selling) your home. There are only questions that never seem to get answered.

Women and Real Estate

I'm often asked what changes I see taking place in the real estate industry. A major change in the past generation is that more women are purchasing real estate by themselves. There are more single mothers, divorced mothers, and single women who have good jobs and have become aware of the financial benefits of homeownership. They, too, want to buy their piece of the American Dream.

But women often face special challenges when they purchase property alone. The decision to buy seems fraught with peril, and the financial and other fears that couples are able to share are doubly heavy when one pair of shoulders must carry them. Not all of the female members of the current generation of first-time buyers (who are typically in their twenties and thirties) have been taught that they *can* purchase and maintain property by themselves. Their fears and insecurities are often reinforced by naïve or prejudiced brokers who sometimes forget that they must see beyond the curves; the person they are showing around is first and foremost a first-time buyer—not a man or a woman. Not a person of color. Simply, a first-time buyer.

The good news is that since this book was first published, many more women are feeling strong enough to make a purchase on their own. After they marry, some women are keeping these homes (in addition to a new home they may purchase with their spouse) as investments. It's a good, strong start to a successful financial future.

Malka's Story

There's an old joke in real estate: If you want to get married, buy a studio apartment.

That's what happened to Malka. She rented for years in New York City, but finally decided (after helping me promote the first edition of this book) that enough was enough. She was no longer going to wait to meet the "man of her dreams" before she acquired real estate. After much searching, she bought a one-bedroom, co-op apartment.

Sure enough, within six months, she met Mr. Wonderful. Her apartment was located in the building where his son and ex-wife lived! Talk about close quarters.

After Malka got married, she continued to live in her apartment, and Mr. Wonderful stayed in his. Within six months of taking their vows, they got rid of both homes and moved into a new place together.

Today, women have more opportunities for involvement with real estate than ever before. In earlier, less enlightened times, women had little opportunity to purchase real estate for themselves; in fact, they were prohibited from owning or inheriting real estate in most of the world. Unfortunately, this kind of rampant discrimination continues to flourish in places, such as England, where daughters may still not inherit their fathers' titles of nobility, but, under a revised order of succession, the eldest child of the monarch, whether male or female, will inherit the crown. (Apparently, this will start with Prince William's future children.)

Many women have encountered severe and disheartening discrimination and prejudice when they have tried to buy or sell real estate. When my husband, Sam, and I were shopping for a loan when we were first married, we went first to the bank where my family has had numerous accounts for more than fifty years. The loan officer (a woman!) looked first at my husband's robust lawyer's salary and then at my smaller freelance-writer's income. With a withering look, she said, "Your income doesn't matter. Only your husband's counts." And she continued the meeting, addressing him only.

I was humiliated and ashamed. And at that moment, as I think happens with anyone who experiences hateful prejudice, bias, or bigotry, a little bit of me withered and died.

Unfortunately, this sort of thing happens all the time. Recently, a professional woman who makes an excellent six-figure salary complained that when she took over the bidding process after her fiancé left town, their broker didn't believe she had "really been given the authority to make an offer and counteroffer." This successful first-time buyer was insulted, and rightly so. There are thousands of these cases. I'd like to be able to say that the discrimination is occurring with less frequency, but I'm not sure it is. I have heard from plenty of women who purchased homes successfully. But it's a little more than ironic that the discrimination persists, considering how many women are employed within the real estate industry as brokers, agents, loan officers, and appraisers.

Minority Discrimination

Any discrimination is deplorable. But the reality is that we live in an imperfect world. We must do what we can to surmount obstacles others have put in our path, strive to achieve our goals, and never be active or cooperative in supporting barriers based on discrimination.

During the 1990s, a huge influx of immigrant home-buying families helped boost homeownership to record levels. Studies showed that an immigrant family's desire to purchase a home far exceeds that of an ordinary American household. Everywhere I traveled—in New York, Boston, Atlanta, Texas, California, and, of course, my hometown of Chicago—I met immigrant families who were buying homes only one to three years after arriving in this country. They were working at two or three jobs, in some cases making enormous personal sacrifices, all in the name of homeownership. Some of the stories were truly awe-inspiring.

The number of Hispanic and Asian first-time home buyers has skyrocketed in this decade. Studies show that Spanish-speaking buyers will soon (if they don't already) account for the majority of first-time home buyers in California.

Unfortunately, minorities, and particularly African Americans and Hispanics, receive the brunt of the worst kind of discrimination. Study after study has documented that African Americans seem to be rejected for home loans twice as often as Caucasians.

So far, no one has been able to pinpoint the exact reasons, but there are some good guesses. Some say loan officers "redline" a specific neighborhood or town; they don't make any more loans in those areas because they have a history of a high rate of default. Others say loan officers simply don't like to make loans to minorities because they're typically smaller, less profitable mortgages.

Whatever the reason, if you're a member of a minority, or a woman, you may have to work twice as hard to get your loan. Just remember that homeownership is well worth it. However, if you feel you have a legitimate beef, contact your local office of the Department of Housing and Urban Development (HUD) to file a complaint.

It All Comes Down to You

Your home-buying experience will ultimately be whatever you make of it. As I see it, your job is to remove any obstacle that stands in the way of your ability to purchase property.

Let your broker know that you have the authority and financial wherewithal to make an offer and follow through on it (but don't share too much information about your finances). Don't be afraid to admit what you don't know, but don't appear too weak and indecisive either.

Take control of the process. Take advantage of the huge amount of information and resources available through the Internet. Keep asking questions until you get answers you understand. Don't let the broker take advantage of your time or good nature. Be confident about asserting yourself. Don't allow the broker to force you to make a decision before you're ready. Remember, you have the money. You're doing the buying. You've got all the cards.

If you find yourself talked down to, or treated badly, don't hesitate to confront the managing broker about the situation and ask for help. Switch brokerage firms if you feel your needs aren't being met. There are hundreds of real estate agents and brokers who will be delighted to help you feel good about the process and about yourself, and will just as happily collect their share of the commission when you close on your first home.

And that's what this book is all about: closing on your first home. Allow me to be your tour guide. This book is the road map, and the closing is your final destination

1

How Do I Know
What I Want?

You can't always get what you want. But if you try, sometimes
you just might find you get what you need.

Rolling Stones

The difference between being a wanna-be and a successful home
buyer may boil down to nothing more than knowing the difference
between what you want in a home, and what you can't live without.

It sounds simple, but that difference requires an ability to recognize what's really important to you and compromise on the rest. Unfortunately, the ability to compromise is often lost between two
spouses or partners who forget that they can't afford to satisfy their
every whim.

It might make you feel better to know that an inability to compromise isn't limited to first-time buyers. Each time we buy a home, we
feel that *this* time we're going to get—or should get—everything we
want. We work hard, and deserve it, right? But life doesn't work that
way, and neither does home buying. The first group of questions is
designed to give you some insight into what's really important to you
and your family.

20/20

hindsight

13

SHOULD I MAKE A WISH LIST?
WHAT ABOUT A REALITY CHECK?

First, let's talk about what constitutes a wish list. A wish list is nothing more than a list of everything you've ever dreamed of having in your house: granite or slate kitchen countertops (or perhaps inlaid, stained concrete), a wood-burning fireplace, a three-car garage, a four-person whirlpool, the best school district in your state, a five-minute walk to work, four bedrooms, a master suite with his and her closets, and vaulted ceilings. You get the picture.

The best real estate agents and brokers will ask their first-time buyers to create a detailed wish list of everything they'd love to have in a home, grouped in these four categories:

1. **Location.** Think about where you like to shop, where your children will attend school, where you work, where you worship, and where your friends and family live.

2. **Size.** Think about the number of bedrooms you want, the size of the garden, the extra room you may need for expansion or family flexibility, where you'll do the laundry, and what kind of storage space you need.

3. **Amenities.** Think about the garage, the kitchen and bathroom appliances, a swimming pool, a fireplace, air-conditioning, electrical wiring, a heating system, and hardwood floors.

4. **Condition.** Do you want a home in move-in condition? Or are you willing to contribute some "sweat equity," to borrow a *This Old House* phrase, to build in value?

At first glance, many of these items may seem to conflict with others on the list. You want to be close to a transportation network so it's easy to get around, and yet you want a quiet and peaceful neighborhood. You might want to walk to work, but when you come home, you want your neighborhood to be silent and secure. You want a wide variety of shopping, and yet you need to be close enough to your health club to use it on a regular basis. You want to take advantage of the city, and yet live in the suburbs.

That's what a wish list is all about. If you're honest about what you want, the inconsistencies and conflicts will be easy to spot. Most first-time buyers get confused by all their choices and take on a "kid in a candy store" mentality.

Choosing between different styles of homes is difficult. One broker has, each year, a few first-time buyers who need to see at least one of everything in the area: a California ranch, an old Victorian, an in-town condo, and several new subdivisions. It takes a tremendous amount of time, which is wasted if the buyer decides ultimately to go with a loft.

To help their clients define their needs as well as their wants, some agents and brokers also use a tool called a reality check.

Joanne, a real estate sales associate in New Jersey, asks her first-time buyers very specific questions about what they *need* for survival in their first home. "I just know their pocketbook will not allow them to have everything they want. I tell them they'll begin to get what they want with their *second* home, not the first."

Here are some of the questions Joanne might ask:

- How many bedrooms do you need?
- How many children do you have, or do you plan to have others while you are living in this home?
- Is a garage absolutely necessary?
- Why do you need a home with a basement or attic?
- Do you use public transportation on a daily basis?
- How close to work do you need to be?
- Does driving on a major expressway, or in traffic, make you crazy?
- Do you want to care for a garden, or would you prefer a maintenance-free home?

By asking specific questions about your daily lifestyle, brokers can center in on the best location, home size, and amenities for your budget. They can read between the lines on your wish list.

Wish lists and reality checks have another use. By prioritizing the items on your list, a good real estate agent can tell which items you might be willing to trade off. For example, if the first wish on your list is to have a four-bedroom, two-bath house, and the thirty-eighth item is a wood-burning fireplace, then the broker knows you'd probably prefer a four-bedroom, two-bath house without a fireplace to a three-bedroom, two-bath house with a fireplace.

The bottom line: Unless you win the lottery or are independently wealthy, you're probably going to have to make some trade-offs when buying your first home.

The general rule about new construction these days is that you'll get a brand-new place with new appliances, new windows, and the rest, but you'll likely have to make some trade-offs to swing it. If the average existing home costs $130,000 in a major market, the average price of new construction tops $170,000. If you can spend only $130,000, the trade-offs will generally include the location and the overall size of the home.

And, sometimes, you're going to make a mistake.

Ilyce and Sam's Story

When Sam and I bought our first place together (a vintage Chicago co-op built in the 1920s), we didn't own a car. We lived in the city, overlooking Lake Michigan, and had easy access to public transportation, so we couldn't even envision that one day we might change our minds and purchase a car. Our wish list included a parking place, but it was low on the list, maybe around the twentieth item.

On the other hand, a wood-burning fireplace was pretty high—about number five—on our list. You can guess what happened. When we were given a car a few years later, and began hunting and pecking for parking spaces on the street, we were sorry (particularly on cold, snowy, below-zero Chicago nights) that we didn't have a space in which to park the car. But not as sorry as when we wanted to sell our unit and discovered that most home buyers in that area wouldn't even consider a building that had no parking. Fewer people cared about the fireplace, although we loved it.

You can bet that a two-car garage was near the top of our list for the next home we purchased.

Brokers say the best wish list should include *everything* you want in a home. If your initial list says "nice house, four bedrooms," try asking yourself these questions to stimulate your true desires:

- How often do I go to the city? Suburbs? Country? Where would I rather be?
- How much time do I want to spend driving to work each day?

- Do I have frequent guests? Do I need a separate guest room? A separate bath?

- Do I work from home? Does my spouse or partner? Do we need separate office space?

- Do I want a special play area for my children?

- Will my children take a bus to school, or walk, or will I have to drive them?

- How far away is my house of worship?

- Do I want a garden? Will I raise vegetables? Flowers? Or are trees and decorative shrubs enough?

- Must I have a garage? For two cars? Three cars? Do I need a dedicated parking space? Will a covered outdoor space suffice?

- How far away is the airport? Grocery store? Dry cleaner? Gym? Fire and police stations?

- What is my favorite form of recreation and how far away is it?

- Where does my extended family live? Where do my close friends live? How far away from them do I want to be?

- Do I want a home that is in mint condition (also called "blue ribbon" condition in some parts of the country)? Or, do I want to buy a small house on a large lot and fix it up, or add onto it, over time?

Questions involving lifestyle are crucial components of a wish list. Do you and your spouse like to stay in on Saturday nights? Or do you prefer to be "close to the action"? Will that preference change over the years? Are you a single person or married with children? Are you a single parent? A gay couple? Do you travel frequently? Do you own a car? Do you own a boat, or are you contemplating purchasing one in the near future? Will you want to be within fifteen minutes of a marina?

You can see how personal preferences feed into the list. Each spouse or partner has to create his or her own wish list. Then, together, you negotiate the wishes via a reality check. Use the worksheets that follow.

When you have all your information down on paper, try to organize it into one comprehensive sentence. For example: "I want a four-bedroom, three-bath home with a large garden, a fairly new kitchen, loads of closet space, a wood-burning fireplace, and a two-car garage,

Each spouse or partner should create his or her own wish list and reality check. (See page 20 for how to create a reality check.) After you finish your lists, sit together and work through each item. You'll be able to afford only one home, so you should create one joint wish list and one joint reality check before you start your search.

Wish List

Item	Spouse/Partner	Spouse/Partner
1.	_____	_____
2.	_____	_____
3.	_____	_____
4.	_____	_____
5.	_____	_____
6.	_____	_____
7.	_____	_____
8.	_____	_____
9.	_____	_____
10.	_____	_____
11.	_____	_____
12.	_____	_____
13.	_____	_____
14.	_____	_____
15.	_____	_____
16.	_____	_____
17.	_____	_____
18.	_____	_____
19.	_____	_____
20.	_____	_____

Note: If your list exceeds twenty items, continue on a blank sheet of paper until everything is in writing. Be as specific and detailed as possible. Being specific will make it easier for your agent to assist you in finding the right home.

Each spouse or partner does his or her own reality check. Afterward, you again sit together and work through each item. You'll be able to afford only one home, so you should end up with one list of basic needs.

Reality Check

Item	Spouse/Partner	Spouse/Partner
1.	_____	_____
2.	_____	_____
3.	_____	_____
4.	_____	_____
5.	_____	_____
6.	_____	_____
7.	_____	_____
8.	_____	_____
9.	_____	_____
10.	_____	_____
11.	_____	_____
12.	_____	_____
13.	_____	_____
14.	_____	_____
15.	_____	_____
16.	_____	_____
17.	_____	_____
18.	_____	_____
19.	_____	_____
20.	_____	_____

located within a fifteen-minute commute to the office and church, a short walk from the high school, in such-and-such area."

That's a start. Next, prioritize the items in your wish list and identify any items you'd trade off for others. For example, would you give up a wood-burning fireplace if it meant having a two-car garage? Could you get by with a smaller house if it meant you'd be in a better school district? Would you prefer to be closer to work even though it means giving up a large garden? What if you had to live in a condo but could walk to work?

If a wish list is everything you want in a home, a reality check is everything you can't live without. For example, you may want a four-bedroom home, but you absolutely need three bedrooms. You may want a large garden, but you really need an outdoor area where you can hang out and grill "dogs" and burgers for your friends. Your reality check may repeat many of the items on your wish list, but in pared down versions. Be completely honest about the minimum you will need, to be comfortable in your home.

20/20

hindsight

No two people are exactly alike. No matter how compatible you and your spouse or partner are, you are two individuals who will end up with two different (sometimes completely different) lists. Rather than denigrate each other's wish list or reality check items, try to view the entries as statements of each person's priorities. Some items from each person's column on the worksheets should make their way into the joint wish list and reality check. If the final choices are too one-sided, you're headed for home-buying trouble.

From your reality check list, create a single sentence that represents your basic needs for a home. If you're a single woman, your reality check sentence might be: "I need two bedrooms [mostly for resale purposes], two bathrooms, a dedicated parking space or attached garage, some sort of outdoor living space, twenty-four-hour security in the building, and a twenty-minute (or shorter) drive to work."

These details give your broker something to work with. He or she can take your wish list and begin to match it to homes listed in the local multiple-listing service. Are the wish list and reality check worth the time and effort? Brokers say they are. Even though a good broker will spend an hour or two divining the same information, having a written wish list and reality check will help you to focus on what you really want and what you can't live without.

An honest and complete wish list is a road map to eventually finding the house of your dreams.

> How long you plan to stay in the house you buy will affect everything from where you buy and how you finance the purchase, to the size and location of the property. Although you may have a time line in mind when you create your wish list and reality check ("We won't move until our youngest finishes high school" or ". . . until our home-based business requires larger office space"), later years may bring surprises. I'll talk about time-based planning throughout this book. For now, think carefully about your time line when creating your wish list and reality check.

WHAT DOES "LOCATION, LOCATION, LOCATION" REALLY MEAN?

QUESTION
2

Among real estate industry professionals, "location, location, location" is called the brokers' maxim. It's the credo that all real estate agents live by, and during the days, weeks, and months when your broker helps you search for a home, you're likely to hear this phrase more than once. What does it really mean?

Brokers say that successful buying or selling is linked to the location of a home. You can usually change everything about a home *except* its location.[1] Think about it: You can paint, decorate, gut the interior of the house, replace the asphalt shingles with slate, put on new siding, add a deck, repave the driveway, and plant flowers. The only thing you can't do is move the home to a different location.

If the house of your dreams is located next to a railroad yard, you should probably just go back to sleep. A poor location will severely limit a property's appreciation in value and will hamper your ability

---

[1] Some houses can be literally picked up and moved. People do buy houses that are slated to be torn down and move them to new locations. Mobile homes and manufactured homes that arrive partially prebuilt can be placed on a purchased or rented lot. They are not the kind of home we're talking about here. No one moves an apartment from midtown Manhattan to New Jersey. And no one takes a 150-year-old brick town house from Boston's North End and moves it to Newburyport, Massachusetts.

to sell the property quickly in the future. Look for the reason why a house is priced very low or has been for sale for a long time.

Ed's Story

Ed, a real estate attorney, bought and sold several homes before he bought the one that backed up to the tracks of Chicago's famous elevated train, known as "the El." The 1880s brick two-story house and its nice yard desperately needed some TLC.

But it backed up to the El. Trains run by there every ten to fifteen minutes, and more frequently in rush hour. The whole house shakes as they go by. Ed stood for a while inside the house before he made an offer. He didn't seem to think the trains would be a problem. "You get used to it; I hardly even hear it." So he bought the house.

He proceeded to completely renovate it; he even put in a sauna. When he decided to move to Texas, he put the house on the market. Two years later, it was still for sale, waiting for someone who wanted to spend several hundred thousand dollars for an overimproved house in a good neighborhood, but in a very poor location.

What is a poor location? Defining *poor* is often a matter of taste. To brokers, a poor location means a home may be difficult to sell because it is located:

- Next to a railroad yard.
- Near a toxic waste or municipal garbage dump.
- On top of, or next to, a freeway, expressway, or interstate highway.
- In the center of nightlife activity.
- Near a busy intersection, or on the busiest street in town, even if that street is a comparatively quiet rural lane.
- Next to a school, where fleets of school buses would arrive twice daily, pedestrian traffic will often be heavy, and kids may hang out on the corners at all hours.
- In the midst of gang territory, or in an otherwise high-crime area.
- On a run-down block or in a deteriorating neighborhood.
- In a city, town, or suburb that has significant budget problems, poor public schools, or a teetering local economy.

- Backing up to, or next to, a type of housing that is different from the rest of the neighborhood. For example, if you're looking at a single-family house and all of the other single-family homes back up to other single-family homes, but the one you like backs up to an apartment complex, the resale value could be a problem.

Many people have turned what might normally be called a poor location into a positive benefit. If you buy a home in a run-down neighborhood that is surrounded by yuppie housing, you might be

Location doesn't just refer to the particular suburb or neighborhood in which you live. It also refers to the block on which your home is located, and even to your home's placement on that block. If corner lots are more valuable in your neighborhood, and you live in the middle of the block, that's a geographic factor you're not going to be able to change. Think about how difficult this home may be to sell *before* you make an offer.

When you buy in a new development, you typically look at a large, vacant cornfield with perhaps one or two spec houses (the developer builds and furnishes them to show you what the other homes in the development will be like). From that sampling, you're supposed to extrapolate what the neighborhood will look like. When new construction is involved, location is even more important. Certain lots will be deemed "premier," and the developer will charge a higher fee for them. For example, on a golf course development, lots that face the golf course might be two to three times as costly as lots that face the outside street. Should you buy the more expensive lot? Brokers say it depends on what you want and how much you can afford. If you want to live on a golf course, and a golf course view is important to you, then buy the view. Otherwise, you may be better off purchasing a nice lot that's near the golf course but isn't as expensive. When you look at the developer's master plan for the area, identify which lots are most and least expensive and try to understand the reasoning behind the developer's pricing strategy. That could be important information when you decide to sell.

able to turn a nice profit as the neighborhood improves over the years. Being located next to a noisy high school may guarantee you peace and quiet throughout the summer months and make it easy for you to frequently check on your child's welfare.

A good location, on the other hand, is one that allows the owner to thoroughly enjoy every aspect of his or her home. It will be located close, but not too close, to shopping, restaurants, work, transportation, good schools, and major traffic arteries. A good location is one that you can easily sell to someone else, which gives you additional flexibility (not to mention peace of mind). If, when you're looking for a home, you're faced with the choice between a beautiful home in a lousy location, or a slightly smaller and less beautiful home in an excellent location, which one will you choose?

HOW DO I FIGURE OUT WHERE I WANT TO LIVE?

Finding the right location is a problem for many buyers, not just first-timers. In part, the answers lie where your bank account meets your wish list. Neighborhoods being what they are, you can almost certainly find something in your price range in an area in which you'd want to live. For example, I'm sure you could find an affordable one-bedroom condo in a suburb that also includes million-dollar homes. Some buildings in Manhattan that contain apartments costing $10 million or more are right next to buildings in which the apartments go for a tiny fraction of that amount. But if you need three bedrooms, an expensive suburb or building will most likely be out of your price range. The point is, you can find something affordable in nearly every neighborhood. Whether it meets your needs is another story.

Your first goal is to find a suburb or neighborhood that offers homes that meet your needs, at a price you can afford. Sometimes, the easiest way to find what you're looking for is to cross out options that are flawed. Start by asking your broker to cross-match your price range with your reality check list. That should instantly narrow your choices of suburbs or neighborhoods. Next, take a close look at those areas that meet these criteria, and apply some of the features of your wish list: Is one in a better school district? Is another closer to work? Does one have more character, or better shopping? Is one located on a golf course? Is one nearer (or farther away from) your parents or in-laws?

When your choices are narrowed down to two or three suburbs, neighborhoods, or streets, take an extensive tour of these areas. Go there at different times. Walk around. Sit on a bench and watch the people go by. They might be your future neighbors. Next, start looking at some of the houses in the neighborhood, perhaps during a Sunday open-house tour. If you begin to see homes you like, in an acceptable and affordable neighborhood, you're on the right track.

The Internet has simplified shopping for a community, particularly for out-of-state home buyers. There are web sites for most major metropolitan areas, and many brokerage sites (both national and local) contain a fair amount of community information. You can also shop for a home by going to a web site and simply keying in some of the items on your reality check list. For example, you can request all listing information for homes that match a particular description (say, four bedrooms, two baths, under $250,000) within a certain location. If nothing comes up that meets your needs, at a price you can afford, it may mean that (1) the neighborhood is too expensive for your price range, (2) the type of housing in which you're interested doesn't exist, or (3) you need to try another web site.

HOW LONG DO I PLAN TO LIVE IN MY FUTURE HOME?

Of all the questions in the book, this may be the single most important one for you to answer. Why? Because the answer directly affects the size, type, and location of the home you buy, as well as the terms of the mortgage you use to finance your purchase.

Times have changed since our parents bought their homes. Chances are, unless they've retired or are in professions that require them to relocate to different parts of the country from time to time, your parents are still living in the home in which you grew up. My mother, Susanne, has lived in the same co-op apartment building for more than 30 years. It was the first and only apartment she and my father purchased. And, though she talks a lot about moving and says she might like to "retire" to Michigan Avenue, in Chicago, my guess is she'll probably be at her current address for some time to come.

Her experience is likely to be quite different from yours. Statistics from the National Association of Realtors (NAR), a national trade association based in Washington, DC, reveal that today, *on average*, renters and homeowners live in their homes only about five to seven years. Then, they move. Many homeowners stay in one place for 10, or even 20, years. But many others sell after two or three years.

How can you estimate how long you're going to live in your home? There's no way to know for sure, but here are some general guidelines, which I like to refer to as the Cycle of Life.

Cycle of Life

If you buy a home when you're young and single, but you are looking toward having a long-term relationship or getting married, it's likely that what you can afford as a single person won't be quite enough space for two. Within five to seven years, you'll probably find a long-term partner or spouse and you will trade your one-bedroom or two-bedroom home for something larger.

If you're a newly married couple and want to have children, you'll probably start a family within a few years of your marriage. Seven years or less later, you'll need additional space as your family (and their stuff, which multiplies exponentially) starts to grow.

If you get divorced or separated, that could mean another move. At that point, in your second or third home, with young children in school, you'll probably settle down for a while. You might even find a house in a good school district and decide to stay there until all your children graduate. If you remarry, you may need to move again.

After your children are grown and out of the house for good, you might decide to sell your big house, take your profits (up to $250,000 for qualified single homeowners, and up to $500,000 for married homeowners, will be tax-free) and move to a smaller condo somewhere warm or perhaps close to some good ski slopes.

A new trend in homeownership is "re-retirement." Seniors are picking up and moving several times during retirement, and they frequently cross state lines to find a different place to call home.

Another possibility is that you'll purchase a second home, to which you may eventually retire. People who are most likely to buy a second home are 55 to 65 years old. They are followed statistically by those aged 45 to 55, and those aged 65 to 75. And those who buy one second home are likely to buy two or three replacement homes during their lifetime.

Moving as a National Pastime

National statistics tell us that the average family will move five to seven times during their lifetime. In addition to accommodating fluctuating family sizes (including grown-up children, grandchildren, and aging parents), buying and selling homes is one of the best ways to accumulate wealth. By repeatedly purchasing homes, fixing them up, and selling them five to seven years later, you should be able to increase significantly the amount of your equity (the cash value you can realize from your home) over the course of your lifetime.

Ted and Susan's Story

Ted and Susan decided they were going to make money by buying fixer-upper properties, investing the time, effort, and cash needed to make them beautiful, and then selling them for a profit.

It's a good plan, and countless home buyers have made use of it. But Ted and Susan were so successful that their profit was hundreds of thousands of dollars from the sale of each home. One purchase was a 6,000-square-foot apartment that had been foreclosed on. They gutted it, updated it, and sold it for more than $2 million. They put that money into a nearby suburban house that cost $2.8 million. Over the next 15 months, they gutted it, did a makeover, and put it on the market for $9.5 million.

As this book went to press, the house was still on the market. They haven't sold it yet, but Susan and Ted are likely to make more than a few bucks in profit from the sale of this home. The Tax Reform Act of 1997, which allows an individual to keep, tax-free, up to $250,000 (up to $500,000 for married couples) in profits from real estate sales, helps homeowners cash in on fixer-upper deals. You might not make millions from the sale of a home you've fixed up, but you'll get to keep a far larger portion today than was possible under earlier tax regulations.

But Wait! There's More . . .

Knowing how long you plan to live in your house is also crucial to choosing the correct mortgage. If you're going to live in your home for only five years, don't take out a 30-year fixed-rate mortgage. The mortgage market has changed drastically in recent years; today, there are excellent options that provide you with the stability of a fixed-rate loan (for as long as you'll need it) at a less expensive interest rate. By choosing an alternative mortgage, such as a two-step mortgage, you might save yourself thousands of dollars over the life of the loan.

If you're going to stay in your home for 10 to 15 years, you might want a 15-year fixed rate mortgage; if you sell the house, after you own it free and clear, you'll have a sizable amount of cash for your next purchase. Or, you might get a 30-year fixed-rate loan and simply add a little extra to your monthly mortgage payment. (It's called *prepaying*, and it can be an excellent way for you to cut down the term of your mortgage and save yourself thousands of dollars in interest.)

If you have questions on mortgages, turn to the financing section of this book, beginning with Question 53.

Look Before You Leap

Before you start to look for a home, think about where you are in the Cycle of Life, and where you'll be, or hope to be, in five or seven years.

- Is marriage, a life partnership, or living with someone else a possibility within five to seven years?

- How many children do you plan to have during the next five to seven years?

- Are your children near or at school age? Have you chosen the school district you want for them?

- Are you likely to be transferred to a different job location within the next five to seven years?

- Do you have an aging parent in another part of the country who may require your close supervision or attention?

• Do you have an aging parent or post-college-age children who might be moving back home with you? Will you need flexible living space that your current home can't provide?

WHAT ARE THE DIFFERENT TYPES OF HOMES?

Your home is supposed to be your castle. But unless your family name is Windsor, it's unlikely you'll end up living in one.

Several basic types of homes are commonly available in all parts of the United States. They may, however, be called by different names. For example, a "two-flat" in Chicago might be called a "two-family" in Boston, or a "duplex" on the west coast.

> If you don't know exactly what you're looking for, or what it is called, don't be shy about asking. Most good real estate agents or brokers would rather work with a knowledgeable buyer, even if they have to fill in the buyer's intelligence gaps along the way. If you plunge ahead, you may think you look smarter, but you'll just end up wasting a lot of your valuable time.

If you decide to buy a home, you'll end up choosing from a condominium, a town house, a cooperative apartment, and a single-family home. Or, you might get a hybrid, or a variation on one of these housing types. Each of these home types has numerous differences, from the rights of ownership to the way the property is maintained. As the saying goes, it's all in the details; knowing the differences among these types of homes is key to making a successful choice.

Condominium

Usually found in urban centers or densely populated suburbs, condos (as they are commonly referred to) became popular in the 1970s when state legislatures passed laws allowing their existence. An apartment building is converted to a condominium by means of a *condominium declaration* (often called a "condo dec"). Newly constructed condominiums must also have a condo dec.

This declaration divvies up the percentage of ownership, defines which areas are commonly held by all owners, determines who is responsible for the maintenance of the property, and states the condo rules.

One of the most important things to remember about a condo is that you don't actually own the unit in which you live. Instead, you own the air space inside the walls, ceiling, and floor of the unit, possibly the plumbing within your unit, and perhaps a parking space. (With newly constructed condos, you sometimes have to buy your parking space separately.) With your neighbors, you also jointly own what's known as the *common elements* of the property, which may include the roof, plumbing, common walls, lobby, laundry room, garden area, and garage.

Condos are not always tall buildings. Condo developments can take the form of town houses, duplexes (condos stacked two-by-two), or four-plexes (condos stacked four-by-four, also known as *quads*). You might get a two-family (or two-flat) house that's been turned into a condo. Or, you can have a single-family, maintenance-free community in which the houses are actually condominiums. Suburban condos tend to be horizontal (long rather than high). City condos tend to be in mid- or high-rise buildings.

New Construction Developers who are building new condos, or renovating an old apartment building to turn it into condos, may keep control of the newly formed condo board or homeowners' association until a certain percentage of the condos have been sold. This can present some difficulty, especially if there is a physical problem with the units (such as a leak) and the homeowners decide to sue the developer. Another issue to think about is that financing new construction can be tricky. Usually, the developer hooks up with a lender to fund the loans. But the national secondary mortgage market leaders (Fannie Mae and Freddie Mac)[2] require that 70 percent of the units be occupied by homeowners before they will fund a loan. So if you decide to refinance before 70 percent of the units are occupied, you may have some trouble. Similarly, if 31 percent of the owners decide to rent their units, you may also have trouble financing or refinancing your unit.

---

[2] The full names given them when they were chartered by Congress are: Federal National Mortgage Association (Fannie Mae) and Federal Home Loan Mortgage Corporation (Freddie Mac). But these companies have since officially adopted their consumer-friendly monikers.

Maintenance   A condo association raises money for maintenance of the common elements through monthly assessments. The building's expenses (including the portion of your monthly payment that goes into the building's emergency reserve account) are tallied, then divided by the percentage of ownership, and then divided by twelve to arrive at the monthly charge. If your annual share of the building maintenance cost is $2,400, you will pay $200 per month in assessments, in addition to the costs of your mortgage and real estate taxes.

> If you choose to buy a condo or a co-op (see below), you must understand that the lender will take into account the extra monthly payment you'll have to make and will readjust the amount it is willing to lend you. For example, the lender might tell you that you can purchase a $160,000 house or a $130,000 condo.

I'm often asked if its fair for a condo building to increase assessments, or levy a special assessment, in the same amount, no matter what the percentage ownership. In other words, should every unit get a $100 per month raise? It depends on what the condo declaration says, but typically, raises or specials will be doled out according to your percentage ownership.

> The condo declaration will divide up the ownership of the property. You, as a condo owner, will own a certain percentage. In many areas, the tax assessor will levy a property tax on your entire condo building. Your share of the tax is typically equal to the percentage of your share of the building. That's why condo owners sometimes have a tougher time protesting their property taxes.

Cooperative Apartment

Before there were condos, prospective homeowners could buy a unit by purchasing shares in a corporation that owned the building in which that unit was located. As my friend David puts it, if you own a condo, you own real estate that you can use to secure a mortgage. If you own a co-op, you own shares in a corporation that owns the real estate in which your apartment is located. The shares give you the right to lease your unit from the corporation. You pay a monthly assessment (often called a lease payment or rent) based on the number of shares you own in the corporation.

One sticky issue with co-ops is control. For many years, co-op boards used their power to reject potential buyers at will and to keep a firm grip on who moved into the building. Unfortunately, a little of that unpleasantness continues to this day, particularly in swanky neighborhoods and in buildings whose owners have, shall we say, certain "attitudes" toward people of color, certain religions, certain occupations, and single parents. In addition, co-op rules often require a higher down payment (between 30 and 50 percent, in cash, is not uncommon), and sometimes refuse to allow purchases financed with a mortgage. Fortunately, many co-ops have relaxed the latter restriction in recent years. If you're looking for an abundance of co-op units, try New York City or Chicago, although a fair number are spread out over the rest of the United States.

Janice's Story

After looking for a home for nearly a year, Janice came upon a co-op conversion located in the town in which she was living. The co-op was asking for a 50 percent down payment, and wanted to see her finances.

"Literally, they asked me to sign a piece of paper that allowed them to do a full credit and financial background check on me. They wanted past addresses, names of references they could call, my current and past jobs, my bank account statements, and my Social Security number," Janice said.

Although Janice had a good amount of cash saved up for her down payment, 50 percent was pushing it just a bit. She decided that the financial obligations with this particular co-op were too onerous, and ultimately declined to make a purchase offer.

In the best light, all of this screening should guarantee a better neighbor, right? But co-op boards sometimes make mistakes, too. In one New York co-op, the board voted in a family that had impeccable credentials. On paper, they had it all: the best schools and best awards, a terrific family history, and glowing letters from the board of the building in which the applicants previously lived. Later, after several incidents involving these particular owners had required that the police be called, board members discovered that the managers of their former residence had been only too glad to be rid of these individuals and had written the letters in an effort to rid themselves of a problem family that had caused tremendous upheaval and unrest.

If you don't "pass the board," as it is commonly called, don't feel bad. Famous celebrities and politicians are often voted down for various reasons. It's illegal for a co-op board to reject you because of your race, religion, or sex, but, more often than not, you'll be told you simply don't have enough money, or there's a "personality" issue. It's hard not to take the rejection personally, but you have to ask yourself whether this kind of place is really right for you.

New Construction Rarely is a co-op built from the ground up these days, although it does happen in New York from time to time. More commonly, you'll see a building converted into a co-op.

Maintenance As in a condo, your monthly assessments cover the general maintenance of the property. But because the corporation pays the real estate taxes as a whole, your share of the taxes is normally included in your monthly assessment. That means your assessment is going to look pretty steep when compared with the bottom line on a condo building assessment notice. For a fair comparison, you'll have to break out the costs. When you look at a co-op listing sheet, remember that the assessment generally includes property taxes.

Aside from New York City brokers, who are intimately familiar with co-ops, many agents and brokers, especially those new to the business, have trouble understanding the concept of co-ops. They may tell you that co-ops aren't a good investment, or try to steer you away for some other reason. Like any type of home, a co-op can be an excellent investment. Sometimes, a co-op price is below that of a comparable condominium apartment, partly because brokers may not understand co-ops and partly because co-ops typically require a larger down payment, which makes them unaffordable or impractical for many first-time buyers. On the other hand, if you own a co-op, selling it may take longer, on average, than selling a condo.

Town House

A town house development can take several different forms, but it usually looks like a group of slender houses attached in a long row. Generally, you share a wall in common with each of your neighbors.

The difference is in the way the property is held. Most row houses built in the first half of the twentieth century are held "fee simple," meaning you hold legal title to your home and the land on which it sits. You are also responsible for the property's real estate taxes, even though you share a common wall with your neighbors. Today, many newly built town homes are constructed as condominiums, complete with a homeowners' association.

New Construction A popular trend in the construction of town houses (and some single-family communities) is a *maintenance-free community*. Essentially, this means that while you own your own property, the homeowners' association manages the exterior and the common elements of the property, and takes care of them for you. If the town houses need painting, there's no need for you to do anything. The homeowners' association will take care of it. On the other hand, they, not you, will typically choose the color.

Maintenance Even if you hold your property fee simple (the way you'd normally own a single-family house), you may have to join a homeowners' association. Your monthly maintenance costs would cover the common areas not immediately on your property, such as a garage, playground, laundry room, and/or swimming pool.

Mobile Homes and Manufactured Housing

Once the poor stepchild of the real estate industry, mobile homes (also known as manufactured homes) have become a way for first-time buyers with few resources to purchase a home and stop paying rent. You might not choose to purchase a mobile home if you can afford a regular home, but you might do so if your only other option is renting.

First, let's talk about what is a mobile home. A mobile home is designed to be transported (hence the term "mobile") in one piece to a plot of land, often within a mobile home park. The park might contain hundreds, if not thousands, of mobile homes. A mobile home comes with bedrooms, bathrooms, a living room, and a kitchen, and might be of standard width (approximately 12–15 feet wide), or of double-wide width (approximately 30 feet wide). Typically, you purchase the mobile home and rent the land.

Mobile homes weren't built too well in the past, which is why they have such a shaggy reputation today. They didn't last long, and they didn't hold up too well. However, several big companies got into the game and started using technology and improved building materials to construct prefabricated homes or manufactured homes. They're still mobile, and can be transported, completely built, to a residence site. But they're of much better quality than earlier models and last a lot longer than mobile homes of the past.

Some mobile home parks have very strict rules, to help increase the value of the homes located there. If the mobile home park in which you're interested has these rules and obviously enforces them, it's good news for your investment.

New Construction   A newly built mobile or manufactured home will last a lot longer than an old one, thanks to certain regulations builders must now follow. Still, even brand-new mobile homes are frequently upended by tornadoes.

Maintenance   Even if you're renting the land, you're typically responsible for the hookups to an electrical cable and a water source, and for sewage disposal and garbage pickup. At the same time, as a homeowner, you'll need to keep your home looking nice so that you'll be able to sell it when you're financially ready to move up into your next home.

Although their quality is improving and mobile homes are becoming more acceptable, we haven't quite seen the day when a mobile home will appreciate faster (or even as fast) than a single-family home, or even a condo or co-op. If you're going to purchase a mobile home, or a manufactured home in a mobile home park, study the values closely, and make sure you're getting what you think you're paying

Single-Family House

Far and away, the most common form of home is the detached, single-family house. Available in all shapes, sizes, and prices, the most common feature among single-family homes is that the house sits by itself, on its own piece of property.

New Construction In some developments, the homes may be clustered together while a large portion of the development sits as open land—a golf course, a nature preserve, or a man-made lake. Again, you'd own your own plot and house fee simple, but you may have to join the homeowners' association and pay monthly dues for the maintenance and insurance of the common areas.

Maintenance Single-family homes can be wonderful! But they can also be a lot of work. As the homeowner, you are responsible for *all* of the expenses associated with ownership and maintenance, including real estate taxes, garbage removal, water, and sewage.

I'm often asked which appreciates fastest: a single-family home, a condominium, or a co-op? The truth is, any of these can appreciate quickly. Your profit depends on how much you pay for the home and what happens to homes in your surrounding neighborhood. Generally speaking, single-family homes appreciate faster than condos or co-ops. However, if you buy a condo that has been foreclosed on and then fix it up, you may realize a gain of 100 percent or more in a short period of time. Or, if you buy a home as a pioneer, in an area that hasn't been developed yet, you may realize an enormous gain if your neighborhood suddenly becomes "hot." It's seductive to think about buying a home and making a fortune on it, but you have to think about whether you'll be comfortable living there, day in and day out. We'll talk more about this later in the book.

SHOULD I BUY A NEW HOME OR AN EXISTING HOME?

Approximately 21 percent of home buyers purchase new houses in a given year. The rest buy used houses. But that number rises or falls depending on the amount of new construction in a given area. For example, as many as 41 percent of home buyers in Phoenix bought new construction in 1998 (most recent numbers available as we went to press)

compared with 12 percent in Cleveland, 10 percent in Los Angeles, and 8.9 percent in San Francisco.
[Source: *Who's Buying Homes in America 1998*
Chicago Title Corporation's annual survey of recent home buyers]

Should I buy a new house? This is one of the questions I'm asked most frequently. It's difficult to answer because where you live, what you can afford, and what your options are factor into any home-buying decision. I have outlined here a few things for you to think about before you make a purchase.

1. New construction generally costs more than existing housing. Typically, you'll pay more for a four-bedroom newly built house than for a similar size home that was built 5, 10, 20, or even 50 years ago. That premium can be partly explained because new houses tend to be larger than homes built 20 years ago. Typically, you'll have two and a half baths in a four-bedroom home. Twenty years ago, it was more common to have four bedrooms and two baths. Fifty years ago, you might have had three bedrooms and only one and a half baths. Today's new construction typically offers central air and loads of appliances, fireplaces, and lofted spaces. You may have a two- or a three-car garage. But when you buy a new house today, you're typically paying a portion of the *impact fees* charged to developers by the community to cover the costs of development (including sewer lines, more roads, and more students in the local schools). If money is an issue, you'll probably want to find an existing house that you can later fix up with all the amenities of a newly built house.

2. The neighborhood may not be established. New construction typically takes place in cornfields. That's because it's difficult to find a vacant, large *infill* plot of land in a city, and it isn't profitable for large developers to build homes piecemeal. Developers purchase acreage farther and farther out from the city center. Whole new communities spring up, but the retail and service development usually lags behind. When you first move into a new community, you might have to drive five miles for a gallon of milk. (And if you have young kids at home, all those milk runs can really add up to extra mileage on your car.) Also, developers sometimes pick less favorable school districts or communities because they offer affordable land. A brand new home may not be in the best school district, or even in a choice suburb. Does that mean you shouldn't buy a home in a new development? No. It simply means that, before you sign the purchase offer, you need to think about where you're going to go shopping, work out, drop off the cleaning, fill up the car, and school your children.

3. Make sure your developer is well funded. One of the dangers in buying new construction early in the life of a project is that the developer may run out of cash before the project is done. If that's the case, your home could plummet in value. Few developers will let you see their financial statements, but be sure to thoroughly research the background of the developer. You shouldn't have trouble with a large, well-known company that has completed various projects, but do your homework. Visit residents who live at other developments the builder has completed. See how well their homes have held up, and ask whether they have any complaints. A series of disgruntled homeowners should be a red flag. Call the local better business bureau and chamber of commerce to check on any complaints. Finally, ask local village officials about their experiences in dealing with this builder.

4. Quality new construction may appreciate at the same speed as, or even more rapidly than, an existing home. If you purchase a home from a reputable, quality developer, and the development itself is a quality project, your home should not only retain its value but also appreciate in value, even though other, newer projects have opened up. But beware: In a low-quality development, homes can come apart faster than they were originally put together.

5. Do you want to live in a new home? Or, do you want to fix up a home? New construction means everything is about as perfect as it's going to get. These days, no matter what the price range, you should be able to customize your home to some degree, take advantage of options and upgrades, and choose your own colors and carpeting. You also get a home specifically designed to your needs. If you require a home office, for example, most new-construction house plans feature a first-floor space that could function as a separate home office. A newly constructed home should require almost no maintenance. (Everything is new.) If you're looking for a house that's virtually maintenance-free (without going into a maintenance-free community, as described earlier), new construction might be perfect for you. But be aware that when you buy new construction, your home will appreciate only as fast as the general area does.

If you are looking to build in value, you'll probably want to choose a fixer-upper home. (See Question 7 for more information on evaluating and purchasing fixer-upper homes.)

> If any real estate deal seems too good to be true, it probably is. If you can't overcome some misgivings about the value you're getting for an investment in a home, don't sign the papers. At a minimum, finish reading this book before you make a final decision on purchasing a home.

SHOULD I BUY A HOME THAT NEEDS RENOVATION? AND, WHAT DO BROKERS MEAN BY "OVERIMPROVED"?

Brokers like to say that three kinds of homes are available from former owners:

1. **Move-in condition.** This is a house that's about as close to perfection as possible. No decorating or renovation is required. All you have to do is move in your furniture (or purchase the sellers' furniture, if that's an option) and start living there.

2. **Good condition.** When you hear brokers refer to a home in this way, it generally means the home's "bones," or structural elements, are in fine shape, and the amenities and appliances are in good working order. On the other hand, you might not like the decor. Gold velvet flocked wallpaper and olive green shag carpeting might be your taste, or it might not. In this type of house, which accounts for most of the homes on the market, you might need to repaint the walls, strip the floors, or replace the carpeting.

3. **Handyman's special or fixer-upper.** With a handyman's special (no offense intended to all of the handy women out there), you can expect to see anything from a home needing minor repairs to a home that requires a gut job to be livable.

When a question involves the advantages and disadvantages of buying a home that needs renovation, the answer depends on how much money you have to spend. Most first-time buyers have limited cash reserves. Usually, the down payment is a stretch, let alone finding money to decorate or renovate a home. Also, fewer people today have the time, know-how, or interest to do much of the renovation themselves, and hiring renovators or decorators can be expensive. If the option of buying a new home is available to you, purchasing new construction can be cheaper and easier in the long run.

If, however, you have the time and cash to put into renovating a home, there are significant advantages to be gained. You might be able to purchase a bigger home in a better neighborhood. Perhaps you can purchase a two-flat or two-family home and fix it up, then rent out one unit and live at a far reduced cost. And, of course, one of the best reasons to buy a fixer-upper is to maximize the investment you make in your home.

Angela and Tom's Story

When Angela and Tom went looking for houses, they realized they couldn't afford to buy anything worthwhile in their top choices for location. So, instead of looking at single-family homes, they looked for a two-family house.

They found one that needed substantial repairs. But, they also could see that the house would make a terrific single-family home, when they could afford to do the renovation and live without the additional rental income.

After six years, and several substantial increases in their annual income due to job changes, Angela and Tom finally had the cash to do the renovation and live without the renter's monthly contribution to the mortgage. Best of all, the neighborhood had appreciated tremendously in value. By renovating their home to just above the neighborhood standard, they were able to significantly increase its value. Today, the house is a showpiece, and Angela and Tom are busy squirreling money away for their young daughter's college education.

But It Doesn't Always Work Out This Well

There are also disadvantages to fixing up a home. Renovation and decorating create mess and chaos; understand ahead of time that during the period of the renovation (and for some time thereafter), your house will never be clean. Construction and renovation almost *always*

take more time (and cost more) than is estimated. And more than one relationship has been known to end during the turmoil and tumult of construction.

When you look at a home that needs renovation or a gut job (stripping a house down to its structural bones or guts), you need to understand exactly how much work would be required and acquire a realistic ballpark estimate of how much that work will cost.

20/20

hindsight

Unless your broker is also a contractor, his or her estimate of renovation costs will likely be dead wrong. Do not rely on his or her estimate. Instead, hire a contractor or architect to tour the home with you before you make an offer. A contractor's or architect's ballpark estimate of renovation and construction costs will be close enough for you to decide how much you want to pay for the home. Just remember, when renovating, expect the unexpected, and add 10 to 15 percent to your expert's ballpark estimate. Renovation almost always costs more, and takes more time, than you think it will. One contractor's best guess: Double the estimated time and add 25 percent to the predicted bottom line, and you won't be sorry.

If you're in a neighborhood where renovated homes sell for $175,000, and you see a house that requires a new kitchen, new electrical wiring, repainting, refinishing of the floors, and three new windows to make it livable, you must estimate the cost of renovation and subtract that amount from the list price. If the house is listed for $175,000 and you figure the renovation will cost $30,000, then the effective list price of that house for you should be $145,000. And, depending on whether the market is fast or slow (i.e., whether it's a buyer's or a seller's market), you might offer something in the high $120,000 range. If, however, every house in the neighborhood needs similar renovations, then $175,000 might be an appropriate price for the property.

Another problem with renovation is that buyers may think they can buy a cheap house and create the house of their dreams. Sometimes that strategy works, but when it doesn't, watch out. When the time comes to sell the house (in five to seven years), you may find you have a white elephant: a house whose value far outstrips the other homes in the neighborhood.

This is called *overimproving* your home. Don't overimprove your home to the point where you'll never be able to get your money out of it. Try to avoid a situation of trying to sell a $400,000 house in a $100,000 neighborhood.

Daniel's Story

Daniel bought a house that needed a new kitchen. He loves to cook, so he put an $18,000 kitchen into a $160,000 house, and planned to do other repair and renovation work. One day, his broker stopped by to say hello and to look at his construction work. After admiring his beautiful new kitchen, the broker cautioned Daniel not to spend so much money that he would want to ask more than $250,000 for the house.

"The neighborhood won't support a house that's worth more than that. I'll have trouble selling it," the broker told Daniel. He hasn't over-improved his house yet, but he must be careful where he spends his renovation dollars—or plan to stay in the house a few extra years until neighborhood values catch up.

Sally and Andy's Story

Sally and Andy make a great living. Together, they earn nearly $550,000 per year. They had owned two previous homes when they decided to buy a 4,000-square-foot condominium in a nice building. They paid $600,000 for the condo and spent another $700,000 completely gutting the place. They created a fancy one-bedroom apartment. The den also functioned as a guest bedroom, and the kitchen was a gourmet cook's delight.

And then one day, at age 48, Sally got pregnant. Realizing that their home wouldn't work for a baby and a nanny, they decided to sell. They put the condo on the market for nearly $1 million, even though no units in the building had ever sold for nearly that much. Had they sold for that price, they would have lost about $300,000 in renovation costs, not to mention another $60,000 in broker's commission.

But the condo didn't sell. And, as we went to press, it still hadn't, even after they lowered the price by another $100,000.

first time
buyer tip

If you're thinking about buying a home that needs renovation, be careful to consider the prices that other renovated homes in your neighborhood are selling for in the marketplace.

2

How Do I Look for a Home?

HOW DO I FIND THE HOME OF MY DREAMS?

QUESTION
8

There are two ways to find the right home: You can work with a real estate broker or you can do it yourself. Most of this book is slanted toward buyers who work with real estate agents or brokers, but let's spend a few minutes examining how you can find a home on your own—and why you might choose to do it that way.

FSBOs

If a seller chooses to sell his or her home without the assistance of a real estate agent or broker, the house is "for sale by owner." You might also see the acronym *FSBO*, which is pronounced "fizz-bo." Homeowners choose to sell their homes themselves for two reasons: (1) they think they can handle all the details, and (2) they won't have to pay a commission to the seller broker.

How many homes are sold as FSBOs? No one really knows. The best studies seem to suggest that anywhere from 15 to 35 percent of homeowners choose to sell without a broker. The National Association of Realtors (NAR) puts the number closer to the 15 percent range, but other industry observers suggest that the true number of FSBOs is quite a bit higher. Some experts suggest that as the Internet matures, the number of FSBOs will naturally increase. (I'll talk more about this in Question 9.)

You'll find FSBOs listed in your local newspaper's real estate classified advertisements under "Houses for Sale." You might also find them listed in alternative newspapers, weekly or monthly neighborhood newspapers, and local magazines. Since 1996, the Internet has exploded with literally thousands of real estate-related web sites. One bunch, dedicated solely to FSBOs, includes Owners (owners.com), the first web site to specialize in homes sold by homeowners. Typically, you can search these sites by location, price, size, and other amenities.

One of the best ways to find a FSBO is to walk around the neighborhoods you've targeted as being acceptable. FSBO homes usually have a sign posted outside, letting prospective buyers know they are for sale.

If you decide you want to tour the inside of a FSBO, simply call the telephone number in the advertisement or on the sign, and make an appointment. The homeowner will then give you a tour of his or her home. This can be awkward; you should be looking for every fault and every reason *not* to buy the home. And yet, you don't want to insult the homeowner, just in case you *do* want to buy the home. Internet listings are helpful here because many web sites allow you to see photos of a home's exterior and interior. As the Internet becomes more developed and technology becomes cheaper, you'll soon be able to download video and audio "tours" of a prospective home.

Going It Alone

Why would you want to look for a home yourself? Frankly, I don't think you should. As a home buyer, you're in the enviable position of having *buyer brokerage* available (the agent owes his or her fiduciary duty to you, not to the seller; see Question 13 for more details), without having to pay for it out of pocket. (The seller still pays the commission.) Why wouldn't you want to have a smart person, who supposedly knows the area and the housing stock, take you around and share a career's worth of knowledge?

The advantage of having a broker seems obvious; yet, I hear more and more stories every day about buyers who are going it alone. Some buyers feel they'll get a better deal from a seller who does not have to pay a commission to a broker. These buyers believe the seller will negotiate down to at least the 6 or 7 percent that would have been paid in commission. This, of course, rarely happens. The way the deal usually plays out is: The seller has overpriced his or her home to begin with, but the buyer doesn't know that because he or she isn't aware of how much homes actually sell for in the neighborhood. All sellers, but particularly FSBOs, tend to be greedy. They're hoping to *save* the 6 or 7 percent, not share it with you, the home buyer. So when you start the negotiations, they may come down 6 or 7 percent, but because they've started out with such a high price, you're still paying more than you should, and you're not really reaping the benefit of the commission savings.

Other buyers like FSBOs because they make them feel as if they are seeing everything that's out there on the market. They aren't. The majority of homes for sale are listed with brokers in a computerized system called a *Multiple Listing Service* (MLS). Access to the MLS used to be restricted to member brokers and their clients. In the days before the Internet, access to the MLS data was so tightly guarded that brokers weren't even allowed to give listing books to their clients to peruse. (Updated telephone-book-size listing books were printed every other week, to include the new listings.) Today, you can find almost all listing information on-line at any number of web sites, including the web site of the National Association of Realtors (realtor.com), Microsoft's HomeAdvisor (homeadvisor.com), HomeShark (homeshark.com), and Yahoo! (yahoo.com), and on brokers' individual sites, which may be listed at the International Real Estate Digest (ired.com).

If you're going to purchase a home that's a FSBO, be sure to hire a good real estate attorney to help you draw up the contract. Even if you live in a state like California, where attorneys typically aren't used, you'll need an attorney because you'll want someone to enforce the disclosures the seller is required to make to you, the buyer. Sellers often do not realize that these disclosures must be delivered at certain times before the deal on the home closes. Also, be sure to hire a professional home inspector to thoroughly scrutinize the home before the closing is scheduled.

New Construction

Many home buyers shop for new construction by themselves. Developers, who have already set aside the amount they must pay as commission to a broker who brings a buyer to the development, love it when a consumer comes without representation. (They generally save the money they would have paid to the buyer broker.) The developer's salespeople love it when someone comes without representation, because they typically get a higher commission or a bonus.

As a buyer, however, you'll find it easier and less time-consuming to go with a buyer broker (or agent) to see a bunch of new construction developments. Developers will tell you that you don't need a broker—but they'll pay the commission should you choose to use one. Here's an important point: *If you don't bring a broker with you to the model, and if you don't protect your broker by signing in under his or her name, you may not be allowed to bring in that broker later. Effectively, you will have no representation in your deal.*

Once in a while, a developer will lower the cost of the new construction by the amount that would have been paid in brokerage commission fees. Mostly, though, this doesn't happen. More likely, extra upgrades will be offered free or at a reduced cost. The truth is, a good broker may be able to extract the same concessions or even more. That's what negotiation is all about.

Again, be sure you have a good real estate attorney who can eyeball your new construction contract. (The standard forms typically favor the builder and give the buyer few, if any, rights or recourse.)

Although it isn't common to hire an inspector for new construction, it's an excellent idea to have someone knowledgeable look in during the four crucial stages of building: (1) after the foundation is poured; (2) after the framing is up; (3) after the house is wired and the plumbing is installed; and (4) just before the walls are closed in. To stay on top of the builder, you'll need someone who can point out mistakes or shoddy workmanship while the home is still under construction and the errors can be remedied. You'll also want to do a final walk-through before closing, and make sure you have a complete *punch list* (your list of items that still need to be finished before the house is completed).

Using a Broker

If you decide you don't want to go alone to look for a place to buy, your other option is to use a broker. Brokers come in all different shapes, sizes, and personalities. The benefits of using a good real estate agent or broker can be significant:

1. **Eyes and Ears.** A good broker is supposed to act as your eyes and ears: prescreening homes on the market, finding out why a home is for sale, and selecting the homes he or she thinks might be right for you.

2. **Less Legwork.** A good broker is supposed to do at least some of the necessary legwork, which means walking through the available homes and eliminating those that won't meet your needs and wants, or your standards.

3. **Guide You.** A good broker will make your appointments for you, chauffeur you around from showing to showing, help you understand the good and bad features of a house, provide you with enough information to create an offer, and then present that offer to the seller and seller broker.

4. **Educate You.** A good broker will educate you about the home-buying process and the local real estate market. He or she should be able to point out the good and the bad, so you can make an informed decision.

Remember, brokers are only as good as you let them be. If you choose to use a broker or agent, you'll have to learn the differences among conventional, buyer, and discount brokers. You'll also have to learn how much to tell your broker, and when complete honesty may not be entirely appropriate (see Question 17).

Everyone comes with "baggage"—a personal collection of aches, pains, and problems. And the older we are, the more baggage we seem to tote around. A home is no different. The older a home is, the more likely that it will have problems, quirks, oddities, and features that seem to make it less than perfect. I'll talk about this more as we move through the home-buying process, but remember this: Buying a home is the American dream, but the reality of the house you choose is what you have to live with.

By tapping into the local MLS, brokers can pull up all kinds of information, including:

- A list of all homes available in your price range or in your desired location.
- The homes' amenities, square footage, most recent tax bill, and number and size of bedrooms and bathrooms.
- How long a particular home has been listed for sale.
- The original price and any later price reduction.
- The home's address and the listing broker's telephone number.
- A photo of the exterior and possibly some of the interior of the home.
- Other pertinent and interesting facts and figures, such as the lot size, the way the house faces, and the listing broker's description.

HOW CAN I FIND A HOME ON THE INTERNET?

Just before the first edition of this book went to press at the end of 1993, I decided to get an e-mail address. Although the World Wide Web was in its infancy (America Online perhaps had 2 or 3 million members—if only I'd bought the stock at that time!), it seemed to me that e-mail would deliver communications a lot faster than the U.S. Postal Service, which perennially seems to have problems getting the mail delivered on time. Also, if e-mail proved easier and faster to send, perhaps more readers would feel comfortable writing to me and asking their own questions.

A few days before the first edition's final press date, I hooked up to America Online and put my e-mail address in the book's preface. I was fortunate in that my e-mail address of choice—my name—was available. (Then again, how many Ilyce Glinks do you know?) In the first year, far more letters came to my post office box (P.O. Box 366, Glencoe, Illinois, 60022) than to my e-mail address (IlyceGlink@aol.com). But, starting in 1995, the amount of e-mail dwarfed the so-called "snail mail" by about 10 to 1. Today, it's about 20 or even 30 to 1. In 1998, I set up my own web site (ThinkGlink.com) as a place for readers to get more information and updates to the books I've written. And the traffic to the site continues to grow.

The use of the Internet as a tool for personal communications, however, has been dwarfed by the incredible speed which with the business community, including the world of real estate, has taken to the World Wide Web. As in other industries, the Internet is forcing profound changes to the core of the real estate industry. These changes are important because they directly affect how you will buy and finance your home.

Until, say, 1996, the way people bought homes had been fairly static for centuries. All of the key information—which homes were listed for sale and how much they cost—resided with a few licensed real estate agents and brokers, who zealously (some might say jealously) guarded it. Access to the information was severely limited. How limited? As late as the late 1980s, books of house listings were printed every other week. Agents who were members of the local MLS (there were typically a dozen or more in a major metropolitan area) would have a copy, and prospective buyers could make an appointment with the agent to see the current listing book. If the agent really liked the client, an old copy of a listing book might be passed along under cover.

You wanted to buy a house? You either worked with a licensed agent or you bought directly from the owner.

In the mid-1990s, computers and the Internet began to open up new opportunities to companies that wanted to move in and disseminate real estate information on a larger scale. The formerly numerous MLSs began to merge into one or two metropolitan units, which cooperated fully with each other and gave all licensed agents who were members (no matter where they were located) access to the data. Now, city brokers could sell houses in the suburbs and vice versa.

Internet companies put everything up on the Web, free to anyone who had a computer and modem. After a few expensive false starts, data about homes that were for sale started getting posted on the Internet for anyone to see. Suddenly, by going to Yahoo! or Realtor .com, consumers could tap into as many as 1.2 million listings and find out the listing price, the number of bedrooms and bathrooms, how much the seller paid in taxes, and all sorts of previously private information.

Both the industry consolidation and the Internet advances were met with a great deal of skepticism and cynicism by both agents and brokers, as well as by real estate reporters who covered the industry.

The key to making any real estate broker happy about the dissemination of the listing data was to put in his or her e-mail address as the contact name for more information about the property—and, *not* to put FSBO properties on the same sites that carry Realtor® listings.

The dissemination of listing data is fine, except that it sets up one of the biggest problems for consumers shopping for a home on the Internet: *If you contact the listing broker for more information about a particular listing and you are either not represented or you do not inform the listing broker at the time of contact that you are represented, there is a very real chance that you will end up in a dual agency situation: The listing broker would not owe his or her loyalty to you or to the seller. You'd be spending the largest amount of money you've ever spent on anything, and no one would be guiding you along the way.* If you don't end up with dual agency, you'll be working with a seller agent, who owes you nothing.

Which brings us to today and to the tens of thousands of real estate-related sites that exist on the Internet.

The Best and the Worst of the Internet

As with any information system, there are some good things and some bad things about using the Internet as a way to shop for a home or a mortgage loan.

The Good News

The Internet is a good place to:

1. **Identify potential cities or neighborhoods.** Mapping sites (like geocities.com) allow you to look at the geographical shape of an area and make selections based on distance to work, to school, or to your house of worship.

2. **Learn more about a particular city or neighborhood.** Many cities have their own sites, which discuss everything from sports and recreational opportunities to cultural offerings, shopping, and restaurants. Various companies—a local

real estate company, for example—may also put neighborhood information up on the Web.

3. **Choose a school district.** Various sites (such as school-match.com) offer links to school ratings programs that rank schools based on an independent evaluation. They also can assist you in finding the right program to meet your children's needs.

4. **Get a taste of what's on the market.** You'll be able to see some, even many, of the homes that are for sale in a given marketplace. Many of the sites offer color photos, 360-degree photos, and video of the interior and exterior of the homes.

5. **Check out the demographics and statistics that define a neighborhood.** Many sites, including Microsoft's HomeAdvisor (homeadvisor.com), offer information on the local population and crime rate in a particular neighboorhood.

6. **Shop around for a home loan.** You can apply on-line to an individual mortgage broker (homeowners.com), a national lender (countrywide.com or norwest.com), or an Internet company that offers a slew of the top lenders from which to choose, including QuickenMortgage (quickenmortgage.com), HomeAdvisor (homeadvisor.com), E-loan (eloan.com), or RealEstate.com (realestate.com).

The Bad News

Unfortunately, the Internet:

1. **Doesn't offer information on every home that's for sale in every neighborhood.** If you rely solely on the Internet when you shop for a home, you're probably missing some, if not a lot, of homes.

2. **Might be out of date.** Although some sites claim to update their information daily, if not several times during the day, the truth is, they can't update anything unless the information has been sent to them from the individual brokerage firms. In some cases, that happens frequently (daily). In other cases, it might happen weekly or even monthly. In a hot sellers' market, like the one we experienced during the latter half of the 1990s, when homes sold in a matter of days (or minutes), keeping listings up to date is tough, if not impossible.

3. **Will steer you toward the seller broker for more information.** The seller broker knows what's going on, but you don't want to end up in a dual agency situation—which might happen if you e-mail a seller broker for more information about a particular listing and you don't mention that you're already represented by a buyer agent. Or you could wind up with no representation at all, if the seller agent continues working only for the seller.

4. **Isn't like walking around a neighborhood.** Getting to know a city or neighborhood through an Internet site is a good idea, but it isn't even close to going to the area in person and experiencing it as a would-be resident. You may like a *house* on the Internet but be horrified by the *neighborhood* once you get there. Until you visit and see for yourself, you'll never really know.

5. **Can't provide you with an electronic closing.** You can shop for a home and a loan on-line, but you'll eventually have to sign real papers and go through a real closing. With any luck, you've actually gone to see the home at least once or twice, and you've followed a home inspector through a general house inspection. As for a true electronic closing, we might get there one day, or we might not.

6. **Can overwhelm you with information.** What the Internet does best is provide you with information so you can make an informed decision on your own. And, you can have access to that information at any time of the day or night. Want to apply for a loan at 3:00 A.M.? No problem. On the other hand, with 30,000+ (some say up to 100,000) real estate-related web sites to peruse, you can get easily overwhelmed if you don't know where to go and what to look for.

The truth is, most of the thousands of real estate web sites are a waste of time. Either the information is duplicated on larger web sites, or the supposedly objective information is provided by someone who wants your business.

Getting Started

By the time you've decided to buy a house, you'll be ready to go full speed ahead. Even the fastest agent won't be quick enough, once you've made the mental commitment to becoming a home buyer. You'll probably want to dive in and help find the perfect home. If you sit back and wait, you'll likely end up frustrated. Take the lead, and assist your broker, but be ready to sit back and listen when he or she has information to share.

When starting your home search, your first stop should be the World Wide Web. Start by searching through the major on-line listing services, such as Realtor.com, HomeAdvisor.com, and iOwn .com. If you don't have access to a computer at home or at work, check out your local library. Most libraries now offer free access to the Internet. You can also access the Internet through on-line cafés, where, for a small hourly fee, you can use their equipment to tap into the Web. In Cambridge, Massachusetts, in the shadow of Harvard University, housing activist Bill Wendel runs Real Estate Café, where you can tap into not only the Internet but Bill's expertise as well (realestatecafe.com).

Each of the national chains, including Century 21 (century21 .com, or keyword Century21 if you're on America Online), Coldwell Banker (coldwellbanker.com), and RE/MAX (remax.com), offers loads of different information, not only about its own national base of listings, but also about the various cities and towns in which it is located. Individual offices sometimes have their own sites that contain local listings. You can get the web site address either by looking at advertisements in your local paper's weekend real estate section, or by calling the office directly. You can also go on-line to the International Real Estate Digest (Ired.com). This site lists many different real estate-related web sites, and often reviews them.

As I discussed earlier, listings on the Web are only as good as the people who input the information and then load it up to the database. Often, the listings are old or sold. By the time you log on, they're gone. Also, and I'll talk about this more in the next couple

No matter how much you think you love a house you found on-line, don't make an offer until you've actually stepped through its portals in person. If you must make an offer, sight unseen, protect yourself by including the regular home inspection, financing, and attorney approval (if applicable in your state) contingencies, in order to protect yourself.

53

of questions, if you contact a listing broker by e-mail and ask for more information on a particular house, you may end up in a *dual agency* situation: The listing broker also becomes your buyer broker. The bottom line is, unfortunately, you'll have no independent representation. (See Question 14 for more details on dual agency.)

The Internet has loads of mortgage information as well. See Question 58 for more information on how to shop and apply for a loan on-line.

QUESTION 10

WHAT IS THE DIFFERENCE BETWEEN A REAL ESTATE AGENT AND A REAL ESTATE BROKER? WHAT IS A REALTOR®?

Real estate professionals go by a few different names, although the distinction shouldn't matter much to you as a first-time buyer. The only caveat here is: Make certain the broker or agent you choose to work with is a licensed real estate professional. All real estate brokers and sales agents are licensed and regulated by each state. Most states have laws that require brokers and agents to post their licenses in a visible place. If you're not certain your agent is licensed, simply ask to see the license. Or, you can call the state agency that regulates real estate agents and brokers in your state and verify that the person is licensed. (See page 382 in the Appendix for a list of regulating agencies in each state.)

What's the difference between a real estate agent and a real estate broker? To the average home buyer or seller, the difference isn't much. To become a real estate agent, an individual must complete the required number of hours of classes and pass the agent's exam. To become a broker, the agent must then take additional classes, have a specified amount of experience in the field (usually a year), and pass another exam. Both agents and brokers are typically required to take a certain number of hours of continuing education courses, and they may also take additional courses to garner a few extra letters after their name.

Having a real estate broker's license confers certain privileges, including the right to open, run, and own a real estate office, and to work independently without an office. A real estate agent must work for a broker, who is responsible for that agent's actions.

Is it better to work with a broker instead of a sales agent? Not necessarily. Although it would seem that a broker may have more experience or be more knowledgeable than an agent, that is not always the case. Plenty of excellent sales agents have chosen not to become brokers because they have no intention of ever running their own office. The experience and knowledge of an agent who has been working in an area for fifteen years will far surpass that of a brand new broker. Find the most experienced professional who can work with you, regardless of whether he or she is an agent or broker.

Realtors® vs. Non-Realtors

What is the difference between a broker who is a Realtor and a broker who is not? A Realtor is a broker or agent who belongs to the National Association of Realtors (NAR) and subscribes to that organization's code of ethics and conduct. There are around 2 million real estate agents and brokers in the United States, of which around 700,000 belong to the NAR.

Is it better to work with a Realtor than a broker or agent who is not a Realtor? Not necessarily. As discussed in the next few questions, you should look for the best, most knowledgeable, and most reliable broker or agent. Don't worry about titles, designations, and how many letters follow his or her name.

> Agents and brokers can assist you equally well in the purchase of property. In fact, an agent with 15 years' experience might be able to better help you than a newer broker, who has far less experience and knowledge of the area.

first time buyer tip

HOW DO I CHOOSE THE RIGHT BROKER?

QUESTION
11

Finding a broker or agent who meets your needs and is compatible with your personality can be tougher than it sounds. Buyers who have the worst experiences are often those who just walk into or call a neighborhood shop and ask for anyone at random. That is *not* how you find a good agent or broker. It might, however, give you a huge headache.

Connie is director of career development and advertising for a real estate firm located in Overland Park, Kansas. She has her broker's license and has sold real estate for more than 14 years. Connie believes every buyer, but especially a first-timer, should carefully interview several agents and brokers. Here are some of her recommendations: "Have them describe to you how they go about assisting a buyer. Try to get a feel for the agents' philosophy on working with buyers. Try to get a feel for their background and experience level. And be sure to ask them for a resume. If you're thinking about letting someone represent you in the transaction, I think it's reasonable to expect to see a copy of their resume."

Connie says she'd be leery of any agent who lets you walk into his or her office and then immediately bundles you into his or her car and shows you homes. The agents need to interview *you*, she says. "And first-time buyers generally need an education on the purchase process and an understanding of what their options are in the transaction."

Although Connie recommends working with a heavily experienced agent (why should you be a guinea pig?), she says brand-new agents sometimes offer excellent service. "That depends on their training and support. It can be a good situation. But more often than not, the more experienced the agents, the more transactions they handle in a year, the more situations they're confronted with, the more insight into the closing process they will have."

Making a Good Match

In addition to looking for an experienced agent, try to find one who suits your personality. If you're an early bird, don't choose someone who is habitually late. If you're allergic to smoking, don't choose a smoker. If you're extremely organized, don't choose a broker who is constantly losing his or her keys. Over time, or on long days of multiple showings, these personality quirks will make you crazy.

It's also important to find someone who won't push you into making a decision before you're ready. You want a broker who will tell you all the facts and will help you compare the differences between properties; you don't want someone who will scare you or pressure you into purchasing a home. Unfortunately, some brokers and agents do pressure buyers to buy. If that happens, you must be tough enough to back away from that pressure and find yourself a new agent. You can also talk with the agent's managing broker about the situation. One of the managing broker's jobs is to smooth out the bumps between agents and brokers and their clients.

Working with a real estate agent is a little like a short-term marriage. Even in the best of circumstances, the pressure will mount and you may not always like what's happening, or how a situation is being handled. You'll be in close proximity for an undetermined amount of time—at least three to six months from start to closing—so it's a good idea to find someone with whom you're compatible.

How do you find a good broker or agent? As in choosing a doctor or an attorney, most people are referred to a broker by friends or a family member—perhaps someone who recently bought or sold a home and had a good experience (make sure it was a *good* experience). If you're moving across state lines and don't know anyone in your hometown-to-be, you may want to contact a relocation company to assist you with the sale of your existing home (if you already own a home) and the purchase of your new home. If your company is moving you, the human resources department may have an ongoing relationship with a broker or brokerage firm in your new location. Although it's certainly wise to interview a broker who is referred by someone you know, also interview several other agents who frequently work in the area you are considering. Aunt Jeanne's suburban agent may not be the most effective person to help you find a downtown loft.

Don't let your mother, father, sibling, or in-laws foist someone on you or try to pressure you into using a family member or friend. If one of your relatives is a real estate agent, by all means sit down and interview that individual. But make sure that's only one of a small handful of agents that you interview before you hire someone. I typically recommend talking to three agents to start, and adding a fourth if you don't feel as though you've found the right person.

Here are a few other suggestions:

1. Open your local newspaper to the real estate section and see who runs the biggest ads, week in and week out.
2. If you ask friends, neighbors, or relatives for referrals, make sure they had a great experience with the agent they used. You

don't want to use someone who won't deliver a good home-buying experience.

3. Visit open houses and spend some time talking to the real estate agents about homes in the neighborhoods. Ask these listing brokers to define what makes a great buyer agent. Ask them who, in addition to themselves, would they want their own children to use.

4. Call your local board of Realtors and ask for the names of agents who sold the most property last year.

Things You Can Do

Despite the horror stories you may have heard, the vast majority of first-time buyers have good, if not great, experiences with their agents. But to ensure you're working with the right person, take on the responsibility of interviewing several agents before you make your final selection. If you simply take a friend's or relative's suggestion, you may find yourself working with the wrong broker, looking in the wrong neighborhoods, and touring homes that are too expensive.

Sixteen Questions You Should Ask Real Estate Agents Before You Hire One

Ask these questions each time you interview a real estate agent:

1. How many years have you been in the real estate business?

2. How many years have you been with this company?

3. How many residential real estate transactions did you complete in each of the past two years?

4. What was the dollar volume of your transactions in each of the past two years?

5. What percentage of your business is with home buyers? What percentage of your home-buyer business is with first-time buyers?

6. How old are your clients, on average? Do they have children?

7. What was the price range of the homes you helped people buy and sell last year?

8. What would you say was the average price of the homes you helped your clients buy and sell?

9. Are you an exclusive buyer broker? Do you ask home buyers to sign an exclusivity contract? Do you charge an up-front fee that is later applied to the commission?

10. What are the primary neighborhoods or communities in which you work?

11. How familiar are you with the schools, crime statistics, and demographics of the various neighborhoods? (Hint: Brokers are forbidden to "steer" you to one neighborhood or another for any reason. For the same reason, they may choose to tell you where to go to get information on crime or schools, but opt not to tell you themselves.)

12. What style of home do you most frequently work with? (If you're looking for a four-family apartment building and the broker is more familiar with single-family houses, it might not be a good fit.)

13. Are you a smoker or a nonsmoker? (If this is important to you.)

14. How many home buyers or sellers do you work with at a given time? (You're trying to find out how much time you'll get from the agent.)

15. How frequently will I hear from you? How do I reach you? Can I e-mail you? Or phone you at home? Are you planning any extended vacations in the next six months?

16. Do you work with an assistant? Will I be working with the assistant or with you?

You can find out a lot about agents just by the way they answer these questions. If they bristle and seem reluctant to share information with you, that may be a sign of things to come. If they're open and friendly, and you develop a connection on the phone, you may have found someone with whom you'll enjoy working.

Going It Alone

As I've said before, I don't see *any* benefit to purchasing a home without help from a buyer broker. Although more and more buyers tell me they are *shopping* on their own, if they purchase something that's listed on the local MLS, they are not necessarily *buying* on their own. They are buying with the assistance of a dual agent, also known as a *transactional agent*, a *facilitator*, or a *nonagent*, depending on which state you live in, or a seller agent.

What does that mean? They are essentially making the largest single purchase of their life without any representation at all. (For more information on dual agents, transactional agents, facilitators, and nonagents, see Question 14.)

WHAT IS A SELLER (OR CONVENTIONAL) BROKER? WHAT ARE HIS OR HER RESPONSIBILITIES TO ME, THE BUYER?

First things first: There is a wide gulf between a seller broker (also known as a conventional broker) and a buyer broker. A buyer broker (or an exclusive buyer broker) represents the interests of the buyer (see Question 13, on page 64). A seller broker represents the interests of the seller.

It seems obvious, but there's a lot of crossover that makes it confusing.

In theory, the broker works for the person who pays his or her commission. For a seller broker, the seller pays the commission. For a buyer broker, the buyer is responsible for paying the commission.

But wait! Didn't I just say that even when you use a buyer agent, the seller will pay the commission? Yep. And, in practice, that's generally how it works. In many states, any broker who works with a buyer, and is not a dual agent, automatically becomes a buyer broker—even if the commission is paid by the seller. But if, for some reason, the seller doesn't pay the commission, the buyer would then be responsible for paying it.

Since the first edition of this book was published, buyer brokerage has gone mainstream. In the early 1990s, there were more conventional brokers than buyer brokers. Today, buyer brokerage has been accepted by the National Association of Realtors (NAR) and written into state statutes. We'll talk more about this in Question 13.

When a seller or conventional broker brings a buyer to a deal, the broker is also called the *subagent*. Even though a subagent will take you, the buyer, around to see various houses, and will appear to work in your best interests, your broker is still a seller broker. He or she has a fiduciary responsibility to the seller, rather than to you, the buyer. A seller broker is required by law to represent the seller's best interest, not the buyer's. These distinctions have caused a tremendous amount of confusion for buyers, who quite naturally assume that the person taking them around, showing them houses, telling them the inside scoop, and buying them coffee and dinner, works for them.

Let's be clear on one point: If you haven't hired a buyer broker and signed an exclusivity contract with him or her, and if you're not living in a state that mandates buyer brokerage, you're most likely working with a seller or conventional broker.

In many states, subagency has been eliminated. In these states, if an agent is working for a buyer, he or she is a buyer agent. If the agent is working for the seller, he or she is a seller agent. That clears up some of the confusion. If the subagent (the person who brings the buyer to the table) or the buyer broker is also the listing broker, he or she is known as a dual agent.

Agency Disclosure

It's all so confusing—far more than it needs to be. To counteract some of the confusion, many states have adopted "agency disclosure" laws that require brokers to disclose to the buyer the person(s) they actually represent in a given deal. In some states, brokers and agents must make that disclosure in writing. If you live in a state that requires a written disclosure form, you might get something that looks like the form shown in Appendix III.

When you sign the form, you're saying that you understand who is working for you, and whether the agent is working for you or for the seller. *If you don't understand what the form says or what it means, don't sign it.*

Things a Seller's Agent Cannot Do for You

If you're a buyer working with a subagent, there are certain things a seller broker may not do, according to the law. Regulations vary slightly from state to state. In general, he or she:

1. **Cannot tell you what to offer for the property.** Because they work for the seller, subagents are supposed to help the seller get his or her list price. If you're in an extremely hot market, like the one during the latter half of the 1990s, you may pay list price or even above list price. In a soft market (one that favors the buyer), you'll probably pay less than list price, perhaps a lot less. Either way, how much you pay will put you in conflict with the obligation the seller broker has to the seller.

2. **Cannot tell you which home to buy if you are deciding between two choices.** A seller broker works for each seller and may work for multiple sellers. If a seller broker, for example, shows you five houses in a given day, he or she has technically worked for five sellers. That's confusing, but it boils down to this: If you like two homes, the seller broker actually works for two sellers simultaneously, and so should not help you choose one home over the other. (Can you see now why buyer brokerage is so much more appealing?)

3. **Cannot point out the defects of a home, unless they are material, hidden defects.** The seller broker cannot say anything or do anything that will influence you not to buy a property. Material hidden defects must be disclosed, however, because they are not visible to the naked eye. For more information on seller disclosure, see Question 44.

4. **May provide you with comparable data only upon request.** A seller broker must provide you with all the information you need to come up with a reasonable offer. So, ask your broker (buyer or seller) to provide you with a list of "comps" detailing how much other homes in the neighborhood, similar in size and amenities to the one you like, sold for in the past six months. Also ask the broker to provide you with a list of current similar listings and their list prices. It's important to know the difference between the asking and the selling prices of homes in the area. Finally, ask for the average number of list days. This will help you figure out whether you're in a fast market (seller's market) or a slow market (buyer's market).

Some seller brokers will give you all these things without your asking for them. It's understandable why they do it: They rely on referrals to make their business grow. If every client refers two buyers or sellers, the agent's or broker's client list pyramids. After a few

years, he or she could have a client list numbering in the hundreds.
Seller brokers work toward these goals:

- They *want* you to have a good experience when you buy a home.
- They *want* the whole process to be easy.
- They *want* you to like them.
- They *want* you to refer your friends to them.

Before you start believing that conventional brokers won't be able to help you buy a home as effectively as a buyer broker, let me reassure you: That is not always the case. For years, conventional brokers were the only game in town. They've helped millions of buyers successfully purchase homes. But if you have a choice, go with a buyer agent or broker.

Many seller brokers pride themselves on being full-service firms, and because they have every incentive to close the deal—after all, they get paid only at the closing—they should be delighted to provide you with the names of various mortgage brokers, inspectors, and attorneys. Ask for several recommendations for each service. In that way, you can properly interview some prospective attorneys or inspectors and choose the best person for the job. Be aware that many real estate companies now own mortgage firms. Undoubtedly, they'll give you the name of their in-house or affiliated lender, who may or may not give you a great deal. But you won't know that until you shop around and compare prices.

The various changes in state laws governing brokers who are subagents of the seller require that you be more aware of the shifting nature of the relationship. However, a good broker (whether a buyer or seller broker) will be responsive to your needs. That puts the onus on

Remember, you want to work with the very best broker you can. A seller broker may be a better choice for you than a buyer broker who doesn't really know the particular neighborhood that is of interest to you. But typically, any broker who works with a buyer is now considered a buyer agent, barring any dual agency.

63

you to be well informed about what you want and how you intend to get it.

QUESTION 13

WHAT IS A BUYER BROKER? WHAT IS AN EXCLUSIVE BUYER AGENT? SHOULD I USE ONE?

We've established that the broker works for the person who pays the commission. Traditionally, that's the seller. But, for an increasing number of buyers, the conventional broker's role poses a conflict of interest. The buyers ask: How can a broker have my best interest at heart when he or she is being paid by the seller? How can a broker help me find the best property at the best price when he or she is bound legally and financially to serve the seller's best interest?

If you find yourself having these qualms about traditional brokerage, you may want to consider buyer brokerage. Although buyer brokerage has been around for nearly 20 years, it only became popular in the latter half of the 1990s, when many states around the country changed their laws to designate buyer agency. Under the new laws, if you're a buyer and are working with a broker, that broker automatically becomes a buyer broker. If you're a seller, the broker functions as a seller broker.

But we're getting a little bit ahead of ourselves. A buyer agent (or broker) is ethically and legally bound to put the buyer's interests ahead of all else in a real estate transaction. The buyer agent owes his or her fiduciary duty to the buyer, not to the seller—*even if the seller will ultimately pay the agent's or broker's commission.*

The duties of a buyer broker are not at all dissimilar to the services of a nice seller broker. The buyer broker will hunt for homes that are appropriate for your needs and budget. He or she will help you negotiate every facet of the contract, striving to get you the best price and terms. Some buyer brokers will even help you find the best mortgage and the most favorable terms for homeowner's insurance. The buyer broker will help with any of the other niggling closing details and will show up at the closing to collect his or her check.

A buyer broker may want you to sign an *exclusivity agreement.* This agreement states that you will not work with any other buyer agents within a defined period of time. As with all real estate contracts, it is negotiable. The broker may want you to put down a fee of some sort (usually refundable at closing). Whether you pay it is up to you; however, I don't think it's necessary to pay a buyer agent or broker to prove that you're committed to working with him or her. Likewise, I would make sure that the exclusivity agreement includes a definite time limit and allows you to cancel the agreement if you decide not to purchase a home or you find someone else you'd rather work with.

There Are Buyer Agents and There Are Exclusive Buyer Agents

The most common form of buyer's agency is *designated agency*, which means the agent is a buyer agent when working with a home buyer and a seller agent when working with a seller.

But that means your buyer agent might also be a listing agent and may in fact have several homes currently listed for sale that may be right for you. The possible conflict of interest is, of course, that you'll be shown one of these listings and find yourself in a dual agency situation—the same agent is representing both sides in the same transaction. You can ask your buyer agent to assign another agent in his or her office to go through the offer/counter-offer process with you, but the switch may be distressing because (1) you've developed a strong attachment to your buyer agent, and (2) more importantly, you've probably told him or her some personal information about how much you can really spend on a house. If your buyer agent becomes a dual agent, can you trust him or her not to reveal your financial secrets to the seller? That kind of disclosure could really destroy your negotiating power.

> We all tell too much about ourselves to our buyer agents. It just happens because so much time is spent together. Don't lose any sleep if you've let slip some vital piece of financial information. But try not to talk, at any time, about exact numbers, just in case the quoted amount comes back to haunt you.

Another way around the potential dual agency conflict of interest is to hire *an exclusive buyer agent.* An exclusive buyer agent never takes listings and represents only buyers. In the mid-1990s, exclusive buyer agents were viewed with skepticism and scorn by the regular brokerage community. In Massachusetts, for example, there were even stories (which I was unable to verify directly) that exclusive buyer brokers were discriminated against when it came to setting up showings. One exclusive buyer agent claimed he had been assaulted by another real estate agent who was unhappy with his client's bid for a property. The agent physically attacked him!

Fortunately, stories like these are few and far between. Exclusive buyer agency has become much more accepted in recent years, although it remains far more popular on the east and west coasts than in the center or southern sections of the United States. The earlier fear that these agents are "extremists" looking to kill all the deals has dissipated. Best of all, where before you might have found only one or two exclusive buyer agents in an entire metropolitan area, more have joined the ranks so that clients have a larger choice of people with whom they can work.

If you're looking for an exclusive buyer agent (EBA), you might want to check out the National Association of Exclusive Buyer's Agents (naeba.com), a nonprofit organization dedicated to improving the image and numbers of EBAs around the country. The organization can recommend you to members, all of whom must abide by a tough code of ethics. Most EBAs will also be members of the National Association of Realtors (NAR), which didn't even recognize buyer's agency as a legitimate form of real estate agency until the early 1990s.

A Difference in Perception

If you're wondering how a buyer broker might treat you differently from a seller broker, you're not alone. If the seller broker breaks the law by providing you with insights and information about various sellers and their homes, and advises you about which house to bid on and how much to offer, then there may not be a great difference in service. (The seller broker could be liable to the seller for breaching his or her fiduciary duty to the seller. But that's not your concern.)

A buyer broker is completely on your side. He or she is bound by contract and the law to provide you with all of the information you need to buy your dream house at the lowest price possible and on the most favorable terms.

Sharon, a sales agent in west suburban Chicago, says: "When I'm working for the seller, my job is to bring in the best offer. When I'm

66

working as a buyer broker, I feel free to give that kind of advice as well as to suggest different pricing [strategies] my clients may offer."

Experts say buyers generally have trouble with two facets of buyer brokerage: (1) the exclusivity agreement and (2) the payment for services rendered. When a buyer opts for buyer brokerage, he or she is often asked to sign an exclusivity agreement. According to most of these documents, the buyer agrees to work only with the buyer broker for a stated length of time. If the buyer purchases a home within the exclusivity period, he or she will owe the broker a fee.

The arrangement sounds simple enough, but buyers, who are used to changing agents at will, sometimes find the idea of exclusivity disquieting. If you feel that a 90-day exclusivity period is too long, ask for a 30-day term that is renewable. A good buyer broker will understand your nervousness (you're not the first to feel this way) and should be happy to make you feel comfortable. Thirty days will be enough time for you to decide whether you like the buyer broker's service.

Payment of the buyer broker's fee is another issue that buyers struggle with—particularly first-time buyers, who are often short on cash. Be aware that the fee guarantees the buyer broker's loyalty. A buyer broker's fees can be paid as a flat payment, hourly, or as a percentage of the purchase price of the home. This fee is entirely negotiable, but 1 to 3 percent of the purchase price would not be unreasonable.

The Real World

In the real world, a buyer broker's compensation often ends up being paid by the seller. The seller agent agrees to split the commission with the buyer broker, just as the seller agent would agree to split the commission with a conventional broker. The fee issue might come into play if you end up buying a FSBO with the help of your buyer agent. But there, too, it usually gets worked out. Either the seller pays half of the commission (2½ or 3 percent) to the buyer agent, or the purchase price of the home is raised to cover the commission.

Other Issues and Concerns

Do buyer brokers ever pressure their clients to buy something if their exclusivity contract is about to expire? Most brokers say no, but first-time buyers Dawn and Bill don't agree. They had a nasty experience with a buyer broker who applied enormous pressure and even took the couple to court. (The judge threw the broker's case out of court and forced him to pay *both* sides' legal fees.) Some real estate attorneys confide that they've seen some agents present their clients with a choice of four houses and pressure them to purchase one—quickly. Again, reputable agents do not act in this way. Your job is to find a reputable agent.

There are many reasons for choosing to work with a buyer broker, but the most obvious one is hardly ever mentioned. Because the buyer broker is paid by the buyer, he or she is free to bring the buyer to any properties that are available, including FSBOs.

Mark's Story

Mark is an architect who purchases homes and small apartment buildings for rehabilitation and resale. Always on the lookout for a deal, he hired a couple of agents to look for these types of properties in different parts of town.

Mark has had some luck calling sellers directly, but he has directed his agents to pursue FSBO properties. He guarantees them their share of the commission when a deal goes through.

Recently, he closed on a FSBO property using a buyer broker. "The property wasn't listed in the multiple listing service. A conventional broker wouldn't have even found it," he said.

Is buyer brokerage the right choice for you? That depends on how comfortable you are with the concept of exclusivity and with being responsible for the broker's commission. When Mark buys a FSBO property, he makes sure the seller will pay half of the commission his broker is entitled to. If the seller balks, Mark adjusts his offer and pays the commission out of his own pocket.

More buyers, especially first-timers, are choosing buyer brokers because they like having someone represent them. Some companies that transfer their employees from one location to another, and pay their moving costs, ask the relocation company to give their employees a buyer broker option. Even some web sites, which originally gave only the listing broker as a contact, now suggest that you might want to contact your own buyer broker first.

As when making any selection, evaluate the options. Interview a buyer broker and (if it's an option in your state) a conventional broker, and then decide who will be able to help you the most.

WHAT IS A DUAL AGENT? WHAT IS A TRANSACTIONAL BROKER? WHAT IS A NON-AGENT?

QUESTION

14

Dual agency occurs when the same real estate broker or agent represents both sides in the same transaction. A dual agent is the single person who represents both the buyer and the seller in the purchase and sale of a single property.

The problem with dual agency is the inherent conflict of interest in having the same person represent two sides of a single deal. The buyer broker has a fiduciary relationship with the buyer and does everything in his or her power to help the buyer purchase a home for the best possible price and on the best possible terms. How can he or she then also act as a seller broker, trying to get the seller the most money possible? It's impossible for a single broker or agent to represent the best interests of opposing sides in a single transaction—no matter what anyone tries to tell you!

Another form of dual agency occurs when the seller broker and the buyer broker work for the same firm. Although not all states recognize this as dual agency, some do because it's possible that the seller agent and the buyer agent will share confidential information in some informal exchange that could be harmful to their client. The firewall separating buyer agents and seller agents can seem dangerously thin (or nonexistent) in some offices.

Because of the inherent conflicts of interest, the National Association of Realtors (NAR), a nonprofit association of some 700,000 agents and brokers, has tried to give new and more palatable names to dual agency.

Two new terms of choice include *transactional brokerage* and *non-agency*. If your buyer broker happens to bring you to one of his or her listings and you fall in love with it and want to make an offer, the buyer broker may cease to become your broker and may assume the role of a *transactional broker*. This means that the broker will help the transaction through to the close, without having a fiduciary duty to either the buyer or seller.

The problem with transactional brokerage is that the buyers and sellers lose and the broker wins. Neither the buyer nor the seller has a broker dedicated to guiding and advising him or her on the deal, but the seller pays the full commission, as if the seller and the buyer were receiving everything they bargained for from full-service brokers.

Non-agency, another name for transactional brokerage, is more honest. Again, the agent does not work for either the buyer or seller, but shuffles papers back and forth and helps the deal go through.

Is dual agency a bad thing? Sometimes, because the broker knows both sides really well, he or she can help smooth over a difficult situation and find the common ground that permits the deal to happen. In that case, dual agency is a good thing. But when the buyer and seller have developed a trusting, personal relationship with their agent, and then suddenly find themselves nonrepresented by an agent who is stuck in the middle, the lack of representation can cause real problems.

What should you do if you're presented with a dual agency situation? If you're the buyer, you can always request that your agent choose to represent either the seller or you. If the agent chooses the seller, ask the managing broker of the firm to assign another agent to you. You'll then have full representation in the construction and negotiation of your contract.

Whether you're working with a buyer agent or a conventional agent, you may run into an uncomfortable situation, either because there is dual agency or because the agent isn't giving you the kind of service you're expecting. If you've tried to speak to the agent about the situation but are still unsatisfied, you may want to talk to the managing broker of the firm. It's the managing broker's responsibility to make sure that all of the home buyers and sellers are happy with the service they're receiving. The managing broker can sit down with you and your agent and help to work out any problems there may be.

QUESTION 15

WHAT IS THE TYPICAL REAL ESTATE COMMISSION?

Although this is more a question for sellers, it's important for buyers to be aware of how much commission is actually being paid. By law,

there is no standard real estate commission. It's entirely negotiable, and real estate agents must tell you that. They might, however, give you a general range of commissions—say, 5 to 7 percent. More often than not, sellers will offer to pay around 6 percent of the final selling price of the property to their broker, who then gives half of the commission to the subagent who brought the buyer to the table.

(Today, around the country, most multiple listing services recognize buyer brokerage and usually pay half of the commission to the buyer agent.)

Even though the seller typically pays the commission, buyers should be aware of the commission rates and whether they face a buyer's or a seller's market in their area. If it's a seller's market—where the qualified buyers outnumber the homes for sale—the commission percentage might be somewhat below the rate typically acceptable for that area. If the commission is normally 6 percent, it might be 5.5 percent or less, because the demand is high for the seller's property and the seller broker doesn't have to work too hard to make the sale.

You might also see far more FSBOs in a seller's market. If there is a huge demand for property, a seller may (1) put up a web site featuring information about the home, (2) advertise in the local newspaper, and (3) put up a large "For Sale" sign on the front lawn. Savvy sellers will hope that they can get away with paying only half the usual commission to the buyer agent and pocketing the other half—the amount they'd normally pay to the seller agent.

If it's a buyer's market (sellers outnumber qualified buyers), the seller might offer more than the typical commission, to entice brokers to bring prospective buyers to tour the house. If the typical commission is 6 percent, the seller might offer 7 percent; of that amount, 4 percent would go to the agent who brought the buyer to the table. Although most agents won't try to sell you a piece of property just because it has an extra-high commission (or other bonuses) attached, they might bring you to see it.

WHAT IS A DISCOUNT BROKER?
WHEN SHOULD I USE ONE?

The idea that you can buy something for less than the announced price is extremely appealing in America. We have discount clothing stores, food stores, drug stores, and whole towns built up around

71

outlet malls. Is it surprising that the demand for discount real estate brokerage has continued to grow?

Here's the basic concept. The discount real estate broker gives you the sellers' names and the addresses of properties for sale, as listed in the local MLS, but you do all the legwork, look at every home that might possibly be right for you, work out your own mortgage, present your own contract, submit your own counteroffer, arrange for your own inspectors, and do your own walk-through. For your "sweat equity," the discount broker will give you a portion of the commission he or she receives.

Why should the discount broker receive anything if you're doing all the work? Good question. To begin with, the discount broker has access to the MLS, which lists all the properties for sale in the area. That's where you find out all the information about homes for sale, such as their size, price, and number of bedrooms and bathrooms. It's a very useful list to have, and access to all these details is strictly limited to member agents and brokers, and their clients. By sharing the commission with the discount broker, you're essentially buying access to the local MLS.

"But wait!" you say. "What about the Internet? Can't I get all the listings from a web site?"

Possibly. But the amount of information you'll receive generally isn't enough to take any action other than calling your own broker or the listing broker. You typically won't get an address (though, in a few years, competition may dictate that the address of the property must be posted), or specific information about the size of the lot and house, or the amount of last year's tax bill. As the listing information available on the Internet expands, it's possible that these details will become available. But right now, they're not there.

The Dollars and Cents of Discount Brokerage

Here's a look at how the dollars and cents of discount brokerage are calculated.

Discount brokerage firms give back up to 50 percent of their share of the commission at closing. On a $100,000 property, your share might be as much as $1,500, which might well pay the points for your mortgage or cover the cost of repainting the interior of the house after you move in. And although $1,500 may not seem like proper repayment for the effort involved, discount brokers say that some home buyers, particularly first-time buyers, need every nickel to buy a home and are willing to put in the necessary time and effort.

As we discussed earlier, real estate companies that work with the buyer typically receive about half of the commission the seller pays to his or her listing agent's company. If the commission is 6 percent of the final selling price, each side gets 3 percent. In conventional brokerage, the company then splits its 3 percent with the real estate agent, so each side gets 1.5 percent of the selling price.

(In some real estate companies, the split between the company and the agent is quite uneven. A top-producing agent may receive as much as 90 or even 95 percent of the commission received by his or her real estate firm.)

A discount broker splits his or her 3 percent commission with you, the buyer, minus any "extras"—and this is where you need to take care. A discount brokerage firm will put a price tag on *every service* it provides for you, including every telephone call or showing. Usually, a minimum number of showings is included in the deal, but if the broker shows you any additional properties, the fees for these pay-as-you-go services are deducted from your portion of the commission.

As an example, a discount brokerage firm in Chicago deducts between one and four percentage points from the commission refund for *each service* it performs. If a client asks the broker to place follow-up calls to the lender, the company reduces the refund by one percent for each call. If the total possible refund is $1,500, each phone call costs $15.

Sandra's Story

A first-time buyer, Sandra needed to put every penny she had into the purchase of her home. She saw an ad for a discount broker, made an inquiry call, and thought the arrangement sounded like a great deal.

Later, she told me she had been thinking that she'd just do some of the work and would receive about $2,000 back from the agent.

Things didn't turn out quite as she had planned. She faced a really tight seller's market. By the time the discount broker got around to setting up showings, the homes had sold. Sandra spend hundreds of hours scouring neighborhoods, real estate classified advertising, the Internet—anywhere she thought there might be an appropriate home for sale.

After a few short weeks, the discount broker informed her that she had used up her allotment of "free time" and would now be charged for everything the broker had to do, from phone calls to setting up appointments. She would even be charged for the ultimate negotiation of the contract.

"I'd given myself a thorough education of the marketplace, and for that I'm grateful," Sandra said later. "But I also realized the value of a full-service agent in a market that's so tight that you need to be in the inner circle of agents to have any chance at all of a successful bid."

Sandra fired the discount broker and hired a full-service broker who worked with the biggest company in town. Within a few weeks, she'd found a house and made a successful offer to purchase.

first time buyer tip

The general caveat for real estate services holds true here: Don't necessarily use the first broker you find. Try to locate more than one discount broker in your area, and then interview each one at length. Ask for a resume and references. Call those references and ask (1) how much time they put into their home purchase and (2) how much money they received back from the broker. Discount brokerage is best used by home buyers who have a clear idea of what they want, or who have been through the process before. But first-time buyers who are willing to put in a little "sweat equity" might be able to save a little money.

QUESTION 17

HOW MUCH SHOULD MY BROKER KNOW ABOUT THE AMOUNT I CAN AFFORD TO SPEND ON A HOME?

As we discussed earlier in this book, all conventional or seller brokers have a fiduciary responsibility to work on the seller's behalf. That means they must do everything they can (legally, morally, and ethically) to get the seller the highest price from the buyer. Buyer brokers have a written fiduciary responsibility to the buyer. They must do everything in their power to help the buyer purchase the home for the best price possible and on the best possible terms.

The reason for this separation of duties is clear. The seller pays the commission of both brokers—the one who lists and shows the property, and the subbroker who brings the ready, willing, and able buyer to the table.

But because most seller agents act as buyer agents when working with buyers, the whole notion of agency representation is a bit sticky. Play it safe. When it comes to your finances, play your cards extremely close to the vest. Remember this important general rule: **NEVER disclose to your agent the maximum amount you can afford to pay for a home.**

Why? Although any buyer broker is supposed to hold clients' intimate thoughts, feelings, and finances in confidence, your buyer broker may show you one of his or her listings and then become a dual agent. Or, your buyer broker might decide to represent the seller and another buyer broker will be assigned to handle your negotiation. Either way, because your former buyer broker now knows how much you can afford to spend, you may end up spending that amount, even if you didn't intend to.

Mark and Amy's Story

Mark and Amy recently discussed their search for the perfect home on Long Island. Like most first-time buyers, they had a general idea of the process, but only a vague concept of the fine lines the real estate world has drawn between broker–seller and broker–buyer relationships.

Mark and Amy found a beautiful house in a tiny, wooded community on Long Island, about an hour and a half from Manhattan. The house was listed at $350,000. They put in a low-ball offer for $260,000, but told "their" agent (who, in fact, was a seller broker and not a buyer broker) that they would go as high as $300,000.

That turned out to be a strategic mistake. By telling the broker they were willing to spend as much as $300,000 for the property, they were precluded from getting the property for less.

Why? "Their" broker was obligated not only to bring the seller the $260,000 offer, but also to inform the seller that Mark and Amy were prepared to go as high as $300,000. If the seller had responded favorably to the lower bid, he or she might have been persuaded to sell the property for less than $300,000. But once informed that the buyers would go as high as $300,000, the seller had no incentive to make a deal for less than that amount.

If, as required by law, Mark and Amy's broker actually told the seller that the couple was willing to bid as much as $300,000, then their effective bid would have been $300,000 rather than the $260,000 they actually offered.

As it happens, Mark and Amy didn't buy that particular house. After this episode, they changed to a buyer agent and simply didn't disclose any information about their finances.

Exclusive Buyer Brokers and Buyer Agents

As you can see, there is a danger in disclosing any information about your finances to either a conventional or a buyer agent. But what about an exclusive buyer agent (EBA)? An EBA will never represent a seller, so there is no potential conflict of interest, right? That's the general idea.

But it's possible that your EBA will represent other prospective home buyers who are interested in the same neighborhood, home type, and price point that you are. If you make an offer for a house and your EBA has another set of clients who are also interested in that property, you've disclosed how much you can pay for the house. The EBA might (I'm not saying "would," I'm saying "might") let it slip how much you can pay. The other couple may then have a slight advantage when they put together their offer.

Protecting Yourself

The best way to protect yourself is also the easiest way: *Don't disclose your financial situation or intent.* Never tell your broker the top price you'd be willing to pay for a piece of property. Simply reassure him or her that you've been preapproved for a loan and you're interested in looking at homes priced from, say, $200,000 to $250,000. Always assume that any financial information you convey to the broker might be transmitted (perhaps inadvertently) to the other side. If your agent or broker offers to assist you in getting a mortgage (or asks directly to see your financial statements), politely accept the names of a few lenders he or she does business with regularly, and then decline to go into specifics.

Although I hope nothing bad happens to you in your search for and purchase of a home, the best protection is to prepare for the worst.

For more information on figuring out how much you can spend on a home, see Question 26, on page 102.

Brokers often tell me that they can't represent a home buyer effectively if they don't know how much the buyer(s) can spend on a home. I'm not sure that's true. Some of the best agents I know simply like to be in complete control of the situation, and that includes knowing about their client's finances. But wanting to know and needing to know are separate issues. Just because you're asked how much you can afford to spend doesn't mean you have to give out a top number. Also, just because you've been told you can spend a certain amount doesn't mean you'll want to go that high. As long as you can truly afford to spend whatever range you give your agent (getting preapproved for a loan is a good way to go), then the agent needn't know anything else.

HOW DO I KNOW WHETHER MY BROKER IS DOING A GOOD JOB?

Whether you use a buyer broker or a conventional agent, his or her first point of business is to assist you in finding a property that's suitable and affordable.

A broker or agent is doing a good job if he or she listens closely to your wants and needs and asks you thoughtful follow-up questions that prompt further introspection and explanation. Whether the agent is doing a good job becomes more apparent once you start seeing some homes. Do the homes you're being shown match up with what you've told the broker you want and need? Do they match up with the priorities on your wish list and reality check?

If your broker is totally off the mark, you might then assume he or she hasn't been paying attention. Or, perhaps you didn't communicate effectively and honestly with him or her. If you aren't honest with yourself about what you want and need, it will be hard to discuss your wishes openly with someone else, and your broker may end up showing you the wrong kind of property. (See Question 1 for more details about a wish list and a reality check.)

Get Clued In

Here are some ways to know whether your broker is doing a good job:

1. Do you feel the broker is paying attention to you? Or, does his or her attention wane when you're speaking?

2. Does the broker ask you a lot of questions? Has he or she ever asked why you're looking for, say, a four-bedroom home or one that has an exercise studio? By asking, the broker may be able to better understand your motivations.

3. If you've worked with the broker several times and all the properties you've been shown were not even close matches to what you'd hoped you would see, you might have a problem.

4. If you're working with a buyer broker, and the seller suddenly seems to know your every move during the negotiation, your broker might be spilling the beans (perhaps unwittingly) and violating his or her fiduciary duty to you, the buyer.

5. If your broker never returns your phone calls, or takes several days to do so, that's a clear signal that he or she is not being conscientious.

If It Isn't Going Well, Take Action

If you decide that the agent assigned to you isn't doing a good job, don't hesitate to speak with the agent's managing broker. One of the most important functions of the managing broker is to make sure the customers of the firm are happy. If you're not satisfied with the response you receive from the managing broker, feel free to file a complaint with the agency that regulates real estate agents in your state. (See the Resources section, on page 378, for a list of all state real estate agencies and commissions.)

Unless you've signed a buyer brokerage exclusivity agreement, you have the option to find another agent or broker at any time. Most agents will allow you to break an exclusivity agreement if you're really unhappy; they don't want you to cut into their future business by discussing with referrals how unhappy you are. But if you can't break your exclusivity agreement, or the agent wants you to pay him or her an additional fee to break the agreement, simply wait out the expiration date of the contract. No one can make you work with someone you don't like.

HOW CAN I HELP IN THE SEARCH FOR A HOME IF I USE A BROKER?

Brokers across the country say that the most important thing you can do is *be honest* about what you really want in a home and what you actually need.

Most buyers think they're being honest, but they may not turn their vision into usable information for the broker. You can say you need a four-bedroom house, but if you don't tell the broker that you need the fourth bedroom for an office, you're not being as helpful as you could be. Why? A house may have other spaces for an office—such as a third-floor attic that offers privacy—but they may not meet the official definition of "bedroom."

After honesty, brokers ask that buyers be flexible with their time and responsive to their calls. If a broker agrees to spend an entire Saturday with you, and sets up a day of showings, it's extremely frustrating if you decide to cancel on Friday night or, worse, on Saturday morning.

It's perfectly acceptable to cancel if there is a true emergency. If that's the case, communicate the emergency to the broker, and reschedule. But remember, weekends are prime time for real estate agents. If time is set aside for you and you cancel, it's lost time to the agent. It would be hard to reschedule new showings for other clients on such short notice.

Here's a list of tips on home buyer etiquette:

1. **Be honest.** Whether you're telling the broker what you really want or need in a home, or telling the agent specifically why you did or did not like a particular home, if you're not being honest and open, you're making the job tougher than it has to be.

2. **Be available.** If you're going to be out of town on business, or tied up in meetings, let the broker know the times when you won't be available to look at property or talk about prospective homes. On the other hand, return your agent's calls promptly, and have a back-up number in case the agent calls with an urgent

79

message about a property. Perhaps an answer to your offer has been forwarded, or a new "hot" property has come on the market in the neighborhood you prefer.

3. **Show loyalty.** Agents like loyal buyers. Don't work with two full-time agents at the same time. The real estate community is small, and word gets around fast. Also, if you've taken up six months of an agent's time, and things are going well, it's not nice to suddenly switch to your relative or to a discount broker to close the sale. Legally, of course, you may have the right to switch at any time (barring an exclusivity agreement). But that doesn't make it right. If you want to use Aunt Edna for the closing because she'll give you a portion of her commission back, use her for the entire process. Don't waste another broker's valuable time.

Helping Out

As we discussed earlier, if you're like every other first-time buyer, the moment you decide to seriously look for a home, you'll be energized—if not consumed—by the process. You'll want to do everything in your power to find the right home *fast!*

You can help your agent by looking through the Internet at properties that might be for sale, and scouring the real estate "For Sale" ads in the local paper. If your broker has a good handle on the local market, he or she has probably seen most of the properties for sale. But if you see something interesting in the paper, ask about it.

You'll probably be tempted to visit some open houses as you walk around the neighborhood. That's fine, but when you're registering in the visitors' books, be sure to sign, after your name, "As represented by [your agent]." That's called "protecting the broker." By signing in as someone's client, you're putting the seller and his or her agent on notice that you are represented. If you don't indicate your broker at an open house, and you later try to go back with your agent and make an offer, the seller broker might put up a fight and say that you were his or her client for that particular house (which makes the listing broker a dual agent who is entitled to the entire commission). Make sure you sign in your broker at each and every open house.

Finally, you can help your agent by trying to learn everything you can about the neighborhoods you've chosen. Walk around and try them on for size. Visit the local grocery store, dry cleaner, schools, and parks. Drive around at various times of the day so you can experience "rush hour" traffic. Get a feel for the people who live and work there. Educate yourself rather than relying on your broker for lessons.

HOW SHOULD I INTERPRET THE HOME DESCRIPTION IN THE LOCAL NEWSPAPER OR IN BROKER LISTING SHEETS?

QUESTION
20

The key to understanding real estate ads is to assume that the broker is putting the best face on a bad situation.

I'm not saying that there aren't some fabulous homes out there. There are, and they may be worth every penny of their list price. And I'm also not saying that brokers are being dishonest. Most of them aren't.

But if Mr. Smith's apartment has a four-inch-wide view of the ocean, sandwiched between two towers, I'll bet you even money that Mr. Smith's broker will put "ocean view" somewhere in the newspaper ad.

Brokers know that most people want to have a good view from their windows—even if they're going to be away at work during the day and will see it only at night and on weekends. (I've always been amazed at people who want to have a view of Lake Michigan or any other body of water. At night, it's completely black and you can't see anything anyway.) Usually, the most expensive property is congregated around whatever view is the star attraction: In Chicago, it's Lake Michigan; in Boston, it's the Charles River; in San Francisco, it's the bay; in New York . . . well, in New York, everything is expensive. But the Manhattan buildings that overlook Central Park are *really* expensive.

When you read an advertisement, how do you distinguish between an apartment that really has a great view and one that has the four-inch-wide strip of blue? How can you tell a home that's really in move-in condition from one that needs to be completely redecorated?

That's the tough part. But remember: The broker will usually be very specific about a true feature. If the kitchen is new with top-brand appliances, the ad may say, "Gourmet kitchen with top appliances." If the view really does include Lake Michigan (or Central Park, or the river, or the bay, or whatever), the ad will say so.

Be Sure to Read Between the Lines

If you don't know a specific building or neighborhood particularly well, try to read between the lines of an advertisement. Here's a list of key phrases to watch out for, and what they may mean (in a tough, cynical world):

Phrase	*What It Might Mean*
Fantastic View	Could be the best view of your life; or, there might be little, if any, view, and you might have to crane your neck out the window to see it.
Treetop View	The apartment is about four floors up. During the summer, your view may be blocked by leaves.
Just Renovated	Probably needs a minimal amount of redecorating—unless the seller's red walls and chintz everywhere don't agree with your ideas about good taste.
Move-In Condition	May be in pristine condition, or you may just need to paint.
Needs Work	Could mean the home needs anything from new paint and carpeting to major structural renovation.
Handyman's Special	Probably a gut job; it's likely the home needs serious renovations and may even be unlivable.
"As Is" Condition	The home may have some serious problems that will emerge in a home inspection report; the house may be filthy, and the seller doesn't want to clean it up; or, the seller simply wants to be done with the deal, without having a prospective buyer try to negotiate the price down because of

Phrase	*What It Might Mean*
	the condition of the house; or, a combination of all three possibilities.
Bright and Sunny	Maybe the home has a southern exposure, or maybe every room is painted bright yellow, or maybe the ceilings have 10,000 watts' worth of lightbulbs, all of which are turned on during the showings.
Dollhouse	A word brokers often use to describe a home that is too small to accommodate a growing family; it may also be too small to accommodate a regularly sized individual.
Oversized Rooms	Don't expect Queen Elizabeth's great-hall; could mean truly large rooms or anything measuring more than nine-by-nine feet.
Street Parking	The broker is telling you the home doesn't come with a parking space and implying that you can park easily on the street. However, if the home is located in a congested metro neighborhood, or an area that doesn't permit street parking from 2:00 A.M. to 6:00 A.M., or an area that doesn't allow parking on the street in case of a "snow emergency" (any amount over two inches), don't believe it unless you see for yourself. It isn't always easy or desirable to park on the street.
Deeded Parking Space	You get a parking space. It could be indoors, outdoors but covered, or simply outdoors, but it's yours—even if it is too small for your vehicle.
Round-the-Clock-Security	Could mean a twenty-four-hour doorman (though brokers usually say this), a nighttime security person patrolling the premises, a monitored television security system, or a buzzer system.
Newer Mechanicals	Might have been replaced last year or five years ago. You may have to replace some

Phrase	What It Might Mean
	expensive mechanical systems within five years.
Newer Roof	You may have to replace the roof within five years, or it may be just fine.
Needs New Roof	During your showing, don't be surprised to find signs of water damage from recent roof leaks. Check for brown water marks on the ceilings and for buckling hardwood floors. Next question: Does the roof need a "tear-off," where several layers of old roofing must be pried off and replaced? Or, could you, for a lot less money, add another layer of asphalt shingles?
Oversized Lot	In Chicago, which has one of the smallest "regular" lot sizes in the country, an oversized lot could mean something as small as 30 by 125 feet. (A standard lot in Chicago is 25 by 125 feet, so you'd be getting a few extra blades of grass.)

What About Square Feet?

The concept of square footage requires explanation. As you tour different homes, brokers will give you a listing sheet for the property. On it you'll see that the size of the unit is given in square feet. You'll remember from your high school geometry class that a square foot is a two-dimensional square measuring one foot by one foot. You'll often see it expressed as $1' \times 1'$ or $10' \times 10'$ (a room measuring 10 feet by 10 feet, or 100 square feet).

Entire homes are measured the same way. But the actual square footage of a home, as presented on paper, can be a bit deceptive. Over the years, I've received dozens of letters from readers who felt that the square footage of their home was misrepresented, and they paid a larger amount because they thought the house was actually bigger than it is.

Pricing a home based on its square footage isn't the best way to go. Consider it only along with other methods of determining value. Here's why.

If your listing sheet says a particular home has 2,000 square feet, you may assume it's a big house. But when you get there, it may not feel that large. Why? Because a home's square footage is often calculated by measuring the exterior perimeter of the home. So, in addition to losing the interior wall space, you also lose the exterior wall space. Although it doesn't sound like much, it can be. You'll also lose space to closets (people don't count the square footage of a small closet, but it can add up), mechanicals, and chimney vents.

Brokers want you to think you're getting the most for your money, so they'll put down, as a home's square footage, the largest number that they can get away with. In my former residence, a vintage co-op built in the 1920s, our unit was listed as having as few as 1,700 square feet and as many as 2,300 square feet. The difference in measurement—600 square feet—is an entire condominium in New York City!

Don't rely on the listing sheet for an accurate assessment of a home's true square footage. If you want to know how many square feet are in the home, either measure the house's exterior, or ask whether the sellers have an architectural plan of the unit. After a while, you'll have a sense of how big 2,000 square feet really is, and you will be able to "guesstimate" how large other homes are, based on how big they feel.

Developers have their own set of tricks for increasing a house's square footage on paper. For example, some developers will include an attached garage when calculating square footage. Others will include the attic, or a crawl space, or the basement, whether it is or isn't finished. What is the true measure of square footage? Again, you should measure around the perimeter of the house or condo, and use that as a base. Also, garages (whether attached or not), basements, unfinished attic spaces, and other spaces that are not legal under the local building code, are typically not included in the square footage assessment. Use the architectural drawings that accompany the information kit the developer has prepared, and make your own determination of size.

If you make an offer based on a certain price per square foot, and later find out that the unit doesn't have quite that much space, don't beat yourself up about it. Remember, if the house was big enough for you when you thought it had 2,000 square feet, it's still probably big enough even if it has only 1,850 square feet.

3

How Do I Identify What I Need Versus What I Like in a Home?

Knowing which of two or three different properties is right for you is the key to *selectivity*. In the next few chapters, we'll talk about ways to hone your natural sense of selectivity and apply it toward your home purchase.

HOW DO I BECOME SELECTIVE WHEN CHOOSING A HOME? HOW DO MY WISH LIST AND REALITY CHECK HELP ME?

QUESTION
21

The issue of selectivity is very tough if you're a first-time buyer. Nearly every home is going to look at lot better than the cramped one-bedroom apartment you've been renting for the past five years (or better than your old room at home, where you've been living rent-free since college).

But it's important not to jump at the first house that appears to meet your needs. Why? Because in addition to meeting your basic needs, you might be able to get a few things you want. And if the house later turns out not to have met as many needs as you first thought, you'll be glad you gave yourself a few days to get over that first rush of house-adrenaline.

Joanne's Story

Joanne set up ten showings for a couple who were first-time buyers. The couple went to the first home and fell in love with it. They wanted to make an offer on the spot. But Joanne, an agent in Pompton Plains, New Jersey, has a policy: Never let a first-time buyer purchase a home at the first showing.

"First showings are all about emotion," she says. "You have to get some distance and some perspective before choosing the right home."

Joanne showed the rest of the homes to the couple. They liked three of the ten, including the first. And then they had to choose. They ended up choosing the first, but for reasons that hadn't even occurred to them when they first decided it was "*the* home."

Relatives and friends can lend perspective. Mike, a sales associate in York, Pennsylvania, says family members can help first-time buyers become more selective about a home, especially if they come to the first showings and feel that they're part of the process. "If they come only for the second showing, they feel compelled to find something wrong with the house," Mike explains.

But learning how to be selective doesn't just mean relying on your friends or relatives to tell you which way to turn. Listening to their advice and opinion (especially if it conflicts with yours) will help develop your selectivity (particularly if you become choosy about whose advice you're going to take). But selectivity is also about defining and refining your own tastes and trusting your own judgment. It's about putting aside emotion in favor of reason and logic.

Starting the Process

You start the process by determining how much you know about the type of home you'd like to buy. Let's say you aren't sure whether to live in a condo, buy a ranch home, or purchase new construction. You shouldn't limit yourself the first time out. Have your real estate agent show you a wide variety of homes: a ranch, some condominiums, a town house, and a subdivision under construction. Compare the styles and feel of each environment. Once you've identified which housing style you like best—maybe it's the subdivision under construction— have your broker set up a showing of a handful of houses that fall into your price range, size, location, and amenity requirements.

Next, you need to compare what you like and dislike about each of the homes you've seen. After each showing, Joanne provides her buyers with a listing sheet that includes a photograph of each home. "When we get back in the car, I immediately ask them to write down what they liked and didn't like about the house. After they've seen five or six homes, I ask them to prioritize the top two or three they're most interested in," Joanne says.

Joanne recommends that you look at the properties that come closest to your needs and wants. Then, begin to eliminate those that don't add up. Try to limit the list of homes you love to no more than two or three. If another "fabulous" home comes up, compare it to the others you love, and try to identify the *new* top two.

When you're in a hot seller's market, the process of learning how to be selective might mean that homes in which you're interested wind up selling to other parties. That's because homes move faster than you do. It's painful to lose a house that might be right, but it's more painful to purchase a home quickly, just for the sake of doing it, and then realize that it isn't right.

Selectivity isn't easy. It forces you to make decisions about what you like and don't like. Also, some of the issues aren't clear-cut. Each home will have pluses and minuses: One may be in a good school district; another might have four oversized bedrooms and a nice backyard. Your wish list and reality check can help. If you've been honest about your priorities, and you understand that reality will temper the amenities you'll get with your first home, the lists should help you step back and take most of the emotion out of the decision. (For more information on how to make a wish list or reality check, see Question 1, on page 14.)

Billy's Story

As a young lawyer fresh out of law school, Billy found himself with a huge salary and no deductions. He'd lived in rental apartments all his life (his parents had never bought a home) and decided to purchase a home before his work assignments got too busy.

A heavy caseload kicked in immediately at the law firm, and Billy ended up taking quick looks (if that) at apartments, and making blind offers. He relied on his agent to do the looking, and then made an offer based on the agent's assessment of how good or bad the condo was.

Needless to say, it wasn't a great way to go. Billy ended up buying a condo that's just so-so.

QUESTION 22

WHEN I GO TO A SHOWING, WHAT SHOULD I LOOK FOR?

The most important thing you can do at a showing is to step back and view the home objectively. For your purposes, the house, condo, or town house isn't a home; it's a physical dwelling with four walls, a floor, and a roof. Brokers say first-time buyers often get caught up in the moment. There's a rush of attention thrust upon them, and brokers are willing to do almost anything to get them to like the properties they're visiting.

Mary, a sales agent in San Antonio, Texas, says she tries to have people look dispassionately at the homes that are for sale. She tells her first-time buyers to inspect everything—every nook and cranny, every corner of the house. Pick up the rugs to inspect the condition of the floors, she urges. Open every door. Poke through the closets.

"I actually prefer to show a vacant house rather than one with furniture in it, because by the time the buyers get halfway through, they're looking at the antique sewing machine, not the bones of the house. Inevitably, conversation turns to the great bedspread or grandfather clock," Mary says.

For some people, seeing through the decoration is the hardest part of buying the right home. If you have an aversion to bright colors, prints, checks, or plaids, and you see a house with blue, yellow, and orange walls, you may have trouble focusing on how beautiful the structure of the home is because you're repulsed by the decoration. Your emotional reaction might be to turn and walk right out the door, but you would miss a potentially terrific home simply because the present owner has different taste.

Sara and Jeff's Story

Sara and Jeff are minimalists. It's an understatement to call their taste "spare," because it almost looks like no one lives in their home. They prefer white walls, hardwood floors or white carpeting, and a few pieces of starkly designed furniture and artwork arranged in a room. Living in their home is quiet and peaceful, Jeff says. It's almost a zenlike experience.

So imagine their frustration when they went house hunting and viewed brightly colored rooms, loud-print wallpaper, and more mess and clutter than they'd ever seen. They looked at beautiful homes, but were unable to visualize how a can of white paint would help a red room become an area they'd enjoy living in.

Eventually, they purchased a loft in a commercial building that was being renovated and converted into residential units. They found it easier to deal with blueprints than with reality.

Your First Showing

When you schedule your first showing, you're looking for a home that meets your basic needs:

1. **Is it within the right distance to work, church, family, and friends?**
2. **Does it have enough bedrooms and bathrooms?**
3. **Is there enough storage space?**
4. **Is there parking?**
5. **Is it safe?**
6. **Is it in the right school district?**

If the home meets the basic requirements, then start to look for how many wish list items it includes. (NOTE: These are my suggestions and are to be used as an example. Go back to your own wish list and reality check, to remind yourself about what's important to you.)

1. **Is there an extra bedroom and/or bathroom?**
2. **Is there a double vanity in the second bathroom?**
3. **Is there a garden or deck?**
4. **Is there a separate laundry room?**
5. **Is there a basement or crawl space? Is it convertible into usable space?**
6. **Is the garage attached?**
7. **Can the kids walk to school and after-school activities?**

8. **Is there a wood-burning fireplace or a gas fireplace?**
9. **What is the condition of the house: its appliances, roof, foundation, walls, mechanicals, wiring, and so on?**

Remember, start with general items and then get more specific.

If you're having trouble remembering which home had more of the features you want, or are finding it difficult to rank the homes based on their amenities, try this simple rating system. Assign five points to each of the top five items on your wish list and reality check. Assign one point to the remaining items on each list. As you go through each house, check off all the features that match your wish list and reality check. Add up the points, and put that number at the top of the listing sheet. This method should help you to rank, nonemotionally, the homes you've seen. If you want to be more specific, make a few copies of your wish list and reality check, and attach the checked-off copies to the individual listing sheets.

HOW CAN I REMEMBER EACH HOME WHEN I'VE SEEN SO MANY?

It's difficult to keep all the homes straight in your head, particularly if you've toured more than ten houses. Brokers know that after buyers see just five or six homes, their recall of each one becomes confused, and it's not unusual to visit ten or more open houses in one Sunday afternoon. New subdivision designers know that prospective buyers might visit as many as five different subdivisions and tour five to eight model homes at each one, in a single weekend. That's 25 to 40 model homes to keep straight—a virtually impossible task!

Is your head swimming yet? You need to create a method to control the real estate madness. Here are a few suggestions for keeping the houses organized in your mind:

1. **Keep a written log.** You can include the date you saw the house, the time of the showing, and who was there (your broker, the seller broker, the owner, your mother, your father-in-law, and so on). I suggest you purchase a spiral-bound notebook

and keep a dated log of each house you've seen. You can either attach listing sheets here or keep them in a three-ring binder (see my later suggestion).

2. **Photocopy and enlarge maps of the areas in which you're most interested.** As you go through an area, use a yellow high-lighter to mark the streets you've looked at. Use a different-colored highlighter (red, blue, or green) to mark the various homes you've actually seen in the area. You'll also want to mark the local schools, shopping, transportation routes, and houses of worship. When my husband, Sam, and I were looking for the house in which we now live, Sam marked the train lines and train stations in red. We only have one car, so he knew he'd be walking to the train station, and about a half-mile was the maxi-mum distance he was willing to go.

3. **Put to good use the listing sheet you've been given.** A list-ing sheet should contain all of the important information about a house: list price, size, lot size, number of bedrooms and bathrooms, and any extra amenities. Choose a few specific or spectacularly memorable things you notice in the house (lime-green kitchen, beautiful greenhouse, attached four-car garage, sauna in basement, pine floors, plastic imitation-wood paneling in basement), and write them down on the back of the listing sheet. Sketch out the floor plan. Either staple these listing sheets into your spiral-bound notebook, or invest in a cheap three-ring binder. Punch holes in your listing sheets and orga-nize them by date. If a house sells, note the selling price. If you don't receive a listing sheet, create one based on what you saw during the showing.

4. **Staple a completed wish list and reality check to the listing sheet.** It should help to remind you what attracted you to the house in the first place.

5. **Create your own photo reference file.** Invest in, or borrow, an instant-print camera and a few packs of film. Or, buy cheap film and use a roll per day when you go to showings. Some in-terior and exterior photos of each house will surely jog your memory later that evening, or even a few weeks later. Be sure to mark the photos with the address of each house. Better yet, sta-ple them to your listing sheet. (Be sure to ask the listing agent for permission to take an interior photo. You do not need any-one's permission to take an exterior photo of a home.)

6. **Make videos; they're even better.** If you take along a video camera, you have the opportunity to record your comments and feelings about a house as you film its interior and exterior, as well as the surrounding neighborhood. A video will give you a heightened sense of your feelings toward the house. (Again, ask permission. Some sellers are understandably nervous about having someone carry away a video of the interior contents of their home.)

7. **Go digital.** With a digital camera (they're getting cheaper and better by the day), you can actually download your photos onto your computer and keep an electronic record of the homes you viewed. You'll always know where the file is (especially if you give it a name you'll remember), and you'll be able to send photos of the homes you've seen to your relatives and friends. You can also pull down, from the Internet, photos of the homes that you've seen. Sites such as Realtor.com (realtor.com) and HomeAdvisor (HomeAdvisor.com), among others, often show photos of homes that are listed for sale.

8. **Give all future residents a chance to express their feelings.** If you're buying the home with another person (spouse, significant other, business partner, child, parent, friend), be sure the other people involved have a chance to write down what they

new construction tip

Many developers will put together information packets that explain the concept behind the subdivision, and will offer floor plans of the various models offered for sale. There may be four to eight (or more) different models for sale, and you may visit that many model homes, so it may be tough to keep everything straight. Model home designers, also known as "merchandisers," go out of their way to create something memorable that will also make you feel at home. An empty-nester couple might see themselves in a house that has the master bedroom on the first floor and guests' rooms upstairs. A family with young children might remember a house that has a bedroom with two cribs (for the twins the imaginary mother is expecting). By taking photos of the exterior and interior of the model homes, you'll be able to personalize each information package. This should help you keep the subdivisions—and their developers—apart.

think about the house. Purchasing a house with other people means buying by committee; you don't get to make a unilateral decision. If you have children over the age of eight (or perhaps younger, and precocious), they will have definite likes and dislikes about a house. I'm not telling you to rely solely on their judgments, but they should certainly be included in the process, perhaps at the second or third showing.

HOW DO I KNOW WHEN IT'S TIME FOR A SECOND SHOWING?

QUESTION 24

Whether you go for a second showing depends on your reaction to a particular home. If the house appears to meet your needs and wants, and you like the design and "feel" of it as a home, your agent may set up a second showing.

Brokers say you'll know when you're ready for a second showing. It usually happens after you've seen four or five houses. You may have followed all the suggestions for remembering which house is which, but you can't seem to place that one house you remember really liking. Or, you still like a particular house better than all the others you've seen, and you want to go back for an extended look.

Brokers may schedule first showings twenty minutes apart so that you can see five to six homes in a morning or afternoon, including travel time. Fifteen minutes should be enough time for you to decide whether the home is a possibility. You'll say either "Maybe" or "Forget it." (As you get further along the path, you may be able to make up your mind in five minutes or less, but that's a lot of pressure to put on a first showing, when you're new to the game.)

Second showings are longer; they start at about a half-hour in length. During a second showing, you'll want to confirm that the things you liked about the house in your first visit are still appealing. Or, you may decide that the house really isn't right and cross it off your list. If you like the house, the second showing is the time to begin examining the home's structure and mechanicals. Although you'll hire a professional inspector to do a home inspection, be aware that each inspection will set you back between $200 and $450. If you know what to look for, you can spot problems early on and save yourself some money.

Here are some physical things to check out during a second showing:

1. **Overall impression of the exterior.** Does the house seem in good shape? Is it sound? Step back: Are the lines of the house straight? Does the roof sag? If the house is brick, is the mortar between the bricks cracked or chinked? Is the paint peeling? Is the aluminum siding dented, dirty, or in really good shape? Is the sidewalk cracked around the house? Does it appear to pitch in toward the house (which might cause leaking into the basement) or slope away from the house?

2. **Roof.** Are the shingles curling or lifting? Ask the agent (or owners, if they're there) how old the roof is, and whether there have been any problems. A new roof, if properly installed, should last between 15 and 25 years. If the house has a tile or slate roof, it could last for 50 to 100 years, or longer, but it might be expensive to fix or replace.

3. **Windows and door frames.** Are they in good shape? Are there storm windows? Has the caulk dried out and pulled away? Are they cracked? Can you feel air blowing in? Are the frames square? Are there cracks in the plaster above the door frames?

4. **Overall impression of the interior.** Does the home appear to be sound? Do the wood floors creak when you walk on them? Are they pitched in any one direction? Are the stairs shaky? Is the kitchen or bathroom linoleum or tile floor peeling or bubbled? Are there discolored patches on the walls or ceiling? Are there other signs of leaks? Is the plaster cracked? Is the paint or wallpaper peeling? Are the walls and ceiling straight? Do doors, cupboards, and drawers open easily? Is the house clean?

5. **Attic or crawl space.** Is there insulation? Has it been laid out properly? Is there a fan? Are there air leaks? Is there poor ventilation?

6. **Plumbing and electricity.** Turn on all the faucets in the sinks, showers, and bathtubs. Flush the toilets. Is everything working? Do they drain well? How's the water pressure? Does the water have a funny smell? Does the home use city water or have its own well? Do the lights seem to work? Check the fuse box or circuit breaker. Are there enough electrical outlets? Or is everything connected with extension cords? Are there enough telephone jacks?

7. **Basement.** Are there cracks in the walls or foundation? Does it smell musty, stale, or damp? Does the basement leak? Is the house in a flood plain? (The listing agent may or may not know the answer to this question. You may have to find out independently by visiting the local village or city hall.)

8. **Mechanicals.** How old are the hot water heater and furnace systems? Is there an air-conditioning system or are there window units? How old are the window units and do they come with the house? Does the listing agent have any information on the heating, electricity, or water bills?

9. **Pests.** Is there evidence of termites? Cockroaches? Mice? Check any wooden beams for tiny holes or piles of sawdust.

Seat Yourself

Second showings take the selectivity issue we've been talking about a step further. In a second showing, you should sit down on the furniture and try to imagine living in the home. You should look around and think about where you would put *your* furniture. Ask yourself these questions:

- How would you feel about coming home to this house after a hard day's work?
- Where would you relax?
- Can you see yourself cooking in the kitchen?
- Will your armoire fit into the living room?
- Is the bedroom quiet enough for sleeping?
- Open up the windows and listen to the sounds of the neighborhood. Are there noisy wind chimes? Children? Dogs? Dump trucks? Airplanes? Is the house on a flight path? Are you listening to a nearby or distant highway? Local traffic? Frequently used train tracks? Are there other noises?
- Do you feel relaxed in the house?

At this point, you might be able to make up your mind about the house. For some first-time buyers, the second showing clinches their decision and they make an offer. However, other first-time buyers need a third, or even a fourth, showing.

Third Showings

After living in our co-op for a few years, Sam and I decided to sell it and buy a house. We put the apartment on the market, and one couple came and looked at it on five separate occasions.

The rule of thumb is: If you don't have a contract in hand when you come for the *fifth* showing, don't come at all. If you ask for a third showing, the brokers and seller are naturally going to think you're really interested. They're going to expect you to make a serious offer.

If the third showing comes and goes and there's no offer, the seller is going to begin to get impatient. If you then call and ask for a fourth showing, the brokers will have to persuade the seller to go along with it. It takes a lot of work to prepare a house for a showing. The seller has to clean up the house, pack everyone off, and basically clear the decks. It's a major maneuver because most of our homes don't look like those featured in *Architectural Digest* or *House Beautiful*. (My apologies to those of you who maintain homes to these standards.)

By the time you ask for a fifth showing, the seller has given up on you and is more interested in the next prospective buyers who are scheduled to visit. If you put in an offer after a fifth showing, the seller may not treat it very seriously (especially if it's a low-ball offer) because you've wasted his or her (and everyone else's) time.

I can hear you howling, "But I wanted to be sure! It's a big investment—the single biggest investment of my life!" That's true, but five showings is a great inconvenience to a seller, particularly if there's no offer. I don't want you to rush and make a bad decision. And the seller will deal with whatever happens. But, over time, as you become more familiar with the process of buying a home, your ability to make a decision will naturally speed up.

By the way, our fifth-showing buyer never made an offer. We eventually took the home off the market and lived there for three more years.

Making an Offer on the First Showing

Some brokers say first-time buyers don't really need a second, third, or fourth showing. They say that if you've been honest with the broker and honest with yourself in filling out your wish list and reality check, the broker will lead you to several homes, each of which will work for you.

Sales agent Mike says he tries to eliminate the need for second showings by picking homes that most closely match the buyer's needs and wants. He does, however, encourage second showings if the buyer initially sees the house at night. "If I've done a good job," he notes, "they'll be ready to make an offer after only two outings. My first-time buyers rarely need to see more than ten properties [to find the one they love]."

Some immigrant first-time buyers, who speak little or no English and work with agents who speak their native language (Coldwell Banker once boasted it had agents who, combined, spoke 75 different languages), get fewer choices than that. My husband Sam has worked with Hispanic buyers who were shown two or three houses and told to choose between them. They were so grateful to be able to buy a house, *any* house, that it didn't even occur to them to ask if there were others on the market that they could look at.

Rarely will two or three homes be enough to see, if you've never bought a home before. (Never let anyone show you just two houses and tell you to choose between them. We'll get to that situation later in the book.) Ten homes might be the right number for some buyers, but 50 or even 110 homes might be the right number for you.

When Sam and I were looking for the house we now own, we looked at perhaps 125 houses over a four-year period. Many were open houses on the weekends. Some were showings. None was right, especially as our way of thinking began to evolve. We changed neighborhoods and locations and finally made our way to a suburb of Chicago, some 17 miles north of where we were originally looking to buy. On the other hand, when we were deciding to purchase a loft for Sam's office, his need to be close to the train, in a certain part of town, and for a certain price, eliminated all but one building. And because that building had only one condo for sale that met the price and size criteria, our choice, in retrospect, was easy.

When you're going through the process of buying a home, it's easy to get sucked into the buyer–broker relationship and start letting the broker make your decisions for you. What you really have to do is step back and analyze whether a particular home is right for *you*. Try not to think about whether the *broker* thinks it's a good choice.

QUESTION 25

WHEN DO I KNOW I'VE FOUND THE RIGHT HOUSE?

What is the most important thing you can learn about buying a home?

There is more than one right home for you.

Reread and remember those two lines. Some buyers get so overcome with emotion that they become fixated on one particular property. The dangers in focusing all of your energy and attention on one property are: (1) you may not get it, or (2) you may overpay for it.

There *is* more than one right home for you.

When you go out looking, try to retain a steady perspective. Don't get emotionally involved with the seductive process of buying a home. Don't get intellectually tangled up in the thousands, or even hundreds of thousands, of dollars you're going to spend. Don't worry about whether you've secured or damaged your prospects for a golden retirement.

Real estate attorneys routinely advise their clients *not* to fall in love with a piece of property. "It's not wise because if you fall in love with a house and then have the inspection and something's terribly wrong, you're going to want to buy the house anyway, and that may not be in your best interests," says one attorney.

Some real estate agents or brokers will seem to encourage you to fall in love with a house. They'll say things like, "Isn't it beautiful?" or "I could spend my whole life here," or "You'll be so happy here," or "Don't you just love this place?"

They want you to fall in love with the house because then you'll buy it. They'll receive their commission and say hello to the next first-time buyer. You, on the other hand, will end up spending the next five to seven *years*, or longer, in that home. And despite the admonitions *not* to fall in love with a home, and *not* to become fixated on one particular piece of property, people do it all the time. Including me.

I fell in love with our vintage co-op with a wood-burning fireplace. We could have bought a newly built house we saw on a huge lot (for Chicago, it was big: about 30 feet by 165 feet) in a nice neighborhood. In the first five years after purchase, it would have nearly doubled in value. But no, I was completely enamored with this twenty-four-hour doorman, no-parking building. I saw all of the pluses and none of the minuses—an oh-so-typical symptom of "first-timeritis."

Ten years, two houses, thousands of newspaper columns, and four books on real estate later, I can tell you that falling in love with a house is exactly the *wrong* thing to do. If you don't keep some objectivity during the buying process, you'll be suckered in before you know it.

About That Objectivity . . .

There is a difference between falling in love with something you've seen and recognizing that you could buy a piece of property and successfully live there for whatever length of time.

Sales agent Joanne says she can tell when her buyers find the right house by the look of joy on their faces. "If they sit down on the couch, it's a good sign. If they're trying to decide where to put their furniture, it's a very good sign. If they've got a special glow on their faces, it's the right house."

You may not be the type to blush easily, but you get the idea. You'll have a chemical reaction to a house that's a good choice. And there may be more than one house to which you respond in this way.

Over time—say, in a few years—the home that's right today may seem small and cramped for your growing family. You'll change, and as your fortunes increase, today's dream home may seem a little like a starter home. You'll reset your sights on a golf course development, or a better neighborhood or school district. Your cozy kitchen will suddenly seem too small for your growing family.

"Where did all that space go?" you'll wonder. And then it will be time to find your next "right" house.

4

How Do I Know
What I Can
Afford to Spend?

HOW MUCH CAN I AFFORD?

How much *house* can you afford?

The answer most real estate experts give is this: If you can afford to rent and you have cash for a down payment, you can probably afford to buy. But the easiest way to find out how much you can afford is to get prequalified or preapproved for your loan.

When you get *prequalified* for your loan, you essentially tell the lender (on the phone, in person, or on-line) how much you earn and what debts you have. The lender crunches those numbers through a formula and comes up with an actual mortgage amount that you can afford to support.

When you get *preapproved*, you may need to provide the lender with documentation: current checking or savings account statements, a recent pay stub from work, and/or perhaps the past two years' income tax forms. If you go on-line for your preapproval, many on-line lenders (e.g., QuickenMortgage.com) do a "lite" version. You need only answer the questions truthfully. The paperwork is done during the verification stage of the loan.

There is a big difference between getting prequalified and being preapproved for a loan. When you are preapproved, the lender is actually committing, in writing, to funding your loan, provided that the house appraises out in value (and assuming that your paperwork checks out). A prequalification carries no commitment from the lender, but you have an idea of what you can afford.

Prequalification

The nice thing about prequalification is that, typically, you do not need to tie yourself in by paying an application fee and actually applying for the mortgage. You can save that until after you've found the home you want to buy, and then you can comparison shop to find the best mortgage deal. Lenders will be delighted to prequalify you in a preliminary way, with no obligation, because they get an opportunity to pitch their wares to you.

Prequalifying is a relatively painless process. The lender will ask you a few simple questions about your debts and assets, and will then apply your numbers to the debt-to-income ratios that are required by lenders on the secondary market. Then, the lender will tell you how much mortgage your income will support.

You may hear about secondary market lenders during the course of your purchase. These are underwriting sources like Fannie Mae and Freddie Mac, which purchase loans from mortgage companies that make loans to consumers like you. By guaranteeing retail lenders a steady source of cash, secondary market lenders help keep the mortgage market "liquid," which keeps mortgages affordable for home buyers. Even though you may see an advertisement for Fannie Mae or Freddie Mac, and perhaps will visit their web sites to get more information about the home-buying process, you won't do business directly with them. For more information about the secondary market, mortgages, and buying a home, visit the web sites at FannieMae.com and FreddieMac.com.

Figure It Out Yourself

If you are paying $600 per month in rent, and you assume the home you're buying will require about $100 per month in real estate taxes and insurance, you're left with $500 per month or $6,000 per year. With annual payments of $6,000, you can manage a $60,000 mortgage, assuming the interest rate is 10 percent. If the interest rate is 7 percent, your annual $6,000 payment will support a mortgage of $85,714.

Three percentage points in the interest rate (the difference between 10 percent and 7 percent) make a huge difference in affordability. Sliding interest rates can drastically affect how much house you can afford to buy. At 4 percent interest, which may be the starting point for some adjustable rate mortgages (ARMs), $500 per month can support a $150,000 mortgage. (Don't forget you have to pay for real estate taxes and insurance too.)

In the past decade, homeownership has become more affordable than at almost any other time since the 1950s. Mortgage interest rates fell from their high of 18 percent in 1982 to 10 percent at the end of the 1980s, and to a range of 6.5 to 8 percent for most of the 1990s.

If interest rates are 10 percent, you can afford to buy a home that costs double your annual income (if you're conservative) or up to two and a half times your annual income. If interest rates are at 7 percent, you may be able to purchase a home that costs more than three times your gross annual income (assuming you have the down payment money and little or no debt).

For example, if your combined family income minus debt payments is $50,000 per year, and the interest rates are at 10 percent (which, by the way, is the historical average), conventional wisdom suggests that you can afford to buy a house that costs around $100,000. If interest rates are 8 percent, your $50,000-per-year income might stretch far enough to buy a home that costs between $150,000 and $190,000, depending on how much you can put down in cash.

Debt-to-Income Ratios

How do mortgage lenders specifically determine how much you can afford to pay? Primary lenders (the retail companies that lend to consumers like you) and lenders on the secondary markets have developed debt-to-income lending ratios through years of trial and error.

All lenders more or less follow the same ratios. They've determined that you can afford to pay between 28 and 36 percent of your gross income in debt service. That means your total outlay for your mortgage principal and interest payments, real estate taxes, insurance, car loan, and credit card payments may not exceed 36 percent of your gross monthly income (your total annual salary divided by 12).

Because the primary lenders have become more sophisticated in dealing with different types of borrowers, and have developed a myriad of creative loan options that can be somewhat personalized for each home buyer, several of the largest secondary market players (which control the way the vast majority of mortgages are made) have somewhat relaxed the 36 percent debt-to-income ratio. Fannie Mae and Freddie Mac, the nation's two largest investors in home mortgages, are federally chartered private corporations mandated to provide financial products and services that increase the availability and affordability of housing for low-, moderate-, and middle-income Americans.

These companies are in competition with each other to purchase, repackage, and resell the largest amount of residential mortgages, so they are continually developing new loan products to help more consumers achieve their homeownership dreams. At the beginning of the 1990s, for example, Fannie Mae decided it would extend the upper limit of the debt-to-income ratio from 36 to as much as 40 or even 42 percent for certain loan products. Freddie Mac quickly jumped in and created loans that do the same thing. On loans backed by the Federal Housing Authority (FHA), the upper limit on the debt-to-income ratios has been extended to as much as 43 percent. For special homeownership programs backed by Community Development Block Grant (CDBG) funds, the ratios can be even higher, with down payment assistance provided.

Although the extra 3 to 6 percent doesn't sound like much, this is ground-breaking stuff. Suddenly, if your family's gross annual income is $50,000, and interest rates are 10 percent, you can buy a house worth $125,000 to $140,000 instead of $100,000—a significant difference in many communities. If interest rates are 7 percent, you may spend up to four times your annual income (depending on how much other debt you're carrying).

Calculating How Large a Loan Payment You Can Carry

Let's leave aside the issue of the down payment for a moment and talk about how much of a monthly loan payment your income will carry. Some experts suggest you should aim to spend 25 percent of your gross monthly income (GMI) on your housing expenses; others say you can spend up to 33 percent. Compared to the 36 to 41 percent of gross monthly income that a lender will allow you to put toward your total debt payment, 25 and 33 percent seem conservative. But the final amount is up to you. You must decide how aggressive you can be without incurring more debt because of your other living expenses.

Get out a pencil and fill in your personal financial facts on the Maximum Monthly Payment Worksheet, on page 107.

Let's say your gross monthly income is $5,000 ($60,000 per year). Multiply by 25 percent or 33 percent:

$$\$5,000 \times .25 = \$1,250 \text{ or } \$5,000 \times .33 = \$1,665$$

Let's say you have a car loan ($150 per month) and you're paying off a credit card balance ($100 per month):

$$\$1,250 - \$250 = \$1,000$$

or

$$\$1,665 - \$250 = \$1,415$$

In this example, you'd be able to spend between $1,000 and $1,415 per month on your principal and interest payments, real estate taxes, and insurance. If real estate taxes are $100 per month ($1,200 per year) and insurance is another $50 per month, that will leave you between $850 and $1,265 to spend on a mortgage.

Here's how to calculate the amount of mortgage you can afford to carry: Multiply the net amount you can spend monthly ($850 to $1,265) by 12 (for an annual mortgage amount), then divide that number by the current prevailing interest rate (say, 8 percent):

25 percent of gross income: $850 × 12 = $10,200 ÷ .08 = $127,500.

33 percent of gross income: $1,265 × 12 = $15,180 ÷ .08 = $189,750.

So how much house can you afford? Assume you add a 20 percent down payment to each of these mortgage amounts (divide $127,500 or $189,750 by 5 and add that number to the total):

$$\$127,500 + \$25,500 = \$153,000$$

$$\$189,750 + \$37,950 = \$227,700$$

According to these calculations, on a $60,000-per-year income, assuming you have 20 percent to put down in cash, you'd be able to afford a home that costs between $153,000 and $227,700.

The 8 percent interest rate allows you to purchase a home between two and a half and nearly four times your income! The lower the interest rates, the more house your hard-earned dollars can buy.

WORKSHEET
Maximum Monthly Payment

1. Gross monthly income from all sources: _____

2. Multiply by the percentage of GMI you
   want to spend (Hint: Multiply by .25 for
   25 percent of your income, .33 for
   33 percent of your income, or .36 for
   36 percent of your income):   × _____

3. Add up your present monthly debt service: _____

   Credit cards   _____

   Car loans   + _____

   School loans   + _____

   Charge accounts   + _____

   Other personal debt + _____

   Total debt: _____

4. Subtract your total debt: − _____

5. Your maximum monthly payment is: _____

Use the worksheet on page 109 to figure out the approximate amount you can afford to spend on a home.

Finding the Comfort Level

Just because you *can* afford to spend up to four times your annual income doesn't mean you *have* to. It's extremely important to find a level of payment that's comfortable for you and your family, based on how you like to spend your money. Although you may be technically able to afford a $150,000 home, making those interest payments might mean that your family will have to give up other luxuries like summer camp or new clothes for school.

> Remember, no one says you have to spend every nickel you have on your home.

Figuring Out Your Budget

Finding your comfort zone is most easily accomplished if you're on top of your expenses. If you know what you spend, you know which expenses can be redirected toward paying the costs associated with home ownership.

The first thing to do is figure out where your paycheck goes each month. Use the Monthly Expenditures Checklist on pages 110–111 to help you determine exactly how you're spending your salary.

But be honest. If you routinely spend $16.99 a week on the newest CD, list that as an expense. If you rent two videos per week, put in the rental tab. If you eat lunch out with your friends four days a week, include the food and the tip. Later, when you're trying to figure out how to save enough money for a down payment, you'll know exactly where to make the cut.

Adding It All Up

Are your monthly expenditures more than your monthly after-tax take-home pay? Are the two numbers closer together than they ought to be? If they are, you're out of balance financially, which could be a problem when you try to get a loan.

25 Percent Gross Monthly Income	33 Percent Gross Monthly Income
GMI _____	_____
× .25 = _____	× .33 = _____
Less: Monthly debt − _____	− _____
= _____	= _____
× 12 months = _____	= _____
Current rate of interest ÷ _____	÷ _____
= _____	= _____

(Amount of mortgage you can afford)

Down payment + + _____	_____
= _____	= _____

(Approximate purchase price of house)

Use this checklist to figure out exactly where your money goes each month. If you have other expenses that aren't listed, add them in at the bottom.

Expenses	Amount Spent Per Month
Rent	_____
Electricity	_____
Gas	_____
Telephone/On-line Fee	_____
Auto Loan/Lease Payment	_____
Auto Insurance	_____
Health Insurance	_____
Renter's Insurance	_____
Life Insurance	_____
Other Insurance	_____
Monthly Savings	_____
Retirement Contribution	_____
Children's Education Fund	_____
Credit Card Debt	_____
School Loans	_____
Other Monthly Debt Payments	_____
Grocery/Pharmacy/Sundry Bills	_____
Weekly Transportation	_____
Care for an Aging Parent or Relative	_____
Charity Contributions	_____
Medical/Dental Bills	_____
Restaurants/Ordering In	_____
Subtotal:	_____

Expenses	Amount Spent Per Month
Entertainment	_____
Health Club/Working Out	_____
Recreation	_____
Child Care/Baby-sitters	_____
Children's Expenses (lessons/camp/clothing, etc.)	_____
School Tuition	_____
Housecleaning Expenses	_____
Vacations (divide your annual expense by 12 to find out the monthly expenditure)	_____
Books/CDs/Tapes/Videos/DVD	_____
Newspaper/Magazine Subscriptions	_____
Laundry/Dry Cleaning	_____
Yard Work/Landscaping	_____
Gifts	_____
Major Purchases (stereo/computer)	_____
Furniture/Decorating	_____
Clothing	_____
Miscellaneous Expenses (morning cup of gourmet coffee, snacks, lottery tickets)	_____
Other _____	_____
_____	_____
_____	_____
_____	_____
Monthly Total	_____

Note: If you're going to enter a clothing purchase under "Clothing," but are carrying it as a debt on your credit card, enter it only once. If you list it under "Clothing," make sure you enter only the amount of interest you pay on your credit card, not the minimum amount due (which includes a tiny bit of principal in addition to all that hefty interest).

An important part of being a homeowner is taking responsibility for your finances. Most first-time buyers (and even some repeat buyers) have to make some trade-offs because homeownership is expensive. By cutting back on your budget now, you'll be steps ahead after you move in and want to spend some more money to dress up the place. Look over the list and begin to determine which expenses can be eliminated or reduced. (For more hints on budgets, credit, and finance, check out my book, *100 Questions You Should Ask About Your Personal Finances.*)

Let's review where you can go to get yourself prequalified and preapproved:

- You can go on-line to QuickenMortgage.com, e-loan.com, Home-Advisor.com, iOwn.com, or other sites that aggregate national lenders who bid on your business. These sites will either prequalify or preapprove you for your loan.

- You can go on-line to a local mortgage broker, who may preapprove you but will probably just prequalify you for your mortgage.

- You can call a national or local lender for a prequalification.

- You can visit a lender's office in person. Face-to-face is nice, but it may actually take longer than if you go on-line, where everything is automated.

Some of the best mortgage programs are available exclusively on-line (see Chapter 8 for more information), but be sure to get everything in writing. Every lender, including on-line lenders, is required to live up to the rules stated in the Real Estate Settlement Procedures Act (RESPA), which is governed by the Department of Housing and Urban Development (HUD). You should get, in writing, a Good Faith Estimate (see Question 68 on page 208) as well as a statement committing to funding your loan (pending the successful appraisal of the property) if you're getting prequalified.

One-Stop Shopping

These days, many decent-sized real estate firms also own related enterprises to which they try to steer business. These side businesses typically include a mortgage brokerage, a title company, home inspectors, alarm companies, housecleaning services, and various other products and services that homeowners typically use.

In addition to selling you a house—or selling your house for you—the real estate agent will also suggest (sometimes gently, sometimes strongly) that you use the brokerage firm's side companies for your other real estate needs. Here are the arguments that will be presented to you:

1. **The price is competitive with any other supplier's fee.** Is it? Have you shopped around? Often, a proprietary or connected firm won't give you the best price until you get a lower quote elsewhere and then go back to negotiate. At that point, unless the firm is willing to beat the price by, say, 5 or 10 percent, you should think about why you'd want to do business with a company that takes an only-when-caught approach to fees.

2. **It's convenient. "I [the broker] will be able to stay on top of them for you."** How good was your broker at staying on top of the details of your purchase or sale? That could be a valuable clue to the attention other details involved in the transaction will get.

3. **"We've used them extensively and they provide good service."** Is it mentioned that the firm gets a fee—known, in rougher times, as a "kickback"—for every home buyer or seller steered toward that company? In some areas, the agent's bonus is determined by how many clients he or she sends to other companies owned by the firm.

The process of looking for a home and shopping for a mortgage is usually stressful, arduous, and time-consuming. I'm all for one-stop shopping to expedite the process, but I strongly believe you'll get the cheapest and best loan after you've shopped around. If nothing else, you'll have the satisfaction of knowing that the best mortgage lender was right under your nose the entire time. Shopping on-line is easy and fast, and studies have shown that you can get a good deal with an on-line lender. But start with the maximum monthly payment worksheet on page 107, and you'll have a pretty good idea of how much you can afford to borrow to purchase your new home.

20/20 hindsight

Real estate companies really, really, *really* want you to use their other services because it's a way for them to build their business and fatten the bottom line without having to pay the costs of bringing in new business. But even if a line on your agency disclosure agreement (or listing agreement, when it comes time to sell your home) says "Check here if you want to use XYZ Title Company," and you check it off, you can always change your mind. Don't ever let anyone try to pressure you into using a product or service that you haven't thoroughly checked out and priced out. Remember, you're the customer.

QUESTION 27

HOW MUCH WILL IT COST TO OWN AND MAINTAIN A HOME?

In the movie *The Money Pit*, Tom Hanks ends up throwing his life savings into renovating his home. Maintaining a home often feels the same way.

Calculating the costs of home ownership appears to be easy: If you can afford your mortgage, insurance, and real estate taxes, you can afford to own a home, right? Unfortunately, that's not always the case. Some costs of home ownership, hidden from renters, can lighten the wallet and break the bank.

Calculating these costs is a lot tougher than predicting your mortgage payments because they're variable by nature and given to change. If your principal, interest, real estate taxes, and insurance (PITI) are the fixed costs of owning a home, utility payments are semifixed, and everything else is a variable.

Here are the *basic* expenses you will be responsible for when you actually buy your home:

- Mortgage payments of principal and interest, paid monthly (or bimonthly, if you have a loan that requires you to make payments every other week).

- Real estate taxes, paid annually or in installments, or paid monthly with the mortgage, if you escrow your insurance and taxes.

- Basic homeowner's insurance, paid monthly with the mortgage, if you escrow your insurance and taxes (an annual or semiannual premium is sometimes paid separately from the mortgage).

- Homeowner's assessments or co-op monthly assessments.
- Utilities, including electricity, gas, cable, satellite, on-line, and so on.
- Trash and garbage collection, including recycling as required by your local municipality.
- Water and sewage (may be billed separately or together).
- Repairs and maintenance of the interior and exterior of the home (includes everything from washing windows to replacing the roof or painting the interior and exterior).
- Landscaping and grounds maintenance (including driveway re-surfacing, as needed, plus all the regular stuff).
- Snow removal (for those living in colder climates).

It is less expensive to keep up with maintenance than to defer it. Plan to put at least $3,000 to $5,000 in a home improvement fund so that you have cash available for emergency repairs or regular mainte-nance. A new roof could cost $3,000; a new hot water heater might cost $600, plus installation. Consider purchasing a home warranty (for existing homes only, not for new construction). It doesn't cover structural problems, but, during the first year you own your home, it will reimburse you for fixing or replacing any appliance or electrical or mechanical system that was working on the day of closing. Best of all, many sellers will pick up the cost of a home warranty as a mar-keting tool. See Question 39 for more information.

The whole point of buying new construction is that you won't have to touch the house for the next ten years, right? That may be true with some things, like the roof, mechanical systems, and appliances (hopefully!), but new construction carries with it a whole other set of problems, including the possibility that the builder didn't install some items properly. You'll find most of these soon after you've moved in. Make sure that the caulking around the bathtubs, show-ers, and sinks stays in place, and don't let exterior painting go for too long. The last thing you want is a nearly brand-new house that looks disheveled and run-down.

How much do these items cost? For some, like landscaping, water, and the utilities, the charges depend greatly on the season and amount of usage. Your mortgage and insurance payments will likely be fixed over their entire term. Utilities will go up and down with the seasons and are likely to drift higher. Repairs and maintenance of the house depend on the condition the home was in when you bought it. If the boiler was on its last legs when you bought the home, you may have to pay for a new one shortly after the closing.

Real Estate Taxes

Real estate taxes are another matter. From every hamlet in the United States, homeowners cry out that their property taxes are too high. Formulas for calculating property taxes differ from state to state, but the general rate that you can expect to pay is anywhere between 1 and 3 percent of the market value of your home.

For example, if your home has a market value of $100,000, you might pay between $1,000 and $3,000 (or more) per year in property taxes, depending on where you live. In Chicago, if you own a $120,000 condo in the Gold Coast (the fanciest part of town), you might pay up to 70 percent more in real estate taxes than a person who owns a $120,000 bungalow on the city's northwest side. Is it fair? Not really. Currently, in California, homeowners pay 1 percent of the sale price of their home, no matter when they bought it. If you paid $100,000 for a California bungalow 25 years ago, you could still be paying around $1,000 in property taxes.

You can't escape property taxes, but you can fight them. See Chapter 12 for some useful information on how to lighten your property tax burden.

General Maintenance

What specific expenses might you encounter in your first few years of home ownership? General maintenance and upkeep of your home can be expensive. Brokers say would-be homeowners often forget to consider the basics for the exterior and interior of the home.

Cold-weather and hot-weather climates exact their own peculiar punishments. Severe winter weather can wreak havoc on driveways, gutters, the roof, and exterior paint, not to mention the time spent shoveling. Depending on the amount of snow, you may want to invest in a snowblower. (Or consider joining your new neighbors to pay for snow removal during the season.) In addition, your driveway may need a coat of sealant from time to time to prevent cracking.

Landscaping and a garden are year-round issues. If you live in the deep South, your garden will require constant care and attention, to avoid its becoming a jungle. In the North, you'll have at least three seasons of gardening.

Another maintenance concern is the exterior upkeep of the home. Brick homes may need expensive tuck-pointing to keep the walls from leaking. Clapboard or shingle houses need painting every few years to stay weather-tight, and may require new shingles or boards from time to time. Even homes with aluminum or vinyl siding have portions that require some painting or, at the very least, washing. (Aluminum or vinyl siding tends to be the cheapest alternative in the long run. Little maintenance beyond an occasional cleaning is required, experts say.)

Repairing or patching the roof can be an ongoing expense. A particularly severe winter or windstorm can rip shingles right off the roof. If you live in the house long enough, you will one day have to replace the roof, though a new roof should last 20 years and usually comes with a warranty.

Hire a professional home inspector or structural engineer to give any home the once-over before you buy. If you're purchasing an older home, an inspection is almost a "must," even if you're buying in "as is" condition. A good inspector (and real estate agent) should point out the age of the home and remind you that you might have to re-place the roof or other appliances and mechanical systems within the next few years.

Maintaining the interior of a home can also be expensive. Older windows may need recaulking or a new sash. You may want to purchase storm windows to improve energy efficiency. Bathroom tiles may need regrouting. If your wood floors have a polyurethane finish, you'll need to buff them down and reapply that finish every two to

117

three years, or risk damaging the floor. Hardwood floors with a wax finish should be cleaned and buffed every two to three years as well.

Older homes may need rewiring, a new hot water heater, or a new furnace right away. Depending on how long you plan to live in the house, odds are you'll replace most of the major mechanical systems. Even newer mechanicals require yearly upkeep, however; filters need to be changed, and systems need to be cleaned. Although basements and attics might seem like ideal storage facilities, they require maintenance as well. Basement walls may require treatment for mold and cracks. Attics may need extra insulation. Other issues may arise as the house—especially a brand-new home—settles.

A good inspector should help pinpoint upcoming maintenance expenses associated with the home, including any pest problems. (For more on inspectors and the inspection process, see Question 45.)

Being a good neighbor means being there in case of an emergency, and helping out if you can. But it also means keeping your home looking good, so that the neighborhood continues to improve and appreciate in value. Maintenance and landscaping are the essence of an unspoken agreement you make when you buy into a neighborhood. If it's a part of the bargain that you aren't willing to keep, perhaps you should rethink your homeownership plans, or purchase a different type of home that doesn't require as much work.

QUESTION 28

WHAT ARE ASSESSMENTS? DO ALL TOWN HOUSES, CONDOS, AND CO-OPS HAVE THEM?

Assessments are fees that you, the owner, pay for the upkeep of property held jointly with other owners. You'll have to pay some sort of monthly or annual assessment if you choose to buy a condo, co-op, or town house. If your single-family home is located in a particular type of subdivision that has common property (a private playground, swimming pool, security gate, clubhouse, and so on), a homeowners' association may assess you for a share of the maintenance of that common property.

Regardless of the type of property you buy, your proportionate share of the upkeep of the property should be assessed based on your percentage of ownership. If you own 1 percent of the property, then your share is 1 percent of the upkeep.

Many different areas and amenities may be part of the common property: a parking garage or parking spaces, recreational amenities (clubhouse, health club or workout facilities, tennis courts, private lake or lagoon), land, the roof and exterior walls (of condos, town houses, and co-ops), lobby, security, doormen, and so on. Part of the upkeep of these common areas includes liability insurance coverage.

Paying Your Assessment

How do you pay an assessment? Assessments are usually billed monthly by the homeowners' association. Some single-family home-owners' associations bill on a yearly basis; some bill twice a year. Whenever the bill comes, you are expected to pay it promptly. If you don't, the association is entitled to bill you for late fees and even to take you to court and force you to sell your home to pay for late assessments.

If you're thinking about buying a town house, condo, co-op, or single-family house that would require payment of an assessment, you should be aware that the lender will consider the assessment to be another fixed expense (like paying down a car loan or credit card balance) and will include the assessment in the debt-to-income ratio. That means you will have less money to spend to buy a home.

For example, if you have $1,000 per month to spend on housing expenses, and the monthly assessment of the condo you've had your eye on is $200, you really have only $800 to spend on your housing expenses.

Another thing: Assessments usually go up. Every condo, co-op, or town house association has a board of directors that oversees the costs, repairs, and maintenance done to the property. The directors have the power to impose "special assessments" to pay for large-scale capital improvements, including a new roof, new deck, new elevators, new windows, tuck-pointing, and a hundred other things.

Protect Yourself: Read

How can you protect yourself? Before you close on a condo, co-op, or town house, request copies of the past two to three years' budgets and board minutes, to familiarize yourself with ongoing issues of maintenance, problems, and long-range planning. You should also request a copy of the current year's budget and the coming year's project budget (if available). Reading board minutes can bore you to tears, or it can be like a juicy gossip rag. You won't know the people, but if you move in, they'll be your neighbors.

Reading the board minutes will quickly get you up to speed on any major capital improvements the board may be planning. You may then have an advantage when negotiating the price of the home. If you read the minutes and find out that the board is planning to levy a three-year special assessment to cover the cost of windows that were replaced five years earlier, you should try to get your seller to lower his or her price to at least recoup some of that cost. (After all, the seller enjoyed the use of those windows for five years.)

When you ask for a copy of the board minutes, you should also request a copy of the rules and regulations of the building. Many properties have pet restrictions, which you'll want to know before making your offer.

5

Putting Together
the Deal

HOW DO I DECIDE WHAT TO OFFER
FOR THE HOME?

If you've been prequalified or preapproved by a mortgage lender, or you've figured out for yourself how much new debt you can manage, you already know your uppermost financial limit. That's the number you can't go beyond unless interest rates change—or unless you earn more, win the lottery, or inherit a bundle.

However, what you can afford to spend has nothing to do with how much a seller is asking for his or her house. The seller wants the highest possible offer. You want to pay the least amount of money. The rest is subject to negotiation.

But we're getting ahead of ourselves. It's important to determine how much a house is worth *before* you make an offer. (This would seem obvious, but plenty of buyers get caught up in the heat of the moment—especially in a hot sellers market—and just offer up a number.)

The answer to the question of worth comes from your broker or agent. He or she has access to the sales data that can tell you what the homes in the neighborhood are selling for, and how long they took to sell. Because of the differences in the fiduciary responsibilities between a buyer broker and a seller broker, however, you'll have to proceed on a slightly different course to get this information and put it to use.

If you're using a buyer broker (I'm assuming he or she is at least competent, if not fabulous), it should be relatively easy to ask the buyer broker for "comps" (sales prices of similar properties that have recently been sold in your neighborhood). Once you have the comps, you and your buyer broker can begin an ongoing discussion about what the comps mean and how they apply to the various homes in which you're interested.

If you're working with a seller broker, he or she is required by law in most states to provide you with everything you need to make an informed decision on how much to offer. However, you may have to specifically request that the seller broker provide you with recent sale comps, as well as the listing prices for similar homes in the neighborhood. You should also request information on the number of days a particular home has been on the market.

What Are Comps?

Comps are homes that have recently been sold and are similar in size, location, and amenities to the home on which you want to bid. Comps give you an idea of what other sellers have been paid for their homes. Finding out the list prices is also important, because comparing the list prices with the sale prices tells you exactly what percentage of their original asking price sellers are getting. (Study after study has found that homes sell, *on average*, for 6 percent below their list price. But that assumes the homes are not overpriced and the market is well balanced with an even number of buyers and sellers. If a home is well priced, it is listed at or just a bit above what comparable homes in the neighborhood have sold for. In the hot sellers' market during the latter half of the 1990s, many sellers received list price—or more—for their homes.)

Here's How It Works

Let's say House A was listed at $100,000 and sold for $96,000 (Seller A received 96 percent of the list price); House B was also priced at $100,000, and sold for $95,000 (Seller B received 95 percent of the list price). House A and House B are nearly identical homes, in more or less the same good physical condition. Seller C, however, put a few extras into House C, such as a wood-burning fireplace and upgraded carpet. House C was priced at $110,000 and the seller received $104,000 (Seller C received 95 percent of the list price).

You are looking at House D, which is in the same condition as Houses A and B, but Seller D is asking $110,000 for the house. Based on the sale prices of other homes in the subdivision, how much would you pay for the house? Sellers A, B, and C received around 95 percent of their list prices, but their homes were competitively priced. Seller D's home is not competitively priced.

If you know that the most you want to offer Seller D for House D is $95,000 (95 percent of $100,000, which is the amount the house should be priced), you have to make a decision about the lower amount that you want to offer initially.

Unless you're in a heated situation where several other parties may be bidding on the house that you want, or if you're in a tight seller's market (sellers are getting almost exactly what they want for their properties, in a very short amount of time), *never offer the list price for a home*. Offer between 5 to 10 percent *below* the maximum price you want to pay for the home. If you've decided you're not going to pay any more than $95,000 for Seller D's home, then you may want to consider an initial offer of $90,000. That's the start of negotiation.

The trick is to know what you want to pay for a property *before* you make your first offer. Your decision should be based on logic and reasoning, not on emotion. If you can't get a clear idea of how much to offer based on the comps your broker has provided to you, then ask him or her for another set of comps. And if your search goes on for more than three months, you'll need another set, because the market continually changes.

If you're working with a buyer broker, feel free to ask what he or she would pay for the house. Buyer brokers, because they owe their fiduciary loyalty to you, the buyer, should be forthcoming with how

If you have a dual agent (representing both sides), a nonagent, or a transactional agent working with you, the effect is the same as with a seller broker. Ask for the information you need and for an explanation of any data you don't understand. Finally, if you feel lost and can't get what you need from your transactional agent, dual agent, or nonagent, you are entitled to go to the managing broker of the firm and ask to have a buyer broker assigned to work with you.

first time buyer tip

much they think a property is worth. If your seller broker is less forthcoming, ask how much he or she would allow his or her children to pay for the home. Remember that the seller broker has a fiduciary responsibility to the seller. According to a strict interpretation of the law, the seller broker can't do anything but suggest you pay the list price.

Making an Offer for New Construction

Making an offer for a home that has yet to be built is, in some ways, more complex than making an offer for an existing house. At least with the existing home, all of the appliances, tile, wall coverings, window treatments, and siding are already there. With new construction, you'll often be buying from blueprints, or perhaps after seeing a model home built and decorated for your viewing pleasure but not to your personal choices of colors and furnishings.

Part of the offer-and-negotiation process includes a myriad of choices—everything from what kind and color of tiles and carpet you want, to whether you want to upgrade to the full basement with the extra tall ceiling and a concrete floor. Do you want to add a fourth bedroom upstairs instead of the double-high entry way? (I think maximizing your interior space is always a savvy choice.) Do you want the three-car garage that offers the future option of making one of the bays into an office?

As a standard rule, developers rarely negotiate down on price, unless they're stuck with a final unit or two that won't sell for whatever reason. More typically, the lowest prices will be offered when the development first opens for business. As sales activity heats up, the price of homes in subsequent phases (you'll often hear about Phase I, Phase II, and Phase III of a development) will rise. Being the first to buy into a new subdivision often means you get the best price and perhaps the best upgrade package on the options that are available.

When you make your offer, you can try to negotiate the developer down on price, but you'll probably have better luck asking for more options and upgrades instead. For example, you might pay full price but receive upgrades on appliances, wiring, and carpet and tile choices. If you're one of the first to buy into a condo development and the parking is being sold separately, you may be able to get the developer to throw in the space for nothing, or to give you two spaces at a discount.

Developers make *a lot* of money on options and upgrades. It's far too easy to walk into a $300,000, four-bedroom, two-and-a-half-bath house and then spend another $100,000 (yes, you read that right) on options and upgrades the salesperson persuades you are must-haves. It's generally easier and cheaper to add these things on in the beginning, but, to gain maximum leverage in your negotiation process, visit competing subdivisions and price out the various packages the other developers are giving to home buyers. (If this process sounds a lot like buying a new car, you're getting the hang of it. The big difference is that new cars depreciate in value and you're hoping that your new home will appreciate.)

Janet's Story

When Janet was in her early thirties, she became editor of a real estate section of a major metropolitan newspaper. After editing the section for a while, she decided that she should stop paying rent and purchase a home instead.

After talking to all of the real estate writers to find out which developer had the best reputation, she settled on a former school that was being converted into condominiums. She was one of the first people to buy in the development, and armed with the information from the writers, she negotiated all kinds of extras and upgrades when she purchased the unit.

Her big coup was getting the developer to throw in her parking space for free. Two weeks later, the developer started charging $15,000 for the spot. Four years later, Janet got married and sold her unit—for a big profit!

HOW DO I MAKE AN OFFER?

There are three basic pieces to an offer: (1) the address or description of the property, (2) the *consideration*, or the price you are prepared to pay, and (3) the date on which the closing will take place.

A valid offer can be written on anything, including a paper napkin, and can read as follows: "I, Ilyce R. Glink, offer to buy 1 Willow Lane for $125,500, to close on July 13, 2002."

Although property has been bought and sold this way for centuries, making an offer today is usually a bit more complex. In some states, it's customary for the broker to use a "Contract to Purchase" form when making an offer. In other states, the broker has a preprinted "Offer for Purchase" form. Whichever form is used, you will generally sit with the broker and discuss all sorts of issues, such as:

1. Contingencies (see Questions 33–36).
2. Earnest money, also known as your *good faith deposit* (see Question 32).
3. Any requests you may have for personal property (such as appliances, lamps, attached bookcases, and so on).

After you fill in and sign the form, your broker will present the offer to the seller and his or her broker. If you are buying a FSBO, you will have to make the presentation yourself. If you don't understand the contract and its implications, *don't sign it.* Consult a real estate attorney first.

As the Internet facilitates the sale of homes, more sellers may try to sell without a broker's help, and save the 5 to 7 percent commission. If 20 percent of homes are sold today without a broker's assistance, in 10 years perhaps 30 percent (or more—although agents don't like to hear that prediction) of homes could be sold by owners. A savvy home buyer needs to know how to make a quality offer that any seller, represented or not, will be happy to accept, and how to sound good in a presentation. Essentially, in a presentation, you go over the offer for purchase with the seller, point by point, discussing things like price, closing date, date of possession, and any contingencies. As long as you're calm and professional, and consult with a real estate attorney ahead of time, you'll do just fine if you end up presenting without the assistance of a broker.

Typically, buyers represented by brokers do not attend the offer presentation. But sometimes they wait nearby.

Leo and Genna's Story

Leo and Genna looked at 50 homes before they found the one they wanted to buy. It was a nice-looking three-bedroom, two-and-a-half-bath house with a big living room, a dining room, and a sun room facing the sunny backyard.

Because there was so much interest in the property, Leo and Genna decided right on the spot (at the first showing) to make an offer. They sat at the kitchen table with their broker and drew up the offer, then waited while the broker went upstairs to present the offer to the sellers.

Although this was their first purchase, Leo and Genna had taken the time to thoroughly investigate the neighborhood and market before looking at homes. These savvy first-time buyers knew almost immediately how much they were going to offer for the house. They had seen many similar homes in the neighborhood, and they knew the range of selling prices over the previous six months. That knowledge enabled them to act fast when the time was right.

The Pressure Cooker

Sometimes, getting what you want hinges on how quickly you're able to act under pressure. Even at its best, making an offer can feel like a pressure cooker. Don't allow yourself to be sucked in to the point where you're no longer able to rationally discuss the offer and its implications. If you're finding yourself dragged along by the current, perhaps against your will, take a time-out. Remember, there is more than one right house for you.

If you're a typical homeowner, you're going to move between five and seven times during your life. There will always be another house. If you fall prey to the notion that a particular home is the only

Making an offer for a newly constructed home often means sitting down with the developer's agent and your agent (if you have one) and working out the price plus the upgrades and options that are to be included in the price. If the developer is mobbed with offers, you may have to make a reservation or be wait-listed for a home, and you may not find out until later whether you are actually going to be able to purchase it.

one for you, you may offer too much for it, thereby making it an imperfect choice.

WHAT GOES INTO THE ACTUAL OFFER TO PURCHASE OR CONTRACT TO PURCHASE?

QUESTION 31

An *offer to purchase* is usually a much simpler document than a *contract to purchase*. Why? Because the contract to purchase must get much more specific about the property's description, fixtures, exclusions, and all the necessary legal language for property transfer, rights to sue for specific performance (if the buyer or seller backs out of the contract on a whim), damages, brokers' fees, and so on.

Every city and state will have its own real estate association or Realtor (member of the National Association of Realtors) to provide standard form contracts for the purchase and sale of real estate. *Although the contracts are similar, real estate law varies from state to state.*

Remember that contracts tend to be written from the seller's perspective. (Originally, all brokers were seller brokers, and remnants of that bias remain.) As a buyer, you need to look over the forms carefully and probably hire a real estate lawyer to help you sort them out. If you're purchasing a FSBO, your attorney should have a contract you can use.

new construction tip

If you're purchasing new construction from a developer or builder, you'll probably use the developer's contract, which will likely be written to favor the developer.

Offer to Purchase

Let's look at an *offer to purchase real estate contract*, which starts out like a letter. It is addressed:

To: [Seller(s) _____

[Date of offer] _____

The property herein referred to is identified as follows: _____

_____ [Fill in the address and/or coordinates of the property.]

I hereby offer to buy said property, which has been offered to me by

_____ [Fill in the name of the seller broker], as your broker, under the following terms and conditions:

The contract allows you to indicate whether you will pay for the property by check or with cash. Next comes how much you will pay for the property, and in what stages:

$_____ is paid herewith as a deposit to bind this offer.

$_____ is to be paid as an additional deposit upon the execution of the purchase and sale agreement provided for below.

$_____ is to be paid at the time of delivery of the Deed in cash, or by certified, cashier's, treasurer's, or bank check.

A statement then tells the seller that the offer is only good until a certain time on a certain date. The seller has until that time to accept the offer, or the offer for purchase becomes invalid. If the seller makes a counteroffer, further negotiation must take place.

When an offer is acceptable, the seller is notified that the offer is contingent upon the execution of the standard purchase and sale agreement.

Next comes the closing date:

A good and sufficient Deed, conveying a good and clear record and marketable title shall be delivered at 12:00 Noon on _____, 2000, at the appropriate Registry of Deeds, unless some other time and place are mutually agreed upon in writing.

After a paragraph in which the buyer promises to forfeit the deposit if he or she does not fulfill his or her obligations, and another that says "Time is of the essence," there is a space to write in any additional terms and conditions, or to attach any riders.

Finally, the document is signed by the buyers, and the receipt for the deposit at the bottom of the page is filled out.

The standard purchase and sale agreement form can be two or three times as long. (See Appendix III for a complete form.)

Real estate attorneys say that most buyers never read the contract that will make them an owner. Although the contract will vary in each state, or even from city to city, most of the main issues and procedures will be similar. *And you should read it.* It represents one of the biggest investments you'll make during your lifetime.

The Contract, Point by Point

A typical completed contract has these (or similar) headings, followed by appropriate information, caveats, prohibitions, or terms:

1. **Parties.** The names of the seller and the buyer.

2. **Description.** The address, title reference, and description of the property. For example: "The land with the buildings thereon, numbered 391 Waverley Avenue, Newton, Middlesex County, Massachusetts, being shown as Lot B on a 'Plan of Land in Newton belonging to Katherine F. Cameron,' E. S. Smithe, Surveyor, dated May 1914, recorded with Middlesex South Registry Deeds Book 4741 and more particularly described in deed to Seller dated May 27, 1977, recorded at Middlesex South Registry Deeds in Book 13200, Page 450."

3. **Buildings, Structures, Improvements, Fixtures.** A general list of the buildings, structures, and improvements that are included with the sale. Before signing, the buyer may wish to delete, exclude, or add some appropriate items—particularly, a list of appliances that the sellers *could* take with them but should be part of the deal: the dishwasher, washer, dryer, and refrigerator. The disposition of some of these items will be decided based on local custom. For example, in downtown Chicago, all appliances stay with the house. In Atlanta, refrigerators, washers, and dryers generally go with the sellers to their new home. (Your agent can fill you in on the local custom if you're not aware of it.)

4. **Title Deed.** Any restrictions, easements (rights other people may have to the use the property or to the restriction of the use of the property), rights, or obligations that the buyer is willing to accept on the title. (If you wish to delete statements that you object to, consult your attorney.)

5. **Plans.** The plans approved by the buyer and recorded in advance by the seller. They should comply with all laws, allowing a clear transfer of the title.

6. **Registered Title.** A system, in some states, for registration of title.

7. **Purchase Price.** The exact amounts, stated in words and in numerals, of the deposit or earnest money (that is, money held in trust or escrow by a third party) and the remainder of the money due at the closing.

8. **Time for Performance: Delivery of Deed.** The time, date, and place agreed on for the closing.

9. **Possession and Conditions of Premises.** The statement confirming that the buyer is to receive full possession, free of tenants and occupants, at closing; that the property does not violate any building or zoning laws; and that the buyer is entitled to inspect the premises before the closing.

10. **Extension to Perfect the Title or Make the Premises Conform.** A provision that permits the seller 30 days to correct any problems with the property's title.

11. **Failure to Perfect the Title or Make the Premises Conform.** A statement that the buyer's money will be refunded if the seller fails to deliver good title.

12. **Buyer's Election to Accept Title.** An agreement that if something impairs the property's title, such as a mechanic's or tax lien, the buyer can elect to take the property as is, subject to the lien, and deduct the lien amount from the purchase price. If a disaster occurs, such as a fire, the buyer can elect to take the home as is and be compensated from the insurance proceeds, or take a reduction in the price of the home to cover the damage.

13. **Acceptance of Deed.** An agreement that the deed will be accepted by the buyer, at the closing, only if all duties and obligations under the contract have been fulfilled by the seller.

14. **Use of Money to Clear Title.** The seller's promise to leave behind, at the closing, money needed to pay off any liens against the property.

15. **Insurance.** The seller's promise to maintain a certain amount of insurance on the property until the buyer's homeowner policy takes effect. The amount, which is usually negotiated, should be sufficient to cover the cost of restoring the property after a fire or other disaster.

16. **Adjustments.** A prorated list of expenses (such as water or electricity bills, or property assessments) and of taxes for the portion of the month or year the seller owned the house. The buyer is credited, at the closing, for these expenses.

17. **Adjustment of Unassessed and Abated Taxes.** Taxes that have not yet been assessed for the year. They are usually prorated, based on the prior year's taxes, according to a local formula.

18. **Brokers' Fee.** Who gets the commissions and how much.

19. **Brokers' Warranties.** The brokers' names, and verification that they are licensed.

20. **Deposit.** The escrow agreement and a statement of who will receive the interest on the account.

21. **Buyer's Default and Damages.** An agreement that if the buyer named in the contract should fail to buy the property, the seller keeps the escrow money.

22. **Release by Husband or Wife.** Confirmation that the seller's spouse agrees to release any claim. The release is omitted if the seller is divorced or widowed.

23. **Broker as Party.** A statement that the brokers are a part of the contract.

24. **Liability of Trustee, Shareholder, or Beneficiary.** A valid concern only if one of the parties is represented by a trustee; otherwise, omitted.

25. **Warranties and Representations.** The promises the seller makes to the buyer regarding the condition of the property.

26. **Mortgage Contingency Clause.** A standard clause on some contracts; otherwise, added as a rider. (See Question 34.)

27. **Construction of Agreement.** Legal language that sets up the contract as a contract.

28. **Lead Paint Law.** Under recently enacted federal rules, a requirement that sellers of properties built before 1978 must disclose whether a home may have lead paint, plaster, or other materials. Some states have gone further. In Massachusetts, if a child under the age of six years resides in any residential premises that contains dangerous levels of lead, the owner must remove or cover the paint to make it safe for children.

29. **Smoke Detectors and Other Certifications.** Where required (e.g., in Massachusetts), the seller's agreement to provide certification from the local fire department that the property is equipped with smoke detectors. In Chicago, Illinois, a seller must provide proof of payment for his or her water bills.

30. **Additional Provisions.** Other singular riders.

For an example of a complete contract to purchase, see Appendix III.

Condominium Contracts

The difference between purchasing a condo and purchasing a single-family home is slight. When you purchase a condo, you are buying real estate plus an interest in the common areas managed by the homeowners' association.

Some real estate sales contracts for condominiums contain special provisions that are not applicable to single-family houses. For example, some condo boards have a right of first refusal when a condo unit is sold. This allows the board to purchase the unit if that decision is in the best interest of the condo building. In a sales contract, the seller will agree to procure the release or waiver of any option or right of first refusal. (See Appendix III for a complete contract.)

Co-op Contracts

When you purchase a co-op, you're not really purchasing real estate. You're purchasing personal property in the form of shares in the corporation that owns the building. You become a tenant and pay "rent" (a monthly maintenance assessment fee) for the right to live there. Because of this, co-op contracts are entirely different from condo or single-family contracts.

WHAT IS THE EARNEST MONEY?
WHO HOLDS IT? WHEN DO I GET IT BACK?

The *earnest money*, also known as a *good faith deposit*, is the cash the buyer puts up to show he or she is serious about purchasing the property. The money represents the buyer's commitment to buy, and

133

it acts as an unofficial option on the property. After receiving an earnest money check, the seller will usually stop showing the property and will wait to see whether the buyer can get a mortgage.

Earnest money is important to the transaction because it shows the seller that the buyer is operating in good faith (hence the name, "earnest"). The bigger the deposit, the more the seller is reassured that "This buyer is serious." It also ties the buyer to the property and keeps him or her from looking for additional properties.

How Much Good Faith Do I Have to Show?

Usually, home buyers offer, as earnest money, 5 to 10 percent of the sales price of the house—in cash. The amount is large enough that almost any buyer will think twice about walking away from the house on a whim. The money is typically held by the seller broker.

If you don't have 10 percent in cash, then put down 5 percent. Some buyers attach a $1,000 check to the offer to purchase, to show initial good faith. The rest of the deposit, or earnest money, is due when the contract is signed by both parties, or shortly thereafter.

Who Holds the Earnest Money?

The money typically goes into an escrow account held by the seller broker, but this is largely a matter of local custom or it can be negotiated. The buyer usually is credited for the interest earned on his or her deposit.

When Do I Get the Earnest Money Back?

If the sale goes through, the earnest money (plus interest) is often used as part of the cash down payment given to the seller. If the sale does not go through and the reason is covered by a contingency in the contract (if, for example, the buyer could not get a mortgage), the seller should sign a release of escrow and refund the earnest money to the buyer. The earnest money should also be refunded to the buyer if the sale does not go through because of a problem on the seller's side. If, however, the buyer backs out of the deal for no reason at all, or for a reason that is not covered by a contingency in the contract, return of the earnest money may be subject to negotiation.

What If the Seller Won't Give Back the Earnest Money?

Before a buyer can get back the earnest money, the seller must sign a *release of escrow*. If the buyer and seller disagree over who is entitled to the earnest money, and the attorneys can't resolve the issue, the broker has two options: (1) to hold the money until the disagreement is resolved, or, (2) in some states, to turn over the funds to the state real estate commission or agency for mediation, or to local courts for litigation. Ask your buyer broker to explain your state law and local customs regarding this situation.

In the real world, brokers hate to be put in this position. Even though, legally, they can't release the funds until the seller and buyer have resolved their differences, they become the focal point for everyone's frustration at the situation. But if they turn over the funds to either party before a resolution is reached, they could lose their license.

WHEN I MAKE AN OFFER, WHAT CONTINGENCIES SHOULD I INCLUDE?

QUESTION
33

Ilyce and Sam's Story

When the first edition of this book was released in 1994, my publisher, Times Books, sent me on a book tour. At the same time, we'd grown tired of our 1920s co-op overlooking Lake Michigan in Chicago and were looking to buy a house.

We looked for more than four years, trying to find the right home. In that time, we saw perhaps 125 houses. (Who knows? It could have been a lot more.)

While I was traveling on my book tour, Sam continued house hunting. Homes were selling quickly at that time. During one trip, he found a couple of houses he liked very much. After we talked on the phone and he described one home in detail, he made an offer to the owner.

He included the usual cadre of contingencies, including an attorney approval rider, a financing contingency, and an inspection contingency. But he also included an "Ilyce has to love it" contingency.

> In effect, this special contingency said: When Ilyce comes back into town, she has to come and see the house. If she doesn't like it, we can back out of the deal.
>
> Lucky thing, because I wasn't wild about the house when I saw it. The sellers had accepted the contingency, and we did back out of the deal.

Although the market in the late 1990s was considerably hotter than in the mid-1990s, this kind of contingency is making a resurgence—through the Internet. Couples are now making offers for properties through the Internet—sight unseen (except for 360-degree photos or video of the property available on-line).

In these deals, the "We have to love it when we finally see it" contingency is becoming more popular. (I don't recommend making an offer, sight unseen, on *any* property, but if you're so inclined, I may have a bridge in Brooklyn that you'd be interested in buying.)

Your Everyday, Garden Variety Contingencies

Let's start with a definition: A *contingency* allows you to back out of a contract for a specific reason. Typically, three contingencies accompany a contract to purchase: (1) financing or mortgage; (2) inspection; and (3) attorney approval. They are explained, respectively, in Questions 34, 35, and 36.

Among the many other contingencies that might appear in a contract for purchase are:

- Sale of your prior residence (not applicable to first-time buyers).
- Admittance to certain clubs (for example, if you are buying a home near a private golf course, you might make the purchase contingent on your acceptance to the club).
- Approval by a condo or co-op board.
- Pest inspection, asbestos, radon, lead, water (may be separate contingencies or lumped under "inspection").
- Compliance with building codes.
- Liking it in person, if you have bid on a home sight unseen (or through the Internet).

You can put forward almost any contingency you like, but remember, having odd contingencies, in addition to mortgage, inspection, and attorney approval, could give the seller grounds for refusing your contract.

WHAT IS A MORTGAGE OR FINANCING CONTINGENCY?

A mortgage or financing contingency allows you to back out of the contract to purchase if you cannot get a lender to give you a mortgage commitment.

The contingency will generally require you (1) to be specific about the type of mortgage you are seeking and (2) to seek mortgage approval within a specified period of time, generally 45 to 60 days. You must be reasonable about the mortgage's parameters, and usually you must agree to look for a mortgage at the current prevailing rate of interest.

The contingency is meant to protect you in case you can't find financing. Here is the Massachusetts mortgage contingency used by the Greater Boston Real Estate Board. Remember, this contingency form's wording may not be viable in your state.

FINANCING CONTINGENCY FOR MASSACHUSETTS

In order to help finance the acquisition of said premises, the BUYER shall apply for a conventional bank or other institutional mortgage loan of _____, payable in no less than _____ years at an interest rate not to exceed _____. If despite the BUYER's diligent efforts a commitment for such a loan cannot be obtained on or before _____, 20____, the BUYER may terminate this agreement by written notice to the SELLER(S) and/or the Broker(s), as agent for the SELLER, prior to the expiration of such time, whereupon any payments made under this agreement shall be forthwith refunded and all other obligations of the parties hereto shall end. In no event will the BUYER be deemed to have used diligent efforts to obtain such commitment unless the BUYER submits a complete mortgage loan application conforming to the foregoing provisions on or before _____, 20____. (Provided courtesy of the Greater Boston Real Estate Board.)

The mortgage contingency should be included in the contract. If it is not, be sure to ask your broker or real estate attorney to make it an addendum to the contract.

What do you do if you're in a really tight bidding war, with several other parties all looking for a way to differentiate their bids? If you've been preapproved for your loan, you'll get your financing as long as the house appraises out in value. The lender has committed to it in writing. In an extreme situation, you could change your financing contingency to read that purchase of the home is contingent only upon the house's appraising out in value by the lender's appraiser. The risk is, of course, that the lender will back out of the deal for some reason. With a written commitment, the lender has to follow through, unless the company goes belly-up. This type of financing contingency may give you the edge you need to complete a winning bid. Before you do this, however, consult with your real estate attorney.

QUESTION 35

WHAT IS THE INSPECTION CONTINGENCY?

This contingency gives you the right to have a house inspector examine the property before you close on the purchase.

Again, the purpose of the contingency is to protect you from buying a home that may have serious hidden structural problems or material defects. When you add an inspection contingency to the contract, make sure it covers both the home and the property on which it sits. You might also want to have a separate contingency for each of the following:

• Radon.
• Asbestos.
• Lead.
• Toxic substances.
• Water.
• Pests, including termites, mice, rats, roaches, and so on.

Generally, the inspection contingency will require you to have your inspection done within five to ten days after the offer is accepted

Although a recently passed federal law requires sellers of homes built before 1978 to disclose whether they have lead in their homes, the sellers may not know. If the home you like is old and you're planning to do any renovation work, you may uncover decades-old lead-based paint that could then get sanded into the air, creating a potentially dangerous situation—especially for children. In any hardware store, products are available that will help you test for lead. One of the easiest tools looks like a cigarette butt. Basically, you swab it over a window sill, next to a pipe, or anywhere else you suspect lead. If the test swab turns red, there is lead present. Like asbestos, lead is only dangerous if it is ingested. Babies can and do pick up tiny pieces of paint and put them in their mouth (our first son, Alex, didn't do it, but our second, Michael, couldn't resist). It's worth a few bucks to make sure you know what's lurking in the house you're about to purchase.

by the seller. Otherwise, you may lose the right to withdraw from the contract. Keep this in mind when scheduling your various tests.

A sample inspection contingency addendum is shown below.

INSPECTION CONTINGENCY
FOR MASSACHUSETTS

The BUYER may, at his own expense and on or before _____, 20____, have the property inspected by a person engaged in the business of conducting home inspections. If it is the opinion of such inspector that the property contains serious structural, mechanical, or other defects, then the BUYER shall have the option of revoking the Offer by written notice to the SELLER and/or the Broker, as your agent, prior to the expiration of such time, which notice shall be accompanied by a copy of the inspector's opinion and any related inspection report, whereupon all deposits made by the BUYER to you shall be forthwith refunded and this Offer shall become null and void and without further recourse to any party. (Provided courtesy of the Greater Boston Real Estate Board.)

Some buyers hope that the home inspection will turn up small, fixable problems, so that they can get additional money from the seller at closing. The real purpose of the inspection contingency, however, is to protect you from purchasing property that may have serious, expensive, or unfixable problems. Like the mortgage contingency, the inspection contingency should be either written into the contract or attached to it as a rider or addendum.

When Don't I Need an Inspection?

I'm often asked whether *every* home buyer should have his or her future home inspected. That depends. If, for example, you've been living in your home for the past five years as a renter, and you've been responsible for the entire upkeep of the property, then perhaps you know what problems exist with the plumbing, heating, and electrical systems. Perhaps you know that the back right burner on the stove doesn't work and the air-conditioning compressor is on its last legs.

But most home buyers haven't lived in the property they're going to purchase. They don't even know where the water shut-off valves are. If that's your situation, you should definitely pay for a professional home inspection.

Some brokers say that if you're moving into a condo or co-op apartment building, you have relatively little risk of something big popping up. That's because with a condo you only own what's inside your unit plus a share of the common elements of the property. With a co-op, you don't even own that. You own shares in the corporation that owns your property, and you pay a monthly rental fee (the maintenance or assessment) for the unit that the shares represent.

In a condo or co-op, the only things for which you're responsible are interior electrical work, appliances, plumbing fixtures (sometimes, not even those), and decorating. Your financial liability, should something go wrong, is slight.

You're probably thinking: Why should any condo or co-op buyer pay for a professional inspection? Because a good inspector will tour the *common* elements of the property—look at the building's heating, electrical, and plumbing systems, and check out the roof, the foundation, the parking structure, and the windows. The inspection may save you a full share of the cost of repairing or replacing some common elements shortly after you move in.

When we moved into our co-op, the inspector found that some members of the building's board of directors had tapped in, illegally, to the electrical panel, causing a dangerous overload. Our inspector was required to report it to the city, which fined the building (and made us less than popular). The building eventually corrected the problem, for which it had to assess all of the residents.

By having the inspection, you learn not only how your own property works, but what problems may exist in a condo or co-op—problems you'll have to pay for during the time you live there.

WHAT IS THE ATTORNEY APPROVAL OR ATTORNEY RIDER?

Before you sign any contract or offer, *consult with someone who can advise you about the purchase and its legal consequences.* In some states, that's a real estate attorney's job. In others, your broker will advise you. The attorney contingency or rider essentially gives your attorney the right to make changes to the contract, or to reject a contract that doesn't adequately protect you.

If you are working with a seller broker and that broker is the person who is supposed to advise you of your legal rights under the contract, there may be a serious conflict of interest. If you have *any* qualms about being counseled by your real estate broker or sales agent, consult an attorney. Spending between $250 and $750 for an attorney's guidance is a small price to pay when you're making the biggest investment of your life. When all the fees and costs are pinching your wallet, try to imagine how expensive and time-consuming it would be if something *really* went wrong.

For more information about why attorneys are important, and how to hire a good one, see Questions 41 and 42.

In some states, the offer for purchase is worded in such a way that there is no need for an attorney approval rider. It would say, for example: "This offer to purchase is subject to a contract that is agreeable to both parties." If you aren't sure whether your offer is worded in that way, it is best to attach an attorney rider.

Do not assume that, just because you have an attorney rider, your attorney can remove you from the deal if you suddenly discover you have made a mistake in the offer (usually, offering too high a price for the home). Some attorneys try to cover for their clients' mistakes by rejecting the contract, but this is unprofessional. If you have any questions about the offer or contract, consult an attorney *before* making the offer or signing your name.

The following sample attorney approval contingency is valid in the State of Illinois. Remember, this language may not be valid in your state, but your broker or your attorney should have a rider that will work for you:

ATTORNEY APPROVAL RIDER
FOR STATE OF ILLINOIS

It is agreed by and between the parties hereto as follows: That their respective attorneys may approve of or make modifications, other than price and dates, mutually acceptable to the parties. Approval will not be unreasonably withheld, but, if within _____ days after the date of acceptance of the Contract, it becomes evident agreement cannot be reached by the parties hereto, and written notice thereof is given to either party within the time specified, then this Contract shall become null and void, and all monies paid by the Purchaser shall be refunded. In the absence of written notice within the time specified herein, this provision shall be deemed waived by all parties hereto, and this contract shall be in full force and effect. (Provided courtesy of the Chicago Association of Realtors.)

6

Negotiating the Deal

QUESTION

37

HOW DOES THE NEGOTIATION PROCESS WORK?

Whether you're negotiating to buy or to sell a home, to settle on the terms and conditions of a divorce, or to confirm the salary, benefits, and bonus you'll accept with your new job, negotiation is about give and take.

David Falk, Michael Jordan's agent, says negotiations are most successful when everyone walks away happy. A person who holds a stronger hand usually gives less and takes more, but in a successful negotiation, both sides end up compromising.

That's what you want when you're buying a home. You don't want the seller to take you for a ride, nor do you want to ride the seller, or he or she will begin to like you a lot less and the move will become more difficult. Emotions run high in something as personal as selling a home. When negotiations get tough or reach an impasse, emotions become embittered arms-at-war.

Happy Homeowners

Unlike a judge's settlement, where both sides may end up profoundly unhappy with the result, a successful house negotiation can leave everyone feeling like a winner—and that's the goal! As a buyer, you want the sellers to feel they are getting a fair price for their home. You want them to bask in the glow of having made a good deal so that they will be nice to you when you want to tromp through with the inspector, your spouse, your friends, your decorator, and your parents.

You want that niceness to extend through to the closing, so that the sellers do not make you crazy with all kinds of nonsense at the end. You want them to like you so that they can feel good about selling their home to someone who will love it as much as they have. (As we'll discuss later, the emotional component to homeownership is stronger than for just about any other type of financial investment.)

You also want to feel that you paid a fair price for the home. There is nothing worse than finding out, the day after you've signed the contract, that you overpaid for the house, because the sellers intend to take (or to steal, you may say) items you thought were included with the price. The nastiness can leave a bad taste in your mouth—and in your attitude toward your new home.

Negotiating Fairly

How do you negotiate fairly? How do you end up with good feelings on all sides of the table? First, enlist your broker (or your attorney, if you choose not to work with a broker) to help keep everyone's emotions at bay. Brokers are good at this kind of public relations. It's one of the most important parts of their job. They must present buyers' offers as being worthwhile, not insulting. You must rely on your broker to characterize you as a serious buyer.

After you write up the offer (with your broker's help), it's up to the broker to present the offer to the seller. This is the first step of the negotiation. The broker will take your offer and present it to the seller and, usually, the seller broker. This can take place in an office, but usually your broker will go to see the seller, in the home, where the surroundings are most comfortable. Perhaps over a cup of coffee, your broker will state exactly how much you are willing to pay for the home, the conditions under which you'll purchase it, and the date you propose for the sale.

These days, offers are frequently communicated over the telephone or by fax. Many brokers would still rather bring the offer in person. After all—as my mother, Susanne, the agent, likes to say—this is a very personal business. When your broker leaves, the seller and the seller's broker will discuss the offer.

Unless a full-price offer is made or the seller is quite desperate, a first offer is almost never accepted. Everyone understands that the first offer is a little bit (or quite a lot) below what you expect to pay for the property. The key to a successful negotiation is to remember that it's a psychological game.

In a bidding-war situation, you may get only one opportunity to make an offer. Constructing a best-bid offer can be frightening. You want to get the property, but you don't want to overpay for it. In that case, you'll have to rely on your broker to steer you through, based on his or her knowledge and years of experience in home sales in the neighborhood.

Offer and Counteroffer

Here's how an offer works. Let's say the home is priced at $100,000. You think that price is close but still slightly high. You offer $90,000, or 10 percent less than the asking price. The seller now assumes you'll be willing to compromise somewhere in the middle—say, $94,000 to $96,000. The seller then makes a calculated guess: Are you willing to go up to $96,000? Will you only go up to $95,000? Or will you stop at $94,000? If the seller wants to cut to the chase, he or she may instruct the seller broker to present a "split-the-difference" counteroffer. If accepted, you would pay $95,000 for the property.

Sometimes, negotiations get tough. If the seller thinks the $100,000 price is fair, any reduction may come in very low increments—say, $1,000. Then you have to decide whether you want to match those increments or make a final offer. Making the last offer is like saying "I call" in a card game. The seller might come down $2,500 and say that $97,500 is a final offer, take it or leave it. Or you might put in a take-it-or-leave-it offer of $95,000, and put the ball in the seller's court. If you turn the negotiation into a power struggle, it could quickly turn nasty. Better to keep things at a more even, if not a downright friendly pace, to keep the negotiations moving ahead step by step.

But that doesn't mean you shouldn't play up your strengths. If you can't afford to pay more than $95,000, have your broker tell the seller that you are making your very best offer and while you can't be more flexible on the price, you really love the house and would be more flexible on the closing date. You're never going to know what the seller's hot points are. The closing date may be of more concern than the extra $5,000. There may be a special interest in turning the home over to people who really love it. That's where you can use a seller's emotional attachment to his or her home to great advantage.

The Low-Ball Bid

If you decide you love a home that's too expensive no matter how you cut your budget, you have a choice. You can either walk away and say you'll come back to a house like that later in your life, or you can make a low-ball offer.

There is no industry definition of a low-ball offer, but several things can be said to describe one:

1. It is usually more than 10 percent below the asking price of the home.
2. A seller usually finds it insulting, which means the seller broker must plead with the seller to reconsider and make a counteroffer.
3. It gives a decidedly negative cast to the negotiation process.

Sometimes, a low-ball offer works; at other times, it doesn't. A lot depends on the presentation of the broker and the desperation of the seller. Another key factor is whether you're in a buyer's market or a seller's market. If you're in a hot seller's market (too many buyers for the homes that are available for sale), expect to pay close to, at, or in excess of the list price for the home. An acceptable low-ball bid in an evenly paced market might be considered highly insulting in a hot market. In fact, many sellers wouldn't even respond to such a bid, even though you might be perfectly willing to raise your initial offer.

For example, if you decide to offer $80,000 for a home priced at $100,000, and you enclose with your offer comps of similar homes in the neighborhood that recently sold for $75,000, the seller may consider your offer. But if you offer $50,000 for a house that's well priced at $100,000, few sellers would even dignify your offer with a response. As a potential buyer, you have the right to make whatever offer you want, and your broker must present that offer to the seller. But that doesn't mean you won't tick off the seller.

Bidding Wars

A bidding war occurs when more than one buyer is interested in purchasing the same home. In the last half of the 1990s, the market all over the United States was so hot that bidding wars erupted over properties that sellers couldn't sell even a year or two earlier.

Usually, the seller broker will ask for bids from the interested parties. The broker will then present the bids to the seller, who will decide which offer to respond to. Often, you'll find out there is another interested party and your broker will encourage you to make your very best bid—in other words, no negotiation. If you want to offer $95,000, then that's what you put in the bid. If you think the other interested party is going to offer $95,000, and you really want the house, offer a little more.

The key problem with the negotiation step in the home-buying process is that it's extremely pressured. Your broker will tell you to stay close to the telephone so that you won't miss "The Call." You'll be on pins and needles, wondering whether your bid is going to be accepted or rejected. Try not to get so worked up about your bid that you can't concentrate on anything else. Take a walk. See a movie. Get your mind off it. By putting some space between you and your offer, or between you and the whole negotiation process, you gain some much-needed perspective.

Marla and David's Story

Marla and David were certain that they'd never be able to buy a home. They had enough cash to make a significant down payment and to cover the closing costs, fees, and cash reserves lenders require. They had excellent credit and had even been approved for a mortgage.

What was killing them was the heat of the market.

Every time they wanted to make an offer, the house was sold before they could even see it. If they were lucky enough to get their bid considered, it was one of several bids in a hotly contested bidding war.

After losing six houses in bidding wars and another half dozen before they could even place a bid, Marla and David sat down for a long talk. They discussed their strategy for finding and bidding on houses, and they evaluated their broker's approach.

They decided to become much more aggressive. They told their broker that she had to almost anticipate the market and become much more aggressive in finding properties for them earlier. They vowed also to be much more aggressive when they put together an offer.

They got the next house they bid on.

Aggressive Negotiation Survival Strategies

Marla and David used some of the following strategies when they put together their final, winning bid. Some sellers and brokers may find a few of these strategies too aggressive—or offensive and even unethical—but they may help you capture the home of your dreams. Use them sparingly, and only when you're facing a relentless seller's market.

1. **Don't be afraid to initially offer the list—or a higher— price.** Yes, you're telling the seller you'll pay at least that much for the home. And you may even go up from there. But nothing gets a seller's attention like an offer that contains the number he or she was hoping to see.

2. **Remove as many contingencies as you can.** The first contingency to go should be your financing contingency—*if* you've been approved for a loan (and have received the lender's commitment in writing), and *if* you're sure that the house is going to appraise out and the lender won't go out of business before you close. In an aggressive situation, some brokers advise their clients that being preapproved is the same as being an all-cash buyer. The next contingency to go should be the inspection contingency. Unless you're worried about a structural element like the foundation or roof, most flaws can be corrected later and paid for as you go. Finally, if you have to, let go of the attorney approval rider. Although your attorney (if you're in a state that uses attorneys) can still negotiate your

148

contract language for you, he or she can't yank you out of a deal simply because the contract doesn't protect you. A tough situation calls for tough measures.

3. **Make an open-ended offer.** If the seller agent calls around for a "best bid," make an offer that really counts. Some extra-aggressive folks have won houses in tough bidding wars by offering to pay $1,000, $5,000, or a specific percentage more than the highest bid. For example, instead of proposing a price, your offer might read: "The buyer agrees to pay 2 percent more than the highest alternative bid."

4. **Offer to let the seller choose the closing time.** If you line up your ducks ahead of time, you may be able to close within a week or two, rather than in two to three months. Let the seller choose a suitable closing time, no matter how it may conflict with your schedule.

5. **Create several offer packages and allow your broker to pick the one that gets the job done.** In a multiple bid presentation, the buyer brokers will often present one after another, allowing each broker to hear the others' bids. Although it's not strictly ethical, some brokers tell their buyers to create multiple offers, which they carry in separate envelopes in their briefcase. They angle to be the last to make a presentation. After hearing the other bids, they simply pull out of their briefcase the bid that tops all others.

Real estate markets can change on a dime. It's rare that a hot buyer's market or hot seller's market will last for years, although, as I write this, we're in our fourth year of the hottest seller's market ever—and it was preceded by a six-year buyer's market in the western and northeastern portions of the United States. The bottom line is: Markets do change and real estate has cyclical highs and lows. If you're overly aggressive, you risk purchasing property at an all-time high price (especially if you're going to hold the property for only a short period of time), and then watching your home lose half of its value overnight (as happened in Boston, New York, and southern California). Consider stepping aside for a few months and waiting until the heat subsides. If it doesn't cool down, you should at least be able to look at the market unemotionally, and with a more seasoned eye.

20/20

hindsight

> When you're doggedly looking for a home to buy, and you've been disappointed again and again, it's easy to start feeling as though you'll never find the right house—or, even if you find it, you'll never be able to buy it. The truth is, plenty of houses come on the market every day. If you don't get a particular house, another will come along that will seem even more wonderful and perfect than the house you lost. Remember, there will always be another house.

Negotiating into the Future

It's hard to imagine a negotiation for anything—an art auction, real estate, a lawsuit—that wouldn't take place in person, or at least over the telephone. But that's what appears to be happening.

During the late 1990s, the success of e-bay (ebay.com), an Internet-based auction site for just about anything from old stuffed animals and trading cards to furniture, has led to an explosion of on-line negotiation. Everyone's trying to help everyone buy things electronically. There's even a site that allows two sides in a lawsuit to negotiate toward the middle. Each side sends an offer (what will be paid or accepted) into the site, and the two sides get closer and closer until they're $5,000 or less apart. Then, the computer finds the right number in the middle. Both parties pay relatively little and save hundreds, if not thousands (or a percentage of the winnings), in attorneys' fees.

In November 1993, going on-line and getting an e-mail address from America Online was about the last thing I did before the first edition of this book went to press. At that time, I couldn't have imagined that, by the end of the 1990s, millions of people would go on-line to peruse all homes that are listed for sale with Multiple Listing Services (MLS) nationwide. I didn't dream people would make offers for homes they'd seen only on the Internet. I could barely imagine buyers and owners getting excellent, complete information about the mortgage process, let alone applying on-line for a home loan.

We've essentially seen the beginnings of a revolution in the way real estate is bought and sold. I'm guessing that by the time I next update this book, on-line mechanisms will be available to help buyers and sellers negotiate the *price* of a home as well.

If you stumble upon such a site, beware. It's all well and good to do things yourself (and, I believe, you can efficiently and successfully conduct about 95 percent of your personal financial life yourself), but having a buyer broker assist you in the negotiation process can be well worth it.

A good broker or agent will keep you from paying too much for a home, even if, in your home-buying zeal, you're bound and determined to do so. The titans of the Internet world have not yet been able to replace a human touch. And until someone finds a way to replace it, you're best off negotiating for your home the old-fashioned way—personally.

HOW DO I MAKE A COUNTEROFFER?

QUESTION
38

Unless an offer is for the list price, and sometimes even if it is, a *counteroffer* is the next event after the initial contract is presented. You (the buyer) make the offer. The seller responds by countering your offer with another offer. Any response from you or the seller, after the initial offer presentation, is a counteroffer.

Making a counteroffer is actually simpler than making the first offer because you're in the driver's seat. The seller's response to your offer means that the seller believes you are a serious buyer and that your offer is within a valid range.

Before responding to the seller's counteroffer, make sure you understand the psychological implications behind it. In making your counteroffer, you can either match the seller's decrease in price with an equal increase, or jump up more to make the seller feel better about the deal. The choice is yours.

After you've decided how much to offer in this next round, talk to your broker. It's usually unnecessary to draw up an entirely new

After you make your counteroffer, you'll be hard-pressed to do anything until you get a response, through your broker. To make sure you hear something soon, consider limiting the time in which your offer is valid. If you put down specific terms—"This offer expires within 24 hours," or ". . . by the end of the business day on Wednesday"—you will force the seller to respond within your time frame, not his or hers.

first time

buyer tip

contract, although customs vary from state to state and county to county. At this stage, the broker usually modifies the existing offer and calls the seller broker, who relays the new offer to the seller.

QUESTION 39

WHAT IS A HOME WARRANTY? WHAT KIND CAN I GET FOR NEW CONSTRUCTION? WHAT ABOUT A PREVIOUSLY-OWNED HOME?

The concept of a home warranty sounds pretty good: If something breaks, or the foundation cracks, or the roof leaks, all you have to do is call an 800 number and someone will come out and fix it for free. All you'll pay is the service premium (also known as a deductible) of $35–$150.

Another cliché unfortunately holds true: If it sounds too good to be true, in most cases, it is.

Although existing and new home warranties should work this way in theory, in practice you will often incur extra headaches and extra expenses on the road to fixing your problem.

There are two types of home warranties: a new home warranty for new construction, and a homeowner's warranty for previously-owned homes. Let's look at new construction first.

New Home Warranties

New construction usually means you'll be the first person to live in your newly-built home. And, today, many developers are building semicustom homes; they allow you to choose your own architectural style, decor, cabinetry, floor coverings, appliances, and bathroom fixtures. You may even have a choice of options—a basement, a sun room, an attic, a two- or three-car garage, an extra bedroom—and upgrades—carpeting, floor coverings, cabinetry, fixtures, and so on.

In the past, developers of new construction provided a new home warranty backed by one of two or three organizations whose combined pool of money covered structural problems with new homes. It worked pretty well until a rash of undercapitalized, sleazy developers built shoddy homes and didn't put in enough money to cover the problems. That left one of the organizations short of funds and unable to pay the claims. In the past few years, two other warranty companies stepped in to fill this gap. Recently, they resumed providing new home warranties for new construction. Unfortunately, these collective pools of cash may not be enough to pay off every claim.

But real estate attorneys say that reputable developers of new construction will often back up their own work, and this should be one of the criteria for your selection of a new home. Usually, the developer will provide a door-to-door warranty for one year on nearly everything in the home. Part of this warranty is covered by the manufacturers of the home's new appliances and mechanical systems. The developer might also extend the warranty for specific major components, such as the roof, hardwood floors, or fireplace, to five or ten years.

I can't stress this enough: It's vital to know exactly what kind of service your developer will provide to you once you've bought his or her home, and what structural items and mechanical systems have what kind of warranty. If the developer refuses to warrant anything, watch out. That refusal might mean that the developer is sleazy, or has built a shoddy project, or has something to hide.

Juanita's Story

Juanita bought a town house in a new development on the west side of Chicago. After she moved in, she started having problems with a few minor leaks, which caused her floorboards to buckle.

The paint in one of her bathrooms started peeling, and the deck didn't look like it was connected correctly. She contacted the architect, who happened to buy a unit in the same development (a good sign, I'd say). Before the architect could respond to her complaints and concerns, Juanita hired a professional home inspector to go through her unit, pointing out all the things that weren't built right.

Juanita sent a three-page letter to the architect, the developer, and the developer's attorney. The home inspector's final conclusion was that fixing all of the little problems would cost about $1,000, but his report was scary to Juanita, and nothing the developer could say would make it right.

Juanita had lived in the unit for a year, but she decided she wanted out. The developer said fine, he'd buy back the unit and pay for some of her closing costs. He intends to fix the relatively minor problems and resell the unit—for an additional $60,000.

What Juanita didn't realize was that the price of her town home had skyrocketed in the year she'd lived there, giving the developer a huge return on his investment.

In Juanita's case, everyone ends up a winner. Juanita gets her money back. She bought from a quality developer who backed up his product. The developer is happy because he'll resell the town house and make a huge profit. The architect is happy because she no longer has a neighbor in the development who's unhappy with the work. Bottom line: It's incredibly important to buy from a quality developer, one who will back up the product a year or more after sale.

If you buy new construction, check out other homes built by the same developer. How have the homes withstood the test of time? Are the homeowners really happy with their residences? If you're buying in an established—or semiestablished—subdivision, knock on doors and ask the owners what they like and dislike about their home. Ask about everything from how well the mechanical systems work to how quickly the developer fixed items on the punch list (a list of items not finished to your satisfaction by the closing). Check out other, older subdivisions the developer has built. What complaints, if any, turn up? Check for complaints that may have been filed against the developer with your local chamber of commerce, the Better Business Bureau, and the state attorney's office. Remember: "The best defense is a good offense." Find out ahead of time what you're up against.

The time to reaffirm that your new home has a warranty is when you're negotiating for the home. Your attorney can step in and request a new home warranty, then make it a condition of buying the home. At the very least, not having a home warranty for new construction means you have no recourse (other than expensive litigation) if something goes wrong.

Existing Home Warranties

The majority of first-time buyers choose to buy previously owned homes that are available for resale. As we've discussed, these older homes are also referred to as "existing" homes in real estate jargon.

About 20 years ago, several companies began providing home warranties for preowned homes. Although this type of homeowner warranty was slow to catch on at first, it has grown by leaps and bounds in the past few years, fueled by our increasingly litigious society and some recent court rulings that have placed more responsibility on the seller to disclose problems in the home. More than a million existing home warranties were purchased in 1998; about half of them were for homes in California. In other parts of the country, the ratio of existing homeowners who purchase warranties ranges from 8 to 20 percent.

Unlike new construction warranties, which cover all types of problems, including expensive structural problems, existing home warranties are actually service contracts. Many people confuse them with insurance; in many states, they are indeed regulated by the state department of insurance.

Like service contracts, existing home warranties cover the costs to repair or replace a broken appliance or plumbing system over and above a deductible amount, which the home warranty industry refers to as a service fee. But the warranties are limited in scope. A typical policy covers the furnace, air-conditioning, kitchen appliances, water heater, trash compactor, electrical system (fuses and interior wiring), and interior plumbing. Commonly, separate warranties must be purchased for refrigerators, washers, and dryers, not to mention swimming pools and spas.

But there are serious exclusions. For example, if a pipe bursts because something gets stuck inside it and the pipe can't withstand the resulting water pressure, the cost of repairing the damaged pipe would be covered. But if a pipe bursts because it freezes, the cost is not covered. Homeowner warranties also don't cover preexisting problems. If an appliance works on the day of the closing, it's covered. Otherwise, it's not. And the warranties don't cover everything in the home. Most important, they do not cover structural problems, such as a crack in the foundation walls or the basement floor, or a leaky roof. Industry experts say the warranties are designed to cover appliances and plumbing and electrical systems that are in working condition when the home is sold.

Usually, the seller purchases a home warranty and pays for it out of the closing proceeds. The buyer is responsible for the service fees, should there be any need to call the toll-free number. Sometimes, a seller broker will purchase the warranty for the buyer. And, increasingly, buyers who are not given a warranty with the home are

purchasing one themselves. The cost runs from less than $200 to more than $400 for a year of coverage.

Neither buyers nor sellers pay much attention to the service fee, but it gets charged every time, and buyers have to foot that bill. On some home warranties, the deductible or service fee can run as much as $150 per call. Most service fees range from $35 to $75 per call.

Are existing home warranties worth it? "If you look at a home in terms of the kinds of things that can go wrong in the first year, it's a pretty good deal [for the buyer]," says a spokesperson for the Home Warranty Association of California. "It's inevitable in a resale house: Some things are going to break down. Water heaters can explode. Furnaces can go out. Air conditioners can break. Without a home warranty, you'd probably spend $1,000 to repair a furnace or $2,500 to replace it," he adds.

One individual, who was starting up a home warranty company (there are fewer than 10 nationwide that provide coverage, but there are a couple dozen operating exclusively in California), says his research showed that new homeowners living in an existing home called the toll-free number at least once during the year. If that's true, and you can get the seller to pick up the bill, there's no reason *not* to have a home warranty.

20/20 hindsight

Don't mistake a home warranty for homeowners' insurance coverage. A home warranty typically only lasts for the first year you live in your home. Generally, coverage cannot be extended. The warranty doesn't cover the types of damage itemized in a homeowner's insurance policy, nor does it have the liability component. The simplest way of putting it is this: Neither new home warranties nor existing home warranties are insurance. They are by-products of the insurance industry. You still need to buy a homeowner's insurance policy.

WHAT DOES THE CONTRACT REALLY SAY AND WHAT ARE MY OBLIGATIONS UNDER IT?

The real estate contract, also called a purchase and sale agreement or an offer to purchase, contains certain provisions that deal with the transfer of title to property between two parties. It also has certain provisions that deal with what happens to the property if it's destroyed before the deal is closed.

Price and title (the actual ownership interest in a house) are most important. Why? Because you have to know what you're buying and how much you're paying for it. Specifically:

- With a single-family house, you're usually buying a house, the measured plot of land on which the house is built, and the things inside it, such as a heating or cooling system, kitchen and bathroom facilities, and perhaps a refrigerator or dishwasher.

- With a condo, or some town houses, you are buying the space within the walls, floor, and ceiling of a building that has generally the same things as a single-family house.

- With a co-op, you're buying shares in a corporation that owns the property. These shares are equal to the unique value of your unit. (You're technically "renting" your unit and anything within it.)

The sellers are supposed to deliver to you good title to the house, condo or town house, or co-op. If they're including personal property in the sale, like a washing machine or refrigerator, they must give you good title to these items as well.

How are the sellers going to guarantee and deliver good title?

Let's first define *good title*. Ownership with good title means the individual who owns the property owns it free of defects, easements, liens, and prior mortgages (the current mortgage does not affect good title), and free from any matters that would impair the use of the home as a residential dwelling.

Basic Elements of a Contract to Purchase

The basic elements of a contract include: the assurance of good title, the deed, conveyance (that is, transfer to your ownership) of personal property such as bookshelves or light fixtures, notification of the method of paying for the property, the selling price, and where the closing will take place. Other elements of the contract are of slightly less importance.

Of all the basic issues, title is the most important. The following example may illustrate one problem.

Sarah and Bob's Story

The Indiana Dunes, on the southern tip of Lake Michigan, is a beautiful stretch of sand and water, punctuated, at times, with a glimpse of the far-off skyline of Chicago. Generations of Chicago and Indiana residents have gone there to rest, play, and enjoy the shore.

Several years ago, Sarah and Bob decided to purchase a vacation house at the Indiana Dunes. They agreed to pay $200,000 and signed the contract. In the contract, the seller sold them the house with a Quit Claim Deed, which essentially sold Sarah and Bob every interest he owned in the house.

Everything would have been fine, had Sarah and Bob bothered to do a title search on the property before they purchased it. What they would have found might have made them change their minds. But they were so enamored of the idea of spending weekends and summers in their new vacation home that they neglected to learn what was going on in the community. If they had been reading the local papers, they would have known why the seller was willing to sell them the property in what seemed to them to be a great deal.

The seller sold them a house he owned on land he had leased from the federal government, and the government had decided not to renew the land leases for some of the homes in the Indiana Dunes. This decision, which reversed generations of policy, was made to protect the shore from becoming too populated too close to the beach. Homeowners like Sarah and Bob, some of whom had recently paid big bucks for vacation homes on the beach, had bought limited occupancy; the government leases had just ten years left before they ended.

At a price tag of $200,000 and with only ten years left to live there, Sarah and Bob were facing a steep tab of $20,000 per year. They could never resell the property and recoup their investment, so they tried to fight the decision, but to no avail.

A purchase and sale agreement usually requires the seller to give the purchasers a warranty deed. That document warrants that the seller has good title to the property and will defend the buyer against others who may claim to have an ownership interest in the home. If the seller has only a leasehold interest in the property, then he or she can sell only that leasehold interest, and not title to the property.

Under a typical purchase contract, the buyer is obliged to purchase the property, for a certain amount of money, at a certain time, provided the seller guarantees good title.

Checking out the title for problems, liens, and encumbrances is the only way to ensure that you'll never have a long-lost relative or friend of the seller laying claim to your home. And to make sure you don't lose out if someone does "pop out of the woodwork" waving a title claim, purchase an owner's title insurance policy that will protect you from unknown claims or matters affecting title to your home.

SHOULD I HIRE A REAL ESTATE ATTORNEY? SHOULD I SIGN ANYTHING BEFORE MY ATTORNEY REVIEWS IT?

QUESTION
41

No state requires a home buyer to hire a real estate attorney. In fact, real estate professionals in some states—California, Arizona, and Indiana, for example, actively discourage the use of an attorney. Instead, buyers and sellers are encouraged to rely on real estate brokers and the local title company to close the deal.

Whether you need a real estate attorney depends on how familiar you are with the workings of the real estate industry. I've talked to attorneys and brokers all over the country, and, except in a few states like California, they overwhelmingly recommend that first-time buyers use attorneys.

There are several good reasons. Real estate attorneys:

- Are the only people involved in the transaction who do not have a vested interest in seeing you close on the deal. Real estate brokers and mortgage lenders, for example, don't get paid until the deal closes.
- Act as buffers, removing emotion from the deal.
- Can negotiate the finer points of the deal for you.

159

- Can protect you from getting a bad deal if problems arise or the negotiation turns nasty.
- Can work with the real estate brokers to organize and finalize details of the closing.
- Can work with the lender to make sure documentation is prepared correctly and is sent to the closing at the right time.
- Can explain the legal consequences of the deal and any terms you may not understand.
- Are a good buy for the money, because they usually work for a fixed fee.
- May be able to get you a reduced fee from the title company (which works on volume).
- Track all the little details that ensure a smooth closing.
- Provide you with a closing book that neatly organizes all the documents involved with your house closing.

Penny Wise, Pound Foolish

You may think you're making a smart move by not hiring a real estate attorney and saving yourself the fee. But when you consider that

In the interests of full disclosure, I want you to know that I'm married to a real estate attorney. For more than a dozen years, I've watch Sam help literally thousands of individuals purchase or sell their homes. Most of the time, the deals go pretty well, but there's always a possibility that something will crop up. In one case, the sellers, who were angry about moving, ripped out all of the wiring in the house just before the closing. Recently, a real estate broker contacted a homeowner about selling to her clients, and then persuaded the seller to give a "loan" to the buyer's mother-in-law, who then gifted the funds to the buyers. Not illegal, per se, as long as it was disclosed to the end lender. (The mortgage broker was in on the deal, too.) Some home buyers and sellers don't know what they're doing, or they fall prey to a bad-apple real estate agent or mortgage lender who uses them to further a personal agenda. There are bad real estate attorneys, too. But a good real estate attorney successfully negotiates the minefield of homeownership, helping you to buy or sell—and to enjoy the experience.

your home is a $60,000, $100,000, or $200,000 investment, trying to save $400 to $600 isn't so smart. Some people might be able to research all of the minutiae involved in selling or buying a home and save themselves some expense. But the vast majority of us don't do this on a daily basis, and we won't be prepared to deal with the consequences if something out of the ordinary happens or we've overlooked a detail.

What would you do, for example, if your seller dies the day before the closing? Or if your buyer lost his or her job the week before the closing and could no longer qualify for the mortgage on his or her new home? What if a long lost relative of the seller turns up a few days before the closing and lays claim to the home?

Even if you're buying a $100,000 home, the attorney's fee is minuscule. On a bad deal, that fee could save you a tremendous amount of heartache, not to mention money to fix whatever problems crop up.

No one hires an attorney for the good times. Protect yourself in case your dream of homeownership turns into a nightmare.

Signing on the Dotted Line

You can sign any contract, as long as it contains the absolute right for your attorney to review the document and approve it before it can go into effect. If the contract or document does not contain that absolute right, then *do not sign it* unless you're sure you understand all of its provisions.

As I mentioned earlier, most attorney riders give your attorney a limited right to cancel the contract on the basis of his or her review of it. If you're going to use a real estate attorney and you're not sure you understand the terms of the contract you're signing—for example, if you're not sure there is an absolute right for your attorney to review and approve the document—then show it to your attorney *before* you sign it.

HOW DO I FIND A REAL ESTATE ATTORNEY? HOW MUCH SHOULD HE OR SHE CHARGE ME?

QUESTION
42

Not all real estate attorneys are competent, let alone good. And it's important to find one who will help, rather than hinder, the deal. Finding a good real estate attorney is like finding a good broker. First, you should ask your broker and friends for recommendations.

161

You want someone who is experienced and has handled a minimum of 50 closings within each of the past three years. If you're purchasing new construction, or building a new home on land that you already own, it's important to hire an attorney who is very familiar with new construction contracts and can protect you in case the developer defaults, or builds a shoddy product that doesn't conform to the governing construction code.

After you get several names, call and ask the attorneys how much they charge and what they will do for that fee. Don't be embarrassed to ask about fees. It's crucial that you know how much you're getting for your money.

How They Charge

Some attorneys (especially those in medium size or large law firms) charge by the hour. In the largest firms, you can expect to pay $150 to $300 per hour, depending on who does your closing. (The young associates have the cheaper hourly rates, and the senior partners charge the most.) You'll also be charged for photocopies, facsimiles, computer research, and the time it takes to actually travel to and attend the closing.

My husband, Sam, says that if a buyer calls and tells him, "My closing is a piece of cake," Sam always raises his fee. He knows, from years of doing residential real estate closings, that these are the deals that tend to have all the problems. The reason: The home buyer often has an unrealistic expectation of what is involved in a home closing, and may have unknowingly created problems that Sam will have to untie. Even "easy" real estate deals are technical and complicated to close successfully.

Other attorneys, especially solo practitioners, charge a flat fee that will range from $350 to more than $1,000, depending on what you're buying. It's not unusual for attorneys to charge more for new construction, especially if the deal won't close for a year or more. A lot of extra work is involved in one of those deals. Also, if you're buying a very large or expensive home, you'll typically be charged a higher flat fee because of the work involved in negotiating the contract. Try to

Looking solely at how much attorneys charge for their services is not necessarily the best way to choose your attorney. For this biggest investment of your life, ask yourself whether you feel comfortable telling this person all the intimate details of your financial life. It's vital that you feel comfortable with, and perhaps even a bit close to, your attorney.

first time buyer tip

find an attorney who will charge you a flat fee for his or her time. In that way, if there is a problem with the closing, you won't be charged for all those extra hours.

Think About This

When you're interviewing your attorney, listen carefully to his or her responses to these questions:

1. **How busy are you right now? How many house deals are you handling?** Some real estate attorneys handle upward of 300 transactions per year. That means they basically don't have time to sneeze—or, you're working with an associate, a paralegal, or an assistant. You want someone who has enough time available to handle not only the closing, but the entire transaction. Think about it this way: Do you want to feel like you're relaying messages to a doctor through a nurse or a secretary, or do you want to talk to the doctor directly?

2. **How many closings do you do each year?** Make sure your attorney completes at least 50 residential real estate closings each year. You will then know that he or she has the necessary experience in residential transactions. Don't hire your cousin the litigator, or your friend Harold, who negotiates airplane leases for a living. These folks probably didn't even do their own house deals.

3. **How much do you charge?** If it seems as though the attorney isn't charging enough, he or she may be part of a network of attorneys who do their own title work. In that case, they also get compensated by a title company that employs real estate attorneys to do title work if you choose to work with that

title company. Is it a bad thing? Perhaps not. If something goes wrong with the title, the attorney could be liable. Either way, you won't know what the story is until you ask.

4. **Are you doing any deals that would conflict with mine right now?** It's happened more than once. A buyer calls up an attorney and finds out that the same attorney (or law firm) is already representing the seller. No attorneys worth their salt will suggest they can handle both sides of the same transaction, *even* if you agree to sign a document that says you know the situation and you approve it. If there is a conflict, ask for a referral to another real estate attorney, preferably in another firm.

5. **Do you have an engagement letter I can review?** Attorneys should present you with an engagement letter that outlines the things the attorney will do to help you negotiate and close on your real estate transaction. The letter should also state the fee. Better attorneys do this; all attorneys should. Ask the attorney you select to prepare one for you to sign.

The old cliché is true: You get what you pay for.

If you're hiring an attorney to handle your new construction purchase, make sure at least one-third of the attorney's practice is new construction. Not all new construction is the same. For example, a single-family home in a development in the far suburbs is going to be different from a loft restoration in an urban area. There are practical differences in each type of development. Make sure the attorney you choose knows how to handle your developer, no matter where you're buying. As a bonus, if you hire an attorney who has done a lot of work for buyers in the development in which you're purchasing a home, you'll get someone who already knows the legal lay of the land, has already seen and read through the condo declaration, and knows where the developer may be willing to kick in a few extra upgrades or items. Hiring that attorney could make the deal go much more smoothly.

When Complications Arise

If a deal is really complicated, you will almost certainly need an attorney, no matter where you live. Sam once worked on a house closing that seemed pretty ordinary until he found out there were ten lenders. He had to negotiate a separate deal with each lender until they were all satisfied. The extremely complicated closing took ten hours. Someone at the closing called it an "hour per lender" deal.

After you hire the attorney, the general idea is to let him or her do the job. If the attorney advises you on certain points, take the advice. If he or she tells you to do something, do it. The attorney knows the ins and outs of real estate law much better than you do.

> Hiring a real estate lawyer is *not* the same thing as having your Uncle Harry, the tax attorney, do your real estate closing. Real estate law is specialized. Uncle Harry may be a whiz at writing wills, or leasing airplanes, or finding creative places to put your money, but he may get you nailed to the wall in two minutes if he doesn't truly understand the finer points of real estate law.

SHOULD I CLOSE AT THE BEGINNING, THE MIDDLE, OR THE END OF THE MONTH? WHY DOES IT MATTER?

The date you choose for your closing will be a point of negotiation between you and the seller. The issues you need to consider are *personal timing* and *money*. Here are some points to help you clarify why timing is everything:

- Set the closing date according to when your current lease ends. If you're living in an apartment, it's foolish to close when you still have six months left on your lease, unless you can easily sublet your apartment or you have an escape clause. If you close at the beginning of a month and your lease expires at the end of the month, and you don't need to do any work in your new home, you'll be paying double rent for one month, which can be costly. Poor timing is one of the biggest mistakes a home buyer can make. (See Appendix I for a list of other common mistakes a home buyer makes.)

- If you close at the beginning of a month, the lender will require you to prepay the interest on your loan from the day of closing to the end of the month. Therefore, the cash you need at the earlier closing date will be more than the amount you would need at an end-of-the-month closing. For example, if you close April 15, you'll have to prepay your mortgage from April 15 to April 30. If you close April 30, you pay only one day's mortgage interest.

- If you're trying to decide whether to close on December 31 or January 2, remember that, at tax time, you take deductions for your house in the year of the closing, even if it's on the last day of the year. If you close on December 31, the points you pay at the closing, plus any prepaid interest, are deductible on your income tax statement for that year. However, make sure, if you choose to close on December 31, that your deductible costs will be greater than the standard deduction allowed to you by the IRS. Talk to your accountant or someone familiar with these real estate tax issues, and find out how they might affect your situation.

The last week of the month is the busiest time for title and escrow companies (not to mention moving companies). If you decide to close at the end of the month, be sure your attorney schedules the closing well in advance. Otherwise, you might find that the title or escrow company is booked up and can't accommodate your closing.

Paying in Arrears—Except for Sub-Par (Also Known as Sub-Prime) Loans

Mortgage interest and principal payments are paid in arrears—that is, you pay on July 1 for money you've borrowed in June. If you close April 15, you would pay a half-month's mortgage interest, in cash, at the closing. You would then pay nothing until June 1, when you would pay the interest for the month of May. On July 1, you pay interest for the month of June. And so on.

The reason: Your loan payments are computed at a certain rate, and that rate remains constant, like a fixed-rate loan. The lender must manually compute the amount of interest from the day of the closing to the end of the month.

This would change only if you're getting a *sub-par* loan. Most home buyers are rated in the excellent or good credit category, and lenders will grade these borrowers "A" or possibly "A–," which means they have had a few problems in their credit history, but nothing serious.

If you have serious credit problems, but still have enough credit to get a loan, you might fall into the B, C, or D category of sub-par lending. You may then have to prepay the interest on your loan before you even borrow the money. If you close on June 15, you have to prepay your interest through the end of the month. Then, instead of waiting until August 1 to make your next mortgage payment, you might be required to pay it on July 1. From then on, you pay a month ahead.

If a lender is going to require this payment schedule on your loan, it should be fully explained to you and written into your loan documentation. If you get a sub-par loan, ask your lender to fully explain your payment schedule.

If your lease expires the same day as your closing, be sure you have a back-up place to live, just in case you don't close on the property—even if it means moving to a hotel or back home with the folks for a few nights. Sometimes, properties just don't close. In new construction, the house might flunk its final inspection. Or, more likely, the work isn't done yet and a Certificate of Occupancy can't be issued. Either way, make sure you're protected, even if it means paying for an additional month of rent.

WHAT IS SELLER DISCLOSURE?
HOW DOES IT AFFECT ME?

At the beginning of the 1990s, the term *seller disclosure* was virtually unknown. As the decade ended, it became a buzzword.

Essentially, seller disclosure requires a home seller to disclose any known *material latent defects* in his or her property. That bit of jargon means the seller must disclose if his or her property has any hidden or unseen defects, or problems, that could adversely affect the value of the property.

Buyers like seller disclosure because it tells them, up front, about the condition of the property. Some sellers like disclosing the defects, because it protects them from the buyers' discovering the defects during an inspection and then asking for money to fix the problems. Other sellers don't. They feel uncomfortable with the formal process of baring their home's soul, so to speak.

As a buyer, you want to find out everything you can, in advance, about the condition of the home. If you run into a seller disclosure form (and it is increasingly likely that you will), the form will ask detailed—or not so detailed—questions about the condition of the home. If the seller answers the questions honestly (there usually is an option for "don't know," which is completely useless to a home buyer), you will learn about such problems as water in the basement when it rains. The seller, of course, will say the price of the house takes into account these problems. You will then have to decide whether the house is worth the asking price if it also needs a new roof and a new furnace or air-conditioning system.

Remember, anything about the purchase and sale can be negotiated. Whether you get it depends on how desperately the seller wants to sell, and current market conditions.

The History

Here's a little bit of recent history to explain the hoopla over seller disclosure. Although it seems as though state law should cover seller disclosure, in most states it does not—at least, not specifically.

In 1987, California passed a law that codified the questions the seller must answer. In addition, the buyer, the seller, and the agent for the seller must sign off that they have reasonably inspected the property and disclosed any defect.

By 1992, only California and Maine had some sort of formal regulation requiring sellers to disclose any hidden material latent defects in the property. In Maine, the broker must ask specific questions that the state has designated. The broker is required to gather this information at the time the property is listed and provide the information, in writing, to the buyer prior to, or during, the preparation of an offer.

In 1992, Coldwell Banker, a national real estate company, announced a new policy that required all sellers listing property with the company to fill out and sign disclosure forms no matter what the state required. Although some sellers weren't thrilled with the prospect of having to fill out a form that asks specific questions about the house, land, and neighborhood, buyers are generally glad to have it.

State law in Illinois prior to 1993, was silent on the issue. In effect, if a defect was hidden in the house and the seller knew about it but didn't say anything to anyone about it, the buyer was stuck with the problem. Caveat emptor: Buyer beware. If, however, the seller told his or her broker about the hidden defect, the broker was obligated to inform the buyer.

But by the mid-1990s, things were changing. In Illinois, sellers must now fill out a 22-question seller disclosure form.

The National Association of Realtors (NAR) would like to see some form of seller disclosure mandated by every state. According to the NAR's legal counsel, one of the largest areas of controversy in

20/20

hindsight

Although seller disclosure forms cause consternation for both buyers and sellers, wouldn't you rather know what's going on *before* you buy a home, and not after you move in? Each state requires a slightly different form of disclosure, but all states require that sellers answer questions truthfully about the physical state of their home. Ask very specific questions about any problems or defects the home might have now or has had in the past. For example, you might ask whether there has ever been leaking or moisture or flooding in the basement. If the answer is "yes," ask what caused these problems and whether they were fixed. You can ask the real estate agent, but chances are he or she won't know the real answers. The agent might say, "Not to the best of my knowledge," which doesn't help you at all. To protect yourself, ask the seller these questions directly. Don't be shy about asking for a copy of the proof of payment if the seller indicates the problem has been fixed. In that way, you'll have the name of the contractor or vendor if you have a similar problem in the future.

the process of buying and selling homes is the failure to disclose defects in a property. The majority of after-closing lawsuits, where the plaintiffs are unhappy buyers, involve an alleged failure to disclose some condition affecting value or desirability.

The finger is usually pointed first in the direction of the broker, and then at the seller. Because the NAR protects the interests of brokers, it feels that sellers, rather than brokers, should shoulder the responsibility for disclosing defects in their house. As the NAR's attorney has said: "The agent has the duty to disclose factors that [he or she] can observe with a reasonably diligent inspection. The broker doesn't live there. Seller disclosure forces those issues to be addressed."

Ask your broker if your state requires seller disclosure, and whether the seller needs to make that disclosure in writing. You should also ask the seller to answer specific questions about the condition of the property *before* you make an offer to purchase.

QUESTION 45

DO I NEED A HOME INSPECTION? HOW DO I FIND A REPUTABLE HOME INSPECTOR?

The quick answer is YES! Except in a rare situation—for example, you're buying a home from your parents, or you have lived in the house and know it intimately—savvy agents always advise their buyers to have the home inspected by a professional inspector or someone who is knowledgeable about construction matters and the various issues involved in residential properties.

But hiring an expert doesn't excuse you from looking at the home carefully before you get to the inspection stage. Remember, the inspector will charge you between $250 and $400 (or more) for each inspection. By keeping a sharp eye out for the items on the following list, you may be able to spot some major problems and eliminate a potential property *before* you pay an inspector.

The Home Buyer's Watch List

When you start visiting homes, watch out for:

- **Wet, clammy, sticky, smelly basements.** A damp feel to a basement can hint at water seepage caused by improperly graded soil or an improperly laid foundation.

- **Cracks in the basement.** A visible crack line in the interior of the basement or on the exterior foundation could point to more-than-normal settling. Or, the house may have been built on new landfill, a hill, or an improperly graded site. It could also point to an area prone to earthquakes or earth movement during heavy rains.

- **Bad smells.** If a house smells bad, it may have a biological problem, like mold growing inside the ductwork or behind vinyl wallpaper. Mold on walls can be scrubbed away with bleach and water, or other cleaners, but you may have to rip out ductwork to get at the mold inside.

- **Poorly fitted ductwork.** Heating and cooling systems can be problematic, especially if the original work was done in a slip-shod way. Check the duct lines to see that they fit snugly and securely.

- **Discolored spots on walls and ceilings.** Discoloration could be the result of a water problem—a leak from the roof, the walls, or the pipes. Beware of a fresh paint job, particularly in the top floor of the house. It may be covering up a problem.

- **Improperly fitted skylights.** Skylights, which are now extremely popular, are usually one-piece preassembled units that are popped into a hole in the roof. Check for discoloration, peeling paint, or other signs that a skylight was improperly fitted or may be leaking.

- **Damp attic.** Poor attic ventilation can lead to moisture being trapped in the upper recesses, causing dry rot or condensation. The underside of the roof should never be wet.

- **Insulation.** Does the house have adequate insulation? If not, you could be looking at a fortune in heating and cooling expenses. If the home has insulation, ask about "the R factor" (the higher the number, the better), and be sure the insulation is facing the correct way.

- **Sloppy masonry work.** Has the homeowner tried to personally patch up the masonry? It could be a sign of a larger problem. If you're looking at new construction, sloppy masonry and detail work can mean that other work was also done in a slipshod way.

- **Do-it-yourself electrical work.** Proper electrical wiring is a must, to avoid future problems that could be costly to fix as well as a serious safety concern. If the electrical box is a mess, it could mean trouble for you.

- **Poorly graded landscaping.** Does the landscaping slope away from the house (the high point should be against the house)? If so, great. If the landscaping is sloping toward the point where the house connects with the ground, or if the walk around the side of the home is pitched toward the home, it's a good bet there has been or will be a problem of leakage into the basement. Water is a very damaging substance (think about the Grand Canyon), and the constant pressure of water (and melting snow) moving toward the house can cause tremendous damage to the foundation.
- **Fuzzy windows.** If the home has double-paned or thermal-paned windows, and the windows appear to be fuzzy or full of condensation, the seal has been broken. That means the windows are no longer working properly and will ultimately have to be replaced—and that can cost quite a chunk of money.

There are hundreds of potential hazards when purchasing a home, and most buyers have no idea where to begin to look for problems. That's why it's so important to have the proper inspections completed before the expiration of the inspection clauses. You never know a home unless you've lived in it. Besides, most people aren't particularly familiar with the structure and mechanicals of a house, town house, or condo. The roof may look fine, but a house inspector may see peeling shingles and notice water marks from leaks on the ceiling. A house inspector can be yet another voice helping you to distance your emotions from the purchase of the home.

new construction tip

Consider hiring a professional home inspector even if you're buying a new home. Why? Because a house may be new, but that is not a guarantee that it was built correctly. Inspectors have shared stories with me about new construction projects that have had outlets wired incorrectly, and ground fault interrupters that aren't connected at all. They've seen balconies that were not fully bolted into the side of the building, hot water faucets that feed only cold water, and dishwashers that aren't bolted into the cabinet (so they rock side to side and the water pipes get loosened and leak).

If you're a new construction buyer and you're planning to hire a home inspector at the end of the project, consider, instead, hiring an inspector at the four critical junctures of the home-building process: (1) after the foundation is poured; (2) after the house is framed; (3) after the house has been wired and plumbed (before the walls get finished); and (4) before you close. Coordinate with the builder or developer to make sure you can bring through the home inspector and that someone from the development company will be available, on site, to answer any questions. When interviewing an inspector for this task, make sure he or she has done *new construction* inspections before.

Finding an Excellent Home Inspector

After you've received the right to have the home inspected (through the inspection clause attached to the contract), you have to hire a home inspector or put together your home inspection team (to conduct multiple inspections for pests, toxic substances, and the general condition of the home).

If you look in your local telephone book, you'll find dozens, if not hundreds, of entrepreneurs calling themselves "professional home inspectors." Some of them are what they say, some of them aren't.

Some of the most qualified home inspectors are members of the American Society of Home Inspectors (ASHI), a nationwide, non-profit professional association founded in 1976. ASHI only admits as members those home inspectors who have performed at least 750 home inspections according to the ASHI Standards of Practice, or 250 inspections in addition to other licenses and experience. Applicants must also pass a written exam, receive approval on at least three sample inspection reports, and perform a satisfactory home inspection before a peer review committee. In fact, ASHI is now consulting with many state legislatures that are thinking of passing laws to license home inspectors. (Currently, only a handful of states license home inspectors.)

Where can you find a good inspector? Ask your real estate broker for a list of suggestions. When you call the inspectors:

- **Compare fees.** An inspection should cost from $250 to $500 (or more), depending on the size of the home. Ask what's included in the fee and how long the inspection should take. Be prepared to allow at least two hours for a thorough inspection of a moderate size property.

- **Compare telephone manners.** The inspector should be courteous and knowledgeable. Ask for a list of specialized inspectors you might call (for radon, asbestos, electromagnetic power, water quality, pest control, and so on). Ask whether the inspector is bonded, licensed, and insured. Is the inspector a member of ASHI or another professional inspection association? Ask for references, and then call them.

- **Make sure you'll receive a written report.** You should receive the report either on site (many inspectors now do their report on a hand-held computer that plugs into a printer in their car) or by fax or e-mail that day or within 24 hours. Be clear on when you'll receive the report, and what kind of report you can expect. Will it be only a checklist, or will the inspector write his or her overall view?

When you've found your inspector, have him or her come to the property before the expiration of the right-to-inspection clause in your contract. You will usually have to have your inspection done within five days from the time you sign the contract. Don't wait until the last day, in case it's raining or the inspection needs to be rescheduled.

For home buyers living in the northern half of the United States, snow can pose huge problems for home inspectors. If there's a big snow the night before your home inspection, the inspector will be limited in what he or she can do. The inspector may be able to brush off enough snow to see a small piece of the roof, but he or she will not be able to make a thorough assessment, nor will it be possible to ascertain the condition of the landscaping. A heavy rain can also make it difficult to properly inspect a home. Also, you can't truly test an air-conditioning system in the winter, or a heating system in the summer. Finally, try not to have the inspector come after dark. You want him or her to inspect the entire property's exterior and interior spaces. Daylight makes the process easier.

When you interview a home inspector, make sure he or she plans to inspect the entire house, top to bottom, inside and out. If the inspector balks at inspecting the basement, crawl space, attic, garage, or any other areas, find someone else. If the inspector tells you these places will be inspected and then balks when actually at the site, call his or her supervisor, or consider ending the home inspection at that point. The home inspector clearly isn't doing his or her job, nor is he or she giving you what you're paying for. At this point, you may have to ask the seller for an extension on the inspection contingency. Be sure you get the extension in writing.

The Inspection Report

At the end of the inspection, or perhaps the next day, the inspector will give you a report of what's wrong with the house. The report should be complete and it should be written. Ideally, the report should include the inspector's written remarks as well.

Be Sure to Tag Along

If you're smart, you'll go to the inspection and walk around with the inspector. Ask a lot of questions as you go along. The inspector should be happy to explain everything to you. It's an excellent opportunity to get to know the home you're buying and to learn what to watch out for in the future.

Watch Out for This Trick

If a qualified, licensed, and bonded house inspector tells you that the property you're considering may need $20,000 worth of repairs within the next five years, it should change the way you think about it. Is the property still a bargain? Should you look elsewhere? Can you afford to buy a home that will need such a substantial cash outlay within such a short period of time? Is the house a great deal anyway? (If your contract has an inspection contingency, you should be able

175

to terminate the contract and get your earnest money back. Then you can search for another home.)

If the home inspector offers to complete any work he or she recommends to you, politely decline the offer. It doesn't happen too often, but the inspector could be suggesting there is trouble where there is none, simply to drum up more business, such as a second "follow-up" inspection.

The Inside Skinny on Home Inspectors

Over the years, I've received loads of mail from disgruntled home buyers who believe they hired second-rate inspectors who did a lousy job. And I've also received loads of mail from disgruntled home inspectors who feel they are being picked on for no good reason.

I believe the truth lies somewhere in the middle. Sometimes, home inspectors miss things that they should have found. Some home buyers have unrealistic expectations about the home they're buying. All home buyers have to understand this truism: *Old houses have old problems. The older the house, the more problems it will have.*

Brand-new and recently built homes have problems, too, but when a house passes its fifteenth birthday, unless it has been flawlessly maintained, there will be problems that need to be addressed and corrected as the years go on. That's just part and parcel of homeownership. If you're not ready for that responsibility, either buy a new house or continue to rent for a while.

You need to find a qualified home inspector who won't scare you needlessly. (Some home inspectors make old grout sound like the roof is caving in.) But you also need one who will tell you the truth and not kowtow to agents who refer business but expect "favors" in return. (If that sounds to you like a conflict of interest waiting to happen, pat yourself on the back. That's exactly how it works in many places.)

I believe that a home inspector should stand behind the reports he or she has written for clients. Many don't; their written inspection forms are nothing more than checklists offering the options of "Good," "Fair," "Poor," and "Recommend Specialist for Further Inspection." If there are too many referrals to specialists, you may

176

wonder what added value the home inspection provides. (If the inspector only recommends you to specialists without identifying a real problem, the inspection has a diminishing value and may ultimately not be worth the fee you paid.) Besides, *when you sign the agreement for your professional house inspection, you're basically signing away your rights to sue the inspector if he or she has missed something or has made an incorrect assessment.*

I believe that loophole is outrageous. Home inspectors should be required to stand behind what they write. And if they can't, they should have insurance to cover their mistakes. Every home buyer should ask the home inspector whether he or she carries an errors and omissions (E&O) policy, and for what amount. Better home inspectors have these policies.

Home inspectors are not the only individuals who do professional home inspections. Some contractors and structural engineers may also do home inspections and might be available to give you an opinion as to the structural integrity of your home. Contractors and engineers are typically licensed by your state and carry insurance.

Although I recommend that you contact the American Society of Home Inspectors for a referral to an ASHI-certified inspector in your neighborhood (see Resources, on page 378), you should know that ASHI doesn't appear to police its wayward members, enforce its ethics code, or step in to mediate trouble between its member inspectors and homeowners who have had problems. Also, some home inspection companies appear to hire anyone off the street to work for the AHSI-trained owner. You may think you're hiring an ASHI-certified inspector when, in fact, you're not getting what you're paying for.

There are other national organizations that claim to certify home inspectors. Before you hire *any* inspector, check out the requirements for membership and certification in the named organization. If they don't at least meet ASHI's standards, you have to wonder whether the home inspector really knows what he or she is doing. For more information on ASHI's standards, visit its web site at ASHI.com.

The Bottom Line

Despite these caveats, I do think almost every home buyer should have his or her home inspected. Just make sure you're getting what you're paying for.

QUESTION
46

SHOULD I TEST FOR TOXIC SUBSTANCES AND CONTAMINATED WATER?

Formerly a rare addition to contracts, toxic substance inspections—including radon, lead, water, and asbestos—have become a regular part of most real estate contracts. Unfortunately, most home inspectors are not qualified to do specialized tests for toxic substances. You must therefore find inspectors who are specialists, or purchase the appropriate test in your local hardware store.

Here are the major toxic substances for which home buyers conduct inspections these days:

- **Radon.** A study by the Environmental Protection Agency (EPA) stated that 22,000 deaths a year are attributed to radon, a gas that seeps into homes through cracks in the walls or foundation. According to an EPA pamphlet, "Radon is the second leading cause of lung cancer in the U.S., after cigarette smoking. As you breathe it in, its decay products become trapped inside your lungs. As these products continue to decay, they release small bursts of energy that can damage lung tissue and lead to lung cancer. It's like exposing your family to hundreds of chest X-rays each year." Of the home buyers and homeowners who actually check for radon, the EPA estimates around 20 percent will find an unacceptable level. You can purchase an EPA-listed radon gas test kit in your local hardware store, but it may be advisable to have a professional inspector perform the test, which requires two to four days' exposure in the home. (Or, start with a store-bought test and hire a professional if the test indicates higher-than-acceptable levels.) Radon emissions can be fixed, either by sealing the cracks in the basement or crawl space, or by installing an air system that sucks out the gas from beneath the home.

- **Asbestos.** If you're buying new construction or a home built since the mid-1970s, you probably don't have to worry about asbestos. If you are buying an older home, some asbestos is likely in the house. Asbestos can be a microscopic airborne fiber that is ingested through the nose or mouth; it lodges in the lungs and can cause lung cancer. If not disturbed, the threat from asbestos is minimal, if measurable at all. You can hire an asbestos specialist to tell you whether there is asbestos in the home and how much it will cost to have it wrapped or removed (the two ways to abate the threat). Lori, a first-time buyer in Chicago, said she wasn't deterred from buying her home because of asbestos. She and the seller agreed, at the closing, that Lori would receive a cash credit (a payment to the buyer at closing) equal to the price of removing the asbestos.

- **Lead paint.** High levels of lead in paint and water (see below) have been connected with mental and physical developmental problems, particularly in young children. Lead is usually a problem only when ingested or inhaled. Lead paint is most often found in older homes (its use has been banned for more than 20 years) and can simply be covered up. In HUD homes, or those financed with an FHA mortgage, lead paint must be removed or covered over. A test by an outside agency can run between $100 and $300, depending on the number of samples tested. The federal government recently passed a lead paint law that requires sellers of homes built before 1978 (the year lead paint was removed from store shelves) to disclose that there may be lead paint in the house. Your local hardware store has lead tests that look like short, white swabs. You simply swab the painted surfaces; if the swab turns red, there is lead present. Again, the problem with lead paint is only serious if you ingest lead paint chips or dust (for example, during renovation of your home).

- **Lead in water.** High levels of lead in water is another problem, particularly in old homes and apartment buildings. If pipes that were soldered together with lead begin to corrode, lead particles can be released into your water supply. If the water is contaminated at the source (from your local or municipal water supply), you may want to consider buying a filtering system, or looking for another home in a different area. Inexpensive water filtering systems that can be purchased at your local hardware store claim to take out at least 93 percent of all lead in water. This is a much more cost-effective solution than either purchasing bottled water or replacing all of the plumbing lines in your house.

- **Electromagnetic radiation.** One of the most recently discovered potential hazards is electromagnetic radiation from high-voltage power lines. Only a few studies have been done, and the results are mixed. Some seem to show an increased rate of cancer and other unusual diseases in people who live in homes that are located directly underneath high-voltage power lines. Other studies show no increase of cancer or other diseases. Power companies deny any health link, but you may want to avoid the risk that there may be a problem or that other problems will be discovered later.

There's another risk: Property prices may not rise as quickly as in other areas because of the perception that there is a problem—whether or not one actually exists. There is no way to shield yourself from electromagnetic radiation. You must simply find another house to buy. A test for electromagnetic radiation can cost between $100 and $250, depending on the size of the house.

Real estate attorneys advise using this language in your contract: "Sale is contingent upon satisfactory results of the tests." If you don't include this sentence, you could find that you have the right to have the tests done, but not the right to back out of the deal if the house fails to pass the tests to your satisfaction. For more details about legal language that would be appropriate in your area, consult a real estate attorney.

For more information on all of these toxins and more, check out the EPA toxin link at EPA.gov/opptintr/, or call the EPA hotline at (800) SOS-RADO.

QUESTION 47

WHAT IF THE INSPECTOR FINDS SOMETHING WRONG WITH THE HOME I WANT TO BUY?

It's likely that your home inspector or your toxic substance and pest inspectors *will* find something wrong with the property you want to buy. Remember, that's their job. When a problem of any significance is found, you have to ask yourself two questions:

1. **Is the problem fixable or unfixable?**
2. **At what price is the problem fixable?**

180

Here are some examples of *unfixable* problems:

- The house sits on a fault line.
- The house is in a flood plain.
- The foundation is severely cracked (a major crack is one that is wider than an eighth of an inch).
- The house's water supply has been contaminated by the local dump.
- The house is located under electromagnetic power lines.

Almost everything else is fixable—even most kinds of earthquake damage.

But is it affordable or smart to try and fix every problem? Is the house worth it? You can fix a leaky roof or replace it entirely, but is the house worth its $100,000 price plus $5,000 for a new roof? What if the house also needs a new furnace and hot water heater? What if it needs upgraded electricity for a clothes dryer? What if the pipes are old and leaking?

If your inspectors find something wrong with the house, you have two options: (1) withdraw from the contract (provided you have the right inspection contingency) or (2) renegotiate the purchase price to reflect the cost of fixing the items marked on the inspection list. If you decide to withdraw from the contract, have your attorney write the letter. If you decide to go ahead but want to renegotiate the purchase price, talk to your broker and your attorney about what procedure may be customary in your area.

first time
buyer tip

Often, sellers assume that home buyers *want* an inspection to find problems so that they can negotiate a lower price. If this is your strategy to buy the house at a lower price, don't be surprised if the seller refuses to do anything and you're stuck taking the house in "as is" condition. In a hot market, many sellers may be unwilling to do more than the bare minimum, if anything at all. That's a symptom of a strong seller's market. In a buyer's market (there are more homes for sale than there are qualified buyers), you'll have more leverage. You should find, however, that most sellers are happy to do what's reasonable and fair. If that's all you ask for, you shouldn't have too much of a problem.

QUESTION 48

WHAT DO I DO IF THE SELLER OR BROKER HAS MISREPRESENTED THE CONDITION OF THE HOME?

If the inspection reveals that the seller or broker has misrepresented the condition of the home, and you have a properly written inspection contingency, you have the option of walking away from the deal. You may also report the broker's conduct to the state agency that regulates real estate professionals. (See Appendix V for a list of agencies that regulate brokers in all 50 states.)

20/20 hindsight

> You may be upset and frustrated, but you have to consider yourself lucky not to have bought what could easily have turned out to be a lemon of a house. There's nothing more frustrating than living through one home repair crisis after another.

If you find out after you close on the home that the seller or broker has clearly misrepresented the condition of the home, or did not disclose everything that was known or should have been known about the property, you can take either or both of them to court. But be prepared to prove that they had or should have had knowledge of the problem.

Ilyce and Sam's Story

When we bought our co-op, the seller and the seller broker told us that everything was working in the unit. We forgot to test the dishwasher before closing. (Rule No. 1: Always run all the appliances during an inspection.)

The first night we were in the apartment, we decided to turn on the dishwasher. Nothing happened. Sam reached down under the sink and turned the water back on. (The sellers had apparently turned off the water to the dishwasher.) The next morning, we found out why. The dishwasher leaked all over our new downstairs neighbors' kitchen, ruining their window shade.

We were furious. Obviously, the sellers knew that their dishwasher leaked, which is why they turned off the water. Would we have bypassed the unit if we'd known about the dishwasher? Of course not. It cost us only $150 to replace the window shade plus $60 for a plumber to replace the faulty hose.

But we were steamed! We wrote a nasty letter to the sellers and felt much better.

Make sure your inspection contingency allows you to withdraw from the deal if the home inspector gives you an unsatisfactory report on the property. But remember, all homes, even new ones, have problems. And old homes have old and more difficult problems. Keep your expectations in line with what you're buying. If you're buying an older home, don't assume it will be in perfect condition or that the seller will pay to upgrade the house with next century technology. If that's your assumption, you may be better off renting.

— 7 —

Possession and Other Parts of the Offer to Purchase

WHAT IS POSSESSION?

Possession is nine-tenths of the law.

Possession occurs when you actually take control of the home. Most buyers take possession of the home at the closing. The keys and other security devices are handed to the buyer by the seller, who has, by then, moved all of his or her belongings from the home. At that moment, you have the right to do anything you want with *your* house.

Sometimes, possession is given before or after the closing. Let's say you need a place to live, or you want to renovate the home prior to the closing. The seller might let you take possession a few days early, so that you can move in or get started on your remodeling. Many real estate attorneys advise sellers not to allow preclosing possession by the buyer. It's very risky. The buyer might move in and then decide not to close. At that point, the seller becomes a landlord and may have to pursue an eviction proceeding against the buyer.

Usually, possession issues in a residential real estate transaction involve a seller who wants to stay in the house after closing (see Question 50).

Possession and the closing date are closely linked. Sometimes, they're used as negotiation points when money isn't the primary issue. In one case in California, a first-time buyer made a full-price offer for a woman's house, but the woman was having trouble accepting the offer. She hadn't found a place to move her family and was worried. The buyer stretched out the date of the closing, in exchange

184

for a few thousand dollars off the selling price, and the deal went through.

With new construction, you can't close on the house and move in until the builder has obtained a Certificate of Occupancy (COO). This certificate, issued by the local municipality, certifies that the house meets certain basic requirements and that necessities (such as the walls, roof, electricity, plumbing, and other mechanicals) are in place and are working. If you're concerned about the condition of the home and the builder says he has received the COO, ask to see it. If you have any questions, call the local building or planning department that issued the COO. Punch list items (small details that need to be fixed) may still remain, but COOs are issued only when the house is virtually complete.

WHAT IF THE SELLER WANTS TO STAY IN THE HOUSE AFTER THE CLOSING?

When the seller indicates that he or she would like to stay on, after the closing, for a few days or weeks, it's called a *post-closing possession*. There are two issues to consider:

1. **Charging a reasonable daily rate.** If you've got a few weeks to go on your lease, or if Mom and Dad will graciously let you camp out for a few more nights, you might want to grant the post-closing possession. If you do, make it clear that you will charge the seller a reasonable per-diem rate for the extra time he or she is in what will be *your* house. This "reasonable" rate should cover your daily expenses, including the daily cost of your mortgage, homeowner's insurance, and taxes.

2. **Overstaying the welcome.** The risk with letting the seller stay after the closing is that he or she might never leave and you'll have to take legal action. If that happens, charge a high rate for each extra day, so the seller realizes it will be much cheaper to leave.

If the seller does not indicate, during the contract negotiations, a wish to stay past the closing, but then announces at the closing an intent to stay for a while, you may have a problem. Real estate attorneys generally advise buyers to refuse to close unless the seller has moved out. Usually, the threat of not closing is enough to get the sellers motivated to leave.

If you schedule your final walk-through after the sellers have moved out, or while they are moving, you'll know that they're really going to be, or are, gone. The ideal situation is to walk through the property and then go directly to the closing.

If the seller asks to stay in the home after the closing (either because the seller's closing on another home is a couple of days later, or the seller is arranging a move to another city), you can grant the couple of days (a set number) for a modest fee that will cover your daily expenses of ownership. But when those days are up, the seller should pay an increased fee that encourages moving out *fast*. To underline that it's time for the seller to move, a large amount of money should be held back at the closing and placed in an escrow account. In addition, the seller should pay you what it actually costs you to own your home.

If the money is held in escrow, and your seller turns out to be a deadbeat, it's much more likely you'll see that cash.

Calculating a Daily Fee That Will Motivate the Seller

There are several ways to calculate a daily fee that will motivate a seller to move before the closing:

1. Charge the same per-diem rate as an expensive local hotel.
2. Find out the going rent for a home like yours, and divide by 30.

In some areas of the country, it's customary for the seller to retain possession *at no cost* for three to five days after the closing. Your broker or attorney should be able to advise you on local closing customs.

You want the seller to understand that staying in the home will be a very expensive proposition. If all else fails, and the seller continues to stay in your new home, you may have to take legal action. Consult your attorney for advice.

WHEN IS THE RIGHT TIME TO TERMINATE A BUYER'S CONTRACT?

The question you should ask yourself is: Why do I want to terminate the contract to purchase?

If you want to terminate the contract because you're feeling "buyer's remorse" (see Question 52), you can't. That's the tough part about the real estate game. The rules say, when you sign and present the offer, and the seller accepts it, you have made a deal. Unless your inspector finds something wrong with the home, or your attorney rejects the contract, or your lender won't grant you a mortgage, you're pretty much stuck.

Some unscrupulous buyers will tell their attorneys to summarily "reject" a contract if they get cold feet. That's not fair to the seller, who has allowed the potential buyer to tie up the property during the negotiation process. In addition, the seller may be able to sue you for specific performance, making you live up to the deal to which you signed your name.

You may be able to walk away from the contract if you are willing to forfeit your deposit, or earnest money. Most first-time buyers have little cash, so the idea of giving up 5, 10, or 20 percent of the purchase price, or even $1,000, seems a little steep. But it has been done many times before. In this case, the earnest money is either split between the seller and the broker, or the seller gets to keep it all.

Returning the Earnest Money

When you put down a good faith deposit, also known as the earnest money, it's usually deposited in the escrow account of the seller broker. The seller broker may not release that money to you without the seller's permission.

I frequently receive letters in which buyers tell me that a seller broker refuses to release their cash deposit. If you terminate the contract for valid reasons, the seller should sign off on the release of the earnest money. But some sellers don't—just out of spite.

If this happens to you, your next step will likely be to explore your legal options. Talk to your real estate attorney. You may have to file suit in order to shake your money loose.

WHAT IS "BUYER'S REMORSE" AND HOW DO I COPE WITH IT?

"Buyer's remorse" is the sinking feeling in the pit of your stomach that you've made a terrible mistake. It usually occurs the minute, day, or week after your broker presents your offer to purchase or you sign the purchase and sale agreement. It keeps you awake at night, tossing and turning in a cold sweat, as you wonder how you're going to make the payments and you agonize over your choice. Are you buying the right house?

Pam, a broker in Rock Hill, South Carolina, says that if a first-time buyer has buyer's remorse, the only person to blame is the real estate agent. "If the agent has truly done her job and qualified those people, and found out what they really wanted in their first home, then they should be happy," she says. "But if the agent turns a blind eye to their insecurity about buying a home and doesn't try to help them understand the process, it can be very tough."

Susanne's Story

No one is exempt from buyer's remorse—even an industry player.

My mother, Susanne, is one of the top real estate agents in the Chicago area. In some years, she has sold nearly $30 million in property.

But the only home she had ever bought was the one she bought 35 years ago. She'd never even had a mortgage.

Even though she's helped thousands of people successfully buy and sell homes throughout her career, when the time came to buy a condo in a new construction development (that she bought as an investment), and get her first mortgage, she came down with a bad case of buyer's remorse.

Even though we think she made a good investment, she's never quite gotten over it.

Fighting Your Emotions

Buying a home is such an emotional process that first-timers often get overwhelmed. Real estate agent Pam says brokers should be understanding and help clients *know* whether they are making the right decision for the right reason. Brokers should be able to read the personality of a buyer and make sure that the decision is not 100 percent emotion and zero percent common sense.

Pam says that she often helps her distraught first-time buyers with something she calls "The Ben Franklin Close." She advises her buyers to make a list of everything they like about the house and then everything they would change. Seeing the pluses and minuses of a home, she says, encourages a rational decision.

Curing Buyer's Remorse

What's the cure for buyer's remorse? As the sages say, "Time heals all wounds." Give yourself six months in your new home. If you still hate it, you can always turn around and try to sell it. Chances are, after six months to a year, you'll be settled in and feeling a whole lot better.

Your best defense against a bad case of buyer's remorse is preparation. If you haven't already created your wish list and reality check, you should do so. Knowing the difference between what you want in a home and what you can't live without will help you understand the important compromises that have to be made when you purchase your first home. And that's what it is—your *first* home, not your last one.

8

Financing Your Home

QUESTION 53

HOW MUCH CAN I AFFORD TO SPEND ON A HOME?

If you're unsure about how much you can actually spend on a house, you're not alone. Most Americans simply guessestimate the amount. The decision goes something like this: "Let's see, I earn $50,000 a year, and I've been told I can spend 2½ times my annual income on a house, so that means I can spend $125,000. Right?"

Perhaps. If interest rates are 10 percent for a 30-year fixed-rate loan, *and* you have no debt, *and* you have 20 percent in cash to put down on a home, then you can probably spend $125,000 for every $50,000 in income. But if interest rates are 8 percent for a 30-year loan, and you don't carry much, if any, debt, and you still have 20 percent in cash for a down payment, you might be able to spend $150,000 or more on a house. And if interest rates are at 6.5 percent, which they were at the beginning of 1999, you might be able to spend $200,000 or more for every $50,000 in income.

Confused? You're not alone here, either. But it's not that tough to use the formulas that mortgage lenders use to calculate how much house you can afford. Or, you can call a local lender and get prequalified or preapproved for your loan. Even easier is to go on-line at any number of sites and use the calculators. Many sites will do virtually instantaneous loan approvals, such as QuickenMortgage.com, HomeAdvisor.com, and Eloan.com.

The worst thing about guessing how much you can afford to spend is that you might be wrong, which means you're out there looking at homes that are out of your price range. That can only lead to one thing—heartbreak. Once you start looking at homes that are too expensive for your budget, it's awfully hard to settle for what you can afford.

Assets and Debts

Every discussion about how much you can afford should start with assets and debts—how much you have versus how much you owe.

The amount of debt you carry is very important. Conventional loan programs will allow you to spend up to 28 percent of your gross monthly income (GMI) on your mortgage payment and up to 36 percent on your total debt, including your mortgage, car payment, school loan payment, credit card payment, and other consumer debt. If you carry no other debt besides your mortgage, you'll be allowed to spend the full 36 percent of your GMI on your mortgage payment. If, however, you spend 10 percent of your GMI on debt, that will reduce the amount of money you have available for your mortgage each month.

Gross monthly income is different from take-home pay. You might spend 36 percent of your GMI on your total debt, but it may feel like 50 percent or more of your take-home pay, after taxes and your 401(k) contribution have been deducted.

For example, Susie and Don earn $75,000 per year. Their gross monthly income is $6,250 per month. If they have no debt, a lender will allow them to spend up to 36 percent of their GMI, or $2,250 on their mortgage, real estate property taxes, and insurance. But if they are paying $250 per month on their car loan, $200 on a graduate school loan, and $100 on their credit card debt, the amount they can spend on their mortgage is reduced by $550, leaving them with $1,700 per month to spend on their home loan.

That $550 may not seem like a lot, but, as you'll see, it can translate into a huge amount of purchasing power.

When you expect to apply for a mortgage, the two best things you can do are: (1) pay off all of your debt or as much as possible, and (2) make sure your credit is as good as gold. Home buyers who have the best credit history get the best rates and terms for their mortgage.

Prequalification vs. Preapproval

When you get *prequalified* for a loan, you're essentially asking the lender to eyeball your numbers and suggest the amount you can afford to spend on a home. The answer is more than a guess because the lender does this every day.

When you get *preapproved* for a loan, the lender takes a look at how much you earn, owe, and have in the bank. If your financial profile is good, the lender commits, in writing, to funding a loan for a certain amount, pending a successful appraisal of the property.

That's pretty strong stuff; you know ahead of time that the lender will fund your loan up to a stated amount, no matter which house you buy. It makes you an exceptionally strong buyer because the seller knows that you've been approved by a lender and are qualified to buy the house.

The reason we call this step "prequalification" or "preapproval" is that it happens before you actually find the house. Years ago, lenders would only allow buyers to apply for a loan *after* they had found the home they wanted. Today, the lending process is a lot more flexible and buyer-friendly. Prequalification is a free process. Preapproval may cost you a couple of hundred dollars, but some lenders won't charge you until you actually get the loan.

Sellers and their agent will perceive a preapproved home buyer to be "stronger" financially than one who is simply prequalified (although many real estate agents use the terms interchangeably). In a seller's market, where there are more home buyers than homes available for sale, you should get preapproved rather than prequalified for your loan. Being preapproved will allow you to move much faster through the lending process, and time may be critical.

Either way, if you want to know how much you can afford to spend on a home, you can't go wrong.

The World Wide Web of Home Loan Lending

As we start the new millennium, there are literally thousands (and perhaps hundreds of thousands) of sites on the Internet where you can get information on financing your home, use calculators, get prequalified or preapproved for a loan, and actually apply for a home loan.

How far we've come since the first edition of this book! Back then, the World Wide Web was still a pipe dream. America Online had a few hundred thousand subscribers. As this book is published, it is surpassing 20 million subscribers. I didn't include any information about the Web in the first edition because I wasn't sure which sites would survive.

Today, an update to this book wouldn't be complete without Web information.

Thousands of lenders are active on the Web. Many are local mortgage brokers who have found it necessary, and even profitable, to put up a web site to attract home buyers, but who still rely on street traffic and referrals for most of their business.

An exception is Homeowners.com. Dick Lepre created the site in the mid-1990s as a way to service and grow his street and referral traffic. By 1999, the business had grown so much that Dick left his regular lending job to focus all of his energies on Homeowners.com. Now, all of Dick's business originates on the Internet—and business is good.

Another category of Internet lender is a national lender. Countrywide Home Loans and Norwest Mortgage are two of the largest home loan lenders, and they publish active web sites to attract new customers, provide information and interactive tools, and help home buyers to apply or to be prequalified or preapproved for a loan.

Yet another category of Internet lender is the aggregator. An aggregator site offers a choice of a handful or perhaps several hundred lenders. The basic concept is this: When you apply for a loan, your information gets coded (so no one sees your name) and is sent blindly to all of the participating lenders. On a site like QuickenMortgage.com, a handful (at press time, it was six) of the cheapest loans will pop up from among the hundreds or thousands that may be available. Other sites like RealEstate.com, may offer a mortgage "auction" concept, where the lenders bid against each other for your business.

Other Internet lending models may spring up in the future. After all, the Internet as we know it isn't even a decade old. (See Question 58 for more information about applying on-line for a loan.)

First Things First

Before you call a lender or go on-line and start playing around with Internet calculators, you ought to know how lenders go about qualifying you for a loan. The worksheet on page 195 should help you figure it out.

Lenders will require you to have enough cash on hand (in a savings account) to pay at least two months' mortgage payments plus tax and insurance escrow payments. This is called your *reserve*. Lenders will not allow you to spend literally all the money you have on your first home. If your monthly mortgage payment is $1,000, you'll need at least $2,000 in reserve, plus closing costs (if any), to close on your home. Subtract that total from the down payment you've accumulated. (For more information on how much you can expect to pay for closing costs, see Questions 63 and 64.)

Playing the Interest Rate Game

As I said earlier, interest rates have a significant effect on how much you can afford to spend on a home. At 10 percent interest, you might be able to afford twice your income; at 6.5 percent, the amount you can afford might be nearly four times your income.

Everyone wants to buy or refinance when rates are at their lowest. But hardly anyone ever gets that super-low rate. Home buyers and homeowners sit on the fence waiting for rates to drop further and are surprised (and a little hurt) when they realize rates have gone back up and they've missed the trough.

The truth is this: On a $100,000 loan, the difference in interest paid, if the loan carries a 7.5 percent versus an 8.5 percent interest rate, is only about $70 per month. It adds up to $25,000 over the life

1. Calculate your gross monthly income (GMI) from all sources: _____

2. Multiply by one of the following percentages:
   .25 (25%), a conservative amount
   .28 (28%), the conventional amount
   .33 (33%), to allow you some debt payments
   .36 (36%), if you have no debt   × _____

3. Calculate and then subtract your total current monthly debt service:

Credit cards	_____	
Car loan(s)/leases	+ _____	
Charge accounts	+ _____	
School loan(s)	+ _____	
Other personal debt	+ _____	
Total debt service	_____	− _____

4. Subtract any monthly or semimonthly condominium or co-op assessments, or homeowner association fees, if applicable   − _____

5. Maximum available for monthly mortgage payment: _____

6. Subtract your estimated real estate property tax and monthly insurance escrow payment   − _____

7. Net available for monthly mortgage payment: _____

8. Multiply by 12 (months of the year)   ×   12   _____

9. Annual mortgage payment: _____

10. Divide by the current interest rate (____%)   ÷ _____

11. Total amount available for mortgage _____

12. Plus cash available for the down payment (save some for closing costs and two months' reserve)   + _____

13. Approximate amount you can spend on a home: _____

of the loan, but you're probably not going to stay in your first house for the next 30 years. Chances are you'll sell or refinance within five to seven years. In that period of time, the difference in what you'll pay will be negligible, and you can negate it by either prepaying your mortgage or going with an adjustable rate mortgage (ARM) rather than a fixed-rate loan. (An ARM carries a lower interest rate; see Question 77 for information on ARMs.)

In the next few questions, we'll discuss different types of loans, how to choose the right one, and the loan application process.

WHAT IS A MORTGAGE?

If a person agrees to lend you money, he or she is likely to ask you to put up something to collateralize the loan. The collateral must be something equal to or of greater worth than the amount of the loan, so that the lender feels secure in giving you the money.

Here's a formal definition: A *mortgage* is a loan document in which you pledge the title to your home as the collateral. The lender agrees to hold the title (or agrees, in some states, to place a lien on your title) until you have paid back the loan plus interest. The lender gives you the money; in exchange, you agree to make monthly payments of principal and interest, home insurance, and real estate taxes. Most people somewhat mistakenly call this collective amount their "mortgage payment."

A Brief History of Home Loans

The history of mortgages is interesting. Before the Great Depression in the 1930s, we didn't have mortgages as we know them today. Back then, people paid cash for their homes. Or, they would take out very short "balloon" mortgages, on which they would pay interest for maybe five years, and then would owe the entire balance in one huge "balloon" payment.

When the stock market crashed in 1929, people who lost their life savings and were unable to pay back their mortgages lost their homes. Many other people were unable to pay their real estate taxes, and they, too, lost their homes. In 1930, so many people in Cook County (the county in Illinois that includes Chicago) couldn't afford to pay their real estate taxes (less than 50 percent paid), that the city canceled the year's real estate tax collection. To this day, Cook County collects its real estate taxes a year in arrears. In other words, Cook County homeowners paid their 1999 taxes in 2000.

The War Ends

At the end of World War II, many returning veterans had money to spend. The federal government, believing that discharged service personnel were good risks, endorsed a plan to lend them money to buy homes. The plan allowed them to borrow money for 30 years and pay it back slowly, with interest. The program was such a huge success that commercial lenders soon followed suit.

That was the beginning of the modern mortgage industry. Today, trillions of dollars in mortgages are arranged every year and are sold on the secondary market. They are such a stable source of income (less than 4 percent of all mortgages fail or go into default) that investors—huge pension funds, for example—buy mortgages from banks, savings and loans, and mortgage brokers. This puts money back into the system, where it can be lent again.

Some lenders do keep a small percentage of loans in-house. Called *portfolio* loans, they typically have more relaxed qualifications for approval. To find out if your mortgage will be kept or sold, ask the person taking your application what percentage of loans are kept or sold. Remember to ask if *your* loan will be kept or sold. Don't be surprised if the answer is "yes." The vast majority of home loans are resold into the *secondary market*. If your loan is sold, another company may be hired to "service" the loan for the new investor. If your loan

Because almost all loans are resold on the secondary market, you can expect your loan to be among them. In fact, don't be surprised if your loan is sold over and over again. But don't worry. Even if your loan is sold, you don't have to pay back the loan all at once. What the new lender is buying is the right either to service your loan (meaning, to collect the funds) or to hold your mortgage note—or both. If your loan is sold, there will be a period of 60 to 90 days in which records get transferred or merged, and there may be some confusion. Be vigilant and keep calling for more information if you're not sure about your mortgage balance or account. It's up to you to make sure you're paying the right lender.

is not sold, you will continue to pay and deal with the local folks who gave you your loan.

A Big, Scary Scam

One of the more common scams is the mortgage sale scam. Here's what happens. You receive a notice that your loan is being sold and a new company, XYZ Capital, will now collect your monthly mortgage check. You're instructed on official-looking letterhead stationery to send your mortgage payments to the new company.

What you don't realize is that there is no new company. It's a scam. So you send in one, two, or even three-months' worth of payments. And you go on with your life.

Out of the blue, you get a call from your old mortgage company: Why are you 60 or 90 days late in paying your loan? Your credit has been damaged, and even though you've already paid out to XYZ Capital, you still owe your regular monthly payments to your real mortgage company.

You call the Federal Trade Commission (see Resources on page 378 for the telephone number) and file a complaint. But what could you have done to protect yourself ahead of time?

If you receive a letter announcing that your mortgage has been sold, be sure to call up your original lender to confirm that the loan has indeed been sold. Get the name and the toll-free telephone number of the new lender from your original lender. The new lender is required by law to provide a toll-free number that you can call if you wish to check on the status of your account.

That's all it takes. If you find out that the letter you've received is a fake, call the FTC immediately. With any luck, they'll be able to put the scam artist out of business permanently.

HOW DO I GET INFORMATION ON MORTGAGES?

Getting the information is easy. Sorting it all out and choosing the best home loan for your financial situation is a little tougher.

Here are some good sources of information:

1. **Newspapers.** The real estate section of your local newspaper probably has something like a "mortgage watch" column. This

column gives you a list of five or ten local mortgage companies and the loans and rates they are currently offering. As you peruse this list each week, remember that those rates are anywhere from four to ten days old, and the interest rate may have shifted up or down. If you call one of those companies, don't ask for the rate you saw in the newspaper. Instead, ask for the current lowest rate on a 30-year, or 15-year, or 1-year ARM. Mortgage companies advertise heavily in the real estate section. You can call several of those companies to inquire about rates and programs.

2. **Real estate agents and brokers.** Real estate agents usually know which local mortgage companies offer good rates. Your agent's firm probably owns a mortgage company (not to mention a title company, an alarm system company, and perhaps even an appraisal company). Your agent should be prepared to give you a list of at least three different mortgage companies he or she knows are good and responsive, including the one his or her firm owns.

3. **Local lenders.** Visit your local bank, savings and loan, or credit union (credit unions typically have really inexpensive mortgages for their members), and ask for the available free information (they should have gobs of it).

4. **Local housing authority.** A local housing authority is an excellent source of free information. It may also have special programs for first-time buyers. These programs could include down payment assistance or extra-low interest rate loans for families who meet certain income or location requirements. If you qualify, you may be able to get a loan at an interest rate that's well below the market rate.

5. **The federal government.** Write to Consumer Publications, Pueblo, Colorado 81003, and ask for a free information guide. A word of warning, however. These federal publications talk about mortgages in general. They're good as far as they go, which isn't nearly far enough. If you find you have questions after reading through one of these little booklets, call your local mortgage company and get answers.

6. **On-Line sources.** Almost everything you can get in person is now available on the Web. Fannie Mae (HomePath.com or FannieMae.com) and Freddie Mac (FreddieMac.com), the two quasi-private institutions (which trade on the New York Stock

Exchange), have excellent web sites chock-full of information on buying a home and getting a mortgage. Bank Rate Monitor's web site (bankrate.com) is devoted to providing the latest interest rate information for mortgages, as well as car loans and credit cards. Aggregators like HomeAdvisor (HomeAdvisor .com), QuickenMortgage (QuickenMortgage.com), RealEstate .com (RealEstate.com), iOwn.com (iOwn.com), and Eloan (Eloan.com) all provide helpful information, in addition to allowing you to play with calculators and apply on-line. Large national mortgage companies like Countrywide Home Loans (Countrywide.com) and Norwest (Norwest.com) also have excellent information, as do some smaller mortgage brokers, like Homeowners.com (Homeowners.com), which has won several Internet awards for site content. Where should you start? These companies' sites offer good, time-tested information. In fact, information from my books and from years of my columns runs on several of these sites. But new sites are always emerging. To stay on top of the newcomers, try the International Real Estate Digest (Ired.com), which ranks sites and attempts to list and categorize many of the real estate sites out there in Webland.

QUESTION 56

WHAT IS THE DIFFERENCE BETWEEN A MORTGAGE BANKER AND A MORTGAGE BROKER? HOW DO I FIND A GOOD LENDER?

The essential ingredient to a successful purchase is finding a lender whom you can trust and who will walk you through the process. Where do you find such a person? To begin with, it's important to understand that lenders come in all shapes and sizes, and they're called by different names.

- **Mortgage brokers** are involved with the origination side of the business. They take loan applications, process the papers, and then submit the files to an institutional investor, typically a savings and loan (S&L), or a bank, or a mortgage banker, who underwrites and closes the loan. Mortgage brokers usually work with a wide variety of investors who buy loans on the secondary market, providing mortgage bankers and brokers with an almost inexhaustible supply of money with which to make new mortgages—and to offer a wide variety of loan packages. Some mortgage brokers seem to have more lending flexibility and can work with folks who might otherwise have a tough time getting a mortgage.

- **Mortgage bankers** go a step further. They work within the origination side of the business, but they also get involved with servicing the loan and closing the loan in their own name with their own funds. If you went to a bank for a loan, the mortgage banker would take the loan application and lend you the money from the bank's own coffers. Once you closed on the loan, the same company might service your account, collect payments, and make sure your real estate taxes were being paid. Or, the company might sell your loan on the secondary market (to institutional investors) and then relend the money. Mortgage bankers make their money on actually making the loan; you pay fees and points, which the banker pockets. Mortgage bankers might make additional money on the spread between the rate on your loan and the going rate of loans in the secondary market.

Qualities to Look For in a Mortgage Company

How should you select a mortgage company? Pick a company based on its experience, customer service, and recommendations. The one thing you *shouldn't* do is make your decision based solely on which lender is offering the lowest rates. Rates are extremely important, but there is a tremendous amount of competition in today's mortgage market. That means all mortgage brokers and bankers should be offering mortgages at competitive prices. If a company is offering a mortgage package that's well below market rates, beware. (Remember the old cliché: If it sounds too good to be true, it probably is.)

All mortgage companies generally choose from the same pool of institutional investors. A company offering abnormally low rates might make up the difference by increasing closing costs or tacking on additional settlement fees.

Richard, president of a mortgage brokerage in Evanston, Illinois, reminds borrowers that the lowest rates are not necessarily paired with good service (in a perfect world, they might be), and fast, efficient service is essential for a smooth closing.

Make sure the lender you choose will be able to deliver the funds needed to close on your new home. Most lenders offer free pre-printed pamphlets and booklets on the mortgage process. The federal government also offers free (or nearly free) booklets from the aforementioned Consumer Publications Office, Pueblo, Colorado 81003. (See the Resources section, in Appendix IV, for additional places to call or write.)

Choosing the Right Lender for You

Choosing the right lender will take some time and effort, and lots of telephone calls. It takes work because lenders today offer a plethora of mortgage options that are individually tailored to each borrower's financing needs. In major metropolitan areas, there are dozens, if not hundreds, of mortgage brokers and bankers; in smaller communities, the numbers fall proportionately. Still, there should be ample choices of lenders, and fairly stiff competition for your business.

Remember, when you apply for a loan, you're in the driver's seat. You're giving the lender *your* business, not the other way around. If a lender seems condescending or doesn't treat you fairly or with civility, take your business elsewhere.

Starting Out

The first thing to do when you're starting to look for your loan is *find out the current mortgage interest rate.* You want to know the following information:

- The current interest rate lenders are charging for their most common mortgages.
- How many points (a point is 1 percent of the loan amount) they are charging to make the loan.
- The annual percentage rate (APR) of the loan (which adds up all the extra costs and fees, and amortizes that total over the life of the loan).
- What lengths of loans the mortgage company offers: 7/23 (pronounced "seven twenty-three"), 5/25 (pronounced "five twenty-

five), 30-year fixed, 15-year fixed, 5-year balloon, and so on. (For more information on various mortgage types, see Question 75.)

As we discussed in Question 55, the easy way to get this information is to look for a mortgage watch column in your local newspaper, or to go on-line.

Newspapers often track current lending rates because they know many of their readers either own a home or are interested in buying or selling. The mortgage watch column lists a handful of lenders (anywhere from five to more than a dozen) and their current mortgage offerings. Telephone numbers and addresses are usually provided.

Clip out the mortgage watch column for several weeks, compare the prices quoted for various loans, and call up the lenders that seem to have the best deals. At this point, there is no way for you to tell which mortgage banker or broker will be able to give you the best service. All you can go on are price and product.

If you choose to go on-line, you'll have to go to either an aggregator (Eloan.com, HomeAdvisor.com, QuickenMortgage.com, or RealEstate.com), or to an individual lender's web site. Each of these sites should give you the current interest rate and allow you to apply on-line.

The Good, the Bad, and the Ugly

How do you find a good mortgage banker or broker? As with finding a good real estate broker, seek out recommendations from friends and family. Your real estate broker may have excellent suggestions, so be sure to ask for a list of lenders. If you have a real estate attorney, ask him or her for a few names. When you've collected several names, go to their offices and talk to the manager in charge. Look around—some new mortgage brokers work out of their home—and investigate the person with whom you'll be dealing. Find out how long the company has been in business. Ask how many mortgages have been closed in the past year, and for around how much money (a range or an average amount). It's important to work with a company that has a track record.

After you've interviewed some lenders, make sure you go back on-line to compare rates and fees. You may find it easier and faster to apply to an on-line lender. You can't do your entire closing electronically yet, but I'm guessing that by the time I next update this book, you might very well be able to have an electronic settlement.

You should feel entirely comfortable with your lender and your loan officer. If you are uncomfortable at an office that you visit, leave and find another mortgage company. If you're concerned about a firm's track record, or the way it deals with its customers, don't be afraid to approach your local Better Business Bureau, chamber of commerce, or state attorney general's office. You can also contact the Mortgage Bankers Association (MBA) of America (202-861-6554, 1125 15th Street NW, Washington, DC 20005-2766) and ask whether any claims have been filed. Finally, feel free to ask for references, and then call them.

WHO ARE THE PEOPLE INVOLVED WITH MAKING THE LOAN?

After you've compared rates and mortgage products (see Question 75), it's time to go and meet the people who will be guiding your loan through the approval process.

The loan officer, your primary contact, is the person you'll be dealing with all the way through the process, from application to closing.

These days, lenders can approve your loan virtually instantaneously. It takes just a few minutes, once they've electronically entered your information and credit report into the computer. In a fast market, it's great to be able to be approved so quickly, but don't think you'll get your loan right then and there. If an electronic appraisal is done on your property (instead of the lender's sending someone out to physically appraise the home, it's done via electronic data bases), that can be done quickly as well. But in a hot market, the appraisers get backed up and there may be a two- or three-week delay until they can actually get out to survey the home and do the requisite research. Still, over the past five years, the time it takes to apply for and get approved for a loan has dropped dramatically. When you apply, you should know almost immediately whether you'll qualify to buy your home.

Typically, the loan officer will take down all your information and create a file for your application. Next, the loan processor (the loan officer's partner) will order an appraisal of the property, a credit report on your financial status, and a title search. When this information has been obtained, the loan is packaged up and sent to the investor, who makes a decision on whether to approve your loan. All the way through, your contact should be with the loan officer, the person you've dealt with from the very beginning.

Beware of hand-offs. Some companies assign a loan officer to take your application, but then other people whom you have never met continue the process. Make it clear that you don't want a *loan processor.* You want the confidence that comes from having a loan officer who will handle your application through to the end, will care about your needs, and will make sure the deal gets done.

How Do You Know Whether the Loan Officer Is Doing His or Her Job?

Generally (and this includes extremely busy periods of low-interest-rate refinancing), approval of a loan application shouldn't take more than three to four weeks. In the late 1990s, when existing homes sales continued to break records year in and year out, and interest rates fell to their lowest levels in a decade, borrowers complained that it was taking as long as six weeks to get loans approved.

When you're applying for your loan, ask the loan officer how long the approval process should take. If you're hearing about delays in mortgage processing, or if you're getting numerous requests for additional information, then you should start to get concerned. There's nothing wrong with a loan officer's calling to say that four pieces of documentation are still needed for your file. But if you're getting multiple requests for documentation, including repeated requests for the same documents, then the loan officer didn't do his or her job in the beginning.

Unless you have special circumstances—for example, you're self-employed or you trade commodities—the loan officer should ask for everything up front. And you should make every effort to give the loan officer all that is needed to get your application approved.

If any particular issues affect your financial picture, it is wise to discuss them early in the process—preferably, before you put down any money. Some of these issues might include credit problems, previous bankruptcies, divorces, recent job changes, starting your own business, and so on.

Remember, you're the customer. If you're not happy with the service you're receiving from your loan officer, speak up! Ask to talk to the supervisor, or the head of the office. If that doesn't get you anywhere, ask to have your application fee refunded, and find another lender. Even if the lender doesn't refund your application fee, you should switch lenders if you feel uncomfortable or aren't getting the proper service. After all, buying a house is the biggest single investment you'll probably ever make. You want to have around you a team of professionals whom you can count on.

QUESTION 58

HOW DO I APPLY FOR A LOAN? SHOULD I APPLY ON-LINE FOR A MORTGAGE?

Applying for a loan is different from getting prequalified. Prequalification before you buy property involves having a lender analyze your assets, liabilities, and income stream. From these items (which the lender may just take your word on), the lender tells you a dollar amount that you can borrow.

You'll need to actually apply for your loan if you ask to be *pre-approved*. And that's when things change. The lender will want to see documentation and proof that you actually have all the assets and debts you say you have. You will sit down with the loan officer, who will ask you questions and write down the answers. Or, you will sit down at your computer, log on to a web site, and fill out your own application.

Handy Information

Having the following information can speed up the loan process significantly:

- Copies of all bank statements for the past three months.
- Copies of all investment account statements, including stock brokerage accounts.
- Most recent pay stubs for you and your spouse or partner.
- W2 forms for the past two years (for you and your spouse or partner).
- If you're self-employed, the past two years' tax returns plus a profit-and-loss statement for the year to date.
- A gift letter, if part of the money you're using to buy the house has come as a gift from your parents, friends, or other relatives.

Important Decisions

You'll have to make some important decisions at the time of application.

1. What type of mortgage should you choose? Think carefully before you decide which mortgage type is right for you. (See Question 75 for a discussion of different mortgage types.) The type of mortgage you choose depends on two factors: (1) how long you plan to stay in the house, and (2) how much risk you are willing to take.

You'll have to decide whether you're the type of person who likes minimal risk (a fixed loan would probably work well for you), some risk (a two-step loan like a 7/23 or 5/25 might be the ticket), or a lot of risk (adjustable rate mortgages may be a good choice; they even have built-in caps on how high the interest rate can jump each year and over the entire life of the loan). The loan officer should be happy to go over the different mortgage products offered by his or her firm, and to counsel you on which one might be right for your situation.

2. Should you float the rate or lock in? When the lender asks you this question, he or she is really asking whether you want to lock in at the current rate, or gamble that the rates will drop a bit before you close on the loan.

Here's how the float option works. Let's say you go in on Monday and fill out an application. The rate for a 30-year fixed loan is 8 percent. You're scheduled to close in two months. You think interest rates are going to drop in the next 60 days, so you opt to float your loan, meaning that at any point in the next 60 days you can call to lock in the rate. If rates drop, you'll get the lower rate. But if rates go up, you'll have to pay the higher rate. If, however, you think that mortgage rates can't possibly go lower before you're scheduled to close, then it's in your best interest to lock in the rate of your mortgage. Locking in means that whatever the mortgage rate is on the day you make the application, that will be the interest rate you pay on your mortgage.

Locking in or floating the interest rate has nothing to do with what type of mortgage you choose. You can choose to float the rate or lock in on all types of mortgages, including a fixed or adjustable rate mortgage (ARM).

3. How long should the lock be? This sounds like the same question as above, but it's not. When you apply for a loan, the mortgage rate offered by the lender is only good for a specific amount of time. You have to choose how long you want the rate to last, while remembering that *the longer the rate lock, the higher the interest rate.*

Lenders usually offer to hold the rate for 30, 45, or 60 days. You should base the length of the lock on when you're supposed to close on the home. For example, if you apply for a loan 28 days before you want to close, you might choose to hold the rate for 30 days. If you're going to close in 38 days, you might choose to lock in for 45 days.

Lenders will rarely offer to hold a lock for longer than 60 days, but if you need to close quickly, they might manage to approve your mortgage and lock a rate for seven days. The shorter the lock, the more important it is to furnish your lender with everything he or she needs to get your loan going.

The reason lenders don't like to lock in rates for extended periods of time is that interest rates fluctuate daily and often change several times each day. With that much activity, it's difficult for lenders and investors to predict how much interest rates will change over the course of two months. To protect themselves, they limit the length of lock-ins. Just remember, the longer you want the lender to hold the lock, the more you'll pay for that privilege.

If you're buying new construction, it's likely that you're buying off of a blueprint, unless you're buying a developer's spec house. It could take anywhere from four months to two years (in the case of some loft or condo conversions) for the property to be ready. If you've got to wait nine months or longer until closing, don't try to lock in on a rate now. You're far better off waiting until you're only 60 days out from closing, and then watching interest rise and fall until you decide it's a good time to lock in the rate.

4. How many points, if any, do you want to pay? Another decision you'll have to make is how many points you want to pay at the closing. Most first-time borrowers don't realize there is an inverse relationship between the number of *points* (a point is one percentage point of the loan amount) you pay and the interest rate you receive. You may have to pay some points or fees, but the more points you pay, the lower the interest rate. If you pay no points up front, you'll have a slightly higher interest rate, and pay more over the life of the loan.

Points are paid in cash (usually tough for first-time buyers to come by) at the closing, but the federal government allows you to deduct them from your income taxes during the year of the closing. Or you can amortize your points (pay them over the life of the loan), which will ultimately increase your rate.

I'm often asked whether points paid in a refinancing can be deducted for tax purposes. The answer is, unfortunately, no. You must amortize the points over the life of the loan and deduct a portion of the points each year. However, if you refinance your loan, say, in five years, you may deduct any remaining points (the amount that has not yet been amortized) in the year you refinance.

Why might you want to pay additional points? Let's say you decide to close on your home in November. That means you have only one month's worth of mortgage interest to deduct on your tax return for that year. However, if you decide to pay three or four points in cash at the closing, you would have a higher amount to deduct for the year, and you can maximize your deductions. If you decide to pay five points, the lender might lower your rate by a point and a half. That's called "buying down" the loan.

Some developers use a different buy-down to entice first-time buyers to purchase new construction. They'll "buy down" the rate for the first two or three years with cash. This doesn't have anything to do with paying more points up front in exchange for a lower interest rate, though they're both called the same name. You receive two significant benefits from buying down your interest rate: (1) a larger deduction, and (2) a lower interest rate for the life of the loan.

Here's how points work. If you need a $100,000 mortgage, each point is $1,000. If you decide to buy down your loan with five points, you will need $5,000 in cash at the closing, just to cover the points paid to the lender.

Good Faith Estimate of Closing Costs

Every time you put in an application for a loan, the lender is required by the federal Real Estate Settlement Procedures Act (RESPA) to give you a good faith estimate of your closing costs. That sheet of paper should detail every fee you'll likely pay, and add it all up for you. You may even be asked to sign the document, to prove that you've seen it.

Many first-time home buyers feel somewhat deceived by the good faith estimate because the actual costs at closing may be significantly different from the costs originally listed. A good lender's estimate should be very close to the actual closing cost numbers. However, an estimate is an estimate. Last-minute costs may come up at the closing. If you feel that the charges are unusually high, you or your real estate attorney can talk to the lender and renegotiate. If a charge seems unfair or completely outrageous, and it was not on the good faith estimate, you should refuse to pay it.

NEVER walk away from an application without getting a copy of every document you've signed. It is extremely important to be able to document, in writing, every step in the application process. If your lender ever gives you trouble, you'll have to prove what was said and what was signed, and when. Also, signing a document signifies that you've actually read it. Take the time to read all documents involved in the application, and don't be afraid to ask questions of the loan officer. Remember, you're not the first first-time buyer the loan officer has dealt with. And you won't be the last.

hindsight

WHAT KIND OF DOCUMENTATION WILL I NEED FOR MY APPLICATION?

QUESTION 59

If you've spent months searching for the perfect home, the last thing you want is a delay in the mortgage approval process. Unfortunately, a delay in getting approved for your mortgage can push back the closing or be a viable reason for the seller to cancel the purchase contract.

One problem that can cause a delay is faulty or missing documentation. Even after going through pounds of paperwork during the mortgage application process, lenders often request more documentation.

According to one loan officer, most borrowers don't understand exactly how much detailed information the lender will need to approve their loans. Here is a list of documents your loan officer may ask for. Be prepared to provide these documents, or copies of them, at a moment's notice.

1. All W2 forms for each person who will be a coborrower on the loan.
2. Copies of completed tax forms for the past three years, including any schedules or attachments.
3. Copies of one month's pay stubs for each coborrower.
4. Copies of the three most recent statements for every bank account, IRA, 401(k), or stock account that you and your spouse or partner have. Bring a copy of your most recent statement for any other assets you own.

5. A copy of the back and front of your canceled earnest money check. Contact your bank if the check has not yet cleared.

6. Copies of the sales contract and all riders; both brokers' names, addresses, and phone numbers; and the same information for both your attorney and the seller's attorney.

7. If you are selling a current residence, a copy of the listing agreement and, if the home is under contract, a copy of the sales contract.

8. If gift funds are involved, the giver must provide proof that he or she had that money to give; a copy of the giver's most recent bank statement will do. You must then show the paper trail for the money, including a deposit slip. The giver will have to fill out a gift letter affidavit, available from the loan officer, indicating that the funds were a gift and the gift giver does not expect repayment.

9. Complete copies of all divorce decrees.

10. Copies of an old survey or title policy for the home you are buying, if available when you apply for the mortgage, or when it becomes available during the purchase process.

11. If you are self-employed, complete copies of the past two years' business tax returns, and a year-to-date profit and loss statement and balance sheet, with original signatures.

12. A list of your addresses in the past seven years.

13. If you have made any large deposits (i.e., larger than your monthly income) into your bank accounts in the past three months, an explanation, and proof, as to where the funds came from.

14. If you have opened a new bank account in the past six months, a letter explaining the source of the money to open this new account.

15. Addresses and account numbers for every form of credit you have.

16. Documentation to verify additional income, such as Social Security, child support, and alimony.

17. If you have had a previous bankruptcy, a complete copy of the bankruptcy proceedings, including all schedules, and a letter explaining the circumstances for the bankruptcy.

18. For a Federal Housing Administration (FHA) or Veterans Administration (VA) loan, a photocopy of a picture ID and a copy of your Social Security card. Also bring proof of military service for a VA loan.

19. If you have any judgments against you, a copy of a recorded satisfaction of judgment, and copies of documents describing any lawsuits in which you are currently involved.

No-Doc Loans

A loan that requires almost no documentation is commonly referred to as a *no-doc* loan. No-doc loans are for people who either can't, or don't want to, provide the documentation lenders need to process a conventional loan.

If you don't want to produce documentation, you can get a no-doc loan. But be prepared to pay extra for it. Depending on what kind of documentation you do or do not produce, your loan could carry an interest rate that's several percentage points higher than a conventional loan.

WHAT TYPES OF CIRCUMSTANCES MIGHT FOUL UP MY LOAN APPLICATION? HOW CAN I FIX THEM?

Lower rates have led to a crush of business at mortgage lenders' offices. As a result, the application process may take longer than usual. The real problem is that a delay can force you to the wall on the occupancy of your new home and even threaten the terms of your loan, such as the interest rate and the fees the lender charges.

It's vital that you, the buyer, stay on top of things from the day of application through the closing. Often, there are things you can do to help speed the mortgage loan process and meet that pressing deadline.

Any number of things can go wrong during the mortgage approval process: You or the lender can lose documents; the lender may demand more documentation; appraisals may be running late; or verification from banks or from your employer may not be processed quickly enough. Mortgage experts agree that problems can surface with interest rates, points, or the up-front fees a lender charges to make a mortgage loan. In fact, they estimate that as many as 30 percent of all mortgage applications will face some problem with the interest rate or points.

The Rate Lock, and Yet Another Scam

To eliminate the uncertainty of changeable interest rates, borrowers may pay their prospective lender for the privilege of locking in a specific interest rate and number of points (a point is equal to 1 percent of the loan amount). The lock is good for a predefined time, usually 30 to 60 days. You must close on your mortgage before the lock expires, or you lose the preset interest rate.

The mortgage loan process can easily go awry, particularly when interest rates start to fluctuate. Lenders, nervous about their investments and bent on charging the highest interest rate possible, are not as eager to close on their loans as when interest rates are dropping. According to a spokesperson for the Office of Banks and Real Estate, which regulates and monitors mortgage brokers, mortgage bankers, and financial institutions in Illinois, there are many ways for the lender to give you trouble.

"The lender may give you a lock on the interest rate that is intentionally too short, given the current market conditions," she says.

A reasonable lock period is 60 days. Lenders rarely agree to extend a lock to 90 days because of market volatility. But the director says lenders often *"play the float"* with mortgages. Although borrowers think they've locked in a certain interest rate and a certain number of points, lenders will, in essence, gamble with the rate rather than actually lock it in, hoping that interest rates will slip further. If they do go down, the loan officer and the mortgage company will then reap extra profits from the end lender for selling you a mortgage so far above the going rate.

If Rates Go Up

The fun starts when interest rates begin to rise. If a loan officer has been playing the float with a loan, and the rate goes up, he or she will have to pay, out of his or her pocket, the difference between the locked-in interest rate and the current market rate, in order to close on the loan. And because loan officers are loath to pay out, they will often find something "wrong" with an application at the last minute, forcing the borrower to accept a higher interest rate or more points, one loan officer warns.

There are a few things you can do to guard against such situations and to ensure you get the mortgage loan you applied for, within the time frame allotted in your application contract.

- **Two can be better than one.** Some experts recommend that buyers apply for two different mortgages at two different companies. Float the rate with one application and lock in the other. "If you have trouble with one of the lenders, you can always play each against the other," says one loan officer. This method of safeguarding will cost you an additional application fee of $200 to $500, unless you can get the lender to waive the fee until the closing.

- **Get the lock commitment in writing.** Never accept a verbal lock. "That way you'll have proof that the lender went against the bargain," suggests the Illinois attorney general's office.

- **Get hard copies of everything.** Before you walk out the door, make sure you receive copies of anything you have signed during the mortgage application process. Don't let the lender mail the papers to you.

- **Secure a good faith estimate.** Make sure the lender hands you a good faith estimate of closing costs before you sign anything or pay anything.

- **Keep your lifestyle intact.** Don't make major lifestyle changes after the application has been made and before you close on the property. Don't buy a car. Don't increase your indebtedness in any way. Don't change jobs. It's possible that the lender will pull a second credit report just before closing, and these lifestyle changes could sink your application.

- **Keep in touch.** Keep in direct and close contact, at least weekly, with your loan officer throughout the process. Experts say that if you aren't going to be approved for a loan, the lender should know within days—certainly within two to four weeks (four is an extreme case). Typically, lenders can tell you almost instantaneously whether you're approved. Credit reports can be pulled up while you're sitting there. If you aren't approved while you're sitting in the lender's office, call almost daily to see whether the loan officer needs any additional information.

- **Create a paper trail.** When your loan officer tells you he or she has all the documentation required for your loan, immediately send a letter, by certified mail, stating that, per your conversation on whatever date, the loan officer requires no additional information. Keep a copy for yourself as part of your paper trail. Also keep a copy of every bit of paperwork and correspondence between you and the lender.

If, after all this, the loan officer tries to back out of your locked-in rate agreement and force you to take higher rates and points than you originally agreed to, experts suggest you start yelling—literally! The squeaky wheel gets the grease. If the loan officer tries to make you take a higher rate, contact the manager of his or her office. Have your attorney yell for a while, and drag out the closing. A few threats about sending letters to the attorney general's office, the Better Business Bureau, and other consumer-action organizations should persuade the loan officer to back down.

Sometimes, the Problem Isn't the Lender

Bennett's Story

Bennett wasn't really interested in selling his house until he was contacted by an eager real estate agent. The contact came in 1999, in the midst of the hottest seller's market ever. The agent wanted to know how much Bennett wanted for his house.

Bennett quoted a sky-high price, and, much to his surprise, the buyer accepted. But then the appraisal came back, indicating that the house was actually worth about $50,000 more than Bennett had asked. So, much to the buyer's chagrin, Bennett changed his mind.

A week or so later, the agent showed him the appraisal sheet. Bennett saw that the appraiser had located his house in the midst of a much hotter neighborhood, and had used comps (the sales prices of comparable properties in the same neighborhood) from a different neighborhood.

So the deal was on again. But then the buyers didn't have enough money for the down payment. Bennett agreed to lend the buyers $10,000, but to structure the loan so that the mother of one of the buyers was the borrower. The mother, in turn, would gift the money back to the buyers. After the closing, the money would be repaid to Bennett.

Bennett's attorney got wind of the loan deal, and it smelled bad. Sellers are not supposed to give the down payment (or any extra cash) to the buyers "under the table," so to speak. And if a wacky transaction is structured, like this one, the lender has to be notified in advance and approve or reject the deal. By not informing the lender, Bennett and the buyers were on the verge of committing mortgage fraud—which the federal government takes quite seriously.

Bennett's attorney ended up saving the deal, but it took quite a while to sort everything out. The closing was delayed for several weeks.

HOW MUCH OF A DOWN PAYMENT WILL I NEED TO BUY MY HOME?

QUESTION 61

These days, the answer starts at zero percent. You can get loans with nothing down; or loans for which the down payment is a gift from friends and relatives, or is a grant; or loans for which you actually put down the cash.

Zero-down loans and very low down payment loans (you put down 3 percent or less) are relatively new phenomena. As lenders get more comfortable with the idea that the vast majority of people who have no equity in their homes are still good risks, the zero-down mortgage programs will continue to expand.

What You Should Put Down

The standard down payment is 20 percent of the sales price of the home. If the home costs $100,000, a conventional lender would require that you have $20,000 in cash for a down payment, plus closing costs. Lenders ask for 20 percent down because homeowners who have a larger equity stake in a home are less likely to default on the mortgage than homeowners who have a smaller equity stake. If you put down at least 20 percent on your home, you will not need to pay for private mortgage insurance (PMI), which can cost between $45 and $60 per month per $100,000 of loan value.

But lenders recognize that 20 percent of the sales price is a huge amount of cash for most first-time buyers. In San Francisco, a first-time buyer's house might cost as much as $300,000. To put down 20 percent on that house, buyers need to come up with $60,000 in cash for the down payment plus another $10,000 or more in closing costs, fees, and reserves.

As a result, several widely available mortgage options will allow you to put down significantly less. For example, first-time buyers commonly put down 10 or 15 percent of the sales price. Conventional lenders will allow a smaller down payment (anything less than 20 percent) as long as the borrower purchases private mortgage insurance (PMI). PMI is paid monthly, along with your mortgage, until you have about 20 percent equity in the home. The law requires lenders to automatically cancel PMI once the loan-to-value ratio reaches 22 percent. (For more information on PMI, see Question 84.)

If you choose an FHA loan, you can put down as little as 3 percent, of which 2 percent may be a gift from a friend or relative, or a grant from a non-profit organization. (You'll need mortgage insurance, however.) VA loans, which are backed and administered by the Veterans Administration and are available only to qualified veterans of the armed services, have a zero-down option, but these loans tend to be extremely expensive. Very low down payment loan options (3 or 5 percent down) from the VA are more reasonably priced.

A new development is that other nontraditional lenders are jumping into the mortgage game. Merrill Lynch, the brokerage company, offers a loan that allows you to borrow your down payment on a margin account against assets that you hold in brokerage accounts with the company. Fidelity offers a similar program. The idea is: You borrow

20/20

hindsight

Borrowing on margin means that you're essentially using your brokerage account (and the stocks, bonds, and mutual funds it contains) as collateral for whatever you are buying. Sophisticated investors have used margin accounts for years, to fully leverage their holdings and invest money they don't necessarily have readily available. The danger with borrowing on margin is that if your assets in the margin account suddenly drop dramatically in value, you may be called on to sell them at a disadvantageous time, in order to maintain a certain loan-to-value ratio in the margin account. Be sure you fully investigate how these accounts—and their mortgage margin account options—work, before you sign on the dotted line.

100 percent of the cost of the home and pay the going mortgage rate. If you have retirement accounts, or investment assets you don't wish to sell in order to come up with down payment cash, you may wish to investigate these programs. If your accounts are with other financial companies, talk to an account representative about any similar programs that may be offered. I believe many of the larger financial companies will soon offer programs like these for clients who wish to buy or refinance a home.

Putting Down More, Not Less

When might you be required to put down more, rather than less?

In special circumstances, a higher down payment may be required. Some co-ops may require a 30 or 40 percent cash down payment to prove that the resident has the financial means to cover any capital expenses that may be required in the future. Co-ops may require a 60 percent down payment. Requiring a high cash down payment is another way for the co-op to filter out individuals whom the residents choose not to have in their building. Fortunately, most co-ops have done away with the higher down payment requirement in order to make the units more affordable.

Some cash-rich folks (or first-time buyers with trust accounts) don't like the idea that they owe anyone, and can't get used to carrying a mortgage. These folks should put down as much as they can.

In the next question, we'll talk about how to figure out whether you should put down the smallest or largest down payment you can afford.

SHOULD I PUT DOWN THE LARGEST OR THE SMALLEST DOWN PAYMENT POSSIBLE?

QUESTION
62

Your answer to this question depends on three things:

1. How much cash you have lying around.
2. How nervous you are about leveraging your finances.
3. What you plan to do with your cash instead of putting it down on a house.

first time buyer tip

Before we even get started, you should know that there's no "right" answer to this question. Some people can borrow 100 percent of their home's purchase price and invest the rest in obscure technology stocks, and still get eight hours of sleep a night. Other people get the jitters just thinking about an 80 percent loan-to-value ratio. And, for some folks, the question isn't how much to put down (they have trouble scraping together the down payment) but whether to put extra cash they receive after the closing toward paying down their mortgage or invest it monthly in the stock market.

Generally, first-time buyers are squeezed to the hilt. If they can scrape up a 10 percent cash down payment, they consider themselves lucky. But if you have more cash available, there are two schools of thought on the size of the down payment. Some experts feel that you should purchase your home with the smallest down payment possible. This will leave you with some cash for emergencies, decorating, and any renovation work you may want to schedule. By taking out the biggest loan possible you'll have cash to invest elsewhere.

On the other hand, you may want to make a larger down payment, to cut down the size of your monthly mortgage payments—and save yourself the monthly cost of private mortgage insurance (PMI), which can run $45 to $60 for each $100,000 of the purchase price.

The more dollars you put down, the lower the cost of owning the home. Why? You pay less interest over the life of the loan. If you put down 20 percent versus 15 percent, and the difference is $5,000, you should strongly consider putting down the 20 percent because you'll also be saving the PMI cost, which can really add up.

Making the Decision

The real question you need to ask yourself is this: What am I going to do with the money if I don't put it down on the house?

Over the past 70 years, the stock market has returned an average of about 11 percent. This number has been skewed lately because the stock market returned more than 30 percent several years in a row during the 1990s. Housing prices, during the same period, rose about 3 percent a year, although during the latter half of the 1990s, prices nationally rose more than 5 percent for several years running.

220

But that doesn't tell the whole story. In some parts of the country, prices rose more than 100 percent annually.

Let's stick with traditional returns. If you can put down 20 percent and save the cost of PMI, and you get a $100,000 loan, you'll have about $50 per month that you wouldn't otherwise have had, and you can invest it in the stock market. You might even have a larger amount for an initial investment in the market. Your choice comes down to how you feel about leveraging your financing, and whether you'll be able to sleep at night. I recommend putting down 20 percent, if you can. (But if you don't have 20% in cash, plus a bit extra for closing costs and reserves, by all means take the PMI option. While you may pay a bit more for PMI now, it's a cheap price to pay to achieve your homeownership dreams.)

Should You Prepay Your Loan?

The question of prepaying your loan versus investing that extra cash in the market each month is a bit easier to answer.

Every dollar you use to prepay your loan actually earns you the net rate of interest you're paying on your mortgage. For example, if your loan rate is 8 percent, and you don't itemize (you take the standard deduction) on your federal income tax form, every dollar you prepay earns 8 percent—a pretty darned good rate! If you were to invest that same dollar in the stock market (either in mutual funds or individual stocks or bonds), you'd need to earn at least enough to match that return plus the taxes charged on it. If you're in the 15

I firmly believe that buying a house isn't just a decision about where to live. It's a decision about your financial future. Studies show that the younger you are when you buy your first house, the wealthier you're likely to be during your lifetime. When you're buying your first home, or your second, or your third, keep your personal finances in mind. If you buy the right house in the right neighborhood, and it goes up in value over time, you've not only made money, you've enhanced your net worth. And that, in turn, enhances your ability to leverage your wealth. All of these financial concepts, and more, are discussed in my book, *100 Questions You Should Ask About Your Personal Finances*.

first time
buyer tip

221

percent bracket, you'd need to earn about 10 percent on your money to achieve the same return as pre-paying your 8 percent home loan. If you're in the 28 percent bracket, you'd need to earn about 11.5 percent.

I believe in diversification, and a real estate investment (even if it is your own home) is a pretty good counterpoint to the stock market. So I recommend you do a little of each.

If you get a 30-year fixed-rate loan, and you make one additional payment per year, you'll cut your 30-year loan to anywhere between 18 to 21 years. If you make two extra payments per year, you'll cut your loan to less than 15 years. (Of course, you could just get a 15-year loan and save even more money because you'll get a lower rate of interest.) The rest of your extra cash should be used for regular investments in the stock market.

QUESTION 63

WHAT FEES ARE ASSOCIATED WITH A MORTGAGE APPLICATION?

Three fees usually must be paid at the time of a mortgage application:

1. **The application fee,** which can range from zero to $500.
2. **The appraisal fee,** which can range from $200 to $400, depending on where you live.
3. **The credit report fee,** which ranges from $25 to $100.

These fees might be grouped together under the application fee. Many lenders apply part of the application fee toward the appraisal and credit report fees. If you're planning to apply for two mortgages (one fixed, one floating), it's best to try to negotiate the lowest up-front fee possible, or find a lender that has no application or up-front fees.

On-Line Lending

If you apply on-line, you may pay just one, smaller fee—say, $200—which will cover your initial application and credit report. Or, the fee will be applied toward all of your lender fees. You'll usually be asked to pay with your credit card on a secured site.

But that's not all. The next question addresses the entire range of lenders' fees that you'll have to pay in order to close on your loan.

WHAT LENDER'S FEES WILL I BE CHARGED FOR MY MORTGAGE?

Way back when times were simpler, lenders often charged home buyers a flat fee to close on a loan. But as interest rates have fallen and some banks have experienced financial troubles, most lenders have begun charging for many different services that were formerly covered by the flat fee. Some mortgage experts say lenders have sought to make up their lost profits by nickel-and-diming buyers to death.

There has been a push, both from the federal government under the Clinton Administration (which sought to raise homeownership levels to record heights) and from Fannie Mae and Freddie Mac, the two secondary mortgage market leaders, to lower the costs associated with homeownership. By adopting technology and lowering the cost of making a loan, Fannie Mae and Freddie Mac hope to make homeownership available to more Americans.

The Name Game

Not every bank calls every closing cost or fee by the same name, which can make comparing lenders as tough as comparing apples and station wagons.

Lenders are supposed to make it easy for you to know and understand their costs of doing business. At the time of the application, the lender is required, under the federal Truth-in-Lending Law, to provide a written, good-faith estimate of all closing costs. And it's supposed to *accurately* reflect your closing costs. Mortgage brokers recommend that you shop around for the best deals before actually applying for a mortgage. You should also not be afraid to negotiate lower fees, and to ask for a detailed explanation of each one.

> The time to negotiate fees with the lender is *before* you sign your application. Once you've signed the application, it's too late. You've made your deal and will have to live with it.

Lender's Fees

Here are some of the fees that a lender may try to charge you for the privilege of lending you money. The fees cited reflect ranges given by real estate experts across the country, but actual charges may be higher or lower, depending on your individual situation and location:

1. **Lender's points, loan origination, or loan service fees.** The lender's points (a point equals 1 percent of the loan amount) may also be referred to as the service charge. The points are the largest fees paid to the lender. They usually run between 1 and 3 percent of the loan amount. Occasionally, the points will run more than 3 percent, particularly if the borrower chooses to buy down the loan rate. **COST:** Usually zero to 3 percent of the loan, or more.

2. **Loan application fee.** The money charged by the lender for accepting your application for a loan. The application fee is almost never refundable, so you'd better be pretty darned sure you want a loan from a particular lender and will actually be approved for it. **COST:** Usually between $0 and $500.

3. **Lender's credit report.** The lender may actually pull up two credit reports on you. The first will come just after you have filled out the application and paid the fee; if a second report is ordered, it will be pulled just before the closing, to make sure you haven't made any enormous purchases or gotten into credit trouble during the elapsed time. Because they only pay once, most first-time borrowers don't realize there may be two credit checks. **COST:** Usually between $25 and $60 per person. If two people are purchasing the property jointly, the cost will be, say, $50 each, or $100. Sometimes, the charge for the credit report has been known to run as high as $75 each, which is ridiculous, given that it costs the lender $10 to $30 to prepare each report.

4. **Lender's processing fee.** With this fee, the lender passes on to you some of the cost of doing business. The processing fee is charged for processing the loan application. **COST:** Usually between $75 and $200.

5. **Lender's document preparation fee.** The cost of preparing the loan documents needed for the closing. **COST:** $0 to $250.

6. **Lender's appraisal fee.** This is the lender's charge for having the home you want to purchase appraised. Lenders supposedly charge you exactly what they're being charged for the service, which is provided by an outside contractor. A new wrinkle to this equation is an *electronic appraisal*. Lenders

search a huge database for comps (the sales prices of homes that are similar to yours and have been sold recently) and then come up with an approximate appraisal. Electronic appraisals haven't yet been perfected, but they are the future of the industry, except for unusual or extremely expensive homes. **COST:** Usually from $225 to $400. If the lender does an electronic appraisal, you might only be charged $100 (but the lender might pay a fraction of that).

7. **Lender's tax escrow service fee.** This is a onetime charge to set up and service your real estate property tax escrow (see Question 69). The bad news is: You'll be charged this fee even if you decide to pay your own taxes out of your own account. **COST:** From $40 to $85.

8. **Title insurance cost for the lender's policy.** Most title insurers charge a flat fee for the loan policy that will be given to the lender. If you want a title insurance policy that will pay you if there is a problem, there will be an additional, though very worthwhile, fee. **COST:** Between $150 and $350.

9. **Special endorsements to title.** If the lender requires extra title endorsements, the buyer must pick up the cost. Some of these might include a condo endorsement, if you're buying a condo; a planned unit development (PUD) endorsement if you're purchasing a home in a development that has specific zoning characteristics; an environmental lien endorsement (a statement to the lender that the lender's mortgage on the property won't be affected if the government finds an environmental hazard on the property and files a lien against it so that the owners must clean it up); a location endorsement (proof that the home is located where the documents say it is); and an adjustable-rate mortgage (ARM) endorsement. **COST:** $25 to $100 *each*.

10. **Prepaid interest on the loan.** There is a per-day interest charge on your loan from the day of the closing until the last day of the month in which you close. This is paid at the closing because the lender has to calculate it by hand. After you pay, you skip a month and then begin to pay your regular monthly balance—that is, the loan is paid in arrears. **COST:** A separate calculation is required for each borrower, but your lender should calculate it for you and put it on your good faith estimate.

NOTE: The above charges are only the lender's charges for doing business with you. For a list of all the closing costs you can expect, see Question 90.

QUESTION 65

WHAT ARE JUNK FEES?
HOW DO I AVOID THEM?

Mortgage brokers say that some of the lender's costs are legitimate. For example, it costs at least $225 to send someone out to do an appraisal almost anywhere in the country.

But some lenders create "junk fees" purely to increase profits. True junk fees are often difficult to identify because the lender has given them legitimate-sounding names, which can confuse borrowers. As one mortgage banker puts it: "When I see names like 'underwriting fee' and 'commitment fee,' I can tell that these types of fees are being beefed up. When you have an appraisal fee or a credit report fee, you know the lender is being charged by different agencies or companies to do actual things. Those agencies or companies charge the bank, and the customer pays it at the closing. But what is an underwriting fee? If you don't underwrite the loan, you have nothing. Buyers should have the lender explain charges they don't understand, and negotiate to exclude certain extra charges. For example, it's ridiculous to pay for an underwriting fee."

It's even sillier when you realize how today's technology has reduced the lender's time and costs for completing all the necessary tasks. The idea is to pass those savings on to the customer.

Be sure to negotiate the lender's fees before you pay the application fee. After you've completed the application, it's too late to renegotiate. You've structured the deal, and both you and the lender must live up to the application contract.

If you've got the moxie, it's not a bad idea to call several lenders and ask them to submit bids to you on a particular type of loan, listing *all* fees. If you ask ten lenders to do this, three or four might actually do it. Then you can go back to the lenders and pit one bidder against another, knocking out the lenders that can't match the lowest terms. Using this method, you should end up with the best possible mortgage, with the fewest possible points and fees.

226

WHAT IS TRUTH IN LENDING?

Under the 1974 Real Estate Settlement Procedures Act (RESPA), the lender is required, in most circumstances, within three days of receiving your application, to give you or place in the mail to you a Truth-in-Lending statement that will disclose all of the closing costs and fees you'll pay plus the *annual percentage rate* (APR) of your loan. (See Question 67.)

In many cases, the APR will be higher than the interest rate stated in your mortgage or deed of trust note, because the APR includes all fees and costs associated with making the loan. In addition to interest, points, and fees, other credit costs are calculated into the total cost of the loan. The Truth-in-Lending statement also discloses other pieces of useful information, such as the finance charge, schedule of payments, late payment charges, and whether additional charges will be assessed if you pay off the balance of your loan before it is due. This is known as the *prepayment penalty*.

A Quick Word About Prepayment Penalties

Many states do not permit lenders to charge a prepayment penalty. But national lenders and federally chartered banks may be able to attach one to your mortgage. Be certain to ask your lender if prepayment fees are legal in your state.

Prepayment penalties do prohibit you from prepaying your loan for the first two to four years. (You can still make extra payments toward the balance of the loan, but you can't refinance or sell your home.) If you do refinance or sell your home, you'll be subject to a penalty of anywhere from 2 to 4 percent of the entire loan amount. On the plus side, the lender will give you a reduced interest rate if you accept a prepayment penalty. If you're planning on being in your home at least five years, there's very little risk to agreeing to a prepayment penalty, and you'll save some extra cash.

And Now, Back to Our Regularly Scheduled Truth-in-Lending Statement

Some of the information that the lender is required to disclose may not have been finalized by the time the Truth-in-Lending statement is sent. In that case, the lender's statement will say it is an estimate. The lender will *always* provide you with a new Truth-in-Lending statement along with a HUD-1 closing statement at the closing. If you want to know about the charges you'll be paying before the closing, you can call the lender and ask whether all the estimates on the statement were correct.

WHAT IS THE ANNUAL PERCENTAGE RATE (APR)?

Under the Truth-in-Lending law, the lender must tally up all the costs involved in making the loan and amortize them over the life of the loan. The APR is what the loan is actually going to cost you. It includes the interest rate, points, fees, and any other costs the lender charges for doing business. If you go to a bank and look at its percentage rate of interest, it will also have the APR for that loan listed. The difference might be considerable: If the interest rate a bank will charge you for your mortgage is 8 percent, the APR might be 8.75 percent or higher.

The APR is one tool for helping you compare various loans. For example, if Lender A and Lender B each offers you an 8 percent, 30-year fixed-rate loan with one point, the APR for each loan will tell you which loan will cost more.

But keep in mind that a loan that has a lower APR may be better for you than a loan with a higher APR. Also, APR has absolutely no meaning, once you close on your loan.

When you're comparing loans, you're actually better off stripping down the loan to its essential components (basic loan with interest rate, and then costs and fees) rather than using the APR.

WHAT IS A GOOD FAITH ESTIMATE?

Under the terms of the Real Estate Settlement Procedures Act (RESPA) of 1974, when you file your application for a loan, the lender must provide you with a Good Faith Estimate of closing costs.

Usually, the lender will give you the estimate before you leave the office after completing your application, but your loan officer may also legally send it to you within three business days. The Good Faith Estimate is based on the lender's experience of the local costs involved with making a mortgage in your area. Any cost the lender anticipates must be stated—except for a paid-in-advance hazard insurance premium (if any), or other reserves deposited with the lender (hazard and mortgage insurance, city property taxes, county property taxes, and annual assessments). The estimate may be stated as a flat dollar amount or a range. The Good Faith Estimate form must be clear and concise, and the estimates must actually reflect the costs you will incur. It is your right to question any estimate of any cost that is provided in a dollar range rather than a flat fee.

If the lender does keep some funds in reserve, they may or may not be included in the estimate. Be sure to add them into your calculations of closing costs. And remember, closing costs can change. It's a good idea to check with the lender a few days before the closing, to determine the accurate closing cost for each item.

WHAT IS A REAL ESTATE TAX ESCROW?

A real estate tax escrow is an account set up by a lender. Into it goes the amount of money your lender tacks onto your monthly principal and interest payment to cover your real estate taxes. When the tax bill comes up, the lender takes the money out of the escrow account and sends it to the tax collector. A lender will also collect for your homeowner's insurance policy (for non-condo and non-co-op properties), which is included in the fees you pay to the lender to hold in escrow for payment of your real estate taxes and insurance premiums.

Paying It Yourself

Why don't most owners pay their own taxes and insurance? Historically, government institutions that developed the concept of the 30-year fixed mortgage collected additional money for real estate taxes and homeowner's insurance. The default rate due to unpaid real estate taxes was low. As private lenders moved into the market, they followed suit.

Today, every state has legislation that allows lenders to require real estate tax and homeowner's insurance escrows. Real estate taxes are a priority item for lenders; the lien for real estate taxes comes before the lender's mortgage lien. If you default on your loan and the home is sold to pay your bills, your real estate tax bill is paid before anything else, including the lender's mortgage (commonly called the first mortgage). Therefore, it's in the lender's best interest to make sure that property taxes are always paid.

Skeptics will tell you that lenders require escrows because they're a large source of free money. Currently, only a dozen states require lenders to pay interest on escrow accounts, although there is national legislation being bandied about that would force lenders to pay interest on all escrow accounts.

Lenders will tell you that tax and insurance escrows help them protect their investment. They also make the argument that borrowers like being budgeted so they aren't surprised with a huge tax bill once or twice a year. There's some merit to both arguments.

Federal legislation regarding escrows is worded to allow the lender the authority to withhold or impound money to cover taxes and insurance. However, some limitations went into effect in the early 1990s.

Lenders are limited to withholding no more than two months' worth of cushion. And they must provide an itemized statement, similar to a checking account statement, of money coming into your account and bills that are paid.

In other words, if you pay $100 per month to cover your real estate taxes and insurance, your lender may hold only an extra $200—or two months' worth—in escrow.

Fine. So why doesn't your lender pay you interest on that money? Because most states and the federal government don't require lenders to do so.

Lenders argue that escrows are complicated and are an extra burden to them. They say it's expensive for them to keep in touch with each homeowner's bills, all of which are due at different times. However, these services are computerized, and lenders do charge a one-time escrow service fee that should offset some of these costs.

Many lenders insist on a tax escrow, no matter how much equity you have in a house. They may tell you, if you are using an FHA or VA loan, that an escrow is required under the terms of your mortgage agreement. That isn't quite true. Although both FHA and VA loans contain provisions for real estate property and insurance escrows, the lender has the option to waive it.

According to industry professionals, some lenders will not demand an escrow account if you have a low loan-to-value ratio. For example, if you put more than 30 percent down in cash, most lenders will cancel the mandatory real estate tax escrow clause. In many states, lenders must waive the escrow requirement if you pledge a savings account with an amount that would be sufficient to pay your real estate taxes. By pledging the account, you can maintain control over payment of your taxes and receive interest on your money.

If you suggest this option and the lender balks, do not hesitate to say you'll be happy to call the state's attorney to check on the legality of the issue. Faced with that threat, the lender should back down. The exceptions are federally chartered savings banks, which claim they are not required to comply with state laws regulating this part of the lending process.

If you are successful in getting your lender to agree not to require an escrow account, you might find yourself hit with a onetime fee not to have one. That fee can run as high as 1 to 2 percent of the loan amount. In some states, charging this onetime fee may violate state law. Ask your real estate attorney for clarification.

> Not all lenders charge for the privilege of paying your own real estate taxes and homeowner's insurance premiums. You may want to find a lender that doesn't.

When Something Goes Wrong

It's important to realize that escrow accounts can easily go awry. Some lenders have collected enormous sums of money from individual homeowners. One attorney said a lender tried to collect two years' worth of real estate taxes from his client, up front. This is, of course, against the law.

Sara's Story

When I was writing the first edition of this book, I interviewed Sara, who at that time was a first-time buyer who recently moved to the east coast. She told me that the lender to whom her bank sold her mortgage increased her tax escrow by 46 percent. They told her they needed several months' cushion. At first she refused to pay the overage; instead, she sent 8 percent more than her normal payment.

"I heard from everybody, from the computer people all the way to the president of the company. Finally, they started returning my checks. After a few months, they make it hard for you. I finally paid it," Sara said, adding that she had almost 30 percent in equity in her property.

Today, the lender couldn't get away with what it did to Sara. The law clearly states that lenders may hold no more than the equivalent of one year's worth of property taxes plus two months extra.

One thing a lender has is the ability to ruin your credit quickly. Even if you're having trouble getting your message through the lender, don't stop paying your mortgage. Pay everything the lender asks of you while you fight the battle. If you prevail, you'll not only receive your money back, but you'll have kept your credit intact. And in today's electronic market, the ability to get a mortgage is almost solely based on credit history.

QUESTION 70

WHAT IS AN INSURANCE ESCROW?

Federal law allows mortgage lenders to require you to buy enough homeowner's insurance to cover the mortgage amount in case of fire, earthquake, tornado, or other catastrophe. Of course, you'll want to get additional coverage that will also protect your equity in the home, plus the cost of replacing your personal possessions and rebuilding your home to today's standards. (More on this in a moment.)

To ensure that the homeowner's policy insurance premium is paid, lenders often will require homeowners to pay the insurance premiums in the form of monthly payments that are tacked onto the regular mortgage payments of interest and principal. The money goes into an insurance escrow. Once a year, the lender will dip into that fund and pay the insurance premium. Insurance is one of the four parts of PITI—principal, interest, taxes, and insurance—and is a basic cost of homeownership. Overall, the insurance escrow works like the real estate tax escrow, except that you never get rid of it.

Mistakes Home Buyers and Homeowners Make

One of the biggest mistakes home buyers and homeowners make is not getting enough homeowner's or hazard insurance. Getting the right kind and amount of coverage may be expensive, but could be the best investment you ever make.

Arnie and Penny's Story

Arnie and Penny lived in their South Florida ranch home for many years. It had a red tiled roof, stucco walls, and a swimming pool. Palm trees towered over the property, and a neighbor's century-old mango tree dropped buckets of sweet fruit onto their lawn once a year.

It was a quiet, peaceful neighborhood, until Hurricane Andrew struck in 1993, leaving a path of bleak destruction in its wake.

Arnie and Penny's property was badly damaged. The pool was destroyed, a portion of the house collapsed, water flooded everything, and tiles were popping up everywhere.

Fortunately, Arnie and Penny had chosen a type of homeowners' insurance that guaranteed that the insurer would rebuild the home to modern-day standards and building codes. The policy was significantly more expensive than ordinary homeowners' insurance, but it paid not only for the nearly complete rebuilding of their home, but also for their stay in a rental home while the work was being completed.

Arnie and Penny had to go to court to force the insurer to pay up, but in the end, it was worth it: Their claim was paid in full.

As your home appreciates in value, it will become more expensive to rebuild if something happens to it. Make sure your homeowners' policy keeps up with not only your home's increase in value, but also the increase in the number and value of your personal possessions, including furniture, clothing, artwork, and jewelry.

HOW CAN I AVOID SETTING UP A REAL ESTATE TAX OR INSURANCE ESCROW?

Lenders will generally forgo the real estate tax escrow requirement if you meet the following criteria:

1. **Put down 30 percent or more in cash.** Most lenders use a 30 percent cash down payment as the benchmark for deciding whether to forgo the requirement for a real estate tax or insurance escrow.

2. **Pledge an interest-bearing account.** If you promise to keep a certain amount of money (enough to cover a year's worth of taxes) in an account at the lending institution, your lender should allow that instead of an escrow account. But you will likely have to use additional funds, outside of the pledged account, to pay your real estate tax bill.

If you don't meet either criterion, you'll probably have to have an escrow account for real estate taxes. However, if you've built up the required 30 percent equity in your home and your lender doesn't offer a procedure for terminating the escrow, you can try to end your real estate tax escrow the next time you refinance.

Insurance escrows work almost the same way. Lenders almost always require an escrow account for insurance, and the law allows them to require it. Still, you can make this a point of negotiation. Ask your lender what you would have to do to have this escrow waived.

WHAT SHOULD I DO TO MAKE SURE THE MORTGAGE APPLICATION PROCESS GOES SMOOTHLY?

Sometimes, the mortgage process seems to have been set up just to bring out the beast in all of us. It can be a brutal, ego-shattering experience—one that not too many people enjoy. The goal is to make the entire process go as smoothly as possible. You don't want to raise the hackles of your loan officer (or the tone of your own voice), but at the same time, you want to remind him or her that you're in control of the situation.

Here are some specific things you can do to make the process go more smoothly.

1. **Straighten out your finances.** If you don't have a grip on money coming in and money going out (and where, and why), you may be in for a rough time when you apply for a home loan.

David and Denise's Story

David was a doctor and Denise was a second-year medical resident at a Boston hospital when they decided it was time to buy a house. David was making nearly $100,000, and Denise was pulling in close to

$35,000. They figured that, together, they had a decent income and should stop wasting money on rent and start taking advantage of some of the deductions of homeownership.

But when they went to get prequalified, they were in for a rude shock: Together, David and Denise had a *negative* net worth! Together, they had around $80,000 worth of school loans to prepay, plus a car loan and credit card payments. The loan officer told them it would be very difficult for them to be approved.

Realizing the loan officer was probably right, David and Denise went about paying off some of their loans. They made it a priority to pay off their credit card debt and their car loan. They consolidated their school loans and refinanced them at lower rates. They made sure their payments were made on time. They put off buying a second car, and they canceled their planned vacation in Europe and instead chose to drive around New England.

When they went back to the loan officer six months later, their financial portfolio was much improved. The loan officer gave his approval, and David and Denise started looking for a home. When they found one four months later, they sailed through the mortgage application process.

2. Give your credit record a checkup. Everyone's heard the horror stories: Your mother, sister, neighbor, or friend goes to buy a home and the subsequent credit report contains negative or inaccurate credit information. Somewhere along the line, the credit history has been tampered with. Instead of a clean record, there is an $80,000 outstanding bill for a liver transplant (or a lease on a Mercedes, or a student loan, or something equally improbable). The loan officer looks at the outstanding bill and gives you a choice: Clean up the credit problem or no loan. Some choice. And you've probably heard how difficult it is to get a wrong credit history cleaned up. Maybe so, but it's important to try.

Here's what to do: First, order a credit report on yourself. Three major national credit companies will do this: (1) Trans-Union (800-888-4213), (2) Equifax (800-685-1111), and (3) Experian (888-EXPERIAN). For less than $10, each credit bureau will send you your credit report. Depending on the state in which you live, you may even be entitled to receive a copy of your credit report for free.

This is the same information lenders will receive. By getting a copy of your credit report before you apply for a loan, you'll get a first look at any problems or discrepancies that have sprung up.

235

Let's backpedal a moment and talk about credit bureaus. In our computerized, big-brother-like world, credit bureaus generally have exchange agreements with companies that provide credit: Visa, MasterCard, American Express, and other credit cards; department or retail stores such as Bloomingdale's, I. Magnin, Marshall Field's, and Spiegel; and banks, credit unions, and savings and loans.

On a daily, weekly, monthly, or semiannual basis, these companies electronically send all their information to the credit bureau, which stores it in a mammoth database and updates the records of each person on file. When you go to a store like Limited Express and sign up for its credit card, it calls the credit bureau (to do a credit check) to be sure you have enough funds to pay your bills. Banks do it the same way. When you go to apply for a mortgage, the lender wants to know how many debts are outstanding, and what your payment record has been.

Credit bureaus provide that information. They can even tell if you've been paying your taxes or if you have court judgments against you.

Mark and Marlene's Story

Mark and Marlene were first-time buyers in the Seattle area. They had been looking for a home for several months, and finally found the house of their dreams. They had been prequalified (as opposed to preapproved) for their loan, so they knew they could afford the property, and they had the cash for the down payment.

But when they went to apply, they were rejected by the lender. The lender pulled a credit report on the couple and discovered that they had "forgotten" to file their taxes in the two previous years. When he went back to the couple to inform them that they had been rejected for the loan, they were shocked at the news. The lender simply didn't want to have anything to do with them. After all, if they could forget something as significant as their federal taxes, how would they deal with a monthly mortgage payment?

So let's say you've ordered your credit report from Trans-Union and it turns up an erroneous $80 bill from a hospital you've never been to. You realize that this isn't your bill. What do you do? The credit bureau didn't originate the information (remember, all the information is sent to the credit bureau from the companies giving credit), so it probably won't be able to help you. You may even find the credit bureau's response (or lack thereof) to be particularly distressing and frustrating, although a new law administered by the Federal Trade Commission requires credit bureaus to respond to such complaints within 30 days.

> Any correspondence you send to a credit bureau should be typewritten, and sent via registered or certified mail, return receipt requested. You'll then be able to develop a paper trail of what you sent, when you sent it, and who received it.

Go to the Source

Go directly to the source of a credit problem—in this case, the hospital. Ask them to pull up the payment record and try to work out whose bill it actually is. (If it turns out to be yours, pay it.) There should be some identification, other than a name, that can easily solve the problem: a Social Security number, the male/female identification, age, race, and so on.

When you can prove that a credit fault is not yours, the credit originator carrying the error should correct its computers. (A Chicago woman's name was the same as her mother's. Even though the Social Security numbers were different, she had a heck of a time getting the report cleared up because the credit bureau computer kept confusing the names.)

It may take some time for a correction to work its way from a company's computer to your credit bureau. If you've started the process before you've found a home, you shouldn't have too much trouble. But if you've gone to a lender because you've found the house of your dreams, and you discover that your credit is in jeopardy, get a letter from the credit originator that explains that an earlier mistake has been corrected. Get your name cleared as quickly as possible.

If you discover that someone else has been using your credit to purchase property, cars, furs, jewels, or any other items, you will probably have a big problem. Consult your attorney, the state attorney's office, or the local office of the Federal Trade Commission.

3. Gather, ahead of time, all the information you need to give the lender. It's a very good idea to gather all the information the lender will need ahead of time and organize it so that it's easily accessible. If you know in advance that you'll need complete copies of your past two or three tax returns, plus a current pay stub (or a current profit and loss statement if you're self-employed), you'll be able to have that information on hand when the lender comes calling.

4. Know the current lending guidelines. Get a current copy of the lending guidelines for Fannie Mae (HomePath.com or FannieMae.com), Freddie Mac (FreddieMac.com), the Federal Housing Authority (FHA), and, if applicable, the Veterans Administration (for VA loans only). You can get this information at your local Housing Authority, or on the Web.

Although it may seem that a lender's primary job is to disqualify mortgage applicants, the reverse is true. The lender wants to qualify as many applicants as possible (lenders make their money by approving loans), but is restricted by the rules and regulations of a larger, more powerful body—the secondary mortgage market, of which Fannie Mae and Freddie Mac are the leaders.

If you understand that the secondary mortgage market (which will ultimately buy your loan and repay the lender, who will then make another loan) actually controls the lender, it's easier to understand why the lender must ask you again and again for more documentation. Usually, repeated requests for more documentation mean that the lender wants to approve your loan but there are obstacles (like creditworthiness) that must be cleared up.

Think about what your lender is going through. It may help smooth the process.

5. Qualify your lender. Just as you shop for a broker and a new home, it's very important to shop for a lender. Not all lenders are created equal. Loan products, services, style, and personal attention vary greatly. Look for a lender that is best qualified to meet your needs. Look for someone exceptionally well trained and thoroughly knowledgeable in the mortgage type you want to use. Look for someone who is seasoned in the business and can guide you through with a practiced hand.

For example, if you're self-employed and you've only been self-employed for a year, you may be considered to have sub-par credit, even though you may have paid every bill on time in your life. The reason: Lenders need to see that you've been self-employed, maintaining an income for at least two years, and have the tax returns to prove it. At this point, your choices would be to wait until you've been self-employed for two years, or go with a sub-par loan (also known as a B or C loan in the lending industry). Sub-par lending can mean that a piece of your credit is missing, or that you have bad credit. You may pay a little more for this loan, but a lender who works with loans like yours on a frequent basis knows where to go to get your loan funded.

For more information on choosing the right lender, see Question 56.

Most first-time buyers don't know that if they receive money from their parents as a gift toward a down payment, they need a letter from their parents stating that the money is a gift and does not need to be repaid. If your parents or relatives give you money, keep that money in your account six months before you go to apply for a loan. Banks will look at your monthly balances for the past six months. The higher the balance, the more likely you'll be approved for your loan.

HOW DO I GET THE BEST LOAN AT THE BEST RATE ON THE BEST TERMS?

QUESTION
73

The most important thing to remember is that the best loan for you may not be the cheapest loan you're being offered.

Your loan should work for *your* personal financial situation, and that may mean paying a bit more up front for a lower long-term rate, or paying nothing up front for a higher rate. Either way, lenders now offer so many different financial products that it's easy to find the creative solution that's best for you.

After you find it, there are some things you can do to get that loan at the best price possible.

- **Know what you want.** The mortgage market is extremely competitive for *conventional* loans, which, in 1999, meant loans under $240,000. (The amount will adjust upward from time to time.) Look at the real estate section of your local paper and identify the "mortgage watch" column. Call a few of the lenders who appear to offer the lowest rates, and have them bid on your business. You can also go on-line to Bank Rate Monitor's site (bankrate.com) and check out the daily mortgage rate (plus the daily rate on auto loans, credit cards, and a host of other credit products).

- **Stay on top of interest rates.** Interest rates change at least once each day, and sometimes even more frequently. If you decide to float your loan, watch the bond market activity closely. If rates seem to be dropping, react quickly and call in your lock. Then get the confirmation in writing.

- **Watch the points and fees.** The number of points and fees changes frequently. Martha and Ken watched as the number of points required on their loan rose to four and a half and then fell back to two. They locked in at two and a half points. You might also choose a no-point, no-fee loan, but be prepared to carry a higher interest rate over the life of the loan.

- **Consider using a mortgage broker.** Mortgage brokers usually have access to more than a dozen investors, and their job is to do your shopping for you. They can offer a wide variety of choices, but don't be afraid to tell them about other mortgage packages you've discovered elsewhere. Let them offer you a better deal. You'll also want to stay on your guard because end lenders (also known as investors) pay mortgage brokers a fee for every loan they buy (call it a finder's fee). The only problem is that because a lender gets a higher fee for every loan that's above the market rate, your lender has a real incentive to sell you a loan that's more expensive than you'd otherwise have to pay and to profit from the *service fee premium*. Ask your mortgage broker to disclose in writing the service fee premium he or she is being paid by the end lender who will purchase your loan. If it's more than 1 percent of the loan amount, you may be overpaying for your loan.

- **Don't be afraid to negotiate for lower fees.** Ask for detailed explanations of fees, and speak up if you don't like something. With a detailed listing of fees and charges from each lender, you can compare apples to apples, then go back to the lender and ask for the elimination of specific fees.

- **Consult with your real estate attorney *before* you apply for a mortgage.** Some first-time buyers believe a real estate attorney should be called in only if there is a problem. Others call the attorney *after* the deal has been negotiated. The truth is, your real estate attorney should probably be the first person you call after having your offer to purchase accepted, or maybe even before. Real estate attorneys who do a lot of house closings know the people at the title companies, the brokers, and the mortgage players. They can give you resources, point you in the right direction, and guide you toward a successful house closing. If you're living in California or another state where real estate attorneys are not commonly used, you should know your stuff even more thoroughly before you meet with the lender.

When the first edition of this book was published in 1994, loans over $203,000 were considered to be jumbo loans. As we went to press in 1999, jumbo loans ranged from $240,000 to about $600,000. Loans from around $600,000 to $1,000,000 fall into the "super-jumbo" category, and higher home loans are in a separate category altogether. The conventional mortgage amount ($240,000 in 1999) changes every year or so. How much it changes depends on how fast home prices are rising. At press time, the number for the year 2000 was not available, but I have been expecting it to go north of $250,000 the next time the conventional loan amount is adjusted. What's the difference between getting a conventional loan and a jumbo loan? You'll have to pay more fees and a higher interest rate for a jumbo loan. The difference is usually a point (a point is 1 percent of the loan amount), and the loan will carry an interest rate that is about a half-point higher than a conventional loan. You can add another 1¼ to 1½ percent to the interest rate for super-jumbo loans. If you can get a conventional loan, you'll save loads of money down the road.

9

Playing the
Mortgage Game

In this chapter, you'll find answers to your questions about what types of loans exist, how private mortgage insurance helps home buyers to purchase their homes, and what to do if you believe a lender isn't treating you the right way.

WHAT IS AN ASSUMABLE MORTGAGE? HOW IS IT DIFFERENT FROM A SUBJECT-TO MORTGAGE?

Some brokers might show you a property, then lean over and say, "And it's got an assumable mortgage, to boot." You nod, knowingly, but inside you're wondering what's up. The broker is obviously trying to tip you off to something, but you're not exactly sure what's going on.

Here's the answer: With an *assumable mortgage*, the buyer takes over from the seller the legal obligation to make monthly payments of principal and interest to the lender. The lender, assured of getting repaid on the loan, then releases the seller from his or her liability.

How do you find out whether a mortgage is assumable? Most conventional mortgages are not assumable; a *due-on-sale* clause is built into the verbiage of the loan. A due-on-sale clause means that if you sell the home, you immediately owe all of the unpaid mortgage balance to the lender. FHA mortgages are assumable—it's one of the reasons brokers like to show first-time buyers FHA properties.

Another reason you might like an assumable mortgage is that it can be cheaper and easier to assume a loan than to take out a new

242

loan. If you, the buyer, decide to assume the mortgage of the seller and if you can qualify for the loan, you will pay fewer closing costs and fees, and less paperwork needs to be completed.

If you purchase property that is *subject to* an existing mortgage, you, the buyer, must make all future loan payments to the existing lender. However, the seller will continue to be liable on the original loan. There is no formal transfer of obligation or liability, as with an assumable mortgage. If someone tries to persuade you to buy a property subject to a mortgage, make sure the lender can't call in the loan as a result of the transfer of title. If you purchase property subject to an existing mortgage, and the lender, upon receiving notice of the transfer of title, calls in the loan, you, the buyer, could be forced to pay the entire loan off immediately.

WHAT DIFFERENT TYPES OF MORTGAGES ARE AVAILABLE? HOW DO I CHOOSE THE RIGHT TYPE FOR ME?

QUESTION
75

Mortgage lenders around the country currently offer literally hundreds of different mortgage products. In fact, most lenders can tailor a loan that's exactly right for you.

So many options, so little time. The variety may seem overwhelming, but if you start to ask a few questions, you'll soon figure out that your lender is actually offering only six or seven *basic* mortgage types. Lenders say that, in today's world of personalized banking, everyone wants an arrangement that is made to order for his or her specific financial situation.

Making the Right Choice

The right mortgage for you must take into account your current monthly income and what you expect it will be in the future; the assets you currently hold; and how much debt you're carrying; and your debt repayment schedule. Other factors can also influence your mortgage decision. Do you want to pay points (a point is 1 percent of the loan amount) up front, or do you prefer to pay them over the life of the loan? Do you want to gamble that interest rates will stay low, and get an adjustable rate mortgage (ARM)? Or would you feel more comfortable paying a fixed amount each month?

Lenders offer a variety of financing options, simply because today's home buyers want a cure for every ill. For example, if you plan to live in your house for only three to five years, you might consider a two-step loan, also known as a 5/25 (pronounced "five twenty-five") or a 7/23 ("seven twenty-three") mortgage, or a one-year adjustable-rate rather than a fixed-interest-rate mortgage. (These are explained below.)

Here is a quick description of the basic types of mortgages available in the marketplace. A more in-depth discussion of these loans follows in the next few Questions.

- **Fixed-rate mortgage.** The original mortgage arrangement, and the most popular type of loan when interest rates are low, a fixed-rate mortgage charges the same percentage rate of interest over the life of the loan. Homeowners repay the loan with a fixed, monthly installment of principal and interest. Fixed-rate loans can be taken out in a variety of lengths, including 10-year, 15-year, 20-year, and the ever popular 30-year loan. In the mid-1990s, a 40-year version of the fixed-rate loan was introduced. *This loan is a complete waste of time and money.* You won't start building up any appreciable equity in your home until nearly the twentieth year of the loan.

- **Adjustable rate mortgage (ARM).** An adjustable-rate mortgage has interest rates that fluctuate and are pegged to one-year Treasury bills or to a specific index. The initial rate of interest tends to be quite low, and then the rate bumps up between one and two points per year. There is usually a yearly cap of one or two percentage points and a lifetime ceiling cap of around five or six points. The interest rate can also go down. In the late 1980s and early 1990s, ARMs proved to be the best deal around because interest rates sank and then stayed low. Homeowners whose initial interest rate was around 5 percent now have loans at 6.5 to 7 percent and have saved thousands of dollars on their loans.

- **Two-step mortgages.** Also known as 5/25s ("five-twenty-fives") and 7/23s ("seven-twenty-threes"), these are 30-year mortgages that come in two different flavors: (1) convertible and (2) nonconvertible. The 5/25 loan has a fixed-interest rate for the first five years and then it either converts to a 25-year fixed-rate loan (a convertible) or it turns into a 1-year adjustable rate mortgage. The 7/23 loan is adjusted after seven years instead of five years (and would covert to a 23-year mortgage). Both of these loans can be amortized over the entire 30-year period. They are considered more risky than fixed-rate loans, but they are significantly less risky than ARMs during the first five or seven years. As a result, the interest rate is lower than a standard 30-year fixed-rate mortgage, but higher than a one-year adjustable-rate mortgage.

- **FHA mortgage.** Preset spending limits are the hallmark of an FHA mortgage. The loan amounts are set by the median prices of different cities within a particular region. The difference in loan amounts between rural and densely populated areas can vary by as much as $25,000 or more. The best part about an FHA loan is the low down payment required. With some special government-backed loan products, you currently need to put down only 2 percent of the sales price of the home. (I expect this to fall further as mortgage companies become more sophisticated with super-low down payment loans.) However, be prepared: If you put down less than 20 percent, you'll pay a steep mortgage insurance premium. Other up-front costs are part of the bargain and must be considered when choosing an FHA loan. FHA loans are assumable, which means that if you qualify, you could simply take over the payments from your seller and save yourself a lot of cost and hassle.

- **VA loan.** A VA loan is administered by the Department of Veterans Affairs in Washington, DC, and is designed to help qualified veterans of the U.S. armed services buy homes with little or no down payment. In addition, veterans are not allowed to pay points to the lender, although they are responsible for some loan fees. That prohibition sometimes causes a problem because the seller usually gets stuck for the extra bucks. Only veterans who have served a specified number of days and who get a certificate of eligibility from the Department of Veterans Affairs can qualify for a VA loan.

- **Balloon mortgage.** This type of mortgage can be any length at all. Some balloon mortgages require monthly payments of principal and interest; others require only interest. In either case, when the loan comes due (after, say, five or seven years), the loan balance must be repaid in full. Balloon mortgages can be paid in one of two ways: (1) the mortgage can be amortized over 15 or 30 years; the homeowner makes regular payments of principal and interest until the loan term ends, and then either pays off the loan or refinances; or (2) only the interest on the loan (as opposed to interest and principal, as when a loan is amortized) is paid until the end of the loan period. For example, if you borrow $100,000 on a five-year interest-only balloon, the $100,000 is due on the last day of the five-year term. Throughout the five years, you pay only the interest on the money you borrowed.

- **Graduated-payment mortgage (GPM).** The GPM was originally designed for first-time buyers because it offers reduced monthly payments early in the life of the loan. The payments become larger as the loan progresses, and, hopefully, the finances of the borrower improve. Most lenders have steered away from the GPM in recent years as two-step mortgages have become more popular. In fact, FHA eliminated its GPM in 1988. GPMs are complicated loans that require a tremendous amount of paperwork, and ongoing calculations and supervision, which make them more expensive for the lender.

- **Shared-appreciation mortgage.** A shared-appreciation mortgage is a financial concept borrowed from commercial property transfers. The lender offers a below-market rate in exchange for a share in the profits of the home when it is sold. There are significant benefits to this arrangement. As the buyer, you get all the tax benefits, and the lender doesn't make any money unless you do. On the other hand, if the home appreciates greatly, you could end up paying a lot of that profit to the lender. Shared-appreciation mortgages are most commonly coordinated by non-profit associations seeking to help low-income first-time buyers become first-time homeowners. They use community development block grant (CDBG) money to help make up the difference between the amount low- to moderate-income families can afford and the amount of cash competitively priced commercial lenders want to see on a borrower's balance sheet. (See the Appendix for more resource information.)

- **Biweekly mortgage.** The name for this mortgage product comes from the number of payments you make per month: two. Each payment represents half of what a regular monthly payment might be, but because you pay every other week, your total is twenty-six payments, or a thirteenth month, within a calendar year. *Making that thirteenth payment, no matter what form it takes, will significantly cut down the amount of interest you'll pay over the life of the loan.* The trouble with biweeklies is that, although they are easier amounts to pay (especially if you get paid biweekly), the obligation to pay twice a month can be onerous, particularly if money is tight. And, the lender will charge you a hefty sum (as much as several hundred dollars) to set up a biweekly loan. You can achieve the same effect by simply making an extra payment on your loan each year, or dividing that extra payment by 12 and paying the promised amount plus one-twelfth of it every month.

HOW SMALL A DOWN PAYMENT CAN I MAKE? WHERE CAN I FIND A ZERO DOWN LOAN?

QUESTION
76

Not so long ago, if you wanted to buy a house, you had to come up with 20 percent in cash for the down payment. If you were buying a $100,000 house, you needed $20,000 in cash.

Study after study has shown that coming up with the down payment has been one of the toughest obstacles for first-time home buyers to overcome. Scraping together that extra cash each month, on top of rent, utilities, child care, and charge card payments, excluded from the benefits of homeownership people whose finances were marginal.

Things began to change when the FHA started permitting home buyers to purchase homes with 10 percent down, and, later, just 5 percent down. Studies showed that although defaults did increase as home buyers put less and less down on their homes, the actual number was tiny. Apparently, there was a profitable market to tap. Conventional lenders followed suit and began offering 95 percent loan-to-value ratio mortgages. Eventually, the FHA dropped its down payment requirement to just 3 percent. Conventional lenders responded by introducing 97 percent loan-to-value ratio loans.

While the down payments were decreasing, lenders (led again by the FHA) were increasing their debt-to-income ratios. Instead of allowing borrowers to spend only 28 percent of their gross monthly income on the mortgage and up to 36 percent on their total debt, home buyers were permitted to spend in certain loan programs up to 41 percent (or more, in some cases). Industry experts saw that these marginal home buyers (made up of significant numbers of minority and immigrant families) were already spending as much as 50 percent of their gross monthly income on rent—and were making it work.

The FHA decided that home buyers needed to put down only 2 percent on a house. The rest of the down payment could consist of a gift from a family member, or a grant. In response, conventional lenders went a step ahead. The Veterans Administration had always offered qualified veterans a true zero down loan, but the loan was expensive. In the late 1990s, a few conventional lenders began testing true zero down loans to ordinary home buyers. Some of the programs were restricted by either income or area, but others will be made available to all home buyers.

Let's be clear about one thing: Anyone who puts down less than 20 percent in cash on a home will pay either private mortgage insurance (PMI) or FHA mortgage insurance (with an FHA loan). I'll talk more about PMI in Question 84. PMI can be expensive, although the cost has gone down in recent years. And although PMI must be canceled automatically by a lender when the borrower reaches a certain level of equity, it could take a decade or more to reach that point. The lower the down payment, the higher the PMI premiums. They are particularly high if the down payment is below 5 percent. But if paying a high PMI is the only way you can buy a home, it's generally worth it.

Finding a Low Down Payment Loan

Almost any major mortgage banker or broker can do a low down payment loan. If you need the extra lending ratios, you may need to go with an FHA loan. Almost all lenders can and will set up an FHA loan (although it requires a bit more paperwork). When you call a lender or go on-line, check out which loan options are available that require only a 3 percent or 5 percent down payment (or less).

Finding a Zero Down Loan

As we go to press, a few true zero down loans were being made available to home buyers:

1. **Merrill Lynch 100 Home Loan.** This loan can be originated if assets are already being held for the prospective borrower in a Merrill Lynch brokerage account. To get the 20 percent down payment if you have such an account, you'd normally have to

sell these assets (which may include retirement accounts, stocks, or bonds). If you don't want to sell them but still want to buy a house, the Merrill Lynch program allows you to borrow the 20 percent you need for the down payment, and use these assets as collateral. The nice thing is that you'll pay the going 30-year interest rate on the whole 100 percent loan (instead of a much higher interest rate). The danger to this program, and others like it, is that you're essentially borrowing the 20 percent on margin. If your assets suddenly fall in value, the 20 percent part of the loan could be called, and you'll have to come up with the money all at once. The Merrill Lynch program tries to guard against this by only allowing you to borrow against a small portion of your assets. Before you decide on this loan, read the brochures thoroughly and ask plenty of questions.

2. **Fidelity Home Loan Program and Others.** Fidelity, which owns some of the largest mutual funds in the country (including the Magellan Fund, its flagship fund), has set up a program similar to the Merrill Lynch 100 Home Loan. I wouldn't be surprised if, in the next few years, other financial companies develop different lending guidelines to meet the needs of their customers.

3. **Individual bank programs.** Before its merger with Nation's Bank, Bank of America introduced a 100 percent loan that was available to people who met certain income criteria. The loan was specifically designed for the first-time buyer market. The loan may or may not be available when you're in the mortgage market, but other lending institutions may begin to offer other 100 percent loan programs. As lenders begin to understand how these loans work and where consumers who take these loans are most vulnerable financially, I predict that more of these 100 percent loan programs will pop up.

4. **Nonprofit organizations.** Traditionally, nonprofit organizations and housing authorities have used community development block grant (CDBG) funds to help first-time home buyers with either down payment funds or a lower interest rate on the loans. Ask your local Housing Authority what programs are being offered. The programs change frequently, so be prepared to call several times.

20/20 hindsight

The higher your loan-to-value ratio, the higher your monthly costs will be. Sometimes, it's better to not stretch yourself too thin financially. I call this concept *underbuying*. When you're underbuying, you're spending less than you can afford because you choose to make your financial life a bit easier. Brokers will often encourage you to *overbuy*—spend as much as, or even more than, you can comfortably afford today, on the theory that soon you'll be earning more money and will be in a house that is the right size for you and your growing family. Whichever way you go, make sure you think it through first. You'll be using your leverage if you overbuy, but that financial trick won't be worth anything if you can't sleep at night.

QUESTION 77

WHAT IS A FIXED-RATE MORTGAGE? WHAT IS AN ADJUSTABLE RATE MORTGAGE (ARM)?

The original and most popular type of mortgage is the fixed-interest-rate mortgage. The amount of the interest and principal repayment is amortized in equal amounts over the life of the loan. Many homeowners like the financial security of knowing that they will pay exactly the same amount of money each month (excluding property tax or insurance payments to an escrow account) until the loan has been paid off in full.

Although the concept of fixed-interest mortgages hasn't changed much, most lenders now offer borrowers a choice in how long a loan they want. A 30-year mortgage was, and is, the most popular length, but 10-, 15-, and 20-year fixed mortgages have recently become more popular as interest rates have continued to stay relatively low.

Recently, a 40-year loan was introduced. On a $100,000 mortgage, you might save an additional $50 per month if you take a 40-year loan instead of a 30-year loan. But because you incur an additional 10 years of interest payments, it's just not worth it. You're far better off purchasing a less expensive home.

When interest rates are low, borrowers find that a shorter loan length offers a significant financial advantage over the regular 30-year mortgage. Homeowners can save thousands of dollars in interest payments if they shorten the length of the loan by up to 15 years. The shorter the amortization period, the higher the monthly payment; but the extra cash each month repays your loan balance much more quickly, so less interest is paid over the life of the loan.

For example, if you take out a $100,000 30-year mortgage at 8 percent interest, your monthly payments toward principal and interest would be around $730. If that same mortgage was 15 years in length, your monthly payment would be around $940.

You'd end up paying $262,800 in principal and interest over the life of the 30-year loan. You'd pay only $169,200—nearly $100,000 less—over the life of a 15-year loan.

When you get a 15-year loan, the interest rate is usually lower than the rate for a 30-year loan. Even if you prepay your 30-year loan down to the point where it will terminate in 15 years, you'll save more money by going with a 15-year loan because the interest rate on the whole loan is less.

Who Would Benefit from a Fixed-Rate Mortgage?

Buyers who have a limited or fixed income, and those who do not like to gamble with interest rates are usually best served by a fixed-rate mortgage. Buyers who can handle the higher payments and want to pay down their mortgage as fast as possible are best served by a 10-, 15-, or 20-year fixed-rate mortgage. Still, people who choose a 30-year mortgage because of the initial lower payments, but want to pay it off faster, can make an additional mortgage payment per year—a thirteenth payment—and direct the lender to use that money to repay the principal (write "For repayment of principal" on the check). An extra payment a year will significantly lessen the amount of interest you pay over the life of the loan. If you begin in the first

If you want to pay off your 30-year loan in 15 years (or 12 years, or less), you can go on-line to any number of sites, including Homeowners.com (HomeOwners.com), Quicken.com (Quicken.com) or HomeAdvisor.com (HomeAdvisor.com). These and other financial sites have calculators that can help you readjust your amortization schedule so you know how many years you'll cut off your loan if you prepay a certain amount each month. You can also play around with this if you have a Quicken, QuickBooks, or Microsoft Money financial software package.

year and make a thirteenth payment every year on a 30-year mortgage, you'll effectively cut your mortgage from 30 years to between 18 and 21 years, depending on when you pay the extra amount.

Be aware, however, that an extra payment per year does not relieve you of the obligation to meet your monthly payments. Even if you pay a doubled amount in one month, you still must make your regular mortgage payment on time during the next month. Moreover, the thirteenth payment alters the end balance on your account but does not lessen future monthly payments.

I'm often asked if you make a 13th payment on a 15-year loan if you will cut that loan term to 8 years. They answer, unfortunately, is no. Because of the benefits of compounding, this trick only works with 30-year loans. You will, however, be able to shave a few years off your loan term, perhaps cutting your 15-year loan to 11 or 12 years.

Adjustable Rate Mortgages (ARMs)

An ARM is a mortgage with an interest rate that is adjusted at specific times over the life of the loan—usually yearly, or every three or five years. A 10-year ARM is adjusted once every 10 years.

Adjustable rate mortgages are attractive to a variety of buyers because their initial interest rate is much lower than the rates on almost any other type of loan. Interest rates on one-year ARMs tend to start out very low—sometimes as low as 4 or 5 percent. Increases in the rate are generally tied to an economic index, such as 1-, 3-, or 5-year Treasury securities. When the time comes for your loan to be adjusted—whether yearly, every 3 years, or every 5 years—a margin of between 1 and 3 percentage points is tacked onto whatever index the loan is tied to. This is how the lender comes up with your next interest rate.

National Cost of Funds Index

As an example, let's look at one index, the National Cost of Funds, which is based on the average cost of funds for savings and loans. Let's say the National Cost of Funds index is at 6.25 percent. If your lender charges 2.5 percentage points as a margin, your new mortgage interest rate, based on that index, would be 8.75 percent when the loan adjusts.

ARMs are likely to fluctuate with the economy, although you can get an idea of how much your mortgage will adjust by keeping an eye on the prime interest rate, the interest rate the Federal Reserve charges banks, and similar economic indicators. Even if the prime rate soars in the next few years, ARM holders are somewhat protected by a lifetime cap on their loan's interest rate. This cap, usually five or six percentage points over the lifetime of the loan, limits how much the interest rate can go up. With a six-point cap, an ARM starting at 5.25 percent could never go higher than 11.25 percent. Make sure your loan has a lifetime interest-rate cap, and that the annual increase in the interest rate is limited to only one or two percentage points.

Going Down

ARMs, the lenders like to point out, can also readjust downward after the first adjustment period. If that happens, a borrower could reap the benefit of his or her gamble for years to come. Let's say you need a $100,000 loan. You decide on a three-year ARM that has a starting interest rate of 6 percent, a two-point cap per year (the loan can go up only two points a year), and a margin of two and a half points over the Treasury bill to which it is tied.

For the first three years, your annual interest payment is $6,000, or $500 per month. At the end of the three years, let's assume the rate rises to 7 percent (just because the interest rate *can* go up two percentage points doesn't mean it always *will*). You will then pay $7,000 per year, or $583.33 monthly. (This example isn't exactly precise because I haven't amortized the numbers, but it works for straight interest loans. To create your own comparisons using amortized numbers, consult the amortization tables in Appendix VI.)

ARMs versus Fixed-Interest-Rate Loans

Let's compare the $100,000 ARM we've just discussed with a $100,000 30-year fixed interest rate mortgage at 8 percent:

253

Year	ARM	Fixed Rate (8 Percent) Loan
1	$ 6,000	$ 8,000
2	6,000	8,000
3	6,000	8,000
4	7,000	8,000
5	7,000	8,000
6	7,000	8,000
Total	$39,000	$48,000

If you were the borrower in this example, and you had chosen an ARM over a fixed-rate mortgage, you would have saved yourself $9,000 over six years. But what if the ARM had increased over and above the interest rate of the fixed-rate mortgage? If you consider that most folks move or refinance their mortgage every five to seven years, it's unlikely that the interest rate, in that period of time, would have risen enough to overcome the savings gained by using an ARM.

But let's say it does. Your $100,000 ARM is adjusted every year and has a two-point annual readjustment cap with a lifetime cap of 6 percent:

Year	Interest Rate	ARM
1	5 percent	$ 5,000
2	7 percent	7,000
3	9 percent	9,000
4	11 percent	11,000
5	11 percent	11,000
6	11 percent	11,000
Total		$54,000

The ARM would cost $54,000 versus $48,000 for a fixed-rate loan. Assuming that the ARM is readjusted upward at the maximum cap every year, it would cost $6,000 more than the fixed-rate mortgage.

The truth of the matter is: It's impossible to predict long-term interest rates. No one has a crystal ball. In fact, if you bought your present home in 1990, your ARM interest rate would have dropped the first year and held steady somewhere around 6 to 7 percent for the rest of the decade.

As interest rates fall, the spread between ARMs and fixed-rate mortgages drops. As we closed out the 1990s, the spread between a 1-year ARM and a 30-year fixed-interest-rate mortgage was just 1 percent. But because rates were so low (at one point in time, you could have locked in on a 30-year fixed-rate loan for as little as 6.5 percent), more people chose a fixed-rate loan over an ARM. That choice is, in fact, the home buyer's greatest opportunity. If interest rates rise when it comes time to buy your first home, you can simply choose an adjustable loan. If rates then drop after you've owned your home for a while, you can turn around and refinance into a fixed-rate mortgage.

Who Could Benefit from an ARM?

Buyers who carry substantial personal debt (in the form of credit cards, school loans, or a car loan) might benefit from the lower interest rates associated with an ARM, particularly if they can show that they have good job and salary prospects for the future. Lenders generally will allow borrowers' housing expense—the mortgage principal and interest, private mortgage insurance, and property taxes—to equal no more than 28 percent of their monthly gross income (income before taxes), unless they get a higher debt-to-income loan.

For example, if your gross monthly income is $4,000, you could afford monthly mortgage and property tax payments of up to $1,120. All debt, including installment and revolving loans (credit cards, car payments), should not exceed 36 percent of your gross income, most lenders say. Conventional lenders have recently begun stretching the upper limit of the debt-to-income ratio to around 40 percent, and only FHA goes above that. Lenders never calculate a loan on the basis of future earnings, but they might be willing to stretch the required qualifications beyond the normal parameters if, for example, you are a fourth-year medical student with a guaranteed residency in the near future, or a third-year law student with a job offer.

(When lenders stretch the requirements for prospective borrowers, they usually keep the loan within the institution's portfolio—they don't resell the loan on the secondary mortgage market. In that way, they needn't worry about Fannie Mae and Freddie Mac requirements, and they have additional lending flexibility.)

Ask Yourself: How Long Do You Plan to Stay?

How long you plan to stay in your new home will have an effect on what home you buy, where you buy it, and how you plan to pay for it.

If you know you're going to stay in a home for only five to seven years, you may want to get an ARM. Lenders acknowledge the strong probability that, compared to a fixed-rate loan, an ARM will end up with a lower interest rate over the entire term of the loan.

WHAT IS A TWO-STEP MORTGAGE?
WHAT IS A BALLOON MORTGAGE?

A two-step mortgage, a hybrid of the adjustable rate mortgage (ARM) and fixed-rate mortgages, is a relatively new invention. Also known as a 5/25 ("five twenty-five") or a 7/23 ("seven twenty-three"), it combines the relative steadiness of a fixed-rate mortgage with some of the risks and rewards of an ARM.

Two-step mortgages come in two varieties: convertible and nonconvertible. With a convertible two-step mortgage, a 5/25 or 7/23 loan has a fixed interest rate for the first five or seven years, then converts into a fixed-rate mortgage for the remaining 25 or 23 years, respectively. A nonconvertible two-step mortgage means that the 5/25 or 7/23 has a fixed interest rate for the first five or seven years, and then converts into a one-year adjustable rate mortgage (ARM) and is adjusted each year for the remaining 25 or 23 years of the loan term.

Let's look at the convertible version in a little more detail. A 5/25, for example, is a 30-year loan that has a fixed interest rate for the first five years and then has a onetime adjustment that determines what the rate will be for the remaining 25 years of the loan. As with other 30-year loans, it's amortized over 30 years. The 7/23 works the same way, but is set at a fixed-interest rate for seven years, and then adjusts once for the remaining 23 years of the loan.

Lenders keep their eyes on the trends of homeownership. If the average homeowner will sell or refinance his or her home every five to seven years, there is less need for 30-year loans. Instead, these hybrid loans allow the homeowner to start off at a much lower interest rate, which will be adjusted once during the life of the loan. If you choose a 7/23, it's more than likely that you'll move before the rate adjusts—or soon thereafter—which will allow you to take full advantage of the first seven years of lower-than-average interest rates.

As with ARMs, the onetime adjustment for both of these loans is tied to an economic index. The increase would be based on the status of the index at the end of the five- or seven-year term. Above the index rate, the lender often tacks on a margin, usually in the neighborhood of one to three points. If the index is at 5 percent at the end of seven years, and you have a three-point margin on your loan, your new rate would be 8 percent.

Let's compare the savings on a 5/25, a 7/23, and a 30-year fixed loan. We'll assume the loan amount is $100,000, and the interest rates are 7 percent (5/25), 7.5 percent (7/23), and 8 percent (30-year fixed). After five years, you would have paid $35,000 for the 5/25, $37,500 for the 7/23, and $40,000 for the 30-year fixed loan. If you moved or refinanced within the five years you held a 5/25 mortgage, you saved yourself $5,000. Even if you stayed through the sixth year and the rate went up to 8 percent, you saved $5,000 for the first five years.

Who Could Benefit from a 5/25 or 7/23?

First-time buyers who do not plan to stay in their homes for more than five or seven years would save thousands of dollars in interest by going with this type of loan, because the initial rate is lower than for fixed-rate loans.

Ideally, you'll sell your home or refinance your mortgage either before or just after the rate adjusts upward. (The rate can also adjust downward, as some buyers who opted for an ARM in recent years have happily discovered.) Even if you stay in your home 10 years with a 7/23, the overall loan rate you pay may be far less than if you had chosen a fixed-rate loan. The rate on a two-step mortgage can be a full percentage point (or more) below the rate on a 30-year fixed-rate mortgage.

Two-step mortgages have become extremely popular, as homeowners (particularly first-time buyers) have begun to realize that they don't need the long-term steadiness of a fixed-rate mortgage. Unlike their parents, they most likely won't spend 30 years in the same home.

Balloon Mortgages

Before 30-year fixed-interest-rate mortgages were invented (we're talking about the pre-Great Depression era), everyone who bought a home and didn't pay cash had a balloon mortgage. Essentially, the buyer would borrow money at the exorbitant interest rate of about 3 or 4 percent for a short period of time (anywhere from one to five years). During the loan term, only the interest on the loan was paid, in monthly or semiannual installments or as one annual payment of interest. At the end of the loan term, the borrower owed the entire principal in full.

If you had borrowed $10,000 at 4 percent interest for five years (remember, a brand new car cost less than $2,000 in those days), you would have owed only $400 in interest per year, or $2,000 in interest over the life of the loan (the interest was paid separately). At the end of five years, you would still have owed the $10,000 in principal. It was simple and easy, and usually everyone paid off the balance. The concept of a balloon mortgage allowed time to scrape together the cash needed to actually purchase the property.

As I explained earlier, balloon mortgages worked fine until the Great Depression, when folks lost all their savings and couldn't pay the interest on the money they borrowed, let alone meet the balloon payments. After World War II, the federal government began a program that offered returning veterans an opportunity to purchase a home and pay it off over 30 years. That was the beginning of the 30-year fixed mortgage. When the 30-year mortgage was successful and became the mortgage of choice, the balloon mortgage became an infrequently used financial vehicle.

Who Could Benefit from a Balloon Mortgage?

With so many financing tools available today, only a few people choose to purchase a home with a balloon mortgage. Sometimes, co-ops (remember, you don't buy a co-op, you buy shares in a corporation that owns the building and then lease your unit) may be purchased with a balloon mortgage, or another special financing tool, because the shares held are personal property (like a refrigerator, clothes, or your typewriter), not real property (like real estate).

In addition, the interest rate on a five-year balloon (some banks offer a 10-year or 15-year balloon mortgage) might be less than some other financing options. A few buyers will choose it, especially if they know they might sell within the balloon's time period.

WHAT IS AN FHA MORTGAGE?
WHAT IS A VA LOAN?

QUESTION
79

A Federal Housing Administration (FHA) loan is often called "the first-time buyer's mortgage." The reason is clear: FHA loans require a much smaller down payment than conventional loans. It's common to have an FHA loan with only 5 percent down (or less), whereas conventional lenders prefer to see a 20 percent cash down payment, which is often too steep for most first-time buyers. (Conventional lenders will allow you to purchase a home for less than 20 percent down, but you'll have to pay private mortgage insurance. You'll pay the FHA's version of mortgage insurance if you get an FHA loan with less than 20 percent down.)

Everyone Qualifies for FHA Loans

Some mortgage seekers wrongly assume that an FHA loan is a government-sponsored handout; that is, you have to be at a certain income level to qualify. That's not true. There are no income requirements for obtaining an FHA loan, and you don't have to be a first-time buyer.

Instead, the only restriction is the amount of money you can borrow. The chart that follows shows the FHA loan limits as we went to press:

1999 FHA Loan Limits

Size of Unit	Continental United States		Alaska, Guam, Hawaii, and the Virgin Islands
	Standard Limits	High-Cost Areas	
Single family	$115,200	$208,800	$313,200
Two family	147,708	267,177	400,765
Three family	178,176	322,944	484,416
Four family	221,448	401,375	602,062

Be advised that these numbers change frequently. You can check out the latest loan limits by going on-line to the web site of the Department of Housing and Urban Development (hud.gov) and then clicking through to "Buying a Home."

web

resources

259

Loans for properties that contain more than four units are considered to be investment properties. As an investor (even if you plan to live in one of the units), you'll pay a higher interest rate if you purchase, say, a six-unit building than if you purchase a four-unit building.

FHA loan limits are not fixed within a metropolitan area. Instead, a metro area that covers several counties might encompass various FHA loan limits. Generally, expensive suburbs have higher loan amounts, and more rural areas (where prices are assumed to be lower) are allowed smaller loan amounts.

The most attractive feature of FHA loans is that the borrower needs less than 5 percent of the loan amount as a down payment. If the property is a single-family house (the phrase "single-family house" includes condos, co-ops, town homes, and multiunit buildings that have four or fewer units), however, the loan comes along with a steep mortgage insurance premium. Just because these government-backed loans are available to all homeowners doesn't mean FHA loans are freebies. *An FHA loan can be more expensive than a conventional loan.* FHA lenders require the same debt-to-income ratio that is applied to fixed-interest loans or ARMs. The big difference is the size of the down payment. If a house costs $100,000, an FHA loan would require the buyer to come up with perhaps just $2,000 in cash—far less than conventional lenders would require.

Who Could Benefit from an FHA Loan?

Cash-strapped first-time buyers are the logical beneficiaries. Another advantage is that FHA loans are assumable, which allows the next buyer to have lower costs when purchasing the property, because he or she isn't taking out a new loan. When buyers assume an FHA loan, lenders are allowed by law to charge a few hundred dollars, plus regular loan origination points and fees for items such as a credit report. There is typically no appraisal, however, which can save a buyer around $275.

FHA loans are also a good choice for people who have had credit problems or bankruptcies in their past. The federal government does not regard these past financial problems in the same light as a private lender would. As long as the debt-to-income ratios are met and the

If you have severe negative information on your credit history, including a bankruptcy, court judgments, or charge-offs, and you have been slowly rebuilding your credit history, an FHA loan may be the only option available to you. Some lenders will try to entice you with offers of getting a loan within a year of bankruptcy, but what you won't be told is that the interest rate you'll pay is about the same as charging your house on a credit card! An FHA loan can fill in the gap until your credit is considered good enough for a conventional lender.

borrower/former bankruptee can pay the mortgage insurance premium (which can be steep), he or she can qualify. As one lender puts it, an FHA loan is a good way to begin to rebuild a credit history. The idea behind the FHA loan is to provide an outlet for people who do not have access to other financial outlets.

VA Loans

One of the many benefits that comes along with joining a branch of the armed services is the Veterans Administration (VA) loan—the helping hand Uncle Sam offers when it comes time to buy a house. The Department of Veterans Affairs, in Washington, DC, guarantees loans for veterans, allowing them to purchase homes at favorable lending terms, with no down payment.

The VA started the program at the end of World War II, and since the program began in 1945, more than 13 million veterans have obtained loans worth more than $360 billion. A spokesperson for the VA estimates that more than 4 million VA loans are currently outstanding. Although the program has changed some since its inception, VA loans generally restrict the amount of money the veteran is obliged to pay for his or her loan. However, the veteran is required to pay some closing costs, including a VA appraisal, a credit report, a survey title, recording fees, a 1 percent loan-origination fee, and a VA funding fee.

The VA funding fee is the expensive part. Except for a brief period during the 1960s, when it was used to distinguish "Cold War" veterans from those who had put in wartime service, there used to be no funding fee for obtaining a VA loan. However, in 1981, a .5 percent funding fee was reinstated. (Disabled veterans who receive compensation were, and continue to be, exempt from the fee.) In 1984, the funding fee was increased to 1 percent; in 1990, it was raised to 1.25 percent. As of October 1, 1993, veterans taking out their first no-down-payment loan were required to pay a 2 percent funding fee to the Department of Veterans Affairs. Veterans taking out their second or third no-down-payment loan were required to pay a funding fee of 3 percent.

These fees are for zero down loans. If a veteran chooses to put down 5 or 10 percent of the sales price, the funding fee is reduced.

For a long time, a VA loan was the only zero down option available. Another plus of the program was that the VA worked closely with veterans who had trouble with their finances subsequent to getting a VA loan. In many cases, the VA took over these loans and homes, which is why the VA loan default rate was so high. But this type of loan was available only to qualified veterans of the armed services, which didn't help the rest of the home-buying population.

The recent introduction of super-low down payment loans and the new zero down payment loans reduces the need for a VA loan, which has grown to be far more expensive than conventional financing. But there are other benefits: The loans are assumable (a buyer can take it over from the seller for very little money—an added incentive for the veteran-as-seller), and the VA has a policy of "forbearance," which means "worthy" veterans experiencing a temporary economic setback are somewhat protected against foreclosure. In rare instances, where a lender has decided to foreclose on such a "worthy" veteran, the VA has stepped in and paid off the lender, putting the loan in its portfolio. Today, you can choose from several VA loan programs, including fixed and adjustable rate mortgages. Lenders, buyers (veterans), and sellers may openly negotiate who will pay the loan's discount points. In the past, a veteran was not allowed to pay any points to the lender.

Here are the four types of loan programs approved by the VA:

1. **Traditional fixed-rate mortgage.** A standard fixed-rate loan. Each payment is fixed over the life of the loan and is made up of principal and interest.

2. **Graduated payment mortgage (GPM).** With this loan, smaller than normal payments are required for the first few years (typically, five years). These payments gradually increase each year, and then level off, after the end of the "graduation period," to larger-than-normal payments for the remaining term of the loan.

3. **Buydown.** The builder of a new home or seller of an existing home may "buy down" the veteran's mortgage payments by paying a large lump-sum payment up front at the closing. The lump sum is used to pay off a percentage of the payment due each month for the first few years of the loan (typically, one to three years).

4. **Growing equity mortgage (GEM).** This little-used repayment plan provides for a gradual annual increase in the monthly payments, where all of the increase is applied to the principal balance. The annual increases in the monthly payment may be fixed (for example, 3 percent per year) or tied to an appropriate index. The increases to the monthly payment result in an early payoff of the loan (11 to 16 years for a typical 30-year mortgage). Most home buyers who can afford a GEM opt for a 15-year loan, to gain a lower interest rate.

Who Might Benefit from a VA Loan?

They are expensive, but VA loans might be just the ticket for veterans who are currently—or perennially—running short of cash. VA loans are often sold on the secondary market, so their upper loan limit usually matches the Fannie Mae and Freddie Mac upper loan limits ($240,200 in 1999). If you're a reservist with six years of duty behind you, you're now eligible for a VA loan. The catch is, you'll pay a funding fee that's three-quarters of a percent higher than the fee charged your active-duty compatriots.

To apply for a VA loan, simply take your eligibility certificate to a lender. You're eligible for a VA loan if you served 90 days of wartime service in World War II, the Korean War, the Vietnam era, or the Persian Gulf War, and were not dishonorably discharged. You are also eligible if you served between six months and 24 months of continuous active duty from 1981 through today, and were not dishonorably discharged. Check with your VA loan office for more details on eligibility.

WHAT OTHER SORTS OF MORTGAGES ARE OUT THERE? WHAT ARE ARTICLES OF AGREEMENT?

Demand for complicated, expensive mortgages like the graduated-payment mortgage (GPM) has fallen along with interest rates. Some of the newly invented mortgages—like the two-step loans and ARMs—are easier to work with and require far less paperwork and attention.

But just in case these loans ever come back into fashion, here's the scoop: A graduated-payment mortgage is a step-payment mortgage that starts out with a low interest rate. Each year, the rate increases a certain number of percentage points until the loan levels out at a higher, fixed rate.

The problem with GPMs is that they require a lot of individual calculations, and each loan must be structured to the specifics of each borrower. That's not cost-effective. Mountains of paperwork made these loans expensive to maintain and adjust. They have essentially been replaced by the 5/25, 7/23, and one-year ARMs.

Who Could Benefit from a GPM?

With affordability at its highest levels in 25 years, there is hardly any interest in this mortgage, a trend that real estate banking experts believe will continue. People used to want a GPM because it meant that they could qualify for the loan at the lower interest rate. The problems started when the loan began to readjust upward. Essentially, borrowers were locking themselves into higher payments down the road. If their projected income didn't match the actual increase in interest payments, the borrowers had trouble.

Many families couldn't handle the steep interest payment shock, so the problem of nonpayment of additional interest was solved with programs like *negative amortization*. With negative amortization (an arcane financial technique), the actual payment increase was limited, and anything that was due in excess of the fixed payment was added to the total amount of the loan. Sounds good, but the borrower would end up paying interest on interest in a potentially never-ending cycle.

It was bad for banking and depressing for the homeowner, who felt he or she would always be in debt.

A Buy-Down Mortgage

A buy down is a financing technique that lets someone other than the buyer pay cash up front to the lender so that the first few years of the loan will be less costly. As buy downs have become more popular through the years, lenders across the country have begun to offer their own tailor-made versions of this loan.

The principle is simple. Typically the seller or the developer if you're buying new construction, or a relative of the buyer) buys down the mortgage rate, allowing the buyer to qualify for a below-market mortgage. With a 3-2-1 buy-down mortgage, the first year would be assessed at three percentage points below the note rate. That rate is good only for the first year. In the second year, the buyer pays interest at a mortgage rate two points below the note rate; in the third year, the mortgage rate is one point below the note rate. Thereafter, the mortgage interest rate is set at the original note rate.

The concept of buy downs is similar to both the ARM and the two-step mortgages: The rate starts lower and goes higher. But, unlike those other mortgages, the buy down is artificially deflated by the seller or another third-party source. The seller makes up the discount that is given to the buyer.

This type of mortgage does offer another option. A first-time buyer can often combine the buy down with an option like the ARM and enjoy a super-cheap first few years. If you get a buy down and combine it with a 5/25, it can put you significantly ahead of the market.

Here's how it works for simple interest: If the buyer takes out a $100,000 loan at 8 percent interest, the annual interest payment would be $8,000, or $666.67 per month. But with a 3-2-1 mortgage, the buyer would pay only 5 percent interest the first year ($5,000, or $416.67 per month), 6 percent interest the second year ($6,000, or $500 per month), and 7 percent interest the third year ($7,000, or $583.33 per month). The total savings would be $6,000 for the buyer. The seller picks up the additional mortgage cost, which is generally paid in cash to the lender at the closing. Then, every month for the first three years, the lender takes a portion of the money received at the closing and adds it to the amount the buyer sends in.

265

The Buy Down's Effect on a $100,000 Loan

Year	Buy Down Interest Rate	Buy Down Monthly Payment	Regular Interest Rate	Regular Monthly Payment
1	5 percent	$416.67	8 percent	$666.67
2	6	500.00	8	666.67
3	7	583.33	8	666.67
4	8	666.67	8	666.67

Total savings for the buyer: $6,000 over the first three years of the loan.

Eric's Story

When Eric, a certified public accountant, and his wife put their home up for sale, they offered to buy down the mortgage of whoever bought the property.

Steve, a first-time buyer, was the winning bidder on the property. Unfortunately, Steve didn't understand the concept of a buy down mortgage. At first, he refused Eric's offer for the buy down; later, he saw the benefit and accepted.

The buy down saved Steve approximately $4,500 on his loan.

A Purchase Money Mortgage

A purchase money mortgage is another type of seller-provided financing. With a purchase money mortgage, the seller offers to give a first mortgage to you, the buyer. In taking over the role normally played by a bank or savings and loan, the seller secures the loan with a down payment, and you pay the seller monthly installments of principal and interest. You get title to the property, but the seller has a lien on the property.

If you default on the mortgage, the seller can reclaim the property. A purchase money mortgage can work well for you because you don't pay any points or other costs to obtain the loan. The seller enjoys an excellent return on his or her funds.

See Question 81 for more information on seller financing.

Articles of Agreement

With articles of agreement, you enter into an installment agreement to buy a home over a specified period of time. The seller keeps legal title, and you receive equitable title, which means you receive an interest in the property but you do not own it. The benefit to you, the first-time buyer, is that the seller will usually accept a much smaller down payment (perhaps 5 percent of the sales price of the home) and will still feel comfortable with the arrangement.

Remember that, with articles of agreement, the seller retains title to the property until you've paid off the loan. If you default on your loan payments to the seller, the seller need only evict you to reclaim possession of the home.

Purchasing a home through articles of agreement can work very well for some home buyers. But it is extremely important that the buyer consult with an attorney who will look after his or her interests. Documents will need to be recorded to protect the buyer's *ownership interest* in the property, which is being built up through regular principal and interest payments.

Howard and Emily's Story

Howard and Emily had owned a condo for years, but when they wanted to sell, they couldn't get anyone interested in their neighborhood, which had fallen on hard times. So they put an ad in the newspaper, offering to sell their property for $3,000 down.

Sally saw the ad, checked her bankbook, and realized she had enough cash to buy the apartment. She moved in and paid Howard and Emily as if they were the bank. Over time, when she was able to afford a regular loan, she paid off the loan held by Howard and Emily. Until then, Sally got a tax deduction, which helped her save more money.

Although an articles-of-agreement purchase seems similar to a lease with an option to buy, the two methods of buying a home are completely different. With the articles of agreement, Sally does not own the home, but because she is paying the real estate taxes and making payments to the seller with interest, she gains the tax benefits. (Real estate taxes and interest are tax-deductible.) If Sally had leased the home with an option to buy, Howard and Emily would have retained ownership of the home until Sally exercised her option. But because they would have paid the real estate taxes, they, not Sally, would have had the tax benefits.

WHAT IS SELLER FINANCING?

QUESTION 81

One of the most flexible sources of real estate financing can be the seller of the property you want to buy. Why are sellers interested in providing financing? For many sellers, the return on their investment (in your mortgage) will be far greater than the amount they can get in the open marketplace. In addition, sellers who provide financing sometimes sell their properties more quickly.

As a home buyer, you should be interested in seller financing because (1) by eliminating any potential red tape that could slow down or mar the closing, it allows you to close more quickly, and (2) you might get financing at a below-market interest rate. Not every seller will help you purchase his or her home. Look for a seller who is ready to trade down to a smaller property or, perhaps, retire to a rental community. Other sellers are likely to need your cash to purchase their next home.

Judith and Scott's Story

First-time buyers Judith and Scott fell in love with a house that was for sale. Unfortunately, with their combined salaries (at the time, she sold advertising for a magazine and he was a second-year medical resident), they couldn't qualify for a mortgage that was large enough to let them make ends meet.

Although Judith and Scott knew it meant scrimping and saving, they were sure they could afford the payments. They went to their seller and asked her to take back a second mortgage. She agreed and offered them a rate that was a half point cheaper than the rate they got for their first mortgage. They closed on the house. A year and a half later, when interest rates dropped, Judith and Scott refinanced and paid off the seller.

When it works, seller financing works beautifully. But consider the experience of Karen, a regular reader of my column, "Real Estate Matters."

Karen's Story

Karen was eager to sell her California bungalow. On the advice of her real estate agent, she took back the mortgage for the buyers.

That was the beginning of four years of problems with the buyers. They missed several loan payments (and finally stopped paying them altogether). They twice failed to pay their property taxes. They declared bankruptcy to avoid foreclosure. They refused to pay the cost of Karen's bankruptcy attorney, plus court costs. And, finally, they committed hazard (homeowner's) insurance fraud—twice!

They finally left, and Karen reclaimed possession of the house. It was a disaster inside. She had to spend thousands of dollars to fix it up.

In the course of the past four years, the housing market in her neighborhood skyrocketed. Karen was able to resell the house at a tidy profit. But even that money, she says, wasn't worth the agony of dealing with a pair of irresponsible buyers.

Seller financing isn't for everyone. And, even though it's touted as being a win–win situation for everyone (buyer, seller, and agent), it doesn't always work out that way. Home buyers should recognize that sellers have to protect themselves. If you're seeking seller financing, be ready to allow the seller access to your credit history via a credit report. A savvy seller will also request financial references, the name of the person you report to at work, and perhaps will do a background check.

Seller Financing Options

Seller financing comes in many forms. The seller can:

- **Provide all the financing and take a straight first mortgage** (eliminating the need for a conventional lender). This is called a *purchase money mortgage*.
- **Take back a second mortgage, to help you scrape together the down payment.**
- **Buy down your mortgage, to enable you to qualify for more house.**

> • **Arrange a purchase by articles of agreement** (an installment purchase). You'll receive an interest in the home, which becomes yours after you pay off the seller in full.

Whatever form the seller financing takes, it's in your best interest to explore this possibility. However, beware of a difficult seller who will constantly call you for his or her money. That kind of overbearing behavior is difficult to stomach. If you do opt for seller financing, keep the transaction at arm's-length.

WHAT IS A B-C LOAN? WHERE DO I GET ONE?

Almost all home buyers who apply for a loan will be graded A or A–. Grade A borrowers have perfect or very good credit reports, have been in their jobs for two years (or more), and always pay their bills on time. Lenders estimate as many as 90 to 95 percent of all borrowers qualify for the Grade A or A– category.

So who is a B or a C borrower?

"It could be anyone walking down the street," says Joe, president of a B-C lending company. He likes to share the story of Ed and Vivian as an example of how anyone, including you, your parents, or your next door neighbor, could fall on hard times quite unexpectedly.

Ed and Vivian's Story

Ed and Vivian were just three years away from paying off the mortgage on their home when the Northridge, California, earthquake hit in 1994. Although their own home was not badly damaged, Ed's printing business almost collapsed.

Due to severe damage sustained in the earthquake, his three largest clients closed up shop, virtually overnight, and moved out of California. Without the income from these three clients, Ed's once-profitable business started running in the red. With the business unable to sustain itself, the couple eventually filed for bankruptcy.

But their story has a relatively happy ending. Ed and Vivian went to see a sub-par lender, also known as a B-C lender. This lender helped them to refinance their home, and they used the equity to pay off their debts and get Ed's business going again. Within two years, Ed and Vivian were back on their feet. Their business was once again thriving, and they were able to refinance their higher-interest-rate loan for a conventional mortgage.

Ed and Vivian are a typical B-C loan couple, says Harvey, a sub-par lender. "It's someone who, through no fault of their own, got downsized and lost their job. It's someone who went from a decent income to unemployment and couldn't make monthly credit card payments. Or, they've been 30 days late, twice in the past year."

Good people who have a bad credit problem, is how Rick, another mortgage banker, describes B-C applicants. "If you've had a bankruptcy any time within the past seven to 10 years, or if you've had medical-bill problems, or other situations where your credit score is so low you can't get a mortgage through the regular channel," then you may be right for a B-C loan.

You may also be a B-C borrower if you own too many pieces of investment property, need a "no-document" loan because you don't wish to disclose all of your income, have been self-employed for too short a period of time, or are purchasing a unique piece of property that doesn't fit into the secondary lending market's A-borrower mold.

There have always been small mom-and-pop lending shops that catered to folks who had major problems with their credit, but the B-C industry has only really come into its own in recent years, as credit scoring has evolved into a fine art, Rick says.

Credit scoring drives the entire sub-par market. Rick adds that the credit scoring model has improved to the point where a lender can pull up a credit report and guess, with at least an 85 percent accuracy rate, whether the borrower should get the loan.

B-C lending depends on different criteria than those you can offer if you have good or only slightly tarnished credit.

If you have cash but a low level of credit, a B-C lender might be able to help you. The most important component of a B-C loan is the loan-to-value ratio. If you're hardly putting down anything, it will be difficult to find a legitimate B-C lender who can help you.

The types of late payments you've made are important, too. You get a much heavier ding for a late payment on a mortgage than for a late installment on your student loan or on a local department store's charge card. (The order of importance for late payments is: mortgage, car loans, credit cards, student loans, and charge cards.) Other important components are: your credit score, any collection accounts you have, and whether you've gone bankrupt.

Surprisingly, neither your income (other than making sure you can afford the monthly payments) nor your job history counts for much.

Mortgage experts say that the B-C lending business is all about risk-based pricing. The bigger risk the bank takes, the more you pay.

For example, an A borrower might get a $240,000 loan for zero points at 7.5 percent, from a conventional lender. A B borrower would pay zero points and 10.5 percent for the same loan. A C borrower would pay zero points and 12.5 percent.

Almost every B-C loan is tailor-made. For example, on a B-C loan, you can pay additional points and lower your rate. Five points (a point is 1 percent of the loan amount and is fully deductible in the year you purchase your house) could lower your interest rate from 10.5 percent to 8.5 percent.

Your loan-to-value ratio also has an impact on the interest rate your loan carries and the points and fees you'll pay. If you get a loan that has an 80 percent loan-to-value ratio (you only have 20 percent equity), you'll pay more than if you get a 60 percent loan-to-value ratio loan, and have 40 percent equity.

Bad Apple Lending

Because B-C lending has been a small-time business, unacceptable practices have become commonplace. In a typical setup, a home buyer who has fairly good credit but doesn't understand the process, or doesn't speak English as their native language, or hasn't been through a mortgage process before, will sit down with a lender. The buyer's credit report will get pulled up, and the lender will see two or three late payments over the course of the past few years.

The lender will make a big deal about these late payments and will tell the borrower that he or she no longer qualifies as an A borrower. But wait—the lender does have a loan for which he or she can qualify.

The only catch? The loan carries a much higher interest rate. But if the borrower makes good and keeps the loan for six months, the broker will be able to refinance it into a lower rate loan.

According to lenders, what's happening is that an A or an A– borrower is getting shoved into a B loan, which is hugely profitable to the broker. Then, in six months, the broker refinances the loan into another slightly-above-market rate, which is so much lower than the first rate that the customer believes he or she is getting a great deal and good service. The bad apple lender could pocket $10,000 or more on such a transaction.

Legitimate mortgage bankers and sub-par lenders can't pull that scam because their companies require them to try and *raise* the

Many lenders believe that all loans, no matter whether the borrower is classified A, A–, B, C, or D, will soon move to risk-based pricing. People who have the best credit scores will then get the best deal on loans. Right now, if you have had, say, two late payments, you get the same mortgage deal as someone who has never been late with a payment. Because credit score modeling continues to be refined, and the technology continues to improve, every borrower will soon pay exactly what he or she should, depending on an individual credit report. If nothing else, this possibility is an added incentive to keep your credit as clean as possible.

borrower's grade. "If they're an A, they go to the regular side of the table. If they're a B, or any of the fine gradations of B or C, they get moved over to the B-C side of the table," Rick says.

Harvey explains, "We view our loans as credit repair loans because we tell the customer, 'You've had challenges in the past, so we'll take your debts, consolidate them for you, reduce your monthly payments, give you a fixed rate for 24 to 36 months, and the opportunity to get back on your feet.' In 12 to 36 months, their credit is repaired by their hard work and they can go elsewhere."

WHY ARE SOME LENDERS WILLING TO GIVE ME A MORTGAGE FOR 125 PERCENT OR 130 PERCENT OF THE HOME'S SELLING PRICE?

QUESTION
83

As competition continues to shake out the mortgage industry (and bring down costs for consumers), lenders are under pressure to develop new loans and new products that will satisfy consumers' demands.

Relatively new entries to the product mix are 125 percent and 130 percent home loans.

How can you borrow more than a home is worth? Good question. There is one legitimate way to do this, and several other choices you should avoid.

The Good 125 Percent Loan

If you are purchasing and renovating a house, you may borrow up to 125 percent of the value of the house, as long as the home will appreciate in value to at least the complete cost of the renovation.

You'll be jumping through several additional hoops to get this loan, which is offered by the FHA. You'll have to submit your plans, plus a contractor's estimate, for review and approval by the lender before your loan can be funded. But it's a nice way to finance your home improvement costs at your regular mortgage rate.

New Construction

What if you already own a piece of land and want to finance the construction of your home? You'll have a couple of options. With a construction-to-own loan, the lender will give you a loan based on appraisals of how much the finished house will be worth. If you paid cash for the land or you inherited the property, you may be able to take out a loan against the vacant lot and use that money to build your home. Consult with your local lender for details.

But Stay Away from *These* Loans

The much more common 125 percent and 130 percent loans are designed to entice people who have severe cash and credit problems and want to purchase or refinance their home.

If you're in that category, a lender will give you a loan that has several stages. You'll pay the going mortgage rate—the standard 80 percent loan-to-value ratio (as if you had 20 percent to put down in cash)—for the first part of the loan. The next 20 percent will be financed at a slightly higher rate, perhaps with more points and fees, and with private mortgage insurance. The next 25 or 30 percent will be like charging the money on your credit card. You can expect to pay anywhere from 12 to 18 percent interest (or more) for this part of the loan.

Essentially, you're getting three loans, and when you average the costs of the segments, you'll see that you're paying through the nose for the privilege.

Who should get these loans? No one. They're inherently risky, particularly for someone who's in a precarious financial position. And, more often than not, quality lenders don't offer them. Shady, bad apple lenders offer them as a solution for whatever credit problems are affecting your credit report. Also, the IRS has ruled that you may only deduct the interest on a mortgage loan up to 100 percent of your home's value.

274

WHAT IS PRIVATE MORTGAGE INSURANCE (PMI)? HOW DO I GET RID OF IT?

QUESTION
84

Private mortgage insurance (PMI) is often a necessary expense when you're buying a house and you have less than 20 percent to put down in cash. Although it's expensive, PMI allows you to purchase a home with a small down payment, and it helps the lender resell your mortgage on the secondary market to an institutional investor.

By definition, PMI is additional insurance designed to protect lenders from individuals who default on their loans and who have less than 20 percent equity in their property. Mortgage experts say that, compared to home buyers who put down the traditional 20 percent of the purchase price, those who make small down payments are more likely to default on their home loans. Therefore, lenders require those riskier buyers to purchase PMI, which insures lenders against the extra risk—and ensuing cost—of foreclosure.

Most states have regulations prohibiting lenders from making a loan in excess of 80 percent of the purchase price without PMI. The difference between putting down 20 percent and, say, 15 percent or even 10 percent, wouldn't seem to make a substantial difference, but a spokesperson for the Mortgage Bankers Association of America (MBA), a nonprofit organization serving the needs of lenders nationwide, says that 20 percent provides a necessary cushion for both home buyers and lenders: "If I put down 20 percent and lose my job, and the house has declined in value, I can still sell it and pay off the mortgage and come out even or with a little bit of cash. But if I've only put down 5 percent in the same set of circumstances, then I'll come out of the deal owing money."

Although it is expensive, PMI has its upside for buyers, too. About 30 percent of home buyers, most of them first-timers, can't put together enough cash for a 20 percent down payment. With PMI, many people can purchase property years earlier than they otherwise could have managed. Buyers who are required to purchase PMI have to pay for that additional security, but they gain from being able to get a mortgage with much less cash up front. This is considered a plus by many real estate experts, who argue in favor of buying a home with as little cash as possible.

First-time buyers often wonder whether every lender charges for PMI. (Not all lenders advertise it.) "If a customer calls me and says a lender doesn't charge PMI, I ask them to check the interest rate," says Ray, a mortgage banker. "It's always one quarter or three-eighths of a percent higher than ours. And you'll be paying it for the life of the loan."

PMI Is Getting Cheaper

Since the first edition of this book was published, several important things have occurred that will ultimately make it less expensive for home buyers to carry PMI.

First, a new law was passed. The Homeowner's Protection Act of 1998 requires all lenders who granted loans after July 29, 1999, to provide consumers with an explanation of how they can cancel their PMI policy. There are three ways to do it:

1. If you believe your home has reached the 20 percent equity threshold, you may hire an appraiser to appraise the value of your home. If indeed you have passed the 20 percent equity market, your lender must cancel your PMI payments.

2. Each monthly mortgage payment consists of both principal and interest. Each bit of principal you repay goes to build up your equity. Starting with loans originated after July 31, 1999, lenders must inform borrowers annually that they may cancel their PMI once they have reached the 20 percent equity threshold. On a 30-year loan, you might hit the 20 percent threshold somewhere around the tenth year. If you prepay your loan, you'll cross the threshold a lot faster.

3. If you do not request a cancellation of your PMI premium after you've gained 20 percent equity, your lender is now required to cancel your PMI when you hit the 22 percent equity threshold. This will be done whether or not you request it.

You don't have to wait for the 10-year date if the value of homes in your neighborhood has risen quickly. If home prices rise an average of 3 percent each year, you may reach the 20 percent level in six to seven years, rather than waiting until 10 years. Or, if you bought a house in certain neighborhoods in southern California in 1998, for example, your house might have doubled in value by the spring of 2000.

Canceling PMI as soon as possible can save you hundreds of dollars per year and thousands of dollars over the life of your loan. If you set aside the money you save each year (which could reach $300 to $500 per $100,000 in loan amount), and use it to prepay your loan, you'll save not only a few thousand dollars on the principal but perhaps tens of thousands of dollars in interest.

The Cost of PMI

The premium price depends on the purchase price of the home and the type of mortgage you've selected (fixed 30-year, fixed 15-year, ARM, 7/23, or balloon). You can expect to pay anywhere from $40 to $50 per month for every $100,000 of loan amount.

Canceling Your PMI Premiums

You don't have to pay PMI throughout the whole life of the loan, unless you've opted to put the cost of PMI into the interest rate of your loan. If that's the case, you'll have to refinance to get rid of it.

When you close on your loan, the lender is required to give you information on how to cancel your PMI payments when you've reached the magic 20 percent equity threshold. Once you've reached the threshold (either under the terms of your loan or because your home has increased in value), you may request (and pay for) an appraisal of your home. If the appraisal shows that your home's value, when combined with the equity you've built up with your regular mortgage payments plus any prepayments, puts you at the 20 percent equity level, the lender must cancel your PMI payments.

Lenders must tell you at the closing exactly how many years and months it will take for you to pay off enough of your loan to cancel PMI. Their schedule won't include any rise in your home's equity, which could shorten the time frame considerably. Each year, your mortgage service must provide you with a phone number that you can call for information about canceling your PMI.

277

If you do nothing, the lender is required to cancel your PMI when your loan-to-value ratio has reached 22 percent.

FHA Loans

Frequently, home buyers wonder whether they have to pay private mortgage insurance if they get an FHA loan. The answer is no. But that doesn't mean you're not paying for some form of mortgage insurance.

All government loans require mortgage insurance, which they refer to as MI. But because you're getting a government loan, you get the government version of PMI. Unlike PMI, however, you can *never* cancel your mortgage insurance on an FHA loan, even if you reach a 50 percent loan-to-value ratio. *The only way to cancel MI on an FHA loan is to refinance into a conventional loan.*

If your lender balks at canceling your PMI, contact the department or agency that regulates mortgage lenders in your state. If your lender is federally chartered, you can call the U.S. Department of the Treasury's Office of Thrift Supervision, or the Federal Deposit Insurance Corporation.

How to Get a Low Down Payment Loan Without PMI

There is one way to get a low down payment loan without paying for private mortgage insurance. It's called an 80/10/10 ("eighty-ten-ten") or an 80/15/5 ("eighty-fifteen-five") loan.

The concept here is that you're essentially getting two loans simultaneously, a regular 80 percent loan-to-value ratio first mortgage, and a home equity loan. With an 80/10/10, the first mortgage is for 80 percent of the sales price of the home, the home equity loan is for an additional 10 percent of the cost, and the final 10 percent represents your down payment. With an 80/15/5, the home equity loan is for an additional 15 percent of the cost of the home, and you put down 5 percent.

There are pluses and minuses to the 80/10/10 loans. The good thing is that you don't pay PMI. And, because home equity loans to $100,000 are tax-deductible, you can deduct the interest you pay. Private mortgage insurance is never tax-deductible.

Unfortunately, the interest on the home equity loan tends to be higher than on a regular loan, which means you'll pay more in interest. But because the interest is tax-deductible, the numbers work out almost even between a PMI low down payment loan and an 80/10/10.

Who's a good candidate for an 80/10/10? If you work for a company that pays a good bonus once a year, and you know that the size of your next bonus will allow you to entirely pay off the home equity portion of the loan, you may want to go with an 80/10/10. You'll be able to get a conventional size mortgage a lot faster, and you'll save yourself the cost of PMI.

Before you make this important decision, talk to your lender, think about how long you'll be paying off this loan, and work out the numbers.

HOW DOES PRIVATE MORTGAGE INSURANCE (PMI) DIFFER FROM MORTGAGE INSURANCE (FHA) AND MORTGAGE/CREDIT INSURANCE?

QUESTION 85

As we've discussed in Question 84, private mortgage insurance is required whenever you put down less than 20 percent on a house. All lenders will require you to have it. The lower your down payment, the higher your PMI premium.

FHA mortgage insurance (also referred to as MI) is the government version of PMI. It is required on all FHA loans, no matter how much you put down in cash, and you can never cancel it. The only way to get rid of MI on an FHA loan is to refinance out of that loan into a conventional loan.

Credit insurance, also referred to as mortgage insurance, is an entirely different matter. This insurance is designed to pay off your bills in case you die or are incapacitated. Depending on the kind of insurance you get, it will pay off either your credit card bills or your entire mortgage.

Sound good? It isn't. Credit insurance and mortgage insurance are extremely expensive. And you're paying a lot of money for a declining liability. Every month, when you write a check to the credit card company or to your mortgage lender, your check includes principal and interest. So, each month, your principal balance due falls a bit.

Suppose you take out mortgage insurance that will pay off a $100,000 loan if you die before paying for the loan. If it's a 30-year loan, and you don't die during those 30 years, you will have paid off your mortgage before taking advantage of the policy. If you then let the policy lapse, you get nothing in return for 30 years' payments. If you die 15 years into your $100,000 mortgage, the balance due may be only $70,000, but you've still been paying for $100,000 in coverage. After the insurance pays off the balance of the $100,000 mortgage, you might expect that your survivor will get the extra $30,000 in cash, right?

Not likely. You've forfeited that $30,000. If you're worried about how your spouse or partner will manage the bills after you've gone, consider buying term life insurance. It's a whole lot less expensive than mortgage or credit insurance, and you'll get everything you're paying for. Also, your surviving spouse or partner will have the option to use the funds in any way he or she wants. Perhaps paying off the mortgage at that time wouldn't be in his or her best interest. Term life insurance provides options that aren't available with mortgage or credit insurance.

20/20

hindsight

One of the things we do to show our family and friends how much we love them is to plan ahead in case the unthinkable happens. Planning for how your loved one will be able to stay in the home you're buying (if that's what you both feel would be best if the unthinkable were to happen) requires your careful consideration and preparation.

QUESTION

86

WHAT IF I'M REJECTED FOR A LOAN?

After all the hours spent searching for the perfect home, negotiating the purchase price, working with an attorney to perfect the contract, and applying for a mortgage, it's extremely disappointing and frustrating to be rejected for a loan. But before you give up and decide you'll never be able to afford a home, you should know that hundreds of people get rejected for loans every day. Sometimes it's their fault, and sometimes lenders reject them for reasons that seem to defy logic or comprehension.

Sam once had a client who was rejected for a loan by several lenders. Her ex-husband had declared bankruptcy, but because her name was on some of the credit card accounts, her credit was tarnished along with his. Another first-time buyer was rejected because she had just bought a new car. The lender she applied to for her mortgage decided that her debt-to-income ratios were out of whack. A third first-time buyer couple was rejected by a handful of lenders because the husband truthfully stated that his business was being sued for $100,000. Because the lawsuit was ongoing, the lenders decided a loan was too big a risk.

Let's look at eleven reasons why you might be rejected for a loan.

1. Credit Report Problems

When you apply for a mortgage, or any other type of loan, the bank or mortgage broker will pull up your credit report. This report includes all of your financial information: every credit card, the balance due, and your payment record; your current and past addresses; any bankruptcies or other credit problems; your bank and money market accounts; any outstanding loans; and a host of other credit information. The credit report is used to determine whether you're a good credit risk.

Numerous types of credit report problems (which may or may not be your fault) would cause a lender to reject your application for a loan. If you've ever missed or been late with a credit card payment, or defaulted on a prior mortgage or a school or car loan, it will probably show up on your credit report. If you've filed for bankruptcy within the past seven years, that will be indicated on your credit report. If you haven't paid your taxes, or a judgment has been filed against you (perhaps for nonpayment of spousal or child support), those facts and the amounts involved will be listed. Failure to pay your landlord, doctor, or hospital may turn into a black spot on your credit report.

Credit report companies get their information about you from sources that extend credit: department stores, lenders, banks, and credit card companies. The information is updated on a periodic basis—sometimes daily, sometimes annually. People actually enter the information into the company's computer, so there is a good chance that a mistake has been made somewhere along the line.

If the credit report contains errors, you should contact the credit bureau immediately. A recent law requires credit bureaus to deal with written requests to correct errors within 30 days.

If you feel that your credit report is wrong, experts say it's best to take up the error with the organization or company that is claiming you owe it money. Try to find documentation that proves the mistake, and have it corrected as quickly as possible. If there is a more serious problem, such as a bankruptcy filing or a judgment against you, or if you've not filed your income tax returns or "forgotten" to pay back a school loan, you may have a more difficult time getting a lender to approve your loan application. If you've been late paying your bills, regroup by paying in full and on time for six months to a year, to prove to the lender that the late payments were an aberration. Be sure all your taxes are paid in full and on time.

2. Inconsistencies in Information

Sometimes, lenders find inconsistencies between how a loan application is filled out and the information their loan officer discovers. If you say your income is $45,000 annually and the lender calls your employer for verification and finds out that you earn only $30,000, that's probably grounds for rejection. The lender figures that if you've lied about something as basic and easily verifiable as your income, you may have lied about something more important.

Most lenders, upon discovering minor inconsistencies (if you say your income is $45,000 and it's really $44,500), will ask you about them and give you a chance to explain. Others won't. The bottom line is: Be straight with the lender. Answer his or her questions honestly, and if you don't know the answer to a question, say so. Don't make anything up. If you get rejected for providing false or misleading information, consider the lost application fee a cheap lesson. Honesty is always the best policy.

3. Employed Less than Two Years

Lenders like to see that you're earning a stable income. They like consistency. They like knowing that someone has been employing you and will continue to employ you. That's why most lenders will generally reject you for a loan if you've been employed less than two years by your current employer.

As with most rules, however, there are exceptions. If you're a secretary making $25,000 a year, and the company across the hall offers you a job as an executive secretary for $35,000, most lenders will be delighted to see you take the job and earn the extra income, even if you're only a couple of weeks away from a closing. Why? Because lenders like lateral moves (the same job for better pay at a competing company) or ascents up the corporate ladder (from vice president to president). Although you're changing jobs, you're changing for the better, and the lender should understand your motivation.

If, however, you spend a year as a mechanic, then become a short-order chef for six months, then move into used-car sales, the lender may reject your application, even if you've moved up in income. Too much movement; not enough consistency.

4. Being Self-Employed

What if you're self-employed? Being self-employed adds an extra twist to the process of getting a mortgage because lenders don't view self-employed workers as being as stable as those who are employed by others. (Although the good news is, you can't be fired!)

Lenders will rarely approve a mortgage unless you have been self-employed for at least two years. When you apply for the mortgage, you'll have to bring profit-and-loss statements, as well as your last two tax returns. The lender won't look at your gross income. Net income (gross income minus expenses) is what's important. Remember this when you're looking for a home, because you may be overestimating the amount of money you'll be able to borrow. For example, if you have gross earnings of $75,000 and expenses of $50,000, a lender will consider your income to be $25,000, even though you may feel you can spend more. Some mortgage brokers specialize in getting loans for self-employed people. They work with lenders who keep these loans in their portfolio and therefore have more relaxed lending policies.

If you're self-employed for less than two years, back away from the application and wait until you have been running your own business for at least two years. Or, find a lender who specializes in placing loans of this type. If you're employed but all or most of your salary is from commission, you may also be a good candidate for rejection, especially if you've been at it less than two years. Try to speak to your mortgage lender before you're ready to apply. Also, avoid paying any fees up front, so that if you aren't approved, you won't lose any money.

My husband, Sam, once represented a man who had taken a new commission-only sales job about six months before making an offer on a home. Although the man was pulling in an excellent salary, he couldn't find a lender who would approve a mortgage. After several weeks of making the rounds to no avail, the man was offered a better job for even more money, in Boston. Thanks to his mortgage contingency, he backed out of the purchase (without penalty) and decided to move his family to Boston.

5. Losing Your Job

If your application is denied based on job loss, wait until your job prospects change and you've been employed at the new job for several months. Then reapply. Try to find something in the same field, for about the same (or more) money; otherwise, you may be subjected to the two-year employment rule. If you lose your job shortly before the closing, it can mean an instant rejection of your loan application. If you're married and your spouse earns enough money to support the mortgage payments, the lender may approve the loan anyway.

6. Unapproved Condo Building or New Development

Sometimes you'll get rejected for a loan and you won't even be the problem. Institutions that buy loans on the secondary market have a specific set of guidelines that lenders must follow. One of these guidelines is the *70 percent rule* for condominiums. Lenders like their home buyers to purchase condos in buildings in which owners occupy at least 70 percent of the building. Why? For stability. Lenders believe that homeowners take better care of property than renters do. This makes sense; owners have more of a stake in a property than renters.

Historically, condo buildings that have a high percentage of renters can lose their value. If you're rejected because of the 70 percent rule, you may want to seek out other lenders who will keep your loan in their own portfolio (instead of reselling it on the secondary market to Fannie Mae or Freddie Mac), and who may be more flexible on this rule.

If the building is less than 50 percent owner-occupied, you may want to rethink your purchase. Or you may want to seek out a lender that has made loans to homeowners in that building.

Buyers who purchase new-construction town houses and condominiums may also have a tough time finding a lender who will approve their loan. Conventional lenders like to see development projects that have been in existence for more than two years. They like to see a new-construction project more than 50 percent owner-occupied before they'll grant a loan; otherwise, the project could go into default and the properties might drop in value (an anathema to a lender, who wants to protect the investment). If you get rejected for a loan for your new town house or condo purchase, check with the developer. Developers can usually arrange for a financing package from a lender who will keep the loans in-house for one to two years, and then resell them on the secondary market.

7. Low Appraisal

Some people get rejected for loans because the property they want to buy doesn't "appraise out." When lenders say a home doesn't appraise out, they mean that the bank's appraiser has determined that the home is worth less than the buyer is ready to pay for it. Let's say you're ready to offer $150,000 for a home, with 20 percent ($30,000) as a cash down payment, which is all the savings you have in the world. You're counting on the bank to lend you the additional $120,000 to purchase the home. But when the bank receives the appraiser's report, the home is valued at $120,000, and the bank will lend you only 80 percent (or $96,000). You need to come up with an additional $24,000, in cash, to close on the home.

If you can't sew up the $24,000 gap yourself, the lender will reject your loan application.

8. Adding New Debt

Some buyers think they'll be able to get away with making a large purchase after they've been approved for a mortgage. For example, if you get approved for your loan, and two weeks before the closing you buy a new Corvette that will require hefty monthly installments, the lender's going to know. How? Few people realize that lenders often do two credit checks: before they approve your loan, and before you close on it. Lenders are increasingly watching out for folks who incur large new debts that may interfere with their repayment of the mortgage. Don't buy a new car just before the closing. Wait until after you close.

9. Refusal to Provide New Documentation

If the loan officer calls you up and asks for additional documentation, by all means provide it. Refusal to provide information is grounds for loan application rejection. If the loan officer continually asks for additional information, or asks you to send material you've already sent, this may be indicative of an extremely disorganized and pressured office. Or you may have another problem.

10. The Gambling Game

This isn't an official scam, but it happens often enough that first-time buyers, repeat buyers, and homeowners looking to refinance their loans should be aware of it. As you have now seen, there are plenty of reasons why a loan application might not be approved. One problem that doesn't get much media attention is this: Some loan officers gamble with your locked-in interest rates, hoping to put more money in their own pockets.

Although that sounds surprising (it is) and perhaps illegal (technically, it is, but it's isn't enforced as long as the lender lives up to the lock agreement), a little explanation might help you understand why some loan officers could be gambling with your rate.

To eliminate the uncertainty of changeable interest rates, borrowers may pay their prospective lender for the privilege of locking in a specific interest rate and number of points (a point is equal to 1 percent of the loan amount). The lock is good for a predefined time, usually 30 to 60 days. When you lock in your rate, you must close on your mortgage before the lock expires, or you lose the preset interest rate. Experts say that the mortgage loan process can easily go awry, particularly when interest rates are headed upward. Lenders, nervous about their investments and eager to charge the highest interest rate possible, are not as eager to close on their loans as when interest rates are dropping.

Here's how it works: Although you think you've locked in at a certain rate with a certain number of points, lenders will, in essence, gamble with the rate rather than actually lock it in, hoping that interest rates will slip further. This is called "playing the float." The loan officer and the mortgage company will then pocket the difference between the new current interest rate and the rate you locked into.

The problems start when interest rates begin to go up instead of down. If the loan officer has been playing the float with your loan, and the rate goes up, he or she will have to pay, out-of-pocket, the difference between your locked-in interest rate and the current market rate, in order to close on the loan. And because loan officers are loath to pay out, they will often find something "wrong" with your application at the last minute (new documentation is needed, and so on), forcing you to accept a higher interest rate or more points, says one loan officer.

If you feel that your loan rejection is without merit, and you can prove that you sent all the information required, you may want to complain to your state regulatory body. Remember, the squeaky wheel gets the grease. Make sure you are heard, loud and clear.

11. Racial Rejection

Recent investigations and surveys of the mortgage banking industry seem to prove that, compared to Caucasians, minorities, specifically African Americans, are twice as likely to be rejected for a loan. And that makes people very angry. If you feel you've been rejected for a loan simply because of your race, sex, or religion, you will want to file a complaint with your state attorney general's office, the state office that regulates the mortgage banking industry, and other regulatory agencies, including the Department of Housing and Urban Development (HUD). If the rejection is for an FHA loan, notify your local Housing Authority office.

In Appendix V, you'll find contact information for the departments and commissions that regulate mortgage lenders and real estate brokers in all 50 states.

10

Before You Close

QUESTION 87

WHEN SHOULD I SCHEDULE MY PRECLOSING INSPECTION? WHAT DO I DO IF I DISCOVER SOMETHING IS DAMAGED OR MISSING?

Patty and Frank's Story

Patty and Frank agreed to buy a $300,000 condominium from David and Marla. When they negotiated the contract, David and Marla agreed to leave all the fixtures, including light fixtures, refrigerator, sconces, and bookcases that were attached to the wall. Everything was so friendly that Patty and Frank decided to forgo the preclosing inspection. They didn't need to walk through the apartment because David and Marla assured them that everything was in order.

After the closing, everyone shook hands, and David and Marla handed over the keys. Patty and Frank went over to their new condo, opened the door, and discovered that it had been stripped bare: no light fixtures, no refrigerator, no sconces, and huge holes in the wall where the bookcases had been ripped out. They were, understandably, heartbroken.

While David and Marla certainly should have lived up to the contract (they could be sued), Patty and Frank should have taken it upon themselves to have a final walk-through of the apartment before closing.

Never Leave Anything to Chance (or Good Will)

Most first-time buyers don't realize that they should ask for a preclosing inspection. Just about everyone is coached to ask for an initial inspection and to hire a licensed house inspector who can point out what's wrong with the home. But too many first-time buyers aren't told that *they should request the right to a second, preclosing inspection.*

To avoid getting burned, schedule the walk-through as close to the actual closing as possible, certainly within the 24 to 48 hours prior to the closing. *If possible, the sellers should have already moved out.* The whole point of the walk-through is to protect yourself and your future property from sellers who aren't as nice as they seem to be, or who are actually as nasty as they appear. By inspecting the premises, you're making sure the seller has lived up to his or her agreements in the sales contract. And if he or she hasn't, you want to know about it in advance of the closing so that remedies (both monetary and otherwise) can be agreed on or implemented before money changes hands.

Look For the Details

What should you look for in a preclosing inspection? To start with, make sure that the condition of the home hasn't changed since you signed the contract several months earlier. Remember, you probably negotiated for the home some 60 to 90 days before, and you have spent the past weeks arranging for your mortgage, packing, and preparing to move. As Patty and Frank discovered, a lot can change in 60 days. And you don't want any surprises at the closing—or afterward.

Here is a general checklist for your walk-through:

- Turn on every appliance.
- Open every door—to a room, a closet, or a cabinet.
- Make sure nothing is broken.
- Be certain everything the seller agreed to leave is actually there and is in good shape.
- Be certain that when the sellers moved out, they did no damage to the home.

It's vital that you turn on every appliance that's being left in the home, including the dishwasher. As you may recall from an earlier discussion, Sam and I learned the hard way. Our story bears repeating.

Sam and Ilyce's Story

When Sam and I were closing on our prewar vintage co-op, we decided to have a final walk-through. We had been in the unit several times, and we knew that we would make some significant cosmetic improvements, so we weren't too worried about the condition of the walls and wallpaper, the flooring, and so on.

But when we walked in, the apartment was a mess. Our sellers were a retired couple who had lived in the unit for 25 years and had a huge accumulation of stuff. Boxes were stacked everywhere. Clothes had been taken from closets and laid down. Furniture had been moved. It was difficult to actually walk through the apartment and look at things. But we plodded along.

When we got to the kitchen, we opened the fridge, and it seemed cold and relatively clean, though at least 20 years old. When we got to the dishwasher, we said to ourselves, "Well, we'll probably replace this soon after closing, so why bother testing it out?" Our sellers, hovering around us, assured us everything worked. We felt as if we were in the way, so we left.

We closed on the unit and moved our stuff in that afternoon. That night, after unwrapping a stack of dishes, Sam suggested we test out the dishwasher. We put a load in and started to run it, but nothing happened. Sam reached under the sink and found the water valve. Sure enough, it had been shut off. ("Now why would they shut off the water?" Sam said to himself.) Sam turned on the water and started the dishwasher. Then, we went to sleep. It was about 3:00 A.M.

We woke up around 7:00 A.M. to banging on the door. In our bathrobes, we opened the door to find one of the co-op's engineers and our new downstairs neighbor. She complained that we had ruined her ceiling and window shade, and who knows what else, all because our dishwasher leaked.

It cost us around $150 to replace our neighbor's window treatment, and another $70 or so to have someone come out and replace the dishwasher's hose. (We never had another problem with the dishwasher, but I can tell you that I never used it without some sense of concern.)

Years later, Sam and I still discuss whether our old sellers actually knew that the dishwasher leaked. Regardless, we know we should have tested the dishwasher while we were there, and let it run a full cycle.

Don't Be Shy

It's equally important to open every door. Don't be afraid to poke your head into your seller's messy closets. You're looking for anything unusual or broken. Finally, be certain that everything the seller agreed to leave is actually in place and in the apartment. Check your contract if you're not sure whether a window air conditioner was part of the agreement, or whether the window shades or curtains are supposed to be left. If the seller asks you at the preclosing inspection if he or she can take additional items, simply say, "I have to check with my attorney." That will give you time to think about whether you want to keep or give away that chandelier.

Another Sam and Ilyce Story

When we went to our preclosing inspection for the 1880s farmhouse, in which we now live, our sellers were in the process of moving out. There were boxes everywhere, and it was extremely difficult to move through the house.

Our seller looked out onto the backyard and motioned toward the swings set. "My son built that," he said.

We looked out and nodded. "It's a fine piece of work," Sam said.

"My grandchildren just love playing on it," our seller said.

"I can imagine they do," I said, looking over the fine construction hosting two swings, a sandbox, and a long, blue slide. The top of the slide was built like a small fort, with straight sides. I imagined little children climbing up to the top and hiding out, then escaping down the slide.

"If you're not going to use it, would you mind if we took it with us?" our seller asked.

Sam and I looked at each other and smiled. We didn't have children at the time (we now have two), but we were planning to put that swings set to great use during the next few years.

"I'm sorry," I told our seller. "But we do plan to use it. It stays."

To replace that set with one of the same quality would have cost us, at the time, more than $700. I wasn't ready to ante up that kind of money so that our seller could have a ready-made play area for his grandchildren in his new home.

New Construction Walk-Through

If you're buying new construction, you'll be looking for different things on your walk-through. Before closing, you will want to be sure that everything the developer promised to do and to put in is actually there (and working). This includes any sod or plantings, doorknobs, a doorbell, window screens, fixtures, appliances, and so on.

Be sure that everything works, in every room. Take a hair dryer or radio with you and test each electrical socket. You can buy a simple device that tells you whether a socket has been wired correctly. Make sure everything has been painted and is in working condition. Turn on the water in the showers and sinks, and flush the toilets. If there is a garage, make sure the electric door opener works.

With new construction, there are always a few last-minute items that need to be finished, and, even with honest effort, it may not be possible for the contractor or developer to complete them before the closing. That's why you need a *punch list*—a list of all items that need to be fixed in the home before you consider it completely finished. During your preclosing inspection, write down every situation that needs attention: a loose tile in the master bath; a wall that wasn't painted; an electrical outlet that doesn't work; a tree that should have been planted in the side yard. Have your attorney or broker present the punch list to the developer at the closing, or before the closing, and have the developer agree to fix these items (in writing) before you actually close. Most developers should be happy to comply with any reasonable request.

Attendance Is Mandatory

Who should go with you to your walk-through? My mother, Susanne, makes it a point to go to almost all of her clients' walk-throughs. She says she helps the buyer remember what was where, amid the mess and muck of moving. It goes without saying that you, the buyer (or buyers, if you're buying with someone else), should attend the walk-through. You should ask your broker to be there. Beyond that, the seller or the seller broker may attend. Sometimes, if the buyer is out of town, the buyer's attorney will attend.

If the seller attends and you notice that certain things are missing, try to avoid a confrontation. Have your broker speak to the seller or the seller broker, to confirm what was written in the contract.

Some buyers like to have a professional house inspector attend the preclosing inspection. I think that's overkill in most cases. The preclosing inspection isn't about finding a leaky oil tank. You should be looking for things like a gash in the wall caused by the L-shaped sofa as it was moved out of the home. That gash is something you could ask the sellers to fix before closing, or they could give you a credit for the damage.

Missing in Action

What should you do if you discover something's missing or damaged during the preclosing inspection? Make a list of anything that doesn't seem right to you, and call your attorney immediately after you leave the home. You can also call your broker. Your attorney may telephone the seller's attorney before the closing, or may present a list of items at the closing. Either way, the list will have to be resolved before you'll agree to close on the house.

The list gives you some leverage because, as anxious as you are to move, the sellers are equally anxious and have most likely found another place to live. Perhaps they are scheduled to close on a new home shortly after you buy theirs. At this point, most sellers, and their attorneys, will find a way to make everyone happy. The seller may offer you $45 instead of fixing the back door. He or she might offer you $600 for the washer and dryer their movers took "by accident." Or the seller might say, "Forget it, I'm not fixing the east window screen."

The bottom line is this: The preclosing inspection or walk-through gives you your last opportunity to make sure that the property is in the same condition (except for normal wear and tear) as the day you bought it. It's important that you take full advantage of that opportunity.

WHEN SHOULD THE SELLER MOVE OUT?

Unless there are some extraordinary circumstances, make sure the seller is completely out of the home before you close the deal. That doesn't mean the end of the business day, as in, you close at 10:00 A.M. and the seller's out by 5:00 P.M. Your new home isn't a business. Getting the seller out by the closing means that if you're scheduled to close at 10:00 A.M., the seller is packed and gone by 9:59 A.M.

After closing (and getting all of his or her money), the seller has little, if any, incentive to move out. If you close and pay money to the seller, and then the seller decides not to leave, you may have a real problem getting the seller out. The seller no longer has any interest in the property once the deed changes hands. An unscrupulous seller might be inclined to inflict damage (if the transaction has been a bit hostile), or may be less than careful when moving his or her items out of the home. The best way to protect your property is to make sure the seller is out before you exchange cash for keys.

Buyers and sellers sometimes make other arrangements. For example, suppose the seller has had the home on the market for a long time—say, a year—and within that year, the seller went out and bought another home and moved. The house you're buying would then be vacant and perhaps empty of furniture. The seller, unless he or she is in a high income bracket, will want to close as quickly as possible, to end the burden of paying two mortgages (on your house and the new house). You don't want to close until your apartment lease is up (to avoid paying both rent and mortgage), but you do want to get in a little early to do some painting. Would the seller mind? It doesn't hurt to ask. If the seller seems to hesitate, offer to "rent the house for a few days before closing," for a nominal daily fee.

The earliest the seller would probably want to let you into a house would be two to three weeks before closing. Still, there's not much risk for a seller in this situation. Time marches forward quickly to the closing.

There's greater risk for you, the buyer, if the seller wants to stay in the house *after* the closing. Let's look at why a seller might want to do this:

1. **No place to go.** The seller may not have found anywhere to live. This is the most dangerous situation for you, because there is no end in sight for the seller's continued residence. It could last a few days, a few months, or indefinitely. Also, you're going to be coming from somewhere else, and you will want to—or have to—move into your house.

2. **Bad timing.** The seller isn't scheduled to close on his or her new home until a few days after your closing. Most sellers are going to turn around and buy something new. In a perfect world, the sellers would attend your closing while they simultaneously closed on their new house. However, this isn't a perfect world, and the sellers will usually want to close first on your home (so that they can use the funds to purchase their new home). You might be scheduled to close on your house on a Friday, and the seller is scheduled to close on his or her new place on Monday and may ask to "rent" your house for the weekend. If you can spend a few extra days in your current abode, and if the seller will pay you the daily rate you want, then that's fine. However, just so you know, the seller could close on his or her new place a few days ahead of your closing by using a financial

product known as a "bridge loan." A bridge loan is a short-term loan that allows the seller to borrow enough money to close on his or her new home before the old home is sold. Some sellers get into trouble by buying a new home before they try to sell their original home. If that happens, and they use a bridge loan to fund the new purchase, they could end up paying the equivalent of three mortgages simultaneously: (1) their original home mortgage, (2) the new home mortgage, and (3) their bridge loan.

3. **Change of heart.** Sometimes, after fixing up a house for sale, the seller decides he or she doesn't really want to move after all. Ideally, this change of heart will come before the seller has accepted an offer. But it has been known to happen a day or so before the closing.

Paying the Piper

How much should you charge for each extra day the seller stays in the home? First, calculate exactly how much the home costs per day.

Add up your monthly mortgage (principal and interest), taxes, and insurance premiums, and divide the total by 30. That number is your *average* minimum out-of-pocket cost to own and maintain the home each day. Let's say you have a $100,000 mortgage that costs you $666.67 per month. And let's say your real estate tax bill is $3,000 per year, or $250 per month, and your insurance premium is $35 per month. Your calculation would be:

$$\$666.67 + \$250 + \$35 = \$951.67 \text{ (monthly cost of the home)}$$

$$\$951.67 \div 30 = \$31.72 \text{ (daily cost of the home)}$$

It would cost you $31.72 per day for PITI (principal, interest, taxes, and insurance), which is generally the most expensive part of homeownership. If you think that $31.72 is too cheap as a daily fee and will not encourage the seller to have a short after-closing stay, increase the daily fee by as much as you think is necessary. A few dollars more per day for electricity, heat, gas, water, sewer, and garbage pickup wouldn't be out of line. Also, if there are any assessments (for condos, co-ops, and town houses), those fees should also be included. A fee of $50 or $75 per day starts to add up pretty quickly.

295

If the seller is staying on in the house, the daily fee and the length of the after-closing stay should be negotiated before the closing. Include a stiff daily penalty for each day the seller stays in the house past the agreed-on deadline for departure. You, or your attorney, should make it completely clear to the seller and his or her attorney that the seller will not receive all the proceeds from the closing until he or she has moved out of the house and you've had a chance to walk through the house and to verify that the house is still in good condition and that the appliances and plumbing are still in working order. Make sure this special "move out" escrow is set to go before the closing.

When to Hold Back Money at the Closing

How much money should be held back at the closing? It's a good idea to retain enough cash to cover the payment due for the after-closing stay, plus at least another 10 days' worth. *Usually, this amount is equal to 2 to 3 percent of the purchase price of the home*, although it may be subject to local custom. If you give the seller all the money at the closing and the seller stays on in the house, you may have to sue to collect your daily fee from the seller. The money should be given to your real estate broker, the title company, or an unassociated third party, and held in an escrow account.

QUESTION 89

WHAT EXACTLY IS THE CLOSING? WHERE IS IT HELD?

By now you've probably heard about "The Closing," which is also called "The Settlement," depending on where you live in the country. (For purposes of this book, I refer to the closing, but if you're hearing "settlement," rest assured that the two terms mean the same thing.)

Real estate industry professionals talk about The Closing as if it were (1) a hit show on Broadway, or (2) a huge black hole in outer space, capable of sucking buyers, sellers, brokers, lawyers, inspectors, money, and mortgages into a netherworld blender, out of which finally pops a deed that has the buyer's name on it. Those are the two extremes. After it's over, you and your broker will describe your closing as either a dream or a nightmare. Rarely have I heard closings described as being somewhere in the middle.

Let's start at the top. Why do we have the closing? One attorney put it this way: If you were the seller, would you take the buyer's personal check, fold it up, put it in your pocket, and then hand the buyer the deed to your house? Of course not. You would want some security that the check was really going to clear. Conversely, you, the buyer, want some reassurance that the deed you're being given is actually the seller's to give. Your lender, worried that you will take bad title to the home, which could mean trouble down the pike for your home loan, also wants that same reassurance. The broker wants some security that he or she will actually get paid the commission. The attorney wants to know his or her fee will be paid.

Everyone wants to be protected. From that motivation, today's closing or settlement evolved. "Closing a transaction" has always described the point in time when the deal is completed. One party has paid another for certain rights, privileges, property, or goods and services. When the passing of money or other consideration has occurred, and the goods and services have been received, a deal is deemed closed—kaput, finished.

Around the country, closings are generally held at the office of the title company, which issues title insurance for the buyer and the lender. The title company researches the chain of title to the home. Your attorney reviews the information furnished by the title company to make sure you will get "good" title to the home when you close. Once the title issues have been resolved (that is, if they need to be resolved), the title company will insure the title in your name—with any exception shown on the policy—in the amount of the purchase price. But remember, lender's title insurance covers the *lender's* losses on the property, if some outside claim to the title is eventually upheld. If you want to protect *your* interests, you will have to purchase a separate title policy that insures against your losses.

A title or escrow company facilitates the closing by providing a forum for the exchange of documents and the releasing of funds. Generally, the title company acts as an agent for the lender; it works to protect the lender's best interest. The seller usually selects which title company will be used, because he or she generally pays for title insurance. (Who actually will pay for the title insurance policy is dictated by local custom.) If the title company can act as agent for the lender, and close the transaction, the closing will take place at the offices of the title company. Otherwise, the closing may take place at the office of the lender, or another location acceptable to the lender.

In several states, including California and New York, it's more common to have what's known as an escrow closing. In this case, the title company acts for the benefit of both parties, using a document called an "escrow agreement." The title company will only disburse money after certain steps take place. For example, in an escrow closing, the title company will send someone to the recorder's office (where deeds are recorded). Once the transfer of title has been accomplished, the title company will allow the closing to take place. If there are any problems along the way, the title company returns the closing funds to the buyer and seller, and records a deed from the buyer back to the seller.

20/20

hindsight

In states that have escrow closings, typically no one attends the type of "closing" that is familiar to folks in the northern and eastern parts of the country. With an escrow closing, don't expect to go to one place and sign a lot of documents. Instead, you provide the escrow company with your money, paperwork, and set of instructions, as does the other side. After the instructions from both parties are carried out, monies are collected, checks are cut, and monies are disbursed, the deal is considered closed. It may happen when you expect it, or it may take some extra time.

The Closing

From the buyer's perspective, the closing generally consists of three activities:

1. Review and signing of loan documents. In the first phase of the closing, you, the buyer, must review and sign all the loan documents provided by the lender. There may be seven to 20 documents, or more, including the actual mortgage, note, affidavits, Truth-in-Lending statements, estimate of closing costs, and the escrow statement letter, which outlines how much will be paid into the real estate tax and insurance escrows.

2. Exchange of documents among the buyer, the seller, and the title (or escrow) company. The second phase of the closing focuses on the relationship among you (the buyer), the seller, and the title company. There is an exchange of documents that must be signed by you and the seller, and of other documents that require the additional signature of the title company's representative. Depending on your local customs (and the home you buy), the seller will provide certain documents for your inspection and your verification that they are correct:

- The deed.
- The bill of sale.
- An affidavit of title.
- Any documentation that may have been required in the contract, including paid water bills, certificates of compliance with laws pertaining to smoke-detection equipment, lead paint, or termite or radon inspection (these items will vary from state to state, and even from county to county).
- Condo assessment full-payment certificate.
- Co-op assessment full-payment certificate.
- Insurance certificate.
- Property survey (except for condos and co-ops).

You may have anywhere from a handful of documents to a dozen or more that will require both your signature (and your spouse's or partner's) and the seller's signature. After you have finished with these documents, the title company will have more papers for you to sign. These documents generally relate to the title, or are forms that the title company must send to the Internal Revenue Service regarding the purchase and sale of the home. Your documentation may include:

- The RESPA (Real Estate Settlement Procedures Act) "HUD-1" statement, which outlines who provides the money and from which sources, and details how the money gets paid out. This document is signed by you, the seller, and the title company.
- Disclosure statements about construction contracts or any agreements entered into, within the past three to six months, for

work to be done on the property. This is to ensure that there are no outstanding mechanics' liens that could be placed on the property.

- Disclosure statement about any tenants or other persons who occupy the property, other than the buyer or seller.
- Statements about any other matters that could ultimately affect the title to the property, such as lawsuits.

Many of these documents are signed and notarized. (Each state and county has particular quirks regarding documentation. For example, any document that will be recorded in Hawaii must be typed and signed in black ink only. Otherwise, it will not be accepted. In other parts of the country, the notary stamp must be embossed.) After the documents are notarized, the closing can proceed to the final step: disbursement.

3. Disbursement of funds. When all the documents have been signed, dated, and notarized, the title company can proceed with the disbursement of funds. It will take the money from you, the buyer, and cut checks to the seller, the seller's lender (if applicable), the brokers, the title company, and the attorneys. Because everyone usually gets paid out of the closing proceeds, it's easy to see why the title company doesn't accept personal checks, even for a few pennies. Title companies accept only cashier's or certified checks, or a wire transfer, because they are equivalent to cash.

And If No Lender Is Involved?

Good question. Almost all first-time buyers will have some sort of financing involved with their purchase, simply because it's expensive to buy a home (even a home that costs $30,000), and most first-time buyers don't have that kind of cash stuffed inside their mattresses. If there's no lender, or if the seller is acting as the lender, through seller financing, the buyer and seller can sit down together and exchange and sign documents. Or, they can have the title company act as an intermediary in an escrow closing. The closing may take less time (most closings that involve financing generally take between 30 minutes and two hours) and will certainly have fewer steps overall.

In my answers to the next few questions, I'll dissect some of the more complicated pieces of the closing, and explain in more detail why they're important.

WHAT ARE MY CLOSING COSTS LIKELY TO BE?

As I explained in Questions 63 and 64, lenders charge certain fees for giving you a mortgage. Every lender won't demand every fee, but the charges can quickly add up. In addition to the lender's fees, the other closing costs that need to be added up include: title fees, recording fees, city and state transfer taxes, and so on. The lion's share of the buyer's closing costs is generated by the mortgage. The lender's points (a point equals 1 percent of the loan amount), which may also be referred to as the service charge, the discount points, or the origination fee, are the largest fees paid to the lender. They usually run between 1 and 3 percent of the loan amount. Occasionally, the points will run more than 3 percent, and there are some loans available with zero points.

(Remember that for every extra point you pay up front, the lender will decrease the interest rate of the loan. If you have the cash and are planning to stay in the home for a long time, you might want to pay three points, to get the lowest interest rate possible. The points are fully deductible on your income tax return in the year you buy your home. On the other hand, if you're strapped for cash today, but you know that, down the line, your prospects for a higher income are good, you may want to go with zero points and a slightly higher interest rate, and then refinance down the line.)

If you've been reading this book start to finish, you know that when it comes to calculating closing costs, your lender is supposed to make it easier for you by giving you a written *good faith estimate* of all closing costs. This estimate is supposed to accurately reflect the buyer's closing costs. "But a lot of times, people are surprised when they actually get to the closing," says Neil, a real estate attorney. "The Truth-in-Lending law is supposed to take the surprise away, but it doesn't require that the lender explain what the costs are used for and where they are going." If the loan officer taking your application doesn't do a good job of explaining what happens at the closing and what the charges are going to be, you might not feel so good when the big day arrives.

Closing Costs

Here's a list of your closing cost responsibilities. Remember, not every charge will apply to your loan, and your actual fee may be higher or lower, depending on your specific situation. Ask your real estate attorney or broker to walk you through this list and identify how much each item might cost. On page 303 is a worksheet that you can fill in when you get your own finalized closing costs.

1. **Lender's points, loan origination, or loan service fees**— usually 0 to 3 percent of the loan, or more.
2. **Loan application fee**—$0 to $500.
3. **Lender's credit report**—$25 to $75.
4. **Lender's processing fee**—$75 to $250.
5. **Lender's document preparation fee**—$50 to $250.
6. **Lender's appraisal fee**—$225 to $400 (less if your lender uses an electronic appraisal).
7. **Prepaid interest on the loan**—paid per day until the end of the month in which the closing occurs.
8. **Lender's insurance escrow**—about 15 to 20 percent of the cost of the homeowner's insurance policy for one year.
9. **Lender's tax escrow**—about 33 to 50 percent of annual property taxes, depending on the time of year you close. (This is paid just at the closing. After the closing, you will begin to make regular real estate tax and insurance escrow payments as part of your monthly mortgage payment.)
10. **Lender's tax escrow service fee, a fee to set up the tax escrow**—$40 to $95.
11. **Title insurance cost for lender's policy**—$150 to $350, based on the dollar amount of the home you buy. The cost to the buyer for title insurance may be relatively small because the seller may have paid a basic fee to the title company, and the lender's policy is issued simultaneously. In many parts of the country, it is the seller's responsibility to ensure that the home is owned free and clear, so the seller picks up most of the cost of title insurance. When you refinance, you'll find that the cost for title insurance goes up substantially. If you purchase a $100,000 house, your title insurance cost might be

WORKSHEET
Closing Costs

Name _____

Property Address _____

Closing Date _____

1. Lender's points, loan origination, or loan service fees _____
2. Loan application fee _____
3. Lender's credit report _____
4. Lender's processing fee _____
5. Lender's document preparation fee _____
6. Lender's appraisal fee _____
   a. Second appraisal (if required) _____
7. Prepaid interest on the loan _____
8. Lender's insurance escrow _____
9. Lender's tax escrow _____
10. Lender's tax escrow service fee _____
11. Title insurance cost for lender's policy _____
12. Special endorsements to the title _____
13. House inspection fee(s) (unpaid) _____
   a. House reinspection fee (if needed) _____
14. Title/escrow company closing fee _____
   a. Special endorsements to the title _____
15. Recording fees, of deed or mortgage _____
16. Local city, town, or village property transfer tax _____
   a. County transfer tax _____
   b. State transfer tax _____
17. Flood certification fee _____
18. Your attorney's fee _____
   a. Lender's attorney's fee (if any) _____
   b. Other fee _____ _____
   c. Other fee _____ _____
   d. Other fee _____ _____
   e. Other fee _____ _____

Total Closing Costs _____

a flat $150. If you refinance that house, your title insurance may skyrocket to $415. That reflects the additional $265 that the seller paid to ensure that you received good title to his or her home.

12. **Special endorsements to the title**—$25 to $100 each. Depending on the type of property you pick, your lender may request that special endorsements be added to the title. If the lender requires an environmental lien endorsement, it may cost $25. A location endorsement proves the house is located where the documents say it is. If you choose an adjustable-rate mortgage, that may be another $70 endorsement, depending on the title company. If the property is a condominium, there may be a condo endorsement. For a town house, there may be a planned-unit development (PUD) endorsement. As you can see, three or four extra endorsements can really add to your closing cost tab.

13. **House inspection fees (unpaid)**—$250 to $400.

14. **Title/escrow company closing fee**—$200 to $500.

15. **Recording fees, for the deed or the mortgage**—$25 to $75.

16. **Local city, town, or village property transfer tax; county transfer tax; state transfer tax.** The charges that you, the buyer, will pay vary from city to city, and state to state. In Illinois, for example, the seller picks up the county tax ($.50 per $1,000 of sales price) and the state tax ($1.00 per $1,000 of sales price). In Chicago, the buyer picks up the city transfer tax (a hefty $3.75 per $500 of sales price). There may be other special taxes on high-end property. And certain kinds of property, such as co-ops, may, under certain circumstances, be exempt from property transfer taxes. In general, property transfer taxes can range from nothing to $5.00 per $1,000 of sales price, or you may be assessed a flat fee of $25 or $50 per transaction.

17. **Flood certification fee**—$10 to $50. A fee you'll pay to determine whether the home you're buying is in a flood plain.

18. **Your attorney's fee**—if you need an attorney, fees generally start at $250. Although some attorneys in large firms charge an hourly rate, there are loads of real estate attorneys who do house closings for a flat fee, and then may charge a small amount extra, depending on whether your deal turns out to be particularly complicated or difficult. NOTE: If you live in

an escrow closing state, like California, you won't be paying an attorney's fee because you won't be using an attorney. But you will be paying higher escrow closing fee.

18. **Condo move-in fee**—a building charge that can run from nothing to more than $400.

19. **Association transfer fees**—often required for condominium and town house buyers. This fee can range from nothing to more than $200.

20. **Co-op apartment fees**—sometimes, small fees are required by co-op associations for transferring shares of stock (remember, with a co-op, you're not buying an apartment; you're buying shares in a corporation that owns the building in which your apartment is located), or doing name searches. These fees can range from $50 to more than $200 or a percentage of the sales price.

21. **Credit checks by the board of a condo or co-op building.**

(Just so you don't think the seller gets off scot-free, he or she will also pay a long list of closing costs, including: survey, $150 to $300 (in some areas of the country, the buyer may pay this fee, too); title insurance, $150 to $500 plus; recording release charges for the mortgage, $23 to $45; broker's commission, usually 5 to 7 percent of the sales price; state, county, and city transfer taxes; paid utility bills, including water, sewer, or electricity, $10 to $25; credit to the buyer of unpaid real estate taxes for the prior year or current year, depending on the way your state collects property taxes; attorney's fee, $250 and up; and FHA fees and costs, depending on the loan amount.)

Due to a change in the federal tax regulations, when you sell your home, your gains will be subject to capital gains tax only if they exceed $250,000 (if you're single) or $500,000 (if you're married). If your profit exceeds these limits, you may pay taxes at the long-term capital gains rate. And you no longer need tell the IRS about the sale of your home unless it exceeds these levels. Any tax that you owe on the sale of your home would be due on April 15 of the year *following* the year in which you sold your home.

Use the closing costs worksheet on page 303 to figure out exactly how much you'll be paying in closing costs.

QUESTION
91

WHAT IS A TITLE SEARCH? WHAT IS TITLE INSURANCE? WHY DO I NEED THEM?

How do you prove you own something? Generally, you have a bill of sale, or the certificate of title to the item—let's say it's a car—that's registered in your name with the appropriate state agency. If anyone inquires about who owns that cherry red Ford Mustang, the state can tell them it's you. Proving that a seller owns a particular home, however, is a little more difficult. Lenders will not allow you to purchase a home without proof that it actually belongs to the person who is selling it. How do you prove the seller owns the home you want to buy? You conduct a title search.

During a title search, the examiner looks at the chain of title of a home, working backward from owner to owner until it reveals the date when the land was granted or sold by the government to the original owners or developers. If the title has been recorded correctly, you should be able to trace the lineage of a piece of land all the way back to when that area of the country was settled. (As with many of our laws, we derive our methods of recording title from the English system, in which some records of property ownership stretch back a thousand years or more.)

How the title search is carried out varies from county to county, and depends on what kinds of records have been kept. Public records that may affect a property's title include records of deaths, divorces, court judgments, liens, taxes, and wills. Public records in a wide variety of county and city offices must be examined, including those in the recorders of deeds, county courts, tax assessors, and surveyors. While many local governments are in the process of computerizing their records, some title searches are performed manually. Someone may spend hours poring over different documents in various offices. If the municipality in which you are buying is computerized, title searches can be done in a matter of minutes.

Title searches are conducted by lawyers, title companies, or title specialists, to discover whether there are any problems—called "clouds" in the industry—with the title. The lender wants to know if any liens (claims made against a property, by a person or tax assessor, for payment of a debt) or judgments (by a court of law) or easements (known or unknown rights) have been filed against the property, and whether they might prevent the buyer from receiving good title.

Roberta and Dave's Story

Roberta and Dave bought a house in a suburb of Chicago. They had the land surveyed, but when they moved into the house, they discovered that, years earlier, a neighbor had built a garage, and it occupied about 10 feet of the back end of their property. The survey should have noted that the garage encroached on their property. The title Roberta and Dave received to the land wasn't "good" title because the encroachment creates a defect on their title. In other words, someone was making use of their land without their permission. If Roberta and Dave had bought title insurance, their insurer (if it failed to catch the encroachment) would have reimbursed them for the portion of land that they paid for but to which they didn't receive good title.

You Need Title Insurance

If your insurer notes an encroachment, you, the buyer, are considered to have been notified of the defect and must approach the seller about it before the closing. A title search looks for any clouds on the title to the home. Title insurance protects you and the lender against any mistakes or errors or omissions made by the individual performing the search. If you buy a home and a long-lost relative turns up later with irrefutable evidence (say, a recorded deed from the property's original owner) that she actually owns the home, you'll have to turn over the home to the long-lost relative. A title search should turn up this kind of information, but whoever conducts the search may miss an important piece of evidence. The lender then finds that it has lent you money to purchase a property from someone who didn't really own it. Title insurance protects you, the buyer, from any losses associated with the cost of any errors made. It also protects the lender's interest.

Title insurance is paid as a onetime premium; the cost is based entirely on the sales price of the home. In many communities, the seller pays for the cost of the title search because he or she wants to guarantee that you, the buyer, will receive good title to the home. The lender will insist that you pay for, or obtain from the seller, title insurance that covers the lender. The lender may not insist that you get an owner's policy, which will compensate you if there is an error (the title insurance protects the lender against errors), but it's a good idea. If you purchase the owner's policy from the same source that provides title insurance for the lender, you may be able to get a discounted rate. In addition, ask your real estate attorney if he or she works regularly with a title company. Attorneys can sometimes flex an economic muscle (they may do a lot of house closings, and the title company may be eager to encourage their business) to get you a discounted rate. Finally, if the seller has owned the home for only a short period of time—say, a few years—you may be able to get a discounted policy by checking with the seller's original title company. They may be able to give you a "reissue" rate, at a significantly lower premium.

QUESTION 92

WHAT IS RESPA? WHAT DOES THE RESPA STATEMENT LOOK LIKE?

In 1974, Congress decided Americans were suffering from abuses in the title industry. Title companies were giving kickbacks to real estate agents and brokers who referred buyers to settlement agencies. Mortgage lenders were paying fees to real estate agents who steered business to them. And the consumer was being bartered like pork bellies.

Congress decided buyers should be free to choose their own title company or settlement agency, and should have more power in the entire transaction. The Real Estate Settlement Procedures Act (RESPA) was passed to address these issues.

Section 8 in the RESPA code is the kickback provision, according to the Mortgage Bankers Association of America (MBA). It makes it a crime to pay or receive any money, or give or receive anything of value, to another person for the referral of any real estate settlement services, which includes making a mortgage loan. (Your broker cannot legally receive money for referring you to Jones Mortgage Company down the street.)

Sections 4 and 5 of the RESPA code deal with disclosure. Mortgage companies must tell you, before you take their mortgage, how many loans they resell on the secondary market. They are also required to tell you when they are actually selling your mortgage. Finally, the company that buys your mortgage must disclose all sorts of information, including a telephone number and the name of a person you can contact if there is trouble with your loan. (These disclosures form the basis of the stack of documents you must sign, sometimes in quadruplicate, before you can close on the property.)

RESPA, which is regulated by the Department of Housing and Urban Development (HUD), also requires that lenders give their prospective borrowers a copy of a HUD information booklet within three days of receiving the loan application. Lenders must also, within three days, give the good faith estimate (GFE) of what the buyer's closing costs will be. There's another disclosure that mortgage companies are required to make: the HUD-1 settlement statement, which outlines exactly what monies come in and how they are distributed. This is a closing document that you will have to sign. It is filled out by the title company after all the numbers have been called in.

The HUD-1 statement is instructive for both buyers and sellers because it shows exactly where the money comes from and where it is going. The buyer's and seller's costs are itemized side by side. It also neatly wraps up a lot of the issues we've been talking about. (See Appendix III for a complete form.)

The first line of the "Summary of Borrower's Transaction" indicates the contract sales price. The settlement charges, or closing costs, are on the next line. On the middle of the page, there is a line for the deposit, or earnest money, and another line for the principal amount of the new loan. Your application fee will also be listed. Finally, any extra city, county, and (perhaps) real estate taxes will be listed. Everything is totaled up at the bottom, where you'll see the amount of cash you'll need to close the deal.

On the seller's side, we see the contract sales price at the top. Then comes his or her settlement charges, or closing costs. Another line details the payoff of the seller's first mortgage loan (including who holds that loan). The earnest money is listed next (it has been paid to the seller, sometimes with interest), and the title indemnity charge (title insurance). Finally, adjustments for items unpaid by the seller, including any city, county, or real estate property taxes, are recorded. The bottom line indicates how much cash the seller will receive from the deal.

Page two details exactly what settlement charges, or closing costs, the buyer and seller are paying, and to whom. For example, a $225 charge may be paid to Randy Appraisal Company for a home appraisal. You may have paid $45 for a credit report and $300 for a mortgage application. (The problem with finding all of this out at the closing is that it's a little too late to start shopping around for another mortgage company if you find yours has added onerous charges that it didn't disclose on the good faith estimate. "Of course," wonders one first-time buyer, "once you go through all the work and actually get to the closing, who's going to quash the deal for an extra $100 here or there?")

A separate page, which isn't part of the HUD-1 statement but is given out by some title companies, looks at disbursements. Who gets what money. Whose name is on the check. Ten to 15 checks may be written at the closing, for title insurance, for city or county stamp taxes, for inspections, for the real estate broker, for the mortgage insurance premium, for the real estate attorney, for paying off any other mortgages or liens, for the seller, and for others. Usually, within 30 days after the closing, the bank releases the real estate tax and insurance escrow proceeds (if any) to the sellers. They no longer need real estate tax and insurance escrow for a property they've sold.

Some folks feel that RESPA is a waste of time. Others find the disclosures and the HUD-1 statement to be useful to consumers. When you go to the closing, you can decide for yourself.

Keep handy a file that contains a copy of all the information you've given to your lender, plus all of the documentation you've received in return. Note especially the good faith estimate. If you get to the closing, or the day before the closing, and you see that the lender has added all sorts of charges and fees above and beyond those quoted in the good faith estimate, you (or your attorney, if you're in a state that uses attorneys) should have an immediate conversation with the lender about these extra charges, and why they've been added to your account. Feel free to whip out the initial good faith estimate and compare the two statements. The lender shouldn't be more than $25 over the good faith estimate. If the numbers come in over that, there could be a serious problem.

QUESTION 93

DO I NEED HOMEOWNER'S INSURANCE? WHAT SHOULD IT COVER?

If you need a loan to buy your home, you will be required to purchase homeowner's, or hazard, insurance. The reason is simple: Lenders want to know that you're protecting their investment from harm. When you take out a mortgage, you're pledging your home as collateral for the loan. The papers you sign say that if you default on the mortgage, the lender may begin foreclosure proceedings and take over the home. The lender's primary concern is to protect the value of the home. Issues of concern to the lender are damage by fire, water, tornado, or flood, or a tree crashing in through the roof. Let's say you have no insurance, you have a $100,000 loan, and there's a fire. In a few hours, the lender's $100,000 has disappeared in a puff of smoke.

There's almost no way (unless you have seller financing and the seller either foolishly or unwittingly fails to insist on it) that you'll get a mortgage without purchasing enough home or hazard insurance to

The amount of insurance you carry should cover the cost of replacing your home *today*, not when you bought it 10, 20, or even 35 years ago. If you are doing a lease with an option to buy, you should carry renter's insurance that would cover the cost of replacing your personal possessions if they become damaged, stolen, or destroyed in some kind of catastrophe. As part of the option agreement, you should require the owner to carry enough homeowner's insurance to rebuild the house to current building code requirements. This way, you're protected if it were to burn to the ground before you pick up your option. Make sure you see a copy of the policy and a paid premium before you move into the property.

Condos and co-ops have different types of insurance because the property's common elements—a hallway, an interior staircase, the elevators, the roof, a laundry room, or landscaping in common areas—must be covered separately. Typically, co-op or condo associations will hold a building insurance policy that covers the common elements of the property and will satisfy your lender's desire for a "building policy." But don't be confused. This policy does not cover you. You will still need a separate policy that meets your lender's requirements as well as your own.

cover at least the amount of money the lender has given you. (You'll have to bring to the closing a piece of paper that says you've purchased a policy for at least a year, and that it's effective on the day of the closing or earlier.)

Even without the mortgage requirement, you should carry homeowner's insurance. In addition to the mortgage, you have a significant personal investment in your home. On a $100,000 property, you may have put down $10,000 to $20,000 in cash. You may have paid between $3,000 to $5,000 in closing costs. Plus, you may have decorated or renovated the interior of the home, or built an addition. You have personal possessions. What goes up in flames can be worth double or triple what you actually owe the lender.

What Kind of Insurance Is Available?

The insurance industry offers this assortment for homeowners:

Type	Coverage
HO2	Most perils, except floods, earthquakes, war, and nuclear accidents
HO3	All known perils (with a few exclusions)
HO4	Renter's insurance; similar in scope to HO2, but geared toward renters, not homeowners
HO6	Homeowner's insurance for condos and co-ops
HO8	Special insurance for older homes, but rarely used

Choosing the Best Kind of Coverage

In some ways, homeowner's insurance is the easiest type of insurance to purchase. You basically decide (1) what you want to cover and (2) how much you're willing to pay as a deductible amount on any claim. These items will dovetail into a policy that's right for you.

What kind of coverage should you get? Most people purchase a general policy that covers the house and its contents. Condominium and co-op owners need their own unique policies, but they still cover the unit and its contents.

Homeowner's Insurance Perils

According to the Insurance Information Institute, a nonprofit information group for the property/casualty insurance industry, your homeowner's policy should cover the 18 perils contained in the following list (a *peril* is a calamity from which you're trying to protect yourself):

- Fire or lightning.
- Windstorm or hail.
- An explosion.
- An aircraft or car ramming through the wall or ceiling of the home, or damaging walkways, lawns, a pool, or other features of the property.
- Smoke.
- Vandalism and malicious mischief.
- Theft.
- Breakage of glass constituting part of the building, such as windows or skylights.
- Falling objects; damage from weight of snow, sleet, or ice; collapse of building(s).
- Sudden and accidental tearing apart, cracking, burning, or bulging of a steam or hot water heating system or of appliances for heating water.
- Freezing of plumbing, heating, or air-conditioning systems and/or household appliances.
- Sudden and accidental damage from artificially generated currents to electrical appliances, devices, fixtures, and wiring (TV and radio tubes are not included, if you happen to have an old one lying around).

Floods, earthquakes, and mud slides are never covered by a regular homeowner's policy. A "riot of civil commotion" may or may not be covered. If you want coverage, you'll have to purchase a separate policy for each of these risks. A "land disturbance" may or may not be covered. What about a chemical or paint spill? Damage from wild animals? Backed-up sewers and drains? Blood stains? Scorching without fire? What about the additional living expenses you'll have to pay if your home is demolished and must be rebuilt? Be sure to ask.

Comparing Policies

When comparing policies, you'll want to look at the deductible, the property and possessions covered, and what type of coverage you're buying. *Replacement insurance* guarantees that the insurer will pay for the cost of replacing the home as it stands today, up to the amount of your coverage. *Guaranteed cost replacement* coverage promises to rebuild your home no matter what the cost, and it has a rider built in, to take care of inflation. A *cash-value* policy will reimburse you based only on your property's current market value—not what it would cost to build it new. Today, guaranteed cost replacement has been somewhat limited. Insurers might only pay to rebuild your home up to 120 to 125 percent of your policy amount. It's up to you to stay on top of how much it will cost to rebuild your home.

Replacement cost insurance for contents may only reimburse you for the actual, depreciated value of the items. If you paid $2,000 for a sofa 10 years ago, and the insurance company says it's worth only $1,000 today, but it will cost $3,000 to purchase another one just like it, you'll have to cough up the extra cash to buy a new one.

Pay attention to the cost-per-square-foot calculations. Your insurance company might estimate that replacing your home will cost only $60 per square foot. In reality, only the cheapest construction can cost that little. Replacing your home the way it is, with all the tile, hardwood floors, wallpaper, marble, and granite you may have will cost far more. A more realistic estimate is $100 to $175 per square foot, depending on where you live. For a high-end home, expect to pay upward of $200 per square foot.

Other Types of Coverage

Some places call it *code-and-contention* coverage. Others call it *building code* coverage or an *ordinance-and-law* rider. The intent is to cover the cost of meeting new building codes that may have gone into effect after your home was built, and that apply to any new homes. If you lack code coverage, your insurer will probably pay only what it would cost to rebuild your old home in its original condition. Because you can't do that, you'll pay the rest to bring the house up to code. Some companies include code coverage in their basic policies, but if you don't ask, you won't know.

If there have been changes in zoning, you may be out of luck—unless you have zoning coverage. For example, you live in a beach house, and the zoning law was changed to restrict any new development on the beach. If your home burns down, you might find yourself unable to rebuild on your site. That's where zoning insurance kicks in. It ensures that you can rebuild where you want to go. The policy should state that you can build your exact house, no matter what the cost, on a different lot. If that statement is missing, choose another policy.

You should also have a policy that covers the cost of replacing your foundation. (Seems obvious, but some insurance companies don't include it.) A *personal articles rider* is the official name for extra coverage of your expensive jewelry and fine art. Make sure you have current appraisals to support your claim. And, don't forget home office coverage. If you run a business out of your home, you'll need a rider to cover that business.

If you have a home office, you may also need special liability coverage for your home-based business. Check with your insurance agent about adding an umbrella rider to your homeowner's policy, for additional liability coverage.

Pictures speak louder than words. If your home is destroyed, the last thing you'll want to do is try to prove what you owned and when you bought it. Take a video camera and record everything in your home. Make sure you date it with a current newspaper in the screen, and then go around your home, inside and out. Back up the video with close-ups of jewelry, furs, rugs, and fine art. Put the tape, the photos, and any appraisals in a safe deposit box outside your home.

They Want to Know *What?*

When you contact an insurance agent to get a homeowner's insurance policy (or if you do it via the Web), you'll need to provide the insurer with some basic information about your home. Here are some of the questions you'll be asked:

1. What is the complete address of your home (or the home you'll be buying)?

2. What is your home made of? (Homes made of aluminum siding or shingles are typically considered to be made of wood.)

3. Is your home one story? Two stories? Split level? Other?

4. How many rooms are there?

5. What was the listing price of your home? What was the purchase price?

6. How old is your home? When was it built? What kinds of major improvements does it have (like a new roof, or new mechanicals)?

7. What is the square footage of your home? (Multiply the length by the width and then multiply that number by the number of livable stories. Typically, attics, basements, and attached garages don't count.)

8. How far away is the nearest fire department? The nearest fire hydrant?

9. Does the home have security devices, including smoke detectors, alarm systems, security lighting, deadbolt locks, or carbon monoxide detectors?

10. Is your home located on a flood plain?

11. Are there other structures on the property (a garage, guest house, or cabana)?

12. Do you own a dog?

13. Do you have any valuable jewelry, fine art, furs, antiques, or silverware? Do you typically keep large amounts of cash in the house? (You may need special insurance riders to protect these items.)

14. What kind of deductible do you want to pay? (The higher the deductible, the lower your premium.)

15. Do you have a business on the premises? (Typically, a home-owner's insurance policy either does not include a home-based business or offers extremely low coverage. If you have a business based at home, you may want to purchase a home business rider or a rider for your computers and other electronic devices.)

16. How much liability insurance do you want? (Typically, a homeowner's policy includes a certain amount of liability coverage. But in these litigious times, you may prefer increased coverage.)

By knowing the answers to these questions ahead of time, you'll speed up the time it takes to find the best deal.

Discounts and Deductions

Although homeowner's insurance is getting more expensive (a direct result of a recent spate of disasters that cost insurance companies huge losses), there are ways to cut down on your costs. If you move or refinance, you might be tempted to poke around and see what else is out there. If you've got a good record, you should find plenty of options. You might even cut your premium by up to 35 to 50 percent. Here are some ideas:

1. **Shop around.** Once you have insurance, you'll be tempted to stay the course unless something happens, but you may be able to lower your premiums simply by shopping around. If you can't lower them, at least you'll feel good knowing you got the best deal. Direct writers of homeowner's insurance include American Express (800-535-2001), Amica (800-242-6422), GEICO (for auto, home, or boat insurance, 800-841-3000) and USAA (800-531-8100). They do their selling over the phone. If you qualify, you'll save, big time, on the commissions. Even with a great policy, you might be able to drop your premium further with one of the ideas given here.

2. **Raise your deductible.** Some insurance companies will drop you if you make more than two claims in a year. Make sure your insurance covers you for catastrophes, and plan on picking

up the cost of the everyday expenses. Raising your deductible from $250 to $500 might enable you to shave 12 percent off your premiums. Raise your deductible to $1,000 and your savings may double.

3. **Tout your improvements.** If you've put on a new roof, and it's made of a flame-repellent material, you might have earned yourself a discount. A new plumbing system, new wiring, or a new heating system might also qualify.

4. **Get connected.** A home security system might qualify for a small discount of 3 to 5 percent. But connect it to the local police and fire station, and you might lower your premium by up to 15 percent annually. If you put in a sprinkler system or smoke detectors, you might get smaller discounts.

5. **Grow old.** If you're over the age of 55, you can probably get a discount.

6. **Educate yourself.** Your insurance company may offer an education program or brochures that will allow you to lower your premium once you've attended or read the material.

7. **Buy your home and auto policies from the same insurer.** Some companies that sell homeowner's, auto, and liability coverage will take 5 to 15 percent off your premium if you buy two or more policies from them.*

8. **Insure your home, not the land it sits on.** If a tree falls in your backyard, chances are it won't hurt anything except the grass. Don't include the value of your land when you're figuring out how much homeowner's insurance you need.

9. **Stop smoking.** The Insurance Information Institute says smoking accounts for more than 23,000 residential fires a year. Quit. Not only will you save on your homeowner's insurance, but you'll probably save a bundle on health insurance (and health-related costs, not to mention the cost of the tobacco products you won't have to buy during your lifetime).

10. **Is group coverage an option?** Professional, nonprofit, and alumni organizations often offer discounts for association members.

---

*Some states don't allow discounts on premiums. Why? Most likely it's because the state insurance lobby is strong, and deductions lower the insurers' profits. Ah, politics.

11. **Stick around.** If you've kept your coverage with the same insurer for years, you should ask for special consideration. Some companies will give discounts of up to 6 percent if you've been a policyholder for six years or more.

12. **Look around.** Your home is an appreciating asset. Some items in your home are depreciating as the years go by. If you're carrying special riders for certain items, you may be able to reduce your coverage if they've lost their original value. If you've sold items covered by riders, instruct your insurance company to remove the rider from your policy.

13. **If all else fails, move.** According to a study by the nonprofit Insurance Research Council, it costs insurers 42 percent more to cover losses in a city than it does to settle claims for those who live five miles outside the city limits. City dwellers may be paying double the amount that nearby suburbanites pay for their insurance. But before you put your home up for sale, consider this: The 6 percent sales commission you would have to pay to sell your home more than makes up the difference in city-vs.-suburb insurance premiums for a long, long time.

resources

The Insurance Information Institute publishes a small book called *How to Get Your Money's Worth in Auto and Home Insurance*, which describes the process of buying the proper insurance coverage.

Floods and Earthquakes

If you live in a flood plain (check with the local municipality for flood plain information), your lender will require you to have flood insurance. You can only buy flood insurance from the federal government, although most agents sell the policies. The average annual cost is about $300 for $100,000 worth of coverage, and the maximum limits as we go to press are $250,000 for the structure of your home and $100,000 for the contents. Finished basements are not covered by federal flood insurance policies, except for basics like the washer, dryer, furnace, and air-conditioning units. You'll take the loss on any carpeting and wood paneling, not to mention items you may have stored, down there. The cost of your policy depends on the value of your home, construction costs, and where your home is located. If it's close to a shoreline, you'll pay a lot more money for your policy.

Frankly, flood insurance is about the cheapest kind of insurance you can purchase, and it's well worth the few hundred bucks you'll spend. Your regular homeowner's insurance won't cover anything if you get flooded because of a rising body of water, and that includes an 18-inch rainstorm. (If your basement floods because your sump pump failed, your regular insurance company will probably pay. Ask your insurance agent, to be sure.) Only 20 percent of folks who live in a flood plain have flood insurance.

For details and referrals to agents, call the Federal Emergency Management Agency (FEMA) at 800-427-4661, or check out its web site at fema.gov.

Earthquakes

Earthquake insurance, unlike flood insurance, is offered through private insurers—typically, as added coverage (called an *endorsement*). But the recent spate of earthquakes has made this insurance very difficult to buy and relatively expensive. This helps to explain why only about 10 percent of homeowners living in earthquake areas have earthquake insurance. You can purchase earthquake insurance through your insurance agent, but it is not available everywhere (by law, insurers in California must offer earthquake insurance). The cost depends on where you live (whether you are close to a fault line), what type of home you have, and whether the structure incorporates modern anti-earthquake technology. In some areas that are highly seismic (except California), earthquake coverage may not be available at any price.

Some Final Thoughts

When you put together your final homeowner's policy, don't forget these items:

- **College may not be covered.** Some policies cover your kid's stuff when he or she is away at school. Some don't. Be sure to ask.

For a few extra dollars, you can get a rider that will fully cover Junior, plus all the hotshot computer equipment he's bringing with him, against things that happen in a college environment.

- **Make sure your stuff is fully insured.** Most policies will reimburse you up to half the face value of your policy. If you have a $300,000 homeowners' policy, most insurers will pay up to $150,000 for you to replace your personal belongings. If that's not enough, investigate additional coverage to fill the gap.

- **Under the umbrella.** The general liability portion of a regular homeowner's policy is pretty small. Consider getting additional coverage that will give you an overriding umbrella liability policy—just in case.

- **Don't make this mistake.** As the years go on, make sure you continue to update your policy to reflect the true cost of rebuilding your home. For a regular house that doesn't include perks like granite countertops in the kitchen, and limestone bathroom tile, you should expect to spend $100 to $125 per square foot to rebuild and refurnish your home. If you buy a 2,500-square-foot house today, and it burns to the ground tomorrow, the cost to rebuild your home to current building standards could range from $250,000 to over $300,000—even if you paid less than that to purchase it. If your home does have the granite countertops, four or five bathrooms, or a fancy kitchen, you can expect to pay $150 to $200 per square foot, or $275,000 to $500,000. Will it always be this much? If you live in a small town, or in a condominium or co-op, you may pay less. In an expensive city, you can expect to pay more. And as the years go on, the price will move only in one direction.

HOW SHOULD I HOLD TITLE TO MY NEW HOME?

When Janet and Scott recently bought a house in a suburb north of Chicago, they wondered how they should hold title. Scott, a pediatrician just starting his own practice, was well aware of the litigious nature of society. Industry statistics tell him that he is likely to be targeted in a medical malpractice suit over the course of his career as a doctor. Scott was worried that if someone sued him and won, the settlement could take away his and Janet's home.

Other homeowners have the same concerns. Whatever business you're in, there may come a time when your home may be in jeopardy.

If you declare bankruptcy, your creditors may be able to attach a lien against your house, possibly even forcing you to sell it. There may be a judgment against you. *The time to think about how to protect your home, your largest investment to date, is now, before you buy it.*

How you *hold title*—the ownership of your real estate—is important. Too often, the way in which title is held is an afterthought. Many buyers aren't even asked what their preference is.

If you're married, you often get joint tenancy with rights of survivorship. If you're single, you hold property in your own name.

But there are other ways of holding title that might help you in certain situations.

For example, should something go wrong and one spouse or partner gets sued professionally, the recorded ownership of your home can mean the difference between the house's being sold to pay off a judgment, and your being allowed to live there until you choose to sell.

Your ownership of your home and other assets can have important estate considerations as well.

When title to a property is at issue, all things aren't equal for married spouses and those partners who are unmarried. In many situations, partners who are unmarried will need to consult with an estate planner or real estate attorney, to make sure their interests and those of their partner are protected under state law.

Here are some of the ways you may hold title to your home, and the effect each one may have on your estate.

Individuals

If you're a single person, your options for holding title to your home are rather limited. You may hold title to your property as an individual, or you may hold it in one of a variety of trusts.

If you hold the property in your own name and a creditor comes after you, the creditor may be able to force the sale of your home to pay off your debt. If you die while holding property in your own name, even if you name your heir in your will, your will (and the property you own) will go through probate and be subject to probate fees.

If you're an individual, the best way to avoid probate is to put your property in a trust. You might also ask your tax or estate attorney if a corporation or limited liability company might be a good choice.

Joint Tenancy

Joint tenancy with rights of survivorship is the most common way married couples hold property, but two nonrelated individuals may also own a piece of property as joint tenants.

The nice thing about joint tenancy is that it allows you and the co-owner to each own the property as a whole. If you own property as joint tenants with rights of survivorship, your share in the property is immediately transferred to your surviving spouse or partner upon your death. Your share is subject, however, to any debts, claims, and expenses you've left behind.

You should also consider the estate planning issues attached to how your surviving partner will inherit your half of the property. Depending on state law, your spouse would inherit your half (married couples are usually assumed to own property equally) at a stepped-up basis. Your half of the property would be revalued as of the date you die, and your spouse would inherit it at its current value.

If you and your surviving partner are not married, the property would be divided based on how much each partner contributed to the purchase of the property. For example, if you each contributed 50 percent of the cost, then your surviving partner would inherit your half of the property and get the stepped-up basis.

If you can't prove how much each of you contributed, state law may attribute total ownership to the partner who dies first. That mandate may have serious estate implications. Consult an estate or tax attorney for details and advice.

The key words to look for when you're considering joint tenancy are "with rights of survivorship."

Tenancy in Common

Tenancy in common allows each person to own his or her piece of the same property separately.

For example, you may own 40 percent, your spouse or partner may own 40 percent, and your parents may own 20 percent, but each co-owner may use and enjoy the whole property. You can't be restricted to using just the 40 percent of the property that you own (if that area can even be defined). And, you may sell your share of the property to anyone you choose. The sale would be similar to selling stock in a corporation.

Tenancy in common is available to married couples or to two or more individuals, but it's not usually used for property purchased by married couples. When you die, your share of the property goes through probate before it is distributed according to your will.

Tenancy by the Entirety

Tenancy by the entirety is similar to joint tenancy in that it has rights of survivorship. However, it is available only to married couples.

The key difference between tenancy by the entirety and joint tenancy is this: If you own property as tenants by the entirety, both spouses must agree before the property becomes subject to one spouse's creditors.

Neither spouse can do anything that would create a claim or lien on the marital property. And, as long as the couple is married, and owns the property, tenancy by the entirety protects the interest of each spouse in the marital home.

For example, if your spouse gets sued, the creditors could not force the sale of the residence, because you and your spouse each own the whole property. The creditors can only prevail if the marriage is severed, or the other spouse consents to the claim, or the property is sold and a claim can be attached to the proceeds.

Tenancy by the entirety is not available in every state. Again, it is only for married couples.

Think About a Trust

The only way you can avoid probate (other than holding it as joint tenants with rights of survivorship) is to put your property into a trust. Here are some alternative ways to hold title that may also affect important estate planning issues.

Land Trust

A land trust is a legal creation. The sole asset in the trust is the property you are buying, and you are the beneficiary of the trust.

At one time, a land trust might have been used to obscure the identity of the beneficiary. Today, that veil has largely been lifted. Individuals, two or more buyers, married couples, and children may be the beneficiaries of a land trust.

There are no estate tax advantages to a land trust, and the trust is available in only a few states, but if there is a successor beneficiary, the property will pass directly to that individual, avoiding probate.

Qualified Personal Residence Trust (QPRT)

This is another type of trust that allows you to discount the future value of your home and possibly save on the gift and estate taxes you'd otherwise owe.

Here's how it works. You set the term of the trust, and place your home into it. You're allowed to live in the home for the term of the trust. The beneficiaries of the trust (your heirs) will receive the home when the term of the trust expires.

If you put your house in a QPRT for five years, your beneficiaries will own your house at the end of the five years. If you're still living and you want to stay in your home, you'll have to rent it.

The benefit of a QPRT is that the IRS allows you to discount the future value of the house according to a preset schedule. You'll pay gift tax on a much lower amount, which will cost you less than the estate tax.

If, however, you die before the QPRT term expires, the property reverts back to you. You'll be credited for any gift taxes you've paid, but you will have lost the fee you paid to an attorney to set up the QPRT.

If you survive the term, however, a QPRT can be helpful in planning your estate. Typically, you are allowed to set up only two QPRTs, one for your primary residence and a second for a vacation home.

Living Trust

A revocable living trust is another way to pass assets from one generation to another and avoid probate.

You set up a trust, and then transfer assets, such as your home or stocks, into the trust. You may name beneficiaries and leave a list of instructions for the trustee who will administer the trust.

For many people, trusts take the place of wills. Also, living trusts aren't public documents, so the privacy aspect is appealing.

But because you retain complete control of the assets in a living trust, it does nothing to lower the estate taxes you may eventually owe.

Family Limited Partnership

By creating a family limited partnership, parents can pass along pieces of their property to their children (or anyone else) by making them small limited partners of a partnership that owns the property.

Limited partners traditionally don't manage the property or have an active role in it. This limited role (hence the name) allows you to discount their share of ownership, which results in lower estate and gift taxes when the property is transferred.

Another value to a family limited partnership is that it allows individuals to give property to their heirs over time, in small amounts, which is less expensive than deeding over small pieces of a particular property.

Unless you own a large ranch, plantation, or other significant residential property, you probably wouldn't use a family limited partnership. Traditionally, they're used to pass down commercial, industrial, or other types of real estate.

Estate Considerations

If you're unsure about the best way to hold title to your property, consult with a real estate attorney, estate planning attorney, or accountant, who can explain the ins and outs of each type of ownership. There may be some very real reasons to go one way or another, and you should be thoroughly informed before you close on your home. One reason might be the amount of total assets you and your spouse or partner own. Although you may want to share title equally with your spouse, if you have joint assets that exceed $1.25 million (going to $2 million in 2006), holding property as joint tenants may not be the economically savvy choice. Tax-wise, or estate-wise, it may be better for you to be sole owner of the property, or to place it into a trust. Emotionally, it may be difficult for you and your spouse to accept an unequal ownership of assets. For detailed explanations, your financial planner can help you work through the various options.

Community Property States

The community property states are: Arizona, California, Idaho, Louisiana, Nevada, New Mexico, Texas, Washington, and Wisconsin. If you live in a community property state, and are married, every asset you purchase during the marriage is assumed to be owned equally between you and your spouse.

Let's say you purchase a house as an investment during the course of your marriage. Only your name is on the deed. When you die, your spouse is assumed to own half of that property. The ownership of the property is divided equally between your spouse and your estate.

Very special issues are involved with community property, especially if you later move to a state that doesn't allow it but still own property in a community property state. Check with your estate attorney or estate planner for details.

11

The Closing

QUESTION 95

WHO SHOULD ATTEND THE CLOSING?
WHAT SHOULD I DO IF I CAN'T BE THERE?

The closing presents for your signature some of the most important legal contracts you'll ever sign. You're promising to pay thousands of dollars in exchange for a place to call home. I'm willing to bet that this will be the largest single investment of your life, which is why it's probably a good idea for you to attend the closing.

(If you live in an escrow state, like California, you may not have a "closing" that matches the description here. You may give a list of instructions to the escrow company, and then go in and sign all of the documents described here. The seller, usually separately, will also go to the escrow company with a list of instructions and sign the necessary documents. When the lists of instructions have been completed, the escrow company will conduct the actual closing and will then call you to come and pick up the keys to the house. Usually, this happens on a preset date, but it could happen at any time within a two- to three-week period.)

For a buyer, a closing is like a command performance. All of the buyers—you, your spouse if you have one, or any partners who are going into the transaction with you—must attend. There are two compelling reasons for you to attend: (1) you have to sign your name a dozen or more times on various documents, and (2) you have to read those documents to make sure everything is in order.

Who else generally attends the closing? If you're in a state where attorneys are involved, your attorney and the seller's attorney will be present. The seller broker and the subagent or buyer broker (who are very interested in making sure that everything goes smoothly up until the final papers are signed and the final checks—including theirs—are cut) will often attend. There will generally be a title officer (if you are closing at a title company) or other closing agent, and there may be a representative from the lender. Sometimes, the lender will bring along an attorney. Whether the sellers attend is up to them. You need to be present to sign documents, but sellers' documents can be signed ahead of time.

Even when you mark your calendar two to three months in advance, there can be a last-minute scheduling conflict with the closing. An important business trip comes up, or someone gets sick, or perhaps a family member passes away and you want to attend the funeral in another state. Whatever comes up, call your attorney and see if you can juggle the closing date. It may be possible, especially if the seller already owns another home, or the seller is taking back financing or moving to an interim home before going to a permanent residence. Moving the closing up or back a few days is the least onerous way to deal with a scheduling conflict.

If you cannot change the date of closing—if, for example, the seller is closing on his or her new property that same day and requires the proceeds from the sale—consider assigning a *power of attorney* to someone who can step into your shoes and sign your name legally at the closing. A power of attorney is a legal right given to someone (usually an attorney) to act on another person's behalf. Usually, it is limited to a single transaction, but an elderly parent or relative may give a power of attorney when he or she is no longer able to manage his or her affairs.

When you are purchasing a home, you're better off giving the power of attorney to someone who is familiar with the transaction. If the only person who knows the details is your attorney, and he or she is willing to accept that designation, then that's who should have it. If a friend or family member is familiar with the transaction, then that person should be designated.

In most cases, it's not smart to give your real estate broker the power of attorney. Many brokers work for and represent the seller, so there's a potential conflict of interest. You wouldn't give power of attorney to the seller, but if you give it to the seller broker, in effect you would be doing just that. If your broker is a buyer broker, then you may want to discuss power of attorney. But remember, no matter who the broker represents, he or she is not a disinterested third party. Most brokers have a significant amount of money riding on the outcome of a closing. If something comes up at the closing (see Question 97), you want the person who holds your power of attorney to look out for your best interests, not his or her own.

Find out ahead of time whether your lender will allow your documents to be signed with a power of attorney. Ask what power-of-attorney form is required. Many lenders will not accept power-of-attorney signatures on their documents. Instead, you'll need to presign your document if, for whatever reason, you can't attend the closing.

QUESTION 96

WHAT ARE PRORATIONS?

Let's say that Ginny makes an offer to purchase Maureen and Mike's home. In the two months leading to the closing, some bills come due that must be paid. Maureen and Mike pay the water bill (which comes every six months), the second installment of real estate taxes (they're due in March and September), and the gas bill (which comes once every two months). On the day of the closing, Maureen and Mike's attorney tells Ginny the dollar amount of her share of these prorated expenses.

Almost every closing has some costs prorated, simply because we don't pay for our housing needs on a daily basis. Can you imagine trucking on down to the county clerk's office to pay your real estate taxes *every day?* What about your electric bills? Water bill? Association dues? Many of these costs are spread out over a long period of time. Depending on where you live, you pay your real estate taxes once or twice a year. It isn't fair for Maureen and Mike to have paid an entire year's worth of property taxes, if they live in the house for only nine months of that year. Likewise, if Ginny bought the home just before the second installment of taxes was due, it wouldn't be fair for her to pay for six months' taxes, when she would have only three months in the home.

A little bit of math evens things out for everyone. How do you calculate prorations? Identify the calendar days covered by the bill, and then divide the bill amount by that number of days. That gives you a daily fee. Then multiply that fee by the number of days up to and including the closing. For example, let's say Maureen and Mike's property taxes are $2,000 for the year. Two installments, of $1,000

330

each, are due on March 15 and September 15. Each $1,000 represents 183 days' payment (it's actually 182.5, but we'll round up):

$$\$1,000 \div 183 = \$5.46 \text{ per day.}$$

If the closing is on September 16, Maureen and Mike have already paid the real estate property taxes for the rest of the calendar year. At the closing, Ginny would have to reimburse them for each day, to the year-end, that she's going to live in the house. From September 17 to the end of the year is 106 days. Multiply 106 by the $5.46 daily fee:

$$106 \text{ days} \times \$5.46 \text{ daily fee} = \$578.76.$$

Ginny would owe Maureen and Mike $578.76 at the closing. The method can work in reverse also. Let's say the closing is on September 14. On September 15, Ginny pays the $1,000 real estate tax bill. It's 76 days from July 1 to September 14. Multiply 76 by the $5.46 daily fee:

$$76 \text{ days} \times \$5.46 \text{ daily fee} = \$414.96.$$

If the closing was on September 14, Maureen and Mike would owe Ginny $414.96 for their share of property taxes.

Asking for a Bit More

In some states, it's common to ask the previous owners to pay a little extra in real estate taxes above the daily fee, because, in many areas, property taxes rise each year and the exact amount for the next bill may not be known. Instead of asking for the daily fee multiplied by the number of days, the buyer may ask the seller to put up 110 percent of the daily fee to cover any increases. In our example, the daily fee of $5.46 would be increased to $6.01 to cover any increase in taxes.

Your real estate attorney (or your broker, if you're in a state where attorneys are not used for house closings) will calculate prorations for every bill that has some sort of shared time arrangement, including gas bills, water bills, assessments to homeowners' associations, and real estate taxes. This also includes any insurance policies (above and beyond hazard insurance required by the lender) or service agreements the buyer will have to pay for. Any bill can be prorated using basic math.

(Generally, telephone service is shut off when an owner vacates a home, and the new owners must start their own account. The local electric company will generally change the name on the service the day of the closing, and will then begin billing the new owners.)

Some attorneys draw up a reproration agreement. If the sellers reimburse the buyer for more than the actual bill, the buyer and seller may agree to recalculate the bill to reflect the actual amount paid. Here's how it works: If you thought the bill was going to be $100 and the seller's share was 25 percent, the seller would have paid you $25. But if the actual bill ends up being only $80, the seller's share is only $20, so you would owe the seller $5 (which is paid after the closing, when the recalculation is done).

Yet Another Escrow Account

Proration money is sometimes kept in escrow (by a disinterested third party), but this usually happens only with substantial amounts of money. The escrow manager then makes payments to the buyer, based on the bills that come in, and will return any extra money to the seller. The important thing with prorations is that the seller must pay all of his or her costs before the closing is complete. Otherwise, you may have to chase the seller to get your fair share.

Local custom dictates who pays for, and who receives the benefit for, the day of the closing. Your attorney, broker, or closing agent should be able to advise you on local custom.

WHAT DO I NEED TO BRING WITH ME TO THE CLOSING? WHAT IF SOMETHING GOES WRONG AT THE CLOSING?

The simple answer, "Bring yourself," won't quite do here. You also need to bring money. I suppose you could bring cash, but a cashier's or certified check is preferred. You must also bring your homeowner's insurance certificate (to prove you have it) and any documents the lender requires (these should have been spelled out in the commitment for the loan).

On the day before the closing, check with your attorney to see how much money you should have the check made out for. It's not a disaster if you bring too much; the title company can cut a check to you for the difference. The problem comes if you have too little. In that case, you may find the closing stretched out as you run all over town trying to convert a personal check into a cashier's check. You may also wire transfer funds but you'll need to get the proper information to know where, and to what account, to wire the money. And bring a favorite pen. You'll be signing your name quite a few times.

Usually, the check you bring to the closing can be made out to your name and endorsed to the title company at the closing.

Don't forget to do your preclosing walk-through with the developer. At this walk-through, you should make a list of all items that need to be fixed, finished, or corrected. This list, also known as the *punch list*, should be signed by the developer, and include the date by which the developer agrees to complete all the items on the list.

When Something Goes Wrong at the Closing

Just when you think you've crossed the finish line, it seems to move farther away. That's how a closing sometimes feels. You solve one problem and another crops up. And another. And another.

When Janet bought her condo, she discovered that the loan amount on the loan document was incorrect. And then she noticed that some of the documentation didn't have her correct address! Leo and Genna's loan agreement also had an incorrect amount. At the last minute, the developer who built Bart and Michelle's town house refused to put $1,500 into escrow to cover the sod and landscaping that was supposed to be part of the deal. One buyer refused to close on a condo for 24 hours because the sellers—who didn't live there anymore—couldn't find their mailbox key.

There are at least ten reasons why a closing won't happen, or will be delayed for a few days, or will be stretched out:

333

1. **Money problems.** Money problems are one of the most frequent reasons home sales may not close on time. For example, if you're transferring money by wire, it's always a possibility that the money will get tied up, or there will be a delay in the processing of the wire transfer. Sometimes, the numbers don't add up and a buyer will find that he or she is short. Lenders and title companies don't take personal checks, so you may have to run across town to get a personal check converted into a certified or cashier's check.

2. **Missing loan package.** If the lender's documents aren't there, you're not closing. If the loan package has to come from out of state, and it's shipped via overnight delivery, it's always possible that the package will be lost or delayed. If documents are missing from the loan package, they may have to be sent by messenger or faxed over to the closing. In addition to the extra time, the lender may try to charge you for the messenger service or even for use of the fax. You should vigorously refuse to pay these charges, particularly if it was the lender who made the mistake.

3. **Disagreement about documents.** Read all of the documents carefully. The loan company may try to slip something in, or may make changes to the documents that you didn't agree to.

4. **Incorrect loan documents.** Nothing can create greater problems than incorrect information on loan documents. Check to be sure that you're actually getting the amount of money you agreed to, and that your address, phone number, and other personal information are all correct. Be certain the interest rate is correct. Bring inconsistencies and wrong information to the attention of the lender. New documents may have to be drawn up, or the lender may try to get by with correction fluid.

5. **Last-minute requests.** Sometimes, the lender will make a last-minute request for documentation at the closing. At Leo and Genna's closing, the lender requested a copy of the canceled deposit check. To safeguard against time-wrenching delays, it's a good idea to bring everything with you to the closing.

6. **Walk-through problems.** If you do the final walk-through (ideally, after the seller has moved out) and find that some items are missing or damaged, it must be brought up at the closing. This is the time to negotiate with the seller (or the

seller's attorney or broker, if the seller is not at the closing) for remuneration. You and the seller should agree to a settlement before you close.

7. **Title problems.** Last-minute title problems may creep up. A long-lost relative turns up, or the title company discovers the real estate taxes haven't been paid. A contractor may have filed a mechanic's lien. Insist that these title issues are resolved before you'll close on the home. You don't want to inherit someone else's problems.

8. **Someone dies.** It doesn't happen too often, but you should know what can happen if either you or the seller dies after the contract is signed and before the closing. If the seller dies after signing the contract, the estate must go through with the sale. However, it may be difficult to close on time, particularly if the seller dies close to the day of the closing, or if the estate is in probate court. If you die, the seller may be able to force your estate to continue with the sale, although, in the real world, sellers may not force the issue. Check with an attorney for further details about your rights in your state.

9. **Catastrophe strikes.** In the days (or should I say, nights) before the closing, nearly every first-time buyer has a nightmare about his or her new home being destroyed before the paperwork is finalized. Fire, flood, earthquake, lightning—you name it. What happens if a fire actually consumes the home you're supposed to purchase tomorrow? In most cases, depending on what the contract says, you wouldn't have to close if something major happened to the home. Or, you can elect to close and take the insurance proceeds (after the seller's lender has been paid off, and if the home is underinsured, that could mean little or nothing for you). If you have already taken possession of the home when disaster strikes, you may lose the right to terminate the purchase and be forced to close. Again, have your attorney advise you of your rights.

10. **Seller's deal falls through.** Usually, sellers take the money from the sale of their home and use it to pay for another home. Your seller is likely to do the same. But if the seller's deal (for any number of reasons) falls through, he or she may have no place to go and might have second thoughts about the closing. In other words, the seller might refuse to vacate the home. If this happens, you have three options: (1) don't close until he

or she moves out; (2) close and force the seller out, which is emotionally, physically, and legally difficult; (3) hold back money from the closing, to ensure that the seller gets out by a certain time, and attach a stiff daily penalty for every day he or she remains in the home. Make that incentive *very* stiff, so that the seller will want to move rather than stay. The daily penalty should be so stiff that it would be cheaper for the seller to put all of his or her belongings in storage and go to a hotel.

Timing the Closing

How long should the closing last? As we discussed earlier, most closings take less than an hour. One attorney estimates that 10 percent of his closings take less than 30 minutes, an additional 50 percent take less than an hour, another 30 percent take less than 90 minutes, and 10 percent take less than two hours. So 90 percent of all closings happen in less than two hours. And the final 10 percent? They could take 10 hours, or 10 days, or never happen at all. But most closings happen. And when yours is over, and the last fire has been put out, you'll own your very own home.

Congratulations!

WHAT SHOULD I GET FROM THE SELLERS AT THE CLOSING?

You've signed your name so often your arm is about to drop off. You've tallied up the numbers, made fast and furious calls to reassure your office that you're still living and breathing, and are wired from cup after cup of stale coffee. The last thing to do is to get the keys to your new home from the seller.

Keys are pretty important, and they require a bit of good faith. After all, when the seller hands you the keys at the closing, you don't know whether they work or not. You won't find out until much later, perhaps even next spring, that the seller forgot to give you the keys (or combination) to the toolshed lock. Or the combination on the bicycle room. Or the key to your storage locker.

At the closing, the seller is supposed to turn over *all* keys to the home: front- and back-door locks, any dead-bolt locks, window locks, interior door locks, shed or storage room locks, or locks on any part of the property. The seller should also give you the combinations you may need to open particular locks. Mailbox keys and garage-door openers are supposed to be included.

If you're purchasing new construction, you may not get your keys at the closing. The developer, or the developer's representative, will give you a letter indicating where your keys can be picked up. Usually, the broker for the development will have the keys.

And If They Don't Work?

Just in case your seller doesn't have any good faith left at the end of the closing, the brokers (if you used one) can be marshaled in to help the situation. If the brokers have participated, it's likely that they have a set of working keys. They should give you those keys to the home, which you can then use to check against the keys the seller has given you. If the seller refuses to turn over the keys, perhaps your first call should be to the local locksmith.

Sam once handled a closing for sellers who had moved out of state several months earlier. The seller broker had the condo keys, and the sellers left their mailbox key with a neighbor. On the day of closing, the buyer refused to close until the mailbox key had been delivered. The sellers, reached by telephone during the closing, told the buyer to call the neighbor. The buyer did call, but the neighbor wasn't there. After hemming and hawing for the better part of a day and a half, the buyer finally decided to have a locksmith come and make a new key for the mailbox. Fine. But he wanted the sellers to pay for the locksmith. The sellers refused. He closed anyway.

Have your attorney or broker make sure the seller has brought all of his or her keys to the closing.

HOW DOES MY DEED GET RECORDED?

What is a deed? A deed is the physical manifestation of the title to your home. Holding title is an amorphous concept—it's not like holding a handful of dirt and saying, "I own this land." To give you something to show for your money and efforts, our legal system (based on the English system of real estate law) has sanctioned deeds, or pieces of paper that say you own a specific piece of property at a specific address.

As part of the process to formalize your ownership, you have the deed recorded. This gives legal recognition—in other words, puts the world on notice—of your ownership of the property. Anyone can go to the office of the recorder of deeds and find out that you own your home. The deed becomes part of the public record. And your ownership becomes part of the property's chain of title. If a title company looked up your property now, after the closing and after the deed has been recorded, your name would come up as the official owner.

Recording Your Deed

How does a deed get recorded? If you're closing at a title company, the title company may record the deed. Or, the title company will deliver the deed to you, and you will have to take it to your local recorder of deeds office. It's as simple as that. But you want to make sure that the deed is recorded properly, and that your correct name, address, and other information are listed. When real estate tax bills are sent out, they are sent to the name and address listed at the recorder's or assessor's office. If there's a problem with your home or with your tax bill, a notice will be sent to the address listed at the recorder's or assessor's office. If the address, or your name, is incorrectly listed, you may never get your property tax bill or any notices, and you could lose your property.

Make sure your deed is recorded correctly and the information is listed correctly. Verify that the proper authorities have your correct address for tax bills. Mark down the days you're supposed to receive your tax bill (you should find this out at the closing). If you don't receive it, call the recorder's (or real estate tax bill collector's) office to find out why. Nonpayment of property taxes is an easy (and quick) way to lose your property. Make sure it doesn't happen to you.

My Story

In the preface to this book, I invite readers to contact me. I give my e-mail address (IlyceGlink@aol.com), my web site address (ThinkGlink.com), and my post office box (P.O. Box 366, Glencoe, Illinois 60022).

Years ago, when I first got this post office box, I used to receive tax bills for someone else's property. I normally receive a bucketful of mail (the post office employees laugh when I come to pick up my mail), so I sometimes just slit open every piece of mail first, and then look at it. That's how I accidentally came to open one of these real estate tax bills.

The property was located on the south side of Chicago. The address for the tax bill was listed as my box (under someone else's name).

Every six months, another tax bill would come. I returned each one, unopened, since I now knew to look for that particular shape. One day, a different sort of letter came to the box. It was a notice from the assessor's office that the property was being auctioned for unpaid property taxes. A few months later, another notice came notifying the owner that the property has been sold.

In the past few years, I haven't received any notices for this property. Nor have I ever heard from the original owner. I have often wondered whether he thought about his property and what happened to it, or simply lost track and forgot about it. I'll never know.

If you move out of your home but keep it as an investment property, make sure to (1) change the address of your tax bill, and (2) keep paying your taxes. Otherwise, you could lose your home.

HOW SHOULD I PREPARE FOR THE MOVE TO MY NEW HOME?

If you feel that you're the only family moving to a new house, maybe you don't know the right people. One out of every five families moves each year (this includes owners and renters). Forty-five percent of these moves happen during the summer, according to the American Movers Conference (AMC), the interstate moving industry's national trade association, which represents some 1,200 moving companies worldwide. (It just *seems* as though everyone is moving on the same day that you are.)

resources

There are dozens of details to think about when you move, even if your new house is just across town. It pays to plan and be organized. Several free or inexpensive (about 50 cents to $1 each) consumer publications about moving are available. I recommend:

- *Guide to a Satisfying Move* and *Moving with Pets and Plants*, published by the American Movers Conference.
- *Helpful Tips in Planning Your Interstate Move* is published by the Interstate Commerce Commission, as is *When You Move: Your Rights and Responsibilities.* Regulated household-goods movers are required to furnish a copy of *When You Move* to prospective customers.

Planning Your Move

Here are some things to think about when planning a move:

1. **Don't take everything with you.** Sort through everything, and throw out, give away, or sell things you don't need anymore. When you've gotten to the bare minimum, start packing.

2. **Save those old newspapers.** As soon as you get your mortgage, start saving old newspapers for wrapping delicate objects like china and glassware. You may want to double- or triple-wrap each piece, so stack away about three times as much newspaper as you think you'll need. If you don't want to rewash the plates after you move, buy packages of plain newsprint or tissue paper for the initial wrap and then put newsprint over that. Or, you can buy an extra large size plastic wrap for the initial wrap, followed by newsprint.

3. **The interim move.** Will your new home be ready on time? Do you need an interim move? Will you be storing your furniture? If you're moving across state lines, it's best to store your belongings near your new home, not your old one. If you need something from storage, you should be able to get it quickly and easily.

4. **Schedule repair or renovation work ahead of time.** If you need repair, decorating, or renovation work done on your new house, and have the extra float time, get busy scheduling the work four to six weeks before you move. If you're planning to paint or decorate, you may want to have that work done before you've unpacked most things and settled into your new home.

5. **Get your new utility accounts.** Three weeks before the move, you'll want to contact your local utility companies (telephone, electricity, cable, gas, water) and inform them of your move. Arrange to have these services cut off at the end of your moving day (if you're moving in the afternoon, it would be nice to be able to drink water and use the bathroom, not to mention the telephone). Don't forget to arrange the hookup of utilities to your new home.

6. **Reserve the elevators.** If you're moving to a condominium or a co-op, you'll need to schedule your move-in day with the building's management. Generally, large condos (those with an elevator) require you to "reserve" the freight elevator for your move. Do this way ahead of time, or the day on which you'd like to move may already be booked. There may be a fee for having the building maintenance workers "oversee" your move. Ask the building manager about moving-in rules, and don't be surprised if you're asked to pay a fee.

7. **Discontinue delivery services.** Two weeks before your move, set a date for discontinuing your delivery services for newspapers, milk, dry cleaning, or laundry. If you're moving to a new state, your broker may be able to offer advice on employing these services in your new town.

8. **Change-of-address cards.** About two weeks before your move, you'll have to fill out and mail your change-of-address cards. Your local post office can give you some cards to fill out, or you may want to have change-of-address cards preprinted. If you receive Federal Express or UPS packages for your home-based business, you'll want to inform these companies of your change of address as well.

9. **Moving with pets.** If you're moving with pets, you may need to take some special precautions, according to the AMC. Pets cannot be shipped on moving vans. They should travel with

you and wear special identification tags with your name, address, and telephone number, and the name of an alternative relative in case you can't be located. If you decide to ship your pet by air, make the arrangements ahead of time. If you move across state lines, nearly every state has laws on the entry of animals. Write to the State Veterinarian, State Department of Animal Husbandry, or other state agency for information. Most states require up-to-date rabies shots for dogs and cats. If you're moving to Hawaii with your pet, you'll have to quarantine the animal for 120 days. Some pets must have an entry permit issued by the destination state's regulatory agency. Finally, your new town (or condo or co-op) may have restrictions on the number of dogs or cats that can live at one residence. If this might be a problem for you, check with your new city or village council.

10. **Moving with plants.** You generally won't have a problem if you're moving house plants, but some states do require you to have them inspected by an authorized state Department of Agriculture inspector. Plants are susceptible to shock when moving, and it may be dangerous to move a plant if it is exposed to temperatures below 35°F or above 95°F to 100°F for more than an hour. The AMC says plants can tolerate darkness for up to a week, but it's best not to store them. Cuttings of your favorite houseplants, while convenient, will not last as long or as well as potted plants.

Finding the Right Moving Company

As many as eight weeks before your moving day, you'll probably need to find a moving company. Shop around and compare prices. Try to use a licensed, insured, and bonded mover. Be careful of overcharges, and if you're moving across state lines, find out how much the company charges per mile. It's better to get a flat fee, if that's possible.

Movers are required to prepare an *order for service* for each customer. Keep a copy of this document; it shows the terms of the initial agreement with the mover. Next, the mover must issue a *bill of lading*, which is the legal contract between the customer and the mover. It is very important, so keep it handy during the move. The Interstate

Commerce Commission warns "not to sign the bill of lading until comparing it with the order of service to be sure that all services ordered are correctly shown."

A *binding estimate* requires the mover to bill only at the price agreed to for the specific services needed. If you make any changes or increase the amount that is being moved, it may void the estimate, which should be in writing and attached to the bill of lading. With a binding estimate, you must pay the mover with cash, a certified check, or a money order, unless you have prearranged to use a credit card. In a *nonbinding estimate*, the final price for the move will not be known until everything has been weighed, and transportation charges have been calculated. Request a copy of the mover's policy on inconvenience or delay (in case the truckers get lost) in advance of the move.

Make sure you and the mover understand when your household furniture is supposed to be picked up, and when it is supposed to be delivered. Do not accept a promise like, "We'll be there as soon as possible." Get definitive dates and make sure they are in writing. If the mover cannot meet the pickup or delivery dates, he or she is required to notify you by telephone or telegram, or in writing. If you're going across country, be sure to ask the mover to notify you of the charges for the move.

Licensed movers are responsible for loss or damage to your property. You should have a list of all the items being moved. Number your boxes, and make a list of the contents of each box. Label them clearly with your name and new address and telephone number. You and the mover should agree about the contents being shipped, and make sure the inventory list reflects your mutual understanding. At the time of delivery, note any items that are damaged or missing, and ask the mover for a liability claims form. Finally, you and the mover should agree on the amount of liability the mover will assume for loss or damage to your property.

The mover's liability is limited to 60 cents per pound, so it's wise to add extra insurance if your goods are particularly valuable. The mover can provide you with added coverage, but be sure you understand what's protected and for how much. You must declare the value of your goods with the mover before the move. Otherwise, the mover is required to value them at a lump-sum equivalent to $1.25 times the weight of the shipment. If your goods weigh 4,000 pounds, the mover is only required to value them at $5,000. Check with your homeowner's or renter's policy to see what's covered.

hindsight

If you have a distant or complicated move, it's best to purchase some additional insurance over and above the minimum tagged for your order. Also, invite the mover to inspect the contents of your house. The mover's representative should know how long the move will take, what it will cost, and how big a truck you'll need. You can also negotiate the price of the move with the mover. Ask them, for example, to throw in the wardrobes (large boxes in which you hang your clothes instead of folding and packing them) for free. You'll also want to purchase your own packing tape for 50 cents a roll, instead of using the mover's tape at $2 per roll. (You won't believe how many rolls your movers will go through, even if you already have everything boxed up.) If possible, hand-carry all valuables, such as cash and jewelry. If you have delicate objects, such as art works, glasswork, china, or crystal, the movers may not insure it unless they pack it themselves (which is an additional charge). Finally, know where each box should be placed in your new home. The movers can put everything in the basement, but your unpacking will go a lot more quickly if they put each box in the room in which it is needed. Give each room an identifying letter, and mark a letter on each box. If your new home has more than twenty-six rooms, use AA, BB, and so on, for the remaining rooms.

———12———

Happily Ever After

You'd like to think that you'll live happily every after in your new home. But life isn't a fairy tale. Here's some advice on what to do if something should prove amiss with your home after you close and move in, and on how to lower your property tax bill. Finally, I've added a few thoughts on how to recognize when it might be time to sell your home and buy another.

Discovering Problems After You Close

The first thing to consider is the problem itself. What happened? Did the boiler blow up? Did a pipe burst? Did the electrical system catch on fire? Is there asbestos in the home? Did you fall through the floor? Did the roof leak? Did the dishwasher break? Did the ceiling paint crack?

If you've bought a *new* home, I think you have a right to expect that everything will work beautifully for a long time. But if something goes wrong, you'll be happy if the builder has provided you with a new home warranty, which covers various items in the home for different periods of time. For example, if your new dishwasher breaks within the first year, the warranty will cover that. If the roof leaks within five years, the warranty may cover that, too.

If you've bought an older or preowned home, you have to realize that some things are going to break. Other items may work, but not well or reliably. Each home is different. Each building has its own rhythms. If something goes wrong, you'll have to fix it, unless your seller or the seller broker purchased a homeowner's warranty plan for your older home. (If you live in California, more than 70 percent of the homes are sold with a warranty plan.) If you have a warranty, you'll be able to have your problems fixed (for the first year) and all you'll be responsible for is the deductible (or service fee). (See Question 39 for more specific information on homeowner's warranties.)

The next question you have to ask is: Did the seller and seller broker know about the problem and simply "forgot" to tell you about it? Or is it possible they didn't realize there was a problem? Is it a case of puffery, where the broker may have said, "This house is perfect! You'll love it."

Common sense should tell you that when a broker says, "This house is perfect," he or she doesn't mean everything in the home is in perfect working order. (Or maybe that *is* what was meant, but you'd be foolish to take that claim seriously.) But if the seller and the seller broker told you the furnace was new, and a week after moving into the home you discover it's old, covered with asbestos, and just had a paint job, that could be a problem. If you were told the house was freshly painted and you find out it wasn't, that could be a problem. If you were told the house's roof did not leak, and a day after the first rain your living room looks like a swimming pool, that could be a problem.

Disclosure laws vary from state to state, but most sellers are required to tell you about "known, material defects" that could affect the value of the home. (I put "known, material defects" in quotes because, typically, the legal standard you need to prove is that the seller knew there were material, or serious, defects in the property that were not disclosed to you.) In some states, homeowners have successfully sued their sellers for not disclosing that someone was murdered in their home, or that a former owner died of AIDS. In some states, not disclosing that your house is haunted could be a real problem for the seller. (Nope, I'm not making that up.)

The bottom line is, if you feel you've been wronged, or lied to, in the purchase of your new home, you'll need to consult an attorney to learn about the legal rights and remedies you have in your state.

But if you have outsized expectations that everything will work perfectly in your home forever, you're setting yourself up for a series of disappointments that may erode your enjoyment of your new home.

How to Lighten Your Property Tax Load

When you decided to become a homeowner, you probably understood that real estate taxes are about as inevitable as death. You'll eventually get to the end of your mortgage payments, but you'll pay property taxes as long as you own this house or any other house.

The good news is, you can do a few things to keep your property taxes as low as possible. According to tax professionals, county and city or township governments often make mistakes when they assess property. The nonprofit National Taxpayers Union (NTU), a taxpayers' advocacy group based in Washington, DC, indicates that approximately 60 percent of all homeowners are overassessed; in other words, in every group of 100 angry taxpayers who think their taxes are too high, sixty are overpaying. Of those sixty, says NTU, only 2 percent appeal their real estate taxes. But, of the 2 percent who do appeal, *50 to 80 percent* (the figures vary, based on the source) receive some reduction in their property taxes. Those are good odds.

(More recent studies seem to indicate that more people are filing appeals of their tax assessments. The anecdotal evidence appears to prove this true: In 1999, property tax bills in Cook County, Illinois, were delayed by several weeks because so many homeowners filed appeals.)

Appealing your property taxes is not a difficult process, but it requires a bit of ingenuity, perseverance, and organization. And the reward—a lower tax bill—is eminently worthwhile.

How worthwhile? That depends on each house. Jim Siudut, an accountant and real estate tax specialist who has produced a video called "Fight Higher Real Estate Taxes and Win," says he saved himself $1,500 in one year. The next year, he saved himself an even greater amount because the rise in his property taxes was keyed to a lower assessed valuation. (See the glossary at the end of this section for definitions of relevant terms.)

The key to a successful reduction of your property taxes is solid evidence, presented clearly and concisely. Siudut says all homeowners should make sure they're being correctly assessed, especially if their property taxes are high or they have received steep increases in recent years. The time to appeal is when you get your assessment notice—not when your tax bill arrives.

The assessment notice details your home's current and past assessed valuation, and its current estimated market value. It should also list your property's physical characteristics. In other words, if you have four bedrooms and two bathrooms and an attached two-car garage, the notice should say that.

The estimated market value is the price the assessor's office attaches to your property, based on surveys and studies of neighboring properties. The assessment is a percentage (usually set by law) of the estimated market value.

It's important to remember that after you receive your assessment notice, you have a limited time to file an appeal—usually thirty to sixty days, depending on the county's policy. If you are not satisfied with your judgment, you may appeal all the way up to your state's Supreme Court.

In North Carolina, for example, any taxpayer who is dissatisfied with the assessment made by the county assessor should arrange immediately for an informal meeting with the assessor to explain why he or she thinks the amount is excessive. If a satisfactory conclusion cannot be reached, the taxpayer can appeal to the County Board of Equalization and Review (Board of County Commissioners) and request a hearing. A taxpayer who questions the decision of the county board may file an appeal with the State Property Tax Commission within thirty days of the date the decision was mailed by the board. That decision may be appealed to the Court of Appeals and, ultimately, to the North Carolina Supreme Court.

To effectively appeal your assessment, you'll need the current and the prior year's tax bills (for new homeowners, the prior bill should be available at the local tax assessor's office), the current assessment notice, the current property survey, the purchase contract or closing statements (if you purchased your home within the past five years), a copy of any building plans, an itemized account of expenses (for any improvements made to the property), and any recent appraisals.

To analyze your assessment, you'll need the following data: your property record card; a list of comparable homes ("comps"), and their property record cards, sale dates, and prices. Experts recommend that you check with a local real estate agent or broker for some of this information. Agents and brokers should be happy to oblige because it's a good opportunity for them to market their services to potential customers.

The first step is to go to the county assessor's office and take a look at your property record card. Identify it by matching the parcel number or permanent real estate index number of your property with the number on your tax bill. The card lists the physical characteristics of your property, including the number of bedrooms, bathrooms, and fireplaces; garage size; square footage; and lot size.

Many overassessments result from factual errors. The assessor's office may say that your house has four bedrooms when it actually has only three. Check the description carefully. Factual errors are the easiest to document and to appeal. If you find a factual error, you'll need either blueprints or a property survey to "prove" your claim. Your evidence should include recent color photographs of the inside and outside of your house. Or, you can ask the assessor's office to send someone to reexamine your house.

Besides checking for factual errors, Jim Siudut uses four tests to determine whether property has been overassessed: (1) an assessment ratio test; (2) a market test; (3) an equity test; and (4) an environmental factors test. Gary Whalen, a real estate broker and tax consultant who has written a book called *Digging for Gold in Your Own Backyard: The Complete Homeowner's Guide to Lowering Your Real Estate Taxes*, refers to property overassessments due to factors other than factual errors as "judgmental errors."

Assessment Ratio Test

"In any county, the assessment is based on the home's market value. The assessment ratio is a percentage of market value. What you want to do is determine whether or not your assessment ratio is in line with that of comparable homes in your neighborhood," Siudut says.

Gathering comparable data is the most time-consuming part of appealing your property taxes. Siudut and Whalen recommend that you look for properties that have sold within the past two years and are similar to yours in size and amenities. When you have the exact addresses of these comps, ask the assessor's office for the properties' record cards. Compare the assessed valuation of each comp with its sale price to see whether the assessor comes close in determining the correct market value. Did the homes sell for less money than their market value? What percentage did the assessor use to determine the assessed valuation (before the multiplier was applied)? Compare this with the percentage used on your property.

Experts say homeowners' biggest misconception is that they think they can use only market value as a basis. The key test to fairness is *uniformity*, not market value.

Market and Equity Tests

The law of uniformity also helps homeowners construct appeals based on market and equity tests. Homes in the same neighborhood should be assessed at the same rate, in proportion to their size and amenities.

Siudut's market test compares the assessment per square foot with those of comps in the same neighborhood. To gain an accurate square footage account, measure from your house's exterior walls. Next, find eight to ten comps; you should then end up with at least four that have lower assessments per square foot. To find out the assessment per square foot, divide the assessed value by the number of square feet in the property.

Like the market test, the equity test compares the value of other homes similar in age and amenities. Again, the idea is to find comps that have been assessed at a lower rate than yours.

Level out the value of the homes by adding or subtracting the value of amenities that are not uniformly present in each house. For example, if your house doesn't have a fireplace, but the comps you've selected do, subtract $1,500 from your assessed valuation. A local real estate agent can help you determine the appropriate value for each amenity.

Environmental Factors Test

Did the state recently build a nuclear power plant close to your property? Did the railroad just add a new switching station down the street? Are a large number of people in your neighborhood out of work because a plant closed down? Is a new garbage dump being planned within a couple of miles of your home?

These are environmental factors that could lower your property's market value. (As a new home buyer, you remembered the broker's maxim, "Location, location, location," and would never buy a house next to a garbage dump.) If you put these factors to work for you, Siudut says, you might be able to lower your assessment. Document these changes and how they might work against property values in the neighborhood. Use articles and editorials from your local newspapers, and include evidence of any television and/or radio reports. Clip these together to give added weight to your appeal.

Whalen and Siudut recommend combining any errors—both judgmental and factual—to get the biggest reduction.

"If you're organized and present a clear case, it does not substantially increase the assessor's workload," Siudut says. "The more organized and focused you are, the easier you make their job, and the easier it is to get that reduction."

When researching your case, don't be afraid to ask the person behind the desk for help. Homeowners should also apply for all the exceptions to which they're legally entitled: senior citizens, homestead, homestead improvement, disabled, or disabled veterans. The assessor can reduce your equalized assessed valuation within a range from $2,000 to $50,000, depending on the benefits you're entitled to.

A Glossary of Tax Terms

Here are a few tax terms you should know:

Assessed Valuation The value placed on property for tax purposes and used as a basis for division of the tax burden. It is a percentage of the amount that is deemed the home's fair market value.

Assessment Ratio The percentage of your home's fair market value that an assessor uses to determine the property's assessed valuation. The ratio can vary from county to county.

Notice of Revision A notice mailed to the property owner after a property has been reassessed.

State Multiplier Also known as the **state equalization factor,** this is a number the state assigns to each county, depending on the assessment ratio the county uses to calculate assessed valuation. The multiplier either raises or lowers the assessed valuation to the state-mandated level of 33.33 percent of market value. The multiplier ensures that taxpayers in each of the state's counties pay the same amount proportionately in property taxes.

Tax Rate The rate at which property is taxed, usually stated per hundred dollars of the property's value.

Uniformity The legal principle that governs property tax assessments. It states that all property in a given area must be assessed at the same level; that is, you should not be assessed at a higher rate than your next-door neighbor. The principle of uniformity is the basis for many successful assessment appeals.

The Next House: Knowing When It's Time to Move On

Although you may think you'll live in your first home forever, odds are you'll be looking for another home within five to seven years.

Why do people move? There are dozens of reasons. They marry, have children, bring an aging parent or relative into their home, change jobs, care for grandchildren, divorce, get sick, or simply decide they want to live somewhere else.

How will *you* know when it's time to move on? You may start to feel cramped or confined in your present space, within and outside the structure. Your house may seem frayed at the edges. Your child may need special services available only in another school district.

Typically, you'll become aware that a subtle dissatisfaction comes over you whenever you walk into your home.

If that happens, start creating a new wish list and reality check. Your list may be quite different from the one you compiled when you moved into your home. Your goal is to identify objectively the qualities you now feel you need and want in a home.

When you've identified what you want and need, you can go about fixing up your current home and preparing to show it to prospective buyers. For more information on how to make the most of your sale, check out my book, *100 Questions Every Home Seller Should Ask*, as well as updates and further information available on my web site, at ThinkGlink.com.

Appendix I
The Top 10 Mistakes First-Time Buyers Make

Borrowing from one of my favorite performers, David Letterman, I've created a top 10 list of things first-time buyers tend to do when they are searching for a home. Brokers call them "mistakes." These are not egregious errors, but if, for example, timing problems are not worked out, or the wrong size home is purchased, or time is wasted looking at unaffordable homes, these mistakes make the process of home buying a little more time-consuming and heart-wrenching. They can also cause problems down the line, when it's time to sell the home.

I can't tell you how many times I've heard first-time buyers exclaim "Not me!" when faced with the possibility of having made mistakes. Reading about them in this Appendix—presumably, after you've read the whole book—might help you head 'em off at the pass. You may not see yourself doing everything on this list, but brokers agree that the average first-time buyer makes at least one of the following errors.

1. Incorrectly Timing Your Move. As a first-time buyer, you have probably been renting until now. If so, the best time to close on a house is when your current lease ends. Don't sign another year-long lease if you expect to buy a home before that lease period expires. If you can't time your closing correctly, approach your landlord about a shorter lease—say, three to six months—or, alternatively, a month-to-month lease. Another option is to ask your landlord to include in your new lease an escape clause that will allow you to get out of your lease with 30 or 60 days' notice.

2. Looking at Homes You Can't Afford. First-time buyers often hear that they can buy a home that costs up to two and a half times their combined income. If interest rates stay in the 6 to 7 percent range, you might even be able to push that number to three, or three and a half, times your combined income. But first you have to factor in your debts (credit cards, mortgage, and so on), property taxes, insurance premiums, private mortgage insurance (PMI), and the down payment. If you look at homes you can't afford, you'll get spoiled. When you finally come to your senses and start looking at homes within your price range, they probably will disappoint you. For example, if you've been looking at four-bedroom homes with attached garages in plush suburbs, a three-bedroom home in a so-so neighborhood with street parking is going to seem "not quite nice enough." To save yourself some heartache, get prequalified through a local lender. There's no cost or obligation, and the lender will tell you exactly how much house you can afford to buy.

3. Buying the Wrong Size Home. Many first-time buyers, especially those who are single and in their late twenties and early thirties, purchase one-bedroom condominiums. What they don't realize is how likely it is they will meet someone, fall madly in love, and marry. Unless you marry a next-door neighbor who has a condo you can combine with yours, your one-bedroom, one-bath apartment will soon seem too small. For the same price, and possibly even at or near the same location, your dollars might buy a two-bedroom, two-bath apartment, which would give you additional flexibility. Before you buy property, think about how long you intend to live there. Is this a five-year home? A ten-year home? The home you intend to die in, years from now? The average American family changes its residence every five to seven years. If you're in your twenties, allow for significant changes in your lifestyle within five to seven years. Buy smart by planning for those changes ahead of time.

4. Buying in a Neighborhood You Know Nothing About. Some first-time buyers fall in love with a house in a neighborhood that is inappropriate for them. Never forget that you'll have to travel through the neighborhood to get to and from your home. Is it a nice neighborhood? Is there graffiti on every wall? Are there gangs? Is there a neighborhood crime watch group? Are the neighbors your age? Are there families around the same age as yours? Is it a transient neighborhood, or do families stay there forever? To avoid making this mistake, spend a lot of time in a neighborhood before you buy there. Drive to and from the house you like. Sit in your car and watch the people who might be your future neighbors come home from work. Listen to how loudly they or their children play their favorite rock music. Walk to the local bar, restaurant, grocery store, and cleaners. Think about whether you'll be as happy in this neighborhood as you might be in the house.

5. Operating on a First-House-Is-Best Basis. If you're leaving behind a cramped, one-bedroom rental, almost any home will look good. Try to avoid jumping at the first home you see. Look at five, ten, or even twenty houses to see what's available on the market, within your spending range. Season your eyes by inspecting different types of homes: condos, town houses, duplexes, and single-family houses. When you've narrowed down your choices to three or four, visit them again. By the time some form of objectivity returns, you should be able to make a sensible choice. Completely impulsive decisions do not usually work out, and you could wind up paying dearly for your impulsiveness.

6. Buying a Property That's Difficult to Resell. Although you say you don't mind that the property backs up to the local railroad, you will when it comes time to sell the home. It's unlikely that you'll be able to easily persuade another buyer that life is quiet and peaceful at that address. Try not to buy a home that will be difficult to resell. You may think you'll live there forever, but you probably won't. Most first-time buyers sell within five to seven years. Before you buy a home, think hard about how you would sell it. Walk yourself through, and point out all the negatives. Describe them out loud. Then ask your agent or broker how long it would take him or her to sell it.

7. Overextending Your Budget. A lender who prequalifies you for a loan may tell you that you're able to afford a $100,000 home, but keep in mind that buying in that price range may stretch your budget beyond your comfort zone. To avoid feeling pinched or losing ground financially, it's important to understand how you spend *all* of your money. You may be comfortable spending 35 percent of your take-home pay on rent, or you may prefer to spend less—say, 25 percent. Write down every amount that you spend (down to that last piece of bubble gum) for two months. Can you live without buying your favorite group's latest CD? Would you feel uncomfortable knowing that you can go out to dinner only once a month? Or that you must eliminate your yearly vacation, or your children's summer camp or piano lessons? As a homeowner, you'll have additional expenses besides your mortgage payment. There will be maintenance and upkeep bills, plus property taxes. If you buy a condo, there will be assessments. Buying a less expensive home will give you greater peace of mind, allow for savings, and permit a few extras.

8. Being Indecisive. When you're searching for the right house, you should take all the time you need. Don't let a broker or a seller bully you into making a decision before you're ready. Ask to see five, ten, twenty, or even fifty homes, if you haven't found one you love. Indecisiveness takes over when you find a home you would like to live in, but you're afraid of making the commitment. First-time buyers often lose two or three potential homes because they can't bring themselves to actually make an offer. Or they might find two wonderful properties and face a tough choice. If you're afraid, admit your fear and conquer it by talking with your broker. You're not the only first-time buyer who has had trouble making up his or her mind.

9. Choosing the Wrong Mortgage. Many first-time buyers have heard from their parents that the only mortgage to get is a thirty-year fixed-interest-rate loan. That's because the generation ahead of yours didn't have the tailor-made financial options that buyers have today. Consider choosing an adjustable-rate mortgage (ARM) to take advantage of super-low interest rates. Or, pick a ten- or fifteen-year fixed-interest-rate loan, which will allow you to maximize your mortgage interest deduction *and* save you hundreds of thousands of dollars in interest. You might also want to look into a two-step mortgage, which combines a little of the risk of an ARM with the dependability of a fixed-rate loan. Explore all the options. Have your lender show you, on paper, how much each option will cost you and how it compares with the others.

10. Underinsuring the Property. First-time buyers know they have to buy home insurance to cover their mortgage. Sometimes they forget to increase the coverage of that insurance as the neighborhood improves and the home appreciates in value, or they neglect to insure the contents of their home. Think about how much it would cost you to replace your furniture, clothing, books, CDs, artwork, and pots and pans. Add up everything and then tack on the cost of actually rebuilding your residence (a single-family home or a town house) if it were to burn to the ground. Add on your mortgage costs, which would still have to be paid. That's how much insurance you should buy.

Appendix II

5 Simple Things You Can Do to Make the Home-Buying Process Easier

1. Get Preapproved for Your Loan. Getting preapproved is the only way to ensure that you're searching in the right price bracket. Too often, people search for homes in a price range they can't afford, either because they don't understand how the numbers work, or because they imagine that they're going to negotiate the seller down to a more affordable number. Not knowing the true costs involved, or holding out false hope of a negotiation miracle is a haphazard approach to spending several hundred thousand dollars. Instead, spend time with a mortgage lender, either on-line or in person, and get preapproved for your loan.

2. Work with a Great Buyer Broker. Would you invest $100,000 in a stock just because you got a hot tip on a cold call? Of course not. But people go out every day and spend hundreds of thousands of dollars on a home without consulting a licensed buyer broker. This is foolish, particularly when consulting a buyer broker typically won't cost you money from your own pocket. You need someone who can advise you on the neighborhood, the regional demographics, and the sales history of homes similar to yours in the neighborhood of your choice.

3. Know the Neighborhood before You Make an Offer. You don't just live in a house, you live in a neighborhood. If you think you've found your new home, spend time walking around the area at all times of the day and night, *before* you make your offer. Chat with your prospective neighbors about their experiences in the neighborhood. Pay a visit to the local dry cleaners, supermarket, or coffee shop. Stop in at the local police headquarters and inquire about the local crime rate. Pay a visit to the nearby schools and observe. No matter how much information is on the Internet, learning first-hand about your future neighborhood can only be done in person.

4. Protect Yourself. Make sure your contract has the right contingencies and the right language, so that you're properly protected. If attorneys are used in the state in which you are purchasing a home, then use one. If attorneys aren't used, consider hiring one anyway, so that you have an adviser who doesn't have a vested interest in seeing the deal close. Buy enough homeowner's insurance, and make sure to increase it as the value of your home—and its contents—increases. Stay on top of your purchase so that there are no unpleasant surprises.

5. Have Reasonable Expectations. If you buy an older home, understand, before you close, that it's not going to be in perfect condition, even if the seller has recently gutted and renovated the whole property. When home buyers pay list (or over list) prices, it's understandable that they might expect something nearing perfection. However, as a home inspector friend of mine likes to say: "All homes have problems, but older homes have older problems." If you expect perfection in an existing home, you're likely to end up disappointed.

Appendix III
Contracts

Most sellers will expect your *offer to purchase* (also known as a *sales contract*) to be accompanied by the "standard package" of contingencies, including attorney approval (if this applies in your state), financing or mortgage, and inspection. Because these three contingencies are so common these days, I've included samples here. This rider is copyrighted by the New York State Association of Realtors, Inc., and is used with permission.

I've also included copies of several other contracts. These forms are copyrighted by the California Association of Realtors and are used only in California. I've reprinted them here with the permission of the California Association of Realtors.

Please note: You may find it useful to examine these contracts, disclosures, and addendums, but they may not include the exact language that will protect you in your state. Ask your real estate attorney or broker for the correct forms for your state.

359

RIDER TO PURCHASE AND SALE CONTRACT
FOR RESIDENTIAL PROPERTY

RIDER ANNEXED TO CONTRACT OF SALE BETWEEN _____ **, AS**

SELLER, AND _____ **, AS BUYER, DATED:** _____ **.**

POSSESSION OF PROPERTY

1.   (Select one of the following):

A. Property shall be delivered vacant and broom clean on title closing, [yes, SELLER'S initials ___].

B. If SELLER remains in possession of property following closing of title, SELLER shall deposit the sum of $_____ to guarantee SELLER'S removal therefrom within three (3) business days after title closes and the delivery of the property to BUYER in the condition required by this Agreement. SELLER is hereby obligated to pay to BUYER the sum of $_____ for each and every day SELLER remains in possession of the property beyond such guaranteed date of removal. All adjustments shall be made as of the date of delivery of possession. This clause shall survive the delivery of a deed herein, but shall in no event be construed as creating a relationship of landlord and tenant. _____ is hereby authorized to release this deposit at the end of the first business day subsequent to the offer of possession of the property to BUYER. In the event the SELLER'S attorney or _____ receives actual notice of any claim of the breach of this paragraph, SELLER'S attorney or _____ shall not release said deposit until such claim is resolved. [yes, SELLER'S initials ___]

INSPECTIONS & TESTS

2.   Buyer may have the premises inspected by a Professional Engineer, Architect or qualified house inspector, to be obtained and paid for by the (BUYER) (SELLER) within _____ calendar days after the date of acceptance of this contract or (other) _____. Buyer may cancel the contract if such inspection shows structural damage which would require an expenditure of $500.00 or more to repair.

3.   BUYER may inspect premises for the presence of hazardous materials, as defined by Federal and NYS Law, by a Licensed Professional Engineer or Environmental Engineer to be obtained and paid for by the (BUYER) (SELLER) within _____ calendar days from the (date of acceptance of contract) or (other) _____. Inspection will be considered acceptable if any such material is found to be within generally accepted guidelines or the estimated total remediation costs do not exceed $_____.

4.   Buyer may conduct a radon test to determine if premises meet minimum USA EPA standards to be obtained and paid for by the (BUYER) (SELLER) within ____ days from (the date of acceptance of contract) or (other) _____. If premises do not meet said minimum standards, BUYER may cancel this contract.

5.   The Purchaser shall have the right to have the premises inspected for the purpose of determining the existence of termite or other wood destroying insect infestation or damage. The cost of said inspection shall be borne by the Purchaser.

In the event termite damage or other wood destroying insect infestation or damage is found, a copy of the report issued by the termite company or other written notice shall be served upon Seller's attorney within fifteen (15) days from the date of this contract. Upon receipt of such notice by the Seller, the Seller may do one of the following:

A.   treat the termite or wood destroying insect condition and damage, if any, with a company acceptable to Purchaser at Seller's own cost and expense in which event the Purchaser agrees to consummate this transaction pursuant to the further terms hereof; or

B.   terminate this Contract by refunding the sums paid hereunder by the Purchaser. Notice of Seller's intent to exercise either option shall be served upon the Purchaser within four (4) days after the receipt of the termite report by certified mail, return receipt requested. If the Seller treats the condition, they shall only employ a licensed exterminator who is authorized to apply pesticides at the premises, and Seller shall deliver to the Purchaser a one (1) year guarantee for said work at or prior to closing of title. The Purchaser shall be permitted on the premises at all times during the application of pesticides.

In the event the Purchaser shall fail to have the premises inspected or fails to serve said written notice postmarked no later than fifteen (15) days from the date of this Contract, the Purchaser shall be deemed to have waived the provisions of this Rider, and this Contract shall remain in full force and effect.

6.   In the event any of the above tests and/or inspections which are to be obtained by the buyer are not performed within the time period stated, the tests and/or inspections are deemed waived. SELLER agrees to fully cooperate and permit timely access to premises for the purpose of required inspection and/or tests with all utilities operational at SELLER'S expense.

7.   If this contract is canceled by buyer due to unsatisfactory inspection report(s) as set forth above, the down payment paid by the buyer shall be refunded to buyer upon cancellation of the contract.

ATTORNEY'S APPROVAL CLAUSE

8.   This agreement is contingent upon BUYER and SELLER obtaining approval of this agreement by their attorney as to all matters contained therein. This contingency shall be deemed waived unless BUYER'S or SELLER'S attorney on behalf of their client notifies

_____, in writing, of their disapproval of the agreement no later than five (5) business days after this contract has been signed by both the SELLER and the BUYER. If BUYER'S or SELLER'S attorney so notifies, then this agreement shall be deemed canceled, null and void, and all deposits shall be returned in full to the BUYER.

BUYERS: _____   SELLERS: _____

_____   _____

_____   _____

(telephone number)   (telephone number)

ADDITIONAL RIDER TO PURCHASE AND SALE CONTRACT FOR RESIDENTIAL PROPERTY

RIDER ANNEXED TO CONTRACT OF SALE BETWEEN _____, **AS SELLER, AND** _____, **AS BUYER, DATED:** _____.

MORTGAGE CONTINGENCY AND EXPENSE

A.   BUYER and SELLER agree that this contract shall only be binding on the BUYER if the BUYER is able to obtain a Conventional or _____ mortgage loan. Said loan shall be obtained solely at the BUYER'S expense. The mortgage loan will be in the sum of $_____ for _____ years at the prevailing rate of interest. The BUYER agrees to apply to an institutional lender including a mortgage banker, mortgage broker or other NYS licensed lender for a first mortgage loan in the above amount. Such application shall be made with due diligence and dispatch upon receipt of a copy of this contract signed by the SELLER. Should BUYER be unable to obtain such a mortgage after due diligent and proper effort on or before _____, 19____ then either party to this contract may elect to cancel the same and upon the return of all monies paid on account of the purchase price pursuant to this contract to the BUYER, this contract shall be canceled null and void and of no further force and effect.

B.   It is hereby further agreed that if the proposed lender issuing the commitment shall fail or refuse to close the loan for any reason other than the BUYER'S default or the BUYER'S failure to act in good faith, then and in that event this Contract shall be deemed canceled and both parties shall be and are hereby released and discharged from all liability hereunder, except that the down payment hereunder shall be promptly refunded to BUYER.

C.   If for any reason BUYER fails to obtain the mortgage described in paragraph 3a above, BUYER shall apply for a mortgage in the sum of $_____ on a no income verification basis.

D. It is agreed that in the event the mortgage referred to herein is approved by the proposed mortgagee in a lesser amount than that set forth in this contract, then in such event, the SELLER shall have the option of reducing the price in the exact amount of the difference between the mortgage granted and the mortgage provided for herein to the effect that the cash investment of the BUYER shall be the same amount as originally contemplated in this contract. In the event the SELLER exercises said option, the BUYER shall not be released from the contract and shall consummate the transaction on the altered terms.

E. A mortgage commitment shall otherwise be considered firm and unconditional even though it contains a condition requiring the sale of the BUYER'S present home prior to closing. The BUYER waives any such condition as an inducement to Seller to enter into this contract. In addition, BUYER acknowledges that it is their sole obligation to extend, at their sole expense, the mortgage commitment until the date of closing as set forth herein, including any reasonable adjournments.

VA AND FHA FINANCING

It is expressly agreed that, notwithstanding any other provisions of this contract, the BUYER shall not be obligated to complete the purchase of the property described herein or to otherwise, in those cases involving a VA Loan, if the contract purchase price or cost exceeds the reasonable value of the property established by the Veterans Administration or in those cases to be insured by the Federal Housing Administration unless the Lender delivered to the BUYER, a written statement issued by the Federal Housing Commissioner setting forth the appraised value of the property (excluding closing costs of not less than $_____ which statement the Lender hereby agrees to deliver to the BUYER promptly after such appraised value statement is made available to the Lender. The BUYER shall, however, have the privilege and option of proceeding with the consummation of this contract without regard to the amount of the appraised valuation made by the Federal Housing Commissioner or reasonable value established by the Veteran's Administration. In those cases involving FHA, the appraised valuation is arrived at to determine the maximum mortgage the Department of Housing and Urban Development will insure. HUD does not warrant the value or the condition of the property. The BUYER should satisfy himself/herself that the price and the condition of the property are acceptable.

BUYER and SELLER acknowledge receipt of LEAD BASED PAINT HEALTH HAZARD DISCLOSURE BULLETIN 312-218 SC235 issued by the United States Government printing office.

BUYERS: _____   SELLERS: _____

_____   _____

_____   _____

(telephone number)   (telephone number)

CALIFORNIA ASSOCIATION OF REALTORS®

BUYER'S INSPECTION ADVISORY

Property Address: _____ ("Property")

IMPORTANCE OF PROPERTY INSPECTION: The physical condition of the land and improvements being purchased are not guaranteed by either Seller or Brokers, except as specifically set forth in the purchase agreement. For this reason, Buyer should conduct a thorough inspection of the Property personally and with professionals, who should provide a written report of their inspections. If the professionals recommend further investigation, tests, or inspections, Buyer should contact qualified experts to conduct such additional investigations, tests, or inspections. **Disclosure duties:** The law requires Seller and Brokers to disclose to Buyer all material facts known to them which affect the value or desirability of the Property. In sales involving residential dwellings with no more than four units, Brokers have a duty to make a diligent visual inspection of the accessible areas of the Property, and to disclose the results of that inspection. However, as some Property defects or conditions may not be discoverable from a visual inspection, it is possible neither Seller nor Brokers are aware of them. **Buyer duties:** Buyer has an affirmative duty to exercise reasonable care to protect himself or herself, including discovery of the legal, practical and technical implications of disclosed facts, and the investigation of information and facts which are known to Buyer, or are within the diligent attention and observation of Buyer. **Property inspections:** Brokers do not have expertise, and therefore cannot advise Buyer on many items, such as soil stability, geologic conditions, hazardous substances, structural conditions of the foundation or other improvements, or the condition of the roof, heating, air conditioning, plumbing, electrical, sewer, septic, waste disposal, or other system. The only way to accurately determine the condition of the Property is through an inspection by an appropriate professional selected by Buyer.

YOU ARE ADVISED TO CONDUCT INSPECTIONS OF THE ENTIRE PROPERTY, INCLUDING BUT NOT LIMITED TO THE FOLLOWING:

1. **GENERAL CONDITION OF THE PROPERTY, ITS SYSTEMS AND COMPONENTS:** Foundation, roof, plumbing, heating, air conditioning, electrical, mechanical, security, pool/spa, and other structural and non-structural systems and components, built-in appliances, any personal property included in the sale, and energy efficiency of the Property. (Structural engineers are best suited to determine possible design or construction defects, and whether improvements are structurally sound.)
2. **SQUARE FOOTAGE, AGE, BOUNDARIES:** Square footage, room dimensions, lot size, age of improvements, and boundaries. Any numerical statements regarding these items are APPROXIMATIONS ONLY, and have not been and cannot be verified by Brokers. Fences, hedges, walls, retaining walls, and other natural or constructed barriers or markers do not necessarily identify true Property boundaries. (An appraiser, architect, surveyor, or civil engineer is best suited to determine respectively square footage, dimensions and boundaries of the Property.)
3. **SOIL STABILITY/GEOLOGIC CONDITIONS:** Existence of fill or compacted soil, or expansive or contracting soil, susceptibility to slippage, settling or movement, and the adequacy of drainage. These types of inspections are particularly important for hillside or sloped properties, but the referenced conditions may also exist on flat land. (Geotechnical engineers are best suited to determine such conditions, causes, and remedies.)
4. **ROOF:** Present condition, approximate age, leaks, and remaining useful life. (Roofing contractors are best suited to determine these conditions.)
5. **POOL/SPA:** Whether there are any cracks, leaks or operational problems. (Pool contractors are best suited to determine these conditions.)
6. **WASTE DISPOSAL:** Type, size, adequacy, capacity and condition of sewer and septic systems and components, connection to sewer, and applicable fees.
7. **WATER AND UTILITIES; WELL SYSTEMS AND COMPONENTS:** Water and utility availability, use restrictions, and costs. Adequacy, condition, and performance of well systems and components.
8. **ENVIRONMENTAL HAZARDS:** Potential environmental hazards, including asbestos, lead-based paint and other lead contamination, methane, other gases, fuel, oil or chemical storage tanks, contaminated soil or water, hazardous waste, waste disposal sites, electromagnetic fields, nuclear sources, and other substances, materials, products, or conditions. (For further information, read the booklet "Environmental Hazards: A Guide for Homeowners and Buyers," or consult an appropriate professional.)
9. **EARTHQUAKE AND FLOOD; INSURANCE AVAILABILITY:** Susceptibility of the Property to earthquake hazards and propensity of the Property to flood. These and other conditions may affect the availability and need for certain types of insurance. (Geologist, Geotechnic Engineer and insurance agents are best suited to provide information on these conditions.)
10. **GOVERNMENTAL REQUIREMENTS AND LIMITATIONS:** Permits, inspections, certificates, zoning, other governmental limitations, restrictions, and requirements affecting the current or future use of the Property, its development or size. (Such information is available through appropriate governmental agencies and private information providers. Brokers are not qualified to obtain, review, or interpret any such information.)
11. **RENTAL PROPERTY RESTRICTIONS:** Some cities and counties impose restrictions which may limit the amount of rent that can be charged, the maximum number of persons who can occupy the Property, and the circumstances in which tenancies can be terminated. Deadbolt or other locks and security systems for doors and windows should be examined to determine whether they satisfy legal requirements (Local government agencies or locksmiths, respectively, can give information about these restrictions and requirements.)
12. **NEIGHBORHOOD, AREA, SUBDIVISION CONDITIONS; PERSONAL FACTORS:** Neighborhood or area conditions, including schools, proximity and adequacy of law enforcement, crime statistics, the proximity of registered felons or offenders, fire protection, other governmental services, proximity to commercial, industrial or agricultural activities, existing and proposed transportation, construction and development which may affect noise, view, or traffic, airport noise, noise or odor from any source, wild and domestic animals, other nuisances, hazards, or circumstances, protected species, wetland properties, historic or other governmentally protected sites or improvements, facilities and condition of common areas of common interest subdivisions, and possible lack of compliance with any governing documents or Homeowners' Association requirements, conditions and influences of significance to certain cultures and/or religions, and personal needs, requirements and preferences of Buyer.

> Buyer acknowledges and agrees that Brokers: (a) Do not guarantee the condition of the Property; (b) Shall not be responsible for defects that are not known to Broker(s) or are not visually observable in reasonably and normally accessible areas of the Property; (c) Cannot verify information contained in inspection reports, square footage or representations made by others; (d) Do not guarantee the performance of others who have provided services or products to Buyer or Seller; (e) Do not guarantee the adequacy or completeness of repairs made by Seller or others; (f) Cannot identify Property boundary lines; and (g) Do not decide what price a buyer should pay or a seller should accept. Buyer agrees to seek desired assistance from appropriate professionals.

YOU ARE STRONGLY ADVISED TO INVESTIGATE THE CONDITION AND SUITABILITY OF ALL ASPECTS OF THE PROPERTY. IF YOU DO NOT DO SO, YOU ARE ACTING AGAINST THE ADVICE OF BROKERS.

By signing below, Buyer acknowledges receipt of a copy of this document. Buyer is encouraged to read it carefully.

_____   _____
Buyer Signature   Date   Buyer Signature   Date

Buyer(s) (Print Name(s)) _____

Current Address _____

Published and Distributed by:
REAL ESTATE BUSINESS SERVICES, INC.
a subsidiary of the CALIFORNIA ASSOCIATION OF REALTORS®
525 South Virgil Avenue, Los Angeles, California 90020

REVISED 4/98

Page ___6___ of _____ Pages.

OFFICE USE ONLY
Reviewed by Broker
or Designee _____
Date _____

PRINT DATE

BUYER'S INSPECTION ADVISORY (BIA-14 PAGE 1 OF 1)

CALIFORNIA
ASSOCIATION
OF REALTORS®

EXCLUSIVE AUTHORIZATION TO ACQUIRE REAL PROPERTY
BUYER BROKER COMPENSATION CONTRACT

1. **AGENCY AGREEMENT:** The undersigned _____ ("Buyer")
grants _____ ("Broker")
the exclusive and irrevocable right, on the terms specified in this Agreement commencing on (date) _____
and expiring at 11:59 p.m. on (date) _____, to represent Buyer in acquiring real property. Broker,
individually or through an associate-licensee, (an individual licensed as a real estate salesperson or broker who
works under the Broker's real estate license) agrees to exercise due diligence and reasonable efforts to fulfill the
following authorizations and obligations. Buyer agrees that Broker's duties are limited by the terms of this Agreement,
including those limitations set forth in paragraph 5.

2. **PROPERTY:**
Type of acquisition:(check all that apply) ☐ purchase ☐ lease ☐ exchange ☐ option ☐ other _____
Type of property: (check all that apply) ☐ residential ☐ residential income ☐ commercial ☐ industrial ☐ vacant land ☐ other _____
General description: _____
_____
Price range: $_____ to $_____
General location: _____
Other: _____

3. **BROKER AUTHORIZATIONS:** Buyer authorizes Broker to: (i) locate and present selected properties to Buyer,
present offers authorized by Buyer, and assist Buyer in negotiating for acceptance of such offers; (ii) assist Buyer with the financing
process, including obtaining loan pre-qualification; (iii) provide guidance to help Buyer with the acquisition of property; (iv) upon
request, provide Buyer with a list of professionals or vendors that perform the services described in paragraph 6C; (v) schedule and
attend meetings and appointments with professionals chosen by Buyer; and (vi) obtain a credit report on Buyer at Buyer's expense.

4. **BROKER OBLIGATIONS:** For property transactions of which Broker is aware, and not precluded from participating by Buyer, Broker,
either directly or indirectly through an authorized person, shall provide and review forms to create a real property contract ("Property
Contract") for the acquisition of a specific property ("Property"). With respect to such Property, Broker shall: (i) if the Property contains
residential property with one-to-four dwelling units, conduct a reasonably competent and diligent, visual inspection of the
accessible areas of the Property only (excluding any common areas), and disclose to Buyer all facts materially affecting the value or
desirability of such Property that are revealed by this inspection; (ii) deliver or communicate to Buyer any disclosures, materials or
information received during this agency by, in personal possession of, or personally known to the individual licensee(s) working with
Buyer; (iii) facilitate the escrow process, including assisting Buyer in negotiating with seller. Unless otherwise specified in writing, any
information provided through Broker in the course of representing Buyer has not been and will not be verified by Broker. Broker's
services are performed in compliance with federal, state and local anti-discrimination laws.

5. **SCOPE OF BROKER DUTY:**
   A. While Broker will perform the duties described in paragraph 4, Broker recommends that Buyer select other professionals, as
      described in paragraph 6C, to investigate the Property through inspections, investigations, tests, surveys, reports, studies and
      other available information ("Inspections") during the transaction. Buyer agrees that these Inspections, to the extent they exceed
      the obligations described in paragraph 4, are not within the scope of Broker's agency duties. Broker informs Buyer that it is in
      Buyer's best interest to obtain such Inspections.
   B. Buyer acknowledges and agrees that Broker: (i) Does not decide what price Buyer should pay or Seller should accept; (ii) Does
      not guarantee the condition of the Property; (iii) Shall not be responsible for identifying defects that are not known to Broker and
      either (a) are not visually observable in reasonably accessible areas of the Property or (b) are in common areas; (iv) Does not
      guarantee the performance, adequacy or completeness of Inspections, services, products or repairs provided or made by seller
      or others to Buyer or Seller; (v) Cannot identify location of boundary lines or other items affecting title; (vi) Cannot verify square
      footage, representations of others or information contained in Inspection reports; (vii) Cannot provide legal or tax advice
      regarding any aspect of a transaction entered into by Buyer in the course of this representation; and (viii) Will not provide other
      advice or information that exceeds the knowledge, education and experience required to perform real estate licensed activity.
      Buyer agrees to seek legal, tax, insurance, title and other desired assistance from appropriate professionals.
   C. Broker owes no duty to inspect for common environmental hazards, earthquake weaknesses, and geologic and seismic
      hazards. If Buyer receives the booklets titled "Environmental Hazards: A Guide for Homeowners and Buyers," "The
      Homeowner's Guide to Earthquake Safety," or "The Commercial Property Owners Guide to Earthquake Safety" they are
      deemed adequate to provide Buyer with information contained in the booklets and Broker is not required to provide Buyer with
      additional information about those items, other than known hazards on or affecting the Property.

Buyer and Broker acknowledge receipt of copy of this page, which constitutes Page 1 of _____ Pages.
Buyer's Initials (_____) (_____)   Broker's Initials (_____) (_____)

Published and Distributed by:
REAL ESTATE BUSINESS SERVICES, INC.
a subsidiary of the CALIFORNIA ASSOCIATION OF REALTORS®
525 South Virgil Avenue, Los Angeles, California 90020

REVISED 4/99

OFFICE USE ONLY
Reviewed by Broker
or Designee _____
Date _____

EQUAL HOUSING
OPPORTUNITY

PRINT DATE

EXCLUSIVE AUTHORIZATION TO ACQUIRE REAL PROPERTY (AAP-11 PAGE 1 OF 4)

Buyer: _____ Date: _____

6. BUYER'S OBLIGATIONS:

A. Buyer agrees to timely view or consider properties selected by Broker and to negotiate in good faith to acquire a property. Buyer further agrees to act in good faith toward the completion of any Property Contract entered into in furtherance of this Agreement. Within **5 days** from the execution of this Agreement, Buyer shall provide relevant personal and financial information to Broker to assure Buyer's ability to acquire Property as described. If Buyer fails to provide such documentation, or if Buyer does not qualify financially to acquire Property, then Broker may cancel this Agreement in writing. Buyer has an affirmative duty to protect him/herself, including discovery of the legal, practical and technical implications of discovered or disclosed facts, and investigation of information and facts which are known to Buyer or are within the diligent attention and observation of Buyer. Buyer has an obligation to, and agrees to, read all documents provided to Buyer. Buyer agrees to seek desired assistance from appropriate professionals, selected by Buyer, such as those referenced below.

B. Buyer shall notify Broker in writing if Buyer requests information on, or has any concerns regarding, any particular area of interest or importance to Buyer.

C. The following list of items represents many areas that typically warrant Inspections by other professionals.

GENERAL CONDITION OF THE PROPERTY, ITS SYSTEMS AND COMPONENTS: Foundation, roof, plumbing, heating, air conditioning, electrical, mechanical, security, pool/spa, and other structural and non-structural systems and components, built-in appliances, any personal property included in the sale, and energy efficiency of the Property. (Structural engineers are best suited to determine possible design or construction defects, and whether improvements are structurally sound.)

SQUARE FOOTAGE, AGE, BOUNDARIES, TITLE: Square footage, room dimensions, lot size, age of improvements, and boundaries. Any numerical statements regarding these items are APPROXIMATIONS ONLY, and have not been and cannot be verified by Brokers. Fences, hedges, walls, retaining walls, and other natural or constructed barriers or markers do not necessarily identify true Property boundaries. Public records may not contain accurate information or all information affecting title. (An appraiser, architect, surveyor, or civil engineer is best suited to determine respectively square footage, dimensions and location of boundaries and other title matters of the Property.)

SOIL STABILITY/GEOLOGIC CONDITIONS: Existence of compacted, expansive or contracting soil, fill, susceptibility to slippage, settling or movement, and the adequacy of drainage. Inspections for these types of conditions are particularly important for hillside or sloped properties, but also relevant for flat land. (Geotechnical engineers are best suited to determine such conditions, causes, and remedies.)

ROOF: Present condition, approximate age, leaks, and remaining useful life. (Roofing contractors are best suited to determine these conditions.)

POOL/SPA: Whether there are any cracks, leaks or operational problems including related equipment and components. (Pool contractors and soil engineers are best suited to determine these conditions.)

WASTE DISPOSAL: Type, size, adequacy, capacity, fees, connection and condition of sewer and septic systems and components.

WATER AND UTILITIES; WELL SYSTEMS AND COMPONENTS: Water and utility availability, use restrictions, and costs. Adequacy, condition, and performance of well systems and components.

ENVIRONMENTAL HAZARDS: Potential environmental hazards, including asbestos, lead-based paint and other lead contamination, methane, radon, other gases, fuel, oil or chemical storage tanks, contaminated soil or water, hazardous waste, waste disposal sites, electromagnetic fields, nuclear sources, and other substances, materials, products, or conditions. (For further information, read the booklet "Environmental Hazards: A Guide for Homeowners and Buyers," or consult an appropriate professional.)

EARTHQUAKE AND FLOOD; INSURANCE AVAILABILITY: Susceptibility of the Property to earthquake hazards and propensity of the Property to flood. These and other conditions may affect the availability and need for certain types of insurance. (Geologist, geotechnic engineer and insurance agents are best suited to provide information on these conditions.)

GOVERNMENTAL REQUIREMENTS AND LIMITATIONS: Permits, inspections, certificates, zoning, other governmental limitations, restrictions, and requirements affecting the current or future use of the Property, its development or size. (Such information is available through appropriate governmental agencies and private information providers. Brokers are not qualified to obtain, review, or interpret any such information.)

RENTAL PROPERTY RESTRICTIONS: Some cities and counties impose restrictions which may limit the amount of rent that can be charged, the maximum number of persons who can occupy the Property, and the circumstances in which tenancies can be terminated. Deadbolt or other locks and security systems for doors and windows should be examined to determine whether they satisfy legal requirements. (Local government agencies or locksmiths, respectively, can give information about these restrictions and requirements.)

NEIGHBORHOOD, AREA, SUBDIVISION CONDITIONS; PERSONAL FACTORS: Neighborhood or area conditions, including schools, proximity and adequacy of law enforcement, crime statistics, the proximity of registered felons or offenders, fire protection, other governmental services, proximity to commercial, industrial or agricultural activities, existing and proposed transportation, construction and development which may affect noise, view, or traffic, airport noise, noise or odor from any source, wild and domestic animals, other nuisances, hazards, or circumstances, protected species, wetland properties, historic or other governmentally protected sites or improvements, facilities and condition of common areas of common interest subdivisions, and possible lack of compliance with any governing documents or Homeowners' Association requirements, conditions and influences of significance to certain cultures and/or religions, and personal needs, requirements and preferences of Buyer.

Buyer and Broker acknowledge receipt of copy of this page, which constitutes Page 2 of _____ Pages.
Buyer's Initials (_____) (_____) Broker's Initials (_____) (_____)

OFFICE USE ONLY
Reviewed by Broker
or Designee
Date _____

REVISED 4/99

EQUAL HOUSING OPPORTUNITY

PRINT DATE

EXCLUSIVE AUTHORIZATION TO ACQUIRE REAL PROPERTY (AAP-11 PAGE 2 OF 4)

Buyer: _____ Date: _____

7. **AGENCY RELATIONSHIPS:**
   A. DISCLOSURE: If the Property includes residential property with one-to-four dwelling units, Buyer acknowledges receipt of the "Disclosure Regarding Real Estate Agency Relationships" form.
   B. BUYER REPRESENTATION: Broker will represent, as described in this Agreement, Buyer in any resulting transaction.
   C. (1) POSSIBLE DUAL AGENCY WITH SELLER: (C(1) APPLIES unless C(2) is initialed by both Buyer and Broker.)
      If Buyer is shown property listed with Broker, Buyer consents to Broker becoming a Dual Agent representing both Buyer and seller with respect to those properties. In event of Dual Agency, Buyer agrees that: **(a)** Broker, without the prior written consent of Buyer, will not disclose to a seller that Buyer is willing to pay a price greater than the offered price; **(b)** Broker, without the prior written consent of a seller, will not disclose to Buyer that a seller is willing to sell property at a price less than the listing price; and **(c)** Other than as set forth in **(a)** and **(b)** above, a Dual Agent is obligated to disclose known facts materially affecting the value or desirability of the property to both parties.
   OR (2) SINGLE AGENCY ONLY: (Applies only if initialed.)
      Broker agrees to act as the exclusive agent of Buyer in any resulting transaction, and not as a Dual Agent. Buyer understands that this election will prevent Broker from showing Buyer those properties which are listed with Broker or from representing Buyer in connection with those properties. Buyer's acquisition of a property listed with Broker shall not affect Broker's right to be compensated under paragraph 8.
      ☐ (Broker to check if applicable:) Broker represents buyers exclusively and does not list property.
      Broker's Initials _____ Buyer's Initials _____ / _____
   D. OTHER POTENTIAL BUYERS: Buyer understands that other potential buyers, through Broker, may consider, make offers on, or acquire the same or similar properties to those Buyer is seeking to acquire. Buyer consents to Broker's representation of such other potential buyers before, during, and after the term of this Agreement, or any extension.
   E. CONFIRMATION: If the Property includes residential property with one-to-four dwelling units, Broker shall confirm with Buyer the agency relationship described above, or as modified, in writing, prior to or coincident with the execution of a Purchase Contract.

8. **COMPENSATION TO BROKER:**
   NOTICE: The amount or rate of real estate commissions is not fixed by law. They are set by each Broker individually and may be negotiable between Buyer and Broker.
   A. AMOUNT OF COMPENSATION: Buyer agrees to pay to Broker, irrespective of agency relationship:
      (Check (1) or (2). Do NOT check both.)
      ☐ **(1)** _____ percent of the acquisition price, or $ _____ . (Applies to _all_ types of acquisitions checked.)
   OR ☐ **(2)** Pursuant to the compensation schedule attached as addendum _____ .
   B. BUYER OBLIGATION TO PAY COMPENSATION: Buyer is responsible for payment provided in this Agreement. **However, if anyone other than Buyer compensates Broker for services covered by this Agreement, that amount shall be credited against Buyer's obligation to pay compensation.** If the amount of compensation Broker receives from anyone other than Buyer exceeds Buyer's obligation, the excess amount shall be disclosed to Buyer, and, if allowed by law, ☐ paid to Broker, ☐ credited to Buyer, or ☐ other _____ .
   C. BROKER RIGHT TO COMPENSATION: Broker shall be entitled to the compensation provided for in paragraph 8A above:
      (1) If Buyer enters into an agreement to acquire Property described in paragraph 2, on those terms or any other terms acceptable to Buyer during the term of this Agreement, or any extension.
      (2) If, within ___ **calendar days** after termination of this Agreement or any extension, Buyer enters into an agreement to acquire Property described in paragraph 2, which property was introduced to Buyer by Broker, or for which Broker acted in Buyer's behalf. The obligation to pay compensation pursuant to this paragraph shall only be required if, prior to or within **5 (or ☐ ____) days** after expiration of this Agreement or any extension, Broker gives Buyer a written notice of those properties which Broker introduced to Buyer, or for which Broker acted in Buyer's behalf.
   D. PAYMENT OF COMPENSATION: Compensation is payable:
      (1) Upon completion of the transaction, through escrow;
      (2) If acquisition is prevented by default of Buyer, upon Buyer's default;
      (3) If acquisition is prevented by a party to the transaction other than Buyer, when Buyer collects damages by suit, settlement, or otherwise. Compensation shall equal one-half of damages recovered, not to exceed the above compensation, after first deducting the unreimbursed expenses of collection, if any.
   E. COMPENSATION INSTRUCTIONS: In any acquisition resulting from this Agreement, Buyer shall execute and deliver instructions to escrow holder irrevocably assigning compensation to Broker.
   F. "BUYER" includes any person or entity, other than Broker, related to Buyer or who in any manner acts on Buyer's behalf to acquire Property which satisfies the conditions set forth in paragraph 2.
   G. OTHER _____

   H. Broker has no obligation to compensate any other broker for the acquisition of Property described in paragraph 2 except
   _____ .
   This Agreement does not apply to Buyer's acquisition of any property listed in the exceptions above during the time Buyer is obligated to compensate another Broker.

Buyer and Broker acknowledge receipt of copy of this page, which constitutes Page 3 of _____ Pages.
Buyer's Initials (_____) (_____)   Broker's Initials (_____) (_____)   **REVISED 4/99**
PRINT DATE

OFFICE USE ONLY
Reviewed by Broker or Designee _____
Date _____

EQUAL HOUSING OPPORTUNITY

EXCLUSIVE AUTHORIZATION TO ACQUIRE REAL PROPERTY (AAP-11 PAGE 3 OF 4)

Buyer: _____   Date: _____

9. **MEDIATION:** Buyer and Broker agree to mediate any dispute or claim arising between them out of this Agreement, or any resulting transaction, before resorting to arbitration or court action, subject to paragraph 11 below. Mediation fees, if any, shall be divided equally among the parties involved. If any party commences an action based on a dispute or claim to which this paragraph applies, without first attempting to resolve the matter through mediation, then that party shall not be entitled to recover attorney's fees, even if they would otherwise be available to that party in any such action. THIS MEDIATION PROVISION APPLIES WHETHER OR NOT THE ARBITRATION PROVISION IS INITIALED.

10. **ARBITRATION OF DISPUTES: Buyer and Broker agree that any dispute or claim in Law or equity arising between them regarding the obligation to pay compensation under this Agreement which is not settled through mediation, shall be decided by neutral, binding arbitration, subject to paragraph 11 below. The arbitrator shall be a retired judge or justice, or an attorney with at least 5 years of residential real estate law experience, unless the parties mutually agree to a different arbitrator, who shall render an award in accordance with substantive California Law. In all other respects, the arbitration shall be conducted in accordance with Part III, Title 9 of the California Code of Civil Procedure. Judgment upon the award of the arbitrator(s) may be entered in any court having jurisdiction. The parties shall have the right to discovery in accordance with Code of Civil Procedure §1283.05.**

    "**NOTICE: BY INITIALING IN THE SPACE BELOW YOU ARE AGREEING TO HAVE ANY DISPUTE ARISING OUT OF THE MATTERS INCLUDED IN THE 'ARBITRATION OF DISPUTES' PROVISION DECIDED BY NEUTRAL ARBITRATION AS PROVIDED BY CALIFORNIA LAW AND YOU ARE GIVING UP ANY RIGHTS YOU MIGHT POSSESS TO HAVE THE DISPUTE LITIGATED IN A COURT OR JURY TRIAL. BY INITIALING IN THE SPACE BELOW YOU ARE GIVING UP YOUR JUDICIAL RIGHTS TO DISCOVERY AND APPEAL, UNLESS THOSE RIGHTS ARE SPECIFICALLY INCLUDED IN THE 'ARBITRATION OF DISPUTES' PROVISION. IF YOU REFUSE TO SUBMIT TO ARBITRATION AFTER AGREEING TO THIS PROVISION, YOU MAY BE COMPELLED TO ARBITRATE UNDER THE AUTHORITY OF THE CALIFORNIA CODE OF CIVIL PROCEDURE. YOUR AGREEMENT TO THIS ARBITRATION PROVISION IS VOLUNTARY.**"

    "**WE HAVE READ AND UNDERSTAND THE FOREGOING AND AGREE TO SUBMIT DISPUTES ARISING OUT OF THE MATTERS INCLUDED IN THE 'ARBITRATION OF DISPUTES' PROVISION TO NEUTRAL ARBITRATION.**"

    Buyer's Initials _____/_____   **Broker's Initials** _____/_____

11. **EXCLUSIONS FROM MEDIATION AND ARBITRATION:** The following matters are excluded from mediation and arbitration hereunder: **(a)** A judicial or non-judicial foreclosure or other action or proceeding to enforce a deed of trust, mortgage, or installment land sale contract as defined in Civil Code §2985; **(b)** An unlawful detainer action; **(c)** The filing or enforcement of a mechanic's lien; **(d)** Any matter which is within the jurisdiction of a probate, bankruptcy or small claims court; and, **(e)** An action for bodily injury or wrongful death, or for latent or patent defects to which Code of Civil Procedure §337.1 or §337.15 applies. The filing of a court action to enable the recording of a notice of pending action, for order of attachment, receivership, injunction, or other provisional remedies, shall not constitute a violation of the Mediation of Disputes and Arbitration of Disputes provisions.

12. **TIME TO BRING LEGAL ACTION:** Legal action for breach of this Agreement, or any obligation arising therefrom, shall be brought no more than two years from the expiration of this Agreement or from the date such cause of action may arise, whichever occurs first.

13. **ADDITIONAL TERMS:** _____
_____

14. **ATTORNEY'S FEES:** In any action, proceeding, or arbitration between Buyer and Broker regarding the obligation to pay compensation under this Agreement, the prevailing Buyer or Broker shall be entitled to reasonable attorney's fees and costs, except as provided in paragraph 9.

15. **ENTIRE CONTRACT:** All understandings between the parties are incorporated in this Agreement. Its terms are intended by the parties as a final, complete and exclusive expression of their agreement with respect to its subject matter, and may not be contradicted by evidence of any prior agreement or contemporaneous oral agreement. This Agreement may not be extended, amended, modified, altered or changed, except in writing signed by Buyer and Broker. In the event that any provision of this Agreement is held to be ineffective or invalid, the remaining provisions will nevertheless be given full force and effect. This Agreement and any supplement, addendum or modification, including any copy, whether by copier, facsimile or electronic, may be signed in two or more counterparts, all of which shall constitute one and the same writing.

Buyer acknowledges that Buyer has read, understood, and received a copy of this Agreement.

Date _____ at _____, California   Date _____ at _____, California

Buyer _____   Buyer _____

Telephone/Fax/Email _____   Telephone/Fax/Email _____

Address _____   Address _____

City _____ State ____ Zip _____   City _____ State _____ Zip _____

Date _____ at _____, California   Telephone/Fax/Email _____

Broker (Firm) _____   Address _____

By (agent) _____   City _____ State _____ Zip _____

This form is available for use by the entire real estate industry. It is not intended to identify the user as a REALTOR®. REALTOR® is a registered collective membership mark which may be used only by members of the NATIONAL ASSOCIATION OF REALTORS® who subscribe to its Code of Ethics.

PRINT DATE

REVISED 4/99

┌─ OFFICE USE ONLY ─┐
Reviewed by Broker
or Designee _____
Date _____

EXCLUSIVE AUTHORIZATION TO ACQUIRE REAL PROPERTY (AAP-11 PAGE 4 OF 4)

CALIFORNIA
ASSOCIATION
OF REALTORS®

SELLER FINANCING ADDENDUM AND DISCLOSURE
(California Civil Code §§2956-2967)

This is an addendum to the ☐ Residential Purchase Agreement, ☐ Counter Offer, or ☐ Other _____

_____ , ("Agreement"), dated _____ ,

On property known as _____ ("Property"),

In which _____ is referred to as Buyer,

And _____ is referred to as Seller.

Seller agrees to extend credit to Buyer as follows:

1. **PRINCIPAL; INTEREST; PAYMENT; MATURITY TERMS:** ☐ Principal amount $ _____ , interest at _____ % per annum, payable at approximately $ _____ per ☐ month, ☐ year, or ☐ other _____ , remaining principal balance due in _____ years.

2. **LOAN APPLICATION; CREDIT REPORT:** Within 5 (or ☐ _____) Days After Acceptance: (a) Buyer shall provide Seller a completed loan application on a form acceptable to Seller (such as a FNMA/FHLMC Uniform Residential Loan Application for residential one to four unit properties); and (b) Buyer authorizes Seller and/or Agent to obtain, at Buyer's expense, a copy of Buyer's credit report. Buyer shall provide any supporting documentation reasonably requested by Seller. Seller may cancel this Agreement in writing if Buyer fails to provide such documents within that time, or if Seller disapproves any above item within 5 (or ☐ _____) Days After receipt of each item.

3. **CREDIT DOCUMENTS:** This extension of credit by Seller will be evidenced by: ☐ Note and deed of trust; ☐ All-inclusive note and deed of trust; ☐ Installment land sale contract; ☐ Lease/option (when parties intend transfer of equitable title); OR ☐ Other (specify) _____

_____

THE FOLLOWING TERMS APPLY ONLY IF CHECKED. IF NOT CHECKED, THE TERM IS NOT PART OF THE SELLER FINANCING.

4. ☐ **LATE CHARGE:** If any payment is not made within _____ Days After it is due, a late charge of either ☐ $ _____ , or
☐ _____ % of the installment due, may be charged to Buyer. NOTE: On single family residences which Buyer intends to occupy, Civil Code §2954.4(a) limits the late charge to no more than 6% of the total monthly payment due and requires a grace period of no less than ten days.

5. ☐ **BALLOON PAYMENT:** The loan will provide for a balloon payment, in the amount of $ _____ , plus any accrued interest, which is due on _____ (date).

6. ☐ **PREPAYMENT:** If all or part of this loan is paid early, Seller may charge a prepayment penalty as follows (if applicable): _____
_____ Caution: Civil Code §2954.9 contains limitations on prepayment penalties for residential one to four properties.

7. ☐ **DUE ON SALE:** If any interest in the Property is sold or otherwise transferred, Seller has the option to require immediate payment of the entire unpaid principal balance, plus any accrued interest.

8.* ☐ **REQUEST FOR COPY OF NOTICE OF DEFAULT:** A Request for a copy of Notice of Default under Civil Code §2924b will be recorded. If Not, Seller is advised to consider recording a Request for Notice of Default.

9.* ☐ **REQUEST FOR NOTICE OF DELINQUENCY:** A Request for Notice of Delinquency, as defined in Civil Code §2924e, to be signed and paid for by Buyer, will be made to senior leinholders. If Not, Seller is advised to consider making a Request for Notice of Delinquency. Seller is advised to check with senior leinholders to verify whether they will honor this request.

10.* ☐ **TAX SERVICE:**
A. Tax service will be arranged to report to Seller if property taxes on the Property become delinquent. If Not, Seller is advised to consider retaining a tax service, or to otherwise determine that property taxes are paid.
B. ☐ Buyer, ☐ Seller, will be responsible for the initial and continued retention of, and payment for, such tax service.

11. ☐ **TITLE INSURANCE:** Title insurance coverage will be provided to both Seller and Buyer, insuring their respective interests in the Property. If Not, Buyer and Seller are advised to consider securing such title insurance coverage.

12. ☐ **HAZARD INSURANCE:**
A. The parties' escrow holder or insurance carrier will be directed to include a loss payee endorsement adding Seller to the property insurance policy. If Not, Seller is advised to secure such an endorsement, or acquire a separate insurance policy.
B. Property insurance does not include earthquake or flood insurance coverage, unless checked:
☐ Earthquake insurance will be obtained; ☐ Flood insurance will be obtained.

13. ☐ **PROCEEDS TO BUYER:** Buyer will receive cash proceeds at the close of the sale transaction. The amount received will be approximately $ _____ , from _____ (indicate source of proceeds). Buyer represents that the purpose of such disbursement is as follows: _____

14. ☐ **NEGATIVE AMORTIZATION; DEFERRED INTEREST:** Negative amortization results when Buyer's periodic payments are less than the amount of interest earned on the obligation. Deferred interest also results when the obligation does not require periodic payments for a period of time. In either case, interest is not payable as it accrues. This accrued interest will be paid by Buyer at a later time, and may result in Buyer owing more on the obligation than at its origination. The credit being extended to Buyer by Seller will provide for negative amortization or deferred interest as indicated below. (Check A, B, or C. CHECK ONE ONLY.)
☐ A. All negative amortization or deferred interest shall be added to the principal _____ (e.g., annually, monthly, etc.), and thereafter shall bear interest at the rate specified in the credit documents (compound interest);
OR ☐ B. All deferred interest shall be due and payable, along with principal, at maturity;
OR ☐ C. Other: _____

15. ☐ **ALL-INCLUSIVE DEED OF TRUST; INSTALLMENT LAND SALE CONTRACT:** This transaction involves the use of an all-inclusive (or wraparound) deed of trust or an installment land sale contract. That deed of trust or contract shall provide as follows:
A. In the event of an acceleration of any senior encumbrance, the responsibility for payment, or for legal defense is: _____
_____ ; OR ☐ Is Not specified in the credit or security documents.
B. In the event of the prepayment of a senior encumbrance, the responsibilities and rights of Buyer and Seller regarding refinancing, prepayment penalties, and any prepayment discounts are: _____ ;
OR ☐ Are Not specified in the documents evidencing credit.
C. Buyer will make periodic payments to _____ (Seller, collection agent, or any neutral third party), who will be responsible for disbursing payments to the payee(s) on the senior encumbrance(s) and to Seller.
NOTE: The Parties are advised to designate a neutral third party for these purposes.

16. ☐ **TAX IDENTIFICATION NUMBERS:** Buyer and Seller shall each provide to the other their social security numbers or taxpayer identification numbers.

17. ☐ **OTHER CREDIT TERMS:** _____

18. ☐ **RECORDING:** The documents evidencing credit (paragraph 3) will be recorded with the county recorder where the Property is located. If Not, Buyer and Seller are advised that their respective interests in the Property may be jeopardized by intervening liens, judgments, encumbrances, or subsequent transfers.

19. ☐ **JUNIOR FINANCING:** There will be additional financing, secured by the Property, junior to this Seller financing. Explain: _____
_____

* (For Paragraphs 8-10) In order to receive timely and continued notification, Seller is advised to record appropriate notices and/or to notify appropriate parties of any change in Seller's address.

Buyer and Seller acknowledge receipt of copy of this page, which constitutes Page _____ of _____ Pages.

Buyer's Initials (_____) (_____)   Seller's Initials (_____) (_____)

Published and Distributed by:
REAL ESTATE BUSINESS SERVICES, INC.
a subsidiary of the CALIFORNIA ASSOCIATION OF REALTORS®
525 South Virgil Avenue, Los Angeles, California 90020
PRINT DATE

REVISED 10/98

┌─ OFFICE USE ONLY ─┐
Reviewed by Broker
or Designee _____
Date _____

SELLER FINANCING ADDENDUM AND DISCLOSURE (SFA-14 PAGE 1 OF 2)

Property Address: _____ Date: _____

20. SENIOR LOANS; ENCUMBRANCES: The following information is provided on loans and/or encumbrances that will be **senior** to Seller financing. NOTE: The following are estimates, unless otherwise marked with an asterisk (*). If checked: ☐ A separate sheet with information on additional senior loans/encumbrances is attached.

	1st	2nd
A. Original Balance	$ _____	$ _____
B. Current Balance	$ _____	$ _____
C. Periodic Payment (e.g. $100/month):	$ _____/_____	$ _____/_____
Including impounds of:	$ _____/_____	$ _____/_____
D. Interest Rate (per annum)	_____ %	_____ %
E. Fixed or Variable Rate:	_____	_____
If Variable Rate: Lifetime Cap (Ceiling)	_____	_____
Indicator (Underlying Index)	_____	_____
Margins	_____	_____
F. Maturity Date	_____	_____
G. Amount of Balloon Payment	$ _____	$ _____
H. Date Balloon Payment Due	_____	_____
I. Potential for Negative Amortization? (Yes, No, or Unknown)	_____	_____
J. Due on Sale? (Yes, No, or Unknown)	_____	_____
K. Pre-payment penalty? (Yes, No, or Unknown)	_____	_____
L. Are payments current? (Yes, No, or Unknown)	_____	_____

21. BUYER'S CREDITWORTHINESS: (CHECK EITHER A OR B. Do not check both.) In addition to the loan application, credit report and other information requested under paragraph 2:

A. ☐ No other disclosure concerning Buyer's creditworthiness has been made to Seller;

OR B. ☐ The following representations concerning Buyer's creditworthiness are made by Buyer(s) to Seller:

Borrower: _____	Co-Borrower: _____
1. Occupation _____	1. Occupation _____
2. Employer: _____	2. Employer: _____
3. Length of Employment _____	3. Length of Employment _____
4. Monthly Gross Income: _____	4. Monthly Gross Income: _____
5. Other: _____	5. Other: _____

22. ADDED, DELETED OR SUBSTITUTED BUYERS: The addition, deletion or substitution of any person or entity under this Agreement or to title prior to close of escrow shall require Seller's written consent. Seller may grant or withhold consent in Seller's sole discretion. Any additional or substituted person or entity shall, if requested by Seller, submit to Seller the same documentation as required for the original named Buyer. Seller and/or Brokers may obtain a credit report, at Buyer's expense, on any such person or entity.

23. CAUTION:

A. If the Seller financing requires a balloon payment, Seller shall give Buyer written notice, according to the terms of Civil Code 2966, at least 90 and not more than 150 days before the balloon payment is due if the transaction is for the purchase of a dwelling for not more than four families.

B. If **any** obligation secured by the Property calls for a balloon payment, Seller and Buyer are aware that refinancing of the balloon payment at maturity may be difficult or impossible, depending on conditions in the conventional mortgage marketplace at that time. There are no assurances that new financing or a loan extension will be available when the balloon prepayment, or any prepayment, is due.

C. If **any** of the existing or proposed loans would require refinancing as a result of a lack of full amortization, such refinancing might be difficult or impossible in the conventional mortgage marketplace.

D. In the event of default by Buyer: (1) Seller may have to reinstate and/or make monthly payments on any and all senior encumbrances (including real property taxes) in order to protect Seller's secured interest; (2) Seller's rights are generally limited to foreclosure on the Property, pursuant to Code of Civil Procedure 580(b); and, (3) the Property may not have sufficient equity to protect Seller's interests because Property may have decreased in value.

If this two-page Addendum and Disclosure is used in a transaction for the purchase of a dwelling for not more than four families, it shall be prepared by an Arranger of Credit as defined in Civil Code §2957(a). (The Arranger of Credit is usually the agent who obtained the offer.)

Arranger of Credit - Print Firm Name		By			Date
Address	City	State	Zip	Telephone	Fax

BUYER AND SELLER ACKNOWLEDGE AND AGREE THAT BROKERS: (A) WILL NOT PROVIDE LEGAL OR TAX ADVICE; (B) WILL NOT PROVIDE OTHER ADVICE OR INFORMATION THAT EXCEEDS THE KNOWLEDGE, EDUCATION AND EXPERIENCE REQUIRED TO OBTAIN A REAL ESTATE LICENSE; OR (C) HAVE NOT AND WILL NOT VERIFY ANY INFORMATION PROVIDED BY EITHER BUYER OR SELLER. BUYER AND SELLER AGREE THAT THEY WILL SEEK LEGAL, TAX, AND OTHER DESIRED ASSISTANCE FROM APPROPRIATE PROFESSIONALS. BUYER AND SELLER ACKNOWLEDGE THAT THE INFORMATION EACH HAS PROVIDED TO THE ARRANGER OF CREDIT FOR INCLUSION IN THIS DISCLOSURE FORM IS ACCURATE. BUYER AND SELLER FURTHER ACKNOWLEDGE THAT EACH HAS RECEIVED A COMPLETED COPY OF THIS DISCLOSURE FORM.

Buyer (Signature)		Date	Seller (Signature)		Date
Address			Address		
City	State	Zip	City	State	Zip
Telephone	Fax		Telephone	Fax	
Buyer (Signature)		Date	Seller (Signature)		Date
Address			Address		
City	State	Zip	City	State	Zip
Telephone	Fax		Telephone	Fax	

This form is available for use by the entire real estate industry. It is not intended to identify the user as a REALTOR®. REALTOR® is a registered collective membership mark which may be used only by members of the NATIONAL ASSOCIATION OF REALTORS® who subscribe to its Code of Ethics.

Page _____ of _____ Pages.

REVISED 10/98

OFFICE USE ONLY
Reviewed by Broker
or Designee _____
Date _____

SELLER FINANCING ADDENDUM AND DISCLOSURE (SFA-14 PAGE 2 OF 2)

CALIFORNIA
ASSOCIATION
OF REALTORS®

RESIDENTIAL PURCHASE AGREEMENT
(AND RECEIPT FOR DEPOSIT)
For Use With Single Family Residential Property — Attached or Detached

Date _____, at _____, California,
Received From _____ ("Buyer"),
A Deposit Of _____ Dollars $ _____, toward the
Purchase Price Of _____ Dollars $ _____,
For Purchase Of Property Situated In _____, County Of _____
California, Described As _____ ("Property").

1. **FINANCING:** Obtaining the loans below **is a contingency** of this Agreement. Buyer shall act diligently and in good faith to obtain the designated loans. Obtaining deposit, down payment and closing costs **is not a contingency**.
   A. **BUYER'S DEPOSIT** shall be held uncashed until Acceptance and then deposited within **3 business days** after .. $ _____
      Acceptance or ☐ _____, ☐ with Escrow Holder,
      ☐ into Broker's trust account, or ☐ _____, by ☐ Personal Check, ☐ Cashier's Check,
      ☐ Cash, or ☐ _____
   B. **INCREASED DEPOSIT** shall be deposited with _____ .. $ _____
      within _____ **Days After Acceptance, or** ☐ _____
   C. **FIRST LOAN IN THE AMOUNT OF** _____ $ _____
      NEW First Deed of Trust in favor of LENDER, encumbering the Property, securing a note payable at maximum
      interest of _____ % fixed rate, or _____ % initial adjustable rate with a maximum interest rate cap of
      _____ %, balance due in _____ years. Buyer shall pay loan fees/points not to exceed _____
      ☐ FHA ☐ VA: Seller shall pay (i) _____ % discount points, (ii) other fees not allowed to be paid by Buyer,
      not to exceed $ _____, and (iii) the cost of lender required repairs not otherwise provided for in
      this Agreement, not to exceed $ _____
   D. **ADDITIONAL FINANCING TERMS:** _____ $ _____
      _____
      ☐ seller financing, (C.A.R. Form SFA-14), ☐ junior or assumed financing, (C.A.R. Form PAA-14, paragraph 5)
   E. **BALANCE OF PURCHASE PRICE** (not including costs of obtaining loans and other closing costs) to be deposited . $ _____
      with escrow holder within sufficient time to close escrow.
   F. **TOTAL PURCHASE PRICE** .... $ _____
   G. **LOAN CONTINGENCY** shall remain in effect until the designated loans are funded (or ☐ _____ **Days After Acceptance,** by which time Buyer
      shall give Seller written notice of Buyer's election to cancel this Agreement If Buyer is unable to obtain the designated loans. If Buyer does not
      give Seller such notice, the contingency of obtaining the designated loans shall be removed by the method specified in paragraph 16B.)
   H. **LOAN APPLICATIONS; PREQUALIFICATION:** For NEW financing, with 5 (or ☐ _____) **Days After Acceptance,** Buyer shall provide Seller
      a letter from lender or mortgage loan broker stating that, based on a review of Buyer's written application and credit report, Buyer is prequalified
      for the NEW loan indicated above. If Buyer fails to provide such letter within that time, Seller may cancel this Agreement in writing.
   I. ☐ **APPRAISAL CONTINGENCY:** (If checked) This Agreement is contingent upon Property appraising at no less than the specified total
      purchase price. If there is a loan contingency, the appraisal contingency shall remain in effect until the loan contingency is removed. If there
      is no loan contingency, the appraisal contingency shall be removed within 10 (or ☐ _____) **Days After Acceptance.**
   J. **ALL CASH OFFER:** If this is an all cash offer, Buyer shall, within 5 (or ☐ _____) **Days After Acceptance,** provide Seller written verification
      of sufficient funds to close this transaction. Seller may cancel this Agreement in writing within **5 Days After:** (i) time to provide verification expires,
      if Buyer fails to provide verification; or (ii) receipt of verification, if Seller reasonably disapproves it.
2. **ESCROW:** Close Of Escrow shall occur _____ **Days After Acceptance** (or ☐ _____ (date). Buyer and Seller shall deliver signed
   escrow instructions consistent with this Agreement ☐ within _____ **Days After Acceptance,** ☐ at least _____ **Days before Close Of Escrow,**
   or ☐ _____. Seller shall deliver possession and occupancy of the Property to Buyer at _____ AM/PM, ☐ on
   the date of Close Of Escrow, ☐ no later than _____ **Days After date of Close Of Escrow, or** ☐ _____
   _____. Property shall be vacant, unless otherwise agreed in writing. If transfer of title and
   possession do not occur at the same time, Buyer and Seller are advised to (a) consult with their insurance advisors, and (b) enter into a written
   occupancy agreement. The omission from escrow instructions of any provision in this Agreement shall not constitute a waiver of that provision.
3. **OCCUPANCY:** Buyer ☐ does, ☐ does not, intend to occupy Property as Buyer's primary residence.
4. **ALLOCATION OF COSTS:** (Check boxes which apply. If needed, insert additional instructions in blank lines.)
   GOVERNMENTAL TRANSFER FEES:
   A. ☐ Buyer ☐ Seller shall pay County transfer tax or transfer fee. _____
   B. ☐ Buyer ☐ Seller shall pay City transfer tax or transfer fee. _____
   TITLE AND ESCROW COSTS:
   C. ☐ Buyer ☐ Seller shall pay for **owner's** title insurance policy, issued by _____ company.
      (Buyer shall pay for any title insurance policy insuring Buyer's **Lender,** unless otherwise agreed)
   D. ☐ Buyer ☐ Seller shall pay escrow fee. _____ Escrow holder shall be _____.
   SEWER/SEPTIC/WELL COSTS:
   E. ☐ Buyer ☐ Seller shall pay for sewer connection, if connection required by Law prior to Close Of Escrow.
   F. ☐ Buyer ☐ Seller shall pay to have septic or private sewage disposal system inspected. _____
   G. ☐ Buyer ☐ Seller shall pay to have domestic wells tested for water potability and productivity. _____
   OTHER COSTS:
   H. ☐ Buyer ☐ Seller shall pay Homeowners' Association transfer fees. _____
   I. ☐ Buyer ☐ Seller shall pay Homeowners' Association document preparation fees. _____
   J. ☐ Buyer ☐ Seller shall pay for zone disclosure reports. _____
   K. ☐ Buyer ☐ Seller shall pay for Smoke Detector installation and/or Water Heater bracing. _____
      Seller, prior to close of escrow, shall provide Buyer a written statement of compliance in accordance with state and local Law, unless exempt.
   L. ☐ Buyer ☐ Seller shall pay the cost of compliance with any other minimum mandatory government retrofit standards and inspections required
      as a condition of closing escrow under any Law. _____
   M. ☐ Buyer ☐ Seller shall pay the cost of a one-year home warranty plan, issued by _____
      with the following optional coverage: _____ Policy cost not to exceed $ _____.
   PEST CONTROL REPORT:
   N. ☐ Buyer ☐ Seller shall pay for the Pest Control Report ("Report"), which, within the time specified in paragraph 16, shall be prepared by
      _____, a registered structural pest control company. _____
   O. **(1)** Buyer shall have the right to disapprove the Report as specified in paragraph 16, UNLESS any box in 4 O (2) is checked below
   OR (2) (Applies if any box is checked below)
      (a) ☐ Buyer ☐ Seller shall pay for work recommended to correct conditions described in the Report as **"Section 1."**
      (b) ☐ Buyer ☐ Seller shall pay for work recommended to correct conditions described in the Report as **"Section 2,"** if requested by Buyer.

Buyer and Seller acknowledge receipt of copy of this page, which constitutes Page 1 of _____ Pages.
Buyer's Initials (_____) (_____) Seller's Initials (_____) (_____)

Published and Distributed by:
REAL ESTATE BUSINESS SERVICES, INC.
a subsidiary of the CALIFORNIA ASSOCIATION OF REALTORS®
525 South Virgil Avenue, Los Angeles, California 90020
PRINT DATE

REVISED 4/99

┌─ OFFICE USE ONLY ─┐
Reviewed by Broker
or Designee _____
Date _____
└───────────────────┘

EQUAL HOUSING OPPORTUNITY

RESIDENTIAL PURCHASE AGREEMENT AND RECEIPT FOR DEPOSIT (RPA-14 PAGE 1 OF 5)

Property Address: _____ Date: _____

5. PEST CONTROL TERMS: If a Report is prepared pursuant to paragraph 4N:
   A. The Report shall cover the main building and attached structures and, if checked: ☐ detached garages and carports, ☐ detached decks, ☐ the following other structures on the Property: _____
   B. If Property is a unit in a condominium, planned development, or residential stock cooperative, the Report shall cover only the separate interest and any exclusive-use areas being transferred, and shall not cover common areas, unless otherwise agreed.
   C. If inspection of inaccessible areas is recommended in the Report, Buyer has the option, within **5 Days After** receipt of the Report, either to accept and approve the Report by the method specified in paragraph 16B, or to request in writing that further inspection be made. If upon further inspection no infestation or infection is found in the inaccessible areas, the cost of the inspection, entry, and closing of those areas shall be paid for by Buyer. If upon further inspection infestation or infection is found in the inaccessible areas, the cost of inspection, entry, and closing of those areas shall be paid for by the party so designated in paragraph 4O(2)a. If no party is so designated, then cost shall be paid by Buyer.
   D. If no infestation or infection by wood destroying pests or organisms is found in the Report, or upon completion of required corrective work, a written Pest Control Certification shall be issued. Certification shall be issued prior to Close Of Escrow, unless otherwise agreed in writing.
   E. Inspections, corrective work and Pest Control Certification in this paragraph refers only to the presence or absence of wood destroying pests or organisms, and does not include the condition of roof coverings. Read paragraphs 9 and 12 concerning roof coverings.
   F. Nothing in paragraph 5 shall relieve Seller of the obligation to repair or replace shower pans and shower enclosures due to leaks, if required by paragraph 9B(3). Water test of shower pans on upper level units may not be performed unless the owners of property below the shower consent.

6. TRANSFER DISCLOSURE STATEMENT; LEAD-BASED PAINT HAZARD DISCLOSURES; NATURAL HAZARD DISCLOSURES; SUBSEQUENT DISCLOSURES; MELLO-ROOS NOTICE; CANCELLATION RIGHTS:
   A. Within the time specified in paragraph 16A(1), if required by law, a Real Estate Transfer Disclosure Statement ("TDS"), Federal Lead-Based Paint Disclosures and pamphlet, ("Lead Disclosures"), and Natural Hazard Disclosure Statement ("NHD") shall be completed and delivered to Buyer, who shall return signed copies to Seller.
   B. In the event Seller, prior to Close Of Escrow, becomes aware of adverse conditions materially affecting the Property, or any material inaccuracy in disclosures, information, or representations previously provided to Buyer (including those made in a TDS) of which Buyer is otherwise unaware, Seller shall promptly provide a subsequent or amended disclosure, in writing, covering those items, **except for those conditions and material inaccuracies disclosed in reports obtained by Buyer.**
   C. Seller shall (i) make a good faith effort to obtain a disclosure notice from any local agencies which levy a special tax on the Property pursuant to the Mello-Roos Community Facilities Act; and (ii) promptly deliver to Buyer any such notice made available by those agencies.
   D. If the TDS, the Lead Disclosures, the NHD, the Mello-Roos disclosure notice, or a subsequent or amended disclosure is delivered to Buyer after the offer is signed, Buyer shall have the right to cancel this Agreement within **3 days** after delivery in person, or **5 days** after delivery by deposit in the mail, by giving written notice of cancellation to Seller or Seller's agent. (Lead Disclosures sent by mail must be sent certified mail or better.)

7. DISCLOSURES: Within the time specified in paragraph 16A(1), Seller shall (i) disclose if Property is located in any zone identified in 7A and provide any other information required for those zones; (ii) if required by law, provide Buyer with the disclosures and other information identified in 7B; and, (iii) if applicable, take the actions specified in 7C. Buyer shall then, within the time specified in paragraph 16, investigate the disclosures and information, and other information provided to Buyer, and provide written notice to Seller of any item disapproved.
   A. ZONE DISCLOSURES: Special Flood Hazard Areas; Potential Flooding (Inundation) Areas; Very High Fire Hazard Zones; State Fire Responsibility Areas; Earthquake Fault Zones; Seismic Hazard Zones; or any other federal, state, or locally designated zone for which disclosure is required by Law.
   B. PROPERTY DISCLOSURES AND PUBLICATIONS: Earthquake Guides (and disclosures), Environmental Hazards Booklet.
   C. ☐ (If checked:) **CONDOMINIUM/COMMON INTEREST SUBDIVISION:** Property is a unit in a condominium, planned development, or other common interest subdivision. Seller shall request from the Homeowners' Association ("HOA"), and upon receipt provide to Buyer: copies of any documents required by Law; any pending or anticipated claims or litigation by or against the HOA; a statement containing the location and number of designated parking and storage spaces; and copies of the most recent 12 months of HOA minutes for regular and special meetings, if available. (C.A.R. Form HOA-11)
   D. NOTICE OF VIOLATION: If, prior to Close Of Escrow, Seller receives notice or is made aware of any notice filed or issued against the Property, for violations of any Laws, Seller shall immediately notify Buyer in writing.
   E. DATA BASE DISCLOSURE: NOTICE: The California Department of Justice, sheriff's departments, police departments serving jurisdictions of 200,000 or more and many other local law enforcement authorities maintain for public access a data base of the locations of persons required to register pursuant to paragraph (1) of subdivision (a) of Section 290.4 of the Penal Code. The data base is updated on a quarterly basis and is a source of information about the presence of these individuals in any neighborhood. The Department of Justice also maintains a Sex Offender Identification Line through which inquiries about individuals may be made. This is a "900" telephone service. Callers must have specific information about individuals they are checking. Information regarding neighborhoods is not available through the "900" telephone service.

8. TITLE AND VESTING:
   A. Within the time specified in paragraph 16A, Buyer shall be provided a current preliminary (title) report (which is only an offer by the title insurer to issue a policy of title insurance, and may not contain every item affecting title). Buyer shall, within the time specified in paragraph 16A(2), provide written notice to Seller of any items reasonably disapproved.
   B. At Close Of Escrow, Buyer shall receive a grant deed conveying title (or, for stock cooperative or long-term lease, an assignment of stock certificate or of seller's interest), including oil, mineral and water rights, if currently owned by Seller. Title shall be subject to all encumbrances, easements, covenants, conditions, restrictions, rights, and other matters which are of record or disclosed to Buyer prior to Close Of Escrow, unless disapproved in writing by Buyer within the time specified in paragraph 16A(2). However, title shall not be subject to any liens against the Property, except for those specified in the Agreement. Buyer shall receive an ALTA-R owner's title insurance policy, if reasonably available. If not, Buyer shall receive a standard coverage owner's policy (e.g. CLTA or ALTA with regional exceptions). Title shall vest as designated in Buyer's escrow instructions. The title company, at Buyer's request, can provide information about availability, desirability, coverage, and cost of various title insurance coverages. THE MANNER OF TAKING TITLE MAY HAVE SIGNIFICANT LEGAL AND TAX CONSEQUENCES.

9. CONDITION OF PROPERTY:
   A. EXCEPT AS SPECIFIED IN THIS AGREEMENT, Property is sold "AS IS," WITHOUT WARRANTY, in its PRESENT physical condition.
   B. (IF CHECKED) SELLER WARRANTS THAT AT THE **TIME POSSESSION IS MADE AVAILABLE TO BUYER:**
   ☐ **(1)** Roof shall be free of leaks KNOWN to Seller or DISCOVERED during escrow.
   ☐ **(2)** Built-in appliances (including free-standing oven and range, if included in sale), heating, air conditioning, electrical, mechanical, water, sewer, and pool/spa systems, if any, shall be repaired, if KNOWN by Seller to be inoperative or DISCOVERED to be so during escrow. (Well system is not warranted by this paragraph. Well system is covered by paragraphs 4G, 12 and 16.)
   ☐ **(3)** Plumbing systems, shower pans, and shower enclosures shall be free of leaks KNOWN to Seller or DISCOVERED during escrow.
   ☐ **(4)** All fire, safety, and structural defects in chimneys and fireplaces KNOWN to Seller or DISCOVERED during escrow shall be repaired.
   ☐ **(5)** Septic system, if any, shall be repaired, if KNOWN by Seller to be inoperative, or DISCOVERED to be so during escrow.
   ☐ **(6)** All broken or cracked glass, torn existing window and door screens, and multi-pane windows with broken seals, shall be replaced.
   ☐ **(7)** All debris and all personal property not included in the sale shall be removed.
   ☐ **(8)** _____
   C. PROPERTY MAINTENANCE: Unless otherwise agreed, Property, including pool, spa, landscaping and grounds, is to be maintained in substantially the same condition as on the date of Acceptance.
   D. INSPECTIONS AND DISCLOSURES: Buyer's right to inspect the Property and disapprove of its condition based upon items discovered in Buyer's Inspections, which are not covered by paragraph 9B, shall be governed by the procedure in paragraphs 12 and 16. Disclosures in the TDS and items discovered in Buyer's Inspections do NOT eliminate Seller's obligations under paragraph 9B, unless specifically agreed in writing. **WHETHER OR NOT SELLER WARRANTS ANY ASPECT OF THE PROPERTY, SELLER IS OBLIGATED TO DISCLOSE KNOWN MATERIAL FACTS, AND TO MAKE OTHER DISCLOSURES REQUIRED BY LAW.**

Buyer and Seller acknowledge receipt of copy of this page, which constitutes Page 2 of _____ Pages.

Buyer's Initials (_____) (_____) Seller's Initials (_____) (_____)   **REVISED 4/99**

OFFICE USE ONLY
Reviewed by Broker or Designee _____
Date _____

RESIDENTIAL PURCHASE AGREEMENT AND RECEIPT FOR DEPOSIT (RPA-14 PAGE 2 OF 5)

Property Address: _____ Date: _____

10. **FIXTURES:** All EXISTING fixtures and fittings that are attached to the Property, or for which special openings have been made, are INCLUDED IN THE PURCHASE PRICE (unless excluded below), and shall be transferred free of liens and "AS IS," unless specifically warranted. Fixtures shall include, but are not limited to, existing electrical, mechanical, lighting, plumbing and heating fixtures, fireplace inserts, solar systems, built-in appliances, window and door screens, awnings, shutters, window coverings, attached floor coverings, television antennas, satellite dishes and related equipment, private integrated telephone systems, air coolers/conditioners, pool/spa equipment, garage door openers/remote controls, attached fireplace equipment, mailbox, in-ground landscaping, including trees/shrubs, and (if owned by Seller) water softeners, water purifiers and security systems/alarms, and _____
FIXTURES EXCLUDED: _____

11. **PERSONAL PROPERTY:** The following items of personal property, free of liens and "AS IS," unless specifically warranted, are INCLUDED IN THE PURCHASE PRICE: _____

12. **BUYER'S INVESTIGATION OF PROPERTY CONDITION:** Buyer's Acceptance of the condition of the Property is a contingency of this Agreement, as specified in this paragraph and paragraph 16. Buyer shall have the right, at Buyer's expense, to conduct inspections, investigations, tests, surveys, and other studies ("Inspections"), including the right to inspect for lead-based paint and other lead-based paint hazards and investigation of the sex offender data base under paragraph 7E. No Inspections shall be made by any governmental building or zoning inspector, or government employee, without Seller's prior written consent, unless required by Law. Property improvements may not be built according to codes or in compliance with current Law, or have had permits issued. Buyer shall, within the time specified in Paragraph 16A(2), complete these Inspections and notify Seller in writing of any items reasonably disapproved. Seller shall make Property available for all Inspections. Buyer shall: keep Property free and clear of liens; indemnify and hold Seller harmless from all liability, claims, demands, damages and costs; and repair all damages arising from Inspections. Buyer shall carry, or Buyer shall require anyone acting on Buyer's behalf to carry, policies of liability, worker's compensation, and other applicable insurance, defending and protecting Seller from liability for any injuries to persons or property occurring during any work done on the Property at Buyer's direction, prior to Close Of Escrow. Seller is advised that certain protections may be afforded Seller by recording a notice of non-responsibility for work done on the Property at Buyer's direction. At Seller's request, Buyer shall give Seller, at no cost, complete copies of all Inspection reports obtained by Buyer concerning the Property. Seller shall have water, gas and electricity on for Buyer's Inspections, and through the date possession is made available to Buyer.

13. **FINAL WALK-THROUGH; VERIFICATION OF CONDITION:** Buyer shall have the right to make a final inspection of the Property within 5 (or _____) Days prior to Close Of Escrow, NOT AS A CONTINGENCY OF THE SALE, but solely to confirm that Repairs have been completed as agreed in writing, and that Seller has complied with Seller's other obligations.

14. **PRORATIONS AND PROPERTY TAXES:** Unless otherwise agreed in writing, real property taxes and assessments, interest, rents, HOA regular, special, and emergency dues and assessments imposed prior to Close of Escrow, premiums on insurance assumed by Buyer, payments on bonds and assessments assumed by Buyer, and payments on Mello-Roos and other Special Assessment District bonds and assessments which are now a lien shall be PAID CURRENT and prorated between Buyer and Seller as of Close Of Escrow. Prorated payments on Mello-Roos and other Special Assessment District bonds and assessments and HOA special assessments that are now a lien but not yet due, shall be assumed by Buyer WITHOUT CREDIT toward the purchase price. Property will be reassessed upon change of ownership. Any supplemental tax bills shall be paid as follows: (1) For periods after Close Of Escrow, by Buyer; and, (2) For periods prior to Close Of Escrow, by Seller. TAX BILLS ISSUED AFTER CLOSE OF ESCROW SHALL BE HANDLED DIRECTLY BETWEEN BUYER AND SELLER. Exceptions: _____

15. **SALE OF BUYER'S PROPERTY:**
A. This Agreement is NOT contingent upon the sale of Buyer's property, unless paragraph 15B is checked.
OR B. ☐ (If checked) This Agreement IS CONTINGENT on the Close Of Escrow of Buyer's property, described as (address) _____
_____ ("Buyer's Property"), which is
(if checked) ☐ listed for sale with _____ Company, and/or
(if checked) ☐ in Escrow No. _____ with _____ Escrow Holder, scheduled to Close Escrow on _____ (date). Buyer shall deliver to Seller, within 5 Days After Seller's request, a copy of the contract for the sale of Buyer's Property, escrow instructions, and all amendments and modifications thereto. If Buyer's Property does not close escrow by the date specified for Close Of Escrow in this paragraph, then either Seller or Buyer may cancel this Agreement in writing.
After Acceptance:
(1) **(Applies UNLESS (2) is checked):** Seller SHALL have the right to continue to offer the Property for sale. If Seller accepts another written offer, Seller shall give Buyer written notice to (i) remove this contingency in writing, (ii) provide written verification of sufficient funds to close escrow on this sale without the sale of Buyer's Property, and (iii) comply with the following additional requirement(s) _____
_____
If Buyer fails to complete those actions within 72 (or _____) hours After receipt of such notice, Seller may cancel this Agreement in writing.
OR ☐ (2) (APPLIES ONLY IF CHECKED:) Seller SHALL NOT have the right to continue to offer the Property for sale, except for back-up offers.

16. **TIME PERIODS/DISAPPROVAL RIGHTS/REMOVAL OF CONTINGENCIES/CANCELLATION RIGHTS:**
A. **TIME PERIODS:** The following time periods shall apply, unless changed by mutual written agreement.
(1) **SELLER HAS:** 5 (or ☐ _____) Days After Acceptance to, as applicable, order, request or complete, and 2 Days After receipt (or completion) to provide to Buyer all reports, disclosures, and information for which Seller is responsible under paragraphs 4, 6, 7A, 7B, 7C, and 8.
(2) **BUYER HAS:** (a) 10 (or ☐ _____) Days After Acceptance to complete all Inspections, investigations and review of reports and other applicable information for which Buyer is responsible, with an additional 7 Days to complete geologic Inspections, and 10 (or _____) Days after Buyer's receipt of Lead Disclosures pursuant to paragraph 6A(1) to complete Inspections for lead-based paint and lead-based paint hazards. WITHIN THIS TIME, Buyer must either disapprove in writing any items, (including, if applicable, the pest control Report under paragraph 4O(1)) which are unacceptable to Buyer, or remove any contingency or disapproval right associated with that item by the active or passive method, as specified below; (b) 5 (or ☐ _____) Days After receipt of (i) each of the items in paragraph 16A(1); and (ii) notice of code and legal violations under paragraph 7D, to either disapprove in writing any items which are unacceptable to Buyer, or to remove any contingency or disapproval right associated with that item, by the active or passive method, as specified below.
(3) **SELLER'S RESPONSE TO BUYER'S DISAPPROVALS:** Seller shall have 5 (or ☐ _____) Days After receipt of Buyer's written notice of items reasonably disapproved, to respond in writing. If Seller refuses or is unable to make repairs to, or correct, any items reasonably disapproved by Buyer, or if Seller does not respond within the time period specified, Buyer shall have 5 (or ☐ _____) Days After receipt of Seller's response, or after the expiration of the time for Seller to respond, whichever occurs first, to cancel this Agreement in writing.
B. **ACTIVE OR PASSIVE REMOVAL OF BUYER'S CONTINGENCIES:**
(1) ☐ **ACTIVE METHOD** (APPLIES IF CHECKED): If Buyer does not give Seller written notice of items reasonably disapproved, removal of contingencies or disapproval right, or notice of cancellation within the time periods specified, Seller shall have the right to cancel this Agreement by giving written notice to Buyer.
(2) **PASSIVE METHOD** (Applies UNLESS Active Method is checked): If Buyer does not give Seller written notice of items reasonably disapproved, or of removal of contingencies or disapproval right, or notice of cancellation within the time periods specified, Buyer shall be deemed to have removed and waived any contingency or disapproval right, or the right to cancel, associated with that item.
C. **EFFECT OF CONTINGENCY REMOVAL:** If Buyer removes any contingency or cancellation right by the active or passive method, as applicable, Buyer shall conclusively be deemed to have: (1) Completed all Inspections, investigations, and review of reports and other applicable information and disclosures pertaining to that contingency or cancellation right; (2) Elected to proceed with the transaction; and, (3) Assumed all liability, responsibility, and expense for repairs or corrections pertaining to that contingency or cancellation right, or for inability to obtain financing if the contingency pertains to financing, except for items which Seller has agreed in writing to repair or correct.

Buyer and Seller acknowledge receipt of copy of this page, which constitutes Page 3 of _____ Pages.
Buyer's Initials (_____) (_____) Seller's Initials (_____) (_____) **REVISED 4/99**

OFFICE USE ONLY
Reviewed by Broker
or Designee _____
Date _____

RESIDENTIAL PURCHASE AGREEMENT AND RECEIPT FOR DEPOSIT (RPA-14 PAGE 3 OF 5)

Property Address: _____ Date: _____

D. CANCELLATION OF SALE/ESCROW; RETURN OF DEPOSITS: If Buyer or Seller gives written NOTICE OF CANCELLATION pursuant to rights duly exercised under the terms of this Agreement, Buyer and Seller agree to sign mutual instructions to cancel the sale and escrow and release deposits, less fees and costs, to the party entitled to the funds. Fees and costs may be payable to service providers and vendors for services and products provided during escrow. Release of funds will require mutual, signed release instructions from both Buyer and Seller, judicial decision, or arbitration award. **A party may be subject to a civil penalty of up to $1,000 for refusal to sign such instructions, if no good faith dispute exists as to who is entitled to the deposited funds (Civil Code §1057.3).**

17. **REPAIRS:** Repairs under this Agreement shall be completed prior to Close Of Escrow, unless otherwise agreed in writing. Work to be performed at Seller's expense may be performed by Seller or through others, provided that work complies with applicable laws, including governmental permit, inspection, and approval requirements. Repairs shall be performed in a skillful manner with materials of quality comparable to existing materials. It is understood that exact restoration of appearance or cosmetic items following all Repairs may not be possible.

18. **WITHHOLDING TAXES:** Seller and Buyer agree to execute and deliver any instrument, affidavit, statement, or instruction reasonably necessary to comply with federal (FIRPTA) and California withholding Laws, if required (such as C.A.R. Forms AS-11 and AB-11).

19. **KEYS:** At the time possession is made available to Buyer, Seller shall provide keys and/or means to operate all Property locks, mailboxes, security systems, alarms, and garage door openers. If the Property is a unit in a condominium or subdivision, Buyer may be required to pay a deposit to the HOA to obtain keys to access the HOA facilities.

20. **LIQUIDATED DAMAGES: If Buyer fails to complete this purchase by reason of any default of Buyer, Seller shall retain, as liquidated damages for breach of contract, the deposit actually paid. However, if the Property is a dwelling with no more than four units, one of which Buyer intends to occupy, then the amount retained shall be no more than 3% of the purchase price. Any excess shall be returned to Buyer. Buyer and Seller shall also sign a separate liquidated damages provision for any increased deposit. (C.A.R. Form RID-11 shall fulfill this requirement.)** Buyer's Initials _____/_____ Seller's Initials _____/_____

21. **DISPUTE RESOLUTION:**

    A. **MEDIATION:** Buyer and Seller agree to mediate any dispute or claim arising between them out of this Agreement, or any resulting transaction, before resorting to arbitration or court action, subject to paragraphs 21C and D below. Mediation fees, if any, shall be divided equally among the parties involved. If any party commences an action based on a dispute or claim to which this paragraph applies, without first attempting to resolve the matter through mediation, then that party shall not be entitled to recover attorney's fees, even if they would otherwise be available to that party in any such action. THIS MEDIATION PROVISION APPLIES WHETHER OR NOT THE ARBITRATION PROVISION IS INITIALED.

    B. **ARBITRATION OF DISPUTES:** Buyer and Seller agree that any dispute or claim in Law or equity arising between them out of this Agreement or any resulting transaction, which is not settled through mediation, shall be decided by neutral, binding arbitration, subject to paragraphs 21C and D below. The arbitrator shall be a retired judge or justice, or an attorney with at least 5 years of residential real estate law experience, unless the parties mutually agree to a different arbitrator, who shall render an award in accordance with substantive California Law. In all other respects, the arbitration shall be conducted in accordance with Part III, Title 9 of the California Code of Civil Procedure. Judgment upon the award of the arbitrator(s) may be entered in any court having jurisdiction. The parties shall have the right to discovery in accordance with Code of Civil Procedure §1283.05.

    "**NOTICE: BY INITIALING IN THE SPACE BELOW YOU ARE AGREEING TO HAVE ANY DISPUTE ARISING OUT OF THE MATTERS INCLUDED IN THE 'ARBITRATION OF DISPUTES' PROVISION DECIDED BY NEUTRAL ARBITRATION AS PROVIDED BY CALIFORNIA LAW AND YOU ARE GIVING UP ANY RIGHTS YOU MIGHT POSSESS TO HAVE THE DISPUTE LITIGATED IN A COURT OR JURY TRIAL. BY INITIALING IN THE SPACE BELOW YOU ARE GIVING UP YOUR JUDICIAL RIGHTS TO DISCOVERY AND APPEAL, UNLESS THOSE RIGHTS ARE SPECIFICALLY INCLUDED IN THE 'ARBITRATION OF DISPUTES' PROVISION. IF YOU REFUSE TO SUBMIT TO ARBITRATION AFTER AGREEING TO THIS PROVISION, YOU MAY BE COMPELLED TO ARBITRATE UNDER THE AUTHORITY OF THE CALIFORNIA CODE OF CIVIL PROCEDURE. YOUR AGREEMENT TO THIS ARBITRATION PROVISION IS VOLUNTARY.**"

    "**WE HAVE READ AND UNDERSTAND THE FOREGOING AND AGREE TO SUBMIT DISPUTES ARISING OUT OF THE MATTERS INCLUDED IN THE 'ARBITRATION OF DISPUTES' PROVISION TO NEUTRAL ARBITRATION.**" Buyer's Initials _____/_____ Seller's Initials _____/_____

    C. **EXCLUSIONS FROM MEDIATION AND ARBITRATION:** The following matters are excluded from Mediation and Arbitration: (a) A judicial or non-judicial foreclosure or other action or proceeding to enforce a deed of trust, mortgage, or installment land sale contract as defined in Civil Code §2985; (b) An unlawful detainer action; (c) The filing or enforcement of a mechanic's lien; (d) Any matter which is within the jurisdiction of a probate, small claims, or bankruptcy court; and (e) An action for bodily injury or wrongful death, or for latent or patent defects to which Code of Civil Procedure §337.1 or §337.15 applies. The filing of a court action to enable the recording of a notice of pending action, for order of attachment, receivership, injunction, or other provisional remedies, shall not constitute a violation of the mediation and arbitration provisions.

    D. **BROKERS:** Buyer and Seller agree to mediate and arbitrate disputes or claims involving either or both Brokers, provided either or both Brokers shall have agreed to such mediation or arbitration, prior to or within a reasonable time after the dispute or claim is presented to Brokers. Any election by either or both Brokers to participate in mediation or arbitration shall not result in Brokers being deemed parties to the Agreement.

22. **DEFINITIONS:** As used in this Agreement:

    A. "**Acceptance**" means the time the offer or final counter offer is accepted in writing by the other party, in accordance with this Agreement or the terms of the final counter offer.

    B. "**Agreement**" means the terms and conditions of this Residential Purchase Agreement and any counter offer.

    C. "**Days**" means calendar days, unless otherwise required by Law.

    D. "**Days After . .**" means the specified number of calendar days after the occurrence of the event specified, not counting the calendar date on which the specified event occurs.

    E. "**Close Of Escrow**" means the date the grant deed, or other evidence of transfer of title, is recorded.

    F. "**Law**" means any law, code, statute, ordinance, regulation, or rule, which is adopted by a controlling city, county, state or federal legislative or judicial body or agency.

    G. "**Repairs**" means any repairs, alterations, replacements, or modifications, (including pest control work) of the Property.

    H. "**Pest Control Certification**" means a written statement made by a registered structural pest control company that on the date of inspection or re-inspection, the Property is "free" or is "now free" of "evidence of active infestation in the visible and accessible areas".

    I. **Section 1** means infestation or infection which is evident. **Section 2** means present conditions likely to lead to infestation or infection.

    J. **Singular and Plural** terms each include the other, when appropriate.

    K. **C.A.R. Form** means the specific form referenced, or another comparable form agreed to by the parties.

23. **MULTIPLE LISTING SERVICE ("MLS"):** Brokers are authorized to report the terms of this transaction to any MLS, to be published and disseminated to persons and entities authorized to use the information, on terms approved by the MLS.

Buyer and Seller acknowledge receipt of copy of this page, which constitutes Page 4 of _____ Pages.
Buyer's Initials (_____) (_____)   Seller's Initials (_____) (_____)   **REVISED 4/99**

RESIDENTIAL PURCHASE AGREEMENT AND RECEIPT FOR DEPOSIT (RPA-14 PAGE 4 OF 5)

Property Address: _____ **Date:** _____

24. **EQUAL HOUSING OPPORTUNITY:** The Property is sold in compliance with federal, state, and local anti-discrimination Laws.

25. **ATTORNEY'S FEES:** In any action, proceeding, or arbitration between Buyer and Seller arising out of this Agreement, the prevailing Buyer or Seller shall be entitled to reasonable attorney's fees and costs from the non-prevailing Buyer or Seller, except as provided in paragraph 21A.

26. **SELECTION OF SERVICE PROVIDERS:** If Brokers give Buyer or Seller referrals to persons, vendors, or service or product providers ("Providers"), Brokers do not guarantee the performance of any of those Providers. Buyer and Seller may select ANY Providers of their own choosing.

27. **TIME OF ESSENCE; ENTIRE CONTRACT; CHANGES:** Time is of the essence. All understandings between the parties are incorporated in this Agreement. Its terms are intended by the parties as a final, complete, and exclusive expression of their agreement with respect to its subject matter, and may not be contradicted by evidence of any prior agreement or contemporaneous oral agreement. **This Agreement may not be extended, amended, modified, altered, or changed, except in writing signed by Buyer and Seller.**

28. **OTHER TERMS AND CONDITIONS,** including ATTACHED SUPPLEMENTS:
☑ Buyer Inspection Advisory (C.A.R. Form BIA-14) _____
☐ Purchase Agreement Addendum (C.A.R. Form PAA-14 paragraph numbers: _____
_____
_____
_____

29. **AGENCY CONFIRMATION:** The following agency relationships are hereby confirmed for this transaction:
Listing Agent: _____ (Print Firm Name) is the agent of (check one):
☐ the Seller exclusively; or ☐ both the Buyer and Seller.
Selling Agent: _____ (Print Firm Name) (if not same as Listing Agent) is the agent of (check one):
☐ the Buyer exclusively; or ☐ the Seller exclusively; or ☐ both the Buyer and Seller.
Real Estate Brokers are not parties to the Agreement between Buyer and Seller.

30. **OFFER:** This is an offer to purchase the Property on the above terms and conditions. All paragraphs with spaces for initials by Buyer and Seller are incorporated in this Agreement only if initialed by all parties. If at least one but not all parties initial, a counter offer is required until agreement is reached. Unless Acceptance of Offer is signed by Seller, and a signed copy delivered in person, by mail, or facsimile, and personally received by Buyer, or by _____, who is authorized to receive it, by (date) _____, at _____ AM/PM, the offer shall be deemed revoked and the deposit shall be returned. Buyer has read and acknowledges receipt of a copy of the offer and agrees to the above confirmation of agency relationships. If this offer is accepted and Buyer subsequently defaults, Buyer may be responsible for payment of Brokers' compensation. This Agreement and any supplement, addendum, or modification, including any photocopy or facsimile, may be signed in two or more counterparts, all of which shall constitute one and the same writing.

> Buyer and Seller acknowledge and agree that Brokers: (a) **Do not decide what price Buyer should pay or Seller should accept; (b) Do not guarantee the condition of the Property; (c) Shall not be responsible for defects that are not known to Broker(s) and are not visually observable in reasonably accessible areas of the Property; (d) Do not guarantee the performance or Repairs of others who have provided services or products to Buyer or Seller; (e) Cannot identify location of boundary lines or other items affecting Property title; (f) Cannot verify inspection reports, square footage or representations of others; (g) Cannot provide legal or tax advice; (h) Will not provide other advice or information that exceeds the knowledge, education and experience required to obtain a real estate license. Buyer and Seller agree that they will seek legal, tax, insurance, title, and other desired assistance from appropriate professionals.**

BUYER _____   BUYER _____

31. **BROKER COMPENSATION:** Seller agrees to pay compensation for services as follows:
_____, to _____, Broker, and
_____, to _____, Broker,
payable: **(a)** On recordation of the deed or other evidence of title; or **(b)** If completion of sale is prevented by default of Seller, upon Seller's default; or, **(c)** If completion of sale is prevented by default of Buyer, only if and when Seller collects damages from Buyer, by suit or otherwise, and then in an amount equal to one-half of the damages recovered, but not to exceed the above compensation, after first deducting title and escrow expenses and the expenses of collection, if any. Seller hereby irrevocably assigns to Brokers such compensation from Seller's proceeds, and irrevocably instructs Escrow Holder to disburse those funds to Brokers at close of escrow. Commission instructions can be amended or revoked only with the written consent of Brokers. In any action, proceeding or arbitration relating to the payment of such compensation, the prevailing party shall be entitled to reasonable attorney's fees and costs, except as provided in paragraph 21A.

32. **ACCEPTANCE OF OFFER:** Seller warrants that Seller is the owner of this Property, or has the authority to execute this Agreement. Seller accepts the above offer, agrees to sell the Property on the above terms and conditions, and agrees to the above confirmation of agency relationships. Seller has read and acknowledges receipt of a copy of this Agreement, and authorizes Broker to deliver a signed copy to Buyer.

If checked: ☐ **SUBJECT TO ATTACHED COUNTER OFFER, DATED** _____.

SELLER _____ Date _____

SELLER _____ Date _____

(____/____)   ACKNOWLEDGMENT OF RECEIPT: Buyer or authorized agent acknowledges receipt of signed Acceptance on (date) _____,
(Initials)   at _____ AM/PM.

Agency relationships are confirmed as above. Real Estate Brokers are not parties to the Agreement between Buyer and Seller.

Receipt for deposit is acknowledged:

Real Estate Broker (Selling Firm Name) _____ By _____ Date _____

Address _____ Telephone _____ Fax _____

Real Estate Broker (Listing Firm Name) _____ By _____ Date _____

Address _____ Telephone _____ Fax _____

REVISED 4/99
Page 5 of _____ Pages.

OFFICE USE ONLY
Reviewed by Broker
or Designee _____
Date _____

RESIDENTIAL PURCHASE AGREEMENT AND RECEIPT FOR DEPOSIT (RPA-14 PAGE 5 OF 5)

CALIFORNIA
ASSOCIATION
OF REALTORS®

DISCLOSURE REGARDING
REAL ESTATE AGENCY RELATIONSHIPS
(As required by the Civil Code)

When you enter into a discussion with a real estate agent regarding a real estate transaction, you should from the outset understand what type of agency relationship or representation you wish to have with the agent in the transaction.

SELLER'S AGENT

A Seller's agent under a listing agreement with the Seller acts as the agent for the Seller only. A Seller's agent or a subagent of that agent has the following affirmative obligations:
To the Seller:
    A Fiduciary duty of utmost care, integrity, honesty, and loyalty in dealings with the Seller.
To the Buyer and the Seller:
    (a) Diligent exercise of reasonable skill and care in performance of the agent's duties.
    (b) A duty of honest and fair dealing and good faith.
    (c) A duty to disclose all facts known to the agent materially affecting the value or desirability of the property that are not known to, or within the diligent attention and observation of, the parties.

An agent is not obligated to reveal to either party any confidential information obtained from the other party that does not involve the affirmative duties set forth above.

BUYER'S AGENT

A selling agent can, with a Buyer's consent, agree to act as agent for the Buyer only. In these situations, the agent is not the Seller's agent, even if by agreement the agent may receive compensation for services rendered, either in full or in part from the Seller. An agent acting only for a Buyer has the following affirmative obligations:
To the Buyer:
    A fiduciary duty of utmost care, integrity, honesty, and loyalty in dealings with the Buyer.
To the Buyer and the Seller:
    (a) Diligent exercise of reasonable skill and care in performance of the agent's duties.
    (b) A duty of honest and fair dealing and good faith.
    (c) A duty to disclose all facts known to the agent materially affecting the value or desirability of the property that are not known to, or within the diligent attention and observation of, the parties.

An agent is not obligated to reveal to either party any confidential information obtained from the other party that does not involve the affirmative duties set forth above.

AGENT REPRESENTING BOTH SELLER & BUYER

A real estate agent, either acting directly or through one or more associate licensees, can legally be the agent of both the Seller and the Buyer in a transaction, but only with the knowledge and consent of both the Seller and the Buyer.

In a dual agency situation, the agent has the following affirmative obligations to both the Seller and the Buyer:
    (a) A fiduciary duty of utmost care, integrity, honesty and loyalty in the dealings with either Seller or the Buyer.
    (b) Other duties to the Seller and the Buyer as stated above in their respective sections.

In representing both Seller and Buyer, the agent may not, without the express permission of the respective party, disclose to the other party that the Seller will accept a price less than the listing price or that the Buyer will pay a price greater than the price offered.

The above duties of the agent in a real estate transaction do not relieve a Seller or Buyer from the responsibility to protect his or her own interests. You should carefully read all agreements to assure that they adequately express your understanding of the transaction. A real estate agent is a person qualified to advise about real estate. If legal or tax advice is desired, consult a competent professional.

Throughout your real property transaction you may receive more than one disclosure form, depending upon the number of agents assisting in the transaction. The law requires each agent with whom you have more than a casual relationship to present you with this disclosure form. You should read its contents each time it is presented to you, considering the relationship between you and the real estate agent in your specific transaction.

This disclosure form includes the provisions of Sections 2079.13 to 2079.24, inclusive, of the Civil Code set forth on the reverse hereof. Read it carefully.

I/WE ACKNOWLEDGE RECEIPT OF A COPY OF THIS DISCLOSURE.

BUYER/SELLER _____ Date _____ Time _____ AM/PM

BUYER/SELLER _____ Date _____ Time _____ AM/PM

AGENT _____ By _____ Date _____
       (Please Print)   (Associate-Licensee or Broker Signature)

SEE REVERSE SIDE FOR FURTHER INFORMATION

R E B S
I N C

Published and Distributed by:
REAL ESTATE BUSINESS SERVICES, INC.
a subsidiary of the CALIFORNIA ASSOCIATION OF REALTORS®
525 South Virgil Avenue, Los Angeles, California 90020

REVISED 4/99

OFFICE USE ONLY
Reviewed by Broker
or Designee _____
Date _____

EQUAL HOUSING
OPPORTUNITY

PRINT DATE

FORM AD-11

CHAPTER 2 OF TITLE 9 OF PART 4 OF DIVISION 3 OF THE CIVIL CODE

2079.13 As used in Sections 2079.14 to 2079.24, inclusive, the following terms have the following meanings:
(a) "Agent" means a person acting under provisions of title 9 (commencing with Section 2295) in a real property transaction, and includes a person who is licensed as a real estate broker under Chapter 3 (commencing with Section 10130) of Part 1 of Division 4 of the Business and Professions Code, and under whose license a listing is executed or an offer to purchase is obtained. **(b)** "Associate licensee" means a person who is licensed as a real broker or salesperson under Chapter 3 (commencing with Section 10130) of Part 1 of Division 4 of the Business and Professions Code and who is either licensed under a broker or has entered into a written contract with a broker to act as the broker's agent in connection with acts requiring a real estate license and to function under the broker's supervision in the capacity of an associate licensee. The agent in the real property transaction bears responsibility for his or her associate licensees who perform as agents of the agent. When an associate licensee owes a duty to any principal, or to any buyer or seller who is not a principal, in a real property transaction, that duty is equivalent to the duty owed to that party by the broker for whom the associate licensee functions. **(c)** "Buyer" means a transferee in a real property transaction, and includes a person who executes an offer to purchase real property from a seller through an agent, or who seeks the services of an agent in more than a casual, transitory, or preliminary manner, with the object of entering into a real property transaction. "Buyer" includes vendee or lessee. **(d)** "Dual agent" means an agent acting, either directly or through an associate licensee, as agent for both the seller and the buyer in a real property transaction. **(e)** "Listing agreement" means a contract between an owner of real property and an agent, by which the agent has been authorized to sell the real property or to find or obtain a buyer. **(f)** "Listing agent" means a person who has obtained a listing of real property to act as an agent for compensation. **(g)** "Listing price" is the amount expressed in dollars specified in the listing for which the seller is willing to sell the real property through the listing agent. **(h)** "Offering price" is the amount expressed in dollars specified in an offer to purchase for which the buyer is willing to buy the real property. **(i)** "Offer to purchase" means a written contract executed by a buyer acting through a selling agent which becomes the contract for the sale of the real property upon acceptance by the seller. **(j)** "Real property" means any estate specified by subdivision (1) or (2) of Section 761 in property which constitutes or is improved with one to four dwelling units, any leasehold in this type of property exceeding one year's duration, and mobilehomes, when offered for sale or sold through an agent pursuant to the authority contained in Section 10131.6 of the Business and Professions Code. **(k)** "Real property transaction" means a transaction for the sale of real property in which an agent is employed by one or more of the principals to act in that transaction, and includes a listing or an offer to purchase. **(l)** "Sell," "sale," or "sold" refers to a transaction for the transfer of real property from the seller to the buyer, and includes exchanges of real property between the seller and buyer, transactions for the creation of a real property sales contract within the meaning of Section 2985, and transactions for the creation of a leasehold exceeding one year's duration. **(m)** "Seller" means the transferor in a real property transaction, and includes an owner who lists real property with an agent, whether or not a transfer results, or who receives an offer to purchase real property of which he or she is the owner from an agent on behalf of another. "Seller" includes both a vendor and a lessor. **(n)** "Selling agent" means a listing agent who acts alone, or an agent who acts in cooperation with a listing agent, and who sells or finds and obtains a buyer for the real property, or an agent who locates property for a buyer or who finds a buyer for a property for which no listing exists and presents an offer to purchase to the seller. **(o)** "Subagent" means a person to whom an agent delegates agency powers as provided in Article 5 (commencing with Section 2349) of Chapter 1 of Title 9. However, "subagent" does not include an associate licensee who is acting under the supervision of an agent in a real property transaction.

2079.14 Listing agents and selling agents shall provide the seller and buyer in a real property transaction with a copy of the disclosure form specified in Section 2079.16, and, except as provided in subdivision (c), shall obtain a signed acknowledgement of receipt from that seller or buyer, except as provided in this section or Section 2079.15, as follows: **(a)** The listing agent, if any, shall provide the disclosure form to the seller prior to entering into the listing agreement. **(b)** The selling agent shall provide the disclosure form to the seller as soon as practicable prior to presenting the seller with an offer to purchase, unless the selling agent previously provided the seller with a copy of the disclosure form pursuant to subdivision (a). **(c)** Where the selling agent does not deal on a face-to-face basis with the seller, the disclosure form prepared by the selling agent may be furnished to the seller (and acknowledgement of receipt obtained for the selling agent from the seller) by the listing agent, or the selling agent may deliver the disclosure form by certified mail addressed to the seller at his or her last known address, in which case no signed acknowledgement of receipt is required. **(d)** The selling agent shall provide the disclosure form to the buyer as soon as practicable prior to execution of the buyer's offer to purchase, except that if the offer to purchase is not prepared by the selling agent, the selling agent shall present the disclosure form to the buyer not later than the next business day after the selling agent receives the offer to purchase from the buyer.

2079.15 In any circumstance in which the seller or buyer refuses to sign an acknowledgement of receipt pursuant to Section 2079.14, the agent, or an associate licensee acting for an agent, shall set forth, sign, and date a written declaration of the facts of the refusal.

2079.17 (a) As soon as practicable, the selling agent shall disclose to the buyer and seller whether the selling agent is acting in the real property transaction exclusively as the buyer's agent, exclusively as the seller's agent, or as a dual agent representing both the buyer and the seller. This relationship shall be confirmed in the contract to purchase and sell real property or in a separate writing executed or acknowledged by the seller, the buyer, and the selling agent prior to or coincident with execution of that contract by the buyer and the seller, respectively. **(b)** As soon as practicable, the listing agent shall disclose to the seller whether the listing agent is acting in the real property transaction exclusively as the seller's agent, or as a dual agent representing both the buyer and seller. This relationship shall be confirmed in the contract to purchase and sell real property or in a separate writing executed or acknowledged by the seller and the listing agent prior to or coincident with the execution of that contract by the seller.
(c) The confirmation required by subdivisions (a) and (b) shall be in the following form.

_____ is the agent of (check one): ☐ the seller exclusively; or ☐ both the buyer and seller.
(Name of Listing Agent)

_____ is the agent of (check one): ☐ the buyer exclusively; or ☐ the seller exclusively; or
(Name of Selling Agent if not the same as the Listing Agent) ☐ both the buyer and seller.

(d) The disclosures and confirmation required by this section shall be in addition to the disclosure required by Section 2079.14.

2079.18 No selling agent in a real property transaction may act as an agent for the buyer only, when the selling agent is also acting as the listing agent in the transaction.

2079.19 The payment of compensation or the obligation to pay compensation to an agent by the seller or buyer is not necessarily determinative of a particular agency relationship between an agent and the seller or buyer. A listing agent and a selling agent may agree to share any compensation or commission paid, or any right to any compensation or commission for which an obligation arises as the result of a real estate transaction, and the terms of any such agreement shall not necessarily be determinative of a particular relationship.

2079.20 Nothing in this article prevents an agent from selecting, as a condition of the agent's employment, a specific form of agency relationship not specifically prohibited by this article if the requirements of Section 2079.14 and Section 2079.17 are complied with.

2079.21 A dual agent shall not disclose to the buyer that the seller is willing to sell the property at a price less than the listing price, without the express written consent of the seller. A dual agent shall not disclose to the seller that the buyer is willing to pay a price greater than the offering price, without the express written consent of the buyer. This section does not alter in any way the duty or responsibility of a dual agent to any principal with respect to confidential information other than price.

2079.22 Nothing in this article precludes a listing agent from also being a selling agent, and the combination of these functions in one agent does not, of itself, make that agent a dual agent.

2079.23 A contract between the principal and agent may be modified or altered to change the agency relationship at any time before the performance of the act which is the object of the agency with the written consent of the parties to the agency relationship.

2079.24 Nothing in this article shall be construed to either diminish the duty of disclosure owed buyers and sellers by agents and their associate licensees, subagents, and employees or to relieve agents and their associate licensees, subagents, and employees from liability for their conduct in connection with acts governed by this article or for any breach of a fiduciary duty or a duty of disclosure.

A. **Settlement Statement**

U.S. Department of Housing
and Urban Development

OMB Approval No. 2502-0265

B. Type of Loan

1. ☐ FHA 2. ☐ FmHA 3. ☐ Conv. Unins.	6. File Number:	7. Loan Number:	8. Mortgage Insurance Case Number:
4. ☐ VA 5. ☐ Conv. Ins.			

C. Note: This form is furnished to give you a statement of actual settlement costs. Amounts paid to and by the settlement agent are shown. Items marked "(p.o.c.)" were paid outside the closing; they are shown here for informational purposes and are not included in the totals.

D. Name & Address of Borrower:	E. Name & Address of Seller:	F. Name & Address of Lender:

G. Property Location:	H. Settlement Agent:	
	Place of Settlement:	I. Settlement Date:

J. Summary of Borrower's Transaction		K. Summary of Seller's Transaction	
100. Gross Amount Due From Borrower		**400. Gross Amount Due To Seller**	
101. Contract sales price		401. Contract sales price	
102. Personal property		402. Personal property	
103. Settlement charges to borrower (line 1400)		403.	
104.		404.	
105.		405.	
Adjustments for items paid by seller in advance		**Adjustments for items paid by seller in advance**	
106. City/town taxes to		406. City/town taxes to	
107. County taxes to		407. County taxes to	
108. Assessments to		408. Assessments to	
109.		409.	
110.		410.	
111.		411.	
112.		412.	
120. Gross Amount Due From Borrower		**420. Gross Amount Due To Seller**	
200. Amounts Paid By Or In Behalf Of Borrower		**500. Reductions In Amount Due To Seller**	
201. Deposit or earnest money		501. Excess deposit (see instructions)	
202. Principal amount of new loan(s)		502. Settlement charges to seller (line 1400)	
203. Existing loan(s) taken subject to		503. Existing loan(s) taken subject to	
204.		504. Payoff of first mortgage loan	
205.		505. Payoff of second mortgage loan	
206.		506.	
207.		507.	
208.		508.	
209.		509.	
Adjustments for items unpaid by seller		**Adjustments for items unpaid by seller**	
210. City/town taxes to		510. City/town taxes to	
211. County taxes to		511. County taxes to	
212. Assessments to		512. Assessments to	
213.		513.	
214.		514.	
215.		515.	
216.		516.	
217.		517.	
218.		518.	
219.		519.	
220. Total Paid By/For Borrower		**520. Total Reduction Amount Due Seller**	
300. Cash At Settlement From/To Borrower		**600. Cash At Settlement To/From Seller**	
301. Gross Amount due from borrower (line 120)		601. Gross amount due to seller (line 420)	
302. Less amounts paid by/for borrower (line 220) (	)	602. Less reductions in amt. due seller (line 520) (	)
303. Cash ☐ From ☐ To Borrower		**603. Cash** ☐ To ☐ From Seller	

Section 5 of the Real Estate Settlement Procedures Act (RESPA) requires the following: • HUD must develop a Special Information Booklet to help persons borrowing money to finance the purchase of residential real estate to better understand the nature and costs of real estate settlement services; • Each lender must provide the booklet to all applicants from whom it receives or for whom it prepares a written application to borrow money to finance the purchase of residential real estate; • Lenders must prepare and distribute with the Booklet a Good Faith Estimate of the settlement costs that the borrower is likely to incur in connection with the settlement. These disclosures are manadatory.

Section 4(a) of RESPA mandates that HUD develop and prescribe this standard form to be used at the time of loan settlement to provide full disclosure of all charges imposed upon the borrower and seller. These are third party disclosures that are designed to provide the borrower with pertinent information during the settlement process in order to be a better shopper.

The Public Reporting Burden for this collection of information is estimated to average one hour per response, including the time for reviewing instructions, searching existing data sources, gathering and maintaining the data needed, and completing and reviewing the collection of information.

This agency may not collect this information, and you are not required to complete this form, unless it displays a currently valid OMB control number.

The information requested does not lend itself to confidentiality.

Previous editions are obsolete

Page 1 of 2

form **HUD-1** (3/86)
ref Handbook 4305.2

L. Settlement Charges

			Paid From Borrowers Funds at Settlement	Paid From Seller's Funds at Settlement
700.	**Total Sales/Broker's Commission based on price $**	@ % =		
	Division of Commission (line 700) as follows:			
701.	$	to		
702.	$	to		
703.	Commission paid at Settlement			
704.				
800.	**Items Payable In Connection With Loan**			
801.	Loan Origination Fee	%		
802.	Loan Discount	%		
803.	Appraisal Fee	to		
804.	Credit Report	to		
805.	Lender's Inspection Fee			
806.	Mortgage Insurance Application Fee to			
807.	Assumption Fee			
808.				
809.				
810.				
811.				
900.	**Items Required By Lender To Be Paid In Advance**			
901.	Interest from to	@$	/day	
902.	Mortgage Insurance Premium for		months to	
903.	Hazard Insurance Premium for		years to	
904.			years to	
905.				
1000.	**Reserves Deposited With Lender**			
1001.	Hazard insurance	months@$	per month	
1002.	Mortgage insurance	months@$	per month	
1003.	City property taxes	months@$	per month	
1004.	County property taxes	months@$	per month	
1005.	Annual assessments	months@$	per month	
1006.		months@$	per month	
1007.		months@$	per month	
1008.		months@$	per month	
1100.	**Title Charges**			
1101.	Settlement or closing fee	to		
1102.	Abstract or title search	to		
1103.	Title examination	to		
1104.	Title insurance binder	to		
1105.	Document preparation	to		
1106.	Notary fees	to		
1107.	Attorney's fees	to		
	(includes above items numbers:	)		
1108.	Title insurance	to		
	(includes above items numbers:	)		
1109.	Lender's coverage	$		
1110.	Owner's coverage	$		
1111.				
1112.				
1113.				
1200.	**Government Recording and Transfer Charges**			
1201.	Recording fees: Deed $	; Mortgage $	; Releases $	
1202.	City/county tax/stamps: Deed $	; Mortgage $		
1203.	State tax/stamps: Deed $	; Mortgage $		
1204.				
1205.				
1300.	**Additional Settlement Charges**			
1301.	Survey to			
1302.	Pest inspection to			
1303.				
1304.				
1305.				
1400.	**Total Settlement Charges (enter on lines 103, Section J and 502, Section K)**			

Appendix IV

General Resources

If you need additional help and information, these resources may provide some assistance.

AMERICAN ASSOCIATION OF RETIRED PERSONS (AARP)

611 E Street, N.W.
Washington, DC 20049
(202) 434-2277
aarp.org

Offers information, publications, and an excellent web site on a variety of topics, targeting toward Americans age 50 and older.

BANK RATE MONITOR

bankrate.com

Bank Rate Monitor provides excellent information about interest rates for a wide variety of items, including mortgages, credit cards, and automobile financing. Their best information, free to the public, is on the Web, which offers generally excellent articles about improving personal finances.

CONSUMER CREDIT COUNSELING SERVICE (CCCS)

(800) 388-2227

This organization has offices around the country, and it provides many services to first-time home buyers, including credit and comprehensive housing counseling. These services are confidential and free of charge. More than 1,100 CCCS offices nationwide can prequalify buyers and talk about various mortgage types, and may be able to tap you into affordable housing programs.

CONSUMER FEDERATION OF AMERICA (CFA)

Headquarters:
1424 16th Street, N.W.
Suite 604
Washington, DC 20036
(202) 387-6121
consumerfed.org
No e-mail

This nonprofit educational and research organization represents homeowners, prospective homeowners, and home investors.

CONSUMER PRODUCT SAFETY COMMISSION

Washington, DC 20207
(800) 638-2772
Fax (301) 504-0281
Cpsc.gov
Info@Cpsc.gov

Call the toll-free (800) number to lodge a complaint about the safety of houses and buildings or about issues involving smoke alarms, electrical systems, indoor air quality, and home insulation. You can also get recall information and safety tips. If you negotiate the options successfully, an operator will eventually come on the line to take your complaint.

CONSUMER PUBLICATIONS

Pueblo, CO 81003
Pueblo.gsa.gov

A list of consumer publications is available that may be useful to you as a first-time (or repeat) home buyer.

COUNCIL OF BETTER BUSINESS BUREAUS

Headquarters
4200 Wilson Boulevard
Suite 800
Arlington, VA 22203
(703) 276-0100
BBB.org

This organization is dedicated to consumers and attempts to be an effective national self-regulation force for business. The headquarters personnel can help you find the bureau nearest you.

DEPARTMENT OF HOUSING AND URBAN DEVELOPMENT (HUD)

451 7th Street, S.W.
Washington, DC 20410
Program information: hud.gov
Listings: HUD.org\dchud\

To locate the HUD office nearest to you:
(202) 708-1112
To get program information:
(202) 708-4374
HUD User, a clearinghouse of information:
(800) 245-2691
HUD User, Washington (DC) area only:
(202) 251-5154

This agency provides programs for low-income housing, including public housing and privately owned rental housing. It supports housing-related site development and housing rehabilitation through Community Development Block Grants to state and local governments. It also provides support for the residential mortgage market through the Federal Housing Administration (FHA).

There is a local HUD office in nearly every urban area. If you are located outside an urban area, call the HUD office in your state capital or in Washington (DC) to find the office located closest to you.

DEPARTMENT OF VETERAN AFFAIRS (VA)

Loan Guarantee Service
810 Vermont Avenue, N.W.
Washington, DC 20420
(800) 827-1000
VA.gov
e-mail linked through web site

This federal agency guarantees a portion of home loans to veterans, and regulates the loans' distribution. The VA publishes a free pamphlet about guaranteed home loans for veterans. Call the general number for information on how to contact your local VA office.

The Department of Veterans Affairs also runs a Vendee Financing program, which provides inexpensive financing (with little or no down payment required, and a discount for a cash purchase) of VA-acquired homes. You need not be a veteran to qualify. Check with the Loan Guarantee Service for more information and current qualifications.

FANNIE MAE (FORMERLY FEDERAL NATIONAL MORTGAGE ASSOCIATION)

Headquarters:
3900 Wisconsin Avenue, N.W.
Washington, DC 20016
(800) 7-Fannie
FannieMae.com
HomePath.com

Fannie Mae, the nation's largest source of home mortgage funds, is a congressionally chartered, shareholder-owned company. The company provides lenders with a constant supply of affordable mortgage funds to make available to home buyers. Its special programs increase the availability and affordability of housing for low-, moderate-, and middle-income Americans. If you call the toll-free number, you'll be able to order information packets on Community Homebuyers programs, as well as other first-time buyer information.

FREDDIE MAC

Headquarters:
8200 Jones Branch Drive
MS #409
McLean, VA 22102
(703) 903-2000
FreddieMac.com

Freddie Mac is a stockholder-owned corporation that purchases mortgages from lenders and issues mortgage-backed securities. Chartered by Congress in 1970, it helps finance one in six homes.

HOME INFORMATION CENTER, A UNIT OF THE OFFICE OF AFFORDABLE HOUSING

P.O. Box 7189
Gaithersburg, MD 20898-7189
(800) 998-9999
ComCon.com
Comcon@aspensys.com

Two programs are operative through this organization: The Home Program and Hope 3. The Home Program gives grant money to nonprofit associations. Hope 3 is a single-family-home buyer program using government help properties. For more information on Hope 3, call the 800 number.

INSURANCE INFORMATION INSTITUTE

110 William Street
New York, NY 10038

The Insurance Information Institute is a nonprofit communications, educational, and fact-finding organization dedicated to improving the public's understanding of the property/casualty insurance business.

NATIONAL CENTER FOR HOME EQUITY CONVERSION (NCHEC)

7373 147th Street
Room 115
Apple Valley, MN 55124
Reverse.org

If you're looking for information about reverse mortgages, this is the place to go. NCHEC's Executive Director, Ken Scholen, has written two excellent books about how reverse mortgages work and how to find a good deal.

NATIONAL COUNCIL FOR STATE HOUSING AGENCIES (NCSHA)

444 North Capital Street, N.W.
Suite 438
Washington, DC 20001
(202) 624-7710

NCSHA is an advocacy group for low-income housing. It represents state housing finance agencies in all fifty states, plus Puerto Rico and the Virgin Islands. If you are unable to find your state housing finance agency, write to this organization.

There are hundreds of public agencies that provided financial assistance to first-time home buyers. Generally, there are home-price and family-income limitations. Your state housing agency or real estate agent should be able to point you in the right direction.

NEIGHBORHOOD REINVESTMENT CORPORATION

1325 G Street, N.W.
Suite 800
Washington, DC 20005
(202) 220-2300
NW.org
e-mail: jparker@nw.org

This organization acts as a national network for affordable housing providers. The headquarters personnel can help you locate the neighborhood housing services nearest to you.

RAM RESEARCH

P.O. Box 1700 (College Estates)
Fredrick, MD 21702
Ramresearch.com/csrttrak
/cardtrak.html

Another place to go for information on interest rates.

Appendix V
State-by-State Resource Guide

Unfortunately, the home buying and selling process doesn't always work out exactly the way you hope it will. You may receive bad service from a real estate agent or work with a mortgage lender who isn't exactly on the up-and-up.

If you want to complain to someone and you don't know whose ear you should bend, this list may prove useful. It contains contact information for the agency, division, or department that regulates real estate brokers and mortgage lenders in every state.

The procedures for handling complaints differ from state to state. Remember to keep a paper trail documenting all of your conversations and correspondence, and be sure to get the full name and telephone number of the person who takes your complaint. Ask what process the office has in place for investigating the complaint, and what the likely outcome will be.

ALABAMA

Web site: webserver.dsmd.state.al.us/arec

Complaints about mortgage lenders:

Banking Department
401 Adams Avenue, Suite 680
Montgomery, AL 36130
Telephone: (334) 242-3452

Complaints about real estate brokers:

Alabama Real Estate Commission
1201 Charmichael Way
Montgomery, AL 36106
Telephone: (334) 242-5544
E-mail: arec@dsmd.state.al.us

ALASKA

Web site: state.ak.us

Complaints about mortgage lenders:

Division of Banking, Securities,
   and Corporations
9th Floor, State Office Building
333 Willoughby Avenue
Juneau, AK 99801
Mailing Address:
   P.O. Box 110807
   Juneau, AK 99811-0807
Telephone: (907) 465-2521

Complaints about real estate brokers:
Division of Occupational Licensing
Alaska Real Estate Commission
Frontier Building
3601 C Street, Suite 722
Anchorage, AK 99503-5986
Telephone: (907) 269-8160
E-mail: Grayce_Oakley@commerce.state.ak.us

ARIZONA

Complaints about mortgage lenders:
Arizona State Banking Department
2910 N. 44th Street, Suite 310
Phoenix, AZ 85018
Telephone: (602) 255-4421
Web site: azbanking.com

Complaints about real estate brokers:
Arizona Organization Department of Real Estate
2910 N. 44th Street
Phoenix, AZ 85018
Telephone: (602) 468-1414
Facsimile: (602) 468-0562
Web site: adre.org
E-mail: cdowns@adre.org

ARKANSAS

Complaints about mortgage lenders:
Arkansas State Banking Department
Tower Building, Suite 500
323 Center Street
Little Rock, AR 72201-2663
Att: Don R. Clark, Deputy Commissioner
Telephone: (501) 324-9019
Web site: state.ar.us/bank/

Complaints about real estate brokers:
Arkansas Organization Arkansas Real Estate
    Commission
612 South Summit Street
Little Rock, AR 72201-4740
Telephone: (501) 683-8010
Web site: state.ar.us/arec/arecweb.html
E-mail: arec@mac.state.ar.us

CALIFORNIA

dfi.ca.gov

Complaints about mortgage lenders:
California Department of Corporations
1-800-622-0620
320 W. 4th Street, Suite 750
Los Angeles, CA 90013-1105
Telephone: (213) 576-7500

1390 Market Street, Suite 810
San Francisco, CA 94102-5303
Telephone: (415) 557-3787

980 9th Street, Suite 500
Sacramento, CA 95814-2725
Telephone: (916) 445-7205

1350 Front Street, Room 2034
San Diego, CA 92101-3697
Telephone: (619) 525-4233

Complaints about real estate brokers:
dre.cahwnet.gov/complnt.htm
California Department of Real Estate
(916) 227-0864
2201 Broadway
Sacramento, CA 95818
Telephone: (916) 227-0931

1350 Front Street, Suite 3064
San Diego, CA 92101-3687
Telephone: (619) 525 4192

1515 Clay Street, Suite 702
Oakland, CA 94612-1402
Telephone: (510) 622-2552

320 W. 4th Street, Suite 350
Los Angeles, CA 90013-1105
Telephone: (213) 897-3399

2550 Mariposa Mall, Room 3070
Fresno, CA 93721-1105
Telephone: (559) 445-5009

COLORADO

Complaints about mortgage lenders:
Division of Banking
1560 Broadway, Suite 1175
Denver, CO 80202
Telephone: (303) 894-7575
Web site: dora.state.co.us/banking/

Complaints about real estate brokers:
Colorado Division of Real Estate
1900 Grant Street, Suite 600
Denver, CO 80203
Telephone: (303) 894-2166
Facsimile: (303) 894-2683
Web site: dora.state.CO.us/Real_Estate
E-mail: Gorham.Mike@dora.state.CO.US

CONNECTICUT

state.ct.us/dob/

Complaints about mortgage lenders:
Consumer Credit Division
Connecticut Department of Banking
260 Constitution Plaza
Hartford, CT 06103-1800
Telephone: (860) 240-8200 or (800) 831-7225
E-mail: michael.buchag@po.state.ct.us or
    richard.lalor@po.state.ct.us

Complaints about real estate brokers:
Department of Consumer Protection
Real Estate and Professional Trades Division
165 Capital Avenue
Hartford, CT 06106
Telephone: (860) 713-6135 or (800) 842-2649

DELAWARE

Complaints about mortgage lenders:
Office of the Bank Commissioner
Compliance Staff
555 E. Loockerman Street, Suite 210
Dover, DE 19901
Telephone: (302) 739-4235
Web site: state.de.us/bank

Complaints about real estate brokers:
Department of Administrative Services
Division of Professional Regulation
Real Estate Commission
861 Silverlake Boulevard
Cannon Building, Suite 203
Dover, DE 19904
Telephone: (302) 739-4522 ext.219
Facsimile: (302) 739-2711

FLORIDA

Complaints about mortgage lenders:
Department of Banking and Finance
Division of Financial Investigations
101 E. Gaines Street, Suite 516
Tallahassee, FL 32399-0350
Telephone: (850) 410-9275
Web site: dbf.state.fl.us

Complaints about real estate brokers:
Department of Real Estate
400 Robinson Street
Box 1900
Orlando, FL 32801
Telephone: (407) 245-0800
Facsimile: (407) 317-7245

GEORGIA

Complaints about mortgage lenders:
Department of Banking and Finance
2990 Brandywine Road, Suite 200
Atlanta, GA 30341-5565
Telephone: (770) 986-1269
Web site: state.ga.us/dbf

Complaints about real estate brokers:
Georgia Real Estate Commission
International Tower, Suite 1000
229 Peachtree Street, NE
Atlanta, GA 30303-1605
Telephone: (404) 656-3916
Web site: state.ga.us/Ga.Real_Estate
E-mail: grecmail@grec.state.ga.us

HAWAII

Complaints about mortgage lenders:
Department of Commerce and Consumer Affairs
Financial Institutions Division
1010 Richards Street
Honolulu, HI 96813
Telephone: (808) 586-2820
Mailing Address:
    P.O. Box 541
    Honolulu, HI 96809
Web site: hawaii.gov

Complaints about real estate brokers:

Hawaii Real Estate Commission
1010 Richards Street
Honolulu, HI 96813
Mailing Address:
P.O. Box 3469
Honolulu, HI 96801
Telephone: (808) 586-2643
Web site: hawaii.gov/hirec

IDAHO

Complaints about mortgage lenders:

Department of Finance
2nd Floor
700 W. State Street
Boise, ID 83702
Mailing Address:
   P.O. Box 83720
   Boise, ID 83720-0031
Telephone: (208) 332-8004
Web site: state.id.us/finance/dof.htm

Complaints about real estate brokers:

Idaho Real Estate Commission
P.O. Box 83720
Boise, ID 83720
Telephone: (208) 334-3285

Complaints about banks:

Department of Finance
700 W. State Street
Boise, ID 83702
Mailing Address:
   P.O. Box
   Boise, ID 83720-0031
Telephone: (208) 332-8002

ILLINOIS

Complaints about mortgage lenders and real estate brokers:

Office of Banks and Real Estate
310 S. Michigan Avenue
Chicago, IL 60604
Telephone-Real Estate: (312) 793-3000
Telephone-Mortgage Lender: (312) 793-1454

500 E. Monroe Street
Springfield, IL 62701
Telephone-Real Estate: (217) 785-9300
Telephone-Mortgage Lender: (217) 782-3000
Web site: state.il.us/obr
E-mail: sidwell@bre084rl.state.il.us

Complaints about credit unions:

Department of Financial Institutions
Credit Union Division
100 W. Randolph Street, Suite 15-700
Chicago, IL 60601
or
Credit Union Division
500 Iles Park Place, Suite 510
Springfield, IL 62718
Web site: state.il.us/dfi/

INDIANA

Complaints about mortgage lenders:

Indiana Department of Financial Institutions
Indianapolis, IN 46204
Telephone: (317) 232-3955
Telephone: (317) 232-6684
Web site: dfi.state.in.us/

Complaints about credit unions:

Division of Credit Unions
Indianapolis, IN 46204
Telephone: (317) 232-5851

Complaints about real estate brokers:

Indiana Professional Licensing Agency
302 West Washington, Room EZ034
Indianapolis, IN 46204
Telephone: (317) 232-2980
Facsimile: (317) 232-2312

IOWA

Complaints about mortgage lenders:

Iowa Department of Commerce
Division of Banking
200 E. Grand Avenue, Suite 300
Des Moines, IA 50309-1827
Telephone: (515) 281-4014
Web site: state.ia.us/government/com/

Complaints about credit unions:

Division of Credit Unions
200 East Grand Avenue, Suite 370
Des Moines, IA 50309
Telephone: (515) 281-6514

Complaints about real estate brokers:

Professional Licensing & Regulation Division
Iowa Real Estate Commission
1918 SE Hulfizer Road
Achne, IA 50021
Telephone: (515) 281-3183
Web site:
    state.ia.us/government/com/prof/realesta
    /realesta.htm
E-mail: Irec@max.state.ia.us

KANSAS

Complaints about mortgage lenders:

Office of State Commission
Consumer and Banking
J Hawk Tower, Suite 1001
700 SW Jackson
Topeka, KA 66603
Telephone: (785) 296 3151

Complaints about real estate brokers:

Kansas Real Estate Commission
3 Townside Plaza, Suite 200
120 SE 6th Avenue
Topeka, KA 66603
Telephone: (785) 296-3411
Web site: ink.org/public/krec

KENTUCKY

Complaints about mortgage lenders:

Department of Financial Institutions
1025 Capital Center Drive
Frankfort, KY 40601
Contact: Andy Cubrt
Telephone: (502) 573-3390 or (800) 223-2579

Complaints about real estate brokers:

Kentucky Real Estate Commission
10200 Lynn Station Road, Suite 201
Louisville, KY
Telephone: (502) 425-4273 / (888) 373-3300
Web site: ukcres.gws.uky.edu/krec/
E-mail: grec@ntr.net

LOUISIANA

Complaints about mortgage lenders:

Office of Financial Institutions
8660 United Plaza Boulevard, 2nd Floor
Baton Rouge, LA
Telephone: Jack Tessier (225) 925-4660

Complaints about credit unions:

Credit Union Division
P.O. Box 94095
Baton Rouge, LA 70804-9095
Telephone: (225) 924-4660

Complaints about real estate brokers:

Louisiana Real Estate Commission
9071 Interline Avenue
Baton Rouge, LA 70809
Mailing Address:
    P.O. Box 14785
    Baton Rouge, LA 70898-4785
Telephone: (504) 925-4771

MAINE

Complaints about mortgage lenders:

Department of Professional and Financial
    Regulation
Maine Bureau of Banking
124 Northern Avenue
Gardiner, ME
Telephone: (207) 624-8527
Web site: state.me.us/
Mailing Address:
    Department of Professional and Financial
    Regulation
    Maine Bureau of Banking
    36 State House Station
    Augusta, ME 04333-0036

Complaints about real estate brokers:

Maine Real Estate Commission
Office of Licensing and Registration
35 State House Station
Augusta ME, 04333
Telephone: (207) 624-8603
Web site: state.me.us/pfr/led/rec/index.htm
E-mail: Carol.J.Leighton@State.me.us

MARYLAND

Complaints about mortgage lenders:
Consumer Credit Unit
Division of Financial Regulation
500 North Calvert Street, Room 402
Baltimore, MD 21202
Telephone: (410) 230-6097

Complaints about banks:
Banking Unit
Division of Financial Regulation
500 N. Calvert Street, Room 402
Baltimore, MD 21202
Telephone: (410) 230-6102

Complaints about real estate brokers:
Department of Licensing & Regulation
Maryland Real Estate Commission
500 N. Calvert Street, 3rd Floor
Baltimore, MD 21202
Telephone: (410) 230-6230

MASSACHUSETTS

Complaints about mortgage lenders:
Consumer Assistance Office
Massachusetts Division of Banks
1 South Station, 3rd Floor
Boston, MA 02110
Telephone: (617) 956-1500

Complaints about real estate brokers:
Board of Registration of Real Estate Brokers &
   Salesperson
Massachusetts Real Estate Board
239 Causeway Street, Suite 500
Boston, MA 02114
Telephone: (617) 727-2373
Web site: state.ma.us/reg/boards/re

MICHIGAN

Complaints about mortgage lenders:
Michigan Financial Institutions Bureau
333 South Capitol Avenue, Suite A
Lansing, MI 48909
Telephone: (517) 373-3470

Complaints about real estate brokers:
Consumer & Industry Services
Real Estate Commission
P.O. Box 30018
Lansing, MI 48909
Telephone: (517) 241-9202
E-mail: ann.millben@cis.state.mi.us

Complaints about credit unions:
Credit Union Division
333 South Capitol Avenue
Lansing, MI 48909

MINNESOTA

Complaints about mortgage lenders:
Division of Financial Examinations
133 East 7th Street
St. Paul, MN 55101
Telephone: (651) 296-2135
E-mail: financial@state.mn.us

Complaints about real estate brokers:
Minnesota Commerce Department
Enforcement Department
133 East 7th Street
St. Paul, MN 55101
Telephone: (612) 296-2488 or (800) 657-3602
Web site: commerce.state.mn.us
E-mail: Barb.Lessard@state.mn.us

MISSISSIPPI

Complaints about mortgage lenders:
Department of Banking and Consumer Finance
Banking Division
550 High Street, Suite 304
Jackson, MS 39202
Telephone: (601) 359-1031
Web site: dbcf.state.ms.us/
E-mail: jallison@dbcf.state.ms.us
Mailing Address:
   Banking Division
   P.O. Drawer 23729
   Jackson, MS 39225-3729

Complaints about real estate brokers:
Mississippi Real Estate Commission
5176 Kelle Street
Jackson, MS 39206
Telephone: (601) 987-3969
E-mail: mrec@mrec.state.ms.us

MISSOURI

Complaints about mortgage lenders:
Division of Finance
Att: Geary Steven
P.O. Box 716
Jefferson City, MO 65101
Telephone: (573) 751-3242
E-mail: finance@mail.state.mo.us
Web site: ecodev.state.mo.us/finance/

Complaints about credit unions:
Division of Credit Unions
2410-A Hyde Park Road
P.O. Box 1607
Jefferson City, MO 65102
Telephone: (573) 751-3419
Web site: ecodev.state.mo.us/cu/
E-mail: cu@mail.state.mo.us

Complaints about real estate brokers:
Missouri Real Estate Commission
3605 Missouri Boulevard
Jefferson City, MO 65109
Telephone: (573) 751-4352
E-mail: jcard01@mail.state.mo.us

MONTANA

Complaints about mortgage lenders:
Department of Commerce
Banking and Financial Institutions Division
846 Front Street
Helena, MT 59620
Mailing Address:
    P.O. Box 200126
    Helena, MT 59620
Telephone: (406) 444-2091
Web site:
    commerce.state.mt.us/bnk&fin/index.html

Complaints about real estate brokers:
Montana Board of Realty Regulation
P.O. Box 200513
Helena, MT 59620
Telephone: (406) 444-2961
E-mail: gberger@state.mt.gov

NEBRASKA

Complaints about mortgage lenders:
Financial Institutions Division
Department of Banking and Finance
1200 N. Street, Suite 311
Lincoln, NE 68508
Telephone: (402) 471-2171
Web site: ndbf.org/FIN.HTM
Mailing Address:
    P.O. Box 95006
    Lincoln, NE 68509-5006

Complaints about real estate brokers:
Nebraska Real Estate Commission
1200 N. Street, Suite 402
Lincoln, NE 68509
Telephone: (402) 471-2004

NEVADA

Complaints about mortgage lenders:
Nevada Department of Business and Industry
Financial Institutions Division
Web site: state.nv.us/b&i/fi/

Carson City:
    406 East 2nd Street, Suite #3
    Carson City, NV 89710
    Telephone: (775) 687-4259

Las Vegas:
    2501 East Sahara Avenue, Suite 300
    Las Vegas, NV 89104
    Telephone: (702) 486-4120

Complaints about real estate brokers:
Nevada Department of Business and Industry
Nevada Real Estate Division

Carson City:
    Compliance Division
    1665 Hot Springs Road
    Carson City, NV 89706-0663
    Telephone: (775) 687-6434

Las Vegas:
    2501 E. Sahara Avenue
    Las Vegas, NV 89104
    Telephone: (702) 486-4033

NEW HAMPSHIRE

Complaints about mortgage lenders:

Office of the Banking Commissioner
Banking Department
56 Old Suncook Road
Concord, NH 03301-5127
Telephone: (603) 271-3561
Web site: state.nh.us/banking

Complaints about real estate brokers:

New Hampshire Real Estate Commission
25 Capitol Street
State Annex House, Room 437, 4th Floor
Concord, NH 03301
Telephone: (603) 271-2701

NEW JERSEY

Complaints about mortgage lenders:

Department of Banking and Insurance
Consumer Service Unit
P.O. Box 40
Trenton, NJ 08625-040
Telephone: (609) 984-2777
Web site: state.nj.us/deptserv.html

Complaints about real estate brokers:

New Jersey Real Estate Commission
P.O. Box 328
Trenton, NJ 08625-0328
Telephone: (609) 292-8280
Web site: naic.org/nj/realcom.htm
E-mail: inndeck@superlink.net

NEW MEXICO

Complaints about mortgage lenders:

Regulation and Licensing Department
Financial Institutions Division
725 St. Michael's Drive
Santa Fe, NM 87501
Telephone: (505) 827-7100
Web site: state.nm.us/rld/fid/fidhome.htm

Complaints about real estate brokers:

New Mexico Real Estate Commission
1650 University Drive, NE, Suite 490
Albuquerque, NM 87102
Telephone: (505) 841-9120

NEW YORK

Complaints about mortgage lenders:

New York State Banking Department

Manhattan:
2 Rector Street
New York, NY 10006-1894
Telephone: (212) 618-6951

Albany:
5 Empire State Plaza, Suite 2310
Albany, NY 12223
Telephone: (518) 474-2364 or (518) 473-6160

Syracuse:
333 East Washington Street
Syracuse, NY 13202
Telephone: (315) 428-4049
Web site: banking.state.ny.us/

Complaints about real estate brokers:

Department of State
Division of Licensing Services
84 Holland Avenue
Albany, NY 12208
Telephone: (518) 473-2728

NORTH CAROLINA

Complaints about mortgage lenders:

Office of the Commissioner of Banks
702 Oberlin Road, Suite 400
Raleigh, NC 27605-0709
Telephone: (919) 733-3016
Web site: banking.state.nc.us/
Mailing Address:
P.O. Box 10709
Raleigh, NC 27605-0709

Complaints about real estate brokers:

North Carolina Real Estate Commission
P.O. Box 17100
Raleigh, NC 27619
Telephone: (919) 875-3700
Web site: ncrec.state.nc.us

NORTH DAKOTA

Complaints about mortgage lenders:

Department of Banking and Financial
    Institutions
Schafer Street, Suite G
Bismarck, ND 58501-1204
Telephone: (701) 328-9933
Web site: state.nd.us/bank/

Complaints about real estate brokers:

North Dakota Real Estate Commission
314 E. Thayer Avenue
Bismarck, ND 58501
Mailing Address:
    P.O. Box 727
    Bismarck, ND 58508
Telephone: (701) 328-9749 / (701) 328-9739

OHIO

Complaints about mortgage lenders:

Department of Commerce
Division of Financial Institutions
77 South High Street, 21st Floor
Columbus, OH 43266-0121
Telephone: (614) 644-9573

Complaints about real estate brokers:

Division of Real Estate & Professional Licensing
77 S. High Street, 20th Floor
Columbus, OH 43266
Telephone: (614) 466-4100

OKLAHOMA

Complaints about mortgage lenders:

Oklahoma State Banking Department
4545 N. Lincoln Boulevard, Suite 104
Oklahoma City, OK 73105-3427
Telephone: (405) 521-3653
Web site: state.ok.us/~sbd/

Complaints about real estate brokers:

Oklahoma Real Estate Commission
4040 N. Lincoln Boulevard, Suite 100
Oklahoma City, OK 73105-3427
Telephone: (405) 521-3387

OREGON

Complaints about mortgage lenders:

Oregon Department of Consumer and Business
    Services
Division of Finance and Corporate Securities
350 Winter Street, NE
Salem, OR 97310
Telephone: (503) 378-4140

Complaints about real estate brokers:

Oregon Real Estate Agency
1177 Center Street, NE
Salem, OR 97301-2505
Telephone: (503) 378-4170

PENNSYLVANIA

Web site: state.pa.us

Complaints about mortgage lenders:

Department of Banking
333 Market Street, 16th Floor
Harrisburg, PA 17101-2290
Telephone: (717) 787-2665

Complaints about real estate brokers:

Pennsylvania Real Estate Commission
124 Pine Street
Harrisburg, PA 17105-2649
Mailing Address:
    P.O. Box 2649
    Harrisburg, PA 17101
Telephone: (717) 783-3658
E-mail: ealespa@padof.dof.state.pa.us

RHODE ISLAND

Complaints about mortgage lenders:

Department of Business Regulation
Banking Division
233 Richmond Street
Providence, RI 02903
Telephone: (401) 222-2405
Web site: state.ri.us/manual/data/queries/stdept

Complaints about real estate brokers:

Department of Business Regulation
233 Richmond Street, Suite 230
Providence, RI 02903
Telephone: (401) 222-2255

SOUTH CAROLINA

Complaints about mortgage lenders:
Consumer Affairs Department:
2801 Devine Street
Columbia, SC 29205
Telephone: (803)734-9450
Mailing Address:
    P.O. Box 5757
    Columbia, SC 29250-5757

Complaints about banks:
SC Board of Financial Institutions
Calhoun Building, 3rd Floor
1015 Sumter Street
Columbia, SC 29211
Telephone: (803) 734-2001

Complaints about real estate brokers:
Department of Labor Licensing & Regulation
South Carolina Real Estate Commission
110 Centerview Drive
Columbia, SC 29210
Mailing Address:
    P.O. Box 11847
    Columbia, SC 29211-1847
Telephone: (803) 896-4400
Web site: 11r.sc.edu/rec
E-mail: selmann@zip.11r.sc.edu

SOUTH DAKOTA

Complaints about mortgage lenders:
Division of Banking
Department of Commerce and Regulation
State Capitol
500 E. Capitol Avenue
Pierre, SD 57501-5070
Telephone: (605) 773-3421
Web site: state/sd/us/dcr/bank/BANK-HOM
E-mail: dcrbankI@comm-bnk.state.sd.us

Complaints about real estate brokers:
South Dakota Real Estate Commission
1800 W. Capital Street
Pierre, SD 57501
Telephone: (605) 773-3600
E-mail: larryl@crprl.state.sd.us

TENNESSEE

Complaints about mortgage lenders:
Division of Consumer Affairs
500 James Robertson Parkway, 5th Floor
Nashville, TN 37243-0600
Telephone: (615) 741-4737

Complaints about real estate brokers:
Tennessee Real Estate Commission
500 James Robertson Parkway, Suite 180
Nashville, TN 37243-1151
Telephone: (615) 741-2273

TEXAS

Complaints about mortgage lenders:
State Finance Commission
2601 North Lamar Building
Austin, TX 78705
Telephone: (512) 475-1300

Complaints about real estate brokers:
Texas Real Estate Commission
1101 Camino La Costa
Austin, TX 78752
Mailing Address:
    P.O. Box 12188
    Austin, TX 78711-2188
Telephone: (512) 559-6544 or (800) 250-8732
Web site: trec.state.tx.us
E-mail: webmaster@trec.state.tx.us

UTAH

Complaints about mortgage lenders:
Department of Corporations
P.O. Box 146701
Salt Lake City, UT 84114-6701

Complaints about real estate brokers:
Department of Commerce
Utah Division of Real Estate
160 E. 300 South
P.O. Box 14670
Salt Lake City, Utah 84114-6701
Telephone: (801) 530-6747
Web site: commerce.state.ut.us
E-mail: realest@e-mail.state.ut.us

VERMONT

Complaints about mortgage lenders:
Department of Banking
89 Main Street
Drawer 20
Montpelier, VE 05620-3101
Telephone: (802) 828-3307

Complaints about real estate brokers:
Office of Professional Regulation
Vermont Real Estate Commission
Heritage Building
81 River Street, Drawer 9
Montpelier, VE 05609
Telephone: (802) 828-3256
E-mail: tmcknigh@heritage.sec.state.vt.us

VIRGINIA

Complaints about mortgage lenders:
Department of Banking
Tyler Building
13006 Main Street
Richmond, VA 23219
Mailing Address:
   Bureau of Financial Institutions
   P.O. Box 640
   Richmond, VA 23218
Telephone: (804) 371-9657

Department of Professional and Occupational
   Regulation
3600 W. Broad Street
Richmond, VA 23230
Telephone: (804) 367-8500
Web site: state.va.us/dpor

WASHINGTON

Complaints about mortgage lenders:
Washington Department of Financial
   Institutions
210 11th Avenue, SW, Room 300
Olympia, WA 98504
Telephone: (360) 902-8700 or (800) 372-8303 (in
   Washington)
Web site: wa.gov/dfi/
Mailing Address:
   P.O. Box 41200
   Olympia, WA 98504-1200

Complaints about real estate brokers:
Department of Licensing
Business and Professions Division
Real Estate Program
2000 4th Avenue, W, 2nd Floor
Olympia, WA 98507
Mailing Address:
   P.O. Box 9015
   Olympia, WA 98507-9015
Telephone: (360) 586-4602
Web site: wa.gov/dol/bpd/recom.htm

WEST VIRGINIA

Complaints about mortgage lenders:
West Virginia Division of Banking
1900 Kanawha Boulevard, E
Building #3, Room 3111
Charleston, WV 25305-0240
Telephone: (304)-555-2294
Web site: state.wv.us/banking

Complaints about real estate brokers:
West Virginia Real Estate Commission
2110 Kanawha Boulevard, E
Charleston, WV 25311
Telephone: (304) 558-3919

WISCONSIN

*Complaints about mortgage lenders and real estate
   brokers:*
Department of Regulation and Licensing
P.O. Box 8935
Madison, WI 53708
Telephone: (608) 266-2112
Web site: state.wi.us/agencies/drl/
E-mail: ahall@mail.state.wi.us

WYOMING

Complaints about mortgage lenders:
Division of Banking
Herschler Building 3E
122 W. 25th
Cheyenne, WY 82002
Telephone: (307) 777-7797
Web site: audit.state.wy.us/banking/default.htm

Complaints about real estate brokers:

Wyoming Real Estate Commission
2020 Capital Avenue, Suite 100
Cheyenne, Wyoming 82002-0180
Telephone: (307) 777-7141
Web site: commerce.state.wy.us/b&c/rec/
E-mail: cander2@missc.state.wy.us

Appendix VI

Amortization Tables

The following amortization tables allow you to figure out exactly how much you'll be paying in interest and principal each month. Here's how to use them: First, find the table that reflects the interest rate you're being charged. Next, go to the column that corresponds with the length of your loan. Finally, add up the columns to find the amount of your loan.

For example, let's say you're borrowing $175,000 at 8.5 percent interest for 30 years. If you go to the 8.5 percent table and find the 30-year loan column, move down the column until you find $100,000. You'll see that borrowing $100,000 at 8.5 percent for 30 years will cost you $768.91 per month. Next, move your finger across the $70,000 column. It will cost you an additional $538.24 per month to borrow that $70,000. Finally, find the $5,000 row, and move across until you get to $38.45. Add these numbers up to get your monthly interest and principal payment:

$$\$768.91 + \$538.24 + \$38.45 = \$1,345.60$$

Your monthly amortized principal and interest payment for a 30-year $175,000 loan at 8.5 percent would be $1,345.60.

4.00% Rate

Amount	Term of Loan in Years					
	10	15	20	25	30	40
$ 50.00	$ 0.51	$ 0.37	$ 0.30	$ 0.26	$ 0.24	$ 0.21
100.00	1.01	0.74	0.61	0.53	0.48	0.42
200.00	2.02	1.48	1.21	1.06	0.95	0.84
300.00	3.04	2.22	1.82	1.58	1.43	1.25
400.00	4.05	2.96	2.42	2.11	1.91	1.67
500.00	5.06	3.70	3.03	2.64	2.39	2.09
600.00	6.07	4.44	3.64	3.17	2.86	2.51
700.00	7.09	5.18	4.24	3.69	3.34	2.93
800.00	8.10	5.92	4.85	4.22	3.82	3.34
900.00	9.11	6.66	5.45	4.75	4.30	3.76
1,000.00	10.12	7.40	6.06	5.28	4.77	4.18
2,000.00	20.25	14.79	12.12	10.56	9.55	8.36
3,000.00	30.37	22.19	18.18	15.84	14.32	12.54
4,000.00	40.50	29.59	24.24	21.11	19.10	16.72
5,000.00	50.62	36.98	30.30	26.39	23.87	20.90
6,000.00	60.75	44.38	36.36	31.67	28.64	25.08
7,000.00	70.87	51.78	42.42	36.95	33.42	29.26
8,000.00	81.00	59.18	48.48	42.23	38.19	33.44
9,000.00	91.12	66.57	54.54	47.51	42.97	37.61
10,000.00	101.25	73.97	60.60	52.78	47.74	41.79
20,000.00	202.49	147.94	121.20	105.57	95.48	83.59
30,000.00	303.74	221.91	181.79	158.35	143.22	125.38
40,000.00	404.98	295.88	242.39	211.13	190.97	167.18
50,000.00	506.23	369.84	302.99	263.92	238.71	208.97
60,000.00	607.47	443.81	363.59	316.70	286.45	250.76
70,000.00	708.72	517.78	424.19	369.49	334.19	292.56
80,000.00	809.96	591.75	484.78	422.27	381.93	334.35
90,000.00	911.21	665.72	545.38	475.05	429.67	376.14
100,000.00	1,012.45	739.69	605.98	527.84	477.42	417.94

4.125% Rate

Amount	Term of Loan in Years					
	10	15	20	25	30	40
$ 50.00	$ 0.51	$ 0.37	$ 0.31	$ 0.27	$ 0.24	$ 0.21
100.00	1.02	0.75	0.61	0.53	0.48	0.43
200.00	2.04	1.49	1.23	1.07	0.97	0.85
300.00	3.06	2.24	1.84	1.60	1.45	1.28
400.00	4.07	2.98	2.45	2.14	1.94	1.70
500.00	5.09	3.73	3.06	2.67	2.42	2.13
600.00	6.11	4.48	3.68	3.21	2.91	2.55
700.00	7.13	5.22	4.29	3.74	3.39	2.98
800.00	8.15	5.97	4.90	4.28	3.88	3.41
900.00	9.17	6.71	5.51	4.81	4.36	3.83
1,000.00	10.18	7.46	6.13	5.35	4.85	4.26
2,000.00	20.37	14.92	12.25	10.70	9.69	8.51
3,000.00	30.55	22.38	18.38	16.04	14.54	12.77
4,000.00	40.74	29.84	24.50	21.39	19.39	17.03
5,000.00	50.92	37.30	30.63	26.74	24.23	21.29
6,000.00	61.10	44.76	36.76	32.09	29.08	25.54
7,000.00	71.29	52.22	42.88	37.43	33.93	29.80
8,000.00	81.47	59.68	49.01	42.78	38.77	34.06
9,000.00	91.66	67.14	55.13	48.13	43.62	38.32
10,000.00	101.84	74.60	61.26	53.48	48.46	42.57
20,000.00	203.68	149.19	122.52	106.95	96.93	85.15
30,000.00	305.52	223.79	183.78	160.43	145.39	127.72
40,000.00	407.36	298.39	245.03	213.91	193.86	170.30
50,000.00	509.20	372.98	306.29	267.38	242.32	212.87
60,000.00	611.04	447.58	367.55	320.86	290.79	255.45
70,000.00	712.88	522.18	428.81	374.33	339.25	298.02
80,000.00	814.72	596.77	490.07	427.81	387.72	340.60
90,000.00	916.56	671.37	551.33	481.29	436.18	383.17
100,000.00	1,018.40	745.97	612.59	534.76	484.65	425.75

4.250% Rate

Amount	Term of Loan in Years					
	10	15	20	25	30	40
$ 50.00	$ 0.51	$ 0.38	$ 0.31	$ 0.27	$ 0.25	$ 0.22
100.00	1.02	0.75	0.62	0.54	0.49	0.43
200.00	2.05	1.50	1.24	1.08	0.98	0.87
300.00	3.07	2.26	1.86	1.63	1.48	1.30
400.00	4.10	3.01	2.48	2.17	1.97	1.73
500.00	5.12	3.76	3.10	2.71	2.46	2.17
600.00	6.15	4.51	3.72	3.25	2.95	2.60
700.00	7.17	5.27	4.33	3.79	3.44	3.04
800.00	8.20	6.02	4.95	4.33	3.94	3.47
900.00	9.22	6.77	5.57	4.88	4.43	3.90
1,000.00	10.24	7.52	6.19	5.42	4.92	4.34
2,000.00	20.49	15.05	12.38	10.83	9.84	8.67
3,000.00	30.73	22.57	18.58	16.25	14.76	13.01
4,000.00	40.98	30.09	24.77	21.67	19.68	17.34
5,000.00	51.22	37.61	30.96	27.09	24.60	21.68
6,000.00	61.46	45.14	37.15	32.50	29.52	26.02
7,000.00	71.71	52.66	43.35	37.92	34.44	30.35
8,000.00	81.95	60.18	49.54	43.34	39.36	34.69
9,000.00	92.19	67.71	55.73	48.76	44.27	39.03
10,000.00	102.44	75.23	61.92	54.17	49.19	43.36
20,000.00	204.88	150.46	123.85	108.35	98.39	86.72
30,000.00	307.31	225.68	185.77	162.52	147.58	130.09
40,000.00	409.75	300.91	247.69	216.70	196.78	173.45
50,000.00	512.19	376.14	309.62	270.87	245.97	216.81
60,000.00	614.63	451.37	371.54	325.04	295.16	260.17
70,000.00	717.06	526.59	433.46	379.22	344.36	303.53
80,000.00	819.50	601.82	495.39	433.39	393.55	346.90
90,000.00	921.94	677.05	557.31	487.56	442.75	390.26
100,000.00	1,024.38	752.28	619.23	541.74	491.94	433.62

4.375% Rate

Amount	Term of Loan in Years					
	10	15	20	25	30	40
$ 50.00	$ 0.52	$ 0.38	$ 0.31	$ 0.27	$ 0.25	$ 0.22
100.00	1.03	0.76	0.63	0.55	0.50	0.44
200.00	2.06	1.52	1.25	1.10	1.00	0.88
300.00	3.09	2.28	1.88	1.65	1.50	1.32
400.00	4.12	3.03	2.50	2.20	2.00	1.77
500.00	5.15	3.79	3.13	2.74	2.50	2.21
600.00	6.18	4.55	3.76	3.29	3.00	2.65
700.00	7.21	5.31	4.38	3.84	3.49	3.09
800.00	8.24	6.07	5.01	4.39	3.99	3.53
900.00	9.27	6.83	5.63	4.94	4.49	3.97
1,000.00	10.30	7.59	6.26	5.49	4.99	4.42
2,000.00	20.61	15.17	12.52	10.98	9.99	8.83
3,000.00	30.91	22.76	18.78	16.46	14.98	13.25
4,000.00	41.21	30.34	25.04	21.95	19.97	17.66
5,000.00	51.52	37.93	31.30	27.44	24.96	22.08
6,000.00	61.82	45.52	37.56	32.93	29.96	26.49
7,000.00	72.13	53.10	43.81	38.41	34.95	30.91
8,000.00	82.43	60.69	50.07	43.90	39.94	35.32
9,000.00	92.73	68.28	56.33	49.39	44.94	39.74
10,000.00	103.04	75.86	62.59	54.88	49.93	44.16
20,000.00	206.07	151.72	125.18	109.75	99.86	88.31
30,000.00	309.11	227.59	187.78	164.63	149.79	132.47
40,000.00	412.15	303.45	250.37	219.50	199.71	176.62
50,000.00	515.18	379.31	312.96	274.38	249.64	220.78
60,000.00	618.22	455.17	375.55	329.26	299.57	264.94
70,000.00	721.26	531.03	438.15	384.13	349.50	309.09
80,000.00	824.30	606.90	500.74	439.01	399.43	353.25
90,000.00	927.33	682.76	563.33	493.89	449.36	397.40
100,000.00	1,030.37	758.62	625.92	548.76	499.29	441.56

4.500% Rate

Amount	Term of Loan in Years					
	10	15	20	25	30	40
$ 50.00	$ 0.52	$ 0.38	$ 0.32	$ 0.28	$ 0.25	0.22
100.00	1.04	0.76	0.63	0.56	0.51	0.45
200.00	2.07	1.53	1.27	1.11	1.01	0.90
300.00	3.11	2.29	1.90	1.67	1.52	1.35
400.00	4.15	3.06	2.53	2.22	2.03	1.80
500.00	5.18	3.82	3.16	2.78	2.53	2.25
600.00	6.22	4.59	3.80	3.33	3.04	2.70
700.00	7.25	5.35	4.43	3.89	3.55	3.15
800.00	8.29	6.12	5.06	4.45	4.05	3.60
900.00	9.33	6.88	5.69	5.00	4.56	4.05
1,000.00	10.36	7.65	6.33	5.56	5.07	4.50
2,000.00	20.73	15.30	12.65	11.12	10.13	8.99
3,000.00	31.09	22.95	18.98	16.67	15.20	13.49
4,000.00	41.46	30.60	25.31	22.23	20.27	17.98
5,000.00	51.82	38.25	31.63	27.79	25.33	22.48
6,000.00	62.18	45.90	37.96	33.35	30.40	26.97
7,000.00	72.55	53.55	44.29	38.91	35.47	31.47
8,000.00	82.91	61.20	50.61	44.47	40.53	35.97
9,000.00	93.27	68.85	56.94	50.02	45.60	40.46
10,000.00	103.64	76.50	63.26	55.58	50.67	44.96
20,000.00	207.28	153.00	126.53	111.17	101.34	89.91
30,000.00	310.92	229.50	189.79	166.75	152.01	134.87
40,000.00	414.55	306.00	253.06	222.33	202.67	179.83
50,000.00	518.19	382.50	316.32	277.92	253.34	224.78
60,000.00	621.83	459.00	379.59	333.50	304.01	269.74
70,000.00	725.47	535.50	442.85	389.08	354.68	314.69
80,000.00	829.11	611.99	506.12	444.67	405.35	359.65
90,000.00	932.75	688.49	569.38	500.25	456.02	404.61
100,000.00	1,036.38	764.99	632.65	555.83	506.69	449.56

4.625% Rate

Amount	Term of Loan in Years					
	10	15	20	25	30	40
$ 50.00	0.52	$ 0.39	$ 0.32	$ 0.28	$ 0.26	$ 0.23
100.00	1.04	0.77	0.64	0.56	0.51	0.46
200.00	2.08	1.54	1.28	1.13	1.03	0.92
300.00	3.13	2.31	1.92	1.69	1.54	1.37
400.00	4.17	3.09	2.56	2.25	2.06	1.83
500.00	5.21	3.86	3.20	2.81	2.57	2.29
600.00	6.25	4.63	3.84	3.38	3.08	2.75
700.00	7.30	5.40	4.48	3.94	3.60	3.20
800.00	8.34	6.17	5.12	4.50	4.11	3.66
900.00	9.38	6.94	5.75	5.07	4.63	4.12
1,000.00	10.42	7.71	6.39	5.63	5.14	4.58
2,000.00	20.85	15.43	12.79	11.26	10.28	9.15
3,000.00	31.27	23.14	19.18	16.89	15.42	13.73
4,000.00	41.70	30.86	25.58	22.52	20.57	18.31
5,000.00	52.12	38.57	31.97	28.15	25.71	22.88
6,000.00	62.55	46.28	38.37	33.78	30.85	27.46
7,000.00	72.97	54.00	44.76	39.41	35.99	32.03
8,000.00	83.39	61.71	51.15	45.04	41.13	36.61
9,000.00	93.82	69.43	57.55	50.67	46.27	41.19
10,000.00	104.24	77.14	63.94	56.30	51.41	45.76
20,000.00	208.48	154.28	127.88	112.59	102.83	91.53
30,000.00	312.73	231.42	191.83	168.89	154.24	137.29
40,000.00	416.97	308.56	255.77	225.18	205.66	183.05
50,000.00	521.21	385.70	319.71	281.48	257.07	228.81
60,000.00	625.45	462.84	383.65	337.77	308.48	274.58
70,000.00	729.69	539.98	447.59	394.07	359.90	320.34
80,000.00	833.94	617.12	511.53	450.36	411.31	366.10
90,000.00	938.18	694.26	575.48	506.66	462.73	411.87
100,000.00	1,042.42	771.40	639.42	562.95	514.14	457.63

4.750% Rate

Amount	Term of Loan in Years					
	10	15	20	25	30	40
$ 50.00	$ 0.52	$ 0.39	$ 0.32	$ 0.29	$ 0.26	$ 0.23
100.00	1.05	0.78	0.65	0.57	0.52	0.47
200.00	2.10	1.56	1.29	1.14	1.04	0.93
300.00	3.15	2.33	1.94	1.71	1.56	1.40
400.00	4.19	3.11	2.58	2.28	2.09	1.86
500.00	5.24	3.89	3.23	2.85	2.61	2.33
600.00	6.29	4.67	3.88	3.42	3.13	2.79
700.00	7.34	5.44	4.52	3.99	3.65	3.26
800.00	8.39	6.22	5.17	4.56	4.17	3.73
900.00	9.44	7.00	5.82	5.13	4.69	4.19
1,000.00	10.48	7.78	6.46	5.70	5.22	4.66
2,000.00	20.97	15.56	12.92	11.40	10.43	9.32
3,000.00	31.45	23.33	19.39	17.10	15.65	13.97
4,000.00	41.94	31.11	25.85	22.80	20.87	18.63
5,000.00	52.42	38.89	32.31	28.51	26.08	23.29
6,000.00	62.91	46.67	38.77	34.21	31.30	27.95
7,000.00	73.39	54.45	45.24	39.91	36.52	32.60
8,000.00	83.88	62.23	51.70	45.61	41.73	37.26
9,000.00	94.36	70.00	58.16	51.31	46.95	41.92
10,000.00	104.85	77.78	64.62	57.01	52.16	46.58
20,000.00	209.70	155.57	129.24	114.02	104.33	93.15
30,000.00	314.54	233.35	193.87	171.04	156.49	139.73
40,000.00	419.39	311.13	258.49	228.05	208.66	186.30
50,000.00	524.24	388.92	323.11	285.06	260.82	232.88
60,000.00	629.09	466.70	387.73	342.07	312.99	279.45
70,000.00	733.93	544.48	452.36	399.08	365.15	326.03
80,000.00	838.78	622.27	516.98	456.09	417.32	372.61
90,000.00	943.63	700.05	581.60	513.11	469.48	419.18
100,000.00	1,048.48	777.83	646.22	570.12	521.65	465.76

4.875% Rate

Amount	Term of Loan in Years					
	10	15	20	25	30	40
$ 50.00	$ 0.53	$ 0.39	$ 0.33	$ 0.29	$ 0.26	$ 0.24
100.00	1.05	0.78	0.65	0.58	0.53	0.47
200.00	2.11	1.57	1.31	1.15	1.06	0.95
300.00	3.16	2.35	1.96	1.73	1.59	1.42
400.00	4.22	3.14	2.61	2.31	2.12	1.90
500.00	5.27	3.92	3.27	2.89	2.65	2.37
600.00	6.33	4.71	3.92	3.46	3.18	2.84
700.00	7.38	5.49	4.57	4.04	3.70	3.32
800.00	8.44	6.27	5.22	4.62	4.23	3.79
900.00	9.49	7.06	5.88	5.20	4.76	4.27
1,000.00	10.55	7.84	6.53	5.77	5.29	4.74
2,000.00	21.09	15.69	13.06	11.55	10.58	9.48
3,000.00	31.64	23.53	19.59	17.32	15.88	14.22
4,000.00	42.18	31.37	26.12	23.09	21.17	18.96
5,000.00	52.73	39.21	32.65	28.87	26.46	23.70
6,000.00	63.27	47.06	39.18	34.64	31.75	28.44
7,000.00	73.82	54.90	45.71	40.41	37.04	33.18
8,000.00	84.36	62.74	52.25	46.19	42.34	37.92
9,000.00	94.91	70.59	58.78	51.96	47.63	42.66
10,000.00	105.46	78.43	65.31	57.73	52.92	47.39
20,000.00	210.91	156.86	130.61	115.47	105.84	94.79
30,000.00	316.37	235.29	195.92	173.20	158.76	142.18
40,000.00	421.82	313.72	261.23	230.93	211.68	189.58
50,000.00	527.28	392.15	326.54	288.67	264.60	236.97
60,000.00	632.73	470.58	391.84	346.40	317.52	284.37
70,000.00	738.19	549.01	457.15	404.13	370.45	331.76
80,000.00	843.64	627.44	522.46	461.86	423.37	379.16
90,000.00	949.10	705.87	587.76	519.60	476.29	426.55
100,000.00	1,054.56	784.30	653.07	577.33	529.21	473.95

5.000% Rate

Amount	Term of Loan in Years					
	10	15	20	25	30	40
$ 50.00	$ 0.53	$ 0.40	$ 0.33	$ 0.29	$ 0.27	$ 0.24
100.00	1.06	0.79	0.66	0.58	0.54	0.48
200.00	2.12	1.58	1.32	1.17	1.07	0.96
300.00	3.18	2.37	1.98	1.75	1.61	1.45
400.00	4.24	3.16	2.64	2.34	2.15	1.93
500.00	5.30	3.95	3.30	2.92	2.68	2.41
600.00	6.36	4.74	3.96	3.51	3.22	2.89
700.00	7.42	5.54	4.62	4.09	3.76	3.38
800.00	8.49	6.33	5.28	4.68	4.29	3.86
900.00	9.55	7.12	5.94	5.26	4.83	4.34
1,000.00	10.61	7.91	6.60	5.85	5.37	4.82
2,000.00	21.21	15.82	13.20	11.69	10.74	9.64
3,000.00	31.82	23.72	19.80	17.54	16.10	14.47
4,000.00	42.43	31.63	26.40	23.38	21.47	19.29
5,000.00	53.03	39.54	33.00	29.23	26.84	24.11
6,000.00	63.64	47.45	39.60	35.08	32.21	28.93
7,000.00	74.25	55.36	46.20	40.92	37.58	33.75
8,000.00	84.85	63.26	52.80	46.77	42.95	38.58
9,000.00	95.46	71.17	59.40	52.61	48.31	43.40
10,000.00	106.07	79.08	66.00	58.46	53.68	48.22
20,000.00	212.13	158.16	131.99	116.92	107.36	96.44
30,000.00	318.20	237.24	197.99	175.38	161.05	144.66
40,000.00	424.26	316.32	263.98	233.84	214.73	192.88
50,000.00	530.33	395.40	329.98	292.30	268.41	241.10
60,000.00	636.39	474.48	395.97	350.75	322.09	289.32
70,000.00	742.46	553.56	461.97	409.21	375.78	337.54
80,000.00	848.52	632.63	527.96	467.67	429.46	385.76
90,000.00	954.59	711.71	593.96	526.13	483.14	433.98
100,000.00	1,060.66	790.79	659.96	584.59	536.82	482.20

5.125% Rate

Amount	Term of Loan in Years					
	10	15	20	25	30	40
$ 50.00	$ 0.53	$ 0.40	$ 0.33	$ 0.30	$ 0.27	$ 0.25
100.00	1.07	0.80	0.67	0.59	0.54	0.49
200.00	2.13	1.59	1.33	1.18	1.09	0.98
300.00	3.20	2.39	2.00	1.78	1.63	1.47
400.00	4.27	3.19	2.67	2.37	2.18	1.96
500.00	5.33	3.99	3.33	2.96	2.72	2.45
600.00	6.40	4.78	4.00	3.55	3.27	2.94
700.00	7.47	5.58	4.67	4.14	3.81	3.43
800.00	8.53	6.38	5.34	4.74	4.36	3.92
900.00	9.60	7.18	6.00	5.33	4.90	4.41
1,000.00	10.67	7.97	6.67	5.92	5.44	4.91
2,000.00	21.34	15.95	13.34	11.84	10.89	9.81
3,000.00	32.00	23.92	20.01	17.76	16.33	14.72
4,000.00	42.67	31.89	26.68	23.68	21.78	19.62
5,000.00	53.34	39.87	33.34	29.59	27.22	24.53
6,000.00	64.01	47.84	40.01	35.51	32.67	29.43
7,000.00	74.67	55.81	46.68	41.43	38.11	34.34
8,000.00	85.34	63.79	53.35	47.35	43.56	39.24
9,000.00	96.01	71.76	60.02	53.27	49.00	44.15
10,000.00	106.68	79.73	66.69	59.19	54.45	49.05
20,000.00	213.36	159.46	133.38	118.38	108.90	98.10
30,000.00	320.03	239.20	200.06	177.57	163.35	147.15
40,000.00	426.71	318.93	266.75	236.76	217.79	196.20
50,000.00	533.39	398.66	333.44	295.95	272.24	245.25
60,000.00	640.07	478.39	400.13	355.14	326.69	294.30
70,000.00	746.74	558.12	466.82	414.33	381.14	343.35
80,000.00	853.42	637.86	533.50	473.52	435.59	392.40
90,000.00	960.10	717.59	600.19	532.71	490.04	441.45
100,000.00	1,066.78	797.32	666.88	591.90	544.49	490.50

5.250% Rate

Amount	Term of Loan in Years					
	10	15	20	25	30	40
$ 50.00	$ 0.54	$ 0.40	$ 0.34	$ 0.30	$ 0.28	$ 0.25
100.00	1.07	0.80	0.67	0.60	0.55	0.50
200.00	2.15	1.61	1.35	1.20	1.10	1.00
300.00	3.22	2.41	2.02	1.80	1.66	1.50
400.00	4.29	3.22	2.70	2.40	2.21	2.00
500.00	5.36	4.02	3.37	3.00	2.76	2.49
600.00	6.44	4.82	4.04	3.60	3.31	2.99
700.00	7.51	5.63	4.72	4.19	3.87	3.49
800.00	8.58	6.43	5.39	4.79	4.42	3.99
900.00	9.66	7.23	6.06	5.39	4.97	4.49
1,000.00	10.73	8.04	6.74	5.99	5.52	4.99
2,000.00	21.46	16.08	13.48	11.98	11.04	9.98
3,000.00	32.19	24.12	20.22	17.98	16.57	14.97
4,000.00	42.92	32.16	26.95	23.97	22.09	19.95
5,000.00	53.65	40.19	33.69	29.96	27.61	24.94
6,000.00	64.38	48.23	40.43	35.95	33.13	29.93
7,000.00	75.10	56.27	47.17	41.95	38.65	34.92
8,000.00	85.83	64.31	53.91	47.94	44.18	39.91
9,000.00	96.56	72.35	60.65	53.93	49.70	44.90
10,000.00	107.29	80.39	67.38	59.92	55.22	49.89
20,000.00	214.58	160.78	134.77	119.85	110.44	99.77
30,000.00	321.88	241.16	202.15	179.77	165.66	149.66
40,000.00	429.17	321.55	269.54	239.70	220.88	199.55
50,000.00	536.46	401.94	336.92	299.62	276.10	249.44
60,000.00	643.75	482.33	404.31	359.55	331.32	299.32
70,000.00	751.04	562.71	471.69	419.47	386.54	349.21
80,000.00	858.33	643.10	539.08	479.40	441.76	399.10
90,000.00	965.63	723.49	606.46	539.32	496.98	448.98
100,000.00	1,072.92	803.88	673.84	599.25	552.20	498.87

5.375% Rate

Amount	Term of Loan in Years					
	10	15	20	25	30	40
$ 50.00	$ 0.54	$ 0.41	$ 0.34	$ 0.30	$ 0.28	$ 0.25
100.00	1.08	0.81	0.68	0.61	0.56	0.51
200.00	2.16	1.62	1.36	1.21	1.12	1.01
300.00	3.24	2.43	2.04	1.82	1.68	1.52
400.00	4.32	3.24	2.72	2.43	2.24	2.03
500.00	5.40	4.05	3.40	3.03	2.80	2.54
600.00	6.47	4.86	4.09	3.64	3.36	3.04
700.00	7.55	5.67	4.77	4.25	3.92	3.55
800.00	8.63	6.48	5.45	4.85	4.48	4.06
900.00	9.71	7.29	6.13	5.46	5.04	4.57
1,000.00	10.79	8.10	6.81	6.07	5.60	5.07
2,000.00	21.58	16.21	13.62	12.13	11.20	10.15
3,000.00	32.37	24.31	20.43	18.20	16.80	15.22
4,000.00	43.16	32.42	27.23	24.27	22.40	20.29
5,000.00	53.95	40.52	34.04	30.33	28.00	25.36
6,000.00	64.74	48.63	40.85	36.40	33.60	30.44
7,000.00	75.54	56.73	47.66	42.47	39.20	35.51
8,000.00	86.33	64.84	54.47	48.53	44.80	40.58
9,000.00	97.12	72.94	61.28	54.60	50.40	45.66
10,000.00	107.91	81.05	68.08	60.66	56.00	50.73
20,000.00	215.82	162.09	136.17	121.33	111.99	101.46
30,000.00	323.72	243.14	204.25	181.99	167.99	152.19
40,000.00	431.63	324.19	272.34	242.66	223.99	202.92
50,000.00	539.54	405.23	340.42	303.32	279.99	253.65
60,000.00	647.45	486.28	408.51	363.99	335.98	304.38
70,000.00	755.36	567.33	476.59	424.65	391.98	355.10
80,000.00	863.26	648.37	544.68	485.32	447.98	405.83
90,000.00	971.17	729.42	612.76	545.98	503.97	456.56
100,000.00	1,079.08	810.47	680.85	606.65	559.97	507.29

5.500% Rate

Amount	Term of Loan in Years					
	10	15	20	25	30	40
$ 50.00	$ 0.54	$ 0.41	$ 0.34	$ 0.31	$ 0.28	$ 0.26
100.00	1.09	0.82	0.69	0.61	0.57	0.52
200.00	2.17	1.63	1.38	1.23	1.14	1.03
300.00	3.26	2.45	2.06	1.84	1.70	1.55
400.00	4.34	3.27	2.75	2.46	2.27	2.06
500.00	5.43	4.09	3.44	3.07	2.84	2.58
600.00	6.51	4.90	4.13	3.68	3.41	3.09
700.00	7.60	5.72	4.82	4.30	3.97	3.61
800.00	8.68	6.54	5.50	4.91	4.54	4.13
900.00	9.77	7.35	6.19	5.53	5.11	4.64
1,000.00	10.85	8.17	6.88	6.14	5.68	5.16
2,000.00	21.71	16.34	13.76	12.28	11.36	10.32
3,000.00	32.56	24.51	20.64	18.42	17.03	15.47
4,000.00	43.41	32.68	27.52	24.56	22.71	20.63
5,000.00	54.26	40.85	34.39	30.70	28.39	25.79
6,000.00	65.12	49.03	41.27	36.85	34.07	30.95
7,000.00	75.97	57.20	48.15	42.99	39.75	36.10
8,000.00	86.82	65.37	55.03	49.13	45.42	41.26
9,000.00	97.67	73.54	61.91	55.27	51.10	46.42
10,000.00	108.53	81.71	68.79	61.41	56.78	51.58
20,000.00	217.05	163.42	137.58	122.82	113.56	103.15
30,000.00	325.58	245.13	206.37	184.23	170.34	154.73
40,000.00	434.11	326.83	275.15	245.63	227.12	206.31
50,000.00	542.63	408.54	343.94	307.04	283.89	257.89
60,000.00	651.16	490.25	412.73	368.45	340.67	309.46
70,000.00	759.68	571.96	481.52	429.86	397.45	361.04
80,000.00	868.21	653.67	550.31	491.27	454.23	412.62
90,000.00	976.74	735.38	619.10	552.68	511.01	464.19
100,000.00	1,085.26	817.08	687.89	614.09	567.79	515.77

5.625% Rate

Amount	Term of Loan in Years					
	10	15	20	25	30	40
$ 50.00	$ 0.55	$ 0.41	$ 0.35	$ 0.31	$ 0.29	$ 0.26
100.00	1.09	0.82	0.69	0.62	0.58	0.52
200.00	2.18	1.65	1.39	1.24	1.15	1.05
300.00	3.27	2.47	2.08	1.86	1.73	1.57
400.00	4.37	3.29	2.78	2.49	2.30	2.10
500.00	5.46	4.12	3.47	3.11	2.88	2.62
600.00	6.55	4.94	4.17	3.73	3.45	3.15
700.00	7.64	5.77	4.86	4.35	4.03	3.67
800.00	8.73	6.59	5.56	4.97	4.61	4.19
900.00	9.82	7.41	6.25	5.59	5.18	4.72
1,000.00	10.91	8.24	6.95	6.22	5.76	5.24
2,000.00	21.83	16.47	13.90	12.43	11.51	10.49
3,000.00	32.74	24.71	20.85	18.65	17.27	15.73
4,000.00	43.66	32.95	27.80	24.86	23.03	20.97
5,000.00	54.57	41.19	34.75	31.08	28.78	26.22
6,000.00	65.49	49.42	41.70	37.29	34.54	31.46
7,000.00	76.40	57.66	48.65	43.51	40.30	36.70
8,000.00	87.32	65.90	55.60	49.73	46.05	41.94
9,000.00	98.23	74.14	62.55	55.94	51.81	47.19
10,000.00	109.15	82.37	69.50	62.16	57.57	52.43
20,000.00	218.29	164.75	138.99	124.31	115.13	104.86
30,000.00	327.44	247.12	208.49	186.47	172.70	157.29
40,000.00	436.59	329.49	277.99	248.63	230.26	209.72
50,000.00	545.73	411.87	347.48	310.79	287.83	262.15
60,000.00	654.88	494.24	416.98	372.94	345.39	314.58
70,000.00	764.03	576.61	486.48	435.10	402.96	367.01
80,000.00	873.17	658.99	555.97	497.26	460.53	419.44
90,000.00	982.32	741.36	625.47	559.42	518.09	471.87
100,000.00	1,091.47	823.73	694.97	621.57	575.66	524.30

5.750% Rate

Amount	10	15	20	25	30	40
			Term of Loan in Years			
$ 50.00	$ 0.55	$ 0.42	$ 0.35	$ 0.31	$ 0.29	$ 0.27
100.00	1.10	0.83	0.70	0.63	0.58	0.53
200.00	2.20	1.66	1.40	1.26	1.17	1.07
300.00	3.29	2.49	2.11	1.89	1.75	1.60
400.00	4.39	3.32	2.81	2.52	2.33	2.13
500.00	5.49	4.15	3.51	3.15	2.92	2.66
600.00	6.59	4.98	4.21	3.77	3.50	3.20
700.00	7.68	5.81	4.91	4.40	4.09	3.73
800.00	8.78	6.64	5.62	5.03	4.67	4.26
900.00	9.88	7.47	6.32	5.66	5.25	4.80
1,000.00	10.98	8.30	7.02	6.29	5.84	5.33
2,000.00	21.95	16.61	14.04	12.58	11.67	10.66
3,000.00	32.93	24.91	21.06	18.87	17.51	15.99
4,000.00	43.91	33.22	28.08	25.16	23.34	21.32
5,000.00	54.88	41.52	35.10	31.46	29.18	26.64
6,000.00	65.86	49.82	42.13	37.75	35.01	31.97
7,000.00	76.84	58.13	49.15	44.04	40.85	37.30
8,000.00	87.82	66.43	56.17	50.33	46.69	42.63
9,000.00	98.79	74.74	63.19	56.62	52.52	47.96
10,000.00	109.77	83.04	70.21	62.91	58.36	53.29
20,000.00	219.54	166.08	140.42	125.82	116.71	106.58
30,000.00	329.31	249.12	210.63	188.73	175.07	159.87
40,000.00	439.08	332.16	280.83	251.64	233.43	213.16
50,000.00	548.85	415.21	351.04	314.55	291.79	266.44
60,000.00	658.62	498.25	421.25	377.46	350.14	319.73
70,000.00	768.38	581.29	491.46	440.37	408.50	373.02
80,000.00	878.15	664.33	561.67	503.29	466.86	426.31
90,000.00	987.92	747.37	631.88	566.20	525.22	479.60
100,000.00	1,097.69	830.41	702.08	629.11	583.57	532.89

411

5.875% Rate

Amount	Term of Loan in Years					
	10	15	20	25	30	40
$ 50.00	$ 0.55	$ 0.42	$ 0.35	$ 0.32	$ 0.30	$ 0.27
100.00	1.10	0.84	0.71	0.64	0.59	0.54
200.00	2.21	1.67	1.42	1.27	1.18	1.08
300.00	3.31	2.51	2.13	1.91	1.77	1.62
400.00	4.42	3.35	2.84	2.55	2.37	2.17
500.00	5.52	4.19	3.55	3.18	2.96	2.71
600.00	6.62	5.02	4.26	3.82	3.55	3.25
700.00	7.73	5.86	4.96	4.46	4.14	3.79
800.00	8.83	6.70	5.67	5.09	4.73	4.33
900.00	9.94	7.53	6.38	5.73	5.32	4.87
1,000.00	11.04	8.37	7.09	6.37	5.92	5.42
2,000.00	22.08	16.74	14.18	12.73	11.83	10.83
3,000.00	33.12	25.11	21.28	19.10	17.75	16.25
4,000.00	44.16	33.48	28.37	25.47	23.66	21.66
5,000.00	55.20	41.86	35.46	31.83	29.58	27.08
6,000.00	66.24	50.23	42.55	38.20	35.49	32.49
7,000.00	77.28	58.60	49.65	44.57	41.41	37.91
8,000.00	88.32	66.97	56.74	50.93	47.32	43.32
9,000.00	99.35	75.34	63.83	57.30	53.24	48.74
10,000.00	110.39	83.71	70.92	63.67	59.15	54.15
20,000.00	220.79	167.42	141.85	127.34	118.31	108.31
30,000.00	331.18	251.14	212.77	191.00	177.46	162.46
40,000.00	441.58	334.85	283.70	254.67	236.62	216.61
50,000.00	551.97	418.56	354.62	318.34	295.77	270.76
60,000.00	662.36	502.27	425.54	382.01	354.92	324.92
70,000.00	772.76	585.98	496.47	445.68	414.08	379.07
80,000.00	883.15	669.69	567.39	509.35	473.23	433.22
90,000.00	993.54	753.41	638.31	573.01	532.38	487.37
100,000.00	1,103.94	837.12	709.24	636.68	591.54	541.53

6.000% Rate

Amount	Term of Loan in Years					
	10	15	20	25	30	40
$ 50.00	$ 0.56	$ 0.42	$ 0.36	$ 0.32	$ 0.30	$ 0.28
100.00	1.11	0.84	0.72	0.64	0.60	0.55
200.00	2.22	1.69	1.43	1.29	1.20	1.10
300.00	3.33	2.53	2.15	1.93	1.80	1.65
400.00	4.44	3.38	2.87	2.58	2.40	2.20
500.00	5.55	4.22	3.58	3.22	3.00	2.75
600.00	6.66	5.06	4.30	3.87	3.60	3.30
700.00	7.77	5.91	5.02	4.51	4.20	3.85
800.00	8.88	6.75	5.73	5.15	4.80	4.40
900.00	9.99	7.59	6.45	5.80	5.40	4.95
1,000.00	11.10	8.44	7.16	6.44	6.00	5.50
2,000.00	22.20	16.88	14.33	12.89	11.99	11.00
3,000.00	33.31	25.32	21.49	19.33	17.99	16.51
4,000.00	44.41	33.75	28.66	25.77	23.98	22.01
5,000.00	55.51	42.19	35.82	32.22	29.98	27.51
6,000.00	66.61	50.63	42.99	38.66	35.97	33.01
7,000.00	77.71	59.07	50.15	45.10	41.97	38.51
8,000.00	88.82	67.51	57.31	51.54	47.96	44.02
9,000.00	99.92	75.95	64.48	57.99	53.96	49.52
10,000.00	111.02	84.39	71.64	64.43	59.96	55.02
20,000.00	222.04	168.77	143.29	128.86	119.91	110.04
30,000.00	333.06	253.16	214.93	193.29	179.87	165.06
40,000.00	444.08	337.54	286.57	257.72	239.82	220.09
50,000.00	555.10	421.93	358.22	322.15	299.78	275.11
60,000.00	666.12	506.31	429.86	386.58	359.73	330.13
70,000.00	777.14	590.70	501.50	451.01	419.69	385.15
80,000.00	888.16	675.09	573.14	515.44	479.64	440.17
90,000.00	999.18	759.47	644.79	579.87	539.60	495.19
100,000.00	1,110.21	843.86	716.43	644.30	599.55	550.21

6.125% Rate

Amount		Term of Loan in Years					
		10	15	20	25	30	40
$ 50.00	$	0.56	$ 0.43	$ 0.36	$ 0.33	$ 0.30	$ 0.28
100.00		1.12	0.85	0.72	0.65	0.61	0.56
200.00		2.23	1.70	1.45	1.30	1.22	1.12
300.00		3.35	2.55	2.17	1.96	1.82	1.68
400.00		4.47	3.40	2.89	2.61	2.43	2.24
500.00		5.58	4.25	3.62	3.26	3.04	2.79
600.00		6.70	5.10	4.34	3.91	3.65	3.35
700.00		7.82	5.95	5.07	4.56	4.25	3.91
800.00		8.93	6.80	5.79	5.22	4.86	4.47
900.00		10.05	7.66	6.51	5.87	5.47	5.03
1,000.00		11.16	8.51	7.24	6.52	6.08	5.59
2,000.00		22.33	17.01	14.47	13.04	12.15	11.18
3,000.00		33.49	25.52	21.71	19.56	18.23	16.77
4,000.00		44.66	34.02	28.95	26.08	24.30	22.36
5,000.00		55.82	42.53	36.18	32.60	30.38	27.95
6,000.00		66.99	51.04	43.42	39.12	36.46	33.54
7,000.00		78.15	59.54	50.66	45.64	42.53	39.13
8,000.00		89.32	68.05	57.89	52.16	48.61	44.72
9,000.00		100.48	76.56	65.13	58.68	54.68	50.31
10,000.00		111.65	85.06	72.37	65.20	60.76	55.90
20,000.00		223.30	170.12	144.73	130.39	121.52	111.79
30,000.00		334.95	255.19	217.10	195.59	182.28	167.69
40,000.00		446.60	340.25	289.46	260.79	243.04	223.58
50,000.00		558.25	425.31	361.83	325.98	303.81	279.48
60,000.00		669.90	510.37	434.20	391.18	364.57	335.37
70,000.00		781.54	595.44	506.56	456.37	425.33	391.27
80,000.00		893.19	680.50	578.93	521.57	486.09	447.16
90,000.00		1,004.84	765.56	651.29	586.77	546.85	503.06
100,000.00		1,116.49	850.62	723.66	651.96	607.61	558.95

6.250% Rate

Amount	Term of Loan in Years					
	10	15	20	25	30	40
$ 50.00	$ 0.56	$ 0.43	$ 0.37	$ 0.33	$ 0.31	$ 0.28
100.00	1.12	0.86	0.73	0.66	0.62	0.57
200.00	2.25	1.71	1.46	1.32	1.23	1.14
300.00	3.37	2.57	2.19	1.98	1.85	1.70
400.00	4.49	3.43	2.92	2.64	2.46	2.27
500.00	5.61	4.29	3.65	3.30	3.08	2.84
600.00	6.74	5.14	4.39	3.96	3.69	3.41
700.00	7.86	6.00	5.12	4.62	4.31	3.97
800.00	8.98	6.86	5.85	5.28	4.93	4.54
900.00	10.11	7.72	6.58	5.94	5.54	5.11
1,000.00	11.23	8.57	7.31	6.60	6.16	5.68
2,000.00	22.46	17.15	14.62	13.19	12.31	11.35
3,000.00	33.68	25.72	21.93	19.79	18.47	17.03
4,000.00	44.91	34.30	29.24	26.39	24.63	22.71
5,000.00	56.14	42.87	36.55	32.98	30.79	28.39
6,000.00	67.37	51.45	43.86	39.58	36.94	34.06
7,000.00	78.60	60.02	51.16	46.18	43.10	39.74
8,000.00	89.82	68.59	58.47	52.77	49.26	45.42
9,000.00	101.05	77.17	65.78	59.37	55.41	51.10
10,000.00	112.28	85.74	73.09	65.97	61.57	56.77
20,000.00	224.56	171.48	146.19	131.93	123.14	113.55
30,000.00	336.84	257.23	219.28	197.90	184.72	170.32
40,000.00	449.12	342.97	292.37	263.87	246.29	227.10
50,000.00	561.40	428.71	365.46	329.83	307.86	283.87
60,000.00	673.68	514.45	438.56	395.80	369.43	340.64
70,000.00	785.96	600.20	511.65	461.77	431.00	397.42
80,000.00	898.24	685.94	584.74	527.74	492.57	454.19
90,000.00	1,010.52	771.68	657.84	593.70	554.15	510.97
100,000.00	1,122.80	857.42	730.93	659.67	615.72	567.74

415

6.375% Rate

Amount	Term of Loan in Years					
	10	15	20	25	30	40
$ 50.00	$ 0.56	$ 0.43	$ 0.37	$ 0.33	$ 0.31	$ 0.29
100.00	1.13	0.86	0.74	0.67	0.62	0.58
200.00	2.26	1.73	1.48	1.33	1.25	1.15
300.00	3.39	2.59	2.21	2.00	1.87	1.73
400.00	4.52	3.46	2.95	2.67	2.50	2.31
500.00	5.65	4.32	3.69	3.34	3.12	2.88
600.00	6.77	5.19	4.43	4.00	3.74	3.46
700.00	7.90	6.05	5.17	4.67	4.37	4.04
800.00	9.03	6.91	5.91	5.34	4.99	4.61
900.00	10.16	7.78	6.64	6.01	5.61	5.19
1,000.00	11.29	8.64	7.38	6.67	6.24	5.77
2,000.00	22.58	17.29	14.76	13.35	12.48	11.53
3,000.00	33.87	25.93	22.15	20.02	18.72	17.30
4,000.00	45.17	34.57	29.53	26.70	24.95	23.06
5,000.00	56.46	43.21	36.91	33.37	31.19	28.83
6,000.00	67.75	51.86	44.29	40.05	37.43	34.59
7,000.00	79.04	60.50	51.68	46.72	43.67	40.36
8,000.00	90.33	69.14	59.06	53.39	49.91	46.13
9,000.00	101.62	77.78	66.44	60.07	56.15	51.89
10,000.00	112.91	86.43	73.82	66.74	62.39	57.66
20,000.00	225.83	172.85	147.65	133.48	124.77	115.31
30,000.00	338.74	259.28	221.47	200.23	187.16	172.97
40,000.00	451.65	345.70	295.29	266.97	249.55	230.63
50,000.00	564.57	432.13	369.12	333.71	311.93	288.29
60,000.00	677.48	518.55	442.94	400.45	374.32	345.94
70,000.00	790.39	604.98	516.76	467.19	436.71	403.60
80,000.00	903.30	691.40	590.59	533.93	499.10	461.26
90,000.00	1,016.22	777.83	664.41	600.68	561.48	518.92
100,000.00	1,129.13	864.25	738.23	667.42	623.87	576.57

6.500% Rate

Amount	Term of Loan in Years					
	10	15	20	25	30	40
$ 50.00	$ 0.57	$ 0.44	$ 0.37	$ 0.34	$ 0.32	$ 0.29
100.00	1.14	0.87	0.75	0.68	0.63	0.59
200.00	2.27	1.74	1.49	1.35	1.26	1.17
300.00	3.41	2.61	2.24	2.03	1.90	1.76
400.00	4.54	3.48	2.98	2.70	2.53	2.34
500.00	5.68	4.36	3.73	3.38	3.16	2.93
600.00	6.81	5.23	4.47	4.05	3.79	3.51
700.00	7.95	6.10	5.22	4.73	4.42	4.10
800.00	9.08	6.97	5.96	5.40	5.06	4.68
900.00	10.22	7.84	6.71	6.08	5.69	5.27
1,000.00	11.35	8.71	7.46	6.75	6.32	5.85
2,000.00	22.71	17.42	14.91	13.50	12.64	11.71
3,000.00	34.06	26.13	22.37	20.26	18.96	17.56
4,000.00	45.42	34.84	29.82	27.01	25.28	23.42
5,000.00	56.77	43.56	37.28	33.76	31.60	29.27
6,000.00	68.13	52.27	44.73	40.51	37.92	35.13
7,000.00	79.48	60.98	52.19	47.26	44.24	40.98
8,000.00	90.84	69.69	59.65	54.02	50.57	46.84
9,000.00	102.19	78.40	67.10	60.77	56.89	52.69
10,000.00	113.55	87.11	74.56	67.52	63.21	58.55
20,000.00	227.10	174.22	149.11	135.04	126.41	117.09
30,000.00	340.64	261.33	223.67	202.56	189.62	175.64
40,000.00	454.19	348.44	298.23	270.08	252.83	234.18
50,000.00	567.74	435.55	372.79	337.60	316.03	292.73
60,000.00	681.29	522.66	447.34	405.12	379.24	351.27
70,000.00	794.84	609.78	521.90	472.65	442.45	409.82
80,000.00	908.38	696.89	596.46	540.17	505.65	468.37
90,000.00	1,021.93	784.00	671.02	607.69	568.86	526.91
100,000.00	1,135.48	871.11	745.57	675.21	632.07	585.46

6.625% Rate

Amount	Term of Loan in Years					
	10	15	20	25	30	40
$ 50.00	$ 0.57	$ 0.44	$ 0.38	$ 0.34	$ 0.32	$ 0.30
100.00	1.14	0.88	0.75	0.68	0.64	0.59
200.00	2.28	1.76	1.51	1.37	1.28	1.19
300.00	3.43	2.63	2.26	2.05	1.92	1.78
400.00	4.57	3.51	3.01	2.73	2.56	2.38
500.00	5.71	4.39	3.76	3.42	3.20	2.97
600.00	6.85	5.27	4.52	4.10	3.84	3.57
700.00	7.99	6.15	5.27	4.78	4.48	4.16
800.00	9.13	7.02	6.02	5.46	5.12	4.76
900.00	10.28	7.90	6.78	6.15	5.76	5.35
1,000.00	11.42	8.78	7.53	6.83	6.40	5.94
2,000.00	22.84	17.56	15.06	13.66	12.81	11.89
3,000.00	34.26	26.34	22.59	20.49	19.21	17.83
4,000.00	45.67	35.12	30.12	27.32	25.61	23.78
5,000.00	57.09	43.90	37.65	34.15	32.02	29.72
6,000.00	68.51	52.68	45.18	40.98	38.42	35.66
7,000.00	79.93	61.46	52.71	47.81	44.82	41.61
8,000.00	91.35	70.24	60.24	54.64	51.22	47.55
9,000.00	102.77	79.02	67.77	61.47	57.63	53.49
10,000.00	114.19	87.80	75.30	68.30	64.03	59.44
20,000.00	228.37	175.60	150.59	136.61	128.06	118.88
30,000.00	342.56	263.40	225.89	204.91	192.09	178.32
40,000.00	456.74	351.20	301.18	273.22	256.12	237.75
50,000.00	570.93	439.00	376.48	341.52	320.16	297.19
60,000.00	685.11	526.80	451.77	409.82	384.19	356.63
70,000.00	799.30	614.60	527.07	478.13	448.22	416.07
80,000.00	913.48	702.40	602.36	546.43	512.25	475.51
90,000.00	1,027.67	790.19	677.66	614.73	576.28	534.95
100,000.00	1,141.85	877.99	752.95	683.04	640.31	594.38

6.750% Rate

Amount	Term of Loan in Years					
	10	15	20	25	30	40
$ 50.00	$ 0.57	$ 0.44	$ 0.38	$ 0.35	$ 0.32	$ 0.30
100.00	1.15	0.88	0.76	0.69	0.65	0.60
200.00	2.30	1.77	1.52	1.38	1.30	1.21
300.00	3.44	2.65	2.28	2.07	1.95	1.81
400.00	4.59	3.54	3.04	2.76	2.59	2.41
500.00	5.74	4.42	3.80	3.45	3.24	3.02
600.00	6.89	5.31	4.56	4.15	3.89	3.62
700.00	8.04	6.19	5.32	4.84	4.54	4.22
800.00	9.19	7.08	6.08	5.53	5.19	4.83
900.00	10.33	7.96	6.84	6.22	5.84	5.43
1,000.00	11.48	8.85	7.60	6.91	6.49	6.03
2,000.00	22.96	17.70	15.21	13.82	12.97	12.07
3,000.00	34.45	26.55	22.81	20.73	19.46	18.10
4,000.00	45.93	35.40	30.41	27.64	25.94	24.13
5,000.00	57.41	44.25	38.02	34.55	32.43	30.17
6,000.00	68.89	53.09	45.62	41.45	38.92	36.20
7,000.00	80.38	61.94	53.23	48.36	45.40	42.23
8,000.00	91.86	70.79	60.83	55.27	51.89	48.27
9,000.00	103.34	79.64	68.43	62.18	58.37	54.30
10,000.00	114.82	88.49	76.04	69.09	64.86	60.34
20,000.00	229.65	176.98	152.07	138.18	129.72	120.67
30,000.00	344.47	265.47	228.11	207.27	194.58	181.01
40,000.00	459.30	353.96	304.15	276.36	259.44	241.34
50,000.00	574.12	442.45	380.18	345.46	324.30	301.68
60,000.00	688.94	530.95	456.22	414.55	389.16	362.01
70,000.00	803.77	619.44	532.25	483.64	454.02	422.35
80,000.00	918.59	707.93	608.29	552.73	518.88	482.69
90,000.00	1,033.42	796.42	684.33	621.82	583.74	543.02
100,000.00	1,148.24	884.91	760.36	690.91	648.60	603.36

6.875% Rate

Amount	Term of Loan in Years					
	10	15	20	25	30	40
$ 50.00	$ 0.58	$ 0.45	$ 0.38	$ 0.35	$ 0.33	$ 0.31
100.00	1.15	0.89	0.77	0.70	0.66	0.61
200.00	2.31	1.78	1.54	1.40	1.31	1.22
300.00	3.46	2.68	2.30	2.10	1.97	1.84
400.00	4.62	3.57	3.07	2.80	2.63	2.45
500.00	5.77	4.46	3.84	3.49	3.28	3.06
600.00	6.93	5.35	4.61	4.19	3.94	3.67
700.00	8.08	6.24	5.37	4.89	4.60	4.29
800.00	9.24	7.13	6.14	5.59	5.26	4.90
900.00	10.39	8.03	6.91	6.29	5.91	5.51
1,000.00	11.55	8.92	7.68	6.99	6.57	6.12
2,000.00	23.09	17.84	15.36	13.98	13.14	12.25
3,000.00	34.64	26.76	23.03	20.96	19.71	18.37
4,000.00	46.19	35.67	30.71	27.95	26.28	24.49
5,000.00	57.73	44.59	38.39	34.94	32.85	30.62
6,000.00	69.28	53.51	46.07	41.93	39.42	36.74
7,000.00	80.83	62.43	53.75	48.92	45.99	42.87
8,000.00	92.37	71.35	61.43	55.91	52.55	48.99
9,000.00	103.92	80.27	69.10	62.89	59.12	55.11
10,000.00	115.47	89.19	76.78	69.88	65.69	61.24
20,000.00	230.93	178.37	153.56	139.77	131.39	122.47
30,000.00	346.40	267.56	230.34	209.65	197.08	183.71
40,000.00	461.86	356.74	307.13	279.53	262.77	244.95
50,000.00	577.33	445.93	383.91	349.41	328.46	306.19
60,000.00	692.79	535.11	460.69	419.30	394.16	367.42
70,000.00	808.26	624.30	537.47	489.18	459.85	428.66
80,000.00	923.72	713.48	614.25	559.06	525.54	489.90
90,000.00	1,039.19	802.67	691.03	628.94	591.24	551.14
100,000.00	1,154.65	891.85	767.81	698.83	656.93	612.37

7.000% Rate

Amount	Term of Loan in Years					
	10	15	20	25	30	40
$ 50.00	$ 0.58	$ 0.45	$ 0.39	$ 0.35	$ 0.33	$ 0.31
100.00	1.16	0.90	0.78	0.71	0.67	0.62
200.00	2.32	1.80	1.55	1.41	1.33	1.24
300.00	3.48	2.70	2.33	2.12	2.00	1.86
400.00	4.64	3.60	3.10	2.83	2.66	2.49
500.00	5.81	4.49	3.88	3.53	3.33	3.11
600.00	6.97	5.39	4.65	4.24	3.99	3.73
700.00	8.13	6.29	5.43	4.95	4.66	4.35
800.00	9.29	7.19	6.20	5.65	5.32	4.97
900.00	10.45	8.09	6.98	6.36	5.99	5.59
1,000.00	11.61	8.99	7.75	7.07	6.65	6.21
2,000.00	23.22	17.98	15.51	14.14	13.31	12.43
3,000.00	34.83	26.96	23.26	21.20	19.96	18.64
4,000.00	46.44	35.95	31.01	28.27	26.61	24.86
5,000.00	58.05	44.94	38.76	35.34	33.27	31.07
6,000.00	69.67	53.93	46.52	42.41	39.92	37.29
7,000.00	81.28	62.92	54.27	49.47	46.57	43.50
8,000.00	92.89	71.91	62.02	56.54	53.22	49.71
9,000.00	104.50	80.89	69.78	63.61	59.88	55.93
10,000.00	116.11	89.88	77.53	70.68	66.53	62.14
20,000.00	232.22	179.77	155.06	141.36	133.06	124.29
30,000.00	348.33	269.65	232.59	212.03	199.59	186.43
40,000.00	464.43	359.53	310.12	282.71	266.12	248.57
50,000.00	580.54	449.41	387.65	353.39	332.65	310.72
60,000.00	696.65	539.30	465.18	424.07	399.18	372.86
70,000.00	812.76	629.18	542.71	494.75	465.71	435.00
80,000.00	928.87	719.06	620.24	565.42	532.24	497.15
90,000.00	1,044.98	808.95	697.77	636.10	598.77	559.29
100,000.00	1,161.08	898.83	775.30	706.78	665.30	621.43

7.125% Rate

Amount	Term of Loan in Years					
	10	15	20	25	30	40
$ 50.00	$ 0.58	$ 0.45	$ 0.39	$ 0.36	$ 0.34	$ 0.32
100.00	1.17	0.91	0.78	0.71	0.67	0.63
200.00	2.34	1.81	1.57	1.43	1.35	1.26
300.00	3.50	2.72	2.35	2.14	2.02	1.89
400.00	4.67	3.62	3.13	2.86	2.69	2.52
500.00	5.84	4.53	3.91	3.57	3.37	3.15
600.00	7.01	5.43	4.70	4.29	4.04	3.78
700.00	8.17	6.34	5.48	5.00	4.72	4.41
800.00	9.34	7.25	6.26	5.72	5.39	5.04
900.00	10.51	8.15	7.05	6.43	6.06	5.67
1,000.00	11.68	9.06	7.83	7.15	6.74	6.31
2,000.00	23.35	18.12	15.66	14.30	13.47	12.61
3,000.00	35.03	27.17	23.48	21.44	20.21	18.92
4,000.00	46.70	36.23	31.31	28.59	26.95	25.22
5,000.00	58.38	45.29	39.14	35.74	33.69	31.53
6,000.00	70.05	54.35	46.97	42.89	40.42	37.83
7,000.00	81.73	63.41	54.80	50.03	47.16	44.14
8,000.00	93.40	72.47	62.63	57.18	53.90	50.44
9,000.00	105.08	81.52	70.45	64.33	60.63	56.75
10,000.00	116.75	90.58	78.28	71.48	67.37	63.05
20,000.00	233.51	181.17	156.56	142.95	134.74	126.11
30,000.00	350.26	271.75	234.85	214.43	202.12	189.16
40,000.00	467.01	362.33	313.13	285.91	269.49	252.21
50,000.00	583.77	452.92	391.41	357.39	336.86	315.27
60,000.00	700.52	543.50	469.69	428.86	404.23	378.32
70,000.00	817.28	634.08	547.97	500.34	471.60	441.37
80,000.00	934.03	724.66	626.26	571.82	538.97	504.43
90,000.00	1,050.78	815.25	704.54	643.30	606.35	567.48
100,000.00	1,167.54	905.83	782.82	714.77	673.72	630.53

7.250% Rate

Amount	Term of Loan in Years					
	10	15	20	25	30	40
$ 50.00	$ 0.59	$ 0.46	$ 0.40	$ 0.36	$ 0.34	$ 0.32
100.00	1.17	0.91	0.79	0.72	0.68	0.64
200.00	2.35	1.83	1.58	1.45	1.36	1.28
300.00	3.52	2.74	2.37	2.17	2.05	1.92
400.00	4.70	3.65	3.16	2.89	2.73	2.56
500.00	5.87	4.56	3.95	3.61	3.41	3.20
600.00	7.04	5.48	4.74	4.34	4.09	3.84
700.00	8.22	6.39	5.53	5.06	4.78	4.48
800.00	9.39	7.30	6.32	5.78	5.46	5.12
900.00	10.57	8.22	7.11	6.51	6.14	5.76
1,000.00	11.74	9.13	7.90	7.23	6.82	6.40
2,000.00	23.48	18.26	15.81	14.46	13.64	12.79
3,000.00	35.22	27.39	23.71	21.68	20.47	19.19
4,000.00	46.96	36.51	31.62	28.91	27.29	25.59
5,000.00	58.70	45.64	39.52	36.14	34.11	31.98
6,000.00	70.44	54.77	47.42	43.37	40.93	38.38
7,000.00	82.18	63.90	55.33	50.60	47.75	44.78
8,000.00	93.92	73.03	63.23	57.82	54.57	51.17
9,000.00	105.66	82.16	71.13	65.05	61.40	57.57
10,000.00	117.40	91.29	79.04	72.28	68.22	63.97
20,000.00	234.80	182.57	158.08	144.56	136.44	127.93
30,000.00	352.20	273.86	237.11	216.84	204.65	191.90
40,000.00	469.60	365.15	316.15	289.12	272.87	255.87
50,000.00	587.01	456.43	395.19	361.40	341.09	319.84
60,000.00	704.41	547.72	474.23	433.68	409.31	383.80
70,000.00	821.81	639.00	553.26	505.96	477.52	447.77
80,000.00	939.21	730.29	632.30	578.25	545.74	511.74
90,000.00	1,056.61	821.58	711.34	650.53	613.96	575.70
100,000.00	1,174.01	912.86	790.38	722.81	682.18	639.67

7.375% Rate

Amount	Term of Loan in Years					
	10	15	20	25	30	40
$ 50.00	$ 0.59	$ 0.46	$ 0.40	$ 0.37	$ 0.35	$ 0.32
100.00	1.18	0.92	0.80	0.73	0.69	0.65
200.00	2.36	1.84	1.60	1.46	1.38	1.30
300.00	3.54	2.76	2.39	2.19	2.07	1.95
400.00	4.72	3.68	3.19	2.92	2.76	2.60
500.00	5.90	4.60	3.99	3.65	3.45	3.24
600.00	7.08	5.52	4.79	4.39	4.14	3.89
700.00	8.26	6.44	5.59	5.12	4.83	4.54
800.00	9.44	7.36	6.38	5.85	5.53	5.19
900.00	10.62	8.28	7.18	6.58	6.22	5.84
1,000.00	11.81	9.20	7.98	7.31	6.91	6.49
2,000.00	23.61	18.40	15.96	14.62	13.81	12.98
3,000.00	35.42	27.60	23.94	21.93	20.72	19.47
4,000.00	47.22	36.80	31.92	29.24	27.63	25.95
5,000.00	59.03	46.00	39.90	36.54	34.53	32.44
6,000.00	70.83	55.20	47.88	43.85	41.44	38.93
7,000.00	82.64	64.39	55.86	51.16	48.35	45.42
8,000.00	94.44	73.59	63.84	58.47	55.25	51.91
9,000.00	106.25	82.79	71.82	65.78	62.16	58.40
10,000.00	118.05	91.99	79.80	73.09	69.07	64.89
20,000.00	236.10	183.98	159.59	146.18	138.14	129.77
30,000.00	354.15	275.98	239.39	219.26	207.20	194.66
40,000.00	472.20	367.97	319.19	292.35	276.27	259.54
50,000.00	590.25	459.96	398.98	365.44	345.34	324.43
60,000.00	708.30	551.95	478.78	438.53	414.41	389.31
70,000.00	826.35	643.95	558.58	511.62	483.47	454.20
80,000.00	944.40	735.94	638.37	584.70	552.54	519.08
90,000.00	1,062.45	827.93	718.17	657.79	621.61	583.97
100,000.00	1,180.50	919.92	797.97	730.88	690.68	648.85

7.500% Rate

Amount	Term of Loan in Years					
	10	15	20	25	30	40
$ 50.00	$ 0.59	$ 0.46	$ 0.40	$ 0.37	$ 0.35	$ 0.33
100.00	1.19	0.93	0.81	0.74	0.70	0.66
200.00	2.37	1.85	1.61	1.48	1.40	1.32
300.00	3.56	2.78	2.42	2.22	2.10	1.97
400.00	4.75	3.71	3.22	2.96	2.80	2.63
500.00	5.94	4.64	4.03	3.69	3.50	3.29
600.00	7.12	5.56	4.83	4.43	4.20	3.95
700.00	8.31	6.49	5.64	5.17	4.89	4.61
800.00	9.50	7.42	6.44	5.91	5.59	5.26
900.00	10.68	8.34	7.25	6.65	6.29	5.92
1,000.00	11.87	9.27	8.06	7.39	6.99	6.58
2,000.00	23.74	18.54	16.11	14.78	13.98	13.16
3,000.00	35.61	27.81	24.17	22.17	20.98	19.74
4,000.00	47.48	37.08	32.22	29.56	27.97	26.32
5,000.00	59.35	46.35	40.28	36.95	34.96	32.90
6,000.00	71.22	55.62	48.34	44.34	41.95	39.48
7,000.00	83.09	64.89	56.39	51.73	48.95	46.06
8,000.00	94.96	74.16	64.45	59.12	55.94	52.65
9,000.00	106.83	83.43	72.50	66.51	62.93	59.23
10,000.00	118.70	92.70	80.56	73.90	69.92	65.81
20,000.00	237.40	185.40	161.12	147.80	139.84	131.61
30,000.00	356.11	278.10	241.68	221.70	209.76	197.42
40,000.00	474.81	370.80	322.24	295.60	279.69	263.23
50,000.00	593.51	463.51	402.80	369.50	349.61	329.04
60,000.00	712.21	556.21	483.36	443.39	419.53	394.84
70,000.00	830.91	648.91	563.92	517.29	489.45	460.65
80,000.00	949.61	741.61	644.47	591.19	559.37	526.46
90,000.00	1,068.32	834.31	725.03	665.09	629.29	592.26
100,000.00	1,187.02	927.01	805.59	738.99	699.21	658.07

7.625% Rate

Amount	\multicolumn{6}{c}{Term of Loan in Years}
	10	15	20	25	30	40
$ 50.00	$ 0.60	$ 0.47	$ 0.41	$ 0.37	$ 0.35	$ 0.33
100.00	1.19	0.93	0.81	0.75	0.71	0.67
200.00	2.39	1.87	1.63	1.49	1.42	1.33
300.00	3.58	2.80	2.44	2.24	2.12	2.00
400.00	4.77	3.74	3.25	2.99	2.83	2.67
500.00	5.97	4.67	4.07	3.74	3.54	3.34
600.00	7.16	5.60	4.88	4.48	4.25	4.00
700.00	8.35	6.54	5.69	5.23	4.95	4.67
800.00	9.55	7.47	6.51	5.98	5.66	5.34
900.00	10.74	8.41	7.32	6.72	6.37	6.01
1,000.00	11.94	9.34	8.13	7.47	7.08	6.67
2,000.00	23.87	18.68	16.27	14.94	14.16	13.35
3,000.00	35.81	28.02	24.40	22.41	21.23	20.02
4,000.00	47.74	37.37	32.53	29.89	28.31	26.69
5,000.00	59.68	46.71	40.66	37.36	35.39	33.37
6,000.00	71.61	56.05	48.80	44.83	42.47	40.04
7,000.00	83.55	65.39	56.93	52.30	49.55	46.71
8,000.00	95.48	74.73	65.06	59.77	56.62	53.39
9,000.00	107.42	84.07	73.19	67.24	63.70	60.06
10,000.00	119.36	93.41	81.33	74.71	70.78	66.73
20,000.00	238.71	186.83	162.65	149.43	141.56	133.47
30,000.00	358.07	280.24	243.98	224.14	212.34	200.20
40,000.00	477.42	373.65	325.30	298.86	283.12	266.93
50,000.00	596.78	467.06	406.63	373.57	353.90	333.66
60,000.00	716.13	560.48	487.95	448.28	424.68	400.40
70,000.00	835.49	653.89	569.28	523.00	495.46	467.13
80,000.00	954.84	747.30	650.60	597.71	566.23	533.86
90,000.00	1,074.20	840.72	731.93	672.43	637.01	600.59
100,000.00	1,193.55	934.13	813.25	747.14	707.79	667.33

7.750% Rate

Amount	Term of Loan in Years					
	10	15	20	25	30	40
$ 50.00	$ 0.60	$ 0.47	$ 0.41	$ 0.38	$ 0.36	$ 0.34
100.00	1.20	0.94	0.82	0.76	0.72	0.68
200.00	2.40	1.88	1.64	1.51	1.43	1.35
300.00	3.60	2.82	2.46	2.27	2.15	2.03
400.00	4.80	3.77	3.28	3.02	2.87	2.71
500.00	6.00	4.71	4.10	3.78	3.58	3.38
600.00	7.20	5.65	4.93	4.53	4.30	4.06
700.00	8.40	6.59	5.75	5.29	5.01	4.74
800.00	9.60	7.53	6.57	6.04	5.73	5.41
900.00	10.80	8.47	7.39	6.80	6.45	6.09
1,000.00	12.00	9.41	8.21	7.55	7.16	6.77
2,000.00	24.00	18.83	16.42	15.11	14.33	13.53
3,000.00	36.00	28.24	24.63	22.66	21.49	20.30
4,000.00	48.00	37.65	32.84	30.21	28.66	27.06
5,000.00	60.01	47.06	41.05	37.77	35.82	33.83
6,000.00	72.01	56.48	49.26	45.32	42.98	40.60
7,000.00	84.01	65.89	57.47	52.87	50.15	47.36
8,000.00	96.01	75.30	65.68	60.43	57.31	54.13
9,000.00	108.01	84.71	73.89	67.98	64.48	60.90
10,000.00	120.01	94.13	82.09	75.53	71.64	67.66
20,000.00	240.02	188.26	164.19	151.07	143.28	135.32
30,000.00	360.03	282.38	246.28	226.60	214.92	202.99
40,000.00	480.04	376.51	328.38	302.13	286.56	270.65
50,000.00	600.05	470.64	410.47	377.66	358.21	338.31
60,000.00	720.06	564.77	492.57	453.20	429.85	405.97
70,000.00	840.07	658.89	574.66	528.73	501.49	473.63
80,000.00	960.09	753.02	656.76	604.26	573.13	541.30
90,000.00	1,080.10	847.15	738.85	679.80	644.77	608.96
100,000.00	1,200.11	941.28	820.95	755.33	716.41	676.62

7.875% Rate

Amount	Term of Loan in Years					
	10	15	20	25	30	40
$ 50.00	$ 0.60	$ 0.47	$ 0.41	$ 0.38	$ 0.36	$ 0.34
100.00	1.21	0.95	0.83	0.76	0.73	0.69
200.00	2.41	1.90	1.66	1.53	1.45	1.37
300.00	3.62	2.85	2.49	2.29	2.18	2.06
400.00	4.83	3.79	3.31	3.05	2.90	2.74
500.00	6.03	4.74	4.14	3.82	3.63	3.43
600.00	7.24	5.69	4.97	4.58	4.35	4.12
700.00	8.45	6.64	5.80	5.34	5.08	4.80
800.00	9.65	7.59	6.63	6.11	5.80	5.49
900.00	10.86	8.54	7.46	6.87	6.53	6.17
1,000.00	12.07	9.48	8.29	7.64	7.25	6.86
2,000.00	24.13	18.97	16.57	15.27	14.50	13.72
3,000.00	36.20	28.45	24.86	22.91	21.75	20.58
4,000.00	48.27	37.94	33.15	30.54	29.00	27.44
5,000.00	60.33	47.42	41.43	38.18	36.25	34.30
6,000.00	72.40	56.91	49.72	45.81	43.50	41.16
7,000.00	84.47	66.39	58.01	53.45	50.75	48.02
8,000.00	96.53	75.88	66.29	61.08	58.01	54.88
9,000.00	108.60	85.36	74.58	68.72	65.26	61.74
10,000.00	120.67	94.84	82.87	76.36	72.51	68.59
20,000.00	241.34	189.69	165.74	152.71	145.01	137.19
30,000.00	362.00	284.53	248.60	229.07	217.52	205.78
40,000.00	482.67	379.38	331.47	305.42	290.03	274.38
50,000.00	603.34	474.22	414.34	381.78	362.53	342.97
60,000.00	724.01	569.07	497.21	458.13	435.04	411.57
70,000.00	844.68	663.91	580.07	534.49	507.55	480.16
80,000.00	965.34	758.76	662.94	610.84	580.06	548.76
90,000.00	1,086.01	853.60	745.81	687.20	652.56	617.35
100,000.00	1,206.68	948.45	828.68	763.55	725.07	685.95

8.000% Rate

Amount	Term of Loan in Years					
	10	15	20	25	30	40
$ 50.00	$ 0.61	$ 0.48	$ 0.42	$ 0.39	$ 0.37	$ 0.35
100.00	1.21	0.96	0.84	0.77	0.73	0.70
200.00	2.43	1.91	1.67	1.54	1.47	1.39
300.00	3.64	2.87	2.51	2.32	2.20	2.09
400.00	4.85	3.82	3.35	3.09	2.94	2.78
500.00	6.07	4.78	4.18	3.86	3.67	3.48
600.00	7.28	5.73	5.02	4.63	4.40	4.17
700.00	8.49	6.69	5.86	5.40	5.14	4.87
800.00	9.71	7.65	6.69	6.17	5.87	5.56
900.00	10.92	8.60	7.53	6.95	6.60	6.26
1,000.00	12.13	9.56	8.36	7.72	7.34	6.95
2,000.00	24.27	19.11	16.73	15.44	14.68	13.91
3,000.00	36.40	28.67	25.09	23.15	22.01	20.86
4,000.00	48.53	38.23	33.46	30.87	29.35	27.81
5,000.00	60.66	47.78	41.82	38.59	36.69	34.77
6,000.00	72.80	57.34	50.19	46.31	44.03	41.72
7,000.00	84.93	66.90	58.55	54.03	51.36	48.67
8,000.00	97.06	76.45	66.92	61.75	58.70	55.62
9,000.00	109.19	86.01	75.28	69.46	66.04	62.58
10,000.00	121.33	95.57	83.64	77.18	73.38	69.53
20,000.00	242.66	191.13	167.29	154.36	146.75	139.06
30,000.00	363.98	286.70	250.93	231.54	220.13	208.59
40,000.00	485.31	382.26	334.58	308.73	293.51	278.12
50,000.00	606.64	477.83	418.22	385.91	366.88	347.66
60,000.00	727.97	573.39	501.86	463.09	440.26	417.19
70,000.00	849.29	668.96	585.51	540.27	513.64	486.72
80,000.00	970.62	764.52	669.15	617.45	587.01	556.25
90,000.00	1,091.95	860.09	752.80	694.63	660.39	625.78
100,000.00	1,213.28	955.65	836.44	771.82	733.76	695.31

8.125% Rate

Amount	Term of Loan in Years					
	10	15	20	25	30	40
$ 50.00	$ 0.61	$ 0.48	$ 0.42	$ 0.39	$ 0.37	$ 0.35
100.00	1.22	0.96	0.84	0.78	0.74	0.70
200.00	2.44	1.93	1.69	1.56	1.48	1.41
300.00	3.66	2.89	2.53	2.34	2.23	2.11
400.00	4.88	3.85	3.38	3.12	2.97	2.82
500.00	6.10	4.81	4.22	3.90	3.71	3.52
600.00	7.32	5.78	5.07	4.68	4.45	4.23
700.00	8.54	6.74	5.91	5.46	5.20	4.93
800.00	9.76	7.70	6.75	6.24	5.94	5.64
900.00	10.98	8.67	7.60	7.02	6.68	6.34
1,000.00	12.20	9.63	8.44	7.80	7.42	7.05
2,000.00	24.40	19.26	16.88	15.60	14.85	14.09
3,000.00	36.60	28.89	25.33	23.40	22.27	21.14
4,000.00	48.80	38.52	33.77	31.20	29.70	28.19
5,000.00	60.99	48.14	42.21	39.01	37.12	35.24
6,000.00	73.19	57.77	50.65	46.81	44.55	42.28
7,000.00	85.39	67.40	59.10	54.61	51.97	49.33
8,000.00	97.59	77.03	67.54	62.41	59.40	56.38
9,000.00	109.79	86.66	75.98	70.21	66.82	63.42
10,000.00	121.99	96.29	84.42	78.01	74.25	70.47
20,000.00	243.98	192.58	168.85	156.02	148.50	140.94
30,000.00	365.97	288.86	253.27	234.03	222.75	211.41
40,000.00	487.96	385.15	337.69	312.05	297.00	281.88
50,000.00	609.95	481.44	422.12	390.06	371.25	352.35
60,000.00	731.93	577.73	506.54	468.07	445.50	422.83
70,000.00	853.92	674.02	590.97	546.08	519.75	493.30
80,000.00	975.91	770.31	675.39	624.09	594.00	563.77
90,000.00	1,097.90	866.59	759.81	702.10	668.25	634.24
100,000.00	1,219.89	962.88	844.24	780.12	742.50	704.71

8.250% Rate

Amount	Term of Loan in Years					
	10	15	20	25	30	40
$ 50.00	$ 0.61	$ 0.49	$ 0.43	$ 0.39	$ 0.38	$ 0.36
100.00	1.23	0.97	0.85	0.79	0.75	0.71
200.00	2.45	1.94	1.70	1.58	1.50	1.43
300.00	3.68	2.91	2.56	2.37	2.25	2.14
400.00	4.91	3.88	3.41	3.15	3.01	2.86
500.00	6.13	4.85	4.26	3.94	3.76	3.57
600.00	7.36	5.82	5.11	4.73	4.51	4.28
700.00	8.59	6.79	5.96	5.52	5.26	5.00
800.00	9.81	7.76	6.82	6.31	6.01	5.71
900.00	11.04	8.73	7.67	7.10	6.76	6.43
1,000.00	12.27	9.70	8.52	7.88	7.51	7.14
2,000.00	24.53	19.40	17.04	15.77	15.03	14.28
3,000.00	36.80	29.10	25.56	23.65	22.54	21.42
4,000.00	49.06	38.81	34.08	31.54	30.05	28.57
5,000.00	61.33	48.51	42.60	39.42	37.56	35.71
6,000.00	73.59	58.21	51.12	47.31	45.08	42.85
7,000.00	85.86	67.91	59.64	55.19	52.59	49.99
8,000.00	98.12	77.61	68.17	63.08	60.10	57.13
9,000.00	110.39	87.31	76.69	70.96	67.61	64.27
10,000.00	122.65	97.01	85.21	78.85	75.13	71.41
20,000.00	245.31	194.03	170.41	157.69	150.25	142.83
30,000.00	367.96	291.04	255.62	236.54	225.38	214.24
40,000.00	490.61	388.06	340.83	315.38	300.51	285.66
50,000.00	613.26	485.07	426.03	394.23	375.63	357.07
60,000.00	735.92	582.08	511.24	473.07	450.76	428.48
70,000.00	858.57	679.10	596.45	551.92	525.89	499.90
80,000.00	981.22	776.11	681.65	630.76	601.01	571.31
90,000.00	1,103.87	873.13	766.86	709.61	676.14	642.72
100,000.00	1,226.53	970.14	852.07	788.45	751.27	714.14

8.375% Rate

Amount	Term of Loan in Years					
	10	15	20	25	30	40
$ 50.00	$ 0.62	$ 0.49	$ 0.43	$ 0.40	$ 0.38	$ 0.36
100.00	1.23	0.98	0.86	0.80	0.76	0.72
200.00	2.47	1.95	1.72	1.59	1.52	1.45
300.00	3.70	2.93	2.58	2.39	2.28	2.17
400.00	4.93	3.91	3.44	3.19	3.04	2.89
500.00	6.17	4.89	4.30	3.98	3.80	3.62
600.00	7.40	5.86	5.16	4.78	4.56	4.34
700.00	8.63	6.84	6.02	5.58	5.32	5.07
800.00	9.87	7.82	6.88	6.37	6.08	5.79
900.00	11.10	8.80	7.74	7.17	6.84	6.51
1,000.00	12.33	9.77	8.60	7.97	7.60	7.24
2,000.00	24.66	19.55	17.20	15.94	15.20	14.47
3,000.00	37.00	29.32	25.80	23.90	22.80	21.71
4,000.00	49.33	39.10	34.40	31.87	30.40	28.94
5,000.00	61.66	48.87	43.00	39.84	38.00	36.18
6,000.00	73.99	58.65	51.60	47.81	45.60	43.42
7,000.00	86.32	68.42	60.19	55.78	53.21	50.65
8,000.00	98.65	78.19	68.79	63.75	60.81	57.89
9,000.00	110.99	87.97	77.39	71.71	68.41	65.12
10,000.00	123.32	97.74	85.99	79.68	76.01	72.36
20,000.00	246.64	195.49	171.99	159.36	152.01	144.72
30,000.00	369.95	293.23	257.98	239.05	228.02	217.08
40,000.00	493.27	390.97	343.97	318.73	304.03	289.44
50,000.00	616.59	488.71	429.96	398.41	380.04	361.80
60,000.00	739.91	586.46	515.96	478.09	456.04	434.16
70,000.00	863.23	684.20	601.95	557.77	532.05	506.52
80,000.00	986.55	781.94	687.94	637.46	608.06	578.88
90,000.00	1,109.86	879.68	773.94	717.14	684.07	651.24
100,000.00	1,233.18	977.43	859.93	796.82	760.07	723.60

8.500% Rate

Amount	Term of Loan in Years					
	10	15	20	25	30	40
$ 50.00	$ 0.62	$ 0.49	$ 0.43	$ 0.40	$ 0.38	$ 0.37
100.00	1.24	0.98	0.87	0.81	0.77	0.73
200.00	2.48	1.97	1.74	1.61	1.54	1.47
300.00	3.72	2.95	2.60	2.42	2.31	2.20
400.00	4.96	3.94	3.47	3.22	3.08	2.93
500.00	6.20	4.92	4.34	4.03	3.84	3.67
600.00	7.44	5.91	5.21	4.83	4.61	4.40
700.00	8.68	6.89	6.07	5.64	5.38	5.13
800.00	9.92	7.88	6.94	6.44	6.15	5.86
900.00	11.16	8.86	7.81	7.25	6.92	6.60
1,000.00	12.40	9.85	8.68	8.05	7.69	7.33
2,000.00	24.80	19.69	17.36	16.10	15.38	14.66
3,000.00	37.20	29.54	26.03	24.16	23.07	21.99
4,000.00	49.59	39.39	34.71	32.21	30.76	29.32
5,000.00	61.99	49.24	43.39	40.26	38.45	36.65
6,000.00	74.39	59.08	52.07	48.31	46.13	43.99
7,000.00	86.79	68.93	60.75	56.37	53.82	51.32
8,000.00	99.19	78.78	69.43	64.42	61.51	58.65
9,000.00	111.59	88.63	78.10	72.47	69.20	65.98
10,000.00	123.99	98.47	86.78	80.52	76.89	73.31
20,000.00	247.97	196.95	173.56	161.05	153.78	146.62
30,000.00	371.96	295.42	260.35	241.57	230.67	219.93
40,000.00	495.94	393.90	347.13	322.09	307.57	293.24
50,000.00	619.93	492.37	433.91	402.61	384.46	366.55
60,000.00	743.91	590.84	520.69	483.14	461.35	439.86
70,000.00	867.90	689.32	607.48	563.66	538.24	513.17
80,000.00	991.89	787.79	694.26	644.18	615.13	586.48
90,000.00	1,115.87	886.27	781.04	724.70	692.02	659.78
100,000.00	1,239.86	984.74	867.82	805.23	768.91	733.09

8.625% Rate

Amount	Term of Loan in Years					
	10	15	20	25	30	40
$ 50.00	$ 0.62	$ 0.50	$ 0.44	$ 0.41	$ 0.39	$ 0.37
100.00	1.25	0.99	0.88	0.81	0.78	0.74
200.00	2.49	1.98	1.75	1.63	1.56	1.49
300.00	3.74	2.98	2.63	2.44	2.33	2.23
400.00	4.99	3.97	3.50	3.25	3.11	2.97
500.00	6.23	4.96	4.38	4.07	3.89	3.71
600.00	7.48	5.95	5.25	4.88	4.67	4.46
700.00	8.73	6.94	6.13	5.70	5.44	5.20
800.00	9.97	7.94	7.01	6.51	6.22	5.94
900.00	11.22	8.93	7.88	7.32	7.00	6.68
1,000.00	12.47	9.92	8.76	8.14	7.78	7.43
2,000.00	24.93	19.84	17.52	16.27	15.56	14.85
3,000.00	37.40	29.76	26.27	24.41	23.33	22.28
4,000.00	49.86	39.68	35.03	32.55	31.11	29.70
5,000.00	62.33	49.60	43.79	40.68	38.89	37.13
6,000.00	74.79	59.52	52.55	48.82	46.67	44.56
7,000.00	87.26	69.45	61.30	56.96	54.45	51.98
8,000.00	99.72	79.37	70.06	65.09	62.22	59.41
9,000.00	112.19	89.29	78.82	73.23	70.00	66.84
10,000.00	124.66	99.21	87.58	81.37	77.78	74.26
20,000.00	249.31	198.42	175.15	162.73	155.56	148.52
30,000.00	373.97	297.62	262.73	244.10	233.34	222.79
40,000.00	498.62	396.83	350.30	325.47	311.12	297.05
50,000.00	623.28	496.04	437.88	406.83	388.89	371.31
60,000.00	747.93	595.25	525.45	488.20	466.67	445.57
70,000.00	872.59	694.46	613.03	569.57	544.45	519.83
80,000.00	997.24	793.66	700.60	650.93	622.23	594.09
90,000.00	1,121.90	892.87	788.18	732.30	700.01	668.36
100,000.00	1,246.55	992.08	875.75	813.67	777.79	742.62

8.750% Rate

Amount	Term of Loan in Years					
	10	15	20	25	30	40
$ 50.00	$ 0.63	$ 0.50	$ 0.44	$ 0.41	$ 0.39	$ 0.38
100.00	1.25	1.00	0.88	0.82	0.79	0.75
200.00	2.51	2.00	1.77	1.64	1.57	1.50
300.00	3.76	3.00	2.65	2.47	2.36	2.26
400.00	5.01	4.00	3.53	3.29	3.15	3.01
500.00	6.27	5.00	4.42	4.11	3.93	3.76
600.00	7.52	6.00	5.30	4.93	4.72	4.51
700.00	8.77	7.00	6.19	5.76	5.51	5.27
800.00	10.03	8.00	7.07	6.58	6.29	6.02
900.00	11.28	9.00	7.95	7.40	7.08	6.77
1,000.00	12.53	9.99	8.84	8.22	7.87	7.52
2,000.00	25.07	19.99	17.67	16.44	15.73	15.04
3,000.00	37.60	29.98	26.51	24.66	23.60	22.57
4,000.00	50.13	39.98	35.35	32.89	31.47	30.09
5,000.00	62.66	49.97	44.19	41.11	39.34	37.61
6,000.00	75.20	59.97	53.02	49.33	47.20	45.13
7,000.00	87.73	69.96	61.86	57.55	55.07	52.65
8,000.00	100.26	79.96	70.70	65.77	62.94	60.17
9,000.00	112.79	89.95	79.53	73.99	70.80	67.70
10,000.00	125.33	99.94	88.37	82.21	78.67	75.22
20,000.00	250.65	199.89	176.74	164.43	157.34	150.43
30,000.00	375.98	299.83	265.11	246.64	236.01	225.65
40,000.00	501.31	399.78	353.48	328.86	314.68	300.87
50,000.00	626.63	499.72	441.86	411.07	393.35	376.09
60,000.00	751.96	599.67	530.23	493.29	472.02	451.30
70,000.00	877.29	699.61	618.60	575.50	550.69	526.52
80,000.00	1,002.61	799.56	706.97	657.71	629.36	601.74
90,000.00	1,127.94	899.50	795.34	739.93	708.03	676.95
100,000.00	1,253.27	999.45	883.71	822.14	786.70	752.17

8.875% Rate

Amount	Term of Loan in Years					
	10	15	20	25	30	40
$ 50.00	$ 0.63	$ 0.50	$ 0.45	$ 0.42	$ 0.40	$ 0.38
100.00	1.26	1.01	0.89	0.83	0.80	0.76
200.00	2.52	2.01	1.78	1.66	1.59	1.52
300.00	3.78	3.02	2.68	2.49	2.39	2.29
400.00	5.04	4.03	3.57	3.32	3.18	3.05
500.00	6.30	5.03	4.46	4.15	3.98	3.81
600.00	7.56	6.04	5.35	4.98	4.77	4.57
700.00	8.82	7.05	6.24	5.81	5.57	5.33
800.00	10.08	8.05	7.13	6.65	6.37	6.09
900.00	11.34	9.06	8.03	7.48	7.16	6.86
1,000.00	12.60	10.07	8.92	8.31	7.96	7.62
2,000.00	25.20	20.14	17.83	16.61	15.91	15.24
3,000.00	37.80	30.21	26.75	24.92	23.87	22.85
4,000.00	50.40	40.27	35.67	33.23	31.83	30.47
5,000.00	63.00	50.34	44.59	41.53	39.78	38.09
6,000.00	75.60	60.41	53.50	49.84	47.74	45.71
7,000.00	88.20	70.48	62.42	58.15	55.70	53.32
8,000.00	100.80	80.55	71.34	66.45	63.65	60.94
9,000.00	113.40	90.62	80.25	74.76	71.61	68.56
10,000.00	126.00	100.68	89.17	83.07	79.56	76.18
20,000.00	252.00	201.37	178.34	166.13	159.13	152.35
30,000.00	378.00	302.05	267.51	249.20	238.69	228.53
40,000.00	504.00	402.74	356.68	332.26	318.26	304.70
50,000.00	630.00	503.42	445.85	415.33	397.82	380.88
60,000.00	756.00	604.11	535.02	498.39	477.39	457.05
70,000.00	882.00	704.79	624.19	581.46	556.95	533.23
80,000.00	1,008.00	805.48	713.36	664.52	636.52	609.40
90,000.00	1,134.00	906.16	802.53	747.59	716.08	685.58
100,000.00	1,260.00	1,006.84	891.70	830.65	795.64	761.75

9.000% Rate

Amount	Term of Loan in Years					
	10	15	20	25	30	40
$ 50.00	$ 0.63	$ 0.51	$ 0.45	$ 0.42	$ 0.40	$ 0.39
100.00	1.27	1.01	0.90	0.84	0.80	0.77
200.00	2.53	2.03	1.80	1.68	1.61	1.54
300.00	3.80	3.04	2.70	2.52	2.41	2.31
400.00	5.07	4.06	3.60	3.36	3.22	3.09
500.00	6.33	5.07	4.50	4.20	4.02	3.86
600.00	7.60	6.09	5.40	5.04	4.83	4.63
700.00	8.87	7.10	6.30	5.87	5.63	5.40
800.00	10.13	8.11	7.20	6.71	6.44	6.17
900.00	11.40	9.13	8.10	7.55	7.24	6.94
1,000.00	12.67	10.14	9.00	8.39	8.05	7.71
2,000.00	25.34	20.29	17.99	16.78	16.09	15.43
3,000.00	38.00	30.43	26.99	25.18	24.14	23.14
4,000.00	50.67	40.57	35.99	33.57	32.18	30.85
5,000.00	63.34	50.71	44.99	41.96	40.23	38.57
6,000.00	76.01	60.86	53.98	50.35	48.28	46.28
7,000.00	88.67	71.00	62.98	58.74	56.32	54.00
8,000.00	101.34	81.14	71.98	67.14	64.37	61.71
9,000.00	114.01	91.28	80.98	75.53	72.42	69.42
10,000.00	126.68	101.43	89.97	83.92	80.46	77.14
20,000.00	253.35	202.85	179.95	167.84	160.92	154.27
30,000.00	380.03	304.28	269.92	251.76	241.39	231.41
40,000.00	506.70	405.71	359.89	335.68	321.85	308.54
50,000.00	633.38	507.13	449.86	419.60	402.31	385.68
60,000.00	760.05	608.56	539.84	503.52	482.77	462.82
70,000.00	886.73	709.99	629.81	587.44	563.24	539.95
80,000.00	1,013.41	811.41	719.78	671.36	643.70	617.09
90,000.00	1,140.08	912.84	809.75	755.28	724.16	694.23
100,000.00	1,266.76	1,014.27	899.73	839.20	804.62	771.36

9.125% Rate

Amount	Term of Loan in Years					
	10	15	20	25	30	40
$ 50.00	$ 0.64	$ 0.51	$ 0.45	$ 0.42	$ 0.41	$ 0.39
100.00	1.27	1.02	0.91	0.85	0.81	0.78
200.00	2.55	2.04	1.82	1.70	1.63	1.56
300.00	3.82	3.07	2.72	2.54	2.44	2.34
400.00	5.09	4.09	3.63	3.39	3.25	3.12
500.00	6.37	5.11	4.54	4.24	4.07	3.90
600.00	7.64	6.13	5.45	5.09	4.88	4.69
700.00	8.91	7.15	6.35	5.93	5.70	5.47
800.00	10.19	8.17	7.26	6.78	6.51	6.25
900.00	11.46	9.20	8.17	7.63	7.32	7.03
1,000.00	12.74	10.22	9.08	8.48	8.14	7.81
2,000.00	25.47	20.43	18.16	16.96	16.27	15.62
3,000.00	38.21	30.65	27.23	25.43	24.41	23.43
4,000.00	50.94	40.87	36.31	33.91	32.55	31.24
5,000.00	63.68	51.09	45.39	42.39	40.68	39.05
6,000.00	76.41	61.30	54.47	50.87	48.82	46.86
7,000.00	89.15	71.52	63.54	59.34	56.95	54.67
8,000.00	101.88	81.74	72.62	67.82	65.09	62.48
9,000.00	114.62	91.95	81.70	76.30	73.23	70.29
10,000.00	127.35	102.17	90.78	84.78	81.36	78.10
20,000.00	254.71	204.34	181.56	169.55	162.73	156.20
30,000.00	382.06	306.51	272.33	254.33	244.09	234.30
40,000.00	509.41	408.69	363.11	339.11	325.45	312.40
50,000.00	636.77	510.86	453.89	423.89	406.82	390.50
60,000.00	764.12	613.03	544.67	508.66	488.18	468.60
70,000.00	891.47	715.20	635.45	593.44	569.54	546.70
80,000.00	1,018.83	817.37	726.22	678.22	650.91	624.80
90,000.00	1,146.18	919.54	817.00	763.00	732.27	702.90
100,000.00	1,273.53	1,021.72	907.78	847.77	813.63	781.00

9.250% Rate

Amount	Term of Loan in Years					
	10	15	20	25	30	40
$ 50.00	$ 0.64	$ 0.51	$ 0.46	$ 0.43	$ 0.41	$ 0.40
100.00	1.28	1.03	0.92	0.86	0.82	0.79
200.00	2.56	2.06	1.83	1.71	1.65	1.58
300.00	3.84	3.09	2.75	2.57	2.47	2.37
400.00	5.12	4.12	3.66	3.43	3.29	3.16
500.00	6.40	5.15	4.58	4.28	4.11	3.95
600.00	7.68	6.18	5.50	5.14	4.94	4.74
700.00	8.96	7.20	6.41	5.99	5.76	5.53
800.00	10.24	8.23	7.33	6.85	6.58	6.33
900.00	11.52	9.26	8.24	7.71	7.40	7.12
1,000.00	12.80	10.29	9.16	8.56	8.23	7.91
2,000.00	25.61	20.58	18.32	17.13	16.45	15.81
3,000.00	38.41	30.88	27.48	25.69	24.68	23.72
4,000.00	51.21	41.17	36.63	34.26	32.91	31.63
5,000.00	64.02	51.46	45.79	42.82	41.13	39.53
6,000.00	76.82	61.75	54.95	51.38	49.36	47.44
7,000.00	89.62	72.04	64.11	59.95	57.59	55.35
8,000.00	102.43	82.34	73.27	68.51	65.81	63.25
9,000.00	115.23	92.63	82.43	77.07	74.04	71.16
10,000.00	128.03	102.92	91.59	85.64	82.27	79.07
20,000.00	256.07	205.84	183.17	171.28	164.54	158.13
30,000.00	384.10	308.76	274.76	256.91	246.80	237.20
40,000.00	512.13	411.68	366.35	342.55	329.07	316.26
50,000.00	640.16	514.60	457.93	428.19	411.34	395.33
60,000.00	768.20	617.52	549.52	513.83	493.61	474.40
70,000.00	896.23	720.43	641.11	599.47	575.87	553.46
80,000.00	1,024.26	823.35	732.69	685.11	658.14	632.53
90,000.00	1,152.29	926.27	824.28	770.74	740.41	711.59
100,000.00	1,280.33	1,029.19	915.87	856.38	822.68	790.66

9.375% Rate

Amount	Term of Loan in Years					
	10	15	20	25	30	40
$ 50.00	$ 0.64	$ 0.52	$ 0.46	$ 0.43	$ 0.42	$ 0.40
100.00	1.29	1.04	0.92	0.87	0.83	0.80
200.00	2.57	2.07	1.85	1.73	1.66	1.60
300.00	3.86	3.11	2.77	2.60	2.50	2.40
400.00	5.15	4.15	3.70	3.46	3.33	3.20
500.00	6.44	5.18	4.62	4.33	4.16	4.00
600.00	7.72	6.22	5.54	5.19	4.99	4.80
700.00	9.01	7.26	6.47	6.06	5.82	5.60
800.00	10.30	8.29	7.39	6.92	6.65	6.40
900.00	11.58	9.33	8.32	7.79	7.49	7.20
1,000.00	12.87	10.37	9.24	8.65	8.32	8.00
2,000.00	25.74	20.73	18.48	17.30	16.63	16.01
3,000.00	38.61	31.10	27.72	25.95	24.95	24.01
4,000.00	51.49	41.47	36.96	34.60	33.27	32.01
5,000.00	64.36	51.83	46.20	43.25	41.59	40.02
6,000.00	77.23	62.20	55.44	51.90	49.90	48.02
7,000.00	90.10	72.57	64.68	60.55	58.22	56.02
8,000.00	102.97	82.94	73.92	69.20	66.54	64.03
9,000.00	115.84	93.30	83.16	77.85	74.86	72.03
10,000.00	128.71	103.67	92.40	86.50	83.17	80.03
20,000.00	257.43	207.34	184.80	173.00	166.35	160.07
30,000.00	386.14	311.01	277.20	259.51	249.52	240.10
40,000.00	514.86	414.68	369.59	346.01	332.70	320.14
50,000.00	643.57	518.35	461.99	432.51	415.87	400.17
60,000.00	772.28	622.02	554.39	519.01	499.05	480.21
70,000.00	901.00	725.69	646.79	605.52	582.22	560.24
80,000.00	1,029.71	829.36	739.19	692.02	665.40	640.28
90,000.00	1,158.43	933.03	831.59	778.52	748.57	720.31
100,000.00	1,287.14	1,036.70	923.98	865.02	831.75	800.35

9.500% Rate

Amount	Term of Loan in Years					
	10	15	20	25	30	40
$ 50.00	$ 0.65	$ 0.52	$ 0.47	$ 0.44	$ 0.42	$ 0.41
100.00	1.29	1.04	0.93	0.87	0.84	0.81
200.00	2.59	2.09	1.86	1.75	1.68	1.62
300.00	3.88	3.13	2.80	2.62	2.52	2.43
400.00	5.18	4.18	3.73	3.49	3.36	3.24
500.00	6.47	5.22	4.66	4.37	4.20	4.05
600.00	7.76	6.27	5.59	5.24	5.05	4.86
700.00	9.06	7.31	6.52	6.12	5.89	5.67
800.00	10.35	8.35	7.46	6.99	6.73	6.48
900.00	11.65	9.40	8.39	7.86	7.57	7.29
1,000.00	12.94	10.44	9.32	8.74	8.41	8.10
2,000.00	25.88	20.88	18.64	17.47	16.82	16.20
3,000.00	38.82	31.33	27.96	26.21	25.23	24.30
4,000.00	51.76	41.77	37.29	34.95	33.63	32.40
5,000.00	64.70	52.21	46.61	43.68	42.04	40.50
6,000.00	77.64	62.65	55.93	52.42	50.45	48.60
7,000.00	90.58	73.10	65.25	61.16	58.86	56.70
8,000.00	103.52	83.54	74.57	69.90	67.27	64.80
9,000.00	116.46	93.98	83.89	78.63	75.68	72.91
10,000.00	129.40	104.42	93.21	87.37	84.09	81.01
20,000.00	258.80	208.84	186.43	174.74	168.17	162.01
30,000.00	388.19	313.27	279.64	262.11	252.26	243.02
40,000.00	517.59	417.69	372.85	349.48	336.34	324.02
50,000.00	646.99	522.11	466.07	436.85	420.43	405.03
60,000.00	776.39	626.53	559.28	524.22	504.51	486.04
70,000.00	905.78	730.96	652.49	611.59	588.60	567.04
80,000.00	1,035.18	835.38	745.70	698.96	672.68	648.05
90,000.00	1,164.58	939.80	838.92	786.33	756.77	729.06
100,000.00	1,293.98	1,044.22	932.13	873.70	840.85	810.06

9.625% Rate

Amount	Term of Loan in Years					
	10	15	20	25	30	40
$ 50.00	$ 0.65	$ 0.53	$ 0.47	$ 0.44	$ 0.42	$ 0.41
100.00	1.30	1.05	0.94	0.88	0.85	0.82
200.00	2.60	2.10	1.88	1.76	1.70	1.64
300.00	3.90	3.16	2.82	2.65	2.55	2.46
400.00	5.20	4.21	3.76	3.53	3.40	3.28
500.00	6.50	5.26	4.70	4.41	4.25	4.10
600.00	7.80	6.31	5.64	5.29	5.10	4.92
700.00	9.11	7.36	6.58	6.18	5.95	5.74
800.00	10.41	8.41	7.52	7.06	6.80	6.56
900.00	11.71	9.47	8.46	7.94	7.65	7.38
1,000.00	13.01	10.52	9.40	8.82	8.50	8.20
2,000.00	26.02	21.04	18.81	17.65	17.00	16.40
3,000.00	39.02	31.55	28.21	26.47	25.50	24.59
4,000.00	52.03	42.07	37.61	35.30	34.00	32.79
5,000.00	65.04	52.59	47.02	44.12	42.50	40.99
6,000.00	78.05	63.11	56.42	52.94	51.00	49.19
7,000.00	91.06	73.62	65.82	61.77	59.50	57.39
8,000.00	104.07	84.14	75.22	70.59	68.00	65.58
9,000.00	117.07	94.66	84.63	79.42	76.50	73.78
10,000.00	130.08	105.18	94.03	88.24	85.00	81.98
20,000.00	260.17	210.36	188.06	176.48	170.00	163.96
30,000.00	390.25	315.53	282.09	264.72	255.00	245.94
40,000.00	520.33	420.71	376.12	352.96	340.00	327.92
50,000.00	650.41	525.89	470.15	441.20	424.99	409.90
60,000.00	780.50	631.07	564.19	529.44	509.99	491.88
70,000.00	910.58	736.25	658.22	617.68	594.99	573.86
80,000.00	1,040.66	841.42	752.25	705.92	679.99	655.84
90,000.00	1,170.75	946.60	846.28	794.16	764.99	737.82
100,000.00	1,300.83	1,051.78	940.31	882.40	849.99	819.80

9.750% Rate

Amount	Term of Loan in Years					
	10	15	20	25	30	40
$ 50.00	$ 0.65	$ 0.53	$ 0.47	$ 0.45	$ 0.43	$ 0.41
100.00	1.31	1.06	0.95	0.89	0.86	0.83
200.00	2.62	2.12	1.90	1.78	1.72	1.66
300.00	3.92	3.18	2.85	2.67	2.58	2.49
400.00	5.23	4.24	3.79	3.56	3.44	3.32
500.00	6.54	5.30	4.74	4.46	4.30	4.15
600.00	7.85	6.36	5.69	5.35	5.15	4.98
700.00	9.15	7.42	6.64	6.24	6.01	5.81
800.00	10.46	8.47	7.59	7.13	6.87	6.64
900.00	11.77	9.53	8.54	8.02	7.73	7.47
1,000.00	13.08	10.59	9.49	8.91	8.59	8.30
2,000.00	26.15	21.19	18.97	17.82	17.18	16.59
3,000.00	39.23	31.78	28.46	26.73	25.77	24.89
4,000.00	52.31	42.37	37.94	35.65	34.37	33.18
5,000.00	65.39	52.97	47.43	44.56	42.96	41.48
6,000.00	78.46	63.56	56.91	53.47	51.55	49.77
7,000.00	91.54	74.16	66.40	62.38	60.14	58.07
8,000.00	104.62	84.75	75.88	71.29	68.73	66.36
9,000.00	117.69	95.34	85.37	80.20	77.32	74.66
10,000.00	130.77	105.94	94.85	89.11	85.92	82.96
20,000.00	261.54	211.87	189.70	178.23	171.83	165.91
30,000.00	392.31	317.81	284.56	267.34	257.75	248.87
40,000.00	523.08	423.75	379.41	356.45	343.66	331.82
50,000.00	653.85	529.68	474.26	445.57	429.58	414.78
60,000.00	784.62	635.62	569.11	534.68	515.49	497.74
70,000.00	915.39	741.55	663.96	623.80	601.41	580.69
80,000.00	1,046.16	847.49	758.81	712.91	687.32	663.65
90,000.00	1,176.93	953.43	853.67	802.02	773.24	746.60
100,000.00	1,307.70	1,059.36	948.52	891.14	859.15	829.56

9.875% Rate

Amount	Term of Loan in Years					
	10	15	20	25	30	40
$ 50.00	$ 0.66	$ 0.53	$ 0.48	$ 0.45	$ 0.43	$ 0.42
100.00	1.31	1.07	0.96	0.90	0.87	0.84
200.00	2.63	2.13	1.91	1.80	1.74	1.68
300.00	3.94	3.20	2.87	2.70	2.61	2.52
400.00	5.26	4.27	3.83	3.60	3.47	3.36
500.00	6.57	5.33	4.78	4.50	4.34	4.20
600.00	7.89	6.40	5.74	5.40	5.21	5.04
700.00	9.20	7.47	6.70	6.30	6.08	5.88
800.00	10.52	8.54	7.65	7.20	6.95	6.71
900.00	11.83	9.60	8.61	8.10	7.82	7.55
1,000.00	13.15	10.67	9.57	9.00	8.68	8.39
2,000.00	26.29	21.34	19.14	18.00	17.37	16.79
3,000.00	39.44	32.01	28.70	27.00	26.05	25.18
4,000.00	52.58	42.68	38.27	36.00	34.73	33.57
5,000.00	65.73	53.35	47.84	45.00	43.42	41.97
6,000.00	78.88	64.02	57.41	53.99	52.10	50.36
7,000.00	92.02	74.69	66.97	62.99	60.78	58.75
8,000.00	105.17	85.36	76.54	71.99	69.47	67.15
9,000.00	118.31	96.03	86.11	80.99	78.15	75.54
10,000.00	131.46	106.70	95.68	89.99	86.83	83.93
20,000.00	262.92	213.39	191.35	179.98	173.67	167.87
30,000.00	394.38	320.09	287.03	269.97	260.50	251.80
40,000.00	525.84	426.79	382.70	359.96	347.34	335.74
50,000.00	657.30	533.49	478.38	449.95	434.17	419.67
60,000.00	788.76	640.18	574.05	539.94	521.01	503.60
70,000.00	920.22	746.88	669.73	629.93	607.84	587.54
80,000.00	1,051.68	853.58	765.40	719.92	694.68	671.47
90,000.00	1,183.14	960.27	861.08	809.91	781.51	755.41
100,000.00	1,314.60	1,066.97	956.75	899.90	868.35	839.34

10.000% Rate

Amount	Term of Loan in Years					
	10	15	20	25	30	40
$ 50.00	$ 0.66	$ 0.54	$ 0.48	$ 0.45	$ 0.44	$ 0.42
100.00	1.32	1.07	0.97	0.91	0.88	0.85
200.00	2.64	2.15	1.93	1.82	1.76	1.70
300.00	3.96	3.22	2.90	2.73	2.63	2.55
400.00	5.29	4.30	3.86	3.63	3.51	3.40
500.00	6.61	5.37	4.83	4.54	4.39	4.25
600.00	7.93	6.45	5.79	5.45	5.27	5.09
700.00	9.25	7.52	6.76	6.36	6.14	5.94
800.00	10.57	8.60	7.72	7.27	7.02	6.79
900.00	11.89	9.67	8.69	8.18	7.90	7.64
1,000.00	13.22	10.75	9.65	9.09	8.78	8.49
2,000.00	26.43	21.49	19.30	18.17	17.55	16.98
3,000.00	39.65	32.24	28.95	27.26	26.33	25.47
4,000.00	52.86	42.98	38.60	36.35	35.10	33.97
5,000.00	66.08	53.73	48.25	45.44	43.88	42.46
6,000.00	79.29	64.48	57.90	54.52	52.65	50.95
7,000.00	92.51	75.22	67.55	63.61	61.43	59.44
8,000.00	105.72	85.97	77.20	72.70	70.21	67.93
9,000.00	118.94	96.71	86.85	81.78	78.98	76.42
10,000.00	132.15	107.46	96.50	90.87	87.76	84.91
20,000.00	264.30	214.92	193.00	181.74	175.51	169.83
30,000.00	396.45	322.38	289.51	272.61	263.27	254.74
40,000.00	528.60	429.84	386.01	363.48	351.03	339.66
50,000.00	660.75	537.30	482.51	454.35	438.79	424.57
60,000.00	792.90	644.76	579.01	545.22	526.54	509.49
70,000.00	925.06	752.22	675.52	636.09	614.30	594.40
80,000.00	1,057.21	859.68	772.02	726.96	702.06	679.32
90,000.00	1,189.36	967.14	868.52	817.83	789.81	764.23
100,000.00	1,321.51	1,074.61	965.02	908.70	877.57	849.15

10.125% Rate

Amount	Term of Loan in Years					
	10	15	20	25	30	40
$ 50.00	$ 0.66	$ 0.54	$ 0.49	$ 0.46	$ 0.44	$ 0.43
100.00	1.33	1.08	0.97	0.92	0.89	0.86
200.00	2.66	2.16	1.95	1.84	1.77	1.72
300.00	3.99	3.25	2.92	2.75	2.66	2.58
400.00	5.31	4.33	3.89	3.67	3.55	3.44
500.00	6.64	5.41	4.87	4.59	4.43	4.29
600.00	7.97	6.49	5.84	5.51	5.32	5.15
700.00	9.30	7.58	6.81	6.42	6.21	6.01
800.00	10.63	8.66	7.79	7.34	7.09	6.87
900.00	11.96	9.74	8.76	8.26	7.98	7.73
1,000.00	13.28	10.82	9.73	9.18	8.87	8.59
2,000.00	26.57	21.65	19.47	18.35	17.74	17.18
3,000.00	39.85	32.47	29.20	27.53	26.60	25.77
4,000.00	53.14	43.29	38.93	36.70	35.47	34.36
5,000.00	66.42	54.11	48.67	45.88	44.34	42.95
6,000.00	79.71	64.94	58.40	55.05	53.21	51.54
7,000.00	92.99	75.76	68.13	64.23	62.08	60.13
8,000.00	106.28	86.58	77.87	73.40	70.95	68.72
9,000.00	119.56	97.40	87.60	82.58	79.81	77.31
10,000.00	132.84	108.23	97.33	91.75	88.68	85.90
20,000.00	265.69	216.45	194.66	183.51	177.36	171.79
30,000.00	398.53	324.68	292.00	275.26	266.05	257.69
40,000.00	531.38	432.91	389.33	367.01	354.73	343.59
50,000.00	664.22	541.13	486.66	458.76	443.41	429.49
60,000.00	797.06	649.36	583.99	550.52	532.09	515.38
70,000.00	929.91	757.59	681.32	642.27	620.78	601.28
80,000.00	1,062.75	865.81	778.65	734.02	709.46	687.18
90,000.00	1,195.60	974.04	875.99	825.77	798.14	773.07
100,000.00	1,328.44	1,082.27	973.32	917.53	886.82	858.97

10.250% Rate

Amount	Term of Loan in Years					
	10	15	20	25	30	40
$ 50.00	$ 0.67	$ 0.54	$ 0.49	$ 0.46	$ 0.45	$ 0.43
100.00	1.34	1.09	0.98	0.93	0.90	0.87
200.00	2.67	2.18	1.96	1.85	1.79	1.74
300.00	4.01	3.27	2.94	2.78	2.69	2.61
400.00	5.34	4.36	3.93	3.71	3.58	3.48
500.00	6.68	5.45	4.91	4.63	4.48	4.34
600.00	8.01	6.54	5.89	5.56	5.38	5.21
700.00	9.35	7.63	6.87	6.48	6.27	6.08
800.00	10.68	8.72	7.85	7.41	7.17	6.95
900.00	12.02	9.81	8.83	8.34	8.06	7.82
1,000.00	13.35	10.90	9.82	9.26	8.96	8.69
2,000.00	26.71	21.80	19.63	18.53	17.92	17.38
3,000.00	40.06	32.70	29.45	27.79	26.88	26.06
4,000.00	53.42	43.60	39.27	37.06	35.84	34.75
5,000.00	66.77	54.50	49.08	46.32	44.81	43.44
6,000.00	80.12	65.40	58.90	55.58	53.77	52.13
7,000.00	93.48	76.30	68.72	64.85	62.73	60.82
8,000.00	106.83	87.20	78.53	74.11	71.69	69.51
9,000.00	120.19	98.10	88.35	83.37	80.65	78.19
10,000.00	133.54	109.00	98.16	92.64	89.61	86.88
20,000.00	267.08	217.99	196.33	185.28	179.22	173.76
30,000.00	400.62	326.99	294.49	277.91	268.83	260.65
40,000.00	534.16	435.98	392.66	370.55	358.44	347.53
50,000.00	667.70	544.98	490.82	463.19	448.05	434.41
60,000.00	801.23	653.97	588.99	555.83	537.66	521.29
70,000.00	934.77	762.97	687.15	648.47	627.27	608.17
80,000.00	1,068.31	871.96	785.31	741.11	716.88	695.05
90,000.00	1,201.85	980.96	883.48	833.74	806.49	781.94
100,000.00	1,335.39	1,089.95	981.64	926.38	896.10	868.82

10.375% Rate

Amount	Term of Loan in Years					
	10	15	20	25	30	40
$ 50.00	$ 0.67	$ 0.55	$ 0.49	$ 0.47	$ 0.45	$ 0.44
100.00	1.34	1.10	0.99	0.94	0.91	0.88
200.00	2.68	2.20	1.98	1.87	1.81	1.76
300.00	4.03	3.29	2.97	2.81	2.72	2.64
400.00	5.37	4.39	3.96	3.74	3.62	3.51
500.00	6.71	5.49	4.95	4.68	4.53	4.39
600.00	8.05	6.59	5.94	5.61	5.43	5.27
700.00	9.40	7.68	6.93	6.55	6.34	6.15
800.00	10.74	8.78	7.92	7.48	7.24	7.03
900.00	12.08	9.88	8.91	8.42	8.15	7.91
1,000.00	13.42	10.98	9.90	9.35	9.05	8.79
2,000.00	26.85	21.95	19.80	18.71	18.11	17.57
3,000.00	40.27	32.93	29.70	28.06	27.16	26.36
4,000.00	53.69	43.91	39.60	37.41	36.22	35.15
5,000.00	67.12	54.88	49.50	46.76	45.27	43.93
6,000.00	80.54	65.86	59.40	56.12	54.32	52.72
7,000.00	93.97	76.84	69.30	65.47	63.38	61.51
8,000.00	107.39	87.81	79.20	74.82	72.43	70.29
9,000.00	120.81	98.79	89.10	84.17	81.49	79.08
10,000.00	134.24	109.77	99.00	93.53	90.54	87.87
20,000.00	268.47	219.53	198.00	187.05	181.08	175.74
30,000.00	402.71	329.30	297.00	280.58	271.62	263.61
40,000.00	536.94	439.06	396.00	374.11	362.16	351.47
50,000.00	671.18	548.83	495.00	467.63	452.70	439.34
60,000.00	805.42	658.60	594.00	561.16	543.24	527.21
70,000.00	939.65	768.36	693.00	654.69	633.78	615.08
80,000.00	1,073.89	878.13	792.00	748.21	724.33	702.95
90,000.00	1,208.12	987.90	891.00	841.74	814.87	790.82
100,000.00	1,342.36	1,097.66	990.00	935.27	905.41	878.68

10.500% Rate

Amount	Term of Loan in Years					
	10	15	20	25	30	40
$ 50.00	$ 0.67	$ 0.55	$ 0.50	$ 0.47	$ 0.46	$ 0.44
100.00	1.35	1.11	1.00	0.94	0.91	0.89
200.00	2.70	2.21	2.00	1.89	1.83	1.78
300.00	4.05	3.32	3.00	2.83	2.74	2.67
400.00	5.40	4.42	3.99	3.78	3.66	3.55
500.00	6.75	5.53	4.99	4.72	4.57	4.44
600.00	8.10	6.63	5.99	5.67	5.49	5.33
700.00	9.45	7.74	6.99	6.61	6.40	6.22
800.00	10.79	8.84	7.99	7.55	7.32	7.11
900.00	12.14	9.95	8.99	8.50	8.23	8.00
1,000.00	13.49	11.05	9.98	9.44	9.15	8.89
2,000.00	26.99	22.11	19.97	18.88	18.29	17.77
3,000.00	40.48	33.16	29.95	28.33	27.44	26.66
4,000.00	53.97	44.22	39.94	37.77	36.59	35.54
5,000.00	67.47	55.27	49.92	47.21	45.74	44.43
6,000.00	80.96	66.32	59.90	56.65	54.88	53.31
7,000.00	94.45	77.38	69.89	66.09	64.03	62.20
8,000.00	107.95	88.43	79.87	75.53	73.18	71.09
9,000.00	121.44	99.49	89.85	84.98	82.33	79.97
10,000.00	134.93	110.54	99.84	94.42	91.47	88.86
20,000.00	269.87	221.08	199.68	188.84	182.95	177.71
30,000.00	404.80	331.62	299.51	283.25	274.42	266.57
40,000.00	539.74	442.16	399.35	377.67	365.90	355.43
50,000.00	674.67	552.70	499.19	472.09	457.37	444.29
60,000.00	809.61	663.24	599.03	566.51	548.84	533.14
70,000.00	944.54	773.78	698.87	660.93	640.32	622.00
80,000.00	1,079.48	884.32	798.70	755.35	731.79	710.86
90,000.00	1,214.41	994.86	898.54	849.76	823.27	799.71
100,000.00	1,349.35	1,105.40	998.38	944.18	914.74	888.57

10.625% Rate

Amount	Term of Loan in Years					
	10	15	20	25	30	40
$ 50.00	$ 0.68	$ 0.56	$ 0.50	$ 0.48	$ 0.46	$ 0.45
100.00	1.36	1.11	1.01	0.95	0.92	0.90
200.00	2.71	2.23	2.01	1.91	1.85	1.80
300.00	4.07	3.34	3.02	2.86	2.77	2.70
400.00	5.43	4.45	4.03	3.81	3.70	3.59
500.00	6.78	5.57	5.03	4.77	4.62	4.49
600.00	8.14	6.68	6.04	5.72	5.54	5.39
700.00	9.49	7.79	7.05	6.67	6.47	6.29
800.00	10.85	8.91	8.05	7.62	7.39	7.19
900.00	12.21	10.02	9.06	8.58	8.32	8.09
1,000.00	13.56	11.13	10.07	9.53	9.24	8.98
2,000.00	27.13	22.26	20.14	19.06	18.48	17.97
3,000.00	40.69	33.39	30.20	28.59	27.72	26.95
4,000.00	54.25	44.53	40.27	38.12	36.96	35.94
5,000.00	67.82	55.66	50.34	47.66	46.20	44.92
6,000.00	81.38	66.79	60.41	57.19	55.45	53.91
7,000.00	94.95	77.92	70.48	66.72	64.69	62.89
8,000.00	108.51	89.05	80.54	76.25	73.93	71.88
9,000.00	122.07	100.18	90.61	85.78	83.17	80.86
10,000.00	135.64	111.32	100.68	95.31	92.41	89.85
20,000.00	271.27	222.63	201.36	190.62	184.82	179.69
30,000.00	406.91	333.95	302.04	285.94	277.23	269.54
40,000.00	542.54	445.26	402.72	381.25	369.64	359.39
50,000.00	678.18	556.58	503.40	476.56	462.05	449.24
60,000.00	813.82	667.90	604.07	571.87	554.46	539.08
70,000.00	949.45	779.21	704.75	667.19	646.87	628.93
80,000.00	1,085.09	890.53	805.43	762.50	739.28	718.78
90,000.00	1,220.72	1,001.84	906.11	857.81	831.69	808.63
100,000.00	1,356.36	1,113.16	1,006.79	953.12	924.10	898.47

10.750% Rate

Amount	Term of Loan in Years					
	10	15	20	25	30	40
$ 50.00	$ 0.68	$ 0.56	$ 0.51	$ 0.48	$ 0.47	$ 0.45
100.00	1.36	1.12	1.02	0.96	0.93	0.91
200.00	2.73	2.24	2.03	1.92	1.87	1.82
300.00	4.09	3.36	3.05	2.89	2.80	2.73
400.00	5.45	4.48	4.06	3.85	3.73	3.63
500.00	6.82	5.60	5.08	4.81	4.67	4.54
600.00	8.18	6.73	6.09	5.77	5.60	5.45
700.00	9.54	7.85	7.11	6.73	6.53	6.36
800.00	10.91	8.97	8.12	7.70	7.47	7.27
900.00	12.27	10.09	9.14	8.66	8.40	8.18
1,000.00	13.63	11.21	10.15	9.62	9.33	9.08
2,000.00	27.27	22.42	20.30	19.24	18.67	18.17
3,000.00	40.90	33.63	30.46	28.86	28.00	27.25
4,000.00	54.54	44.84	40.61	38.48	37.34	36.34
5,000.00	68.17	56.05	50.76	48.10	46.67	45.42
6,000.00	81.80	67.26	60.91	57.73	56.01	54.50
7,000.00	95.44	78.47	71.07	67.35	65.34	63.59
8,000.00	109.07	89.68	81.22	76.97	74.68	72.67
9,000.00	122.70	100.89	91.37	86.59	84.01	81.76
10,000.00	136.34	112.09	101.52	96.21	93.35	90.84
20,000.00	272.68	224.19	203.05	192.42	186.70	181.68
30,000.00	409.02	336.28	304.57	288.63	280.04	272.52
40,000.00	545.35	448.38	406.09	384.84	373.39	363.36
50,000.00	681.69	560.47	507.61	481.05	466.74	454.20
60,000.00	818.03	672.57	609.14	577.26	560.09	545.04
70,000.00	954.37	784.66	710.66	673.46	653.44	635.88
80,000.00	1,090.71	896.76	812.18	769.67	746.79	726.72
90,000.00	1,227.05	1,008.85	913.71	865.88	840.13	817.56
100,000.00	1,363.39	1,120.95	1,015.23	962.09	933.48	908.40

10.875% Rate

Amount	Term of Loan in Years					
	10	15	20	25	30	40
$ 50.00	$ 0.69	$ 0.56	$ 0.51	$ 0.49	$ 0.47	$ 0.46
100.00	1.37	1.13	1.02	0.97	0.94	0.92
200.00	2.74	2.26	2.05	1.94	1.89	1.84
300.00	4.11	3.39	3.07	2.91	2.83	2.76
400.00	5.48	4.52	4.09	3.88	3.77	3.67
500.00	6.85	5.64	5.12	4.86	4.71	4.59
600.00	8.22	6.77	6.14	5.83	5.66	5.51
700.00	9.59	7.90	7.17	6.80	6.60	6.43
800.00	10.96	9.03	8.19	7.77	7.54	7.35
900.00	12.33	10.16	9.21	8.74	8.49	8.27
1,000.00	13.70	11.29	10.24	9.71	9.43	9.18
2,000.00	27.41	22.58	20.47	19.42	18.86	18.37
3,000.00	41.11	33.86	30.71	29.13	28.29	27.55
4,000.00	54.82	45.15	40.95	38.84	37.72	36.73
5,000.00	68.52	56.44	51.18	48.55	47.14	45.92
6,000.00	82.23	67.73	61.42	58.27	56.57	55.10
7,000.00	95.93	79.01	71.66	67.98	66.00	64.28
8,000.00	109.63	90.30	81.90	77.69	75.43	73.47
9,000.00	123.34	101.59	92.13	87.40	84.86	82.65
10,000.00	137.04	112.88	102.37	97.11	94.29	91.83
20,000.00	274.09	225.75	204.74	194.22	188.58	183.67
30,000.00	411.13	338.63	307.11	291.33	282.87	275.50
40,000.00	548.17	451.50	409.48	388.44	377.16	367.33
50,000.00	685.22	564.38	511.85	485.54	471.45	459.17
60,000.00	822.26	677.26	614.22	582.65	565.73	551.00
70,000.00	959.30	790.13	716.59	679.76	660.02	642.84
80,000.00	1,096.35	903.01	818.96	776.87	754.31	734.67
90,000.00	1,233.39	1,015.88	921.33	873.98	848.60	826.50
100,000.00	1,370.43	1,128.76	1,023.70	971.09	942.89	918.34

11.000% Rate

Amount	10	15	20	25	30	40
			Term of Loan in Years			
$ 50.00	$ 0.69	$ 0.57	$ 0.52	$ 0.49	$ 0.48	$ 0.46
100.00	1.38	1.14	1.03	0.98	0.95	0.93
200.00	2.76	2.27	2.06	1.96	1.90	1.86
300.00	4.13	3.41	3.10	2.94	2.86	2.78
400.00	5.51	4.55	4.13	3.92	3.81	3.71
500.00	6.89	5.68	5.16	4.90	4.76	4.64
600.00	8.27	6.82	6.19	5.88	5.71	5.57
700.00	9.64	7.96	7.23	6.86	6.67	6.50
800.00	11.02	9.09	8.26	7.84	7.62	7.43
900.00	12.40	10.23	9.29	8.82	8.57	8.35
1,000.00	13.78	11.37	10.32	9.80	9.52	9.28
2,000.00	27.55	22.73	20.64	19.60	19.05	18.57
3,000.00	41.33	34.10	30.97	29.40	28.57	27.85
4,000.00	55.10	45.46	41.29	39.20	38.09	37.13
5,000.00	68.88	56.83	51.61	49.01	47.62	46.41
6,000.00	82.65	68.20	61.93	58.81	57.14	55.70
7,000.00	96.43	79.56	72.25	68.61	66.66	64.98
8,000.00	110.20	90.93	82.58	78.41	76.19	74.26
9,000.00	123.98	102.29	92.90	88.21	85.71	83.55
10,000.00	137.75	113.66	103.22	98.01	95.23	92.83
20,000.00	275.50	227.32	206.44	196.02	190.46	185.66
30,000.00	413.25	340.98	309.66	294.03	285.70	278.49
40,000.00	551.00	454.64	412.88	392.05	380.93	371.32
50,000.00	688.75	568.30	516.09	490.06	476.16	464.15
60,000.00	826.50	681.96	619.31	588.07	571.39	556.98
70,000.00	964.25	795.62	722.53	686.08	666.63	649.81
80,000.00	1,102.00	909.28	825.75	784.09	761.86	742.64
90,000.00	1,239.75	1,022.94	928.97	882.10	857.09	835.46
100,000.00	1,377.50	1,136.60	1,032.19	980.11	952.32	928.29

11.125% Rate

Amount	Term of Loan in Years					
	10	15	20	25	30	40
$ 50.00	$ 0.69	$ 0.57	$ 0.52	$ 0.49	$ 0.48	$ 0.47
100.00	1.38	1.14	1.04	0.99	0.96	0.94
200.00	2.77	2.29	2.08	1.98	1.92	1.88
300.00	4.15	3.43	3.12	2.97	2.89	2.81
400.00	5.54	4.58	4.16	3.96	3.85	3.75
500.00	6.92	5.72	5.20	4.95	4.81	4.69
600.00	8.31	6.87	6.24	5.93	5.77	5.63
700.00	9.69	8.01	7.28	6.92	6.73	6.57
800.00	11.08	9.16	8.33	7.91	7.69	7.51
900.00	12.46	10.30	9.37	8.90	8.66	8.44
1,000.00	13.85	11.44	10.41	9.89	9.62	9.38
2,000.00	27.69	22.89	20.81	19.78	19.24	18.77
3,000.00	41.54	34.33	31.22	29.67	28.85	28.15
4,000.00	55.38	45.78	41.63	39.57	38.47	37.53
5,000.00	69.23	57.22	52.04	49.46	48.09	46.91
6,000.00	83.08	68.67	62.44	59.35	57.71	56.30
7,000.00	96.92	80.11	72.85	69.24	67.32	65.68
8,000.00	110.77	91.56	83.26	79.13	76.94	75.06
9,000.00	124.61	103.00	93.66	89.02	86.56	84.44
10,000.00	138.46	114.45	104.07	98.92	96.18	93.83
20,000.00	276.92	228.89	208.14	197.83	192.36	187.65
30,000.00	415.38	343.34	312.21	296.75	288.53	281.48
40,000.00	553.83	457.78	416.28	395.67	384.71	375.31
50,000.00	692.29	572.23	520.35	494.58	480.89	469.13
60,000.00	830.75	686.68	624.43	593.50	577.07	562.96
70,000.00	969.21	801.12	728.50	692.41	673.25	656.79
80,000.00	1,107.67	915.57	832.57	791.33	769.42	750.61
90,000.00	1,246.13	1,030.01	936.64	890.25	865.60	844.44
100,000.00	1,384.59	1,144.46	1,040.71	989.16	961.78	938.27

11.250% Rate

Amount	Term of Loan in Years					
	10	15	20	25	30	40
$ 50.00	$ 0.70	$ 0.58	$ 0.52	$ 0.50	$ 0.49	$ 0.47
100.00	1.39	1.15	1.05	1.00	0.97	0.95
200.00	2.78	2.30	2.10	2.00	1.94	1.90
300.00	4.18	3.46	3.15	2.99	2.91	2.84
400.00	5.57	4.61	4.20	3.99	3.89	3.79
500.00	6.96	5.76	5.25	4.99	4.86	4.74
600.00	8.35	6.91	6.30	5.99	5.83	5.69
700.00	9.74	8.07	7.34	6.99	6.80	6.64
800.00	11.13	9.22	8.39	7.99	7.77	7.59
900.00	12.53	10.37	9.44	8.98	8.74	8.53
1,000.00	13.92	11.52	10.49	9.98	9.71	9.48
2,000.00	27.83	23.05	20.99	19.96	19.43	18.97
3,000.00	41.75	34.57	31.48	29.95	29.14	28.45
4,000.00	55.67	46.09	41.97	39.93	38.85	37.93
5,000.00	69.58	57.62	52.46	49.91	48.56	47.41
6,000.00	83.50	69.14	62.96	59.89	58.28	56.90
7,000.00	97.42	80.66	73.45	69.88	67.99	66.38
8,000.00	111.34	92.19	83.94	79.86	77.70	75.86
9,000.00	125.25	103.71	94.43	89.84	87.41	85.34
10,000.00	139.17	115.23	104.93	99.82	97.13	94.83
20,000.00	278.34	230.47	209.85	199.65	194.25	189.65
30,000.00	417.51	345.70	314.78	299.47	291.38	284.48
40,000.00	556.68	460.94	419.70	399.30	388.50	379.30
50,000.00	695.84	576.17	524.63	499.12	485.63	474.13
60,000.00	835.01	691.41	629.55	598.94	582.76	568.95
70,000.00	974.18	806.64	734.48	698.77	679.88	663.78
80,000.00	1,113.35	921.88	839.40	798.59	777.01	758.61
90,000.00	1,252.52	1,037.11	944.33	898.42	874.14	853.43
100,000.00	1,391.69	1,152.34	1,049.26	998.24	971.26	948.26

11.375% Rate

Amount	Term of Loan in Years					
	10	15	20	25	30	40
$ 50.00	$ 0.70	$ 0.58	$ 0.53	$ 0.50	$ 0.49	$ 0.48
100.00	1.40	1.16	1.06	1.01	0.98	0.96
200.00	2.80	2.32	2.12	2.01	1.96	1.92
300.00	4.20	3.48	3.17	3.02	2.94	2.87
400.00	5.60	4.64	4.23	4.03	3.92	3.83
500.00	6.99	5.80	5.29	5.04	4.90	4.79
600.00	8.39	6.96	6.35	6.04	5.88	5.75
700.00	9.79	8.12	7.40	7.05	6.87	6.71
800.00	11.19	9.28	8.46	8.06	7.85	7.67
900.00	12.59	10.44	9.52	9.07	8.83	8.62
1,000.00	13.99	11.60	10.58	10.07	9.81	9.58
2,000.00	27.98	23.21	21.16	20.15	19.62	19.17
3,000.00	41.96	34.81	31.73	30.22	29.42	28.75
4,000.00	55.95	46.41	42.31	40.29	39.23	38.33
5,000.00	69.94	58.01	52.89	50.37	49.04	47.91
6,000.00	83.93	69.62	63.47	60.44	58.85	57.50
7,000.00	97.92	81.22	74.05	70.51	68.65	67.08
8,000.00	111.91	92.82	84.63	80.59	78.46	76.66
9,000.00	125.89	104.42	95.20	90.66	88.27	86.24
10,000.00	139.88	116.03	105.78	100.73	98.08	95.83
20,000.00	279.76	232.05	211.57	201.47	196.15	191.65
30,000.00	419.64	348.08	317.35	302.20	294.23	287.48
40,000.00	559.53	464.10	423.13	402.94	392.31	383.30
50,000.00	699.41	580.13	528.91	503.67	490.38	479.13
60,000.00	839.29	696.15	634.70	604.40	588.46	574.96
70,000.00	979.17	812.18	740.48	705.14	686.54	670.78
80,000.00	1,119.05	928.20	846.26	805.87	784.61	766.61
90,000.00	1,258.93	1,044.23	952.05	906.61	882.69	862.44
100,000.00	1,398.81	1,160.26	1,057.83	1,007.34	980.77	958.26

11.500% Rate

Amount	Term of Loan in Years					
	10	15	20	25	30	40
$ 50.00	$ 0.70	$ 0.58	$ 0.53	$ 0.51	$ 0.50	$ 0.48
100.00	1.41	1.17	1.07	1.02	0.99	0.97
200.00	2.81	2.34	2.13	2.03	1.98	1.94
300.00	4.22	3.50	3.20	3.05	2.97	2.90
400.00	5.62	4.67	4.27	4.07	3.96	3.87
500.00	7.03	5.84	5.33	5.08	4.95	4.84
600.00	8.44	7.01	6.40	6.10	5.94	5.81
700.00	9.84	8.18	7.47	7.12	6.93	6.78
800.00	11.25	9.35	8.53	8.13	7.92	7.75
900.00	12.65	10.51	9.60	9.15	8.91	8.71
1,000.00	14.06	11.68	10.66	10.16	9.90	9.68
2,000.00	28.12	23.36	21.33	20.33	19.81	19.37
3,000.00	42.18	35.05	31.99	30.49	29.71	29.05
4,000.00	56.24	46.73	42.66	40.66	39.61	38.73
5,000.00	70.30	58.41	53.32	50.82	49.51	48.41
6,000.00	84.36	70.09	63.99	60.99	59.42	58.10
7,000.00	98.42	81.77	74.65	71.15	69.32	67.78
8,000.00	112.48	93.46	85.31	81.32	79.22	77.46
9,000.00	126.54	105.14	95.98	91.48	89.13	87.15
10,000.00	140.60	116.82	106.64	101.65	99.03	96.83
20,000.00	281.19	233.64	213.29	203.29	198.06	193.66
30,000.00	421.79	350.46	319.93	304.94	297.09	290.48
40,000.00	562.38	467.28	426.57	406.59	396.12	387.31
50,000.00	702.98	584.09	533.21	508.23	495.15	484.14
60,000.00	843.57	700.91	639.86	609.88	594.17	580.97
70,000.00	984.17	817.73	746.50	711.53	693.20	677.80
80,000.00	1,124.76	934.55	853.14	813.18	792.23	774.63
90,000.00	1,265.36	1,051.37	959.79	914.82	891.26	871.45
100,000.00	1,405.95	1,168.19	1,066.43	1,016.47	990.29	968.28

11.625% Rate

Amount	Term of Loan in Years					
	10	15	20	25	30	40
$ 50.00	$ 0.71	$ 0.59	$ 0.54	$ 0.51	$ 0.50	$ 0.49
100.00	1.41	1.18	1.08	1.03	1.00	0.98
200.00	2.83	2.35	2.15	2.05	2.00	1.96
300.00	4.24	3.53	3.23	3.08	3.00	2.93
400.00	5.65	4.70	4.30	4.10	4.00	3.91
500.00	7.07	5.88	5.38	5.13	5.00	4.89
600.00	8.48	7.06	6.45	6.15	6.00	5.87
700.00	9.89	8.23	7.53	7.18	7.00	6.85
800.00	11.30	9.41	8.60	8.20	8.00	7.83
900.00	12.72	10.59	9.68	9.23	9.00	8.80
1,000.00	14.13	11.76	10.75	10.26	10.00	9.78
2,000.00	28.26	23.52	21.50	20.51	20.00	19.57
3,000.00	42.39	35.28	32.25	30.77	30.00	29.35
4,000.00	56.52	47.05	43.00	41.02	39.99	39.13
5,000.00	70.66	58.81	53.75	51.28	49.99	48.92
6,000.00	84.79	70.57	64.50	61.54	59.99	58.70
7,000.00	98.92	82.33	75.25	71.79	69.99	68.48
8,000.00	113.05	94.09	86.00	82.05	79.99	78.27
9,000.00	127.18	105.85	96.75	92.31	89.99	88.05
10,000.00	141.31	117.61	107.51	102.56	99.98	97.83
20,000.00	282.62	235.23	215.01	205.12	199.97	195.66
30,000.00	423.93	352.84	322.52	307.69	299.95	293.49
40,000.00	565.25	470.46	430.02	410.25	399.94	391.33
50,000.00	706.56	588.07	537.53	512.81	499.92	489.16
60,000.00	847.87	705.69	645.03	615.37	599.90	586.99
70,000.00	989.18	823.30	752.54	717.93	699.89	684.82
80,000.00	1,130.49	940.92	860.04	820.50	799.87	782.65
90,000.00	1,271.80	1,058.53	967.55	923.06	899.86	880.48
100,000.00	1,413.12	1,176.15	1,075.06	1,025.62	999.84	978.32

11.750% Rate

Amount	Term of Loan in Years					
	10	15	20	25	30	40
$ 50.00	$ 0.71	$ 0.59	$ 0.54	$ 0.52	$ 0.50	$ 0.49
100.00	1.42	1.18	1.08	1.03	1.01	0.99
200.00	2.84	2.37	2.17	2.07	2.02	1.98
300.00	4.26	3.55	3.25	3.10	3.03	2.97
400.00	5.68	4.74	4.33	4.14	4.04	3.95
500.00	7.10	5.92	5.42	5.17	5.05	4.94
600.00	8.52	7.10	6.50	6.21	6.06	5.93
700.00	9.94	8.29	7.59	7.24	7.07	6.92
800.00	11.36	9.47	8.67	8.28	8.08	7.91
900.00	12.78	10.66	9.75	9.31	9.08	8.90
1,000.00	14.20	11.84	10.84	10.35	10.09	9.88
2,000.00	28.41	23.68	21.67	20.70	20.19	19.77
3,000.00	42.61	35.52	32.51	31.04	30.28	29.65
4,000.00	56.81	47.37	43.35	41.39	40.38	39.53
5,000.00	71.01	59.21	54.19	51.74	50.47	49.42
6,000.00	85.22	71.05	65.02	62.09	60.56	59.30
7,000.00	99.42	82.89	75.86	72.44	70.66	69.19
8,000.00	113.62	94.73	86.70	82.78	80.75	79.07
9,000.00	127.83	106.57	97.53	93.13	90.85	88.95
10,000.00	142.03	118.41	108.37	103.48	100.94	98.84
20,000.00	284.06	236.83	216.74	206.96	201.88	197.67
30,000.00	426.09	355.24	325.11	310.44	302.82	296.51
40,000.00	568.12	473.65	433.48	413.92	403.76	395.35
50,000.00	710.15	592.07	541.85	517.40	504.70	494.18
60,000.00	852.18	710.48	650.22	620.88	605.65	593.02
70,000.00	994.21	828.89	758.59	724.36	706.59	691.85
80,000.00	1,136.24	947.31	866.97	827.84	807.53	790.69
90,000.00	1,278.27	1,065.72	975.34	931.32	908.47	889.53
100,000.00	1,420.29	1,184.13	1,083.71	1,034.80	1,009.41	988.36

11.875% Rate

Amount	Term of Loan in Years					
	10	15	20	25	30	40
$ 50.00	$ 0.71	$ 0.60	$ 0.55	$ 0.52	$ 0.51	$ 0.50
100.00	1.43	1.19	1.09	1.04	1.02	1.00
200.00	2.85	2.38	2.18	2.09	2.04	2.00
300.00	4.28	3.58	3.28	3.13	3.06	3.00
400.00	5.71	4.77	4.37	4.18	4.08	3.99
500.00	7.14	5.96	5.46	5.22	5.10	4.99
600.00	8.56	7.15	6.55	6.26	6.11	5.99
700.00	9.99	8.34	7.65	7.31	7.13	6.99
800.00	11.42	9.54	8.74	8.35	8.15	7.99
900.00	12.85	10.73	9.83	9.40	9.17	8.99
1,000.00	14.27	11.92	10.92	10.44	10.19	9.98
2,000.00	28.55	23.84	21.85	20.88	20.38	19.97
3,000.00	42.82	35.76	32.77	31.32	30.57	29.95
4,000.00	57.10	47.69	43.70	41.76	40.76	39.94
5,000.00	71.37	59.61	54.62	52.20	50.95	49.92
6,000.00	85.65	71.53	65.54	62.64	61.14	59.91
7,000.00	99.92	83.45	76.47	73.08	71.33	69.89
8,000.00	114.20	95.37	87.39	83.52	81.52	79.87
9,000.00	128.47	107.29	98.31	93.96	91.71	89.86
10,000.00	142.75	119.21	109.24	104.40	101.90	99.84
20,000.00	285.50	238.43	218.48	208.80	203.80	199.69
30,000.00	428.25	357.64	327.72	313.20	305.70	299.53
40,000.00	571.00	476.86	436.95	417.60	407.60	399.37
50,000.00	713.75	596.07	546.19	522.00	509.50	499.21
60,000.00	856.50	715.28	655.43	626.40	611.40	599.06
70,000.00	999.24	834.50	764.67	730.80	713.30	698.90
80,000.00	1,141.99	953.71	873.91	835.20	815.20	798.74
90,000.00	1,284.74	1,072.92	983.15	939.60	917.10	898.58
100,000.00	1,427.49	1,192.14	1,092.38	1,044.00	1,019.00	998.43

12.000% Rate

Amount	Term of Loan in Years					
	10	15	20	25	30	40
$ 50.00	$ 0.72	$ 0.60	$ 0.55	$ 0.53	$ 0.51	$ 0.50
100.00	1.43	1.20	1.10	1.05	1.03	1.01
200.00	2.87	2.40	2.20	2.11	2.06	2.02
300.00	4.30	3.60	3.30	3.16	3.09	3.03
400.00	5.74	4.80	4.40	4.21	4.11	4.03
500.00	7.17	6.00	5.51	5.27	5.14	5.04
600.00	8.61	7.20	6.61	6.32	6.17	6.05
700.00	10.04	8.40	7.71	7.37	7.20	7.06
800.00	11.48	9.60	8.81	8.43	8.23	8.07
900.00	12.91	10.80	9.91	9.48	9.26	9.08
1,000.00	14.35	12.00	11.01	10.53	10.29	10.08
2,000.00	28.69	24.00	22.02	21.06	20.57	20.17
3,000.00	43.04	36.01	33.03	31.60	30.86	30.25
4,000.00	57.39	48.01	44.04	42.13	41.14	40.34
5,000.00	71.74	60.01	55.05	52.66	51.43	50.42
6,000.00	86.08	72.01	66.07	63.19	61.72	60.51
7,000.00	100.43	84.01	77.08	73.73	72.00	70.59
8,000.00	114.78	96.01	88.09	84.26	82.29	80.68
9,000.00	129.12	108.02	99.10	94.79	92.58	90.76
10,000.00	143.47	120.02	110.11	105.32	102.86	100.85
20,000.00	286.94	240.03	220.22	210.64	205.72	201.70
30,000.00	430.41	360.05	330.33	315.97	308.58	302.55
40,000.00	573.88	480.07	440.43	421.29	411.45	403.40
50,000.00	717.35	600.08	550.54	526.61	514.31	504.25
60,000.00	860.83	720.10	660.65	631.93	617.17	605.10
70,000.00	1,004.30	840.12	770.76	737.26	720.03	705.95
80,000.00	1,147.77	960.13	880.87	842.58	822.89	806.80
90,000.00	1,291.24	1,080.15	990.98	947.90	925.75	907.65
100,000.00	1,434.71	1,200.17	1,101.09	1,053.22	1,028.61	1,008.50

12.125% Rate

Amount	Term of Loan in Years					
	10	15	20	25	30	40
$ 50.00	$ 0.72	$ 0.60	$ 0.55	$ 0.53	$ 0.52	$ 0.51
100.00	1.44	1.21	1.11	1.06	1.04	1.02
200.00	2.88	2.42	2.22	2.12	2.08	2.04
300.00	4.33	3.62	3.33	3.19	3.11	3.06
400.00	5.77	4.83	4.44	4.25	4.15	4.07
500.00	7.21	6.04	5.55	5.31	5.19	5.09
600.00	8.65	7.25	6.66	6.37	6.23	6.11
700.00	10.09	8.46	7.77	7.44	7.27	7.13
800.00	11.54	9.67	8.88	8.50	8.31	8.15
900.00	12.98	10.87	9.99	9.56	9.34	9.17
1,000.00	14.42	12.08	11.10	10.62	10.38	10.19
2,000.00	28.84	24.16	22.20	21.25	20.76	20.37
3,000.00	43.26	36.25	33.29	31.87	31.15	30.56
4,000.00	57.68	48.33	44.39	42.50	41.53	40.74
5,000.00	72.10	60.41	55.49	53.12	51.91	50.93
6,000.00	86.52	72.49	66.59	63.75	62.29	61.12
7,000.00	100.94	84.58	77.69	74.37	72.68	71.30
8,000.00	115.36	96.66	88.79	85.00	83.06	81.49
9,000.00	129.78	108.74	99.88	95.62	93.44	91.67
10,000.00	144.19	120.82	110.98	106.25	103.82	101.86
20,000.00	288.39	241.64	221.96	212.49	207.65	203.72
30,000.00	432.58	362.47	332.94	318.74	311.47	305.58
40,000.00	576.78	483.29	443.93	424.99	415.30	407.43
50,000.00	720.97	604.11	554.91	531.24	519.12	509.29
60,000.00	865.17	724.93	665.89	637.48	622.95	611.15
70,000.00	1,009.36	845.76	776.87	743.73	726.77	713.01
80,000.00	1,153.56	966.58	887.85	849.98	830.60	814.87
90,000.00	1,297.75	1,087.40	998.83	956.23	934.42	916.73
100,000.00	1,441.94	1,208.22	1,109.81	1,062.47	1,038.24	1,018.59

12.250% Rate

Amount	Term of Loan in Years					
	10	15	20	25	30	40
$ 50.00	$ 0.72	$ 0.61	$ 0.56	$ 0.54	$ 0.52	$ 0.51
100.00	1.45	1.22	1.12	1.07	1.05	1.03
200.00	2.90	2.43	2.24	2.14	2.10	2.06
300.00	4.35	3.65	3.36	3.22	3.14	3.09
400.00	5.80	4.87	4.47	4.29	4.19	4.11
500.00	7.25	6.08	5.59	5.36	5.24	5.14
600.00	8.70	7.30	6.71	6.43	6.29	6.17
700.00	10.14	8.51	7.83	7.50	7.34	7.20
800.00	11.59	9.73	8.95	8.57	8.38	8.23
900.00	13.04	10.95	10.07	9.65	9.43	9.26
1,000.00	14.49	12.16	11.19	10.72	10.48	10.29
2,000.00	28.98	24.33	22.37	21.43	20.96	20.57
3,000.00	43.48	36.49	33.56	32.15	31.44	30.86
4,000.00	57.97	48.65	44.74	42.87	41.92	41.15
5,000.00	72.46	60.81	55.93	53.59	52.39	51.43
6,000.00	86.95	72.98	67.11	64.30	62.87	61.72
7,000.00	101.44	85.14	78.30	75.02	73.35	72.01
8,000.00	115.94	97.30	89.49	85.74	83.83	82.29
9,000.00	130.43	109.47	100.67	96.46	94.31	92.58
10,000.00	144.92	121.63	111.86	107.17	104.79	102.87
20,000.00	289.84	243.26	223.71	214.35	209.58	205.74
30,000.00	434.76	364.89	335.57	321.52	314.37	308.61
40,000.00	579.68	486.52	447.43	428.70	419.16	411.47
50,000.00	724.60	608.15	559.28	535.87	523.95	514.34
60,000.00	869.52	729.78	671.14	643.05	628.74	617.21
70,000.00	1,014.44	851.41	783.00	750.22	733.53	720.08
80,000.00	1,159.36	973.04	894.85	857.40	838.32	822.95
90,000.00	1,304.28	1,094.67	1,006.71	964.57	943.11	925.82
100,000.00	1,449.20	1,216.30	1,118.56	1,071.74	1,047.90	1,028.69

12.375% Rate

Amount	Term of Loan in Years					
	10	15	20	25	30	40
$ 50.00	$ 0.73	$ 0.61	$ 0.56	$ 0.54	$ 0.53	$ 0.52
100.00	1.46	1.22	1.13	1.08	1.06	1.04
200.00	2.91	2.45	2.25	2.16	2.12	2.08
300.00	4.37	3.67	3.38	3.24	3.17	3.12
400.00	5.83	4.90	4.51	4.32	4.23	4.16
500.00	7.28	6.12	5.64	5.41	5.29	5.19
600.00	8.74	7.35	6.76	6.49	6.35	6.23
700.00	10.20	8.57	7.89	7.57	7.40	7.27
800.00	11.65	9.80	9.02	8.65	8.46	8.31
900.00	13.11	11.02	10.15	9.73	9.52	9.35
1,000.00	14.56	12.24	11.27	10.81	10.58	10.39
2,000.00	29.13	24.49	22.55	21.62	21.15	20.78
3,000.00	43.69	36.73	33.82	32.43	31.73	31.16
4,000.00	58.26	48.98	45.09	43.24	42.30	41.55
5,000.00	72.82	61.22	56.37	54.05	52.88	51.94
6,000.00	87.39	73.46	67.64	64.86	63.45	62.33
7,000.00	101.95	85.71	78.91	75.67	74.03	72.72
8,000.00	116.52	97.95	90.19	86.48	84.61	83.10
9,000.00	131.08	110.20	101.46	97.29	95.18	93.49
10,000.00	145.65	122.44	112.73	108.10	105.76	103.88
20,000.00	291.29	244.88	225.47	216.21	211.51	207.76
30,000.00	436.94	367.32	338.20	324.31	317.27	311.64
40,000.00	582.59	489.76	450.94	432.42	423.03	415.52
50,000.00	728.24	612.20	563.67	540.52	528.78	519.40
60,000.00	873.88	734.64	676.40	648.62	634.54	623.28
70,000.00	1,019.53	857.08	789.14	756.73	740.30	727.16
80,000.00	1,165.18	979.52	901.87	864.83	846.05	831.04
90,000.00	1,310.82	1,101.96	1,014.61	972.93	951.81	934.92
100,000.00	1,456.47	1,224.40	1,127.34	1,081.04	1,057.57	1,038.80

12.500% Rate

Amount	Term of Loan in Years					
	10	15	20	25	30	40
$ 50.00	$ 0.73	$ 0.62	$ 0.57	$ 0.55	$ 0.53	$ 0.52
100.00	1.46	1.23	1.14	1.09	1.07	1.05
200.00	2.93	2.47	2.27	2.18	2.13	2.10
300.00	4.39	3.70	3.41	3.27	3.20	3.15
400.00	5.86	4.93	4.54	4.36	4.27	4.20
500.00	7.32	6.16	5.68	5.45	5.34	5.24
600.00	8.78	7.40	6.82	6.54	6.40	6.29
700.00	10.25	8.63	7.95	7.63	7.47	7.34
800.00	11.71	9.86	9.09	8.72	8.54	8.39
900.00	13.17	11.09	10.23	9.81	9.61	9.44
1,000.00	14.64	12.33	11.36	10.90	10.67	10.49
2,000.00	29.28	24.65	22.72	21.81	21.35	20.98
3,000.00	43.91	36.98	34.08	32.71	32.02	31.47
4,000.00	58.55	49.30	45.45	43.61	42.69	41.96
5,000.00	73.19	61.63	56.81	54.52	53.36	52.45
6,000.00	87.83	73.95	68.17	65.42	64.04	62.94
7,000.00	102.46	86.28	79.53	76.32	74.71	73.42
8,000.00	117.10	98.60	90.89	87.23	85.38	83.91
9,000.00	131.74	110.93	102.25	98.13	96.05	94.40
10,000.00	146.38	123.25	113.61	109.04	106.73	104.89
20,000.00	292.75	246.50	227.23	218.07	213.45	209.78
30,000.00	439.13	369.76	340.84	327.11	320.18	314.68
40,000.00	585.50	493.01	454.46	436.14	426.90	419.57
50,000.00	731.88	616.26	568.07	545.18	533.63	524.46
60,000.00	878.26	739.51	681.68	654.21	640.35	629.35
70,000.00	1,024.63	862.77	795.30	763.25	747.08	734.24
80,000.00	1,171.01	986.02	908.91	872.28	853.81	839.14
90,000.00	1,317.39	1,109.27	1,022.53	981.32	960.53	944.03
100,000.00	1,463.76	1,232.52	1,136.14	1,090.35	1,067.26	1,048.92

12.625% Rate

Amount	Term of Loan in Years					
	10	15	20	25	30	40
$ 50.00	$ 0.74	$ 0.62	$ 0.57	$ 0.55	$ 0.54	$ 0.53
100.00	1.47	1.24	1.14	1.10	1.08	1.06
200.00	2.94	2.48	2.29	2.20	2.15	2.12
300.00	4.41	3.72	3.43	3.30	3.23	3.18
400.00	5.88	4.96	4.58	4.40	4.31	4.24
500.00	7.36	6.20	5.72	5.50	5.38	5.30
600.00	8.83	7.44	6.87	6.60	6.46	6.35
700.00	10.30	8.68	8.01	7.70	7.54	7.41
800.00	11.77	9.93	9.16	8.80	8.62	8.47
900.00	13.24	11.17	10.30	9.90	9.69	9.53
1,000.00	14.71	12.41	11.45	11.00	10.77	10.59
2,000.00	29.42	24.81	22.90	21.99	21.54	21.18
3,000.00	44.13	37.22	34.35	32.99	32.31	31.77
4,000.00	58.84	49.63	45.80	43.99	43.08	42.36
5,000.00	73.55	62.03	57.25	54.98	53.85	52.95
6,000.00	88.26	74.44	68.70	65.98	64.62	63.54
7,000.00	102.97	86.85	80.15	76.98	75.39	74.13
8,000.00	117.69	99.25	91.60	87.98	86.16	84.72
9,000.00	132.40	111.66	103.05	98.97	96.93	95.31
10,000.00	147.11	124.07	114.50	109.97	107.70	105.91
20,000.00	294.21	248.13	228.99	219.94	215.39	211.81
30,000.00	441.32	372.20	343.49	329.91	323.09	317.72
40,000.00	588.43	496.27	457.99	439.88	430.79	423.62
50,000.00	735.54	620.33	572.48	549.85	538.48	529.53
60,000.00	882.64	744.40	686.98	659.82	646.18	635.43
70,000.00	1,029.75	868.47	801.48	769.78	753.88	741.34
80,000.00	1,176.86	992.53	915.97	879.75	861.57	847.24
90,000.00	1,323.96	1,116.60	1,030.47	989.72	969.27	953.15
100,000.00	1,471.07	1,240.67	1,144.96	1,099.69	1,076.97	1,059.05

12.750% Rate

Amount	Term of Loan in Years					
	10	15	20	25	30	40
$ 50.00	$ 0.74	$ 0.62	$ 0.58	$ 0.55	$ 0.54	$ 0.53
100.00	1.48	1.25	1.15	1.11	1.09	1.07
200.00	2.96	2.50	2.31	2.22	2.17	2.14
300.00	4.44	3.75	3.46	3.33	3.26	3.21
400.00	5.91	5.00	4.62	4.44	4.35	4.28
500.00	7.39	6.24	5.77	5.55	5.43	5.35
600.00	8.87	7.49	6.92	6.65	6.52	6.42
700.00	10.35	8.74	8.08	7.76	7.61	7.48
800.00	11.83	9.99	9.23	8.87	8.69	8.55
900.00	13.31	11.24	10.38	9.98	9.78	9.62
1,000.00	14.78	12.49	11.54	11.09	10.87	10.69
2,000.00	29.57	24.98	23.08	22.18	21.73	21.38
3,000.00	44.35	37.47	34.61	33.27	32.60	32.08
4,000.00	59.14	49.95	46.15	44.36	43.47	42.77
5,000.00	73.92	62.44	57.69	55.45	54.33	53.46
6,000.00	88.70	74.93	69.23	66.54	65.20	64.15
7,000.00	103.49	87.42	80.77	77.63	76.07	74.84
8,000.00	118.27	99.91	92.30	88.72	86.94	85.54
9,000.00	133.06	112.40	103.84	99.81	97.80	96.23
10,000.00	147.84	124.88	115.38	110.91	108.67	106.92
20,000.00	295.68	249.77	230.76	221.81	217.34	213.84
30,000.00	443.52	374.65	346.14	332.72	326.01	320.76
40,000.00	591.36	499.53	461.52	443.62	434.68	427.68
50,000.00	739.20	624.42	576.91	554.53	543.35	534.60
60,000.00	887.04	749.30	692.29	665.43	652.02	641.52
70,000.00	1,034.88	874.19	807.67	776.34	760.69	748.44
80,000.00	1,182.72	999.07	923.05	887.24	869.35	855.36
90,000.00	1,330.56	1,123.95	1,038.43	998.15	978.02	962.28
100,000.00	1,478.40	1,248.84	1,153.81	1,109.05	1,086.69	1,069.20

12.875% Rate

Amount	Term of Loan in Years					
	10	15	20	25	30	40
$ 50.00	$ 0.74	$ 0.63	$ 0.58	$ 0.56	$ 0.55	$ 0.54
100.00	1.49	1.26	1.16	1.12	1.10	1.08
200.00	2.97	2.51	2.33	2.24	2.19	2.16
300.00	4.46	3.77	3.49	3.36	3.29	3.24
400.00	5.94	5.03	4.65	4.47	4.39	4.32
500.00	7.43	6.29	5.81	5.59	5.48	5.40
600.00	8.91	7.54	6.98	6.71	6.58	6.48
700.00	10.40	8.80	8.14	7.83	7.68	7.56
800.00	11.89	10.06	9.30	8.95	8.77	8.63
900.00	13.37	11.31	10.46	10.07	9.87	9.71
1,000.00	14.86	12.57	11.63	11.18	10.96	10.79
2,000.00	29.71	25.14	23.25	22.37	21.93	21.59
3,000.00	44.57	37.71	34.88	33.55	32.89	32.38
4,000.00	59.43	50.28	46.51	44.74	43.86	43.17
5,000.00	74.29	62.85	58.13	55.92	54.82	53.97
6,000.00	89.14	75.42	69.76	67.11	65.79	64.76
7,000.00	104.00	87.99	81.39	78.29	76.75	75.55
8,000.00	118.86	100.56	93.01	89.47	87.72	86.35
9,000.00	133.72	113.13	104.64	100.66	98.68	97.14
10,000.00	148.57	125.70	116.27	111.84	109.64	107.94
20,000.00	297.15	251.41	232.54	223.69	219.29	215.87
30,000.00	445.72	377.11	348.80	335.53	328.93	323.81
40,000.00	594.30	502.81	465.07	447.37	438.58	431.74
50,000.00	742.87	628.51	581.34	559.22	548.22	539.68
60,000.00	891.45	754.22	697.61	671.06	657.86	647.61
70,000.00	1,040.02	879.92	813.88	782.90	767.51	755.55
80,000.00	1,188.59	1,005.62	930.15	894.75	877.15	863.48
90,000.00	1,337.17	1,131.33	1,046.41	1,006.59	986.79	971.42
100,000.00	1,485.74	1,257.03	1,162.68	1,118.43	1,096.44	1,079.35

13.000% Rate

Amount	10	15	20	25	30	40
$ 50.00	$ 0.75	$ 0.63	$ 0.59	$ 0.56	$ 0.55	$ 0.54
100.00	1.49	1.27	1.17	1.13	1.11	1.09
200.00	2.99	2.53	2.34	2.26	2.21	2.18
300.00	4.48	3.80	3.51	3.38	3.32	3.27
400.00	5.97	5.06	4.69	4.51	4.42	4.36
500.00	7.47	6.33	5.86	5.64	5.53	5.45
600.00	8.96	7.59	7.03	6.77	6.64	6.54
700.00	10.45	8.86	8.20	7.89	7.74	7.63
800.00	11.94	10.12	9.37	9.02	8.85	8.72
900.00	13.44	11.39	10.54	10.15	9.96	9.81
1,000.00	14.93	12.65	11.72	11.28	11.06	10.90
2,000.00	29.86	25.30	23.43	22.56	22.12	21.79
3,000.00	44.79	37.96	35.15	33.84	33.19	32.69
4,000.00	59.72	50.61	46.86	45.11	44.25	43.58
5,000.00	74.66	63.26	58.58	56.39	55.31	54.48
6,000.00	89.59	75.91	70.29	67.67	66.37	65.37
7,000.00	104.52	88.57	82.01	78.95	77.43	76.27
8,000.00	119.45	101.22	93.73	90.23	88.50	87.16
9,000.00	134.38	113.87	105.44	101.51	99.56	98.06
10,000.00	149.31	126.52	117.16	112.78	110.62	108.95
20,000.00	298.62	253.05	234.32	225.57	221.24	217.90
30,000.00	447.93	379.57	351.47	338.35	331.86	326.85
40,000.00	597.24	506.10	468.63	451.13	442.48	435.81
50,000.00	746.55	632.62	585.79	563.92	553.10	544.76
60,000.00	895.86	759.15	702.95	676.70	663.72	653.71
70,000.00	1,045.18	885.67	820.10	789.48	774.34	762.66
80,000.00	1,194.49	1,012.19	937.26	902.27	884.96	871.61
90,000.00	1,343.80	1,138.72	1,054.42	1,015.05	995.58	980.56
100,000.00	1,493.11	1,265.24	1,171.58	1,127.84	1,106.20	1,089.51

Term of Loan in Years

13.125% Rate

Amount	Term of Loan in Years					
	10	15	20	25	30	40
$ 50.00	$ 0.75	$ 0.64	$ 0.59	$ 0.57	$ 0.56	$ 0.55
100.00	1.50	1.27	1.18	1.14	1.12	1.10
200.00	3.00	2.55	2.36	2.27	2.23	2.20
300.00	4.50	3.82	3.54	3.41	3.35	3.30
400.00	6.00	5.09	4.72	4.55	4.46	4.40
500.00	7.50	6.37	5.90	5.69	5.58	5.50
600.00	9.00	7.64	7.08	6.82	6.70	6.60
700.00	10.50	8.91	8.26	7.96	7.81	7.70
800.00	12.00	10.19	9.44	9.10	8.93	8.80
900.00	13.50	11.46	10.62	10.24	10.04	9.90
1,000.00	15.00	12.73	11.80	11.37	11.16	11.00
2,000.00	30.01	25.47	23.61	22.75	22.32	21.99
3,000.00	45.01	38.20	35.41	34.12	33.48	32.99
4,000.00	60.02	50.94	47.22	45.49	44.64	43.99
5,000.00	75.02	63.67	59.02	56.86	55.80	54.98
6,000.00	90.03	76.41	70.83	68.24	66.96	65.98
7,000.00	105.03	89.14	82.63	79.61	78.12	76.98
8,000.00	120.04	101.88	94.44	90.98	89.28	87.97
9,000.00	135.04	114.61	106.24	102.35	100.44	98.97
10,000.00	150.05	127.35	118.05	113.73	111.60	109.97
20,000.00	300.10	254.70	236.10	227.45	223.20	219.94
30,000.00	450.15	382.04	354.15	341.18	334.79	329.91
40,000.00	600.20	509.39	472.20	454.90	446.39	439.87
50,000.00	750.24	636.74	590.25	568.63	557.99	549.84
60,000.00	900.29	764.09	708.30	682.35	669.59	659.81
70,000.00	1,050.34	891.43	826.34	796.08	781.18	769.78
80,000.00	1,200.39	1,018.78	944.39	909.81	892.78	879.75
90,000.00	1,350.44	1,146.13	1,062.44	1,023.53	1,004.38	989.72
100,000.00	1,500.49	1,273.48	1,180.49	1,137.26	1,115.98	1,099.69

13.250% Rate

Amount		Term of Loan in Years									
		10		15		20		25		30	40
$	50.00	$	0.75	$	0.64	$	0.59	$	0.57	$ 0.56	$ 0.55
	100.00		1.51		1.28		1.19		1.15	1.13	1.11
	200.00		3.02		2.56		2.38		2.29	2.25	2.22
	300.00		4.52		3.85		3.57		3.44	3.38	3.33
	400.00		6.03		5.13		4.76		4.59	4.50	4.44
	500.00		7.54		6.41		5.95		5.73	5.63	5.55
	600.00		9.05		7.69		7.14		6.88	6.75	6.66
	700.00		10.56		8.97		8.33		8.03	7.88	7.77
	800.00		12.06		10.25		9.52		9.17	9.01	8.88
	900.00		13.57		11.54		10.70		10.32	10.13	9.99
	1,000.00		15.08		12.82		11.89		11.47	11.26	11.10
	2,000.00		30.16		25.63		23.79		22.93	22.52	22.20
	3,000.00		45.24		38.45		35.68		34.40	33.77	33.30
	4,000.00		60.32		51.27		47.58		45.87	45.03	44.39
	5,000.00		75.39		64.09		59.47		57.34	56.29	55.49
	6,000.00		90.47		76.90		71.37		68.80	67.55	66.59
	7,000.00		105.55		89.72		83.26		80.27	78.80	77.69
	8,000.00		120.63		102.54		95.15		91.74	90.06	88.79
	9,000.00		135.71		115.36		107.05		103.20	101.32	99.89
	10,000.00		150.79		128.17		118.94		114.67	112.58	110.99
	20,000.00		301.58		256.35		237.89		229.34	225.15	221.97
	30,000.00		452.37		384.52		356.83		344.01	337.73	332.96
	40,000.00		603.16		512.69		475.77		458.68	450.31	443.95
	50,000.00		753.94		640.87		594.72		573.35	562.89	554.93
	60,000.00		904.73		769.04		713.66		688.02	675.46	665.92
	70,000.00		1,055.52		897.22		832.60		802.69	788.04	776.91
	80,000.00		1,206.31		1,025.39		951.54		917.36	900.62	887.90
	90,000.00		1,357.10		1,153.56		1,070.49		1,032.03	1,013.20	998.88
	100,000.00		1,507.89		1,281.74		1,189.43		1,146.70	1,125.77	1,109.87

13.375% Rate

Amount	Term of Loan in Years					
	10	15	20	25	30	40
$ 50.00	$ 0.76	$ 0.65	$ 0.60	$ 0.58	$ 0.57	$ 0.56
100.00	1.52	1.29	1.20	1.16	1.14	1.12
200.00	3.03	2.58	2.40	2.31	2.27	2.24
300.00	4.55	3.87	3.60	3.47	3.41	3.36
400.00	6.06	5.16	4.79	4.62	4.54	4.48
500.00	7.58	6.45	5.99	5.78	5.68	5.60
600.00	9.09	7.74	7.19	6.94	6.81	6.72
700.00	10.61	9.03	8.39	8.09	7.95	7.84
800.00	12.12	10.32	9.59	9.25	9.08	8.96
900.00	13.64	11.61	10.79	10.41	10.22	10.08
1,000.00	15.15	12.90	11.98	11.56	11.36	11.20
2,000.00	30.31	25.80	23.97	23.12	22.71	22.40
3,000.00	45.46	38.70	35.95	34.68	34.07	33.60
4,000.00	60.61	51.60	47.94	46.25	45.42	44.80
5,000.00	75.77	64.50	59.92	57.81	56.78	56.00
6,000.00	90.92	77.40	71.90	69.37	68.14	67.20
7,000.00	106.07	90.30	83.89	80.93	79.49	78.40
8,000.00	121.22	103.20	95.87	92.49	90.85	89.60
9,000.00	136.38	116.10	107.86	104.05	102.20	100.81
10,000.00	151.53	129.00	119.84	115.62	113.56	112.01
20,000.00	303.06	258.00	239.68	231.23	227.12	224.01
30,000.00	454.59	387.00	359.52	346.85	340.68	336.02
40,000.00	606.12	516.01	479.36	462.47	454.23	448.02
50,000.00	757.65	645.01	599.20	578.08	567.79	560.03
60,000.00	909.18	774.01	719.04	693.70	681.35	672.04
70,000.00	1,060.71	903.01	838.87	809.31	794.91	784.04
80,000.00	1,212.25	1,032.01	958.71	924.93	908.47	896.05
90,000.00	1,363.78	1,161.01	1,078.55	1,040.55	1,022.03	1,008.06
100,000.00	1,515.31	1,290.02	1,198.39	1,156.16	1,135.58	1,120.06

13.500% Rate

Amount	Term of Loan in Years					
	10	15	20	25	30	40
$ 50.00	$ 0.76	$ 0.65	$ 0.60	$ 0.58	$ 0.57	$ 0.57
100.00	1.52	1.30	1.21	1.17	1.15	1.13
200.00	3.05	2.60	2.41	2.33	2.29	2.26
300.00	4.57	3.89	3.62	3.50	3.44	3.39
400.00	6.09	5.19	4.83	4.66	4.58	4.52
500.00	7.61	6.49	6.04	5.83	5.73	5.65
600.00	9.14	7.79	7.24	6.99	6.87	6.78
700.00	10.66	9.09	8.45	8.16	8.02	7.91
800.00	12.18	10.39	9.66	9.33	9.16	9.04
900.00	13.70	11.68	10.87	10.49	10.31	10.17
1,000.00	15.23	12.98	12.07	11.66	11.45	11.30
2,000.00	30.45	25.97	24.15	23.31	22.91	22.61
3,000.00	45.68	38.95	36.22	34.97	34.36	33.91
4,000.00	60.91	51.93	48.29	46.63	45.82	45.21
5,000.00	76.14	64.92	60.37	58.28	57.27	56.51
6,000.00	91.36	77.90	72.44	69.94	68.72	67.82
7,000.00	106.59	90.88	84.52	81.60	80.18	79.12
8,000.00	121.82	103.87	96.59	93.25	91.63	90.42
9,000.00	137.05	116.85	108.66	104.91	103.09	101.72
10,000.00	152.27	129.83	120.74	116.56	114.54	113.03
20,000.00	304.55	259.66	241.47	233.13	229.08	226.05
30,000.00	456.82	389.50	362.21	349.69	343.62	339.08
40,000.00	609.10	519.33	482.95	466.26	458.16	452.10
50,000.00	761.37	649.16	603.69	582.82	572.71	565.13
60,000.00	913.65	778.99	724.42	699.39	687.25	678.16
70,000.00	1,065.92	908.82	845.16	815.95	801.79	791.18
80,000.00	1,218.19	1,038.65	965.90	932.52	916.33	904.21
90,000.00	1,370.47	1,168.49	1,086.64	1,049.08	1,030.87	1,017.24
100,000.00	1,522.74	1,298.32	1,207.37	1,165.64	1,145.41	1,130.26

473

13.625% Rate

Amount	Term of Loan in Years					
	10	15	20	25	30	40
$ 50.00	$ 0.77	$ 0.65	$ 0.61	$ 0.59	$ 0.58	$ 0.57
100.00	1.53	1.31	1.22	1.18	1.16	1.14
200.00	3.06	2.61	2.43	2.35	2.31	2.28
300.00	4.59	3.92	3.65	3.53	3.47	3.42
400.00	6.12	5.23	4.87	4.70	4.62	4.56
500.00	7.65	6.53	6.08	5.88	5.78	5.70
600.00	9.18	7.84	7.30	7.05	6.93	6.84
700.00	10.71	9.15	8.51	8.23	8.09	7.98
800.00	12.24	10.45	9.73	9.40	9.24	9.12
900.00	13.77	11.76	10.95	10.58	10.40	10.26
1,000.00	15.30	13.07	12.16	11.75	11.55	11.40
2,000.00	30.60	26.13	24.33	23.50	23.11	22.81
3,000.00	45.91	39.20	36.49	35.25	34.66	34.21
4,000.00	61.21	52.27	48.66	47.01	46.21	45.62
5,000.00	76.51	65.33	60.82	58.76	57.76	57.02
6,000.00	91.81	78.40	72.98	70.51	69.32	68.43
7,000.00	107.11	91.46	85.15	82.26	80.87	79.83
8,000.00	122.42	104.53	97.31	94.01	92.42	91.24
9,000.00	137.72	117.60	109.47	105.76	103.97	102.64
10,000.00	153.02	130.66	121.64	117.51	115.53	114.05
20,000.00	306.04	261.33	243.28	235.03	231.05	228.09
30,000.00	459.06	391.99	364.91	352.54	346.58	342.14
40,000.00	612.08	522.66	486.55	470.06	462.10	456.19
50,000.00	765.10	653.32	608.19	587.57	577.63	570.23
60,000.00	918.12	783.99	729.83	705.09	693.15	684.28
70,000.00	1,071.14	914.65	851.47	822.60	808.68	798.33
80,000.00	1,224.16	1,045.31	973.10	940.12	924.20	912.38
90,000.00	1,377.18	1,175.98	1,094.74	1,057.63	1,039.73	1,026.42
100,000.00	1,530.20	1,306.64	1,216.38	1,175.15	1,155.25	1,140.47

13.750% Rate

Amount	Term of Loan in Years					
	10	15	20	25	30	40
$ 50.00	$ 0.77	$ 0.66	$ 0.61	$ 0.59	$ 0.58	$ 0.58
100.00	1.54	1.31	1.23	1.18	1.17	1.15
200.00	3.08	2.63	2.45	2.37	2.33	2.30
300.00	4.61	3.94	3.68	3.55	3.50	3.45
400.00	6.15	5.26	4.90	4.74	4.66	4.60
500.00	7.69	6.57	6.13	5.92	5.83	5.75
600.00	9.23	7.89	7.35	7.11	6.99	6.90
700.00	10.76	9.20	8.58	8.29	8.16	8.05
800.00	12.30	10.52	9.80	9.48	9.32	9.21
900.00	13.84	11.83	11.03	10.66	10.49	10.36
1,000.00	15.38	13.15	12.25	11.85	11.65	11.51
2,000.00	30.75	26.30	24.51	23.69	23.30	23.01
3,000.00	46.13	39.45	36.76	35.54	34.95	34.52
4,000.00	61.51	52.60	49.02	47.39	46.60	46.03
5,000.00	76.88	65.75	61.27	59.23	58.26	57.53
6,000.00	92.26	78.90	73.52	71.08	69.91	69.04
7,000.00	107.64	92.05	85.78	82.93	81.56	80.55
8,000.00	123.01	105.20	98.03	94.77	93.21	92.05
9,000.00	138.39	118.35	110.29	106.62	104.86	103.56
10,000.00	153.77	131.50	122.54	118.47	116.51	115.07
20,000.00	307.53	263.00	245.08	236.93	233.02	230.14
30,000.00	461.30	394.50	367.62	355.40	349.53	345.21
40,000.00	615.07	525.99	490.16	473.87	466.05	460.27
50,000.00	768.83	657.49	612.70	592.33	582.56	575.34
60,000.00	922.60	788.99	735.24	710.80	699.07	690.41
70,000.00	1,076.37	920.49	857.78	829.27	815.58	805.48
80,000.00	1,230.13	1,051.99	980.32	947.73	932.09	920.55
90,000.00	1,383.90	1,183.49	1,102.86	1,066.20	1,048.60	1,035.62
100,000.00	1,537.67	1,314.99	1,225.41	1,184.67	1,165.11	1,150.69

13.875% Rate

Amount	Term of Loan in Years					
	10	15	20	25	30	40
$ 50.00	$ 0.77	$ 0.66	$ 0.62	$ 0.60	$ 0.59	$ 0.58
100.00	1.55	1.32	1.23	1.19	1.17	1.16
200.00	3.09	2.65	2.47	2.39	2.35	2.32
300.00	4.64	3.97	3.70	3.58	3.52	3.48
400.00	6.18	5.29	4.94	4.78	4.70	4.64
500.00	7.73	6.62	6.17	5.97	5.87	5.80
600.00	9.27	7.94	7.41	7.17	7.05	6.97
700.00	10.82	9.26	8.64	8.36	8.22	8.13
800.00	12.36	10.59	9.88	9.55	9.40	9.29
900.00	13.91	11.91	11.11	10.75	10.57	10.45
1,000.00	15.45	13.23	12.34	11.94	11.75	11.61
2,000.00	30.90	26.47	24.69	23.88	23.50	23.22
3,000.00	46.35	39.70	37.03	35.83	35.25	34.83
4,000.00	61.81	52.93	49.38	47.77	47.00	46.44
5,000.00	77.26	66.17	61.72	59.71	58.75	58.05
6,000.00	92.71	79.40	74.07	71.65	70.50	69.65
7,000.00	108.16	92.63	86.41	83.59	82.25	81.26
8,000.00	123.61	105.87	98.76	95.54	94.00	92.87
9,000.00	139.06	119.10	111.10	107.48	105.75	104.48
10,000.00	154.52	132.34	123.45	119.42	117.50	116.09
20,000.00	309.03	264.67	246.89	238.84	235.00	232.18
30,000.00	463.55	397.01	370.34	358.26	352.50	348.27
40,000.00	618.06	529.34	493.78	477.68	469.99	464.36
50,000.00	772.58	661.68	617.23	597.10	587.49	580.45
60,000.00	927.09	794.01	740.67	716.52	704.99	696.55
70,000.00	1,081.61	926.35	864.12	835.94	822.49	812.64
80,000.00	1,236.13	1,058.68	987.56	955.36	939.99	928.73
90,000.00	1,390.64	1,191.02	1,111.01	1,074.78	1,057.49	1,044.82
100,000.00	1,545.16	1,323.35	1,234.45	1,194.20	1,174.98	1,160.91

Glossary of Real Estate Terms Every Home Buyer Should Know

Abstract (of Title)   A summary of the public records affecting the title to a particular piece of land. An attorney or title insurance company officer creates the abstract of title by examining all recorded instruments (documents) relating to a specific piece of property, such as easements, liens, mortgages, etc.

Acceleration Clause   A provision in a loan agreement that allows the lender to require the balance of the loan to become due immediately if mortgage payments are not made or there is a breach in your obligation under your mortgage or note.

Addendum   Any addition to, or modification of, a contract. Also called an amendment or rider.

Adjustable Rate Mortgage (ARM)   A type of loan whose prevailing interest rate is tied to an economic index (like one-year Treasury Bills), which fluctuates with the market. There are three types of ARMs, including one-year ARMs, which adjust every year; three-year ARMs, which adjust every three years; and five-year ARMs, which adjust every five years. When the loan adjusts, the lender tacks a margin onto the economic index rate to come up with your loan's new rate. ARMs are considered far riskier than fixed-rate

477

mortgages, but their starting interest rates are extremely low, and in the past five to ten years, people have done very well with them.

Agency   A term used to describe the relationship between a seller and a broker, or a buyer and a broker.

Agency Closing   The lender's use of a title company or other party to act on the lender's behalf for the purposes of closing on the purchase of a home or refinancing of a loan.

Agent   An individual who represents a buyer or a seller in the purchase or sale of a home. Licensed by the state, an agent must work for a broker or a brokerage firm.

Agreement of Sale   This document is also known as the contract of purchase, purchase agreement, or sales agreement. It is the agreement by which the seller agrees to sell you his or her property if you pay a certain price. It contains all the provisions and conditions for the purchase, must be written, and is signed by both parties.

Amortization   A payment plan which enables the borrower to reduce his debt gradually through monthly payments of principal and interest. Amortization tables (see Appendix VI) allow you to see exactly how much you would pay each month in interest and how much you repay in principal, depending on the amount of money borrowed at a specific interest rate.

Annual Percentage Rate (APR)   The total cost of your loan, expressed as a percentage rate of interest, which includes not only the loan's interest rate, but factors in all the costs associated with making that loan, including closing costs and fees. The costs are then amortized over the life of the loan. Banks are required by the federal Truth-in-Lending statutes to disclose the APR of a loan, which allows borrowers a common ground for comparing various loans from different lenders.

Application   A series of documents you must fill out when you apply for a loan.

Application Fee   A one-time fee charged by the mortgage company for processing your application for a loan. Sometimes the application fee is applied toward certain costs, including the appraisal and credit report.

Appraisal   The opinion of an appraiser, who estimates the value of a home at a specific point in time.

Articles-of-Agreement Mortgage A type of seller financing which allows the buyer to purchase the home in installments over a specified period of time. The seller keeps legal title to the home until the loan is paid off. The buyer receives an interest in the property—called equitable title—but does not own it. However, because the buyer is paying the real estate taxes and paying interest to the seller, it is the buyer who receives the tax benefits of homeownership.

Assumption of Mortgage If you assume a mortgage when you purchase a home, you undertake to fulfill the obligations of the existing loan agreement the seller made with the lender. The obligations are similar to those that you would incur if you took out a new mortgage. When assuming a mortgage, you become personally liable for the payment of principal and interest. The seller, or original mortgagor, is released from the liability, and should get that release in writing. Otherwise, he or she could be liable if you don't make the monthly payments.

Balloon Mortgage A type of mortgage which is generally short in length, but is amortized over twenty-five or thirty years so that the borrower pays a combination of interest and principal each month. At the end of the loan term, the entire balance of the loan must be repaid at once.

Broker An individual who acts as the agent of the seller or buyer. A real estate broker must be licensed by the state.

Building Line or Setback The distance from the front, back, or side of a lot beyond which construction or improvements may not extend without permission from the proper governmental authority. The building line may be established by a filed plat of subdivision, by restrictive covenants in deeds, by building codes, or by zoning ordinances.

Buy Down An incentive offered by a developer or seller that allows the buyer to lower his or her initial interest rate by putting up a certain amount of money. A buy down also refers to the process of paying extra points up front at the closing of your loan in order to have a lower interest rate over the life of the loan.

Buyer Broker A buyer broker is a real estate broker who specializes in representing home buyers. Unlike a seller broker or conventional broker, the buyer broker has a fiduciary duty to the buyer, because the buyer accepts the legal obligation of paying the broker. The buyer broker is obligated to find the best property for a client,

479

and then negotiate the best possible purchase price and terms. Buyer brokerage has gained a significant amount of respect in recent years, since the National Association of Realtors has changed its code of ethics to accept this designation.

Buyer's Market   Market conditions that favor the buyer. A buyer's market is usually expressed when there are too many homes for sale, and a home can be bought for less money.

Certificate of Title   A document or instrument issued by a local government agency to a homeowner, naming the homeowner as the owner of a specific piece of property. At the sale of the property, the certificate of title is transferred to the buyer. The agency then issues a new certificate of title to the buyer.

Chain of Title   The lineage of ownership of a particular property.

Closing   The day when buyers and sellers sign the papers and actually swap money for title to the new home. The closing finalizes the agreements reached in the sales agreement.

Closing Costs   This phrase can refer to a lender's costs for closing on a loan, or it can mean all the costs associated with closing on a piece of property. Considering all closing costs, it's easy to see that closing can be expensive for both buyers and sellers. A home buyer's closing costs might include: lender's points, loan origination or loan service fees; loan application fee; lender's credit report; lender's processing fee; lender's document preparation fee; lender's appraisal fee; prepaid interest on the loan; lender's insurance escrow; lender's real estate tax escrow; lender's tax escrow service fee; cost for the lender's title policy; special endorsements to the lender's title policy; house inspection fees; title company closing fee; deed or mortgage recording fees; local municipal, county, and state taxes; and the attorney's fee. A seller's closing costs might include: survey (which in some parts of the country is paid for by the buyer); title insurance; recorded release of mortgage; broker's commission; state, county, and local municipality transfer taxes; credit to the buyer for unpaid real estate taxes and other bills; attorney's fees; FHA fees and costs.

Cloud (on title)   An outstanding claim or encumbrance that adversely affects the marketability of a property.

Commission   The amount of money paid to the broker by the seller (or, in some cases, the buyer), as a compensation for selling the home. Usually, the commission is a percentage of the sales price of the home, and generally hovers in the 5 to 7 percent range. There is no "set" commission rate. It is always and entirely negotiable.

Condemnation The government holds the right to "condemn" land for public use, even against the will of the owner. The government, however, must pay fair market price for the land. Condemnation may also mean that the government has decided a particular piece of land, or a dwelling, is unsafe for human habitation.

Condominium A dwelling of two or more units in which you individually own the interior space of your unit and jointly own common areas such as the lobby, roof, parking, plumbing, and recreational areas.

Contingency A provision in a contract that sets forth one or more conditions that must be met prior to the closing. If the contingency is not met, usually the party who is benefitting from the contingency can terminate the contract. Some common contingencies include financing, inspection, attorney approval, and toxic substances.

Contract to Purchase Another name for Agreement of Sale.

Contractor In the building industry, the contractor is the individual who contracts to build the property. He or she erects the structure and manages the subcontracting (to the electrician, plumber, etc.) until the project is finished.

Conventional Mortgage A conventional mortgage means that the loan is underwritten by banks, savings and loans, or other types of mortgage companies. There are also certain limitations imposed on conventional mortgages that allow them to be sold to private institutional investors (like pension funds) on the secondary market. For example, as of 1993, the loan must be less than $203,500, otherwise it is considered a "jumbo" loan. Also, if you are buying a condominium, conventional financing decrees that the condo building be more than 70 percent owner-occupied.

Co-op Cooperative housing refers to a building, or a group of buildings, that is owned by a corporation. The shareholders of the corporation are the people who live in the building. They own shares—which gives them the right to lease a specific unit within the building—in the corporation that owns their building and pay "rent" or monthly maintenance assessments for the expenses associated with living in the building. Co-ops are relatively unknown outside of New York, Chicago, and a few other cities. Since the 1970s, condominiums have become much more popular.

Counteroffer When the seller or buyer responds to a bid. If you decide to offer $100,000 for a home listed at $150,000, the seller might counter your offer and propose that you purchase the home for $140,000. That new proposal, and any subsequent offer, is called a counteroffer.

Covenant Assurances or promises set out in the deed or a legally binding contract, or implied in the law. For example, when you obtain title to a property by warranty, there is the Covenant of Quiet Enjoyment, which gives you the right to enjoy your property without disturbances.

Credit Report A lender will decide whether or not to give you a loan based on your credit history. A credit report lists all of your credit accounts (such as charge cards), and any debts or late payments that have been reported to the credit company.

Cul de Sac A street that ends in a U-shape, leading the driver or pedestrian back to the beginning. The cul de sac has become exceptionally popular with modern subdivision developers, who use the design technique to create quiet streets and give the development a nonlinear feel.

Custom Builder A home builder who builds houses for individual owners to the owners' specification. The home builder may either own a piece of property or build a home on someone else's land.

Debt Service The total amount of debt (credit cards, mortgage, car loan) that an individual is carrying at any one time.

Declaration of Restrictions Developers of condominiums (or any other type of housing unit that functions as a condo) are required to file a condominium declaration, which sets out the rules and restrictions for the property, the division of ownership, and the rights and privileges of the owners. The "condo dec" or "homeowner's dec," as it is commonly called, reflects the developer's original intent, and may only be changed by unit-owner vote. There are other types of declarations, including homeowners' association and town house association. Co-op dwellers are governed by a similar type of document.

Deed The document used to transfer ownership in a property from seller to buyer.

Deed of Trust   A deed of trust or trust deed is an instrument similar to a mortgage that gives the lender the right to foreclose on the property if there is a default under the trust deed or note by the borrower.

Deposit   Money given by the buyer to the seller with a signed contract to purchase or offer to purchase, as a show of good faith. Also called the earnest money.

Down Payment   The cash put into a purchase by the borrower. Lenders like to see the borrower put at least 20 percent down in cash, because lenders generally believe that if you have a higher cash down payment, it is less likely the home will go into foreclosure. In recent years, however, lenders have become more flexible about cash down payments; recently, lenders have begun accepting cash down payments of as little as 5 percent.

Dual Agency   When a real estate broker represents both the buyer and the seller in a single transaction it creates a situation known as dual agency. In most states, brokers must disclose to the buyer and to the seller whom they are representing. Even with disclosure, dual agency presents a conflict of interest for the broker in the transaction. If the broker is acting as the seller broker and the subagent for the seller (by bringing the buyer), then anything the buyer tells the broker must by law be brought to the seller's attention. If the broker represents the seller as a seller broker and the buyer as a buyer broker in the same transaction, the broker will receive money from both the buyer and the seller, an obvious conflict of interest.

Due on Sale Clause   Nearly every mortgage has this clause, which states that the mortgage must be paid off in full upon the sale of the home.

Earnest Money   The money the buyer gives the seller up front as a show of good faith. It can be as much as 10 percent of the purchase price. Earnest money is sometimes called a deposit.

Easement   A right given by a landowner to a third party to make use of the land in a specific way. There may be several easements on your property, including for passage of utility lines or poles, sewer or water mains, and even a driveway. Once the right is given, it continues indefinitely, or until released by the party who received it.

Eminent Domain   The right of the government to condemn private land for public use. The government must, however, pay full market value for the property.

Encroachment   When your neighbor builds a garage or a fence, and it occupies your land, it is said to "encroach on" your property.

Encumbrance   A claim or lien or interest in a property by another party. An encumbrance hinders the seller's ability to pass good, marketable, and unencumbered title to you.

Escrow Closing   A third party, usually a title company, acts as the neutral party for the receipt of documents for the exchange of the deed by the sellers for the buyer's money. The final exchange is completed when the third party determines that certain preset requirements have been satisfied.

Escrow (for Earnest Money)   The document that creates the arrangement whereby a third party or broker holds the earnest money for the benefit of the buyer and seller.

Escrow (for Real Estate Taxes and Insurance)   An account in which monthly installments for real estate taxes and property insurance are held—usually in the name of the home buyer's lender.

Fee Simple   The most basic type of ownership, under which the owner has the right to use and dispose of the property at will.

Fiduciary Duty   A relationship of trust between a broker and a seller or a buyer broker and a buyer, or an attorney and a client.

First Mortgage   A mortgage that takes priority over all other voluntary liens.

Fixture   Personal property, such as a built-in bookcase, furnace, hot water heater, and recessed lights, that becomes "affixed" because it has been permanently attached to the home.

Foreclosure   The legal action taken to extinguish a homeowner's right and interest in a property, so that the property can be sold in a foreclosure sale to satisfy a debt.

Gift Letter   A letter to the lender indicating that a gift of cash has been made to the buyer and that it is not expected to be repaid. The letter must detail the amount of the gift, and the name of the giver.

Good Faith Estimate (GFE)   Under RESPA, lenders are required to give potential borrowers a written Good Faith Estimate of closing costs within three days of an application submission.

Grace Period   The period of time after a loan payment due date in which a mortgage payment may be made and not be considered delinquent.

Graduated Payment Mortgage   A mortgage in which the payments increase over the life of the mortgage, allowing the borrower to make very low payments at the beginning of the loan.

Hazard Insurance   Insurance that covers the property from damages that might materially affect its value. Also known as homeowner's insurance.

Holdback   An amount of money held back at closing by the lender or the escrow agent until a particular condition has been met. If the problem is a repair, the money is kept until the repair is made. If the repair is not made, the lender or escrow agent uses the money to make the repair. Buyers and sellers may also have holdbacks between them, to ensure that specific conditions of the sale are met.

Homeowner Association   A group of homeowners in a particular subdivision or area who band together to take care of common property and common interests.

Homeowner's Insurance   Coverage that includes hazard insurance, as well as personal liability and theft.

Home Warranty   A service contract that covers appliances (with exclusions) in working condition in the home for a certain period of time, usually one year. Homeowners are responsible for a per-call service fee. There is a homeowner's warranty for new construction. Some developers will purchase a warranty from a company specializing in new construction for the homes they sell. A homeowner's warranty will warrant the good working order of the appliances and workmanship of a new home for between one and ten years; for example, appliances might be covered for one year while the roof may be covered for several years.

Housing and Urban Development, Department of   Also known as HUD, this is the federal department responsible for the nation's housing programs. It also regulates RESPA, the Real Estate Settlement Procedures Act, which governs how lenders must deal with their customers.

Inspection   The service an inspector performs when he or she is hired to scrutinize the home for any possible structural defects. May also be done in order to check for the presence of toxic substances, such as leaded paint or water, asbestos, radon, or pests, including termites.

Installment Contract   The purchase of property in installments. Title to the property is given to the purchaser when all installments are made.

Institutional Investors or Lenders   Private or public companies, corporations, or funds (such as pension funds) that purchase loans on the secondary market from commercial lenders such as banks and savings and loans. Or, they are sources of funds for mortgages through mortgage brokers.

Interest   Money charged for the use of borrowed funds. Usually expressed as an interest rate, it is the percentage of the total loan charged annually for the use of the funds.

Interest-Only Mortgage   A loan in which only the interest is paid on a regular basis (usually monthly), and the principal is owed in full at the end of the loan term.

Interest Rate Cap   The total number of percentage points that an adjustable-rate mortgage (ARM) might rise over the life of the loan.

Joint Tenancy   An equal, undivided ownership in a property taken by two or more owners. Under joint tenancy there are rights of survivorship, which means that if one of the owners dies, the surviving owner rather than the heirs of the estate inherits the other's total interest in the property.

Landscape   The trees, flowers, plantings, lawn, and shrubbery that surround the exterior of a dwelling.

Late Charge   A penalty applied to a mortgage payment that arrives after the grace period (usually the 10th or 15th of a month).

Lease with an Option to Buy   When the renter or lessee of a piece of property has the right to purchase the property for a specific period of time at a specific price. Usually, a lease with an option to buy allows a first-time buyer to accumulate a down payment by applying a portion of the monthly rent toward the down payment.

Lender   A person, company, corporation, or entity that lends money for the purchase of real estate.

Letter of Intent   A formal statement, usually in letter form, from the buyer to the seller stating that the buyer intends to purchase a specific piece of property for a specific price on a specific date.

Leverage   Using a small amount of cash, say a 10 or 20 percent down payment, to purchase a piece of property.

Lien   An encumbrance against the property, which may be voluntary or involuntary. There are many different kinds of liens, including a tax lien (for unpaid federal, state, or real estate taxes), a judgment lien (for monetary judgments by a court of law), a mortgage lien (when you take out a mortgage), and a mechanic's lien (for work done by a contractor on the property that has not been paid for). For a lien to be attached to the property's title, it must be filed or recorded with local county government.

Listing   A property that a broker agrees to list for sale in return for a commission.

Loan   An amount of money that is lent to a borrower, who agrees to repay it plus interest.

Loan Commitment   A written document that states that a mortgage company has agreed to lend a buyer a certain amount of money at a certain rate of interest for a specific period of time, which may contain sets of conditions and a date by which the loan must close.

Loan Origination Fee   A one-time fee charged by the mortgage company to arrange the financing for the loan.

Loan-to-Value Ratio   The ratio of the amount of money you wish to borrow compared to the value of the property you wish to purchase. Institutional investors (who buy loans on the secondary market from your mortgage company) set up certain ratios that guide lending practices. For example, the mortgage company might only lend you 80 percent of a property's value.

Location   Where property is geographically situated. "Location, location, location" is a broker's maxim that states that where the property is located is its most important feature, because you can change everything about a house, except its location.

Lock-In   When a borrower signals to a mortgage company that he or she has decided to lock in, or take, a particular interest rate for a specific amount of time. The mechanism by which a borrower locks in the interest rate that will be charged on a particular loan. Usually, the lock lasts for a certain time period, such as thirty, forty-five, or sixty days. On a new construction, the lock may be much longer.

Maintenance Fee   The monthly or annual fee charged to condo, co-op, or town house owners, and paid to the homeowner's association, for the maintenance of common property. Also called an assessment.

Mortgage   A document granting a lien on a home in exchange for financing granted by a lender. The mortgage is the means by which the lender secures the loan and has the ability to foreclose on the home.

Mortgage Banker   A company or a corporation, like a bank, that lends its own funds to borrowers in addition to bringing together lenders and borrowers. A mortgage banker may also service the loan (i.e., collect the monthly payments).

Mortgage Broker   A company or individual that brings together lenders and borrowers and processes mortgage applications.

Mortgagee   A legal term for the lender.

Mortgagor   A legal term for the borrower.

Multiple Listing Service (MLS)   A computerized listing of all properties offered for sale by member brokers. Buyers may only gain access to the MLS by working with a member broker.

Negative Amortization   A condition created when the monthly mortgage payment is less than the amount necessary to pay off the loan over the period of time set forth in the note. Because you're paying less than the amount necessary, the actual loan amount increases over time. That's how you end up with negative equity. To pay off the loan, a lump-sum payment must be made.

Option   When a buyer pays for the right or option to purchase property for a given length of time, without having the obligation to actually purchase the property.

Origination Fee   A fee charged by the lender for allowing you to borrow money to purchase property. The fee—which is also referred to as points—is usually expressed as a percentage of the total loan amount.

Ownership   The absolute right to use, enjoy, and dispose of property. You own it!

Package Mortgage   A mortgage that uses both real and personal property to secure a loan.

Paper   Slang usage that refers to the mortgage, trust deed, installment, and land contract.

Personal Property   Moveable property, such as appliances, furniture, clothing, and artwork.

PITI   An acronym for Principal-Interest-Taxes-and-Insurance. These are usually the four parts of your monthly mortgage payment.

Pledged Account   Borrowers who do not want to have a real estate tax or insurance escrow administered by the mortgage servicer can, in some circumstances, pledge a savings account into which enough money to cover real estate taxes and the insurance premium must be deposited. You must then make the payments for your real estate taxes and insurance premiums from a separate account. If you fail to pay your taxes or premiums, the lender is allowed to use the funds in the pledged account to make those payments.

Point   A point is one percent of the loan amount.

Possession   Being in control of a piece of property, and having the right to use it to the exclusion of all others.

Power of Attorney   The legal authorization given to an individual to act on behalf of another individual.

Prepaid Interest   Interest paid at closing for the number of days left in the month after closing. For example, if you close on the 15th, you would prepay the interest for the 16th through the end of the month.

Prepayment Penalty   A fine imposed when a loan is paid off before it comes due. Many states now have laws against prepayment penalties, although banks with federal charters are exempt from state laws. If possible, do not use a mortgage that has a prepayment penalty, or you will be charged a fine if you sell your property before your mortgage has been paid off.

Prequalifying for a Loan   When a mortgage company tells a buyer in advance of the formal application approximately how much money the buyer can afford to borrow.

Principal   The amount of money you borrow.

Private Mortgage Insurance (PMI)   Special insurance that specifically protects the top 20 percent of a loan, allowing the lender to lend more than 80 percent of the value of the property. PMI is paid in monthly installments by the borrower.

Property Tax   A tax levied by a county or local authority on the value of real estate.

Proration   The proportional division of certain costs of homeownership. Usually used at closing to figure out how much the buyer and seller each owe for certain expenditures, including real estate taxes, assessments, and water bills.

Purchase Agreement   An agreement between the buyer and seller for the purchase of property.

Purchase Money Mortgage   An instrument used in seller financing, a purchase money mortgage is signed by a buyer and given to the seller in exchange for a portion of the purchase price.

Quit Claim Deed   A deed that operates to release any interest in a property that a person may have, *without a representation that he or she actually has a right in that property.* For example, Sally may use a quit claim deed to grant Bill her interest in the White House, in Washington, DC, although she may not actually own, or have any rights to, that particular house.

Real Estate   Land and anything permanently attached to it, such as buildings and improvements.

Real Estate Agent   An individual licensed by the state, who acts on behalf of the seller or buyer. For his or her services, the agent receives a commission, which is usually expressed as a percentage of the sales price of a home and is split with his or her real estate firm. A real estate agent must also be a real estate broker or work for one.

Real Estate Attorney   An attorney who specializes in the purchase and sale of real estate.

Real Estate Broker   An individual who is licensed by the state to act as an agent on behalf of the seller or buyer. For his or her services, the broker receives a commission, which is usually expressed as a percentage of the sales price of a home.

Real Estate Settlement Procedures Act (RESPA)   This federal statute was originally passed in 1974, and contains provisions that govern the way companies involved with a real estate closing must treat each other and the consumer. For example, one section of

RESPA requires lenders to give consumers a written Good Faith Estimate within three days of making an application for a loan. Another section of RESPA prohibits title companies from giving referral fees to brokers for steering business to them.

Realist   A designation given to an agent or broker who is a member of the National Association of Real Estate Brokers.

Realtor   A designation given to a real estate agent or broker who is a member of the National Association of Realtors.

Recording   The process of filing documents at a specific government office. Upon such recording, the document becomes part of the public record.

Redlining   The slang term used to describe an illegal practice of discrimination against a particular racial group by real estate lenders. Redlining occurs when lenders decide certain areas of a community are too high risk and refuse to lend to buyers who want to purchase property in those areas, regardless of their qualifications or creditworthiness.

Regulation Z   Also known as the Truth in Lending Act. Congress determined that lenders must provide a written good faith estimate of closing costs to all borrowers and provide them with other written information about the loan.

Reserve   The amount of money set aside by a condo, co-op, or homeowners' association for future capital improvements.

Sale-Leaseback   A transaction in which the seller sells property to a buyer, who then leases the property back to the seller. This is accomplished within the same transaction.

Sales Contract   The document by which a buyer contracts to purchase property. Also known as the purchase contract or a Contract to Purchase.

Second Mortgage   A mortgage that is obtained after the primary mortgage, and whose rights for repayment are secondary to the first mortgage.

Seller Broker   A broker who has a fiduciary responsibility to the seller. Most brokers are seller brokers, although an increasing number are buyer brokers, who have a fiduciary responsibility to the buyer.

Settlement Statement A statement that details the monies paid out and received by the buyer and seller at closing.

Shared Appreciation Mortgage A relatively new mortgage used to help first-time buyers who might not qualify for conventional financing. In a shared appreciation mortgage, the lender offers a below-market interest rate in return for a portion of the profits made by the homeowner when the property is sold. Before entering into a shared appreciation mortgage, be sure to have your real estate attorney review the documentation.

Special Assessment An additional charge levied by a condo or co-op board in order to pay for capital improvements, or other unforeseen expenses.

Subagent A broker who brings the buyer to the property. Although subagent would appear to be working for the buyer (a sub-agent usually ferries around the buyer, showing him or her properties), they are paid by the seller and have a fiduciary responsibility to the seller. Subagency is often confusing to first-time buyers, who think that because the subagent shows them property, the sub-agent is "their" agent, rather than the seller's.

Subdivision The division of a large piece of property into several smaller pieces. Usually a developer or a group of developers will build single family or duplex homes of a similar design and cost within one subdivision.

Tax Lien A lien that is attached to property if the owner does not pay his or her real estate taxes or federal income taxes. If overdue property taxes are not paid, the owner's property might be sold at auction for the amount owed in back taxes.

Tenancy by the Entirety A type of ownership whereby both the husband and wife each own the complete property. Each spouse has an ownership interest in the property as their marital residence and, as a result, creditors cannot force the sale of the home to pay back the debts of one spouse without the other spouse's consent. There are rights of survivorship whereby upon the death of one spouse, the other spouse would immediately inherit the entire property.

Tenants in Common A type of ownership in which two or more parties have an undivided interest in the property. The owners may or may not have equal shares of ownership, and there are no rights of survivorship. However, each owner retains the right to sell his or her share in the property as he or she sees fit.

Title Refers to the ownership of a particular piece of property.

Title Company The corporation or company that insures the status of title (title insurance) through the closing, and may handle other aspects of the closing.

Title Insurance Insurance that protects the lender and the property owner against losses arising from defects or problems with the title to property.

Torrens Title A system of recording the chain of ownership for property, which takes its name from the man who created it in Australia in 1858, Sir Robert Torrens. While popular in the nineteenth century, most cities have converted to other, less cumbersome, systems of recording.

Trust Account An account used by brokers and escrow agents, in which funds for another individual are held separately, and not commingled with other funds.

Underwriter One who underwrites a loan for another. Your lender will have an investor underwrite your loan.

Variable Interest Rate An interest rate that rises and falls according to a particular economic indicator, such as Treasury Bills.

Void A contract or document that is not enforceable.

Voluntary Lien A lien, such as a mortgage, that a homeowner elects to grant to a lender.

Waiver The surrender or relinquishment of a particular right, claim, or privilege.

Warranty A legally binding promise given to the buyer at closing by the seller, generally regarding the condition of the home, property, or other matter.

Zoning The right of the local municipal government to decide how different areas of the municipality will be used. Zoning ordinances are the laws that govern the use of the land.

Alphabetical Listing
of Websites

Alabama
   (dsmd.state.al.us/arec)
Alaska
   (state.ak.us)
American Association of Retired Persons (AARP)
   (aarp.org)
American Society of Home Inspectors
   (ASHI.com)
Arizona Organization Department of Real Estate
   (adre.org)
Arizona State Banking Department
   (azbanking.com)
Arkansas Organization Arkansas Real Estate Commission
   (state.ar.us/arec/arecweb.html)
ArkansasState Banking Department
   (state.ar.us/bank/)

Bank Rate Monitor
   (bankrate.com)

California
   (dfi.ca.gov)
California Department of Real Estate
   (dre.cahwnet.gov/complnt.htm)
Century 21
   (century21.com)
   (keyword Century21 if you're on America Online)
Coldwell Banker
   (coldwellbanker.com)
Colorado Division of Banking
   (dora.state.co.us/banking/)

Colorado Division of Real Estate
  (dora.state.CO.us/Real_Estate)
Connecticut
  (state.ct.us/dob/)
Consumer Federation of America (CFA)
  (consumerfed.org)
Consumer Product Safety Commission
  (Cpsc.gov)
Consumer Publications
  (Pueblo.gsa.gov)
Council of Better Business Bureaus
  (BBB.org)
Countrywide Home Loans
  (Countrywide.com)

Delaware Office of the Bank Commissioner
  (state.de.us/bank)
Department of Financial Institutions
  (state.il.us/dfi/)
Department of Housing and Urban Development (HUD)
  (HUD.org\dchud\)
Department of Veteran Affairs (VA)
  (VA.gov)

e-bay
  (ebay.com)
E-Loan
  (Eloan.com)
EPA toxin link
  (EPA.gov/opptintr/)

Fannie Mae (formerly Federal National Mortgage Association)
  (FannieMae.com)
  (HomePath.com)
Federal Emergency Management Agency (FEMA)
  (fema.gov)
Florida Department of Banking and Finance
  (dbf.state.fl.us)
Freddie Mac
  (FreddieMac.com)

Georgia Department of Banking and Finance
  (state.ga.us/dbf)
Georgia Real Estate Commission
  (state.ga.us/Ga.Real_Estate)

Hawaii Department of Commerce and Consumer Affairs
  (hawaii.gov)
Hawaii Real Estate Commission
  (hawaii.gov/hirec)

HomeAdvisor
   (HomeAdvisor.com)
Home Information Center, a unit of the Office of
   Affordable Housing
   (ComCon.com)
HomeOwners.com
   (HomeOwners.com)
HomeShark
   (homeshark.com)

Idaho Department of Finance
   (state.id.us/finance/dof.htm)
Illinois Office of Banks and Real Estate
   (state.il.us/obr)
Ilyce Glink
   (ThinkGlink.com)
Indiana Department of Financial Institutions
   (dfi.state.in.us/)
International Real Estate Digest
   (Ired.com)
Iowa Department of Commerce
   (state.ia.us/government/com/)
Iowa Real Estate Commission
   (state.ia.us/government/com/prof/realesta/realesta.htm)
iOwn.com
   (iOwn.com)

Kansas Real Estate Commission
   (ink.org/public/krec)
Kentucky Real Estate Commission
   (ukcres.gws.uky.edu/krec/)

Maine Department of Professional and Financial Regulation
   (state.me.us/)
Maine Real Estate Commission
   (state.me.us/pfr/led/rec/index.htm)
Mapping sites
   (geocities.com)
Massachusetts Real Estate Board
   (state.ma.us/reg/boards/re)
Microsoft's HomeAdvisor
   (HomeAdvisor.com)
Minnesota Commerce Department Enforcement Department
   (commerce.state.mn.us)
Mississippi Department of Banking and Consumer Finance
   (dbcf.state.ms.us/)
Missouri Division of Credit Unions
   (ecodev.state.mo.us/cu/)
Missouri Division of Finance
   (ecodev.state.mo.us/finance/)

Montana Department of Commerce
(commerce.state.mt.us/bnk&fin/index.html)
Mortgage broker
(HomeOwners.com)

National Association of Exclusive Buyer's Agents
(naeba.com)
National Association of Realtors
(realtor.com)
National Center for Home Equity Conversion (NCHEC)
(Reverse.org)
National lender
(Countrywide.com)
(Norwest.com)
Nebraska Financial Institutions Division
(ndbf.org/FIN.HTM)
Neighborhood Reinvestment Corporation
(NW.org)
Nevada Nevada Department of Business and Industry
(state.nv.us/b&i/fi/)
New Hampshire Office of the Banking Commissioner
(state.nh.us/banking)
New Jersey Department of Banking and Insurance
(state.nj.us/deptserv.html)
New Jersey Real Estate Commission
(naic.org/nj/realcom.htm)
New Mexico Regulation and Licensing Department
(state.nm.us/rld/fid/fidhome.htm)
New York State Banking Department
(banking.state.ny.us/)
North Carolina Office of the Commissioner of Banks
(banking.state.nc.us/)
North Carolina Real Estate Commission
(ncrec.state.nc.us)
North Dakota Department of Banking and Financial Institutions
(state.nd.us/bank/)
Norwest
(Norwest.com)

Oklahoma State Banking Department
(state.ok.us/~sbd/)
Owners
(owners.com)

Pennsylvania
(state.pa.us)

Quicken.com
(Quicken.com)
QuickenMortgage
(QuickenMortgage.com)

Ram Research
(Ramresearch.com/csrttrak/cardtrak.html)
RE/MAX
(remax.com)
Real Estate Café
(realestatecafe.com)
RealEstate.com
(RealEstate.com)
Realtor.com
(realtor.com)
Rhode Island Department of Business Regulation
(state.ri.us/manual/data/queries/stdept)

School district
(schoolmatch.com)
South Carolina Real Estate Commission
(11r.sc.edu/rec)
South Dakota Division of Banking
(state/sd/us/dcr/bank/BANK-HOM)

Texas Real Estate Commission
(trec.state.tx.us)

Urban Development
(hud.gov)
Utah Division of Real Estate
(commerce.state.ut.us)

Virginia Department of Professional and Occupational Regulation
(state.va.us/dpor)

Washington Department of Financial Institutions
(wa.gov/dfi/)
Washington Department of Licensing
(wa.gov/dol/bpd/recom.htm)
West Virginia Division of Banking
(state.wv.us/banking)
Wisconsin Department of Regulation and Licensing
(state.wi.us/agencies/drl/)
Wyoming Division of Banking
(audit.state.wy.us/banking/default.htm)
Wyoming Real Estate Commission
(commerce.state.wy.us/b&c/rec/)

Yahoo!
(yahoo.com)

Acknowledgments

There are many people without whose help it would have been impossible to start, let alone finish, this book. I would like to express my heartfelt thanks to the thousands of real estate professionals, experts, industry observers, home buyers and sellers all over the country, who, over the course of the first and second editions of this book, other books, Internet chats, radio programs, television interviews, and hundreds of articles, have given freely of their advice, guidance, counsel, and wisdom, and have honestly shared their experiences.

I am grateful for the counsel and friendship of: my attorney, Ralph Martire, whose mind is wonderfully sharp and witty; my agent, Alice Martell, who helps make a difficult process as easy as pie; and my publisher and editor, Carie Freimuth, whose enthusiasm for these and other projects is so rare, and who makes me feel right at home.

My family continues to put up with the best and worst of this eclectic life I've chosen, offering only their love and support. I especially wish to thank my sisters, Shona Glink Kitei and Phyllis Glink, who are kind, thoughtful, and encouraging, and my mother, Susanne Kraus Glink, one of the best (and top-selling!) real estate agents in Chicago, who introduced me to this crazy business, opened my eyes to some of its deepest, darkest secrets, told me some hilarious (but true!) stories, and repeatedly suggested that I write a book.

Finally, I would never have finished without the unstinting help of my husband and best friend, Samuel J. Tamkin, the world's best real estate attorney, and one hell of an editor, who continues to believe all my wildest dreams will come true.

Index